ELECTRONIC COLLECTION MANAGEMENT

FORMS, POLICIES, PROCEDURES, *and* GUIDELINES MANUAL

with CD-ROM

Rebecca Brumley

Neal-Schuman Publishers, Inc.

New York   London

Published by Neal-Schuman Publishers, Inc.
100 William St., Suite 2004
New York, NY 10038

Printed and bound in the United States of America.

The paper used in this publication meets the minimum requirements of American National Standard for Information Sciences—Permanence of Paper for Printed Library Materials, ANSI Z39.48-1992.

Library of Congress Cataloging-in-Publication Data

Brumley, Rebecca, 1959-
  Electronic collection management forms, policies, procedures, and guidelines manual with CD-ROM / Rebecca Brumley.
      p. cm.
  Includes index.
  ISBN 978-1-55570-663-0 (alk. paper)
  1. Libraries—Special collections—Electronic information resources—Case studies. 2. Electronic information resources—Management—Case studies. 3. Library rules and regulations—Case studies. I. Title.

Z692.C65B78 2009
025.17'4—dc22

                                                          2009007929

For Peaches

I didn't deserve your love and devotion

But, my life was immeasurably happier because of it

CONTENTS

PREFACE

Clear effective policies and procedures are vital to effective management. They are the framework that says what you do and why.

Despite growing library expenditures in the area of electronic resources and the complexity of licensing and managing them, an astonishing number of libraries have few policies in the area of electronic resources management, outdated policies, or ill-conceived and inadequate policies.

Larger libraries often have handbooks that cover only electronic resources, but that neglect important issues such as privacy, copyright, access, licensing, and security. Remember, there is much truth in the old adage "If you can't show a problem patron the policy in writing, the rule doesn't exist."

Today's busy professionals must manage their constantly growing and evolving electronic collection. How to tackle the task? How do libraries like yours manage their electronic resources? What's the best way to expand, modernize, and improve your own policies and procedures in this critical area of library management?

I created *Electronic Collection Management Forms, Policies, Procedures, and Guidelines with CD-ROM* as a collection of the best practices in this field, a practical tool to make your life easier and to offer fresh ideas. To compile this resource, I reviewed and researched thousands of forms, policies, procedures, and guidelines regarding electronic management on library Web sites. I selected and received permission to use more than 600 of the best ones for inclusion both in the printed book and on the accompanying CD-ROM.

ORGANIZATION

The policies, procedures, and forms are assembled into nine broad areas: administration, collection development, electronic equipment and hardware, access to electronic resources, related library services, legal safeguards, issues of special interest to public libraries, today's top job descriptions, and recommended forms. Each of these parts is further divided into key areas of interest, which is how I arranged the actual policy documents. For example, "Electronic Equipment and Hardware" includes the more specific chapter called "Equipment Inventory," which in turn includes the section "Needs Assessment." All policies, procedures, and forms featured in the book are also included on the accompanying CD-ROM so you can utilize the content without rekeying it. As a bonus, where indicated within the text, the CD-ROM provides additional materials not included in the book due to space limitations.

Part I, "Administration," explores cutting-edge and comprehensive policies that regulate electronic resources. This section is a little different from the other sections in that it needs to be read from start to finish. Some technology plans in this section reflect the strategies and goals administrators set. They provide an excellent starting point or serve as a comparison to work you may be doing or need to start. The importance of actually outlining where you want your library to be in one, two, five, or more years cannot be overestimated.

1. "Electronic Resources Plans" presents the ways in which libraries establish goals and achieve objectives, create powerful yet practical mission statements, and define the function, purpose, and scope of resources.
2. "Management Guidelines" considers policies to craft detailed versions of the vision and mission statements as departmental goals, scrutinize staff education, and supervise user training.

3. "Technology Plan Processes" reviews documents, including setting priorities, strategies for success, and creating tech plans.

Part II, "Collection Development," looks at the contemporary state of electronic resources in today's libraries. With the cost of technology comes a responsibility to spend your money with purpose.

4. "Categories of E-Resources" surveys databases and clearly defines e-journals, e-resources, government documents, and off-line resources.

5. "Collection Digitization" features an assortment of policies on deciding the distribution of paper and electronic resources. Policies include archiving, digital library archiving and file formats, general guidelines, and life cycle management.

6. "Departmental Selection, Collection, and Weeding" contains an abundance of useful examples for definitions, electronic-only migration, evaluation and deselection, evaluation and trials, frequency updates, general selection guidelines and criteria, implementation and review, initiation procedures for and integration of new electronic resources, mission, policy purpose, review and reassessment, and scope.

7. "Digital Resources" features goals, licenses, mission, priorities, purpose of collection, responsibility and implementation, retention and renewal, selection criteria, and types of material.

8. "Financial Arrangements" examines committees, consortia, and cooperative agreements; pricing, funding, and group acquisitions; licensed databases and licensing FAQs. It also features negotiation and review guidelines.

9. "Types of Material" tackles books with disks, CDs, CD-ROMs, e-books, DVDs, and videocassettes. Also included are items supporting free Web-based resources, Internet resources, multiple formats, and popular, classical, and spoken-word sound recordings.

Part III, "Electronic Equipment and Hardware," surveys how to create a comprehensive strategy through the use of specific policies to guide selection of equipment and software.

10. "Equipment Guidelines" includes time limits for computer workstations and general workstation policies.

11. "Equipment Inventory" features a sample needs assessment.

12. "Hardware and Software Guidelines" looks at interfaces, network security; software word processing needs assessment, and telecommunications.

13. "Special Equipment Guidelines" examines digital cameras, digital crawl restrictions, and laptop (both public and personal) use guidelines.

Part IV, "Access to Electronic Resources," investigates the often complicated questions of who, when, and under what circumstances patrons/students/guests can use your library's electronic resources. Remember, if you have a problem of access with a user and don't have a policy in writing, you will have trouble enforcing your rules. Be sure to have your policy in writing.

14. "Access Guidelines" looks at the Americans with Disabilities Act (ADA) policies; equitable user access; library responsibilities; service priorities; special status access; staff access to resources; student populations; user access to licensed resources, reserved materials, and other resources; and user resources definitions.

15. "Access Options" considers local and remote access.

16. "User Access Fundamentals" examines passwords, acceptable and unacceptable use of electronic resources, responsible use of licensed resources, and user rights.

17. "Wireless Access" provides general guidelines and examines wireless netiquette.

Part V, "Related Library Services," contemplates some of the basic questions in this area. What links do you allow on your Web site? Do you have a disclaimer? How much are you going to charge for printing? Will you make digital photos? Who can use your media center? How do you schedule your electronic classroom? Do you have IM and Ask guidelines?

18. "Electronic Classrooms" features general guidelines, room use instructions, and room use priorities.
19. "Library Web Site" examines purpose and mission statements, Web site content and evaluation techniques, and e-mail accounts. It also explores guidelines for links as well as links to student groups, outside sources, and user link requests.
20. "Media Center" deals with general guidelines and audiovisual rooms.
21. "Overdue, Lost, or Damaged Electronic Materials" examines fines and fees.
22. "Reproduction of Audio, Print, Scanned, and Graphic Images for Users" delves into photocopying and printing, audiotape duplication, as well as reproduction fees and conditions of use.
23. "Virtual Reference" looks at "Ask Reference" guidelines, FAQs, instant messaging, and mission and privacy statements.
24. "Personalized Information Searching" surveys library blog rules and regulations, personal digital assistants (PDAs), podcasts, and wikis.
25. "Information Literacy" investigates general guidelines, mission and vision statements, and scheduling instruction.

Part VI, "Legal Safeguards," realizes that in this day of rampant plagiarism and privacy headlines, you need to tell your users how you protect them and emphasize their responsibility to give proper credit when using someone else's work. This will save you countless headaches and provide your users with a comfort level by knowing what you do with their information.

26. "Collection of User Information" deals with Internet tracking guidelines, Social Security numbers, and information collected from users and from cookies.
27. "Copyright Restrictions" focuses on reproduction guidelines and permission requests.
28. "Copyright Rules for Specific Materials" features a cache of individual regulations for audiovisual formats, distance learning, images, music, multimedia productions, off-air recordings, reserves, university logo reproduction, and videos.
29. "Fair Use Policies" offers guidelines for downloading and policy statements.
30. "Library Policies" presents compliance with policies, departmental disclaimers, enforcement and sanctions, and library limitation of liabilities.
31. "Principles" surveys intellectual freedom and freedom of speech guidelines, records and the Patriot Act, records and open access, and staff responsibilities to ensure compliance.
32. "User Privacy Protections" considers access to user information limitations, general guidelines, and privacy/no privacy disclaimers.

Part VII, "Issues of Special Interest to Public Libraries," recognizes policy matters required by the public library mission to serve everyone.

33. "Internet Use" examines children's Internet use policies, specifically the Children's Internet Protection Act, and more generally the relationship between parents and children.
34. "Virtual Reference" looks into safety and third-party issues.
35. "Web Site Home Page for Children" explores purpose and mission statements and filters.

Part VIII, "Today's Top Job Descriptions," features 37 specific positions divided into four large arenas. Writing job descriptions can seem even harder than writing policies. I collected a broad array of descriptions for you to compare to your current prerequisites. See what other directors/deans expect.

36. "Administrative" encompasses a range of positions from Adult Services Supervisor/Automation Coordinator to V-CAT Administrator/Technology Coordinator.
37. "Librarians" looks at such jobs as Library Services Librarian for Technical Services, Metadata Librarian, and Virtual Librarian.
38. "Support Staff" covers such positions as Computer Equipment Technician, Information Systems Technician, and Technology Center Assistant.

39. "Technology and Web Site Personnel" describes requirements for Technology Trainer, Webmaster, and Web Programmer.

Part IX, "Treasury of Recommended Forms," brings together useful examples, including an E-Journal Request, a Laptop Liability Form, and an Equipment Rental Agreement. Forms are hard to create from scratch. This section is a collection of helpful ones you can copy or edit to suit your particular needs.

Electronic Collection Management Forms, Policies, Procedures, and Guidelines with CD-ROM ends with a list of Web sites for the libraries who have graciously contributed their work to this book as well as a wide-ranging, inclusive, and comprehensive index.

HOW TO SEARCH

To search for a specific term or subject go to the Index and look up your issue using standard librarian jargon. Each main entry may include several subsets under that topic, but you will quickly come across what you need.

Another search method is to look at the headings on the table of contents. For instance, if you are looking for cooperative arrangements with local libraries for sharing resources, look first for "Collection Development" (Part II), find "Financial Arrangements" (Chapter 8), and then pinpoint your particular topics from among the subheadings, in this case "Consortia" and "Cooperative Agreements."

A COMMITMENT TO SHARING

The rest of the world could learn a thing or two from librarians—especially the commitment to sharing. We share knowledge, resources, ideas, and, yes, copy from each other as we travel through our professional lives. Hundreds of librarians graciously provided what works for them: their policies, job descriptions, and forms. I am always reminded with each book I write what a very wise librarian wrote on her permission in my first book:

> *I eagerly grant permission to use parts of our instruction manual in your new book. Like many policies in many libraries, this guideline distills the wisdom of our peers. If you see your hand in our policy, thank you for your help. If you see your policy or something like it, every librarian who uses it thanks you.*

—Shirley Vonderhaar, Policy Contributor
James Kennedy Public Library, Dyersville, Iowa

It is no doubt that you have more work than time. This guidebook is a solution to one of your duties. Managing day-to-day library responsibilities does not leave much time for paperwork. There simply are not enough hours in the day to devote to policy manuals, record keeping, updating job descriptions, or writing policies, guidelines, technology plans, and other important documents. *Electronic Collection Management Forms, Policies, Procedures, and Guidelines with CD-ROM* makes it easy. I hope we all continue to share what works for us.

ACKNOWLEDGMENTS

I want to thank Charles Harmon, Vice President and Director of Publishing at Neal-Schuman Publishers, for continuing to have faith in the importance of this series of books on job descriptions, policies, guidelines, procedures, and forms in libraries and his faith in me. To my friends Lisa Lipton and John Haley, thank you for your support.

The Alberta Library
Edmonton, Alberta, Canada

Debra A. Blanchard
Athol Public Library
Athol, Massachusetts

Rose Dawson
Alexandria Library
Alexandria, Virginia

Alverno College
Alverno College Library
Milwaukee, Wisconsin

Art Weeks
Ames Public Library
Ames, Iowa

Megan Johnson
Appalachian State University
Belk Library and Information Commons
Boone, North Carolina

Aurora Public Library
Aurora, Colorado

Austin History Center
Austin Public Library
Austin, Texas

Kenneth S. Venet
Barry University
Monsignor William Barry Memorial Library
Miami Shores, Florida

Kyri Freeman
Barstow College
Barstow College Library
Barstow, California

Baruch College/CUNY
Newman Library
New York, New York

Benedict College
Benedict College Learning Resource Center
Columbia, South Carolina

Stephanie Bakos
Berkeley Heights Public Library
Berkeley Heights, New Jersey

Berry College
Memorial Library
Mount Berry, Georgia

Kevin Wayne Booe
Boise Public Library
Boise, Idaho

Boulder Public Library
Boulder, Colorado

Bowdoin College
Bowdoin College Library
Brunswick, Maine

Eric Le Page
Bridgewater State College
Bridgewater, Massachusetts

Brown University
Brown University Libraries
Providence, Rhode Island

Bryant University
Douglas and Judith Krupp Library
Smithfield, Rhode Island

Elliott Shore
Bryn Mawr College
Canaday Library
Bryn Mawr, Pennsylvania

Maryruth F. Glogowski
Buffalo State College
E. H. Butler Library
Buffalo, New York

Canton Public Library
Canton, Michigan

Johanna Bowen
Cabrillo College
Robert E. Swenson Library
Aptos, California

Virginia Rodes, Library Director
Calumet College of St. Joseph
Specker Library
Whiting, Indiana

Carnegie Library of Pittsburgh
Pittsburgh, Pennsylvania

Alan Bogage
Carroll Community College
Carroll Community College Library and Media
    Center
Westminster, Maryland

Anne Marie Casey
Central Michigan University
Charles V. Park Library
Mount Pleasant, Michigan

Charlevoix Public Library
Charlevoix, Michigan

City of Concord Public Library
Concord, New Hampshire

City of Longmont Public Library
Longmont, Colorado

Kay L. Wall
Clemson University
Clemson University Libraries
Clemson, South Carolina

Barbara Burd
Coastal Carolina University
Kimbel Library
Conway, South Carolina

Lisa Stock
College of DuPage
College of DuPage Library
Glen Ellyn, Illinois

Carol Dickerson
Colorado College
Tutt Library
Colorado Springs, Colorado

Arlie F. Sims
Columbia College Chicago
Columbia College Chicago Library
Chicago, Illinois

Columbia University in the City of New York
Columbia University Libraries
New York, New York

Sharon Hoverson
Concordia College
Carl B. Ylvisaker Library
Moorhead, Minnesota

Connecticut State Library
Hartford, Connecticut

Jonelle Prether Darr
Cumberland County Library System
Carlisle, Pennsylvania

Cuyahoga County Public Library
Parma, Ohio

Dakota State University
Karl E. Mundt Library and Learning Commons
Madison, South Dakota

Jeffery Horrell
Dartmouth College
Dartmouth College Library
Hanover, New Hampshire

Davidson College
Davidson College Library
Davidson, North Carolina

Rickie Emerson (former director)
Dorothy Alling Memorial Library
Williston, Vermont

Drexel University
Drexel University Libraries
Philadelphia, Pennsylvania

Patricia L. Thibodeau
Duke University
Medical Center Library and Archives
Durham, North Carolina

Duke University
Perkins Library
Durham, North Carolina

William Miller
Florida Atlantic University
Wimberly Library
Boca Raton, Florida

Bonnie Mitchell
Framingham State College
Henry Whittemore Library
Framingham, Massachusetts

Karen Bosch Cobb
Fresno County Library
Fresno, California

Great Falls Public Library
Great Falls, Montana

Greenville Public Library
Smithfield, Rhode Island

Highline Community College
Highline Community College Library
Des Moines, Washington

Louise S. Sherby
Hunter College City University of New York
Hunter College City University of New York
    Libraries
New York, New York

Indiana University—Purdue University Fort Wayne
Walter E. Helmke Library
Fort Wayne, Indiana

Indiana University South Bend
Franklin D. Schurz Library
South Bend, Indiana

Jefferson County Public Library
Lakewood, Colorado

Johns Hopkins University
Sheridan Libraries
Baltimore, Maryland

Chung Sook Kim
Johns Hopkins University
William H. Welch Medical Library
Baltimore, Maryland

Dr. Charles D. Hanson
Kettering University
Kettering University Library
Flint, Michigan

Lafayette Public Library
Lafayette, Louisiana

William H. Teschek and Bobb Menk
Lane Memorial Library
Hampton, New Hampshire

Diane Courtney
Larchmont Public Library
Larchmont, New York

Lehigh University Libraries
Lending Services
Bethlehem, Pennsylvania

Scott L. Shafer
Lima Public Library
Lima, Ohio

Long Beach City College
Long Beach City College Library
Long Beach, California

Long Island University/ C. W. Post Campus
B. Davis Schwartz Memorial Library
Brookville, New York

Wendell A. Barbour
Longwood University
Janet D. Greenwood Library
Farmville, Virginia

Barbara L. Dimick
Madison Public Library
Madison, Wisconsin

Manitowoc Public Library
Manitowoc, Wisconsin

Pamela A. Price
Mercer County Community College
Mercer County Community College Library
West Windsor, New Jersey

Clifford H. Haka
Michigan State University
Michigan State University Libraries
East Lansing, Michigan

Thomas M. Jones
Middle Georgia Regional Library
Macon, Georgia

Scott R. Anderson
Millersville University
Helen A. Ganser Library
Millersville, Pennsylvania

Beth Fisher
MOBIUS Consortium Office
Columbia, Missouri

Montana State University
Renne Library
Bozeman, Montana

Moraine Valley Community College
Robert E. Turner Library
Palos Hills, Illinois

Board of Trustees, Morton Grove Public Library
Morton Grove Public Library
Morton Grove, Illinois

Naperville Public Library
Naperville, Illinois

Neill Public Library
Pullman, Washington

Michele M. Reid
North Dakota State University
North Dakota State University Libraries
Fargo, North Dakota

Ed Salazar
Northcentral University
Northcentral University Library
Prescott Valley, Arizona

Mary Louise Foster
Northeast Community College
Northeast Community College Library
Norfolk, Nebraska

Northwestern University
Courtesy Northwestern University Library
Evanston, Illinois

Orbis Cascade Alliance
Eugene, Oregon

Linda Sickles
Orion Township Public Library
Lake Orion, Michigan

Orland Park Public Library
Orland Park, Illinois

Ouachita Parish Public Library
Monroe, Louisiana

Owensboro Community and Technical College
Owensboro Community and Technical College
    Library
Owensboro, Kentucky

City of Pasadena
Pasadena Public Library
Pasadena, California

Amanda Maple
Pennsylvania State University
Pennsylvania State University Libraries
University Park, Pennsylvania

Pickaway County District Public Library
Circleville, Ohio

Edra Waterman
Plainfield-Guilford Township Public Library
Plainfield, Indiana

Porter County Public Library System
Valparaiso, Indiana

Donna Reed
Portland Community College
Portland Community College Library
Portland, Oregon

Carlton Sears
Public Library of Youngstown and Mahoning
    County
Youngstown, Ohio

Nancy Miller
River Falls Public Library
River Falls, Wisconsin

Jonathan Miller
Rollins College
Olin Library
Winter Park, Florida

Rutgers University
Rutgers University Libraries
New Brunswick, New Jersey

Randy A. De Soto
Saint John the Baptist Parish Library
LaPlace, Louisiana

Gail M. Staines, PhD
Saint Louis University
Pius XII Memorial Library
Saint Louis, Missouri

Brad Neufeldt
Saint Mary's University College
Saint Mary's University College Library
Calgary, Alberta, Canada

Deborah Robinson
Saint Petersburg College
M. M. Bennett Library
Saint Petersburg, Florida

Sandusky Library
Sandusky, Ohio

Joylene Campbell
Saskatchewan Provincial Library
Regina, Saskatchewan, Canada

The Seattle Public Library
Seattle, Washington

Barbra Nadler
Sharon Public Library
Sharon, Massachusetts

Jay Field, Vice President Technology and Learning Resources
Solano Community College
Solano Community College Library
Fairfield, California

Valerie Sommer
South San Francisco Public Library
South San Francisco, California

State Library and Archives of Florida
Tallahassee, Florida

Lynda Reynolds
Stillwater Public Library
Stillwater, Oklahoma

Tacoma Public Library
Tacoma, Washington

Carol Bailey
Talbot Belmond Public Library
Belmond, Iowa

Tempe Public Library
Tempe, Arizona

Texas A&M Corpus Christi
Texas A&M Corpus Christi Library
Corpus Christi, Texas

Texas State Library and Archives Commission
Austin, Texas

Alkek Library Reference Librarian Staff
Texas State University San Marcos
Albert B. Alkek Library
San Marcos, Texas

Donald H. Dyal
Texas Tech University
Texas Tech University Libraries
Lubbock, Texas

Thomas Jefferson University
Scott Memorial Library
Philadelphia, Pennsylvania

Toronto Public Library
Toronto, Ontario, Canada

Laura Walters
Tufts University
Tisch Library
Medford, Massachusetts

Lance Query
Tulane University
Howard-Tilton Memorial Library
New Orleans, Louisiana

The University of Akron
University Libraries
Akron, Ohio

University of Alberta
University of Alberta Libraries
Edmonton, Alberta, Canada

Gary Freiburger/Arizona Board of Regents
University of Arizona
Arizona Health Sciences Library
Tucson, Arizona

Jan Hart
University of Arkansas for Medical Sciences
University of Arkansas for Medical Sciences Library
Little Rock, Arkansas

Thomas C. Leonard
University of California Berkeley
University of California Berkeley Libraries
Berkeley, California

Library and Center for Knowledge Management
University of California San Francisco
San Francisco, California

Map & Imagery Laboratory, Davidson Library
University of California, Santa Barbara
Santa Barbara, California

Yem Fong
University of Colorado
University of Colorado Libraries
Boulder, Colorado

Marian D. Farley
University of Connecticut
University of Connecticut Libraries
Storrs, Connecticut

Kathleen Webb
University of Dayton
Roesch Library
Dayton, Ohio

Paula T. Kaufman
University of Illinois at Urbana-Champaign
University Libraries
Urbana, Illinois

The University of Iowa
The University of Iowa Libraries
Iowa City, Iowa

Lorraine J. Haricombe
University of Kansas
University of Kansas Library
Lawrence, Kansas

University of Maryland
University of Maryland Libraries
College Park, Maryland

M. J. Tooey
University of Maryland, Baltimore
Health Sciences and Human Services Library
Baltimore, Maryland

Katy Sullivan and Uta Hussong
University of Maryland Baltimore County
Albin O. Kuhn Library and Gallery
Baltimore, Maryland

Dr. Daniel Ortiz
University of Massachusetts Boston
Joseph P. Healey Library
Boston, Massachusetts

University of Miami Libraries
Otto G. Richter Library
Coral Gables, Florida

Paul N. Courant
University of Michigan
University of Michigan Library
Ann Arbor, Michigan

University of Minnesota
University of Minnesota Libraries
Minneapolis, Minnesota

Dr. James Clotfelter
The University of North Carolina at Greensboro
Information Technology Services
Greensboro, North Carolina

University of North Texas
University Libraries
Denton, Texas

University of Northern Iowa
Rod Library
Cedar Falls, Iowa

Jennifer Younger
University of Notre Dame
Hesburgh Libraries
Notre Dame, Indiana

Leslie Weir
University of Ottawa
University of Ottawa Library
Ottawa, Ontario, Canada

University of Oregon
University of Oregon Libraries
Eugene, Oregon

Daniel R. Gjelten
University of Saint Thomas
University Libraries
Saint Paul, Minnesota

Gerald Saxon
University of Texas at Arlington
University of Texas at Arlington Libraries
Arlington, Texas

Merry Burlingham
University of Texas at Austin
Research Services Division
University of Texas Libraries
Austin, Texas

Robert L Stakes
University of Texas El Paso
University Library
El Paso, Texas

John C. McCance
University of the Southwest
Scarborough Memorial Library
Hobbs, New Mexico

Marcia Krautter Suter
The University of Toledo
Carlson Library
Toledo, Ohio

Gretchen N. Arnold
University of Virginia
University of Virginia Health Sciences Library
Charlottesville, Virginia

Lizabeth A. Wilson
University of Washington
University of Washington Libraries
Seattle, Washington

Reference Department
University of West Florida
University of West Florida Libraries
Pensacola, Florida

Maggie Farrell
University of Wyoming
University Libraries
Laramie, Wyoming

W. Walworth Harrison Public Library
Greenville, Texas

Marlys Rudeen
Washington State Library
Olympia, Washington

Wasilla Public Library
Wasilla, Alaska

Karen Albury
Westerville Public Library
Westerville, Ohio

Wisconsin Valley Library Service
Wausau, Wisconsin

Meribah Mansfield
Worthington Libraries
Worthington, Ohio

Part I
Administration

Chapter 1

ELECTRONIC RESOURCES PLANS

GOALS AND OBJECTIVES

Cabrillo College
Robert E. Swenson Library
Aptos, California

Goals and strategies for the Library:

Goal 1: Create sustainable, robust and reliable systems for delivering information resources within a Common User Interface environment

Strategies:

- Upgrade as needed the hardware and operating systems of workstations and servers.
- Upgrade as needed the software used in the delivery of information resources.
- Ensure connectivity for all users
- Explore secure network infrastructure for provision of laptop access to the network within the library building.
- Create a spares inventory for technology and media equipment to minimize disruptions in service and staff work environments.
- Explore debit card readers for non-subscription resources and for pay-for-print services.
- Review on an ongoing basis the sustainability of information workstations and servers in the library. Submit plans for and costs of upgrades to all potential campus funding options.
- Review on an ongoing basis the plug-in configuration for public access workstations

Goal 2: Provide access to non-print resources

Strategies:

- Expand the core of electronic resources as appropriate to support the instruction program at the College.
- Provide for purchasing non computer media in support of instruction.
- Study and make plans for including DVD media and converting to Universal Players for delivery systems.
- Provide for the delivery of video to group rooms in the library.
- Work with instructors to pursue the expansion of Computer Aided Instruction into a supported delivery center.
- Work with instructors to pursue the purchase of software for Computer Aided Instruction
- Add Machine Readable Cataloging (MARC) records to the library catalog for campus owned resources available elsewhere. For example:
- Software available in CTC, TLC
- Audiotape and Video collection in Music Lab
- Children's materials in ECE collections

Goal 3: Support the technological needs of the library's instruction and information literacy program

Strategies:

- Monitor the development of wireless technology for its usefulness to the future delivery of information resources within the library.
- Provide a state of the art library classroom for information literacy sessions.
- Provide Cabrillo instructors with training and assistance for integrating information resources into the curriculum.
- Develop web based tutorials
- Develop courses for delivery over the internet
- Pursue emerging technologies that improve and expand student learning opportunities

Goal 4: Provide timely services to remote users (students, staff and instructors at home; Watsonville Center; SLV Center; Distance Education offerings)

Strategies:

- Provide online ability to generate an interlibrary loan request
- Provide online ability to recommend items for purchase
- Expand reserve services to include scanning and digitizing materials for faculty
- Provide access to electronic reserves
- Plan for the provision of direct and indirect library services at the Wattsonville Center

Goal 5: Provide services to students with special needs

Strategies:

- Where feasible convert all remaining 15" monitors (student and staff) to 17" monitors.
- Provide a second OMNI 3000 Kurzweil reading system
- Review the effectiveness of selected software and maintain the currency of assistive technology software for web access
- Achieve full accessibility of library web pages (meet WAI standards)
- Standardize Web page construction software in the library
- Explore providing a Lynx browser for visually challenged users
- Expand the number of adjustable height workstations to 10% of the available

Goal 6: Support Library Staff Resources and Library Staff Development

Strategies:

- Support a staff intranet that encompasses all active policies and procedures.
- Secure additional staff to support the library technology environment
- Ensure minimally disruptive new technology rollouts through careful planning, timing and training
- Establish an annual review of efficiency of staff workstations and create a staged replacement policy for worn or dated equipment.
- Provide ongoing technical training / retraining for librarians and staff.
- Support conference attendance and training seminars in emerging technologies for staff and librarians.

Goal 7: Secure stable Monetary Resources

Strategies:

- Secure funding for additional staff to support growth of technology services.
- Secure funding for a spares inventory.
- Secure funding for supplies and equipment to support innovations.

- Secure funding to support staff and librarian professional development.
- Secure base budget funding to support the commitment to online full text resources.
- Secure funding for appropriately staged replacement of all workstations as they reach their capacity to deliver.

Greenville Public Library
Smithfield, Rhode Island

Goals, Objectives, and Activities

A. Provide free public access to electronic information resources on the Internet.
    1. To maintain public access computers, especially those with wireless access and laptops. Maintenance schedule, including laptop battery charging is followed.
    2. To continue to loan laptop computers, with wireless Internet and printing capability, to adults for use within the library.
    3. To maintain wireless Internet access and printing within the Library building for our equipment and the public's laptops.
    4. To make available and offer access to a variety of database and e-books that meet the public's need for information. These are available remotely on the library webpage 24 hours a day.
B. Provide free public access to electronic information available on CD-ROM.
    1. The general trend is away from CD-ROM technology and toward databases available via the World Wide Web. Staff will keep abreast of new technology for CD-ROM delivery. At the same time the virtual CD-Rom server will be maintained to assure public access to CD-ROM products. CD products are evaluated annually in January.
    2. To continue to create CD-ROM's which hold the images of materials that are too fragile to let the public use, and make them available to the public.
C. Promote and facilitate access to electronic information sites through the library's home page on the World Wide Web.
    1. To utilize the home page as an information provider by allowing Smithfield residents free access via the home page to library subscription databases, and free databases on the Internet via links. Links are checked monthly.
    2. To provide videoconferences and video access to Library staff via the home page by June 2005.
    3. To maintain 24 hour e-mail reference service and live-chat with reference librarians using Ask Your Library.orgl
    4. To maintain Tutor.com, which is a virtual tutoring service available after school on weekdays via the Library's Web page. It was begun in October 2003.
D. Educate staff and the community on the use of electronic information technology.
    1. To continue to educate library staff on new technologies and software available at the library. There will be at least $500 included in the budget annually for staff education and the technology coordinator will provide at staff workshops and well as individual training as needed.
    2. To offer at least four computer classes per year to adults, utilizing the homework center and its equipment during the fiscal year (July-June).
    3. To offer streaming video instructional movies available via the Library's web site, made by the staff, by May 2006.
    4. Promote homework center to the community for use by non-profit and government agencies (free) and businesses (for a fee) for teleconferencing, computer training, and programs requiring computer projection.
    5. To make available audio books via the library web page by January 2006.

E. Facilitate staff communication.
    1. All staff have e-mail accounts and are trained to use e-mail client software and to attach documents.
    2. Videoconferencing for staff to communicate with other libraries and agencies and to communicate with this Library is available.
    3. Maintain Web based media ordering with shared ordering folders.

F. Secure electronic files and programs by regular back-ups.
    1. Weekly back-ups of all staff files on office computers are made automatically using Retrospect. Checked daily.
    2. The file server is backed up via a tape drive nightly.
    3. There are secondary back-ups made at regular intervals and taken off the premises.

I. Maintain system.
    1. To replace public and staff computers that are more than four years old. We are forced to transition to Windows operating machines by the Champlin Foundations' requirement for obtaining computer grants. The technology coordinator will make sure the transition is seamless and not disruptive. Wireless Macintosh computers will be used as long as possible, to save on the inconvenience and cost of wiring. Other grant sources will be sought to pay for wireless machines that have internal wireless cards.
    2. To keep at least three spare computers and monitors and maintain ghosted images of each computer configuration.

Solano Community College
Solano Community College Library
Fairfield, California

The library has adopted the following objectives to achieve its information technology goals:
- Maintain an automated library system with broad functionality.
- Share the automated library system with other libraries in the area.
- Participate in a governance agreement for cooperative information technology programs.
- Seek to conform to all relevant standards and legal requirements.
- Maintain an "electronic access center" for use by library patrons.
- Use only PCs as remote peripherals, and utilize a multi-tier PC strategy.
- Configure all of the PCs, existing and future, with a Web browser.
- Monitor bandwidth requirements and make adjustments as needed.
- Provide access to a CD-ROM server from all workstations.
- Maintain staff training and patron orientation programs.
- Maintain a bibliographic instruction lab.
- Maintain a spares inventory.
- Use competitive bidding for online reference services.
- Avoid proliferation of the same information in multiple formats.
- Upgrade staff work surfaces to accommodate information technologies.
- Accommodate information technologies when building or remodeling library facilities.
- Maintain an electronic security system.
- Seek funding from external sources.
- Phase in implementation over a four-year period.

These components are discussed in detail on the following pages.

1. Maintain an automated library system with broad functionality.

   The library will maintain an automated library system which supports the internal automation of acquisitions with online ordering; serials control with online claiming; cataloging with authority control and bibliographic utility interface; circulation with off-line back-up, patron telephone and e-mail notification, and telephone renewal; patron access catalog; Z39.50-based linkages to other automated library systems; and interlibrary loan.

   Staff productivity in small libraries usually is not improved when acquisitions and serials control are automated. The automation of acquisitions and serials control will be undertaken in fiscal year 2000/2001 if SNAP, the consortium with which the library shares its automated library system, makes the modules available by then. Automating acquisitions will allow library staff and patrons to determine what is on order regardless of where they are. Patrons will be able to place hold requests so that they will be notified as soon as the needed materials have been received and processed. Automating serials control will allow library staff and patrons to determine the most recent issue received of any serial subscription, and whether a specific issue for which is citation has been found is held and currently available. There is no additional software licensing cost for the acquisitions and serials control functionality.

   Online ordering and claiming will be implemented, but only when EDIFACT is adopted by the book jobbers and subscription agents used by the libraries. EDIFACT is an international standard which links the automated systems of libraries and their suppliers. The industry has been slow to implement EDIFACT because there has been confusion about two older, now obsolete standards: BISAC online ordering and EDI x.12 online claiming. EDIFACT will probably be implemented in fiscal year 2001/2002, or later if CARL, the vendor of the automated library system, or SNAP, does not make it available by then. The cost has not yet been determined.

   The cataloging module will be linked to a bibliographic utility—OCLC for the foreseeable future. If some books are supplied pre-processed, the book wholesaler will be asked to log onto the system and transfer machine-readable records online by FTP, rather than sending records periodically on magnetic media.

   The database will be complete, including not only the book collection, but also bibliographic records for periodicals, course reserves, non-print materials, and electronic resources. The major cost in completing the database is staff time. The target date for completion is the end of fiscal year 2002/2003.

   Circulation will be configured with off-line back-up so that the library can continue to charge and discharge library materials when the host or server is not available. The cost for circulation back-up may be as high as $1,500 unless the library can take advantage of a site license agreement. The implementation will be sought in 2000/2001 as the system will be more vulnerable to failure as it ages.

   Circulation will also include patron telephone and e-mail notification for overdues and recalls. Telephone renewal will be made available. The additional cost is not yet known, therefore, a decision about implementation will be deferred.

   The library will seek to utilize a graphical user interface (GUI) for all staff modules as this has been shown to increase staff productivity. The additional cost is not yet known, but information will be sought from SNAP no later than fiscal year 2000/2001.

   The patron access catalog will be configured with a Web-based user interface as this type of interface is more intuitive than a text-based user interface. The Web-based user interface also has the advantage of being familiar to many users because of its use with the Internet, and it allows a common user interface to a number of sources of electronic information. The text-based user interface will be phased out when the vendor of the automated library system ceases to support it—something that is expected to happen in the next two to three years. There is no additional software license charge for this functionality, but it does require the continued use of PCs as remote peripherals.

Z39.50 linkages will be maintained with other automated library systems. It will be augmented with SuperSearch, an interlibrary loan system maintained by the North Bay Cooperative Library System. At such time as Z39.50 linkages mature and interlibrary loan modules become available from CARL and the vendors of the other systems in the area, it may not be necessary to use SuperSearch.

Rather than maintaining a community information module (also known as information & referral) so that staff and patrons will know which agencies in the community provide what services to whom, and on what terms, the library will rely on campus agencies to place their information on the College's Web site and will rely on the public libraries in the area to provide information about community-based agencies.

Other modules will be considered, but they must be demonstrated to be cost and/or service effective before an investment will be made in them.

The library will emphasize that its reason for automating its internal operations is to improve service to patrons, not to reduce costs. A major way of improving services is to provide rapid access to the resources of the library regardless of where the library user is at the time of the search.

2. Share the automated library system with other libraries in the area.

    Rather than maintaining its own automated library system, the library will share a system with the other academic and public libraries of the area. That will not only make it possible for someone in any library to see the resources of all of the libraries of the area, but will also facilitate the movement of patrons among the public and community college libraries. The library will seek to emphasize its own resources; those of its partner libraries will complement the Solana College collection.

    When software becomes available which allows local holdings to be displayed first, the library will take advantage of it.

    The library will maintain a membership in SNAP, a regional consortium of four public and two community college libraries, which operates a CARL automated library system with broad functionality. The system is located at the Solano County Library. The SCC Library is connected to the central site via a 128 KPBS frame relay circuit. SNAP provides a higher level of staffing for the system than the library could afford on its own. SNAP also maintains a reserve fund so that system upgrades do not require major capital outlays.

    Not only do the libraries participate in sharing an automated library system, they also undertake other cooperative programs through SNAP, including resource sharing and joint subscriptions to online reference services. SNAP is beginning to develop a training program for library staffs.

3. Participate in a governance agreement for cooperative information technology programs.

    Libraries which share information technologies need a written agreement among them which spells out their rights and obligations. The library wishes to be flexible in the content of such an agreement, but has adopted the following terms which it believes should be incorporated for such an agreement:

    a. The automated library system shall consist of all central site hardware and software (CPU, disk drives, tape drives, UPS, etc.), telecommunications network, and remote peripherals (PCs, side printers, light pens, etc.) necessary for the libraries to support their internal operations and access remote electronic resources.

    b. The central site and telecommunications network shall be owned by the consortium; remote peripherals-which is that hardware and software in the individual libraries connected to the telecommunications network C shall be owned by the individual libraries.

    c. The designated service bureau shall be responsible for housing and operating the central site and telecommunications network-a service for which it shall recover reasonable operating costs from the participating libraries.

d. The procurement of hardware and software for the central site and telecommunications network shall be the responsibility of the service bureau.

e. The procurement of the remote peripherals shall be the responsibility of the individual participating libraries. Remote peripherals shall be owned by the individual participating libraries.

f. All applications software modules (acquisitions, serials control, cataloging, circulation, patron access catalog, etc.) available from the vendor selected shall be made available on the automated library system if any one of the participating libraries requires it. However, no participating library shall have to share financial responsibility for the purchase or maintenance of a specialized software module which only one or two participating libraries use.

g. The purchase price of central site hardware and software, and the telecommunications network, shall be apportioned among the participating libraries on the basis of the number of concurrent user licenses they require or another formula agreed upon by the participating libraries.

h. The service bureau shall be responsible for keeping the central site hardware and software, and the telecommunications network under maintenance, including field-maintenance support from the automated library system vendor or a third-party maintenance organization, at least 8:00 a.m. to 5:00 p.m. (local time) weekdays.

i. The maintenance charges for the central site hardware and software, and the telecommunications network, shall be allocated among the participating libraries on the basis of the number of concurrent user licenses they require or another formula agreed upon by the participating libraries. However, no participating library shall be required to pay for the maintenance of hardware or software which it does not use.

j. The service bureau shall be responsible for operating the central site all of the hours any of the participating libraries is open to its users, including evenings and weekends.

k. The service bureau shall have an operator available at the central site between the hours of 8:00 a.m. and 5:00 p.m. daily. The operator need not be dedicated to the automated library system.

l. The service bureau shall have an operator on call by telephone or pager during those hours that any one of the participating libraries is open to its users outside the 8:00 a.m. to 5:00 p.m. weekdays period.

m. The cost of operation of the central site-which shall include the cost of the operators' wages and benefits pro-rated among the automated library system and other systems for which they are responsible; floor space rental; and management overhead shall be allocated among the participating libraries on the basis of the number of concurrent user licenses they require or another formula agreed upon by the participants.

n. A participating library which seeks to withdraw from the Agreement prior to five years of participation shall not be reimbursed for its share of the value of the automated library system unless one or more other libraries is prepared to purchase the capacity surrendered.

o. A participating library which seeks to withdraw from the Agreement prior to five years of participation shall be reimbursed for the amount of its initial capital contribution toward the central site hardware and telecommunications network purchase, less 2 percent per month of system use, if one or more other libraries has agreed to purchase the capacity surrendered.

p. If additional libraries are accepted for participation, they shall be required to pay the same amount for central site hardware and software, and telecommunications network, per concurrent user, or other formula agreed upon by the participants, that the original participants have paid. The amount in excess of the incremental cost of adding these libraries shall be distributed among the initial participating libraries as credits toward future financial obligations in proportion to the number of concurrent user licenses each hold or another formula agreed upon by the participants.

4. Seek to conform to all relevant standards and legal requirements.

    Conformity to all relevant standards is a high priority. All cataloging will conform to the Anglo-American Cataloging Code, Second Edition (AACR2). The database of the automated library system will be developed and maintained in full-MARC format, including bibliographic, authority, holdings, and patron records.

    The vendor of the automated library system will be required to conform to EDIFACT (ISO 9735) for online ordering and claiming. It will also be required to commit to conformity to the Z39.50 linking standard and the Z39.63 interlibrary loan standard (or ISO 10160 and 10161). The library will also expect conformity to the Z39.70 format for circulation transactions within a year of the time it is published.

    The automated library system must support the TCP/IP network protocol and the SMTP electronic mail protocol. The automated library system and the network must conform to IEEE standard 802.3 for 100 Mbps data transmission over Category 5 UTP (unshielded twisted pair) wire and the TIA/EIA 568A95 standard for cable installation.

    UNICODE compliance will be sought to facilitate multi-lingual user interfaces.

    The library will seek to comply with all legal requirements, including the guidelines of the Americans with Disabilities Act (ADA).

5. Maintain an "electronic access center" for use by library patrons.

    An "electronic access center" will be maintained for use by library patrons. It consists of a cluster of PCs which provide access to the patron access catalog and a variety of electronic publications, whether mounted on the local automated library system, local CD-ROM towers, another library's platform, or an online reference service. The resources accessible through the center will complement the library's print collection, rather than replace it. While the most widely consulted electronic publications today are indexes and the full-text of journal articles, an increasingly wider range of electronic sources of information is becoming available.

    The Internet, especially that part of it known as the Worldwide Web, will be available from the "electronic access center," but the emphasis will be on identifying the most appropriate sites, rather than facilitating aimless "surfing." While frequently used useful sites may be identified by an icon, the vast majority will be cataloged and searchable through the patron access catalog. A subject or keyword search will retrieve a bibliographic record for the URL and a "hot link" will make it possible to access the site. The American Library Association has identified nearly 1,000 useful sites and the OCLC database has machine-readable records for almost all of them. Given staff constraints, it may require an externally funded special project to launch the URL cataloging effort.

    The "electronic access center" will be near the reference desk so that staff will be able to observe users who are having difficulty. There will be no fewer than one PC for each 25 persons, or significant fraction thereof, entering the library in the course of a day. As of early 1999, 16 PCs were required.

    Ideally, each PC in the center will have its own side printer, with each PC printer configured with a debit card reader to recover the cost of the printer, paper, and other supplies. Not only is it annoying to have to wait for copies printed on a network printer, but it is confusing when printed pages for two or more patrons cannot be easily differentiated. Network printing, while more convenient for a library to administer, does not offer patrons the level of convenience to which they are entitled. A debit card machine can measure the number of pages, and allows the rate to be adjusted as needed. When configured to accommodate credit cards, the amount to be charged will be determined by the service which the patron accesses.

    Given the high cost of debit card readers ($500-750 each), the library will not consider this approach until the predicted sharp reduction in debit card reader prices occurs. Until then, one or more networked laser printers will be used. When debit card readers are purchased, they will also be installed on photocopiers and microform printers.

Patrons will be allowed to download to their own diskettes, but not allowed to load their software onto these machines.

Security, while a concern, has not been a major problem for libraries. Nevertheless, each PC will be configured with Centurion Guard, Fortress, or another PC security product which controls access to the PCs operating system and utilities. Except for library staff, access to the automated library system will be limited to the patron access catalog. CD-ROM server software is limited and, if properly backed up, can be reloaded in a very short time. The CD-ROMs are not erasable.

The "electronic access center" will be configured to support multimedia access. Multimedia is a combination of television, personal computing, and optical storage, such as CD-ROM or Laserdisc. An enhanced PC which conforms to the multimedia standards can retrieve not only bibliographic files, but also full-text files, still images, audio, and motion images. Audio listening will require earphones, rather than speakers.

The library will equip the "electronic access center" with high-end PCs, typically a model which is at the third-level. It is this level which generally offers the best price/performance. For example, if the latest technology were a Pentium 450, the library would purchase Pentium 350 machines.

At least two "electronic access center" workstations will be ADA compliant, including zoom text, a second keyboard with large keys, and audio with headset.

Insofar as space and available funds permit, PCs will be installed in carrels 48 to 52 inches wide and 30 inches deep. This size provides sufficient space for PCs and printers, in addition to user books and personal possessions. At least two of the carrels will have work surfaces which can be adjusted to accommodate wheelchairs.

The PCs, which will cost $2,000 each or $32,000 for 16, will be acquired as part of general College PC procurements, and will be maintained under the College's general technology support program. Carrels for the "electronic access center" will cost approximately $1,000 each, or $16,000.

6. Use only PCs as remote peripherals, and utilize a multi-tier PC strategy.

"Dumb" terminals—remote peripherals without memory—on the automated library system will not be used on the automated library system. Now that high-end Pentium PCs with printers have dropped to as little as $2,000, it is realistic to use PCs in lieu of $600 terminals. There are two reasons for doing so: PCs can support a wider range of tasks than "dumb" terminals, and the vendors of automated library systems are redesigning their systems to support only PCs as remote peripherals. The redesign will make it possible for the remote peripherals to control the "presentation" of the information on the screen.

"Third-level" PCs, those which are two levels below the highest priced machines, will be specified. In early 1999 that is the Pentium 350 with 32 MB of memory. In fiscal year 2000/2001 the Pentium 400 with 64 MB is expected to be the "third-level" machine. Each will be Multimedia enabled, and will include a Web browser. Insofar as possible, each PC will be configured with a side printer. A three-year onsite warranty will be required.

As new PCs are purchased they will be installed in the "electronic access center" and the machines replaced will be reallocated to other applications which require less robust machines. Typical of such applications is word processing. Older PCs will also be used for circulation charge and discharge—an activity which involves no substantial movement of data. The expectation is that machines will remain in the "electronic access center" for no more than three years.

No more than half of the machines are expected to be usable after five years. The rest will be cannibalized for parts. The machines will be declared salvage after a total of six years regardless of condition.

As of early 1999, the library required a total of 46-48 PCs, all but three of them at least Pentium II/350s. The distribution was two in technical services, three in reference, one in the circulation/reserve office, two in administration, 16 in the "electronic access center," and 19-21 in the bibliographic instruction lab. Three less robust machines were required for circulation charge and discharge. Only two high-end machines were available, as well as the three machines needed for circulation charge and discharge. The 19-21 PCs for the bibliographic instruction lab had been budgeted. The shortfall, therefore, was 22 high-end PCs.

Twenty-two machines will be purchased in fiscal 2000/2001 at a cost of $44,000, $32,000 of which has been included in objective 5. Machines equal to no fewer than 25 percent of the total number deployed will be purchased each year thereafter. The estimated cost is $24,000 per year.

7. Configure all of the PCs, existing and future, with a Web browser.

There is a strong trend toward Web-based user interfaces. Almost all vendors of automated library systems have introduced a Web-based patron access catalog, and many plan to introduce Web-based user interfaces for other modules by 2000. Many online reference services and CD-ROM publishers are also changing to a Web-based user interfaces. The prospect for a common user interface for a wide variety of electronic products and services by 2000 is very good.

CARL's Everybody's Menu Builder will continue to be used. The number of icons on the first screen will be limited, and the Internet will be de-emphasized. Instead, Web sites will be "selected" just as books and periodicals, and icons or pull-down menus will be provided for those which are considered particularly useful. Other useful URLs will be cataloged when resources permit.

Consideration will be given to having the first screen of the "electronic access center" machines provide users the option of specifying the broad subject area of their inquiry: business, consumer affairs, environment, history, literature, science, etc. The next screen will provide the options, with no emphasis on the source of the information: CD-ROM, Web-site, etc. Interdisciplinary resources such as general encyclopedias will appear on each screen.

The cost of moving to Web-based user interfaces is incorporated in the purchase prices of the PCs.

It will be necessary to maintain a Web server in the automated library system to provide access from Web browsers, both within a library and coming in through a Web home page. This need not be separate hardware, but does require software. The software will make it possible to require the entry of a patron ID to gain access to electronic products and services, therefore, limiting such access to registered patrons. The library will seek to use the PIN number required for online registration to authenticate users. This will be a major step forward to providing students participating in distance learning with the same electronic resources as those on the campuses.

The library will consider purchasing "Internet Watchdog," a software package from Charles River Media of Rockland, MA or a similar product for recording the number of times each application, product, or service has been accessed via the Web browser. This will make it possible to determine which resources are most used. This is particularly important in the case of resources for which the library pays a subscription fee. [If the online reference service provides usage data, it will be possible to verify the accuracy of the data]. The cost of the software will be $29.95 per PC. It may be possible to negotiate a site license.

8. Monitor bandwidth requirements and make adjustments as needed.

The number of PCs in the library and their use, including access to the shared automated library system and the Internet, requires an increasing amount of bandwidth. Increasingly, Web sites are adding color, motion, and audio, each requiring additional bandwidth.

The library currently is connected to the automated library system's central site via a 128 Mpbs circuit. Given the fact that half or more of the 46-48 PCs the library will soon have may be accessing the automated library system at one time, there is a need to increase the bandwidth to 256 Kbps. Alternately, all of the PCs in the bibliographic instruction lab will access the system via the Internet. In that case, additional bandwidth will be required for Internet access.

The library will seek to provide an average of 56 Kbps per Internet user. Assuming that as many as half of the library's 46-48 PCs will be accessing the Internet at any one time, there is a need for a T-1 circuit no later than 2001. The cost may be as high as $6,000 per year. At the point that it has 60 PCs installed, but in no event later than 2003, the library will reexamine its bandwidth requirements.

9. Provide access to a CD-ROM server from all workstations.

Electronic publications on CD-ROM will continue to be acquired as some publishers offer only that medium, and others offer more favorable pricing for CD-ROM products than for online services. Insofar as licensing restrictions and prices permit, they will be mounted on a CD-ROM server and made accessible from throughout the campus, and from off-campus. If licensing restrictions or prices make it more cost effective to limit access to the library or the campus that will be done.

If response times for popular titles—especially multimedia titles—deteriorate, one or more 9.0GB hard disks will be connected to the CD-ROM server, and the content of the titles loaded onto it. This will increase the number of concurrent users who can be accommodated and improve response times.

The library's present CD-ROM equipment was purchased in 1996. It will be obsolete by fiscal year 2000/2001. Before that time, CD-ROM drives rated at less than 32x will be replaced as needed with 32x drives—the speed which offers the best price/performance.

A new CD-ROM server will be purchased in fiscal year 2000/2001. It will be specified as "self configuring," meaning that it can be directly connected to a network without having to spend time configuring it. The cost will be approximately $6,500.

10. Maintain staff training and patron orientation programs.

As systems become more complex, staff training increases in importance. Not only will the library purchase staff training from the vendor of each system or product at time of initial purchase, but it will budget for refresher training each year. The typical automated library system requires two days of on-site training per module; refresher training typically is one-half day per module. The cost is approximately $1,500 per day, or $3,000 for refresher training in the core modules.

Training will be limited to groups of six as that provides both hands-on experience and close monitoring by the trainer. If more than six staff need to be trained, the library will have the vendor train a core group, and have that group train the others. That core group will also train new staff as they are hired.

Online reference services also provide training, but it usually is done regionally, rather than on-site at a library. The library will seek to send a group of two to six staff to such training, and will have that group train the others.

CD-ROM products generally come without training, therefore, the library will assign a staff member to become familiar with each product using the manual and hands-on practice. The staff member will then be asked to demonstrate the product to other staff members.

The library will provide regular orientation sessions for patrons. These will be limited to 18-20 persons and will include an overview of the automated library system, the Internet, and CD-ROMs, and the basics of library research in a mixed print and electronic environment. Skills in using specific electronic resources will also be taught. As much as possible, orientation will be undertaken in conjunction with a class assignment and the cooperation of the course instructor. The purpose of the orientation program is "information competency," not "computer literacy." The latter is a College responsibility.

A special effort will be made to orient faculty to electronic resources. Each academic discipline will be invited as a unit to spend 75 minutes in the library for an overview of electronic resources in that academic area.

Other than library courses which are part of the curriculum, training programs will not be offered to patrons, but the library will maintain a roster of campus and community training opportunities.

11. Maintain a bibliographic instruction lab.

The library will maintain a bibliographic instruction lab in which to conduct its staff training, patron orientation, and formal instruction by library staff. It must be possible for classes to come into the library for a group assignment or for orientation without tying up all of the workstations in the library, therefore, a dedicated lab is required.

The present lab, which is outside the library's entrance and limited to word processing, may be retrofitted as an assessment testing center. The new bibliographic instruction lab will have a minimum of 18 to 20 workstations, plus an instructor's station. If space permits, it will be as large as 30 workstations. It will be within the library. Faculty at other community colleges which have bibliographic instruction labs have complained that it is difficult to work with a class when some are in the library and others in a lab away from the library. They wish to work with the entire class a group using all aspects of a library's resources.

While the workstations in the lab will have the same capabilities as those in the "electronic access centers," they will be in addition to the number required by the library attendance formula adopted by the library. The lab will have an instructor's workstation linked to a digital projector so that everyone in the room can see what is on the instructor's screen.

As of early 1999, funds were available for the establishment of the bibliographic instruction lab. The support of the hardware will be funded from the College's general technology support budget.

The bibliographic instruction lab will not be made available as an open lab. Instead, students will be referred to the large open lab being installed on the library's mezzanine. That lab is not planned to be under library control.

12. Maintain a spares inventory.

In order to minimize the impact of having equipment out for repair, especially when it ages, a spares inventory will be maintained. It will include at least two PC, two printers, two light pens or scanners, and one debit card reader at such time as they are installed on printers. When a failure occurs, the failed unit will be replaced from the spares inventory within one hour.

PCs in the spares inventory will be configured with all of the software used in the library. Security software will be used to restrict access to the applications which are suitable for the location in which the spare is placed.

A spares inventory, if established in 2001-2002, will cost approximately $6,000 to establish.

Insofar as possible, the staff member responsible for the bibliographic instruction lab will be responsible for all of the library's PCs. Other full-time library staff will not seek to undertake trouble shooting beyond reboots and clearing of paper jams, and will not repair equipment; instead, maintenance will be referred to the staff member responsible for the PCs. If he cannot resolve a problem in a time manner, repairs will be referred to the College's technology support center.

The library will train several student assistants to check PCs, remote components which are not working, and install working components. One appropriately qualified student assistant will be scheduled for each hour the library is open. Normally, the student assistant will be assigned to shelving library materials or working at the circulation desk, with release for PC hardware duty as needed. Software configuration will not be part of the responsibility of student assistants. Each PC will be configured with a "standard load" which can be turned on selectively using the remote PC management software controlled by the College's technology support center or by security software under the control of an authorized library staff member.

13. Use competitive bidding for online reference services.

The library cannot afford to purchase all of the online reference services which may be of interest to its patrons at their published prices, nor would it want to purchase those not used frequently enough to justify the subscription price. It will, therefore, seek to reduce the cost by undertaking competitive procurements and, insofar as possible, sharing the procurements with other libraries—including SNAP, the North Bay Cooperative Library System, and academic libraries statewide through the Community College League.

It is likely that an online reference service which provides access to the full-text of 1,500 or more periodicals will continue to be of wide interest to both academic and public libraries in the state. SNAP subscribes to EbscoHost, including its Master File, Health File, and Newspaper File. As of early 1999, the library augmented it with Ebsco Academic from its own funds. The sharing of that subscription will be pursued with other academic libraries. Other services which will be considered are those offered by Chadwyck-Healey, IAC, OCLC, OVID, UMI, and H.W. Wilson—several of which offer services which are similar in their content to EbscoHost and Ebsco Academic.

If no partner(s) can be found, the library will pursue a competitive procurement on its own.

While an online reference service provides full-text for many journal titles, many will continue to be supplied from the library's print collection. The identification of what is available from a library's own holdings is facilitated by the serials control module of the automated library system provided that the library maintain records for all of its subscriptions in the database. All holdings, including the most recent check-in information, will then be available to patrons and staff.

Costs for online reference services vary widely, but a useful "rule-of-thumb" is $.50 to $1.00 per anticipated use. As many as 10,000 uses per year are expected by fiscal year 2000/2001 at a cost of approximately $7,500, with a 25-30 percent per year increase thereafter.

14. Avoid proliferation of the same information in multiple formats.

Hundreds of titles are now available in multiple formats, including print, microform, and electronic. A primary format will be chosen for each title using criteria to be developed, and the purchase of the same title in another format will be avoided unless the level of use warrants the additional copy. While the best decision basis would appear to be the latest well established format, the decision has to be made in light of cost. The electronic format is not always the most cost effective. For example, a three-year back file of 300 popular periodicals may cost $30,000 to bind, counting in-house labor costs, plus $1,500 per year to service, for a total five-year cost of $37,500. Or it may cost $25,000 to purchase the same backfiles on microform, including equipment, plus $2,500 per year to service, for a total five-year cost of $37,500. But, the cost per year for the same information on CD-ROM, including the cost of equipment, would be $15,000—plus $3,000 per year for service, for a total five-year cost of $90,000. Access to the full-text of the same titles will be a minimum of $5,000 per year through an online reference service, for a total five-year cost of $25,000.

While an electronic format is the format of the future for many publications, the library will continue to purchase a great deal of printed material and some microform for the next decade.

15. Upgrade staff work surfaces to accommodate information technologies.

Staff who regularly access automated systems in their work cannot be expected to work efficiently at small desks and tables which are filled with PCs, printers, books, and notebooks. Each such staff member will be provided an ergonomically correct desk which has space for each piece of equipment and places the keyboard and monitor at the right visual height and reach. The standard is articulated in the College's Technology Plan.

The cost of upgrading existing workstations is estimated at $3,500. The upgrade will be undertaken in fiscal year 2002/2003.

16. Accommodate information technologies when building or remodeling library facilities.

A standard has already been adopted for data cabling within the library: Category 5 UTP (unshielded twisted pair) wiring which can accommodate data transmission rates of up to 100 Mbps. As new facilities are constructed or remodeling is undertaken, "premises wiring" will be required so that it will not be necessary to continually install wiring to locations where data access is needed.

The availability of "clean" electrical power in all areas where electronic equipment may be installed will also be required. This consists of installing separate conditioned electrical circuits.

It will be assumed that each staff member's desk and each staff member's workstation at a service counter will require a data outlet and a "clean" duplex electrical outlet. All carrels in a reference area will also require similar treatment. Group study rooms will also be wired.

Instructions to architects and/or contractors will specify that fenestration and lighting must minimize glare as glare on display screens is a major source of discomfort and inconvenience. All furniture and equipment must be of ergonomic design.

The cost of the rewiring—both data and electrical—will be approximately $75 per data jack or electrical outlet if undertaken during construction or remodeling; $200-300 if undertaken at another time.

17. Maintain an electronic security system.

Libraries are experiencing significant losses from their collections. It is, therefore, necessary to maintain an electronic security system at the library's entrance/exit.

The targets will be the type that requires de-magnetizing at time of check-out, and remagnetizing at time of check-in. Periodical issues will have targets randomly inserted at time of initial receipt.

An electronic security system does not eliminate losses completely, but anecdotal evidence suggests that the reduction in losses will be at least 50 percent, and as high as 70 percent; therefore, it is cost effective in almost all libraries which have a collection of more than 20,000 volumes.

As the system is already installed, the cost is limited to maintenance and targets for new materials—a total of approximately $750 per year.

Patron self-charging will be considered when the cost of the systems drops below the current price of $26,000 per station ($22,000 to 3M or Kingsley (manufacturers of the self-charging stations) and $3,000 to the vendor supplying the automated library system). Several vendors have begun to develop units which may be priced as low as $5,000. The installation has tentatively been scheduled for fiscal year 2003/2004.

By interfacing a circulation workstation to a "desensitizing" unit, it will be possible for patrons who have no renewals or fines to quickly charge materials and remove the charge on the target in side the materials.

18. Seek funding from external sources.

While it is not realistic to obtain general operating funds from any source other than a library's appropriating authority, there is reason to believe that external funding is available for the capital purchase of information technology and ongoing data communications costs.

Contact will be maintained with the state library agency to determine what funds may be available, and the requirements for applying. This may include both federal and state funds for capital purchases. It may also include some funds for ongoing data communications costs under the Universal Services Fund.

A special effort will be made to identify foundations by conducting an annual database search of foundations which have funded information technology for libraries in the past few years, especially those which have made such funding available in this area or to special needs groups which may be represented in the local population.

The library will adopt the grant application format developed by the National Network of Grant-makers, a consortium of more than 40 foundations which have agreed to a common grant application. The structure of the grant application is very similar to that of hundreds of other foundations, corporations, and federal agencies. It includes a summary sheet, a description of the organization submitting the application, a description of the request, a means for evaluating the success of the project, an overview of the organizational structure of the applicant, financial information, and supporting materials, including published articles about the organization. By adopting this application as "boilerplate," the library will have a foundation for the rapid preparation of grant requests.

19. Phase in implementation over a four-year period.

The components of the Information Technology Plan will be implemented over a four-year period. This amount of time is required not only for financial reasons, but also because library staff cannot be expected to do everything at once.

The plan will be updated each year and a detailed schedule of activities will be drafted. It will include updated specifications and cost figures.

MISSION STATEMENT: FUNCTION IN THE ENTIRE LIBRARY

Lafayette Public Library
Lafayette, Louisiana

The mission of Lafayette Public Library is to enhance the quality of life of our community by providing free and equal access to high-quality, cost-effective library services that meet the needs and expectations of our diverse community for information, life-long learning, recreation, and cultural enrichment.

This policy addresses the use of the Library's electronic resources, including hardware, software, and access to the Internet, databases, and other resources provided to users both inside the library and remotely.

(For additional policies, please see the accompanying CD-ROM.)

PURPOSE AND SCOPE

University of Illinois at Urbana-Champaign
University of Illinois Libraries
Urbana, Illinois

Electronic Information Policy for Library Users
1. Introduction
1.1. The UIUC Library Mission statement:

The University Library exists as an archive of accumulated knowledge, a gateway to scholarship, and a catalyst for the discovery and advancement of new ideas. In fulfilling its obligation to provide knowledge to the University and the scholarly community at large, the University Library collects, organizes, and provides access to recorded knowledge in all formats. The Library Faculty initiates discussions and propose creative solutions to the information challenges facing the University and the scholarly community. The University Library's faculty and staff actively participate in providing quality service, access, instruction, and management of scholarly information.

1.2. The primary purpose of this policy is to detail the rights and responsibilities of consumers of electronic information in the Library.

Given the rapid rate of change within the field of electronic information this document must be regarded as a work in progress. Revision will not only be necessary but desirable.

Underlying Principles

The principles of academic freedom apply in full to the electronic communications and information environment.

The UIUC Library's Electronic Information Policy is part of the University's overall policy structure and should be interpreted in conjunction with other existing policies. Use of the Library's computing and networking services is governed by the policy statement provided in this document, other relevant University policies, and all applicable laws. Individuals using these services should be particularly aware of the policies which apply to discrimination, harassment and equal opportunity and those which apply to the appropriate use of university resources. These and other policies can be found in major University policy documents, including:

- Campus Administrative Manual
- University of Illinois Statutes and the General Rules Concerning Organization and Procedures
- Academic Staff Handbook
- Code of Policies and Regulations Applying to All Students
- University Policy and Rules for Civil Service Staff

Chapter 2

MANAGEMENT GUIDELINES

MISSION STATEMENTS: DEPARTMENTAL GOALS

Indiana University South Bend
Franklin D. Schurz Library
South Bend, Indiana

Electronic resources are collected according to the existing collection development mission and policy: to acquire and maintain the information resources necessary to support the teaching and scholarly mission of the campus.

Baruch College/CUNY
William and Anita Newman Library
New York, New York

CUNY's computer resources are dedicated to the support of the university's mission of education, research and public service. In furtherance of this mission, CUNY respects, upholds and endeavors to safeguard the principles of academic freedom, freedom of expression and freedom of inquiry.

CUNY recognizes that there is a concern among the university community that because information created, used, transmitted or stored in electronic form is by its nature susceptible to disclosure, invasion, loss, and similar risks, electronic communications and transactions will be particularly vulnerable to infringements of academic freedom. CUNY's commitment to the principles of academic freedom and freedom of expression includes electronic information. Therefore, whenever possible, CUNY will resolve doubts about the need to access CUNY computer resources in favor of a user's privacy interest.

However, the use of CUNY computer resources, including for electronic transactions and communications, like the use of other university-provided resources and activities, is subject to the requirements of legal and ethical behavior. This policy is intended to support the free exchange of ideas among members of the CUNY community and between the CUNY community and other communities, while recognizing the responsibilities and limitations associated with such exchange.

STAFF EDUCATION

Greenville Public Library
Smithfield, Rhode Island

The library employs a librarian with the title "technology coordinator," whose duties are to maintain the library's home page, oversee maintenance of the computer equipment, software installation and removal, data entry, planning for technology upgrades, staff training and other duties related to the reference department and technology. The current technology coordinator is trained in Apple OSX and provides staff instruction in Windows XP, Windows 2000, and Macintosh X operating systems. He also provides staff and the public with instruction on the operation of programs, and conducts adult computer classes in the homework center.

Library staff is trained to use AppleWorks 6, Microsoft Office, and Filemaker Pro, which are available in both Windows XP and Macintosh OSX formats for sharing files on different workstation platforms. They have also been trained to use Internet browsers.

Lafayette Public Library
Lafayette, Louisiana

GOALS AND STRATEGIES FOR PROFESSIONAL DEVELOPMENT

A trained staff will be better able to assist the public. A trained staff will be better able to perform library tasks. A trained public will be able to fully utilize the library's technology resources and be better equipped to achieve in life experiences and work or school where knowledge of technology is required or helpful.

The Library's staff is trained on operating and maintaining existing equipment. The Library currently provides training to staff and public on basic Internet and basic Microsoft Office applications. The staff also provides basic assistance via email, telephone, and in-person to those having trouble accessing the online catalog, the databases, the web site, or connecting via the wireless network. As technologies change and staff turnover occurs, a continual training program is necessary to keep 100% of the staff up to date.

Goal #1: Provide for a fully-trained staff on all library technologies.

Strategy #1: Fund and encourage staff attendance at the annual Bayouland Technology Workshop, State Library-sponsored workshops, SOLINET workshops, conference-related workshops, and specific courses through the University of Louisiana's Professional Development program. Provide training in the library's computer lab(s) for staff by key library staff trained as trainers. The Library will offer its training labs and meeting facilities in support of these endeavors.

Goal #2: Provide training classes for the public to help bridge the Digital Divide.

Strategy #2: Staff will develop and present regular classes in our computer labs for basic computing, office productivity applications, Internet, and specialized areas such as genealogy. The Library will work with groups, including the Lafayette Genealogy Society and the St. Pierre Genealogy Society, in these endeavors. The new Regional Libraries will offer distance learning capabilities for enhancing this service.

Goal #3: Encourage and provide funding and training for staff wishing to pursue a Masters in Library and Information Science from Louisiana State University.

Strategy #3: Continue to fund the Tuition Reimbursement program (under Lafayette City/Parish Government PPM 261-12) for full time employees. Work towards funding tuition reimbursement for part time employees. Support the distance learning classroom at the Main Library for such courses. Provide distance learning equipment and data connections in new facilities for such courses.

USER TRAINING

Orland Park Public Library
Orland Park, Illinois

Patron Assistance and Instruction

The Orland Park Public Library's staff may provide assistance to patrons in the use of electronic information networks as time and staff knowledge permits. It may not be possible for staff to evaluate or judge the quality or merits of sites that the patron may access. Printed and online documentation and instructions are available at or near points of services. Formal instruction in particular aspects of electronic information network use may be available.

VISION STATEMENTS: DEPARTMENTAL GOALS

Bryant University
Douglas and Judith Krupp Library
Smithfield, Rhode Island

The Douglas and Judith Krupp Library will continue to utilize information and communication technologies to enhance the access and delivery of information and library services to its users.

The Library in conjunction with the Information Services Division at Bryant University will provide library users with robust equipment and networks which support the current needs of library users and efficient access to information resources.

Equipment for library users includes 72 public workstations, 3 copiers, 2 microfilm readers, 1 open book scanner, 5 public printers, self checkout station, and 10 laptops for loan. Replacement for public computer workstations within the library is on a 4-year replacement cycle. The number of workstations to be replaced will be based on computer lab needs throughout the campus. The library is considered a "computer lab" and all software available to Bryant students is also loaded on library workstations. Bryant is also a "laptop" campus (4th year into program) and this may have an impact on the number of fixed stations needing future replacement. Replacement of major equipment such as the self checkout system and microfilm readers is done via Bryant's special request process. Continued need for such items will be evaluated at the time of replacement. Most library equipment (workstations) including staff equipment is over 3 years old and public workstations may be replaced in the Fall of 2006.

Staff equipment includes workstations, scanners, barcode readers, library material desensitizers and printers. Staff workstations are acquired via the campus roll out policy. Special consideration is given to workstations requiring special needs such as the ARIEL interlibrary loan station. Less expensive equipment, such as barcode readers and scanners will be replaced as needed with general library operating funds.

The campus network infrastructure used by the Douglas and Judith Krupp Library is maintained by the Network Services group within the Information Services Division of which the library is a part. The campus network infrastructure continues to be upgraded and enhanced annually supporting wired, wireless and voice over ip connectivity.

The library will utilize a Content Management System to organize the intellectual output of Bryant University and to highlight Bryant's legacy collections.

Content management systems have been examined since 2003. Systems examined include MIT's D-Space (open source), OCLC's ContentDM (hosted or unhosted options) and Digital Commons (Berkeley Electronic Press). In November 2005 HELIN received a grant from the Davis Educational Foundation to support the above goal. Bryant will begin adding content to this HELIN repository in late winter/early spring of 2006.

The library will use information and telecommunication technologies to enhance information literacy objectives.

Information literacy objectives continue to include a possible online learning component or a complete course which is delivered electronically in a variety of formats including online tutorials, streaming video, etc. Content and delivery production is being done in-house. A couple of "How do I . . ." combination Powerpoint/video clips have been created using both Camtasia and Mediasite Live.

The library will seek ways to deliver educational video content to students and faculty.

Efforts are under way to provide access to educational video collections across campus networks. In 2005 the library purchased 150 digital educational videos and trialed VOD (video on demand) software from Starbak Communications. A trial with Video Furnace will begin in early 2006. In addition to commercial content, library staff are experimenting with ways to deliver library instruction on equipment such as the self-checkout system, e-resources and library services via in-house produced digital video which would be made available via the campus network.

Software and equipment for in-house digital video productions is available on campus via the Information Services Audio Visual Department and the new Communication Center. Staff have access to Camtasia, Mediasite Live and Avid software.

Training for in-house productions is/will be shared by Bryant Audio Visual staff and early library staff adopters.

The library will continue to replace print content with electronic content where possible.

The library subscribes to over 40 electronic databases and this number is increasing each year. These subscriptions provide access to the full text content for over 20,000 journals and other information resources. During the past year a standing order was activated for all e-books published by AMACOM. Additional e-books will be purchased during 2006. Electronic reference acquisitions will be preferred. Funding for new e-content typically comes from money formerly allocated to print sources or from the Bryant special request process. Current e-subscriptions are evaluated annually by library staff. E-usage stats are maintained as well.

Staff training on e-resources is typically provided by the vendor, online tutorials, or via staff exploration.

The library will continue to maintain a robust integrated library system (ILS).

The library will continue to maintain membership in the HELIN (Higher Education Library Information Network) consortium and work with HELIN membership to ensure that the ILS (integrated library system) is meeting the needs of users, collections, and library staff. Annual investigation and discussion of vendor provided enhancements and options will be considered through HELIN Board and committee work.

Open source ILS solutions will be examined over the next five years and the open source software trends in higher education will be monitored. In addition, features and functions of for profit ILS systems should be intermittently examined during the next 5 years.

ILS connectivity and relationships with other campus systems such as Banner, Blackboard, ePortfolio and college portals will also be monitored so that connectivity between systems is seamless and user friendly. Pending issues currently under discussion include the inability to acquire the patron barcode in Banner downloads. Single sign on for users of disparate systems also needs to be addressed.

The viability of individual modules within the ILS such as E-Reserves vs. course management systems such as Blackboard and the Serials Management module vs. e-journal management systems such as Serials Solutions requires examination over the next 5 years.

The library will consider and provide non content related e-services for its users.

New e-services such as federated searching will be considered for use by library users and will be made available based on need, product integrity and funding. Virtual chat room reference is currently in place via Trillian. An E-journal management service was acquired in 2004 year and Article linking services were purchased for 2005-2006.

The library will continue to provide staff with the education needed to support new technologies.

Library staff are encouraged to learn and embrace new technologies both formally and informally. Formal options include courses offered via NELINET, Bryant, Nercomp and other local organizations. Informal training opportunities exist within the HELIN consortium, the Information Services Division at Bryant, and sessions provided by vendors.

In 2006 the library will investigate and provide access to GIS (Geographical Information Systems)

In 2005 an electronic touch screen and large plasma display were installed to accommodate Google Earth and ESRI geographical software. ESRI's Business Analyst product will be examined and possibly acquired in 2006.

This technology plan will be reviewed and updated annually.

Chapter 3

TECHNOLOGY PLAN PROCESSES

PRIORITIES SETTING

Stillwater Public Library
Stillwater, Oklahoma

The 2008-2010 Stillwater Public Library Technology Plan includes nine priorities that work toward providing library patrons with up-to-date devices, content, software, and skills that will meet their information and entertainment needs. In close partnership with the City of Stillwater Information Technology (IT) Department, the Library will strive to meet the following priorities:

Priority 1: Maintain and improve the public catalog and website.

The library will employ new technological resources to improve services provided on the library website.

Priority 2: Prepare for new Sirsi software Symphony and investigate possible new Operating System for the server.

The library software company is releasing a new version of their software which is a major change from our existing system and will require more staff training.

Priority 3: Re-configure library software to email patrons pre-due, overdue, holds, and Interlibrary Loan notices.

Many library customers now have email and automatic electronic notification will enhance our patron contact methods.

Priority 4: Investigate downloadable books.

Access to downloadable materials will allow customers to use personal electronic devices such as MP3 players, computerized readers, and home computers to enjoy their books.

Priority 5: Develop a social networking library policy.

The library needs a policy to institutionalize our stance in regards to social networks accessed via the library.

Priority 6: Investigate building a digital collection.

Digitizing the unique collections of the Stillwater Public Library could be a solution to preservation of these rare items and make these items more accessible to a greater number of people.

Priority 7: Investigate establishing a music listening station.

Many library customers would like to listen to our selection of music before checking out the CDs.

Priority 8: Investigate staff collaborative software.

The library staff works as a team developing programs and content. Email has many deficiencies in this regard and specific collaboration software may enhance staff cooperation resulting in even better library programs for the community.

Priority 9: Investigate new library technologies.

We need to keep apprised of emerging trends and equipment to better serve our library customers.

2008-2010 Technology Plan Priorities

Priority 1: Maintain and improve the public catalog and website.

As a gateway to providing for the informational needs of its users, the Stillwater Public Library website (library.stillwater.org) is a vital resource and must be constantly maintained and improved. The website currently provides an online card catalog (Webcat); eleven databases, four of which are provided by the Oklahoma Department of Libraries; and general library information.

Action Steps

The Stillwater Public Library will:

- Investigate upgrading to a newer SIRSI online card catalog design.
- Explore the purchase of a metaportal software product to streamline accessing information from the Library's catalog and databases.
- Determine the content and cost of additional databases.
- Analyze the website for improvements and receive staff training from the City of Stillwater Information Technology (IT) Department.
- Update the website with new pages to improve the ease of navigation for users.

Projected Costs:

- Staff Training: $1,000-$4,000
- New design: $6,000-10,000
- New databases: $500-$2,000 per database

Priority 2: Prepare for new Sirsi software Symphony and investigate possible new Operating System for the server.

Sirsi has merged with another library software company (Dynix) and is offering a brand new hybrid version (Symphony) which will be radically different than our existing Workflows client version. Our next upgrade will involve much more than an overview of new features. Staff will need to be re-trained for the new software for daily procedures and workflow, server maintenance, and database maintenance. A new Operating System (OS) for the server may have to be purchased to run the Symphony software. The library now uses UNIX, but may have to change to a JAVA based OS. This will involve another major upgrade to the server and will require training for the Technical Services staff.

Action Steps

The Stillwater Public Library will:

- Monitor how new software is working for beta libraries.
- Develop a timeline for the upgrade to Symphony.
- Investigate moving to new server operating system.
- Provide initial and on-going staff training on Symphony and possibly for JAVA.
- Develop and/or find materials and curriculum to meet the needs of staff.

Projected costs:

- Upgrade: $11,000
- Training and staff time: $1,000-5,000.

Priority 3: Re-configure library software to email patrons pre-due, overdue, holds, and Interlibrary Loan notices.

Email notification for patrons should improve item overdues and free up time staff spends calling via telephone and mailing paper notices.

Action steps

The Stillwater Public Library will:

- Generate new texts for pre-due, hold availability and Interlibrary Loan availability on UNIX with v editor software.
- Manipulate the reports module to generate pre-due and holds reports daily and automatically.
- Re-configure our server to send and receive emails and work with City IT department to allow email through their firewalls.

Projected costs:

- Unix consultant: $500

Priority 4: Investigate downloadable books.

Downloadable books can come in many forms, but basically they are Mp3 files. The library could subscribe to a database that offers this format and the customer "checks out" an Mp3 file, or the library could provide "readers" that have a book loaded on them and the customer can take the reader with them.

Action steps

The Stillwater Public Library will:

- Investigate available databases.
- Investigate available readers or takeaways.
- Consider public relations and advertising to let the public know about downloadable books.

Projected Costs:

- Upgraded Netlibrary database: $2,500 minimum
- Overdrive base package database: $2,000
- Takeaways: $300/unit

Priority 5: Develop a social networking library policy.

The public's information and entertainment needs have gone from one-way communication from the library to interactive and collaborative use internet sites such as Wikipedia, librarything, and myspace. The library needs approved policies to deal with any situations that may arise with these new two-way communications.

Action steps

The Stillwater Public Library will:

- Develop a Social Software policy for Library Board approval.

Projected costs:

- In-house: $0

Priority 6: Investigate building a digital collection.

The library has many unique items that will need preserving for the future. One strategy of preservation is to digitize these items. This would allow both preservation and greater access by the public.

Action steps:

The Stillwater Public Library will:

- Investigate using the City of Stillwater's new digital imaging management software.
- Investigate digitizing on our own with flatbed and photocopy scanners.
- Investigate where to put a digital collection.
- Decide on a digitization project.
- Develop a digitization plan.

Projected costs:

- Scanning items: $1,000-2,000
- Cataloging and maintaining collection: $2,000-20,000

Priority 7: Investigate establishing a music listening station.

Customers would like to preview music CDs before checking them out. A music listening center would allow for CD previews.

Action steps:

The Stillwater Public Library will:

- Investigate available listening centers.
- Search out appropriate furniture and location.
- Develop procedures for possible clean-up/re-shelving of CDs.

Projected costs:

- Listening center: $1,500-2,500
- Furniture: $1,000-2,000

Priority 8: Investigate staff collaborative software.

The library staff works as a team developing programming and content. Email has many deficiencies in this regard and specific collaboration software may work to help us work together.

Action steps:

The Stillwater Public Library will:

- Investigate available collaborative software.
- Decide if applicable to library team work.

Projected costs:

- Software: $100-1,000
- Training: In-house or through City IT Department

Priority 9: Investigate new library technologies.

We need to keep apprised of emerging trends and equipment to better serve our library customers. The library will diligently research new technology and trends as they become available. Some areas that are just breaking in 2008 are selfcheck stations, RFID (radio frequency identification), downloadable books/music/films, patron driven content, social network tools, wireless handheld circ computers, e-commerce solutions for patrons.

Action steps:

The Stillwater Public Library will:
- Stay apprised of new technology and innovation.
- Analyze the potentials for our local situation.
- Plan for fast-paced technology change.

Projected costs examples:
- RFID: $50,000
- Self-check station: $30,000
- Downloadable items: $2,500-10,000
- Social networking: $0-20,000

STRATEGIES FOR PLAN SUCCESS

Greenville Public Library
Smithfield, Rhode Island

Connection to the Internet is accomplished via two switches, one wireless Apple Airport base station, and a hub that connects the LAN to the CLAN Internet provider. The current connection is through a T1 line that is maintained by CLAN.

Lafayette Public Library
Lafayette, Louisiana

Telecommunications

A public library is in the communication and information business. Telecommunications is how we deliver much of our information to the public whether it is through the traditional telephone line, wireless services, or through digital lines.

Goal #1: Provide reliable, high speed data transmission lines to ensure reliable connectivity among our libraries and with other libraries and internet sites globally.

Strategy #5: Work with State Library in maintaining and enhancing the State network. Work with the Lafayette City/Parish Government (though its CIO) to standardize, maintain, and enhance the Library network. Monitor network utilization and upgrade bandwidth to areas as warranted by monitoring. Upgrade from Frame Relay to fiber optic connections as service becomes available if cost/benefit warrants. Connect new facilities to the WAN via fiber optic or similar state-of-the-art technologies as affordable to meet the increasing demand of public access and staff access computing.

Strategy #6: Provide dedicated access for Distance Learning and video conferencing so that these bandwidth-intensive applications do not erode the available bandwidth for public and staff for Internet, ILS, Library Web site, email, and Intranet access.

Goal #2: Improve the first interaction most of the public has with the library—the telephone call.

Strategy #7: Improve the phone system, considering the newer VOIP technologies—with its ability to locally manage features and cost considerations. Improve the voice mail system—making it convenient for patrons to leave messages and easy for staff to be alerted to and retrieve messages. Consider a library-wide phone system by the time the Main Library renovations are completed. Continue to select the best long distance and phone service features for the library system, evaluating cost with efficiency.

Goal #3: Minimize technology down time.

Strategy #8: Provide paging services and / or cellular service for IT personnel.

Enhance the staff Intranet with a "help desk" site and improve the web-based submittal of technology service requests. Implement a backup generator at South Regional Library and possibly (depending on budget) at Main Library to power mission-critical technology infrastructure during power or other emergencies.

Goal #4: Improve response to facilities problems or for patron complaints that are escalated to administration or other situations requiring immediate attention.

Strategy #9: Provide paging services and / or cellular service for facilities personnel and administrative personnel.

Goal #5: Improve communication between outreach service and their users.

Strategy #10: Outreach staff is on the road 5-6 hours a day and their users often must leave a message with the receptionist. Communication with the outreach staff while on the road will allow their public to communicate with them at the public's convenience and staff to be reachable by Library personnel for communication of critical messages related to the job. Access to the Library's catalog system while the Outreach staff is on their routes will allow the staff to respond to patron queries in a timely fashion.

Middle Georgia Regional Library
Technology Services Department
Macon, Georgia

STRATEGIC DIRECTIONS, GOALS, OBJECTIVES, AND DESIRED RESULTS

Goal 1: Respond to the needs of patrons by delivering services utilizing traditional and computer-based programs and services, including the Internet.

Objective: Increase the use of computers, Internet and other computer-based information resources.

Desired Results: Provide the patrons in the six counties of the Middle Georgia Regional library with access to Georgia Library PINES Catalog, the Internet, World Wide Web, GALILEO and other electronic databases such as H. W. Wilson, UMI ProQuest, and Encyclopedia Britannica.

Action Required:
1. The library needs to provide the MGRL libraries with updated computers, replacing older models with state of the art computers and peripherals.
2. Monitor, maintain, and upgrade CAT 5 Ethernet wiring in all branches.
3. Monitor, maintain, and upgrade electrical outlets and associated infrastructure to be able to provide the necessary capacity to handle existing and additional computer equipment.
4. Purchase furniture designed to accommodate computer equipment and peripherals.
5. Provide access to the Internet through connections with the Georgia Public Library Service (GPLS) Network. GPLS provides this service to the Georgia public libraries at no cost.
6. Update Webpage.

Evaluation:
1. The installation of CAT 5 Ethernet wiring has been completed at all MGRL library branches. A new library planned for South Bibb County has wiring included in the building program.
2. Internet access via the GPLS Network has been provided in all MGRL library branches.
3. Electrical wiring has been updated in older facilities.
4. Upgrades to computers funded though Gates Library Foundation Grants have been planned for fall 2007.

Goal 2: Train the Library Staff to use Computers, the Internet, and Online Databases.

Objectives:

- A: Train Public Services Staff to use computers, the Internet and other computer based information resources to answer reference questions and assist patrons in the use of the library computers.
- B: Train all Staff members to use computers, the Internet, and software used for collecting statistics, word-processing, database management, email, and records keeping.
- C: Increase the use of computers, Internet, and other computer-based information resources among non-public services staff in automating the various library tasks and procedures.
- D: Develop a train-the-trainer program to insure that at least one person at each branch library is proficient in the use of electronic equipment and programs, competent to instruct patrons and staff and able troubleshoot problems with equipment.
- E: Provide computer classes to staff using in-house training classes.

Desired Results: Take advantage of new technologies to provide traditional and non-traditional public services to patrons. To provide new services to patrons such and Internet browsing, online database searching, use of GALILEO databases, periodical indexes, and accessing other libraries catalogs and databases.

Action Required:

1. Provide access to computer training programs provided by the Georgia Public Library Service, Educational Technology Center, SOLINET, and private computer training seminars such as those sponsored by the American Management Association.
2. Develop in-house training classes on software, operating systems, e-mail, Internet and other applications used in day-to-day operations.
3. Use trainers educated in the workshops funded by the Gates Library Foundation Grant to Libraries and sponsored by the Georgia Public Library Service to conduct in-house training classes and make the trainers available to other public library systems in Georgia.
4. Allow paid time off during business hours for staff attendance at training sessions.

Evaluation: Five staff members attended the GPLS Train-the-Trainer Workshop funded by a grant from the Gates Library Foundation. The trainers have held workshops on the MS-Office Suite, Basic Computer Skills, GALILEO databases, and Internet Searching. We have also hosted workshops sponsored by OIIT, EBSCO and PINES to train staff on various library databases and applications. Five days of Staff Training on the new GPLS PINES Evergreen© software was held in August 2006. Follow-up training sessions are planned for Spring 2007.

Goal 3: Automate Genealogy and Archives Collection.

Objective 1:

- A: Continue to upgrade, maintain, and develop new electronic resources to provide access to Genealogy, Archives and Digitized materials both local and worldwide.
- B: Provide access to the PINES catalog using OPAC workstations and access to Genealogical databases through the Internet as a link from the Library's web page and complete the retrospective conversion of existing materials into PINES and the Georgia Online Library Database (GOLD).

Desired Results: Complete the retrospective conversion of the Genealogy and Archive collections into PINES and GOLD. Maintain and update the PINES and GOLD databases as new materials are added to the collections.

Action Required:

1. Maintain and upgrade cataloging workstations.
2. Train Staff to catalog new materials into the PINES database using the GPLS PINES Evergreen software.

Evaluation:

1. The Genealogy collection has been added to the PINES and GOLD databases.
2. New books and materials are cataloged into PINES and added to GOLD.
3. The retrospective conversion of the collection has been completed. Database MIDDLE GEORGIA REGIONAL LIBRARY cleanup and the addition of unique and problem items are processed as time and budget permits.
4. The addition of archival materials to the database will proceed as time and budget permits.

Objective 2: Digitize local history, archival records, manuscripts, photographs, newspapers, and other sensitive materials.

Desired Results: Provide digital access to local history materials including family records, genealogies, city and county documents, wills, photographs, architectural drawings, newspapers, obituary records, planning and zoning records, maps, archival documents, and other historical records available in the genealogical and historical department, city and county offices, funeral homes, and other local depositories. Many of these records are in fragile or delicate condition, are the only known copy of the source, or may not be accessible to the general public, and may lack indexing or reference sources to the contents. The library would be the central access point to these resources and could provide unlimited access to materials that would be too delicate to handle in the original format.

Action required: Purchase Scanner, Server, Software, Personal Computer, CD-R\RW drives and Zip Drives for digitization, indexing and storage of the database. Start scanning and indexing project. Contact local news media and sources of information to inform the community about the project and to request materials from varies agencies and individuals owing the materials and information to be included in the database. Load database and search software into Server connected to OPAC workstations.

Evaluation:

1. Equipment, software, and computer furniture has been purchased with Library Services and Technology Grant (LSTA) funds and a pilot project have been completed.
2. Demonstration projects focusing on materials in the Genealogy and Archives collections are planned.
3. Develop cooperative projects with Local History Groups, Museums, and Genealogical Societies.

Objective 3: Automate Archives Collection:

Desired Results: Provide access to a catalog of the archives materials through the OPAC stations in the Genealogical and Historical Department. Convert archive records and index using Encoded Archival Description (EAD) software. Add archive records to the Georgia Library PINES and GOLD databases.

Action Required:

1. Purchase software module to add records to genealogy catalog.
2. Train staff to use EAD software.
3. Train staff to convert records to software located on a server running the Windows 2000 Server operating system.

Evaluation:

1. One-third of the Archives collection has been added to the SOLINET database using the GAMMA Project as a model. The remainder of the collection needs to be added.
2. Software for adding the records to the OPAC catalog is being reviewed.
3. Computer workstations have been installed in the department. Additional equipment and upgrades will be added as funds are made available.

Goal 4: Library Web Page.

Objective: Allow 24-hour access to library databases, electronic resources, library policies and the PINES catalog.

Desired Results: Provide Middle Georgia Regional library patrons with access to the library catalog twenty-four hours a day. Allow patrons to use the Internet to place requests for books and to receive answers to reference questions. Provide access to library and other electronics databases via the Internet from patron's home computers.

Action Required:

1. Allow access to library periodical and other electronic databases and resources from the Internet.
2. Develop procedures for answering reference and reserve requests for books via email, chat, instant messaging, or links on the library web page.
3. Update Library Webpage.

Evaluation: Patrons may use the Internet to access the PINES catalog from their personal computers. They may also submit requests for books and ask reference and genealogy questions using a link from the library webpage. Future applications may also allow reference questions and book requests using chat, instant messaging or other interactive software.

Goal 5: Children's Multimedia Computer Center.

Objective: Upgrade computers, equipment, furniture, multimedia products, and provide access to the Internet and other online databases.

Desired Results: Provide the children of the six counties of the Middle Georgia Regional Library System with Internet access, multimedia programs such as books on CD-ROM, educational games, word processing, and access to GALILEO and other online databases. Create an atmosphere for learning for the children of the community by using electronic resources in addition to traditional library resources such as books, magazines, newspapers, and other print media.

Action Required:

1. Upgrade and purchase additional computer workstations, servers, and printers.
2. Purchase CD-ROM and database subscriptions.

Evaluation: Funding from a variety of sources including the Gates Foundation Opportunity Grant in 1999, Bill & Melinda Foundation Grants to Libraries in 2000, LSTA grants from 1999- 2002, and the MGRL library budget provided for the purchase of a multimedia computer center for the Washington Memorial Library and children's computers for each branch of MGRL.

Future plans include the purchase of additional computers to meet patron demands and replace older computers and peripherals.

Goal 6: Children's Internet Protection Act (CIPA).

Objective 1: Purchase and install equipment and software to protect the children of the Middle Georgia Regional Library System from pornography and the problems associated with the availability of Internet pornography in public libraries.

Objective 2: Comply with the provisions of Children's Internet Protection Act (CIPA) to remain eligible for federal funding under the E-rate, LSTA and other federal government programs.

Desired Results: Protect the children accessing the Internet at MGRL library branches from pornography, undesirable Internet content, and other problems associated with the Internet access by minors. Meet or exceed the requirements of the Children's Internet Protection Act (CIPA).

Action Required:

1. Implement the GPLS filtering software.
2. Keep current with changes to and interpretation of CIPA by the legislature and courts.

Evaluation: The Georgia Public Library Service purchased, installed, and maintains Secure Computing SMARTFILTER ® Internet filtering equipment and software on the GPLS Network. The use of the equipment and software is available to the public libraries in Georgia to comply with CIPA requirements. The Middle Georgia Regional Library has availed itself of the software and equipment since it became available in July 2002. Staff will continue to monitor the software and Internet sites to assure that requirements for filtering are met.

Goal 7: Assistive Technology Workstations.

Objective: Purchase equipment and software to assist patrons that are blind or physically impaired.

Desired Results: Provide assistive technology to enable patrons with visual and physical handicaps to access the resources of the library in both print and electronic formats. Remove barriers imposed by traditional library resources, which limit their use, by patrons with visual or other physical impairments.

Action Required: Purchase computers, equipment, furniture, magnifiers, speech synthesizers, screen enlargers, scanners, screen readers and software to convert traditional print and computer sources to a format usable by the visually and physically impaired.

Evaluation: In 1998 an assistive technology grant was used to provide equipment to Washington Memorial Library in Bibb County. The computer and software on this computer are reaching the limits of usability and should be replaced with a new model containing updated versions of accessibility software. In addition an immediate goal is to provide workstations in the main library branch of each county in the region. Long-range goals are to provide at least one assistive technology workstation in each library branch.

Goal 8: Facility and Workstation Security.

Objective: Purchase equipment and software to guard computer equipment, software and peripherals against theft, vandalism, contamination from viruses and other malicious programs.

Desired Results: Prevent loss, damage, and downtime of equipment through available preventive technologies.

Action Required:

1. Purchase equipment to lock down computers and peripherals.
2. Purchase and install anti-virus software.
3. Purchase and install desktop security software.
4. Purchase tracking software to provide additional options for retrieving lost or stolen equipment.
5. Install security cameras and equipment in each branch library of MGRL.

Evaluation: Video cameras and equipment has been installed in the Washington Memorial Library and the city branch libraries in Bibb County. The libraries are monitored using CCTV and software on administrative computers. The purchase of additional cameras and equipment is necessary to monitor the main and branch libraries in the remaining five counties of MGRL.

Anti-virus is installed on all computers and desktop security software is installed on patron access computers.

Goal 9: Upgrade Print collections of Research/Reference Materials to Microfilm, CD-ROM, or Digital editions.

Objective: To purchase equipment to facilitate the conversion of past county/city newspapers contained in the county library affiliate collections and for newspapers in the Washington Memorial Library Genealogical and Historical Room.

Desired Results: Convert the past city/county newspapers of the county library affiliate collections and those of the Washington Memorial Library Genealogical and Historical Room from paper to Microfilm, CD-ROM, or Digitized editions.

Action Required:

1. The library will purchase or lease digital conversion equipment to facilitate conversion from print to Microfilm, CD-ROM, or Digital editions. Alternately, the library will outsource the conversion of the newspapers from print to Microfilm, CD-ROM, or Digital editions.

2. Train library staff on digital conversion procedures.
3. Gather newspapers and other printed organs of the city/county libraries and Genealogical and Historical Room.

Evaluation: Newspapers and printed organs of the city and county libraries are only available in printed versions. Local newspapers and official organs of the cities in which the county libraries are located are unique resources that contain local culture, photographs, obituaries, and other records that document the history of each locale. Many of these records are in fragile or delicate condition, are the only known copy of the source, or may not be accessible to the general public, and may lack indexing or reference sources to the contents. The library would be the central access point to these resources and could provide unlimited access to materials that would be too delicate to handle in the original format.

Goal 10: Wireless LAN Technology.

Objective: Install wireless LAN Technology in the Washington Memorial Library and Main Library of the six counties of the Middle Georgia Regional Library to provide network access to add additional public computers in areas where the architecture and construction of the building makes the installation of conventional CAT-5 wiring difficult if not impossible.

Desired Results: Provide additional public library computers in response to patron demand.

Action Required:

1. Purchase and install appropriate wireless technology.
2. Purchase and install library computer furniture.
3. Purchase and install personal computers.
4. Plan for WI-FI access to patron owned laptop/notebook computers.

Evaluation: Wireless technology and equipment has been installed at the Washington Memorial Library and the Main Branch of the county libraries with Library Services and Technology Grant (LSTA) funds. Additional equipment and upgrades will be added as patron and staff computer usage demands and funds become available.

Goal 11: Telecommunications.

Objective: Provide telephone access to patrons and staff. Provide answers to patron reference and research questions over the telephone. Provide patrons with basic library information using an automated answering system.

Desired Results: Allow patrons to call in reference and research questions via the telephone. Provide callers with library operating hours, days of service and basic information through the use of an automated answering system.

Evaluation: MGRL upgraded telephone service to the main library and branches in 2000. Additional upgrades to the city and county branches are planned.

Action Required:

1. Purchase and install telephone equipment.
2. Lease telephone services.
3. Maintain and upgrade telephone services as budget permits.

Evaluation: The library provides callers with basic information such as days and hours of service when the library is closed. Patrons may call in reference and research questions to the Reference Department at the Washington Memorial Library (Main Library) and each branch of MGRL.

Patrons may also call the Genealogical and Archives for specialized questions on family history and genealogy. The library will add additional equipment and upgrades as patron and staff demands and funds become available. The library participates in the Universal Services Fund program to Schools and Libraries to receive discounted telephone rates and for purchase of new equipment and services.

Goal 12: Georgia Library PINES Database (PINES).

Objective: Meet the requirements for participation in Georgia Library PINES, the statewide library catalog available to public libraries in Georgia. Provide access to the PINES catalog to the patrons of Middle Georgia Regional Library to access books and materials available at MGRL library branches and at participating public libraries in Georgia.

Desired Results: MGRL library patrons have access to the holdings of 252 libraries in 123 counties in Georgia. Patrons with a PINES library card have access to materials beyond what is available on their local shelves and enjoy the benefits of a shared collection of 15 million books, tapes, CDs and videos that can be delivered to their home library free of charge.

Action Required:

1. Purchase and install computers and software for PINES Online Public Access Catalogs (OPAC).
2. Purchase and install computers and software for staff use of the OPAC, Circulation, Cataloging, Reports and other modules of the PINES software.
3. Provide for staff training on the use of the various modules of the PINES software
4. Provide for patron training on the use of the PINES OPAC.
5. Maintain, upgrade, and replace patron and staff computers as funds become available.

Evaluation: Middle Georgia Regional Library has been a member of PINES since its inception in 2000. Future plans are to increase the number of OPACs available for patron use. MGRL will comply with technology and software requirements for membership in PINES.

Goal 13: Workstation and Print Management.

Objective 1: Purchase and install color laser printers in MGRL branches.
Objective 2: Purchase and install print management software in MGRL branches.

Desired Results: Meet patron demand for both color and black & white laser printed copies of research materials. Install workstation and print management software to monitor the number of copies printer and compile computer usage statistics.

Action Required:

1. Purchase and install color and black & white laser printers.
2. Purchase and install workstation and print management software.

Evaluation: Middle Georgia Regional Library currently offers black & white copies on materials from patron access computers. As funds become available color network printers would be purchase for each branch library of the Middle Georgia Regional Library. Workstation management software would also staff to monitor computer usage, compile statistics on use of software applications, Internet usage, as well as monitor the number of patron printouts during a computer session.

TECH PLANS CREATION

Connecticut State Library
Douglas Lord
Hartford, Connecticut

Connecticut State Library Checklist for Technology Plans

A checklist from the Connecticut State Library to help you walk through your library's technology planning process.

The technology plan will, ideally, be an integral part of the overall long range planning of the library. It should reflect how technology will be used to improve the service goals of the library. Contain a description of the strategy for using information technology in the activities of the library, including integration of that technology into the library services;

To qualify as an approved Technology Plan for a Universal Service discount, the plan must meet the following five criteria that are core elements of successful school and library technology initiatives:

(1) the plan must establish clear goals and a realistic strategy for using telecommunications and information technology to improve education or library services;

(2) the plan must have a professional development strategy to ensure that staff know how to use these new technologies to improve education or library services;

(3) the plan must include an assessment of the telecommunication services, hardware, software, and other services that will be needed to improve education or library services;

(4) the plan must provide for a sufficient budget to acquire and maintain the hardware, software, professional development, and other services that will be needed to implement the strategy; and

(5) the plan must include an evaluation process that enables the school or library to monitor progress toward the specified goals and make mid-course corrections in response to new developments and opportunities as they arise.

In addition the plan should:

- Describe all activities eligible for support under the Universal Service provisions;
- Provide for the acquisition and use of:
  - hardware
  - software
  - staff and training needs/development;
  - and describe why each is needed for implementation of eligible services
- Include enough details to enable judgment of the validity of the request for Universal Services in meeting the objectives for use of information technologies in the plan.
- List and describe the telecommunication services your library will be requesting under USF in your plan and ensuring that these telecommunication services are supported by objectives in plan.
- State clearly the time period covered by the plan. Remember that a technology plan may cover no more than three years.
- Include approval by the library's governing authority (Board, municipality, etc.).

When writing your plan you may wish to consider the following components:

Vision statement

The statement should be consistent with the vision statement in the library's overall plan and reflect how the library views the integration of technology for improving library services. How does technology generally facilitate the role of the public library? How does the impact of technology on society affect library management and services? How is the role of the public library changing because of technological advances? What is your vision for technology in the library? What benefits do you anticipate?

Description of the current environment

What is the current technological capacity of the library. What equipment and telecommunications services are already available?

Goals and objectives for using technology in the library

Broad goals form the framework for plan. Each objective should be measurable and lead to necessary action steps.

What administrative functions will be more effective/efficient using technology?

What patron services or programs do you want to provide that require technology or telecommunications capacity?

What type of environment do you want to create? For example: Internet access networked CD-ROM's, administrative LAN, network participation.

What specific skills do you want staff and patrons to acquire?

What kind of technology linkages do you want to establish? For example to: schools or municipal offices, the Connecticut Digital Library, automation consortium, the Internet.

What changes must be made to the facility to accommodate technology/telecommunications?

Strategy or action plan for achieving the goals and objectives

The action steps should be specific enough to justify services and equipment for which you will be seeking USF discounts. Include the specific activities or action steps that must take place to implement the identified goals and objectives. For each action step consider:

- Staffing
- Training
- Budget implications
- Building renovation
- Policies and procedures

Equipment needs: What already exists? What upgrades or purchases will be necessary? Where will equipment be located? How will maintenance be handled?

Software needs (Same as hardware)

Telecommunication /wiring needs: What specific capabilities are required (phone lines, cable drops, location, speed) What upgrades will be necessary to accommodate new technology and meet goals?

+Implementation timelines. What time frame is realistic for each activity?

Part II
Collection Development

Chapter 4

CATEGORIES OF E-RESOURCES

DATABASES

Long Island University
B. Davis Schwartz Memorial Library
Brookville, New York

Selection Process for Online Databases

Recommendations for the purchase of electronic databases are received by the Database Coordinator from the Dean, Library Faculty, faculty from other departments, staff, and students. The Database Coordinator reviews these suggestions, and consults with the Database Coordinators at the other campus libraries within the LIU system prior to presenting recommendations to the Dean of the University Libraries.

Whenever possible, the Database Coordinator sets up a trial of the electronic resource to facilitate a complete evaluation of the product with the criteria set forth below. The trial may be set up by either IP authentication or by password. The information is distributed to all full-time and part-time Library Faculty who may inform the faculty in other departments on campus as part of their responsibilities in the Library's Liaison Program. The information is also posted on the Library's website by the Library Webmaster under the "Trial Databases" heading. If a positive recommendation is received after evaluation of the product during the trial period, the Database Coordinator recommends purchase to the Dean of University Libraries.

The Dean is responsible for reviewing, negotiating and signing all licensing agreements and for all other contractual matters pertaining to the purchase of electronic resources or access to these resources.

Texas State Library and Archives Commission
Austin, Texas

TexShare Core Databases

TexShare enables community colleges, universities, libraries of clinical medicine, and public libraries to broaden the range of materials and services available to their patrons. TexShare's electronic full-text magazine and journal articles supplement resources on the local level. Given the diversity of Texas libraries, the program may not meet all of the electronic information needs of all TexShare member libraries. The TexShare electronic resources collection will provide access to broad multi-topic authoritative full-text content for both advanced scholars and the general public. When possible within budgetary constraints, additional specialized resources in the areas of literature, business, current affairs, science, history, and genealogy are selected which serve the broadest range of citizens.

The TexShare Electronic resources are selected through recommendations of the Electronic Information Working Group (EIWG), which reviews products for the TexShare program, and solicits and reviews input from member libraries. Membership in the Working Group is representative of TexShare member libraries. EIWG decisions are guided by these criteria when making decisions:

- Membership Surveys
- Usage Statistics
- Database Content

- Vendor Reliability
- Best Value

Individual Libraries can participate in the database selection by:

- Sending comments and recommendations to the EIWG
- Sending recommendations about databases to TexShare staff (all comments are forwarded to the EIWG)
- Filling out and submitting database surveys
- Sending comments throughout the statewide database trial period to the EIWG and the TexShare staff

Pasadena Public Library
Pasadena, California

Electronic Databases (Commercial)

Online computerized databases extend the collection by providing timely and versatile access to information in electronic format. Databases are used by the library staff to enhance and supplement reference service. Many of the databases contain specialized information beyond the scope of the library's print collections; others have information that does not exist in print format. Some databases duplicate print sources which are carefully evaluated for retention with consideration to cost, frequency of use, and ease of access to library users. Databases supplied by commercial vendors are accessed by the library staff at their discretion. Customized searches for patrons with specialized needs, such as mailing lists and literature searches, are provided through the library's fee-based service, POINT (Pasadena Online Information Network).

E-JOURNALS

University of Maryland
University of Maryland Libraries
College Park, Maryland

Electronic Access to Scholarly Material

Electronic Journal FAQ's

Are all of the Libraries' journals available in electronic format?

Not all journal titles have an electronic version. The number of titles published electronically, however, is increasing rapidly. So far, UM Libraries provide access to more than 4,000 electronic journals. We pay for subscriptions to more than 6,000 print journals.

Is there a difference in cost between electronic and paper journals? Can't we have access to electronic and print versions of a journal for the same amount of money?

Initially, many e-journals were "bundled" with the print subscription. Sometimes a percentage surcharge was tacked on for electronic access. Consequently, e-journals actually increased our annual subscription costs. Increasingly, publishers are beginning to charge more for bundled print and electronic subscriptions, while charging less for electronic only subscriptions making it more economically advantageous to subscribe to journal collections in electronic format only. For more information regarding this trend and the associated costs to the Libraries please see Moving Beyond Paper 2005: More Journal Subscriptions to be received only in Electronic Form.

Will older issues of electronic journals become available in electronic format? How far back in time are electronic journals available?

> The publisher determines whether or not to make older issues of e-journals available. Because of the trend to move to electronic only access, many publishers have developed e-journal archival plans that ensure long-term access to journals available electronically, but also seek to digitize back issues that, previously, had no electronic equivalent.

> Those publishers that are providing online access to journal backfiles are usually doing so for an additional fee. So it varies as to how many issues of a journal are available online. The availability of backfiles can range from last year to the nineteenth century. For example, the American Physical Society provides backfile access it its titles through Physical Review Online Archive (PROLA).

> In addition, projects like JSTOR, an electronic archive of journals from across the disciplines, are addressing the need for electronic access to back issues and digital archiving of e-journals.

How will the Libraries ensure perpetual access to e-journals? What happens if the publisher goes out of business? What happens if the Libraries cancel then restart an e-journal subscription?

> This is an area of great concern for both libraries and the scholarly community. We examine our license agreements closely to evaluate the terms of long-term access. We prefer products that offer strong archival plans and access to electronic journal content, even if we cancel our subscription. Since we currently license most of our e-journal content, unless we own the paper volumes, we have to be sure that the publisher will provide us with electronic access to the years of the journal for which we had a subscription. Often, in the license agreement, the publisher will specify what happens to our access if we cancel our subscription or if the publisher goes out of business. Publishers may give or sell us the issues on CD-ROM or let us FTP the data to a local server. Many publishers are contracting with another publisher/organization, such as OCLC, Online Computer Library Center, to ensure continued access.

> Libraries and the academic community in general are examining how best to preserve e-journal content to ensure perpetual access. The Andrew W. Mellon Foundation provided grant money for academic libraries to investigate issues in e-journal archiving. Progress is being made and libraries are working with publishers and the academic community on sustainable, technically sound solutions. Some notable initiatives include LOCKSS out of Stanford and E-archive a project run by Ithaka, a non-profit organization dedicated to promoting the use of information technologies in higher education.

Can I download e-journal articles to create my own database or to share them with colleagues?

> Many of our license agreements place restrictions on systematic downloading and printing. For example, a license may forbid the downloading or printing of an entire issue of a journal or it may restrict downloading and printing to academic use. While usually these rules simply reflect copyright law, some licenses are more restrictive. Restrictions are usually described on the journal's website if you have any questions. We prefer to license products that allow you to download articles and store them on your computer for your own use. But, often these articles cannot be distributed to colleagues via a web or ftp website other than the publisher's website.

How do I access electronic journals?

> You can access UM's e-journals from both on and off campus. For off-campus access, please use Research Port . See Off-Campus Access for other ways of accessing e-journals remotely.

> If you don't see the title you are looking for, contact your librarian subject specialist or go to the nearest UM Libraries reference desk.

How does the image quality of electronic journals compare to the paper version? If I print out an e-journal article will it look the same as what I see on the screen?

With the increasing emphasis on e-journals, digital image quality is becoming comparable to paper journals with some e-journals including additional dynamic, hyperlinked graphics. Sometimes, however, there is a difference between the electronic and paper version of the same journal article in terms of the image quality of photographs, tables, and graphs. Due to publisher distribution agreements, an electronic journal article may not contain actual graphs, tables, and photos found in the paper version. Conversely, e-journal articles may include additional text, images, sound, or video, which are omitted from the article's paper counterpart.

Printing e-journal articles is dependent on the quality of your monitor and the resolution of your printer. Printing out an article does not, necessarily, ensure quality comparable to the paper or electronic version of the article. For best results, set your printer at a high resolution when printing e-journal articles containing images, graphs, or tables.

If the library does not subscribe to an e-journal can I request articles through Interlibrary Loan (ILL)? How much does it cost?

Interlibrary Loan (ILL) is a library service that will obtain materials not owned by UM Libraries from other libraries. Unless the request exceeds a certain cost, you do not pay for this service (UM Libraries funds this service). Obtaining articles through ILL is an alternative to subscribing to low use journals. Journal articles requested through ILL will be delivered to your desktop as page images. There is a time limit and copyright restrictions placed on your ILL request. Please see additional services for information on desktop delivery.

Will the paper version of a journal be destroyed because we have electronic access?

Although some current journals will only be acquired in electronic format, the Libraries will not be discarding any of our paper collections. In 2002, the Libraries formulated a policy that dictates the criteria upon which decisions to cancel paper subscriptions are based. Please see Moving Beyond Paper 2005: More Journal Subscriptions to be received only in Electronic Form for more information. We will continue to evaluate publisher packages and individual journals on a case by case basis.

Why don't we have a particular electronic journal I've seen advertised?

Subscribing to e-journal collections is often complex. Some publishers require substantial additional payments and complicated or unreasonable licensing and/or access terms, which place limitations on use. Some packages may have clauses in the license agreement that would prevent the Libraries from cancelling the corresponding paper titles for the duration of the agreement.

Also, our ability to provide comprehensive journal access is affected by the crisis in scholarly communication. This crisis was precipitated by price increases in journal subscriptions that have outstripped the ability of library budgets to pay for them. We are not guaranteed annual budget increases to pay for inflation, much less add new titles. Every year we evaluate our journal subscriptions to try and balance our need to maintain paper titles, purchase added electronic access, and add new titles in paper and electronic formats. For more information about the scholarly communication crisis and how you can help, see Crisis In Scholarly Communication FAQ's.

Duke University
William R. Perkins Library
Durham, North Carolina

Perkins Library System E-Only Journal Exceptions Policy

The E-Only Journal Exceptions Policy was adopted by the Perkins Library System Collections Council on April 25, 2007. This policy adapted from the Cornell University Library E-Only Journal Exceptions Policy will guide the acquisition of new and existing journal titles from July 2007 and on. The guiding principle behind the policy is that all journal subscriptions will be digital unless one or more of the following exceptions are met.

- Function
    1. If the print journal functions better as a browsing journal or current awareness source (e.g., due to interface design in the electronic version)
    2. If the quality of images or graphics is demonstrably poorer in the electronic journal.
    3. If the print has significant artifactual or aesthetic value.
- Electronic Archival Availability
    4. If there is no guarantee that the publisher will continue to provide access to the electronic volumes to which we subscribed in case of future cancellation.
    5. If there is no evidence of an institutional commitment to the journal's long-term preservation.
- Print Retention Responsibility
    6. If Duke University Libraries has either a consortia responsibility to retain a paper copy or another strong responsibility to retain a print archive of this journal title or the subject area to which it belongs.
- Timeliness & Reliability
    7. If there is any delay between publication of print and availability of online content.
    8. If the provider of the electronic journal is unreliable.
- Content
    9. If the content of the print differs from that of the electronic. (e.g., the print version contains significantly more material than the electronic version)
- Use Restrictions
    10. If license restrictions prevent the university community from using the electronic version in a way that differs materially from use of the print version.

Adapted from Cornell University Library. E-Only Journal Exceptions Site.

Texas A&M Corpus Christi
Mary and Jeff Bell Library
Corpus Christi, Texas

Electronic Journals

As stated above, for the purposes of this policy, an electronic journal is defined as being a digital version of a print journal, or a journal-like electronic publication with no print counterpart, made available via the Web, e-mail, or other means of Internet access. The distinction is important to selection decisions and should be one of the first pieces of information a selector considers about an e-journal.

In either case, the following criteria must be considered:

- Content decisions, that is, the decision whether or not the topics covered by a journal support the educational and/or research missions of the library and the university should be made based on the selection criteria outlined in each individual subject collection development policy. Judgments of quality such as whether a journal is considered to be a core title in its discipline may be supported by information contained in Ulrich's or Magazines in Libraries.
- Cost is almost always a consideration in the decision to purchase a new subscription, more so than with monographic purchases because of the recurring financial commitment that a journal subscription requires. At the time that this policy is being written, the Library's serials budget is static. New subscriptions are added rarely and almost always accompanied by an equivalent reduction in some other part of the Library budget (for example the cancelling of an equivalently priced journal subscription or the re-

duction of library services or student assistant hours). For this reason, freely available, open access e-journals are preferred.

- Whether or not the contents of the journal are covered in indexes to which the library subscribes should be seriously considered. The lack of inclusion in library subscribed indexes significantly reduces the usefulness of the journal to library users.

In cases when a journal is available in more than one format (e.g. print and/or microform as well as electronic), the following additional criteria should be considered:

- Does the library subscribe to the journal in any other format?
- Is the selector suggesting that the Library add a subscription to the e-journal in addition to any current subscriptions to the journal in other formats? Or is the selector recommending that the Library purchase a subscription to the e-journal to replace any current subscriptions in other formats? A case could be made for either possibility and there is currently no preference as long as both possibilities are considered.
- Is the fee to upgrade to the e-journal version reasonable? How expensive would it be to cancel the subscription to the print or microform version in favor of a subscription to the e-journal version?
- Is there a preferred format among users? Several ways that this might be determined is by usage statistics or informal comments from users if the library is currently subscribing to the journal in another format. Does expected usage warrant the selection of a particular format or the addition of an additional format?
- Is content in all versions/formats identical? There may be occasions where subscribing to the e-journal version of a journal may be warranted if the content of the e-journal version contains information that is unavailable in the print or microform version.

In cases when the journal is not available in any other format or once a preference for e-journal version is established, the following additional selection criteria should be considered:

- What is the overall quality of the web site? For example,
  - If images, photographs, or other forms of non-test data are essential parts of articles, are the color and detail presented with acceptable clarity and accuracy?
  - Is the site easy to navigate?
  - Are there any especially desirable features present (e.g. tables of contents or alerting services)?
- Is there a restriction on the number of simultaneous users of the e-journal? Preference will be given to those e-journals with no such restriction.
- How are authorized users identified (what is the method of authentication)? Preference will be given to those e-journals that use IP recognition to identify authorized users over those e-journals that use passwords or referring URLs to do so.
- Does the subscription include access to the e-journal's backfiles? Preference will be given to those e-journals that provide access to backfiles of a journal either through open access or as a benefit of owning a current subscription.
- Does the subscription include a guarantee of permanent access to the volumes and issues purchased or will all access cease if (when) the subscription is cancelled? Preference will be given to those e-journals that provide a guarantee of permanent access.
- How reliable is the publisher and how stable is the website where the e-journal is published and archived? Preference will be given to stable publishers who make reasonable efforts to maintain access.
  - Do they appear to make reasonable efforts to maintain the information and upgrade to new storage and access technology as warranted?
  - Is access to the e-journal reliable (e.g. does the server crash all the time)?
  - Does the publisher provide advanced notice of maintenance or other down time?
  - Are electronic issues published/made available in a timely manner? Do they appear before or after receipt of the print version if one exists?
  - Does the publisher provide adequate technical support for their website?

- Is any client side software required to view the content of the e-journal? Preference will be given to those e-journals that do not require special handling or software installations on Library workstations.
- Is the website on which the e-journal is published compliant with ADA accessibility requirements? Preference will be given to those e-journals that are accessible to library users with visual, hearing, and other impairments.
- Is the e-journal included in the Library's electronic journal management system? Currently the library subscribes to EBSCO's A-to-Z Service to manage access to journal subscriptions in all formats and make them available to library users. It is particularly important that the Library be able to provide access to the e-journal through an e-journal management system in order to obtain durable URLs to link to the e-journal because the Library currently lacks the resources to conduct link checking on non-durable URLs. A high preference will be given to e-journals that are accessible through the Library's e-journal management system or that provide access via durable URLs.
- Will the library be required to negotiate and agree to a new license agreement in order to access the e-journal? While this requirement does not preclude the purchase of an e-journal that requires a new license agreement, selectors should be aware that this adds quite a bit of processing time and effort for Periodicals / Electronic Resources staff and make their selections accordingly.
  - Does the license allow for fair use of the journal contents including making the contents available via InterLibrary Loan?
  - Does the license exclude, modify or affect any of the Library's rights under copyright law?
- Are usage statistics provided by the publisher? Preference will be given to those e-journals that provide the Library with usage statistics on which to base decisions about the relative usefulness of the e-journal to Library users.

University of Oregon
Knight Library
Eugene, Oregon

Electronic Journals

I. Purpose

The University of Oregon Libraries supports the instructional and research programs of the University. Toward this aim, the Library collects or provides access to materials in multiple formats, including electronic formats. The challenges to providing access to electronic journals warrant a separate collection development policy focusing on these materials. This policy will provide guidelines for the selection and acquisition of electronic journals as well as the provision of access. Related collection development documents will address procedural concerns in detail.

II. Scope

This policy seeks to address the selection and acquisition of electronic journals accessible via the Internet. This policy covers electronic journals for which the Library gains free access, access at a reduced rate because the Library subscribes to the print, or purchased access to an electronic-only version.

The Library will pursue the purchase of other types of resources as these develop in the future and meet the guidelines outlined herein. This policy also does not address the following electronic resources, which may fall into more than one of the following categories:

- online bibliographic or full-text databases
- offline electronic resources
- Internet resources (monographic in nature)

- Collection development policies for online resources and offline electronic resources address the selection, acquisition, and provision of access for these materials.

III. Principal Access Point and Provision of Access

The Library will provide access to electronic journals which it acquires and/or licenses via the central Library Web page. The Library will maximize access to the Library's electronic journals through several means: cataloging of each e-journal, necessary archiving and/or storage, provision, maintenance, preparation, and loading of necessary software and hardware, and appropriate staff and user support and training for optimal use. Because the Library will catalog e-journals, there will be links to these resources via the Janus Webpac. Additionally, subject specialists or departmental libraries and collections may wish to provide links to these journals via appropriate Web pages.

IV. General Selection Principles

Selection Responsibility: Responsibility for selecting these materials falls to individual subject specialists and the head of collection development as these materials fall into their regular selecting responsibility. Other librarians and library users will offer suggestions to appropriate subject specialists or the head of collection development.

Funding: Ordinarily, the subject content will determine the individual fund. Subject specialists and the head of collection development will determine the appropriate individual funds to use for purchasing electronic journals. As with all other formats, the Library will consider other allocations for those titles deemed major purchases.

Adherence to Other Collection Development Guidelines: The purchase of electronic journals should follow present collecting policies whether general or subject specific policies. Specifically their purchase should adhere to the chronological, geographical, language, and date of publication guidelines set forth in general or subject specific policies. As with other materials subject specialists should also 1) consider present curriculum and research needs, 2) select materials which meet the standards the Library expects of all materials in regard to excellence, comprehensiveness, and authoritativeness, and 3) weigh the purchase of a particular title against other possible acquisitions from material budgets.

Specific Format Criteria: In addition to content, subject specialists should closely consider the criteria listed below when considering the purchase of electronic journals:

- if free, the improvement or enhancement that the resource will give to existing print materials
- the technical requirements necessary to provide access
- the broad accessibility of the resource under present copyright laws and licensing agreements
- the user-friendliness of the resource
- the necessity of archiving and/or availability of archives

It is particularly important to consult available published reviews of electronic journals before their acquisition. Reviews can outline how well a resource meets specific criteria and can provide further insight regarding the resource's overall quality. If reviews are not available, then subject specialists should make an effort to locate other pertinent information about the resource, possibly through listserves, and provide the names of contacts at comparable institutions who are using the resource so that Collection Development may explore possible issues and concerns about a resource.

Subject specialists should not necessarily exclude a title because it does not meet every individual criterion or because it automatically duplicates a print subscription. However, subject specialists should attempt to select resources that adequately meet as many of the selection criteria as is possible. Because this format increases the complexity of acquisition and access, subject specialists should include the detailed list of pre-order guidelines when ordering electronic journals. A sample of this detailed list is appended to this policy.

V. Licensing

The Library will negotiate and comply with vendor licensing agreements. An appended list of pre-order guidelines outlines the necessary details for this negotiation and compliance. The Library will also promote compliance with licensing agreements among its users and among its staff. Because this format increases the complexity of licensing agreements, subject specialists should include the detailed list of pre-order guidelines and the necessary licensing agreement, when available, with any order for electronic journals prior to ordering the title.

VII. Duplicates

The Library will purchase electronic journals which duplicate print subscriptions when:

- one format is unstable
- a cost benefit for purchasing multiple formats exists
- multiple formats meet the different needs of user groups
- the archived format of a resource will not operate with current technology.

VIII. Policy Review

Because of the complex and dynamic nature of providing access to electronic journals, the head of Collection Development, the subject specialists, and other librarians will need to review this policy at least every two years.

University of Maryland, Baltimore
University of Maryland Health Sciences and Human Services Library
Baltimore, Maryland

E-journals: As with print journals, electronic journals require a long-term commitment from the Library in terms of financial resources and human resources to acquire and maintain them. As more and more scholarly journals become available in electronic as well as print versions, the Library must decide whether to maintain both versions or cancel the print when the online version becomes available.

Free with Existing Print Subscription Upon Request: the Library will provide access to the Web version of a print journal to which it subscribes if it meets the following criteria:

- free (i.e, no additional cost beyond that of the print subscription).
- access is provided by IP address and/or proxy server (no passwords).
- no additional software (other than a Web browser) is required.
- licensing terms are acceptable.
- journal is full text, not just abstracts or tables of contents.

Not Included With Existing Subscription: electronic journals which are not included in the cost of a print subscription, as well as resources new to the Library, will be reviewed by the Electronic Resources Committee.

E-RESOURCE DEFINITION

Indiana University South Bend
Franklin D. Schurz Library
South Bend, Indiana

Definition

For selection and collection management purposes, e-resources are defined as works electronically accessible and may include but are not limited to electronic journals, government publications, e-books, or electronic indexes more commonly referred to as databases. They are given the same consideration for selection as all other formats.

The Schurz Library considers all types of electronic resources. The library collects content-rich electronic resources and bibliographic management software (i.e. Endnote, Refworks). Application software such as word processing is purchased and supported by the IUSB campus Information Technologies Department.

Baruch College/CUNY
William and Anita Newman Library
New York, New York

"CUNY Computer resources" refers to all computer and information technology hardware, software, data, access and other resources owned, operated, or contracted by CUNY. This includes, but is not limited to, personal computers, handheld devices, workstations, mainframes, minicomputers, servers, network facilities, databases, memory, and associated peripherals and software, and the applications they support, such as e-mail and access to the internet.

"E-mail" includes point-to-point messages, postings to newsgroups and listservs, and other electronic messages involving computers and computer networks.

Solano Community College
Solano Community College Library
Fairfield, California

Definitions

"Computer and communications systems" includes but it not limited to the District telephone system, voice mail system, computer networks, e-mail system, and access to the Internet.

"User" refers to any District officer, employee, independent contractor, student, or public user authorized to use District computer and communications systems.

"System administrative" is the person responsible for configuring, supporting, and programming a computer or communications system/network and of ensuring its integrity and security.

"Integrity" of the system refers to the proper operation of a system/network, including the compatibility of all components as well as the validity of data contained therein or transmitted thereby.

"Security" refers to the use of passwords and physical devices for allowing only appropriate users to have access at an appropriate level to special data or services via a computer or communications network.

GOVERNMENT DOCUMENTS

Florida Atlantic University
S.E. Wimberly Library
Boca Raton, Florida

Public Guidelines for Government Information in Electronic Formats:

As a Federal Depository Library, the Government Documents Library is committed to free public access to government information, as mandated by 44 U.S.C. §1911. The Government Documents collections and services are available to the public as well as to persons affiliated with Florida Atlantic University (FAU). Service for government information in electronic formats at S.E. Wimberly Library is governed by the federal government's Depository Library Public Service Guidelines for Government Information in Electronic Formats (1998) and by the PC Use Policy for Library Users.

FAU Libraries provides free Internet access to government information from its public computer workstations for accessing government information in electronic formats. In addition, at least one computer workstation is dedicated to documents reference use to ensure availability of federal government information even in times of peak library usage. This workstation is located in the Government Documents Office and has 3-1/4 inch floppy disk/CD-ROM/DVD drives. No password, sign-up, or Florida Atlantic University identification is required to use these workstations, and no Internet filters are installed. All workstations have 3-1/4 inch floppy disk/CD-ROM drives, and downloading of electronic data to disk is encouraged.

The Government Documents Department attempts to maintain computer equipment that meets the latest "Recommended Specifications for Public Access Work Stations in Federal Depository Libraries" as published annually in Administrative Notes.

All workstations have Microsoft Office, Microsoft Word and Microsoft Excel for manipulation of downloaded data. Printing from all workstations is available for a fee set by Library Administration for all public printers in the library, currently 15 cents per page.

The Government Documents Department's CD-ROM collection is located in a cabinet housed in the Government Documents Office. If a CD-ROM requires special software to run, government documents staff will load the CD and any necessary software on a public workstation within one business day, if possible. Most CD-ROMs can also be checked out by users for use on their own workstations. A manual of instructions for loading the library's CD-ROMs is also available for checkout. Exceptions include: Census Bureau publications, reference titles, and high-use items.

The Government Documents Department maintains a web site designed to facilitate access to government information on the Internet as well as to guides for finding and using government information on the Internet. Some Internet sites containing government information require a password which will be provided for users in the Government Documents Offices.

Reference service, including assistance with government information in electronic formats, is available by e-mail at. . . . If necessary, documents shorter than ten pages in length can be sent to library users via fax; longer documents can be mailed. Personal or telephone assistance with using government information in all formats is available in the Government Documents Office from . . . Assistance is available at the general information desk at other times the library is open.

Long Island University
B. Davis Schwartz Memorial Library
Brookville, New York

As of 2005, over 80% of information provided by the federal Government Printing Office is available electronically. The GPO maintains PURLs to these resources which may be accessed free of charge. One exception to the free access policy is to the National Trade Databank; the Department is provided with a password for this resource. The Department maintains its home page and bookmarks for the most useful and effective web sites to locate information generated by all levels of government.

The Department is one of twenty full research depositories of the State of New York. Through 1995, the department received microfiche copies of all the State's copyright-free documents listed in the Checklist of the Official Publications of the State of New York. Due to budgetary constraints, the New York State Library now produces digital publications instead of microfiche. This digitized information is accessible free of charge. In addition, about twenty major reference titles published in paper format are also automatically sent to the department.

Copies in paper format of other New York State publications and quasi-government publications (such as those issued by the Federal Reserve Banks) are solicited through contact with the sponsoring agency and through mail list subscription. Additional reference resources of a non-depository nature are purchased to augment and provide access to the collection.

Retention of the tangible Federal and New York State documents follows the shared acquisitions policy of the LILRC Committee. Federal information is to be kept for a minimum of five years and New York State microfiche distributed to research depositories held permanently. Since digitization of both retrospective Federal and New York documents is not too extensive, tangible documents of publications are retained if they have value for research.

Texas A&M Corpus Christi
Mary and Jeff Bell Library
Corpus Christi, Texas

Government Documents—Electronic resources received through the federal and state depository programs are subject to government mandated requirements, criteria, and conditions unique to those programs. As far as is possible their selection will be based on the criteria described in this policy. In cases of conflict between this policy and government mandated requirements, criteria, and conditions, the government's policies will take precedence.

OFFLINE RESOURCES

University of Oregon
Knight Library
Eugene, Oregon

Off-line Electronic Resources

I. Purpose

The University of Oregon Libraries supports the instructional and research programs of the University. Toward this aim, the Library collects or provides access to materials in multiple formats, including electronic formats. The challenges to providing access to off-line electronic resources warrant a separate collection development policy focusing on these materials. This policy will provide guidelines for the selection and acquisition of off-line electronic resources as well as the provision of access. Related collection development documents will address procedural concerns in detail.

II. Scope

This policy seeks to address the selection and acquisition of off-line electronic resources, primarily those monographic titles available on CD-ROM or floppy disk. These resources may be:
* numeric data files
* textual files
* bibliographic files
* graphic and multimedia files
* courseware/instructional files
* software needed specifically to utilize resources listed above.

The Library will pursue the purchase of other types of resources as these develop in the future and meet the guidelines outlined herein. This policy also does not address the following electronic resources, which may fall into more than one of the following categories:

- online bibliographic or full-text databases
- Internet resources
- electronic journals or serials

Collection development policies for online resources and electronic journals will address the selection, acquisition, and provision of access for these resources.

III. Location

The Knight Library Instructional Technology Center (ITC) will be the central location of most of these resources as well as the central access provider. Other libraries and collections, such as Science, Maps, AAA, Math, Music, Reference, Law, and Government Documents, also house and provide access to off-line electronic resources, appropriate for their individual missions.

IV. Electronic Resources Accompanying Other Formats

Floppy disks and CD-ROMs may accompany other formats—monographs, serials, films, videos, or audio recordings. When possible, the Library will purchase and provide access to these materials in compliance with this policy's guidelines. If off-line electronic resources accompany other primary formats, they will be shelved together in the appropriate location. Procedures for handling electronic resources that accompany print formats are provided in greater detail in a related document, Accompanying Off-line Electronic Resources.

V. General Selection Principles

Selection Responsibility: Responsibility for selecting these materials falls to individual subject specialists and the head of collection development as these materials fall into their regular selecting responsibility. The coordinator for the ITC as well as library users and other individuals will offer suggestions to appropriate subject specialists or the head of Collection Development.

Funding: Ordinarily, the subject content will determine the individual fund. Subject specialists and the head of collection development will determine the appropriate individual funds to use for purchasing off-line electronic resources. As with all other formats, the Library will consider other allocations for those titles deemed major purchases.

Adherence to Other Collection Development Guidelines: The purchase of off-line electronic resources should follow present collecting policies whether general or subject specific policies. Specifically their purchase should adhere to the chronological, geographical, language, and date of publication guidelines set forth in general or subject specific policies. As with other materials subject specialists should also 1) consider present curriculum and research needs, 2) select materials which meet the standards the Library expects of all materials in regard to excellence, comprehensiveness, and authoritativeness, and 3) weigh the purchase of a particular title against other possible acquisitions from material budgets.

Specific Format Criteria: In addition to content, subject specialists should closely consider the criteria listed below when considering the purchase of off-line electronic resources.

- the necessary amount of staff time to provide access, training, and assistance
- the improvement or enhancement that the resource will give to existing print materials
- the long-term viability of resources for preservation purposes
- the long-term usability of a resource's data (10 years or more)
- the broad accessibility of the resource under present copyright laws and licensing agreements
- the compatibility of the resource with existing hardware about to be purchased or already in
- the Library and hardware on the University of Oregon campus
- the availability and adequacy of documentation
- the currency of the resource's information, if deemed necessary for subject matter
- the user-friendliness of the resource

- the ability to network the resource if deemed appropriate
- the replacement policy of the publisher in the event of damage or theft.

It is particularly important to consult available published reviews of off-line electronic resources before their acquisition. Reviews can outline how well a resource meets specific criteria and can provide further insight regarding the resource's overall quality. Subject specialists should not necessarily exclude a title because it does not meet every individual criterion. However, subject specialists should attempt to select resources that adequately meet as many of the selection criteria as is possible. Because this format increases the complexity of acquisition and access, subject specialists should include the detailed list of pre-order guidelines when ordering off-line electronic resources. A sample of this detailed list is appended to this policy.

Selection Tools: In addition to subject-oriented reviewing sources and Choice reviews, subject specialists may consult several sources for current reviews of off-line electronic resources and for general information about the technology. Titles held by the UO Libraries include:

- CD-ROM News Extra
- CD-ROM Professional
- "CD-ROM Review," a regular feature of Library Journal
- Database
- "Multimedia Reviews," a monthly feature of Publishers Weekly
- Online and CD-ROM Review.

VI. Copyright

The Library will comply with the existing copyright laws. The Library will also promote copyright compliance among its users and among its staff.

VII. Licensing

The Library will negotiate and comply with vendor licensing agreements. An appended list of pre-order guidelines outline the necessary details for this negotiation and compliance. Because this format increases the complexity of licensing agreements, subject specialists should include the detailed list of pre-order guidelines and the necessary licensing agreement, when available, with any order for off-line electronic resources prior to ordering the title.

VIII. Provision of Access

The Library will maximize access to the Library's off-line electronic resources through several means:

- cataloging of each resource
- necessary storage
- provision, maintenance, preparation, and loading of necessary software and hardware
- appropriate staff and user support and training for in-building use
- circulation of resources according to ITC circulation procedures.

IX. Gifts

The Library will evaluate and accept gifts of off-line resources that meet the specific format criteria identified herein and that adhere to other collection development guidelines, whether general or subject specific. Gifts of off-line electronic resources should also follow the Library's gifts policy.

X. Replacements

The Library will replace off-line electronic resources using the same criteria for other formats: demand for the resource, cost, and availability from publishers or vendors.

XI. Conversion of Outmoded Off-line Electronic Resources

Off-line electronic resources may operate on computer software and hardware that becomes outdated or obsolete while the resource's information remains valuable. In such cases, the Library will attempt to convert or update off-line electronic resources to a useable format. When conversion of outmoded electronic resources is possible, the Library may decide to convert after examining copyright and licensing of the product, demand for the resource, historical significance and uniqueness of the resource (including cost of the conversion), and availability of the information in another format.

XII. Duplicates

The Library will purchase duplicate copies of off-line electronic resources when demonstrated need and other restrictions indicate that networking or other options for providing access are not adequate or available. The Library also will purchase duplicates of electronic resources or purchase duplicates of print resources in electronic format when:

- the resource has significant historical value
- one format is unstable
- a cost benefit for purchasing multiple formats exists
- multiple formats meet the different needs of user groups
- the archived format of a resource will not operate with current technology.

XIII. Policy Review

Because of the complex and dynamic nature of providing access to off-line resources, the head of Collection Development, the coordinator for the Instructional Technology Center, and other librarians will need to review this policy at least every two years.

Chapter 5

COLLECTION DIGITIZATION

ARCHIVING

Central Michigan University
Central Michigan Universities Libraries
Mount Pleasant, Michigan

Archiving

The CMU Libraries have a legitimate interest in maintaining collection integrity through archives of the electronic resources they have licensed or otherwise acquired. For electronic journals and other similar resources, a license should include permanent rights to information that has been paid for, in the event that a licensed database is subsequently canceled or removed by either the Libraries or the vendor.

In these cases, responsibility for providing archival access should be clearly defined in all agreements and licenses. Government publications and some professional societies and publishers take on the responsibility for data archive security or are in partnership with a university of other entities to archive electronic-only publications. If the information provider does not maintain archival access, the CMU Libraries retain the right to maintain archival access on their own servers and/or to negotiate for formats that are most appropriate for the transfer and storage of archival information.

The Libraries are moving away from ownership in the electronic environment, preferring access via Internet, WWW, etc. whenever possible for ease of use, wider access, and possible cost savings over local maintenance and storage. However, there will be costs, copyright, and licensing issues associated with Internet access. It is not necessary in many instances for the Libraries to own the archival version of electronic products, but ownership can be crucial in certain circumstances, such as when vendors/publishers do not guarantee maintaining archival copies of products that are essential to the research and teaching needs of the University. Archival ownership may not be necessary, for example, for bibliographic databases and certain full-text databases. Bibliographers should use their best judgment in recommending the highest quality medium and must investigate cost/benefit and risk in collaboration with the Head of Collection Development.

Indiana University South Bend
Franklin D. Schurz Library
South Bend, Indiana

Archiving: Strong preference should be given to agreements that allow the library to have access to, or own the content of, the last-held version of the database in perpetuity.

DIGITAL LIBRARY ARCHIVING AND FILE FORMATS

Northwestern University
Northwestern University Library
Evanston, Illinois

Report of the Digital Library Committee's Archiving and File Formats Subcommittee
Introduction to the Subcommittee's work

The Digital Library Committee's Archiving and File Formats Subcommittee (AFF) began work in October 2001. The AFF developed a set of questions based on its original charge (see Appendices A and B) to guide its work. While many digital library archiving policy details relate to questions still evolving within the digital library community at large, the existing body of policies do establish institutional targets required to accomplish current work and outline overall trends that will inevitably help us predict, define and develop the infrastructure, expertise and resources that will be necessary for us to develop and support a trusted digital repository to preserve our collections over time.

The focus was narrowed to accomplishment of three tasks. The first was to identify broad archiving issues and the second to identify areas of responsibility to be assigned to particular library departments for further study and policy creation. The last task was to develop practical standard recommendations for the manner of producing and archiving digital library project data and objects. Tasks one and two are addressed in Part one below, and task three in Part two.

The AFF makes these recommendations to the Digital Library Committee (DLC) for review and revision before they are submitted to the library administration.

Part one: General recommendations

1. INSTITUTIONAL COMMITMENT The library administration must commit support and resources sufficient to sustain long-term management of and access to electronic resources. Digital archiving is expensive but necessary for a research library of our stature.

2. STORING DIGITAL OBJECTS The Information Technology division (NULIT), should assume responsibility for providing and maintaining sufficient storage space for all digital library project data and objects and ensuring that they are properly backed up off-site.

3. MANAGEMENT AND PRESERVATION OF DIGITAL LIBRARY PROJECT FILES The Preservation Department should work with appropriate partners to create policies, guidelines and procedures for long-term management and preservation of digital library project files (described in Section Two below) and data, including preservation metadata. These policies and procedures will include data verification, refreshing or migration. The Preservation Department should assume primary responsibility to work with other partners in order to guarantee that the Library's digital assets can be managed and maintained over time.

4. EXTERNAL PARTICIPATION The library should develop its digital archiving strengths by participating actively in external activities that seek to develop sustainable digital repositories for locally generated or purchased electronic resources. Foci that will benefit the library include: 1) project planning and development, 2) policy and standards development, 3) information management and digital archiving and, 4) resource sharing.

5. ESTABLISHING LIBRARY-WIDE ELECTRONIC ARCHIVING POLICIES The library should expand upon the above responsibilities and the procedures outlined in Section Two below to develop an archiving plan for staff-generated electronic information. This will include publications such as the library's web site, but also extend to administrative documents and other important materials generated by staff in the course of their daily work.

6. UNIVERSITY-WIDE ELECTRONIC ARCHIVING PROGRAM The Library should determine its role in addressing University-wide electronic archiving needs. Electronic records, including online publications and email, fall within the University Archives' collecting scope, but require new procedures and the support of the University in order for the Archives to identify, schedule, store, and provide access to them. The Library's role within the University could be either limited to recommending practices, or expanded to establishing and supporting a comprehensive University-wide electronic archiving program with accompanying levels of financial support. (See the CIC-University Archivists Group's Standards for an Electronic Records Policy at http://www-personal.umich.edu/~deromedi/CIC/cic4.htm)

7. ANNUAL REVIEW In July 2004, the DLC or a group it designates should review and make any necessary updates to this document and procedures outlined in Part two (below). Thereafter, this document should be reviewed annually and should include a new survey of current research.

Part Two: Specific recommendations governing creation and retention of digital library project data and objects

When staff is engaged in a digital library project, successful and on-time completion is the primary focus. It is equally important, however, to retain the information about how a project was executed and the basis on which decisions were made. In addition, if format and file naming decisions are based on expediency or other short-term concerns, there may be a higher price to be paid in the long term. The specific recommendations in Sections A and B, below, direct project managers and project staff how and when to create, and document the process of creating, digital library material.

These general principles are applicable to all phases of digital library project development, and are expanded in Sections A and B, below.

1. When documenting decisions and procedures, follow the same file format standards set forth for digital library objects themselves. The University's standards for supported applications may provide additional guidance if the library guidelines are found to be lacking.

2. Version control is critical; it allows project staff to backtrack within a project cycle to make corrections or changes. Save versions when significant changes are made, keeping these until the project is actually released or published. After the project is complete, it may be possible to eliminate some intermediate versions (saving only samplings of test scans, working prototypes, etc.)

3. All documents and objects must be kept on online (network-accessible) server storage locations provided by NULIT.

4. Two types of information must be collected and retained: 1) documentation of decision-making process and 2) objects created.

5. Use standard file names for all documents and digital objects.

6. Use prescribed technical standards (for capture) and standard file formats.

Section A: Recommended documentation and retention procedures for digital library projects

This section describes decisions to be documented and objects to be retained for each project phase. Examples are illustrative but not exhaustive.

1. Pre-production

The pre-production phase or phases of a digital library project involve such things as project planning, feasibility study, proof-of-concept, and prototype construction. In most cases, the documents to be retained will be administrative in nature: correspondence, reports, budgets and the like.

Decisions documented

a) Project plans and project team creation

b) Budgets

c) Establishment of version-control audit trail

d) Establishment of project space on server and description of online workspace:
   i. Testing/prototype area
   ii. Staging
   iii. Production

Objects saved

a) Test scans or other digitization or markup tests

2. Production

The production phase involves the actual conversion or creation of digital objects. It may be the longest phase in a digital library project, and it may be concurrent with other phases, particularly the metadata phase (3, below). Production may be partially or completely outsourced or may be performed within the library.

Decisions documented

a) Correspondence with vendors (including shipping/invoicing records) or with NUL staff performing digitization

b) RFP and its development, incl. local digitization settings

c) Local production instructions and guidelines

Objects saved

a) Deliverable digital objects

b) Collation data and indexes

c) Test scans—important for documenting the testing/approval process (see below, Post-Production, for deletion of all but samplings of test scans)

d) XML/SGML marked-up text (see also Phase 3, Metadata Generation, for admin/technical metadata)

e) Quality control records

3. Metadata Generation

In the metadata generation phase, data is created that is auxiliary to the digital objects themselves. This includes bibliographic, administrative and technical metadata.

Decisions documented

a) Rationale for schema selection

b) Granularity of metadata

Objects saved

a) Marked-up/ tagged files

b) Intermediate or alternate metadata (such as MARC) or local non-standard formats

c) Conversion utilities

d) DTD or schema

e) Handbook or toolkit for encoding

f) Locally-produced scripts

4. Site Integration and Publication

In this phase, objects and their associated metadata are assembled or packaged in some way for delivery to users.

Decisions documented

a) Creation and development of information infrastructure (documenting what has been done and how).

b) Post-launch corrections, adjustments, bug fixes

Objects saved

a) Mock-ups (not all versions—just working prototypes—but retain all versions until project is actually in production)

b) Supplemental material delivered in addition to digital objects: essays, presentation images, scope notes

c) Publicity materials (digital or Word documents)

d) "Build" files and scripts

5. Post-production

After the project is complete and published, and before much time has elapsed, it is important that the project team produces a summary of the work and cleans the online work areas to remove extraneous material.

Decisions documented

Final report/ project narrative (including the Project Survey template) to summarize the basics—e.g., "the _____ project used _____ for _____; these files are stored _____."

Objects saved

a)   Hand-off document for permanent owner of site

Objects deleted

b)   Surplus test scans, mock-ups

6. Long-Term Storage

While technically occurring after (or post-) production, the preparation of materials for long-term storage and ongoing care for these materials are treated as a separate phase. Data should be refreshed according to policies to be established.

Decisions documented

None

Objects saved

a)   Server back-up on tape

b)   Copy of ALL files in first 5 Phases, burned onto CD or DVD

c)   Index CD (with list of all files)

d)   Off-site storage records and receipts

Section B: Recommended file naming and file format standards

An environment must exist in which long-term archiving can succeed. Two keys to this success are easy identification of objects through regular file naming and using file formats that are most likely to be accessible in the long run.

File Naming Standards

File names may be named either according to a conservative, shortened form for best compatibility with DOS and other older systems, or may follow the longer form. Regardless of the form selected, however, the file naming must follow a certain structure as set forth here.

File name length:
   • Minimum: 8 characters + 3 character extension (some funding agencies may specify a short 8+3 file name structure)
   • Maximum: 31 characters, of which up to 4 may be extension
   • Recommended: 8 characters +[up to] 19 characters + 3 character extension, where 19 is the area for optional elements.

Required elements:
   • Base filename (up to 6 characters)
   • Extension indicating file type (.ext, for example: .jpg or .gif)

Recommended elements:
   • Use code suffix (see below)

Allowed elements:
- Project code: this should follow the base file name but precede the use code

When using the minimum recommended 8 characters +3 character file naming:
- Require use code (suffix)
- Standard MIME type extensions
- Use subdirectories for other variants

To further distinguish between different derivatives of a single object, apply these use codes as suffixes after the base file name and before the extension:

Text and Images:
MS – Master
AH – Access High
AL – Access Low
TH – Thumbnail
PR – Print
Audio/Video
CL – audio/video "clip"
PS – Postage stamp

General notes and rules about file naming:
- For numbering: pad with leading 0 as necessary (e.g., 009, 011, 111)
- Revision codes are not recommended; if necessary, use subdirectories to distinguish between revisions
- Do not use case TO differentiate between VERSIONS
- Do not mix loWERcasE/UpperCaSe
- Special Characters allowed are ~ _ -
- Do not use spaces or special characters other than ~ _ -

File Capture and Formats Standards

These standards duplicate the information available on the Digital Library Committee's Ad Hoc Digitization Standards: Technical Standards for Digital Capture as of July, 2003 (see: http://staffweb.library.northwestern.edu/dl/adhocdigitization/technicalstandards/index.html)

Text collections: technical standards for capture

In cases where text collections are to be digitized, all standards for image capture (see below) should be followed. OCR software generally requires 300 or 600 DPI bitonal images in TIFF format. In-house Optical Character Recognition (OCR) technologies have not been tested to a point where the resulting files may be considered acceptable for long-term storage.

If OCR is employed in ad-hoc projects, it is understood that the resulting recognized, machine-readable text is an access copy only. An uncompressed, TIFF version of each page must also be generated and retained according to image capture standards.

Recognized text in access copies may be delivered in a variety of text formats, including HTML, ASCII Text, and XML in EAD, TEI or other accepted standard depending on the needs of the project. Another option is to use the Adobe Acrobat PDF image + text technology to deliver both an image facsimile and "dirty" (uncorrected) OCR'd text in a single document.

Image collections: technical standards for image capture

As with other types of library collections, collections of image materials should only be subjected to the stress of digitizing once. Therefore, images should be digitized at archival quality in anticipation of a variety of future uses. This is known as a use-neutral approach to digitizing (RLG Guide to Quality in Visual Imaging: http://www.rlg.org/visguides/)

While there is no universal standards for quality image capture per se, Northwestern University Library will adhere to best practices adopted by a recognized leading institution. These standards for NUL digital capture are based on California Digital Library Digital Image Format Standards, 2001 (http://www.cdlib.org /about/publications/CDLImageStd-2001.pdf PDF file).

Note that a digital master must be generated for every object digitized, whether or not a screen and print resolution version is also generated. Resolution digital master files is measured in DPI (dots per inch) to capture as much data contained in the original as possible; a larger original will result in a proportionately larger digital master file.

Surrogate access files, alternatively, are measured by their pixel dimensions, as this determines how the image will display on a monitor.

Scanning resolution in dots per inch is achieved using the following formula:

(Desired pixel dimension) / (Size of original in inches) = Scanning resolution in dpi
For example:
6000 pixels in length / 11 inches in length = 545 dots per inch

Audio collections: technical standards for capture

Approaches to audio digitization may depend somewhat on the quality and format of the original. Extremely low fidelity recordings may not benefit from high frequency capture.

Higher end audio standards, such as the standard for DVD Audio, are still emerging. Therefore, in keeping with a use-neutral and technology-neutral approach, the following standards shall be applied.

Based on the Library of Congress AV prototyping project (http://www.loc.gov/rr/mopic/avprot/audioSOW .html update 3/23/01)

Note that a Digital master must be generated for every object digitized, whether or not service files are also generated.

Purpose
Sample rate
Sample size
Channels
File format(s)
Digital master
96 kHz (strongly recommended)
48 kHz (minimum)
24 bit
Mono or stereo, depending on characteristic of original
WAV uncompressed
Service file (high fidelity)
44kHz
16 bit
Mono or stereo, depending on characteristic of original
WAV or AIFF uncompressed
Service file (lower fidelity)
128 or 256 kbps
Sample size

Mono or stereo, depending on characteristic of original

MP3, QuickTime, Windows Media Audio, or Real Media (ra or rm)

Video collections: technical standards for capture

None of the existing file standards for video are approved for creating digital master copies. Digital video projects produce access copies only.

Based on the Library of Congress AV prototyping project: Video technical issues (http://lcweb.loc.gov/rr /mopic/avprot/avbrief3.html update 10/19/99)

Conclusion

While the procedures and recommendations above are structured to provide specific guidance to digital library project staff, they are generic enough that it may be possible to extend them to other library technology projects. For example, the file naming and file format standards set forth in Part Two, Section B could be adopted by departmental web authors or by individual staff saving documents pertaining to their daily work.

Developing coherent long-term archiving procedures and practices will be critical to the success of all digital library projects at Northwestern. These elements must be completely integrated into the workflow of a number of library departments. These departments, therefore, should have the opportunity to lead archiving policy development at Northwestern, building on the above recommendations and on activities of the international digital archiving community.

APPENDIX A: Charge to the Archiving and File Formats Subcommittee

1. Investigate and analyze digital archiving policies and infrastructure at NU and assess future needs, in light of emerging Library and University initiatives such as digital dissertations and distance learning. Survey digital archives policies and practices at other libraries, and current research and development occurring nationally and internationally.

2. Formulate a digital archiving policy, addressing selection, formats, levels of permanence, security, access, etc., for review, revision and endorsement by the DLC and Library Administration. Archiving issues would also be incorporated into the DLC proposal development and review process.

3. Finalize recommendations to the Library Administration for a plan for a digital archiving program, including requirements and budgets for infrastructure, staffing, and maintenance; and identifying possible sources of external funding.

Members of the subcommittee

APPENDIX B: The AFF began by developing a set of questions, based on its charge, to guide its work:

1. Who will be responsible for enforcing the policies we recommend?
2. What is an acceptable lifespan for electronics (equipment) and physical storage media (CD-R, DVD-R, magnetic tape, etc.)?
3. What should the policy for deleting things be?
4. What should we retain?
5. What are acceptable file formats and compression standards (images, sound, video, text, metadata files but not metadata structures)?
6. Where will these files be stored, including administrative data about the project?
7. What are approved storage locations for each stage of project development?

8. What kinds of backup systems will we need?
9. What is our data refreshing policy and schedule?
10. What are data migration and reformatting (including conversion from digital format to digital format) strategies?
11. What are our file naming conventions? How will we handle legacy project file naming?
12. Will we standardize on software used to create and manage our digital library data? How will this software be purchased and supported in the library?
13. Will we investigate emulation technologies and/or retain old versions of key software to ensure future access?
14. How will we ensure data integrity (periodic testing of stored data, procedures to measure the accuracy of data input, etc.)?
15. What will our data redundancy policy be? Will we have an off-site storage location or expand our current contracts for off-site storage?
16. What are procedures for rescuing data from damaged media or obsolete hardware/software?

Washington State Library
Olympia, Washington

PRESERVATION OF DIGITAL PROJECTS

Issues of Importance

The goals of digitization and preservation must coincide with the goals of the organization. The cost of digitization is too high to consider outside of the context of value and need. Organizations will have to set priorities for digitization and preservation that match its mission, access goals. Costs for creating digital copies of existing collections must be balanced with long-term benefits to the organization.

Washington libraries and cultural institutions have collections that will benefit all residents of the state if they are preserved and offered digitally. Some collections will not be worth the effort to create digital copies. Particularly those materials such as Northwest history books that are available in several Washington library collections. Other collections may not be suited to digitization. An example would be Washington newspapers. They already exist in microfilmed versions and are widely accessible. The technology to create useable digital copies of newspapers is only beginning to be understood. Port Townsend Library has undertaken a pilot project to test methods to digitize the microfilm copy of one year of the Morning Leader newspaper from 1901. (Port Townsend report)

Preservation of digital objects is little understood and no one has yet perfected the methods that will assure that a digital version of any material will survive over time. The National Archives recommends that public records and permanent copies of documents be preserved in an "eye readable" format. Eye readable for the most part is still paper copies or microforms that can be viewed on readers.

Preservation is: prevention of loss (deterioration); renewal of usability (treatment) and extension of usefulness of information content (reformatting).

"Preservation is: resource management, collection management and risk management."

"Preservation is the creation of digital products worth maintaining over time."

"Quality is the value we add to digital products."

"Quality and use combine to make a product worth preserving."

"Digital imaging is more than another way to copy a book, map or photograph. Imaging transforms the original in creating a new artifact with its own value apart from the original."

"Few digital collections will warrant the cost of a comprehensive migration strategy without considering value and use."

"Preservation in the digital world is knowing how to adapt traditional preservation concepts to manage risk."

The Library of Congress has presented a report defining the issues in preservation of objects that are born digital. Perpetual care of digital objects is more challenging than perpetual care of paper. Preservation of "born digital" objects is urgent. (link to LC21 document http://memory.loc.gov/ammem/techdocs/conserv 83199a.pdf)

Options to Consider

Digitization is not preservation. If the goal is to preserve existing collections, then use of traditional preservation methods will mostly be of greater cost benefit. Preservation through acid-free photocopies or preservation-quality microfilm will prove to be more cost effective.

For truly unique, damaged and fragile materials a procedure to conserve and re-house the originals, make digital versions for access and create a database and delivery product can be an effective preservation strategy. A carefully thought out project with quality control procedures can provide long-term benefits for cultural organizations and be cost effective.

Consider if the materials have sufficient value to users to justify digitization and preservation. Can digitization achieve the goals of the organization? Is the cost appropriate and can the staff resources be devoted to the project? If the answer is no for any of these questions then the digitization project is not viable.

Long-term preservation of the digital collection will require an investment in infrastructure and digital content management. Does the organization have the resources to create the infrastructure and management strategy? Where will the funding come from to create such an infrastructure?

Scanning from the originals is always best, unless they are too fragile or damaged to survive handling.

Scanners have been developed for commercial use and are not yet designed for the library and archive market, careful evaluation of the scanner purchase must be considered.

There is no single off-the-shelf solution for either hardware or software appropriate for libraries and historical organizations' preservation and digitization needs.

Project Checklist

Is the organization ready to make the commitment to digital collection building?

Digitization requires handling the originals, do you have procedures in place to minimize damage to the originals?

Will the project include activities to protect and preserve the original documents?

Following scanning, will formerly circulating items be assigned a non-circulating status?

How will the digital masters be protected and preserved?

How will the digital masters be stored?

Has the administrative metadata about the documents and equipment been collected and stored in a permanent medium?

Have you provided for long-term enduring access to the digital files and the metadata?

- Project a lifespan for the digital reproductions.
- Use digitization to its greatest advantage.
- Use traditional techniques and digital conversion together to preserve materials.

- Choose carefully to maximize the strength of traditional and digital technology.

Will the digitized material represent the original as an accurate copy or transcend the original by creating the possibility of uses impossible to achieve with the original?

GENERAL GUIDELINES

Columbia University
Columbia University Libraries
New York, New York

Statement of CUL policy for preservation of digital resources

According to the Columbia University Libraries' Mission Statement (7/22/93):

The Columbia University Libraries provides Columbia faculty, students, and staff with access to information in all subject areas related to the University's academic mission and its goals. The Libraries embraces its time-honored obligations of collecting, preserving, and providing access to collections, not only for the Columbia community but also for scholars and students from throughout the world who require access to the Libraries' unique materials.

Policy:

Digital resources are part of the CUL collections and subject to the same criteria for selection and retention decisions as other media. As such, they are included under the central CUL preservation policy: ensuring that the collections remain available over the long term, through prevention of damage and deterioration; reversing damage where possible; and, when necessary, changing the format of materials to preserve their intellectual content.

As with other parts of the collections, decisions about preservation are made by selectors, curators, and bibliographers as experts on the value of the content, in consultation with the relevant technical experts, including Academic Information Systems, the Library Systems Office, and Preservation. Priorities for preservation action are based on this Policy, the CU Strategic Plan, and available resources. When possible, decisions about the need for long-term retention are made at the time of creation, acquisition, or licensing of digital resources.

For digital resources that are deemed to be of long-term value, preservation can be defined as the actions needed to assure enduring access to the full content of those resources over time. Content has wider implications than simply assuring that a given image can be accessed.

Thus, hierarchical and structural relationships among the files (e.g. the pages of a book) an metadata that make the files usable must be preserved as well as the files themselves, Digital resources may exist in multiple versions. CUL is committed to preserving the archival version: the fullest, highest-quality available version of the resource, whenever possible; and the descriptive, structural, and administrative metadata associated with it.

Scope of preservation responsibility:

1. Responsibility for internal long-term retention and management by CUL/AcIS of:
    a. Digital resources created by CUL for which no other versions exist, and deemed to be of long-term value.
    b. Digital versions of resources reformatted by CUL, and deemed to be of long-term value in digital form.

    c. Unique digital resources which are acquired by CUL (through donation or purchase) as parts of archival/manuscript collections and which are unlikely to be preserved anywhere else.

    d. Digital records (e.g. bibliographic records, personnel records) deemed of long-term value and/or essential to CUL's functioning, and not preserved through any other arm of the university.

2. Responsibility for working externally through consortia action, licensing agreements, etc. to assure that someone (possibly but not necessarily CUL/AcIS) carries out preservation of appropriate commercially available digital resources to assure that CU faculty, staff, and students will have adequate ongoing access to these resources. Particular emphasis should be given to resources which exist in digital form only.

3. Responsibility for informing, consulting, and as appropriate coordinating with other units of Columbia University in the preservation of administrative and other digital resources to assure that CU faculty, staff, and students will have adequate ongoing access to these resources. Included here are digital resources created at CU outside of the Libraries but considered to be part of the digital library (EPIC ventures, others) and of long-term value.

Frequency with which preservation/retention policy for digital materials will be updated:

This policy will be reviewed by at the beginning of each academic year to assure timely updates as technology and experience mature, or more often if need arises.

LIFE CYCLE MANAGEMENT

Columbia University
Columbia University Libraries
New York, New York

Statement of CUL's commitment to lifecycle management

CUL is committed to lifecycle management of its digital resources. Guidelines and procedures for each stage have been or are being developed, and are reviewed as technology changes or other need arises. CUL will participate actively where appropriate in research, development, and implementation of new practices for preservation of digital resources.

- Development of preservation strategies, including consideration of:
  - Degree of integration with storage, backup, and preservation for non-digital library resources.
  - Development and use of decision-making tools (e.g., risk analysis, usage monitoring, probability of loss calculations, cost models, etc.).
  - Maintenance strategies (backups - online and/or offline, monitoring, refreshing, redundancy through mirror sites or caching, etc.).
  - Survival strategies 7(migration, emulation, archeology, etc.).
  - Reliance on outside consulting and archiving services, if any, contract negotiation, etc.
- Selection for long-term retention at time of digitization, acquisition, or licensing; and later reselection for retention if this decision was not made initially:
  - Primary criteria: based on institutional mission, needs, priorities, and reasons for creating or acquiring the resources (related to long-term institutional mission and linked to conversion guidelines): see Selection Criteria for Digital Imaging Projects, http://www.columbia.edu/cu/libraries/digital/criteria.htm.
  - Secondary criteria: based on regional, national, consortia, and international responsibilities.

- Conversion guidelines:
  - CUL follows relevant standards where they have been established and best practice for digital conversion, as documented by Library of Congress, the Research Libraries Group (RLG), the Digital Library Federation (DLF), and other relevant bodies.
  - See: Technical Recommendations for Digital Imaging Projects, http://www.columbia.edu/acis/dl/imagespec.html.
- Metadata creation and management (unique IDs and other descriptive, structural and administrative metadata, including ownership/rights management):
  - CUL follows relevant standards where they have been established and best practice for metadata creation and management, as documented by Library of Congress, RLG, DLF, and other relevant bodies.
  - Digital resources deemed to be of long-term value are tracked through the Master Metadata File (MMF). See: CU Master Metadata File, http://www.columbia.edu/cu/libraries/inside/projects/metadata/.
- Storage (online, offline, redundancy recommendations, etc.):
  - CUL follows relevant standards where they have been established and best practice for storage, as documented by Library of Congress, RLG, DLF, and other relevant bodies.
  - The archival version of the digital resource is preserved in a lossless, non-proprietary format, whenever possible.
  - Storage plan for primary responsibility materials:
    1. Resources currently in use: kept online with regular backup, refreshment, and migration.
    2. Whether online or not: all archival versions (highest resolution, fullest capture, lossless compression) are written to approved storage media and stored off-line in the Library Systems Office (LSO), with a schedule for regular refreshment, and migration.
    3. For archival versions which are not currently online: a duplicate off-line copy is created for storage at a different site.
    4. All versions, online and offline, are tracked through the MMF.
- Access arrangements (database management, Web interface, access reliability, etc.):
  - CUL follows relevant standards where they have been established and best practice for access arrangements, as documented by Library of Congress, RLG, DLF, and other relevant bodies.

Chapter 6

DEPARTMENTAL SELECTION, COLLECTION, AND WEEDING

DEFINITIONS

Texas A&M Corpus Christi
Mary and Jeff Bell Library
Corpus Christi, Texas

Definitions

These definitions are provided to clarify what is meant by the use of the following terms in this policy.

Announcing—making users aware of the availability of, location of, content of, usefulness of, and how to use an electronic resource (usually recently acquired).

Acquiring—purchasing and/or providing access to materials in the Library's collection, including free resources.

Database—A large, regularly updated file of digitized information (bibliographic records, full-text documents, directory entries, images, statistics, etc.), sometimes related to a specific subject or field, consisting of records of uniform format organized for ease and speed of search and retrieval and managed with the aid of database management system (DBMS) software that includes an internal mechanism (search interface) for searching based on proprietary metadata.

Content may be created by the publisher or be an aggregation of material published by other entities. Databases are often accessible online through the Internet.

Electronic Book (e-book, e-library book)—a digital version of a traditional print book, or a book-like electronic publication with no print counterpart, designed to be read on a personal computer or an e-book reader.

Electronic Journal (e-journal, e-magazine, e-zine, e-serial)—a digital version of a print journal, or a journal-like electronic publication with no print counterpart, made available via the Web, e-mail, or other means of Internet access. Includes electronic versions of popular magazines, newsletters, newspapers, and zines.

Electronic Resource—materials that require computer mediation in order to access their content and make it useful.

Evaluating—regularly reviewing the continued usefulness of each electronic resource.

Licensing—controlling the use of a resource by negotiating a formal written contract between a library and a vendor for the lease of one or more proprietary (copyrighted) bibliographic resources, usually for a fixed period of time and usually in exchange for payment of an annual subscription fee or per-search charge.

Maintaining—keeping library electronic resources operable and the information contained within them accessible.

Newsletter—A serial publication consisting of no more than a few pages, devoted to news, announcements, and current information of interest primarily to a specialized group of subscribers or members of an association or organization who receive it as part of their membership available in print and/or online and/or by email. Most periodical indexes and bibliographic databases do not cover newsletter content.

Organizing—the arrangement of resources in order to provide the most effective access to them.

Selecting—Determining which materials should be added to the library collection in order to develop a balanced collection of materials to meet the information needs of university faculty, staff and students in accordance to the library's mission statement and the General Collection Development Policy.

Website—An information resource suitable for the Internet which is accessible through a web browser. The content is formatted with a markup language and often provides navigation to other web pages via (hypertext) links. Websites are differentiated from online databases by their general lack of internal database management system (DBMS) software although they may have a "search this site" box (powered by external software like Google, Yahoo!, Ask.com, etc.) that allows a keyword search of the site.
- Internal websites are sites whose content is created and maintained by library personnel.
- External websites are sites whose content is not created and maintained by library personnel.

United States Department of Agriculture
National Agriculture Library
Beltsville, Maryland

Definition

Electronic resources include remotely accessible files that are openly available on the Internet and those for which the library must pay a licensing fee and negotiate access with the provider. They also include files residing in a variety of storage media. Electronic resources include file types such as:

Bibliographic files. These contain information that leads the user to material. They can be analogous to library catalogs or to printed abstracting and indexing services, or can be sites on the Internet. These files are selected and cataloged in accordance with the NAL Collection Development Policy.

Full text/numeric/graphic files. Home pages may also be included in this category when appropriate. These files are selected and cataloged when in scope for NAL.

Instructional or modeling software. These programs instruct or guide the user through a series of concepts, processes, or models and may be interactive, requiring the user to input data. Such programs include, for example, texts for programmed learning, and modeling and simulation programs. These files may be selected and cataloged at NAL when they address the needs of agricultural researchers.

Applications software. Programs which are intended to manipulate and/or organize the textual or numeric input of the user. Examples of such programs are word processing and spreadsheet programs, database managers, and statistical analysis programs. They are of general applicability and are often widely available. While used by USDA staff, these applications are not cataloged for the NAL collection.

ELECTRONIC-ONLY MIGRATION

Central Michigan University
Central Michigan Universities Libraries
Mount Pleasant, Michigan

INTRODUCTION

Print journals have traditionally been the only format available to libraries, and their longevity and utility have justified the very substantial investments made by the CMU Libraries in acquiring and preserving them.

Now however, electronic journals are increasingly available. As of 2005/2006 the Libraries subscribed to 911 electronic-only periodicals, 1,412 periodicals in both print and electronic formats, and 1,973 in print-only.

The goal of the CMU Libraries is to selectively migrate its print and electronic subscriptions as well as its print-only subscriptions to electronic-only, so that by September 2008 70% of its periodical subscriptions are electronic-only.

In so doing, the Libraries' want to ensure that it is collecting the full equivalent of the journal and can access the purchased electronic content in perpetuity. It is therefore important for the CMU Libraries to clarify the circumstances under which a subscription to only the electronic form of a journal is acceptable. Library Bibliographers will work closely with affected departments in evaluating the appropriateness of such conversions for individual titles.

This policy is intended solely to evaluate when it is appropriate to collect only the electronic form of a journal or periodical, i.e., whether the print format of a title can be cancelled in favor of the online. This policy is not intended to evaluate whether a particular online source should be acquired or not.

CRITERIA

A print journal (or collection of journals) could be discontinued if the electronic equivalent meets all of the following criteria:

Content: The online journal must contain at least the full scholarly content of the print equivalent. For instance, not only should it include all research articles, but it should also include content such as supplements (if included with the print journal subscription), letters, calls for papers and other professional announcements, editorials, job openings, and book reviews.

Timeliness: The full content of each issue should be available online no later than publication of the print.

Format: The electronic journal should be provided as PDF files or an equivalent full-image format identical to the print edition.

Image and Graphics Quality: The quality of illustrative materials (photographs, tables, figures, artistic renderings, etc.) should be of a standard sufficient to meet intended use and should be at least the quality of such images in the print edition. Bibliographers will consult with appropriate departments and will not cancel print if departmental faculty have concerns about images.

Vendor Reliability: The speed of loading/accessing content must meet CMU Libraries' users' expectations. Server downtime should be minimal. Vendors should provide ongoing access if there is a failure and technical assistance when needed.

IP Access: Access to the electronic version should be provided via campus-wide IP address. Access provided should be compatible with Central Michigan university authentication systems.

Printing and Downloading Capability: All content must be printable and downloadable.

Stability: There must be a reasonable guarantee of the stability of the electronic journal. Since stability in aggregated databases cannot be guaranteed, such databases will not be considered a substitute for print journals as part of this process. Electronic journals must be subscribed to from the publisher or equivalent.

Pricing: Migration to electronic-only should be cost effective.

Perpetual access: The CMU Libraries must have perpetual access to all content paid for. The CMU Libraries' are committed to providing our users long term and uninterrupted access to such materials. The CMU Libraries should have the same perpetual access to electronic materials we purchase as we have for our print materials without paying additional fees. However, the concept of "perpetual access" is difficult to pin down in the digital world. Terminology used in the literature also includes "ownership," "sustainability," and "archiving." We will interchangeably use all terms except the last, which can be confused with the more general use of the term.

In particular the CMU Libraries must have a guarantee of perpetual access to paid-for content if we subsequently cancel the electronic journal. Such access must be in the same manner (or equivalent) as provided when we subscribed. It is very important that access continue to be provided in this manner.

Leasing of an electronic journal is not sufficient to allow for the cancellation of the print equivalent.

Such "perpetual access" must be addressed in the license. Suggested language from various Model Licenses follows:

PERPETUAL LICENSE: Licensor hereby grants to Licensee a nonexclusive, royalty-free, perpetual license to use any Licensed Materials that were accessible during the term of this Agreement. Such use shall be in accordance with the provisions of this Agreement, which provisions shall survive any termination of this Agreement. Except in the case of termination for cause, Licensor shall provide the Licensee with access to the Licensed Materials in a usable format substantially equivalent to the means by which access is provided under this Agreement.

After termination of this Agreement (save for a material breach by the Licensee of its obligations under this Agreement) the Publisher will provide (at the option of the Licensee) the Licensee and its Authorized and Walk-in Users with access to and use of the full text of the Licensed Material which was published and paid for within the Subscription Period, either by i) continuing online access to archival copies of the same Licensed Material on the Publisher's server which shall be without charge; or ii) by supplying archival copies of the same Licensed Material in an electronic medium mutually agreed between the parties which will be delivered to the Licensee or to a central archiving facility operated on behalf of the UK HE/FE community or other archival facility (excluding an archival facility of a STM publisher) without charge; or iii) supplying without charge archival copies via ftp protocol of the same Licensed Material.

Perpetual License: Notwithstanding anything else in this Agreement, Licensor hereby grants to Licensee a nonexclusive, royalty-free, perpetual license to use any Licensed Materials that were accessible during the term of this Agreement. Such use shall be in accordance with the provisions of this Agreement, which provisions shall survive any termination of this Agreement. The means by which Licensee shall have access to such Licensed Materials shall be in a manner and form substantially equivalent to the means by which access is provided under this Agreement.

Allowing the CMU Libraries to permanently store our purchased content in a system such as PORTICO (http://www.protico.org) with post-cancellation access will be considered a viable alternative to the above.

License: The license must not be overly restrictive regarding local use; must allow off-campus use by authorized users and walk-in use by visitors; must not be overly restrictive regarding simultaneous users; must allow Interlibrary Loan of content; and allow cancellation of the print. All of the above as well as other licensing terms must be provided in a license for the CMU Libraries to review before a decision will be made.

EVALUATION AND DESELECTION

Texas A&M Corpus Christi
Mary and Jeff Bell Library
Corpus Christi, Texas

Evaluation and Deselection

Databases: Database usage (and cost per search for fee based databases) is reviewed by the Periodicals / Electronic Resources Department monthly. These statistics are currently available to library staff upon request and are occasionally highlighted at reference meetings. Full database reviews using the criteria outlined in this policy currently occur on an irregular basis. Deselection occurs most often based on external conditions such as the exclusion of a particular database from a consortial purchase (like TexShare) or renewal.

E-journals: E-journal usage is reviewed by the Periodicals / Electronic Resources Department monthly. These statistics are currently available to library staff upon request. Full e-journal reviews using the criteria outlined in this policy currently occur on an irregular basis. Deselection occurs most often based on external conditions like a publisher removing their journal from an aggregation (database) or in other ways changing their access model (i.e. requiring that we pay for the online version of a journal that had previously been available for free with the print subscription). E-journal deselection can also occur when a consortia subscription is not renewed.

Websites: Websites are reviewed using the criteria outlined in this policy by the librarian liaisons as they update subject guides and department web pages. This usually occurs annually.

University of Oregon
Knight Library
Eugene, Oregon

Deselection

Different subject areas obviously require different applications of generally accepted deselection principles. Nevertheless, ongoing deselection of Internet resources is a necessity because of the dynamic nature of such resources. These guidelines should provide some suggestions for when to deselect a resource:

1) an Internet resource is no longer available or maintained;

2) the currency and reliability of the resource's information has lost its value;

3) another Internet site or resource offers more comprehensive coverage.

EVALUATION AND TRIALS

Rollins College
Olin Library
Winter Park, Florida

Different vendors offer different conditions for evaluating electronic resources, so it is not possible to establish one rigid evaluation procedure. If the resource is available for a trial period (e.g. trial access to an online resource or a limited duration download), the resource should be examined first by the reference department and then by any interested and relevant departments outside the Library. This sequence is not mandatory, however, as time constraints might require making a resource immediately available for evaluation by all concerned.

Evaluations should be scheduled while classes are in session to ease faculty participation.

Non-library faculty should be advised to compare the resource's usefulness to that of existing print resources and of current electronic resources. When possible, it is advantageous to give evaluators a stronger basis for comparison by arranging concurrent trials for similar resources.

The Electronic Resources Librarian, the Head of Public Services, and/or the Acquisitions Librarian will make formal recommendations based on feedback from both the reference department and non-library faculty and on the criteria listed.

FREQUENCY UPDATE

Indiana University South Bend
Franklin D. Schurz Library
South Bend, Indiana

Policy Review

Because of the changing and dynamic nature of electronic resources, the Electronic Resources Subcommittee will need to review this policy at least every two years.

GENERAL SELECTION GUIDELINES

Dartmouth College
Dartmouth College Library
Hanover, New Hampshire

Making the Decision to Acquire Information in Electronic Format

Selecting an electronic information resource is similar to selecting other formats for the Library's collection. Bibliographers base selection decisions, regardless of format, on relevance to Dartmouth programs, the curriculum, and faculty and student research.

Cost is always a consideration because bibliographers must fund purchases from their respective materials budget, and they must continually balance the cost of information against importance and relevance to the collection.

Several bibliographers may share the cost of a purchase when they conclude a resource is relevant yet too expensive for one bibliographer's budget. Electronic information sources are often more expensive than print and may be appropriate candidates for central funding or split funding.

Points to Consider Before Purchase:
- If there is a choice of formats, consider the advantages and disadvantages to be sure the electronic form is the most useful. Frequency of updates, inclusion of additional information, ability to manipulate data, and the ability to network all add value to the product.
- Consider only fully-documented products with well-known system requirements. Helpful sources in this regard: comments from relevant listservs, vendor presence in the Library community, vendor's reputation, other products owned by the Library from the same publisher or vendor.
- Consider whether the Library has the necessary staff resources and expertise to support the hardware and software, including installation, maintenance, troubleshooting etc.
- From a user services perspective, consider the staff time that may be needed to prepare user guides and to teach faculty and students how to use the product.
- Specify the type of hardware (Mac, IBM or compatible) and hard disk and RAM capacity required.
- Note any video or audio requirements.
- Based on any knowledge of the product gained from the literature, product reviews, conferences etc., evaluate the user interface, any additional product features (downloading, for example) and users' familiarity with the software.
- Investigate potential for saving and manipulating search results (i. e. printing, saving to a disk, to a hard disk, e-mail, or ftp). Also, can the results be imported into a word processing program?
- Check possible exposure to computer viruses resulting from a choice of media and access.

- Look at ways to access archival issues.
- Investigate ways to assure compliance (is monitoring software provided?) with license agreement or copyright requirements.
- Consider the level of access most appropriate for the product (should it be on the campus network? on a LAN? etc.) and consult appropriate people or groups.
- In the case of compact disk databases, consider possible obstacles or constrictions: network speed, cd reader speed, printing bottlenecks.
- Note stability and adequacy of hardware; for example, high-capacity disk drives will be needed to read high-density disks.
- Decide on a location and necessary furniture for optimum access and use; investigate ergonomic considerations in setting up the workspaces
- If an electronic acquisition duplicates a print product currently received, consider whether the print subscription can be cancelled.
- If the product exists in electronic form in the library system, consider whether it could be networked instead of duplicated.

The Product
- Are product reviews available?
- Do relevant listservs exist to query colleagues?
- Is the product user-friendly?
- Can product quality and database content be easily appraised? (can one request a demo?)
- What workspaces are necessary and appropriate?
- What is the currency of content and frequency of updating?
- Could information be supplied by other vendors? If so, what are the advantages and disadvantages of each, including cost?

The Vendor
- What is the reputation of the vendor?
- Do we have other products from the vendor and if so, what are bibliographers' impressions?
- Are terms and conditions of contracts and access arrangements negotiable enough to meet Dartmouth's needs?
- Is customer service and support available?

Necessary Equipment
- What equipment—hardware, printer(s), specialized accessories such as a math co-processor—is needed to run the product?
- Is existing hardware adequate or will new purchase(s) be necessary?
- What software is needed?
- What technical expertise and support is available?
- Is new furniture needed to adequately house the product?

Service After the Sale
- Is equipment maintenance/support/service available?
- Is vendor support available after the sale?
- What is known about hardware reliability?
- Is documentation included and is it adequate?

The Bibliographer's Communication and Decision-Making Environment
- Bibliographer and colleagues with whom he/she consults
- Bibliographer's means of learning about electronic resources
- listservs
- newsgroups

- product reviews
- colleagues
- faculty and student recommendations
- Library committees and departments
- Library groups: LOSC, Internet Resources Subcommittee, Automation, Tecor
- Computing Services: IBM Specialists, Academic Computing Coordinators
- College Attorneys

Budget

As noted earlier previously, bibliographers fund purchases for the collection from their respective budgets. As the cost of electronic information may exceed the ability of one bibliographer to fund it, several bibliographers may collaborate on a purchase. In addition, the Director of Collection Services may be consulted to explore other funding possibilities. In the case of bibliographers working in a library associated with the professional schools, operating with acquisitions budgets separate from Arts and Sciences, these decisions rest with the Department Head, who may in turn consult with the Director of Collection Services.

Information Format and Type:

CD-ROM Databases
- hardware and software requirements
- stand-alone systems
- networked for one location
- networked across zones
- terms and conditions of use, including licensing and contracts

Magnetic Tape Databases
- hardware and software requirements
- constituencies served
- terms and conditions of use, including licensing and contracts

Remotely-Accessible Files
- files are accessible using various tools, including ftp, Gopher, Mosaic
- text, images and data—software and hardware
- requirements at the requestor's workstation

Types of Information Content
- bibliographic, text, numeric, graphic and multimedia

Augmented Collection Services
- tables of contents providers and/or
- document delivery services

Information Access
- Local Access
  - Fileserver Resources
  - Dartmouth Gopher
  - DCLOS, DCIS
- Remote Access
  - Internet-accessible resources such as newsgroups

Commercial online services
- pricing options: discounted for educational use,
- fixed-price, off-peak pricing

Access Tools
- ftp, Mosaic, Gopher, Wais, WWW, Veronica, etc.
- hardware and software requirements to gather and receive data

University of Arizona
Arizona Health Sciences Library
Tucson, Arizona

INTRODUCTION

The AHS Library's current collection development policy governing the funding, selection, acquisition, and retention of library materials and information resources applies to all formats including electronic resources.

When possible, the Library will give priority to the acquisition of electronic resources that offer significant added-value such as uniqueness of information, ease of use, wider accessibility, timely updates and cost-effectiveness.

Partnerships in cooperative acquisitions and cost sharing, both within and outside the University community, e.g., University campus units, other academic and public libraries in Arizona, consortia such as AZHIN, etc., should be pursued when feasible.

Thomas Jefferson University
Scott Memorial Library
Philadelphia, Pennsylvania

Trends in Collections and Publishing

In the 14 years since this policy was last updated there have been several changes in the publishing industry and the types of resources the Library collects. Electronic publishing is a challenging issue facing libraries today as demand for access to resources outside of the Library's physical space increases. Researchers want access to materials at their desktop, students want access from home or their rotation site, and clinicians increasingly want access at their patients' bedside. Electronic resources are also now available in non-bibliographic formats like integrated multi-module drug information products, data sets and databases of genetic sequences and protein structures.

The issues of ownership and perpetual access to any type of electronic resource are not as straightforward as when the Library collected only print materials. For these new materials considerable staff time is spent reading and negotiating access licenses for which there are no national standards. Additional steps necessary to provide electronic access include registering IP addresses and proxy servers, user authentication, creating and maintaining a portal that lists the titles with access and URL maintenance. An example of this complexity is the availability of electronic book-on-demand services, which are changing the traditional way libraries "checkout" books to users.

Publishers and database providers have adopted a variety of pricing models, that can change from year to year, which usually require knowledge about the size and location of the Library's various constituents. Deciding how many simultaneous user licenses to purchase and when it is appropriate to increase the number of licenses are new challenges as well. Changing technologies and obsolete platforms also have an effect on the availability of electronic resources. There is also the problem of differences in the availability of electronic resources among disciplines. As libraries consider moving to more virtual collections, one unfortunate outcome may be that the breadth of their collections will suffer.

There are three possible scenarios in acquiring electronic journals: the title is purchased outright and archival access is available for the years purchased if the title is cancelled; the online access comes with the print subscription, at no additional cost, and should the title be cancelled electronic access is completely lost; the online access is purchased in addition to the print subscription and may or may not be available should the library cancel the title depending on the publisher's policy. In any of these options the impact on the Library's budget is taken into consideration when making a subscription decision.

Open access is a relatively new model of journal publishing that provides immediate and permanent free online access to published peer-reviewed literature. This movement was started as an alternative to commercially published journals whose costs to libraries have skyrocketed in the last several decades. The costs associated with publishing open access articles are typically borne by the author and not libraries in the form of a subscription. In addition to entire journals, special issues or even an individual article(s) in an issue may be open access. Some commercial publishers are experimenting by offering a single title as open access while they determine the impact on their costs and revenue. Initial reluctance by authors to participate in these publications due to concerns about tenure and funding has started to ease and citation impact data is beginning to be collected on some titles. There are avid supporters of the movement in the library community as well as skeptical librarians and publishers who question whether this model can survive long term. It may be years before an answer is available.

The marketplace for knowledge-based resources is also changing. There have been a significant number of publisher mergers in recent years resulting in a reduction of available resources as competition is eliminated, and an overall increase in costs of resources.

Google's plan to digitize the collections of several large academic libraries' collections will offer an alternative method to traditional interlibrary loan for acquiring access to predominantly historical materials. Librarians are following Google's activities with interest as they introduce new search tools and products to the marketplace. Information professionals in libraries welcome many of Google's innovations and are constantly updating services to incorporate the better aspects of web services as they become available.

Just as the radio did not end the practice of people enjoying a live concert or other event, the introduction of electronic resources has not eliminated the need to for print materials. The Library continues to be a vibrant part of the University—as a place for study and work as well as a collection of many types of materials. All of these trends make it a very exciting, if uncertain time for librarians concerned with collection issues.

Texas State Library and Archives Commission
Austin, Texas

TEXSHARE Collection Development Statement

TexShare is founded on the belief of Texas State officials and librarians that citizen health and well-being is furthered by efficient information exchange in all communities and institutions where quality teaching, research excellence, and lifelong learning are valued. The TexShare database program seeks to help meet the information needs of the citizens of Texas, whether they are currently attending the state's colleges and universities or seeking information from their public libraries. TexShare programs contribute to the intellectual productivity of Texans at the participating institutions by emphasizing access to rather than ownership of documents and other information sources.

United States Department of Agriculture
National Agriculture Library
Beltsville, Maryland

Introduction

This policy supplements the Collection Development Policy of the National Agricultural Library. It is shaped by the National Agricultural Library's dual responsibility as a national library and as USDA's departmental library. As a national library, NAL collects material in agricultural subjects comprehensively and serves as library of last resort for other U.S. agricultural libraries. To fulfill its responsibility to USDA, NAL serves the information needs of USDA staff, collects USDA publications, and makes those publications available to library users. NAL will provide access to electronic resources in subjects it collects, with special emphasis on electronic resources published by USDA.

In general, NAL provides access to material in electronic formats when the material contains reports of original research, new scientific findings, information of potential historical value, and information that would support USDA's research, education and regulatory functions. The introductory pages of the Collection Development Policy of the National Agricultural Library provide basic information on NAL's collecting policies. These pages also include definitions of the collecting levels used in the policy and describe the extent to which NAL will collect electronic material at each collecting level. The introductory pages also note that certain kinds of ephemera are excluded from the NAL collection. This exclusion is particularly pertinent to the selection of Internet resources at NAL.

University of Northern Iowa
Rod Library
Cedar Falls, Iowa

ELECTRONIC RESOURCES COLLECTION MANAGEMENT POLICY

Introduction

The Electronic Resources Collection Management policy is part of the Rod Library larger Collection Management policy. This document addresses those aspects of collection development and evaluation decisions which are particular to electronic resources. Such decisions are made in the framework of general policy statements concerning the acquisition and provision of access to resources which are not contained in the Collection Management Policy.

This policy is not intended to address the provision of access to remote electronic resources through links established on the library's World Wide Web home page or through UNISTAR, the online catalog.

I. Types of Electronic Resources

The library acquires selected electronic directories, and bibliographic, full-text, multi-media, and numeric file electronic resources. These include, but may not be limited to:

(1) index and abstract titles which support study and teaching in primary areas of emphasis within the university curriculum;

(2) general reference works and bibliographic tools;

(3) information, textual, or graphical sources in subject areas of significance within the university curriculum;

(4) federal and state depository resources anticipated to be of use to the university and/or larger regional community;

(5) whole books in electronic format when appropriate, and when the electronic format adds particular interest to the text, as in the use of graphics, hypertext, or interactive relationship with the reader;

(6) simulations or game-like resources when the primary intent of these simulations is educational and the material is focused on some aspect of the University curriculum;

(7) sources of basic or core information in subject fields not represented in the university curriculum; and

(8) resources that support faculty and advanced student research.

Satilla Regional Library System
Douglas, Georgia

To provide free and equal access to information, the SRLS and its Board of Trustees endorse the American Library Association (ALA) Code of Ethics, Freedom to Read, and Freedom to View statements as well as the ALA's Library Bill of Rights statement and its interpretations. With these endorsements, the SRLS undergirds citizens' rights to intellectual freedom by allowing access to a free flow of unbiased information that impartially communicates a broad range of ideas. The SRLS Collection will reflect diverse viewpoints, opinions, and cultures shared by both majority and minority members of the communities' citizenry and society as a whole. The existence of any particular viewpoint in the collection is an expression of the library's policy of intellectual freedom, not an endorsement of a particular point of view. The SRLS ensures users' confidentiality with procedures implemented to protect this right.

The SRLS is committed to the following values.

- We value SRLS libraries as public forums, as community facilities for open communication of ideas and information with collections, displays, programs, and services that reflect an array of opinions and view-points.
- We value the SRLS's communities, actively participating in the communities' activities and endeavoring to enhance the quality of life for the communities' citizens.
- We value full and equal access to information provided by the SRLS's Collections, services, and programs.
- We value the collection of and accessibility to information in all formats: print, audio, video and electronic.
- We value our customers by responding to them equally with respectful, accurate, and friendly service to all.
- We value reading and learning by promoting both for all ages.
- We value the privacy of our users by following procedures to keep their transactions strictly confidential.

Although the SRLS refrains from censoring, supporting, or sanctioning any particular view represented in the collection, it has complied with the Children's' Internet Protection Act by installing filters provided by the GPLS. The SRLS does not assume responsibility for information accessed in-house or remotely or checked out by any library user regardless of age. The Library System does not act as the parent or guardian and will not question the appropriateness of the child's selection. This responsibility falls completely and irreversibly to the parent or guardian.

IMPLEMENTATION AND REVIEW

United States Department of Agriculture
National Agriculture Library
Beltsville, Maryland

Implementation

NAL will make electronic resources accessible to its users by:
- Providing bibliographic control through cataloging and indexing electronic resources, as appropriate
- Storing electronic resources, when appropriate
- Circulating electronic resources, whenever possible
- Acquiring and maintaining the software and hardware needed to use electronic resources as long as is practicable
- Providing training and support to staff and users

NAL selectors may choose to acquire more than one format of a work. The decision to do so may be based on technical, economic and service requirements.

NAL may obtain multiple copies of electronic resources when it is in the best interests of service to NAL users.

Electronic resources are subject to the same review by the Weeding and Retention Subcommittee and Collection Development Committee as other library materials.

University of Iowa
University of Iowa Libraries
Iowa City, Iowa

Implementation Responsibilities of the Library

A. The library will comply with the copyright law and will take measures to promote copyright law compliance among its users.
B. The library will optimize access to and utility of electronic resources through the following activities:
    1. Bibliographic control through the cataloging or inventorying of each resource.
    2. Storage for the item, if needed.
    3. Appropriate circulation procedures.
    4. The purchase, maintenance, preparation, and loading of software and hardware necessary to use the resource.
    5. Appropriate staff support and training.
    6. Appropriate user support and training.
C. The Libraries will negotiate and comply with vendor licensing agreements.
    1. In general, it will be the responsibility of the University Libraries acquisitions staff and the Director for Collections and Information Resources to negotiate and sign licensing agreements, in consultation with the appropriate collection management librarian. In cases where an agreement is appropriately negotiated by other staff, it should be reviewed by the Director for Collection Management and Development. In some cases the University Purchasing Department may negotiate and sign agreements. Monographic Acquisitions will maintain a file containing copies of all licensing agreements.
    2. The department or unit which houses or provides access to an electronic resource is responsible for the day-to-day oversight of licensing requirements.
    3. Final responsibility for compliance with licensing agreements rests with the Director for Collection Management and Development, in consultation with the University Purchasing Department and the University Attorney, as may be necessary.

INITIATION PROCEDURES FOR NEW ELECTRONIC RESOURCES

Highline Community College
Highline Community College Library
Des Moines, Washington

Electronic Resources Processing Procedures

E-Resources Management Process

> (participants in process: Collection Development Librarian, Electronic Resources Librarian; Library Acquisitions Technician; Library Systems Administrator; Director of Technical Services; Library Serials Technician)

> Resource Identification: anyone (usually Collection Development Librarian or Electronic Resources Librarian)

> Selection for Investigation: (Collection Development or Electronic Resources Librarian)

Evaluation

> content / interface—Electronic Resources Librarian

license—everyone

technical review—Library Systems Administrator

database maintenance—Library Systems Administrator, Director of Technical Services, Electronic Resources Librarian

Pricing—Electronic Resources Librarian, Library Acquisitions Technician, Library Serials Technician

Ordering—Library Acquisitions Technician

Receiving—Electronic Resources Librarian, Library Systems Administrator, Library Acquisitions Technician

Discovery / Access Management—Library Systems Administrator, Electronic Resources Librarian, Director of Technical Services

Payment—Library Acquisitions Technician

Ongoing evaluation as above plus usage tracking—Electronic Resources Librarian

Renewals / Cancellation—Collection Development Librarian and/or Electronic Resources Librarian

Decision Point—Collection Development Librarian, Electronic Resources Librarian, Library Systems Administrator, Director of Technical Services

Negotiation

Final negotiation—Library Acquisitions Technician

Final license agreement—Library Acquisitions Technician (as agreed ahead of time by all)

INTEGRATION OF NEW ELECTRONIC RESOURCES

Texas A&M Corpus Christi
Mary and Jeff Bell Library
Corpus Christi, Texas

Procedures for acquiring and integrating new electronic resources

Databases:

Trials are often used to evaluate databases. The Periodicals / Electronic Resources department will attempt to arrange a trial of a database at the request of library staff or library users. Working with the Systems department, the trial database is made available on the library web site. Feedback is collected and price information requested and retained until such time as a purchase decision is made.

Once a database to be added to the collection is identified, any site licenses or access contracts are reviewed by the Serials / Electronic Resources Librarian and then negotiated and executed by the University Purchasing Department. Serials / Electronic Resources staff, then work with the database vendor, the librarian liaison to the subject area covered by the database, and the Systems Department to complete a database information sheet on the database. The database information sheet is forwarded to the Systems Department for incorporation into the library databases page. The Serials / Electronic Resources Librarian activates the database in the SFX link resolver and the Metalib federated search engine.

E-journals:

Once an e-journal to be added to the collection is identified, any site licenses or access contracts are reviewed by the Serials / Electronic Resources Librarian and then negotiated and executed by the University Purchasing Department. Serials / Electronic Resources staff, then confirm access (on campus and remote), troubleshoot any errors and add the link to the Periodical Holdings List.

Websites:

Once a website to be included on a resource guide or departmental web page is identified, it should be brought to the attention of the librarian liaison and/or department head that is responsible for the subject area or departmental web pages to which the site is pertinent. Librarian liaisons and/or department heads are responsible for incorporating the site into the resource guides and departmental web pages that they are responsible for maintaining. Web pages are updated in MS Word using the "track changes" feature. Resource Guides updated using MS Word and then saved as PDF documents then edited by the reference librarian in charge of those guides. The changed document is routed to the Systems Department for publishing on the library web site.

MISSION

Satilla Regional Library System
Douglas, Georgia

The SRLS's mission is to serve the region by providing organized access to information in various available formats that meet the citizens' educational, informational, recreational, and cultural needs. The SRLS's vision is to be the port of information access to the region's communities through print, audio, and video formats as well as electronically formatted local data and the World Wide Web. This mission and vision, providing the foremost guiding forces in collection development, initiate broad and ambitious goals and require library roles to change with each user. Many of our users need resources for developing fundamental reading skills and for enhancing educational activities from pre-school through high school. Older SRLS users need children's and parenting information or information to stay competitive in the job market and to plan for financial security. Others use the resources to help them relax and enjoy life. As a vital part of the regional community, the SRLS strives to help citizens achieve personal enrichment for better lives.

Welch Medical Library
Johns Hopkins University
Baltimore, Maryland

The availability of electronic resources opens new vistas for teaching, research, and patient care. Although acquiring materials in digital forms and organizing them for use is both costly and challenging, electronic resources will be a critical element of the Johns Hopkins Medical Institutions and Johns Hopkins Health Systems of the future. The library will meet the demand for broader subject access and for cross-campus access with e-resources.

Material needed on a regular basis will be provided electronically. Remaining print materials will be housed onsite in the Institute of the History of Medicine and off-site in the Libraries Service Center.

POLICY PURPOSE

University of Iowa
University of Iowa Libraries
Iowa City, Iowa

Purpose of This Policy

The University Libraries collect or provide access to appropriate materials in print and non-print media. Currently, electronic formats present libraries with management issues that more traditional formats do not. They may be significantly more expensive to acquire and maintain. They may be physically located in a library or they may be housed elsewhere on campus or at remote locations. They may require additional hardware and software to operate or to access. Because these concerns complicate the selection and the accessibility of such materials within the University Libraries, a policy specifically for electronic formats is needed.

This "Policy for Electronic Resources Management" provides context and guidelines for the University Libraries in the selection, acquisition, provision of access to, and maintenance of electronic resources. It does not address specific procedural issues such as where a particular resource will be located or funding options. These are discussed in related University Libraries documents such as the "Information Arcade Selection Criteria" document produced by the Database Task Force and the "Expensive Purchase Recommendation" guidelines.

Owensboro Community and Technical College
Owensboro Community and Technical College Library
Owensboro, Kentucky

Purpose

The purpose of this electronic resources policy is to provide guidelines for building and maintaining a strong and balanced collection of electronic resources for Owensboro Community and Technical College (OCTC) Library users. Electronic resources specific to OCTC are those electronic resources through the library homepage such as databases containing various periodicals and journals, electronic books, and resources retrieved through the Kentucky Virtual Library (KYVL). This policy reflects the mission of the library, which states: "The Owensboro Community and Technical College library will strive for excellence by providing the highest quality information resources and services for faculty, staff, students, and community users. We will endeavor to achieve this excellence by:

Selecting and making accessible a variety of materials that support the instructional and research needs of our patrons.

Creating a supportive and open environment that reflects our commitment to life-long learning.

Instructing users in effectively accessing and evaluating materials to meet their informational needs.

Maintaining a knowledgeable and professional staff that respects the worth of each individual, while combining our diverse interests and strengths to best serve our patrons.

Working collaboratively with other libraries and institutions to provide resources not available locally."

The policy provides guidance for building and maintaining an effective collection of electronic resources, as well as supplement and adhere to the same elements of the Collection Development Policy of the OCTC Library main collection.

University of Arizona
Arizona Health Sciences Library
Tucson, Arizona

PURPOSE OF THIS POLICY

To offer library users electronic resources relevant to the mission of the Library.

To provide access to information resources that will support the instructional, research, and patient care goals of the Arizona Health Sciences Center, including the Colleges of Medicine, Nursing, and Pharmacy, and the School of Health Professions, and the University Medical Center.

To provide access to information resources to health care providers and others with health information needs throughout Arizona.

To provide access to those resources and to organize and maintain the information in a meaningful manner to fulfill users' needs.

To provide access to those resources and to organize and maintain the information in a meaningful manner to fulfill users' needs.

Northcentral University
Northcentral University Library
Prescott Valley, Arizona

The E-Library Collection Development Plan states the principles and guidelines that Northcentral University follows in the selection and acquisition of electronic materials. The purpose of the policy is to provide consistency among the persons responsible for collection development and communicating library policy to faculty, staff, students, and the community.

RESPONSIBILITY FOR SELECTION

University of Maryland
University of Maryland Libraries
College Park, Maryland

Selection

Primary responsibility for the selection of all electronic materials (including trial offers) for public use rests with the assigned subject selector using the above selection criteria. For electronic resources that are intended primarily for reference use, i.e., indexes, directories, the subject selector will coordinate selection with the Service Plus Coordinator. Requests from other librarians, library staff, faculty or other users should be directed to the relevant subject selector. The subject selector will work in close cooperation with the designated Electronic Information Services staff. If needed the selector will consult as well with the Technical Services division, Information Technology division, Academic Information Technology Services, and with relevant faculty. Issues affecting broader disciplines will be coordinated by the appropriate subject team or teams.

The selector will contact EIS to ask the vendor to determine minimum software and hardware specifications and to arrange for testing of the product (unless the product is under $100). The selector will work with the EIS manager to arrange testing of the product using the electronic resources guidelines for guidance and involving others with relevant subject responsibilities. In addition, EIS will check licensing requirements and estimated costs with the vendor. In any discussions with vendors, selectors need to communicate that they are only requesting information and that final purchase authority rests with Acquisitions. Once an order has been placed, any questions about the status of the order should be directed to Acquisitions.

When the forms have been completed, the selector will send requests to their Team Manager. If the forms are incomplete, they will be returned to the selector.

The Electronic Resources Committee (ERC) develops and reviews policies related to the development of electronic resources. The Committee reviews requests as needed. The Electronic Information Services Manager will determine when ERC review is necessary. The ERC reviews all networked products and is responsible for reviewing products for transfer to other locations (i.e, the Electronic Information Center).

Selectors are responsible for reviewing ongoing products (before renewal) to re-assess for relevance to the collections, currency, ease of use, and cost. When a product no longer has value as part of the collections, it should be reviewed by the selector for deselection. Deselection for serial titles (most databases are treated as serials) must be made on the Serials Cancellation Form or for single-purchase items, the Monograph Transfer/Withdrawal Form. If a selector initiates deselection, notification, including relevant paperwork, must be made to the Electronic Information Services Manager. Any deselection decisions must consider collaborative acquisition and provision of electronic resources. In most instances, the costs of providing the resources are shared among institutions on a usage basis. A deselection decision by the USM Libraries which involves a resource provided in cooperation with USM or other institutions must include substantial justification and sufficient notification to collaborating institutions.

Once a new electronic resource has been cataloged and is available to the public, the selector will assist in promoting the resource to relevant faculty, students, and library staff. If staff training is needed, the subject selector will coordinate the training with the Electronic Information Services Manager. The Electronic Information Services Manager will coordinate overall publicity and training for new electronic resources. As needed announcements are submitted to FYI for campus distribution.

(For additional policies, please see the accompanying CD-ROM.)

REVIEW AND REASSESSMENT

University of Iowa
University of Iowa Libraries
Iowa City, Iowa

Policy Review

The University Libraries Collection Management Committee will review this policy at least every three years, or as needed.

Columbia College
Columbia College Library
Chicago, Illinois

A subscription to a product may be cancelled if:
- Usage statistics are consistently low over a significant period of time.
- The product is no longer cost-effective
- The content provided is no longer meeting the needs of Columbia College Chicago users.
- A competitive or better product becomes available.
- The vendor fails to hold up their end of the agreement and/or provides poor service.
- A product's price inflates such that it no longer is considered affordable.
- The product's content is found to duplicate content in another database.
- A new vendor can deliver a superior product, including a more user-friendly search interface, providing greater and more reliable access at a reasonable cost, or meet other key criteria not being met by current database provider.

Florida Atlantic University
S.E. Wimberly Library
Boca Raton, Florida

Review of Electronic Resources

Electronic resources are reviewed and reassessed before renewal. A resource may be withdrawn from the collection when:

- The resource no longer supports the curriculum and/or research needs of the University.
- The resource is no longer available or maintained.
- The resource is no longer reliable or relevant.
- The resource overlaps or duplicates material in another resource which provides more comprehensive coverage of the subject.
- The information is available in a more suitable format.
- Usage or circulation statistics indicate a declining level of interest.
- Cost is not commensurate with usage.
- The current product becomes obsolete or damaged.
- Budget reductions force cancellation of products.

Long Island University
B. Davis Schwartz Memorial Library
Brookville, New York

The evolving and constantly changing electronic information environment requires that databases and other electronic resources be reviewed frequently throughout the year. The selection criteria used to evaluate resources for purchase are used to determine if a resource should be renewed. Primary among these criteria are the cost effectiveness and continued relevance of resources. Usage statistics are also reviewed to determine if the level of use justifies renewal of the subscription.

Northcentral University
Northcentral University Library
Prescott Valley, Arizona

Electronic resources are reviewed and reassessed before renewal. A resource may be withdrawn from the collection when:

- The resource no longer supports the curriculum and/or research needs of the University.
- The resource is no longer available or maintained.
- The resource is no longer reliable or relevant.
- The resource overlaps or duplicates material in another resource that provides more comprehensive coverage of the subject.
- The information is available in a more suitable format.
- Usage or circulation statistics indicate a declining level of interest.
- Cost is not commensurate with usage.
- The current product becomes obsolete or damaged.
- Budget reductions force cancellation of products.

University of Northern Iowa
Rod Library
Cedar Falls, Iowa

Review of Electronic Resources Subscriptions

Departments administering electronic resources will gather/use statistics on a regular basis, evaluate them, and determine whether currently available products continue to be the best way to meet the needs of library users. Such statistics and relevant analysis will be forwarded to the head of the department and to the Head of Collection Management & Special Services. Evaluation of the continued need for and desirability of maintaining subscriptions or providing access to materials in particular formats will be coordinated by these individuals.

Scope

University of Iowa
University of Iowa Libraries
Iowa City, Iowa

Scope of Policy

A. This policy addresses the selection for acquisition or access of the following types of electronic materials:
    1. Numeric data files.
    2. Textual files.
    3. Bibliographic files.
    4. Graphic and multimedia files.
    5. Courseware/Instructional files.
    6. World Wide Web resources that fall under categories 1-5.
    7. Specific applications software needed to utilize the resources listed above.
    8. The University Libraries will consider the purchase of other types of electronic resources as they are developed, in light of their relevance, appropriateness, and contribution to the Libraries' mission.
B. This policy does not cover general purpose applications software such as authoring programs, gateways programs, reference management programs, productivity programs, and integrated library management programs (e.g., NOTIS).
C. This policy does not cover any resources purchased primarily for staff use.

University of Maryland, Baltimore
University of Maryland Health Sciences and Human Services Library
Baltimore, Maryland

SCOPE

The term electronic resources as used in this policy refers to any source of information which can only be accessed or used via a computer. Electronic resources covered by this policy include, but are not limited to, those intended for addition to the HS/HSL collection, for delivery of educational or research content, for inclusion on the HS/HSL networks or computers, and for remote access (i.e., commercial databases and Internet resources) by HS/HSL clientele. Types of resources include but are not limited to Web or Internet-based, CD-ROM, magnetic tape, floppy disk, and online. Electronic resources needed for operational use by the Library (e.g., word processing, spreadsheet, or presentation software; circulation, cataloging, or acquisitions systems) are not covered by this policy.

Electronic resources must fall within the subject and language scope of the print collection, as stated in the Library's general Collection Development Policy.

Owensboro Community and Technical College
Owensboro Community and Technical College Library
Owensboro, Kentucky

Scope of the policy

"Electronic resources" refer to those materials that require computer access, whether through microcomputer, mainframe, or other types of computers, and that may either be accessed locally or from a remote location. The policy addresses both electronic resources purchased or licensed by the library and free Internet resources. The curriculum needs of the college in the various disciplines and programs, especially classes offered for distant learning students, and information needs of various OCTC faculty, staff, students, and community users are covered. This policy serves all three college campus locations: the main campus, the downtown campus, and the southeast campus.

Types of electronic resources included, but not limited to:

- Online public access catalogs
- Indexing and abstracting databases
- Aggregated databases that include full-text journals and periodicals
- Electronic books
- Reference databases that include directories, dictionaries, encyclopedias
- Web sites
- CD-ROM and/or multimedia products
- Other technologies that may evolve

Welch Medical Library
Johns Hopkins University
Baltimore, Maryland

Format

E-journals: As with print journals, e-journals require a long-term commitment from the library in terms of financial and human resources to acquire and maintain. The library subscribes to an e-journal only if it is full text.

Bundled with Existing Print subscription

The library provides access to the free web version of a print journal to which it subscribes when the access criteria is met.

Print and Online subscriptions

The library continues to provide print subscriptions for high use items and for things that are not yet electronic.

Online-Only

If they are available, all new titles will be subscribed to online only.

If online access is bundled with print, the print issues are not checked in, but are maintained at the library for one year and discarded without binding. If contents of print copies and electronic versions have any differences, then print copies are kept. Where there is a compelling reason, i.e., print is the only choice or intense user demand for paper copies, the library orders print materials.

E-Books: The library will acquire when there is a demand from patrons.

Databases: General information and bibliographic databases are selectively acquired.

CD-ROMs/Diskettes/Other Multimedia: In general these formats are not collected. CD-ROMs that accompany print materials are retained only if the content is supplemental to the text. Web-based multimedia will be collected according to their relevance.

Web sites: These will be selected according to their relevance to the library's collection.

Access

Resources may be accessed in a variety of ways but internet/worldwide web is preferred. The decision to select specific products depends on projected use, licensing requirements, support services either local or remote, and other access issues. Materials must be available on campus and remotely. Reserves and distance learning programs are included. Resources are accessed via the JHU online catalog and/or the library web site.

SELECTION CRITERIA

University of Northern Iowa
Rod Library
Cedar Falls, Iowa

Selection Criteria

Electronic resources, whether serials or monographs, are selected in accordance with many of the same factors used in making selection decisions for library resources in other formats. The subject emphasis and scope of coverage are primary factors in any selection decision; these are considered in the context of established subject collection development policies.

Bibliographers make initial evaluations and recommendations for purchase or provision of access to electronic resources, reviewing recommendations submitted by other members of the library faculty and staff or larger university community. Selection and evaluation of titles for the Reference Collection and Indexes/Abstracts are coordinated by the Reference Collection Management Coordinator. Selection and evaluation of titles within the collecting responsibilities of Special Services units are coordinated by the Head of Collection Management & Special Services.

As appropriate, the administrator of the department(s) or area(s) in which a product would be located evaluates the effect of adding or providing access to that product on the area's existing services and operations. Technical evaluation, including hardware requirements, systems compatibility, and networking requirements is coordinated with the Department of Library Technologies and Systems.

Evaluation of electronic resources also involves specialized, frequently format-specific, factors and technical considerations. Consideration is given to the size of the potential user group, subject and technical relationship to other titles already in the collection or to which remote access is provided, search capabilities, ease of use relative to alternative products, and initial and ongoing costs relative to the anticipated usefulness of the product. Alternative means of access are reviewed in consultation with the Library Technologies and Systems Department, and the need for print/electronic duplication assessed. Search software, operating and network software, licensing restrictions, contractual obligations, hardware availability and compatibility, and vendor support also are evaluated. Likely effects on existing services and operations, including development of staff expertise and the need for patron training in use of a product, are weighed. In some instances, a decision may be made that an electronic resource will be acquired or access provided with only minimal staff assistance to be provided to the public. The potential impact on Interlibrary Loan services is reviewed with the Head of Access Services.

Columbia College
Columbia College Library
Chicago, Illinois

General Criteria

- Subject matter covered is relevant to the Columbia curriculum and needs of primary users (students, faculty and staff)
- Appropriate intellectual level, depth of coverage and quality of information for user population
- Reputable, reliable, and authoritative producer
- Information and updates are current, accurate and complete
- Electronic format provides greater accessibility to information over other formats
- Uniqueness of information
- Formats
  - Citation/abstract databases
  - Full text article databases
  - Full text reference sources online
  - Graphics and multimedia files
  - Ebooks (selective)
- Access
  The following are the preferred methods of access:
  - Delivery via the web
  - Authentication by IP address (rather than passwords or logins)
  - Compatibility with the Library's existing proxy server and software
- User-Friendliness
  Electronic resources should adhere to conventional user expectations such as:
  - Availability of on-screen help and/or tutorials
  - Basic and guided/advanced searching
  - Helpful error messages (i.e., error message indicates specific problem(s) and provides possible alternatives)
  - Ability to print, save, and email results and/or articles
- Cost Considerations
  - Cost-effectiveness (including the availability and cost of updates and backfiles when appropriate)
  - Ability to sustain cost for the foreseeable future
  - Potential usage and/or uniqueness of information justifies cost
- Vendor Considerations
  - Provides responsive customer service and technical support that is available during library working hours
  - Availability and quality of training programs
  - Reputation and business record suggests continued support for the product via updates or new versions
  - Documentation is thorough and clear

- Technical Considerations
  - Meets usual and customary technical standards in the industry
  - Allows for local customizations via system administration access for the Library
  - Product is compatible with the Library's existing and/or future hardware
  - Product is compatible with standard web browsers if accessible via the web
  - Usage statistics are readily available in a user-friendly format (preferably COUNTER** compliant).
- Special Considerations for Online Reference Sources or Subscriptions to Individual Online Journals
  A subscription to or purchase of an individual online reference or journal title will be considered if:
  - The electronic format offers value-added enhancements to make it preferable over, or a significant addition to, its print equivalent. Examples of such enhancements include wider access, flexibility in searching, and frequent updates.
  - It contains or covers the equivalent information compared to the print format.
  - Acquiring the electronic version is cost-effective (e.g., the cost differential is justified by demonstrated or expected increase in use) and provides greater access to users
  - If an electronic resource is acquired in the electronic format, especially with perpetual ownership rights, the Electronic Resources Committee (in conjunction with appropriate Library staff) should determine if the print equivalent should be canceled.

Central Michigan University
Central Michigan Universities Libraries
Mount Pleasant, Michigan

Selection

Resources available via the Internet are proliferating. The Libraries recognizes that careful selection of electronic resources, and availability of these trough the Libraries' catalog will accomplish several objectives:

1) Increase awareness and maximize use of significant sites;

2) Provide value-added access to Internet resources often absent when using various search engines to locate resources;

3) Enhance and expand the Libraries' collection of traditional formats. Selection responsibility of these resources rests with individual Subject Bibliographers and the Head of Collection Development as these materials fall into their regular selecting responsibilities.

Electronic or digital resources considered for acquisition should usually:
- Follow current collection parameters already in place as represented by the currently approved collection development policy statements, individual department policies and other related documents;
- Be available in formats currently accessible by appropriate hardware/software already in the library or available on campus. If the necessary hardware/software is not currently available on campus, purchasing these should be considered along with the resource. Care should be taken when choosing formats to consider the usability (due to format) of the data in the long term;
- Be an enhancement and enrichment of current collections;
- Be substituted for printed information with caution because of the volatility of the information industry;
- Be evaluated in light of other potential acquisitions, and weighed against other possible acquisitions from the materials budget;
- Be evaluated for stability and integrity;
- Allow for the number of simultaneous users appropriate to the resource;
- Allow printing, sharing, downloading within copyright regulations.

Florida Atlantic University
S.E. Wimberly Library
Boca Raton, Florida

Criteria

Cost, including any hidden costs, the possibility of consortia arrangements, and whether the cost is for a one-time purchase or a subscription.

Technical considerations:

- Access by IP recognition, including remote access;
- No requirements for additional or special hardware or software, other than what is freely available and widely used;
- Compatibility across different platforms (PC, Mac, etc.).
- Compatibility with open URL link resolvers and federated searching programs currently utilized by the Libraries (SFX and MetaLib).
- Full-text availability in PDF and/or HTML or SGML as appropriate.
- Compatibility with course management software.
- Trial period available for review of the resource prior to purchase decision.
- Value added enhancements and/or improved access, such as:
  - Availability independent of time or location;
  - Greater functionality, including multiple search indexes;
  - More extensive content;
  - More up-to-date content.
- Should be user-friendly and provide assistance to the user by prompts and menus, context or function specific help screens, or tutorials.
- Updated on a regular basis, if currency is a factor.
- Vendor reliability as to content, business practices, customer and technical support, documentation and training, and notification of content and format changes.
- Should include printing, downloading and email capabilities.
- Availability of Counting Electronic Usage of Networked Electronic Resources (COUNTER) compliant usage data.
- Acceptable license terms.

University of Maryland
University of Maryland Libraries
College Park, Maryland

General Selection Criteria

Selection criteria need to be consistent with the UM Libraries' plans for establishing an electronic information environment.

Electronic resources considered for acquisition should fall within current collecting guidelines as described in the subject collection development policies and other appropriate guidelines.

All electronic materials should be relevant and appropriate to a significant segment of the Libraries' user community and reflect current academic needs and the University's mission. Special attention should be given to electronic resources that provide coverage of underrepresented or high-priority subject areas.

In the selection of electronic materials, the availability of appropriate hardware and software should be considered. For CD-ROM products, consideration also needs to be given as to whether the product is networkable. If additional software needs to be acquired to run the product, this factor should be noted.

If the electronic resource duplicates another resource already available in the Libraries, the proposed electronic resource should offer some value-added enhancement; for example, wider access or greater flexibility in searching. If a product changes format, it should be reevaluated and a selection/retention decision made in the appropriate manner.

In addition to the cost of the product, if any, the following hidden costs need to be considered: licensing fees, hardware, software, staff training and continuing education, cataloging, duplicating support materials, updates, maintenance, and any other costs.

The product should be "user-friendly," that is, provide ease of use and guidance for the user via appropriate menus, help screens, or tutorials.

The product should reflect the quality expected of similar materials in other formats.

Additional selection guidelines are available for

- Free Web-based resources
- Electronic Publications

Longwood University
Greenwood Library
Farmville, Virginia

Electronic Resources

The Library collects materials in a variety of electronic formats including but not limited to CD-ROMs, computer disks, online databases, electronic journals, and electronic texts. Since the acquisition and maintenance of these formats may pose management issues that traditional formats do not, some additional criteria need to be considered in the selection of these materials.

The Electronic Resources Librarian will have primary responsibility for contacting publishers of electronic resources, arranging for trials or demonstrations, and negotiating agreements for the purchase or licensing of electronic resources. The Vice President for Administration and Finance is required to sign all license agreements. The Electronic Resources Librarian is responsible for maintenance of and compliance with these agreements.

Selection Guidelines for Electronic Resources

The following criteria should be considered when selecting electronic resources. Each of these criteria is not necessarily applicable to every electronic format or resource and a negative in any one of them is not necessarily, by itself, a reason not to proceed with the selection.

- General Criteria:
  - Enhances the collection in a way current materials don't, for example, it provides wider access, greater flexibility in searching, more timely information, or more extensive content.
  - Meets customary technical standards in the industry.
  - If duplicating print resources, consideration should be given to weeding the print format or canceling the print subscription.

- General abstracts and indexes will have priority over individual specialized reference tools, although a balance will be sought.
- Product Considerations:
  - Product is considered "user friendly."
  - The following characteristics are examples of "friendliness":
    Online tutorials
    Prompts and menus
    Function-specific help
    Quality keyword searching (novice and expert levels)
    Marking of records
    Helpful error messages
    Index browsing
    Amount of time required for staff and user training is reasonable.
    Manuals, guides, and tutorials are available and useful.
  - Resources are available in formats for which the University owns appropriate hardware and software.
  - If currency is important, the resource is updated often enough to be useful.
  - Published reviews of the resource have been taken into account.
  - Databases with full-text or abstracts preferred to those with citations alone.
  - Textual resources are in the most commonly used and appropriate language for the subject matter.

- Vendor Considerations:
  - Trial period is available.
  - Vendor's reliability and business record suggest continued support for the product via updates or new versions.
  - Vendor-produced documentation is thorough and clear.
  - Software enhancements are included in the purchase or lease price.
  - Customer support is available.
  - Contract doesn't require restrictions such as limitations to access that conflict with the library's policies.
  - Contract permits library to make/obtain digital and or printed copies of content for archiving and use in perpetuity.
  - The resource can be made available in agreement with the Intellectual Freedom statement of the American Library Association, which Longwood University Library fully supports.

- Hardware Considerations:
  - Resource is compatible with existing systems in the library and with the systems used by the University.
  - Sufficient staff expertise and resources exist to maintain the system (upgrades, backups, hardware and software).
  - Security from theft and tampering exists.

- Cost Considerations:
  - Purchase and lease options are compared to determine the most cost-effective option.
  - Plans for any additional costs for future updates or upgrades are considered at the time of the original purchase.
  - The shelf life of the product's storage medium is weighed against replacement costs.
  - Cost requirements for hardware, software, supplies, and staff training time are considered.

Electronic Collection Management Forms, Policies, Procedures, and Guidelines Manual

University of Maryland
University of Maryland Libraries
College Park, Maryland

Introduction

Electronic resources are of increasing importance to faculty and students. With the rapidly growing body of electronic information, what is universally available must be considered in relation to what should be available on the University of Maryland campus. It is therefore clear that successful collection development, regardless of media, will reflect academic priorities already established at the campus level. The Libraries are committed to taking a leadership role in collaborating with academic departments in providing electronic resources to support instruction and research.

The University of Maryland Libraries are also part of the University System of Maryland(USM) library consortium. As part of USM, the Libraries cooperate in the provision of electronic resources to the USM community. As the Libraries and USM continue to explore collaborative efforts, selection criteria should continue to reflect the academic priorities for the campus. Electronic resources cooperatively provided to the USM user community are currently selected by the USM Council of Library Directors and the USM Electronic Resources Committee.

This document provides guidelines for selection and deselection, review and approval, acquisition, cataloging, and preservation of electronic resources. The selection, review and approval process addresses issues concerned with licensing, access vs. ownership, developing industry standards, and physical location of resources. Currently known material types are: CD-ROM, interactive multi-media, machine readable bibliographic, non-bibliographic and full text databases, software, E-journals, and other materials accessible on the Internet and elsewhere.

University of Iowa
University of Iowa Libraries
Iowa City, Iowa

Selection and Acquisition Responsibilities of the Library

A. General Guidelines
  1. The Libraries will select, fund, and make available appropriate electronic resources.
  2. The Libraries will provide monies from its materials budget for the purchase of electronic materials meeting the criteria specified below in sections V.A.6 and V.B.
  3. The collection management librarians will have the primary responsibility for identifying, selecting, and funding through the individual subject fund lines the electronic resources they wish to add to the library collection.
  4. The collection management librarians will have the primary responsibility for negotiating and coordinating funding for applications programs needed to operate specific electronic resources they have selected.
  5. The collection management librarians will have the primary responsibility for selecting for the Gateway to the Internet resources falling under the categories listed in IV.A above.
  6. Very expensive electronic resources of campus-wide utility, such as the Wilson databases, may be purchased with general materials monies. The Collection Management Committee will review such recommendations.

7. The fundamental and primary criteria used for measuring the appropriateness of adding a particular electronic resource to the Libraries' collection will not differ essentially from those criteria used to measure books or any other format. These primary criteria are:
   a. The resource contributes to the Libraries' mission of providing support for instruction and research.
   b. There is demonstrated demand or a potential audience for the resource.
8. If significant additional expenditures or extraordinary arrangements would be required to make the resource available, such as special hardware, a different operating system, or unusual space or maintenance requirements, its acquisition should be justifiable with the strongest possible arguments from Section V.B. below. A mechanism exists for collection management librarians to use individual materials funds to purchase needed equipment, if no other means of obtaining the equipment is available.
9. The public services support required to make a resource available should be given early consideration in the selection process. Collection management librarians should consult with staff of other library departments that may be affected. Aspects of public services support to be considered are:
   a. The need for staff and user training.
   b. The availability and usefulness of manuals, guides, and tutorials from the producer.
   c. The ease of production of a brief guide, if necessary, by University Libraries staff.

If substantial amounts of staff time and effort would be required to make a resource available, its acquisition should be justifiable with the strongest possible arguments based on the criteria in Section B below.

B. Additional Criteria

In addition to the primary criteria in section V.A.6 above, the following criteria specific to electronic resources should be considered. They are not listed in priority order. Not all of the suggested criteria will be applicable in every case.

1. The resource offers some value-added enhancement to make it preferable over, or a significant addition to, other print or non-print equivalents. Examples of such enhancements include wider access and greater flexibility in searching.
2. If the item is an electronic version of a resource in another format, it contains or covers the equivalent information to the extent appropriate and desirable.
3. The resource meets usual and customary technical standards in the industry.
4. If currency is important, the resource is updated often enough to be useful.
5. The production quality is satisfactory for the proposed use.
6. The resource is "user-friendly." Some measures of "friendliness" are:
   a. The existence of introductory screens
   b. The availability of on-screen tutorials
   c. Prompts and menus
   d. Function-specific help
   e. Novice and expert searching levels
   f. Helpful error messages
   g. Ease of exiting from one point in database to another
   h. Index browsing
   i. Searching on index terms without re-typing
   j. Software allows for both printing and downloading
7. Vendor-related issues, such as:
   a. Vendor reliability and business record suggests continued support for the product via updates or new versions.
   b. Vendor-produced documentation is thorough and clear.
   c. Customer support is available from the vendor during library working hours.

    d. Price penalties, if any, for different formats have been investigated.

8. The resource is potentially networkable.
9. Textual resources are in the most commonly used and appropriate language for the subject matter.
10. Published reviews of the resource have been taken into account.
11. A trial period is available for examining the utility and value of the resource before a final commitment is made with the vendor.
12. Access-related issues, such as:

    a. The physical location of the resource, if applicable.

    b. Vendor-required limitations to access.

    c. The resource can be made available in agreement with the Intellectual Freedom statement of the American Library Association, which the University Libraries fully support.

Chapter 7

DIGITAL RESOURCES

GOALS

The University of Texas at Austin
The University of Texas Libraries
Austin, Texas

Within this framework, it is the objective of the library to collect scholarly digital materials in order to provide broad access to relevant scholarly information at every level of granularity including articles, monographs, and large databases. As with all formats, digital material should meet the same subject, chronological, geographical, language and other guidelines as outlined in the library's subject collection policies; and possess the same standards of excellence, comprehensiveness, and authority that the library expects from all of its acquisitions. The library recognizes that different disciplines utilize different formats and different types of information in different ways, and that no one solution is appropriate for every subject or area of study. The ultimate goal of The University of Texas Libraries digital library collection development planning—is to provide seamless cross-linkages between all elements of the digital library whether commercially licensed or locally created, and whether the resources are locally or remotely mounted and serviced.

University of Ottawa
University of Ottawa Library
Ottawa, Ontario, Canada

Goals

It is the objective of the University of Ottawa Libraries to collect scholarly digital materials in order to provide broad access to relevant research at every level of need, including full-text journal literature, books, reference works, databases, geospatial tools, datasets, and other material. This collection is intended to underpin the University of Ottawa Libraries' central role in promoting academic success and lifelong learning.

Digital materials should meet the same selection criteria as outlined in the library's subject collection policies, namely subject, chronological, geographical, and language guidelines, and possess the same standards of excellence, comprehensiveness, and authority that the library expects from all of its acquisitions. The University of Ottawa Libraries recognizes that disciplines are structured in unique ways and that their researchers utilize information and conduct research in their own ways—no single approach is appropriate for all disciplines or areas of research.

One of the key goals in digital library collection development planning is to provide seamless links between all elements of the digital library whether commercially licensed or locally created, and whether the resources are locally or remotely mounted and serviced.

University of Iowa
University of Iowa Libraries
Iowa City, Iowa

Digital Library Services strives to attain these overarching goals:

1. Integration. Develop a full range of digital resources and services that are closely coordinated with each other and well integrated with other library resources and services.
2. Collaboration. Foster diverse collaborations on digital projects both within the University Libraries and with partners on campus and in the broader community.
3. Interoperability. Promote shared technology architectures and standards needed to achieve interoperability and integration among diverse digital information resources.
4. Education. Inform and educate content providers about digital collections, services, and technologies, including intellectual property rights in the digital environment.
5. Infrastructure. Provide a reliable and robust infrastructure to support digital library initiatives.
6. Assessment. Develop a program of regular assessment and measurement to evaluate current programs and to plan for future digital library needs.

LICENSES

Rutgers University
Rutgers University Libraries
New Brunswick, New Jersey

Licensed Digital Resources

The Rutgers University Libraries obtain many indexes, databases, electronic journals, electronic reserves, and other full-text resources through commercial licensing agreements that restrict access to current students, faculty, and staff and all onsite users. Onsite users may gain access, but only current students, faculty, and staff of the university may connect from remote locations.

Library licensing negotiations secure for the Rutgers community the ability to use digital resources for normal educational and research purposes. Basic uses requested are the ability to print, download, and email information and to fill interlibrary loan requests from digital resources. Agreements that preserve copyright fair use and recognize educational and library exemptions in copyright law are sought. Requests to make more extensive use of licensed resources for grants or projects should be directed to Robert Sewell, associate university librarian for collection development and management, or head of distributed technical services.

Authorized Rutgers users comprise all current students, faculty, and staff of the university, wherever they are located, and all onsite users. The Rutgers University Libraries have a secure proxy server that authenticates authorized users for remote access.

Rutgers University sites are defined as every campus location, physical and virtual, as well as remote research and learning locations.

Acceptable uses by authorized Rutgers users are defined as permission to:
• View and search the content of the online resource
• Download individual items or articles for the individual use of an authorized user
• Print individual articles from the online resource for the individual use of an authorized user

If a contract is silent about copying, then standard fair use exceptions might apply.

The Rutgers University Libraries agree to assist in the management of user behavior by making reasonable efforts to ensure compliance with license provisions and by providing appropriate notice of conditions under which access to the licensed materials is granted.

University of Maryland, Baltimore
University of Maryland Health Sciences and Human Services Library
Baltimore, Maryland

LICENSING

With respect to licensing, the Library has the following definitions and expectations:

- The Library's authorized users include the students, faculty, and staff of University of Maryland, Baltimore (UMB) and the University of Maryland Medical Center (UMMC), and all on-site visitors.
- "Site" is defined to include any UMB or UMMC unit, including satellite facilities.
- UMB and UMMC students, faculty and staff should be able to access digital resources from any location.
- The preferred method for authenticating authorized users is via IP address ranges. Individual username and password access is considered only in exceptional cases.
- The number of users in a multi-user license is determined by anticipated demand and available funding.
- The "fair use" provision of the U.S. Copyright Law applies to all formats. The Library expects all licenses and agreements to allow use of the resource for supplying interlibrary loan requests in accordance with the Interlibrary Loan Provision of Section 108 of the U.S. Copyright Law, and the National Commission on New Technological Uses of Copyrighted Works (CONTU) Guidelines.
- The Library expects all licenses and agreements to allow the use of the resource in course reserves (print or digital) by authorized users in connection with specific courses.
- The purchase or leasing of digital information should include provisions for perpetual access to that information.
- Partnerships in cooperative acquisitions and cost sharing of digital resources, both within and outside the University community, are pursued when it is advantageous to do so.
- A vendor's ability to work with these definitions and meet these expectations is an important factor in the evaluation and selection of a digital resource. The Library's prerogative and authority in making sound selection decisions should not be compromised by vendor-defined conditions and constraints.

MISSION

Montana State University
Montana State University Libraries
Bozeman, Montana

Mission

MSU Digital Initiatives serves as the catalyst for the creation, management, and delivery of digital content in support of the MSU Library mission and goals. The initiative provides for the storage and dissemination of digital objects, including text, images, audio, and video in their various digital manifestations and combinations. The MSU Library provides a web presence for digital collections, and provides storage, backup and digital preservation support for all digital content accepted into, or developed by the Library.

University of Michigan
University of Michigan Libraries
Ann Arbor, Michigan

The Digital Library Production Service (DLPS) is part of the University Library's Library Information Technology division. DLPS has three main functions:

1. Digitize library collections: The Digital Conversion Unit within DLPS has staff knowledgeable in the use of flat-bed, overhead and other specialized scanners and photography equipment for digitization.

2. Host online collections: The Information Retrieval unit is responsible for providing access to digitized books and journals, museum images, archival finding aids, bibliographies and catalogs. DLPS staff develop digital library software called DLXS.

3. Provide leadership in digital library development: Through memberships in national and international organizations, such as the Digital Library Federation, the Text Encoding Initiative, and a number of committees, task forces, and working groups, DLPS represents the University of Michigan in the creation of best practices, standards, and cutting-edge research in digital libraries. We provide advice and expertise throughout the University on digital library issues. As part of the Library Information Technology, DLPS is part of initiatives such as the partnership with Google that are changing the nature of libraries and scholarship.

DLPS is funded by the University Library. In addition, DLPS receives funding from grants, and from partnerships with other universities, commercial publishers, and non-profit organizations.

DLPS grew out of the Digital Library Program at the University of Michigan. The unit was formed in 1996 in response to a felt need for production level (twenty four hour a day, seven days a week) support for digital library resources. DLPS was originally jointly funded by the University Library, the Information Technology Division, the Media Union, and the School of Information.

University of Iowa
University of Iowa Libraries
Iowa City, Iowa

Mission

The University of Iowa Libraries' Digital Library Services department facilitates the creation, use, and preservation of digital content by offering a wide array of resources and services to faculty, academic departments, centers and institutes, and librarians in support of teaching, learning, research, scholarship, and creative activities.

Digital Library Services works in close cooperation with other campus units including Information Technology Services in order to coordinate efforts, reduce duplicate infrastructure, and maximize efficient and effective use of campus technology resources. The department provides outreach and leadership for digital initiatives throughout the state and participates locally and nationally in the development of digital library standards and best practices.

PRIORITIES

University of Ottawa
University of Ottawa Library
Ottawa, Ontario, Canada

Digital material is expected to create unique value. This includes: additional content; enhanced functionality; 24 × 7 accessibility; incorporation with teaching technologies; linking with other information resources;

improved resource sharing ability; and ease of archiving. Below are key priorities or strategies in acquiring digital content.

- To purchase digital resources rather than leasing arrangements, wherever feasible, in order to secure permanent access ;
- To acquire digital resources directly from the publisher rather than a vendor or aggregator whenever possible, in order to provide a maximum amount of security and stability in the content available to our users ;
- To privilege the digital format over the print format unless there are valid reasons for doing otherwise, since our user community has come to expect online access wherever available;
- To avoid duplication of format, in order to use our acquisitions budget in a cost-effective manner;
- To acquire digital resources that respond to the needs of faculty and students in an increasingly interdisciplinary environment, since new knowledge is often being created in the confluence of traditional disciplines;
- To acquire digital resources that are appropriate to the strategic areas of development defined by the University, in order to advance the goals of the University and support the researchers working in these areas;
- To pursue opportunities to digitize library print collections as appropriate, in order to broaden access to the richness of research material and advance the potential of open access for scholarship and learning.

The University of Texas at Austin
The University of Texas Libraries
Austin, Texas

Priorities

Priorities should be given to those digital materials that offer significant added value in supporting teaching and research over similar materials in traditional formats, that offer significant opportunities for cost containment, and whose license terms are reflective of the University's academic values. Measures of added value might include: additional content, greater functionality, greater accessibility, improved resource sharing ability, improved linkages with other information tools, ease of archiving, and the enabling of more efficient uses of limited faculty and student time and resources. Licenses should allow the library the flexibility to develop collections that match the University's needs without contractually forcing entangling ties to unwanted products, and without restricting the rights of fair use or the values of academic inquiry. License terms should also be financially sustainable and address archival rights to the resources in question. Materials that meet these and other selection needs, will be given priority over digital material of a more problematic nature.

PURPOSE OF COLLECTION

University of Maryland, Baltimore
University of Maryland Health Sciences and Human Services Library
Baltimore, Maryland

INTRODUCTION

The Health Sciences and Human Services Library of the University of Maryland, Baltimore (UMB) recognizes the growing importance of digital resources to the information needs of its clientele. Digital resources offer faculty, staff, and students the ability to satisfy their information needs from their homes, offices, and other remote locations. They offer distance education opportunities for those who would otherwise not have access to those resources. They have many value-added features not found in other formats, but they also present challenges unique to the digital environment. This policy is to be used in conjunction with the Library's general Collection Development Policy. New resources may be suggested by any UMB faculty, staff, or student, and are submitted to the Digital Resources Committee for consideration.

PURPOSE OF POLICY

This policy describes in detail the Library's goal of providing access to digital information resources that will support the instructional, research, and clinical goals of the University of Maryland, Baltimore, including the Schools of Dentistry, Medicine, Nursing, Pharmacy, Social Work, the Graduate School, and the University of Maryland Medical Center. The Library strives to organize and maintain its digital resources in a meaningful manner to fulfill users' needs.

University of Iowa
University of Iowa Libraries
Iowa City, Iowa

Guiding Principles

The resources and services offered by Digital Library Services are shaped by a commitment to:

Access
Build highly usable and accessible collections to make resources available to as wide a range of researchers, scholars, students, and the general public as possible.

Preservation
Maintain and promote awareness and understanding of preservation of digital collections and take steps throughout the life cycle of digital materials to ensure ongoing access and usability.

Added value
Enhance digital objects with rich descriptive and technical metadata to promote deeper analysis and greater understanding of the collections and materials.

Adoption of standards and best practices
Promote the use of standards, best practices, and open systems whenever possible to ensure longevity of and ongoing access to digital resources.

Respect for intellectual property
Provide mechanisms for managing rights and ensuring only authorized access to restricted resources in order to protect the rights of intellectual property owners and comply with the terms of binding agreements.

Efficient use of resources
Establish partnerships with other campus units, peer institutions, Regents, universities, and other organizations to make best use of available resources.

106

University of Ottawa
University of Ottawa Library
Ottawa, Ontario, Canada

Purpose

Digital library materials are collected to support the mission of the University of Ottawa, namely to support the teaching, learning and research needs of the university community. The purpose of this collection is also to foster an environment in which scholarship and innovation can flourish, and where interdisciplinary research can lead to the development of new knowledge and the furthering of the university's mission.

Montana State University
Montana State University Libraries
Bozeman, Montana

MSU Digital Initiatives Aims To:
- Make materials more accessible, both materials within the libraries and archives as well as material held elsewhere that is relevant to University programs and initiatives.
- Make content of value to faculty and staff for teaching and research readily available in digital formats compatible with instructional technology tools.
- Build digital collections including materials that are unique or less widely disseminated or held by multiple libraries.
- Organize and provide tools for easy identification and navigation of digital content, both locally created and commercially licensed.
- Educate faculty, librarians, and other staff in the creation and effective use of digital content.
- Provide a stable, scalable, and sustainable platform for the delivery and long-term management of digital content.

RESPONSIBILITY AND IMPLEMENTATION

University of Maryland, Baltimore
University of Maryland Health Sciences and Human Services Library
Baltimore, Maryland

RESPONSIBILITY AND LIBRARY DEPARTMENTAL COORDINATION

Evaluation, Selection, Acquisition, Renewal: Coordinated by the Digital Resources Librarian, who chairs the Digital Resources Committee, in conjunction with Collection Development, Information and Instructional Services, Library Administration, and other library departments. Usage statistics, coordinated by the Digital Resources Librarian, serve as an important retention and renewal tool.

Access: Initial access is verified by Digital Resources Librarian, who also troubleshoots subsequent access problems in cooperation with Computing and Technology Services. Web access is ensured by the Web Manager. Access via the catalog is ensured by the Electronic/Continuations Cataloger.

Technical Support and Maintenance: Network connections, installation, and storage (if appropriate) are provided by Computing and Technology Services in collaboration with Enterprise Services and Support.

Staff and User Training: Coordinated by Information and Instructional Services.

Publicity and Marketing: Conducted via e-mail, library newsletter, library web page, personal contacts, etc. by Information and Instructional Services.

IMPLEMENTATION AND REVIEW

This policy will be revised as appropriate to reflect changes in the emerging and constantly changing electronic information environment.

RETENTION AND RENEWAL

University of Maryland, Baltimore
University of Maryland Health Sciences and Human Services Library
Baltimore, Maryland

RETENTION AND RENEWAL

The dynamic nature of the Internet, as well as the speed with which new information-delivery technologies come in and out of vogue, requires that the Library frequently review its digital resources for continuing relevance and cost-effectiveness. In addition to considering each factor in the SELECTION CRITERIA section, the Library also studies usage statistics to determine if the use of a resource justifies its continued maintenance and accessibility.

SELECTION CRITERIA

Northwestern University
Northwestern University Library
Evanston, Illinois

Selection Criteria for Digital Library Projects at Northwestern

The mission of Northwestern University Library is "to provide information resources and services of the highest quality to sustain and enhance the University's teaching, research, professional, and performance programs." To fulfill this mission in the digital age, Northwestern's library must not only acquire resources through purchase, subscription, and loan, but also provide sophisticated electronic access to especially remarkable and often unique content in our collections, taking full advantage of the communications and analysis potential of new technologies. Since the Internet makes Northwestern's digital library collections available everywhere, these projects have implications far beyond our campus. They represent contributions to the far larger digital library now taking shape at the national and international levels. Although the Northwestern community remains our primary audience, the inherently shared nature of digital library collections requires that we take into account larger constituencies—and also, to avoid costly redundancy of effort, be cognizant of existing and prospective projects undertaken by other institutions, consortia, and commercial publishers.

The significant financial and staff resources required to mount and sustain digital library collections mean that a careful selection must be made from among many desirable proposals. What types of projects do we encourage library staff and Northwestern faculty to propose? Here are the chief criteria for selection applied by Northwestern's Digital Library Committee when considering new proposals:

1. Northwestern's Existing Collection Development Priorities: Projects that promise to advance existing goals for library collections will continue to be given the highest priority.

2. Intellectual Value and Uniqueness: Northwestern University Library houses many distinctive collections in many different formats—text, still and moving image, sound, and all possible combinations of these formats. Proposals for digital library projects should make clear the intellectual and scholarly value of the materials involved and also set forth the value that will be added by making these resources available as a digital library collection.

3. Mobilizing Northwestern's Human Resources: Proposals for digital library projects can gain additional weight by incorporating the expertise of specific faculty, library staff, or advanced students.

4. Campus Needs and Exhibits: Recurring curricular needs, exhibits at the library or elsewhere on campus, along with other events, projects, or initiatives at Northwestern may recommend yet other digital library projects.

5. Leveraging Digitally Reformatted Materials: Preservation-based digital reformatting of books, documents, audio, images, and other library materials that are endangered, damaged, or deteriorated provides—in addition to a new physical copy for Northwestern users—digital data files which can form the basis of digital library projects.

6. Protecting and Enhancing Access to Collections: Digitizing collections can enhance access to rare, fragile, endangered, or otherwise inaccessible library collections. In this way, digitizing collections becomes a legitimate tool to achieve both preservation and access goals.

7. Openness to "Opportunistic" Projects: Finally, Northwestern's digital library can include digitized materials that we do not own in physical form. There must be no restrictions made other than those of scholarly value and the practicality of the project.

Even the best proposals can founder if certain formal requirements are not met, especially in the area of rights and permissions, but also if there is a threat of duplication of efforts currently being undertaken elsewhere. These formal issues are addressed in the course of the proposal review process, prior to approving and embarking on a project. The Digital Library Committee has elaborated a list of important parameters—including several "showstoppers"—that must be examined carefully before a project can be approved to proceed.

For all decisions regarding digital library projects, the exploitation of the Internet and the digital medium must clearly add value to the collection at hand and further the scholarly and curricular mission of the Library and the University.

(For additional policies, please see the accompanying CD-ROM.)

TYPES OF MATERIAL

The University of Texas at Austin
The University of Texas Libraries
Austin, Texas

Categories

Digital library materials currently collected by The University of Texas Libraries consist of three broad categories:

1. Purchased or licensed material such as electronic journals or databases. These are generally acquired from a commercial source, a government entity, a non-profit organization, a professional society, or an

institution engaged in furthering scholarly research. In many cases this material is not "physically owned" by the library in the same sense that a printed book or journal may be owned, but instead the library has acquired specific rights to the material on behalf of the library's clientele.

2. Material that has been reformatted (digitized) by The University of Texas Libraries or the University from non-copyrighted print or analog sources, or has been reformatted from copyrighted sources with appropriate permission. In some cases the library may also serve as a repository for material digitized by other libraries, universities, institutions, or individuals. Typically, this material consists of resources from special collections that have been selected for digitization in order to make them more widely available, or deteriorating materials that have been reformatted for preservation reasons. As the use of digital material expands in higher education, the library will increasingly digitize materials on a program-matic basis in order to support the mission of the University and The University of Texas Libraries.

3. Links and pointers to Internet resources of significant scholarly value which are added to the library's catalogs, databases, and networked resources as appropriate.

Observations and Qualifications:

Electronic Journals:

Goals: To license access to a critical mass of high quality electronic journals throughout all subject areas.

Observations: Because the acquisition of any particular electronic journal is staff-intensive and involves the work of many people over a period of months—initial collecting efforts will focus on acquiring a solid core of proven e-journals from respected publishers.

Qualifications: E-journal publishers vary greatly in their familiarity with electronic publishing issues, and in their familiarity with needs of the scholarly and library community. In some cases e-journal publishers have unrealistic expectations as to the prices libraries can afford, and in the technical and format barri-ers they expect libraries to scale in order to access their journals. The library has limited funds and staff time that can be devoted to problematic publishers. In those cases where the content is desirable, but the price and practical barriers are too formidable, we will not pursue the electronic versions of the journal, but will provide access through other formats or delivery mechanisms.

Indexing and Abstracting Databases:

Goals: To acquire the primary database in each subject area, and secondary and tertiary databases as needed by local programs.

Observations: Indexing and Abstracting databases provide valuable discovery tools both for material owned and licensed by The University of Texas Libraries and for other material which may be obtained through Inter-Library Loan or Document Delivery. In some instances these services also provide valu-able links and online access to actual data and full-text resources.

Qualifications: The number of databases relevant to UT-Austin programs is multiplying faster than the library's ability to fund them. Selection of secondary and specialty databases will continue to be limited by available funds for the foreseeable future. The usefulness of a particular database to a discipline or audience group will be measured database by database, particularly against other types of resources that might be purchased with the available funds, and against how it fits in with the library's overall mix of resources and technical platforms, and the database's prospects for long-term utility.

Full-Text Databases:

Goals: To acquire a complete range of full-text databases that serve the university's general and specialized scholarly interests.

Observations: Full-text databases are notable for their ease of use and cost-effectiveness. They typically receive high use and are the least expensive means of providing access to information covered by the database.

Qualifications: These databases must be constantly monitored as the specific resources covered by each database change as publishers renegotiate contracts with the vendor. By their very nature, full-text databases directed at different audiences and designed for different purposes may also have significant overlap in coverage.

Primary Resources:

Goals: Identify selected content that has value for teaching and research at the university, that would benefit from being more widely available in digital form.

Observations: The nature of primary resources used in different disciples varies significantly. The original primary resources may be manuscripts, pamphlets, books, official records, photos, paintings, audio clips, data sets, lab reports, digital files, etc. With all of recorded human history to draw upon, the reformatting of primary resources into digital form presents a wealth of potential material.

Qualifications: This material is available in a number of ways including licensing via commercial vendors, free via the Internet, or via resource sharing agreements with other institutions. The potential use and value of the material must be weighed against its cost and the amount of resources its provision requires. Consultation with faculty, and consideration of the experiences of other institutions with the material is especially valuable in considering selection. When possible, outright purchase of the digital primary resource material should be considered as an option, instead of paying ongoing subscription and maintenance fees. In many cases this primary resource material is being republished from another easily available published format such as microfilm; in these cases the cost of digital primary research materials must be carefully weighed against the potential usage and convenience of digital access.

Digitization of Local Materials:

Goals: Identify local materials whose wider availability would aid university teaching and research, promote scholarship, enrich the arts and sciences, deepen our understanding of human culture, and benefit the citizens of Texas

Observations: Local materials are digitized both to provide wider access, and to preserve them for future generations.

Qualifications: Digitization projects require a significant investment of local resources and are not undertaken lightly. Long-term value to the academic community, congruency with the library and university mission and university mission and areas of interest, and significance to worldwide users of the Internet are all important considerations. Digitization projects are planned in consultation with the Electronic Information Programs Division and the Research Services Division.

Online Books:

Goals: To contract with vendors for permanent online digital rights to selected current academic and trade books.

Observations: These services are new but growing in number. Initially The University of Texas Libraries will purchase rights to reserve items, high circulating popular scholarly items, and convenience books such as reference items or items that are frequently consulted but not pondered at length nor read in depth.

Qualifications: Until these services become reliable, The University of Texas Libraries will continue its general policy of fiscally conservative experimentation.

Alerting and Profiling Services:

Goals: To subscribe to services and databases that can supply e-mail alerts to new articles, publications, and digital resources in a library user's area of interests.

Observations: These types of automated notification services are a way of extending the library's collection development activities outward to encompass newly published material that the library does not yet own, and to more fully involve faculty and students in the dialogue that is the library's collection building effort.

Qualifications: The amount of faculty and student interest in well-developed alerting and profiling services is not known. Current e-mail alerting services are little used.

Electronic Document Delivery and Pay Per View services:

Goals: To contract with vendors for the seamless delivery of material on a cost-per-use basis, that the library does not own and has not previously licensed.

Observations: For the immediate future these electronic services will be mediated through Inter-library Services in order to insure efficiency and to control costs. In the future, unmediated delivery of electronic information directly to the user is a realistic possibility, though access would be controlled via computerized rationing or accounts

Qualifications: The lines between services such as these, and full-text databases, and electronic journals and books, is likely to continue to blur.

Archiving of non-University of Texas web sites:

Goals: To undertake archival responsibilities for non-University of Texas web-based information carefully and with proper consideration for all the issues involved.

Observations: There are considerable intellectual property, copyright, technical, and resource issues involved with archiving a web site. The issues pertaining to serving data that was created on another hardware/software platform are legion, and any archival consideration needs to begin with a finding of whether or not archiving the site in question is technically possible. Consideration for local archiving of a web site also includes obtaining signed legal permission for The University of Texas Libraries to archive and serve the data, and a consideration of whether the library has the resources (staff/hardware/software/etc.) to undertake the project.

Qualifications: Other archival options, such as printing out screens from the web site, cataloging them, and making them available in the library; or relying on national web archival options such as the Alexa project or Library of Congress should also be explored.

Integration of Print and Electronic Resources:

Goals: To promote the integration of print and digital items through bibliographer subject pages, conversion of finding aids into digital form, and through the licensing of resources that intermix citations to multiple formats.

Observations: Integration of formats can be achieved technically through improved discovery and access mechanisms, as well as through the efforts of individual librarians via the creation of bibliographer subject pages, the addition of digital resources to the online catalog, and similar activities.

Qualifications: For the foreseeable future, print and digital resources will both be essential in a successful research library. Collection planning needs to consider both formats.

Overall Multiple User Profiling and Alerting Capability:

Goals: To insure that the various digital library products are capable of responding to profiling and alerting services that the library may create or contract with, so that users may be automatically notified of new information of personal interest.

Observations: Integration of the variety of vendor based products of this nature is currently problematical

Qualifications: Campus usage of these services is low, and whether or not library users would find these services truly useful is unclear.

University of Maryland, Baltimore
University of Maryland Health Sciences and Human Services Library
Baltimore, Maryland

TYPES OF DIGITAL RESOURCES

The Library prefers web-based digital resources in lieu of other types and methods of electronic access.

E-journals: As with print journals, e-journals require a long-term commitment from the Library in terms of financial and human resources to acquire and maintain. As more and more scholarly journals become available in digital as well as print versions, the Library must decide whether to maintain both versions or cancel the print when the online version becomes available. The Library subscribes to an e-journal only if it is full text, not if it has just abstracts or tables of contents. In addition to the Digital Resources Committee, the Journal Review Committee may also review e-journal requests in conjunction with a print journal request.

Free with Existing Print Subscription

The Library provides access to the free web version of a **print** journal to which it subscribes if the following criteria are met access is provided by IP address and /or proxy server (no passwords) licensing terms are acceptable access is not for a limited time or trial basis, except for purposes of evaluation.

Additional Cost to Existing Subscription

E-journals that are not included in the cost of a print subscription are reviewed by the Digital Resources Committee on a case-by-case basis. The Committee uses criteria similar to those used for print journals in addition to the SELECTION CRITERIA listed below.

Online-Only

This category includes those e-journals that are available only online, as well as those which are published in both print and online, but to which the Library is considering only online access. These are reviewed by the Digital Resources Committee on a case-by-case basis. The Committee uses criteria similar to those used for print journals in addition to the SELECTION CRITERIA listed below.

E-Books: The Library selectively acquires e-books if free, if included in a digital resource package (see number 3 below), or if the e-book fills a unique user need.

Aggregated resources: These products typically combine more than one type of digital resource into one package. For example, MDConsult includes both e-journals and e-books. The contents of aggregated products that include both relevant and out-of-scope resources are reviewed on a title-by-title basis by HS/HSL information specialists. Only those resources that are relevant are included in the Library's catalog and on the Library's web page.

CD-ROMs/Diskettes/Other Media: In general, CD-ROMs, diskettes, and other digital media are not collected unless they can be networked and are for reference use. These formats are acquired only occasionally if the content is unique, not available in any other format, and present no technical support difficulties.

CD-ROMs that accompany print material are retained only if the content is supplemental to the text and only at the discretion of the subject specialist.

Databases: General information and bibliographic databases are selectively acquired. Of particular importance to consider for this category are the cost per anticipated use and the interface.

Web sites: These are generally identified and selected by HS/HSL subject specialists according to their relevance to the Library's collection using the Library's Web Site Evaluation Checklist.

University of Ottawa
University of Ottawa Library
Ottawa, Ontario, Canada

Categories

Digital library materials currently collected by the libraries consist of the following categories:
- E journals
- Bibliographic and full-text databases
- Ebooks and other full-text primary sources
- Reference tools
- Image files
- Geospatial material
- Datasets
- Hybrid content (usually involving full-text, image and research or primary tools packaged together)

Chapter 8

FINANCIAL ARRANGEMENTS

COMMITTEES

Dartmouth College
Dartmouth College Library
Hanover, New Hampshire

We recommend that CMDC form a permanent electronic information resources sub-committee to develop a priority list of electronic resources that bibliographers want to acquire for the collection or make accessible to the Dartmouth community. The sub-committee should serve as a resource for bibliographers in answering the questions raised when electronic resources are considered for acquisition.

University of Oregon
Orbis Cascade Alliance
Eugene, Oregon

Committee on Electronic Resources CER

Established 12/18/98

Type of committee: Standing committee

Charge

The Committee on Electronic Resources (CER) meets regularly to discuss new electronic resources (including reference works, full-text databases, and electronic journals), to arrange trials, to review and evaluate product performance, and to determine the level of interest among the represented libraries for both new purchases and renewals. For each product, one or more committee members work as a subgroup to negotiate price and access issues with the vendor. The committee is also responsible for determining an equitable cost distribution that adheres to the principles adopted by the Orbis Council. The chair or designated committee member is responsible for ordering the product, signing the licensing agreement, and working with Orbis and UO (fiscal agent) staff to arrange for payment of the invoice and billing of participating libraries. Council encourages maximum use of email in conjunction with Orbis-funded meetings (see funding policy).

CER is supported by Orbis staff who produce committee meeting minutes, track the status of licensing projects, maintain a CER Web site, maintain key data (e.g., ip address ranges, enrollment), coordinate meetings, and work with UO staff to pay invoices and bill libraries. Requests for additional funding or staff support should be presented to the Orbis Executive Committee.

Timeline

CER is a standing committee. Meeting minutes should be produced and distributed to committee members and Orbis staff for distribution to Council. An annual written report is submitted to Council.

Membership

Members: Each Orbis or Portals member institution may designate one staff person as a member of CER.

Dartmouth College
Dartmouth College Library
Hanover, New Hampshire

The Collection Management and Development Committee is composed of all librarians with subject responsibilities as well as librarians from Acquisitions Services, Bibliographic Control Services, and Circulation Services. The committee meets monthly and is chaired by the Director of Collection Services. Established in 1979, the CMDC oversaw the first preparation of written collection development policies for each subject area of the collection and the creation of the Bibliographer's Manual. In addition to the full monthly meetings, committee members are encouraged to serve on one or more subgroups, which include:

Subgroups:

- Steering Committee
- Collection Policies Group
- Electronic Information Group
- EIG at CMDC May 16, 2001
- Electronic Products Tests: Current Tests : for staff use only
- Electronic Products Tests: Completed Tests : for staff use only
- Considerations for Digital Formats
- Licenses for Electronic Resources: Guidelines for Bibliographers
- Dartmouth College Library Digital Resources License Information
- To view or print the complete database
- To search the database
- Dartmouth Web Journals Test Report Recommendations : Final Draft
- Using Electronic Journals : a trouble-shooting guide for staff
- Preservation Group
- Serials Group

The Committee serves as a forum to discuss collection development activities, to define and solve problems, and to develop strategies for coping with pressures on the materials budgets and with the growth of the electronic information environment. The Committee is charged with the following responsibilities: 1) revise and approve collection development policies written by bibliographers, 2) develop principles and methods to guide the evaluations of collections, 3) establish criteria for review of collections for storage and preservation, 4) decide issues of bibliographic control and access relating to collection management, 5) participate in and contribute to cooperative collection development activities with the Research Libraries Group, 6) monitor the issues and problems which affect costs and maintenance of serials collections, 7) establish ad hoc groups as necessary, to carry out tasks relating to collection management and development, 8) document the policies and procedures of the program, and, 9) maintain awareness of trends and developments in the publishing world and the information marketplace.

CONSORTIA

Tufts University
Tisch Library
Medford, Massachusetts

The Boston Library Consortium (BLC) is a cooperative association of academic and research libraries located in New England. Founded in 1970, the BLC supports resource sharing and enhancement of services to users of the member libraries. Click here to see a list of BLC members.

Most member libraries are open to Tisch Library users for onsite use of materials. Tisch Library adheres to mutually accepted criteria applicable throughout the BLC. Questions concerning operating hours, borrowing privileges and use of the collections at BLC member libraries should be directed to the individual library. Links to individual BLC members are available on the BLC website.

Tisch Library issues BLC Borrower cards to Tufts Arts, Sciences & Engineering applicants. Faculty, staff and students of the Fletcher, Health Sciences and Veterinary Schools can apply for BLC cards at their respective libraries. Borrowing privileges at BLC member libraries are determined by the individual library. All BLC card users are responsible for resolving any charges accrued on their BLC accounts at member libraries, including overdue fines and replacement fees. Any charges incurred by Tisch Library for AS&E BLC card users will be added to the user's Tisch Library account.

BLC card applications are available at Tisch Library's circulation desk. A valid, current Tufts ID must be presented when applying for a BLC card. Completed applications are processed whenever the circulation desk is staffed.

COOPERATIVE AGREEMENTS

Dartmouth College
Dartmouth College Library
Hanover, New Hampshire

Cooperative Arrangements

Electronic information resources are often very expensive. Their acquisition may involve negotiations with publishers or vendors, particularly when networking is involved.

Cooperative development and purchase arrangements negotiated with other institutions stretch our funds and make more services available to the Dartmouth community. At this writing, cooperative projects have been done and are being planned with Middlebury College and Williams College, respectively. The Director of Collection Services helps initiate and manage such arrangements.

Florida Atlantic University
S.E. Wimberly Library
Boca Raton, Florida

The Libraries will cooperate in the purchase or leasing of library materials such as electronic products, machine readable datafiles, government documents, etc., with SEFLIN member libraries, State University Libraries, and other library cooperative arrangements when possible. The Libraries share in the development of digital library cooperative programs such as the SUL Publication of Archival Library & Museum Initiatives

(PALMM), including the Florida Heritage Collection. In an age of developing information technologies, resource sharing activities will need to be reviewed on a continuing basis.

University of Arizona
Arizona Health Science Library
Tucson, Arizona

Collaborations

The library expands and deepens resource availability for its users by collaborations of various kinds. Its participation in University of Arizona initiatives is fundamental but consortial memberships such as the Arizona University Libraries Consortium (AULC) and Arizona Health Information Network (AZHIN) also provide opportunities to maximize resource availability at the least possible cost. The library is a Resource Library within the National Library of Medicine's National Network of Libraries of Medicine program. Interlibrary loan borrowing and lending are provisions of this membership. While collaborations have always been important, in this digital age they are critical.

FUNDING

Indiana University South Bend
Franklin D. Schurz Library
South Bend, Indiana

Funding: The electronic resources of the Schurz Library are an integral part of the reference, reserve, government documents, and general collections. Funds for electronic resources are administered as part of the general library material budget, and in most cases are not assigned to academic departments' library allocations.

Texas State Library and Archives Commission
Austin, Texas

TexSelect

TexShare electronic resources are supplemented through the selection of resources to be included as TexSelect products. TexSelect enables the Texas State Library and Archives Commission to utilize the aggregated purchasing power of the state to leverage the use of local funds to purchase databases at discounted prices.

Recommendations for TexSelect products will be made using similar criteria and procedures as for the TexShare Core Databases. Selection practices for TexSelect will accommodate selections that appeal to a smaller number of member libraries that are highly motivated to subscribe to specialized content. TexSelect products should be useful in more than one type of library, or provide unique content/indexing, and include commitment from the vendor for renewal of TexSelect discounts in future years. Additional criteria are:

• Significant subscription discounts
• Content that supplements what is available in the core databases

Washington State Library
Olympia, Washington

PURSUE THE FUNDING

Grant funding may be available to support the needs of your digital projects. Federal agencies such as the Institute for Museum and Library Services (IMLS), National Leadership Grant program provide dedicated funds to support digital projects in libraries and museums. In Washington State additional IMLS funds are available through grant programs administered by the Washington State Library to assist libraries to complete digital projects.

Writing good grant applications takes experience and planning. Most funding agencies are impressed by well thought out, well planned projects that meet one or more of the funding criteria. It is important to do your homework ahead of writing the grant proposal. Grant requests that clearly prove a need that is documented with survey information or statistical facts will be well received. Most government granting agencies such as IMLS, the National Endowment for the Humanities, (NEH) and the State Library have staff available to assist you with questions concerning your grant application. Make use of that resource; it can save you time and prevent many mistakes in your grant application.

The national funding agencies and the Washington State Library grant funding programs favor collaboration in digital projects. Partnering between museums or heritage organizations and libraries or between libraries is a goal of the funding programs. For libraries of all sizes digital projects that feature collaboration in the use of collections, sharing of staff expertise, or building common access to digital collections are given priority for funding programs.

Using grant funding for a pilot project or a development project is a good way to get started building your organization's digital collections. Over time library and heritage organizations will need to develop resources within organizational budgets to conduct digital projects. Plans should be made to provide resources for digital collections just as print based collections and museum collections are funded.

Options to consider:

When beginning to assemble the materials to write a grant request, ask the funding agencies if they can provide examples of successful grant proposals from past grant cycles. Often you can get many useful ideas from reading a few successful grant proposals. Consider how you will support your request with statistics. Use local examples to support and prove the need. Provide specific information on the impact of the project. Seek community support in the form of partnerships or contributions of time, volunteers or in-kind resources whenever possible. The grant proposal should be built around a clear set of needs and goals, with logical steps outlined. Describe how the project will move toward meeting the need or solving the problem.

Some granting agencies offer planning grants. Consider pursuing funds to complete a planning cycle before pursuing a larger grant to support a complex digital project.

When using a consultant to help prepare a grant proposal, examine examples of successful grants written by the consultant. Ask for and contact references. Good writing skills are essential. Consultants can be useful in helping to focus and clarify a grant project. A consultant could be a wise investment if you are considering a complex or multi-phased grant proposal.

Project checklist:

- Follow grant guidelines closely. Meet each requirement and don't leave out any steps.
- Ask several people to review your grant for common sense and clarity before you submit it.

119

- Make sure your grant application contains a clear and logical budget, with narrative description that explains the costs in each category.
- Supply documentation on how the costs were determined
- Gather statistics to support your request
- Do a survey of stakeholders when possible to demonstrate the need for the project.
- Be sure to include information on how you will evaluate the success of the project.
- Be sure to indicate how your project will meet state or national standards and digital guidelines.
- Review the list of projects that have recently been funded by NEH, IMLS and the State Library to determine if your project will meet the funding criteria.
- For insights into the funding process for digital projects at IMLS see "Digitization Grants and How to Get One: Advice from the Director, Office of Library Services, Institute of Museum and Library Services" in the October 15 edition of "RLG DigiNews," the bimonthly Web-based newsletter of the Research Libraries Group. The Research Libraries Group (RLG) is a not-for-profit membership corporation devoted to the mission of "improving access to information that supports research and learning."

University of Oregon
Knight Library
Eugene, Oregon

Funding: Collection Development will encourage subject specialists to select Internet resources which are free of charge. Selection of free Internet resources will bypass the usual routing of orders through the Acquisitions Department. This situation will foreseeably change as more commercial resources become available via the Internet. At present and in the future, when funding is necessary, the subject content will determine the individual fund. Subject specialists and the head of collection development will determine the appropriate individual funds to use for purchasing Internet resources. As with all other formats, the Library will consider other allocations for those titles deemed major purchases. The Library will also consider trial periods.

Satilla Regional Library System
Douglas, Georgia

Funding, Acquisition, and Cataloging

Materials budgets are allocated through state and local funding with infrastructure provided through State and local tax sources. When the interest accumulation allows, the Coffee County Public Library Endowment Fund provides another source of funds, mainly for the purchase of materials for a specialized purpose. The Director or appointee will order new selections and initiate or renew periodical subscriptions. Then, appropriate information will be provided to the SRLS Bookkeeper for invoice and payment processing. The Director will initial invoice cover sheets as indication of order and payment approval. All collection additions will be cataloged and processed as timely as possible.

GROUP ACQUISITIONS

Columbia College
Columbia College Library
Chicago, Illinois

Requesting New Subscriptions/Acquisitions

All new electronic acquisitions must be requested through the Coordinator of Electronic Resources and the Electronic Resources Committee.

In consultation with faculty, liaisons, appropriate library staff and others (as needed), the Electronic Resources Committee will consider whether or not the product meets the selection criteria outlined in the Electronic Resources Collection Development Policy.

The Coordinator of Electronic Resources will request pricing for the product and investigate consortia purchase options.

The Coordinator of Electronic Resources will request a trial of the product. All trials should be coordinated through the Coordinator of Electronic Resources. This will ensure that the trial is appropriately timed and publicized when necessary.

In consultation with faculty, liaisons, appropriate library staff and others (as needed), the Coordinator of Electronic Resources will solicit feedback and evaluate the product based on the trial.

The Coordinator of Electronic Resources will consult reviews of the product.

The Coordinator of Electronic Resources will consult other subscribers to the product.

Based on cost, perceived need, usage, and the degree to which the electronic resource meets the selection criteria, the committee will: 1) decide whether or not to acquire and 2) if a decision to acquire is made, prioritize its purchase in relation to other electronic resources requested within budgetary constraints.

LICENSED DATABASES

Central Michigan University
Central Michigan Universities Libraries
Mount Pleasant, Michigan

Licensing

When acquiring electronic resources, the Head of Collection Development will negotiate vendor licensing agreements in consultation with the appropriate subject bibliographer(s), Systems, and Technical Service staff. It is also possible that in some cases the University Purchasing Department may negotiate and sign agreements. Collection development will maintain the file containing copies of all licensing agreements. Final responsibility for compliance with licensing agreements rests with the Head of Collection Development, in consultation with the relevant members of the Libraries' DAC, the University Purchasing Department and the University Attorney, as may be necessary.

Information providers should employ a standard agreement that describes the rights of the Libraries and their authorized users in terms that are readable and explicit, and they should reflect realistic expectations about CMU's ability to monitor use and discover abuse. Agreements should contain consistent business and legal provisions, including, for example, indemnification against third party copyright infringement liability, the application of Michigan state laws and the use of Michigan courts of law should that become necessary.

Licenses should permit fair use of all information for non-commercial educational, instructional and research purposes by authorized users. Authorized users are defined as all currently enrolled students (i.e., not former students), faculty, staff on or off campus, or visiting patrons located in the Libraries. License should include interlibrary loan permissions whenever feasible.

Information providers should be able to link their access control mechanisms to CMU's authentication infrastructure; access to their products should not require individual passwords and/or user IDs.

Columbia College
Columbia College Library
Chicago, Illinois

License Agreements

The Columbia College Chicago Library purchases access to or data from publishers who require signed license agreements. When negotiating license agreements, the Library keeps the interests of the user in mind and refrains from purchasing products where use restrictions would seriously impede research or be impossible to enforce. The Head of Collection Management coordinates the review of license agreements and submits the signed license agreement as part of the ordering procedure. The Library will consult with General Counsel to amend vendor license agreements on a case-by-case basis to ensure use is granted to the fullest extent possible.

Florida Atlantic University
S.E. Wimberly Library
Boca Raton, Florida

The FAU Libraries will negotiate the best possible license with each vendor. Each resource may have differing terms and not all preferences may be met. In general, the vendor should provide a standard agreement that describes the terms of the license in easy-to-understand and explicit language. Licenses should include, but are not limited to:

- Broad definitions of authorized users including faculty, students, staff, and walk-in users.
- Broad definitions of authorized sites with permission to access from anywhere via the University's network, including remotely via EZproxy authentication.
- Fair use permission of all information for non-commercial, educational, instructional, and research purposes by authorized users. Other uses permitted under fair use should include ILL, e-reserves, course packs, and virtual reference.
- Pricing model, service fees, and any price caps applicable to multi-year licenses.
- Realistic expectations concerning the Libraries' ability to monitor and detect abuse.
- Provision of perpetual access to the subscribed years.
- Provision for some type of archival copy of the material.
- Warranties that the licensor has the right and authority to license the material.
- Duration of the license and whether automatic renewal is assumed.
- Termination terms. Preference is that termination not be required in writing or more than 30 days in advance of the renewal date.
- A continuous service and scheduled down-time clause.
- Guaranteed anonymity of the users and confidentiality of their information.
- Dispute resolution arrangements.

Rollins College
Olin Library
Winter Park, Florida

All license agreements will be reviewed before signing by the Electronic Resources Librarian and/or the Acquisitions Librarian. Any agreements with terms that conflict with the Electronic Resources Licensing Policy will be referred to the Director of Libraries.

"Click through" or "Shrink wrap" license agreements, also known as "contracts of adhesion," are to be avoided whenever possible, and will be referred to the Director of Libraries.

The Yale LibLicense Database will be used to create license agreements that comply with Licensing Policy as needed.

Licensing policies will be consistent with the "Principles for Licensing Electronic Resources," as ratified by the American Association of Law Libraries, American Library Association, Association of Academic Health Sciences Libraries, Association of Research Libraries, Medical Library Association and Special Libraries Association.

Tufts University
University Information Technology
Somerville, Massachusetts

Policy on Licensing of Electronic Content Resources

General Statement

The license agreements for electronic content are a fact of life in an electronic environment. Many units within the University sign license agreements for access to electronic content. The libraries lead the University in this activity as one of their primary roles is the purchasing or licensing of electronic content resources to support Tufts University's mission of teaching, learning and research. As responsible agents for Tufts, the librarians negotiate licenses that address the institution's needs and recognize its obligations to the licensor. As such, the librarians provide a licensing consulting service to other University units who are licensing content resources whose annual licensing fees exceed $5000.

In order to leverage the financial investment and assure University-wide access and support, the initial procurement process for electronic resources, as defined in this policy, is facilitated by a team of staff from the libraries and the requesting unit. One or several of the libraries may offer to assume the licensing of the resource if it is appropriate for the library collections. The libraries will also serve as a clearinghouse to ensure that the resource is not already available to the Tufts community.

Definition of Electronic Content Resources

An electronic content resource is defined as any publication, database, indexing source, or service made available over the Internet, on CD-ROM, on tape or on any other electronic medium. For the purposes of this policy it includes only those resources whose annual license fee equals or exceeds $5000. It does not include the purchase or site licensing of software to be run on PCs, Macs or time-sharing computers. Individuals should contact Tufts Computing and Communications Services (UIT) for information about site licensing of software.

Review Process

The libraries will serve as a clearinghouse and resource for the licensing of electronic content resources. A review will be conducted with the sponsoring unit based on the following premises:

- One of the library's primary roles is to review electronic databases for licensing decision
- Monitoring is done by the library to ensure the database is available according to the license agreement
- A single license is negotiated for the entire University
- The resource is properly evaluated for content appropriateness which may include comparison with similar resources already licensed as well as monitoring when deselection is appropriate as other databases become available
- The resource is not already available or being negotiated via consortia arrangements such as with the Boston Library Consortium

- The license agreement sets terms that will best serve the community whether they are on or off campus
- The best price is negotiated
- University Counsel will be consulted whenever necessary
- The resource is evaluated for systems compatibility
- Licensing Process

Any University unit outside of the libraries wishing to license or purchase an electronic resource will contact the chair of the ULC Collections and Licensing Committee to evaluate the resource as a possible purchase within the library. The process includes:

1) Review of the resource with the appointed library staff.

2) Determination of who will pay for the resource, a library or the sponsoring units.

3) If it is determined the resource should be licensed by the sponsoring unit, the review team will review the terms of the license, and negotiate new terms if needed. University Counsel may be required in unusual situations.

4) Sponsoring unit signs the negotiated license, sets up the ongoing subscription, and pays for the subscription.

5) To provide off campus access to the Tufts community, request proxy service for the resource through the University Library Technology Services Office (ULTS). ULTS will maintain a central listing on Tufts' homepage of all electronic databases Tufts subscribes to or licenses.

Implementation Plan

The libraries will work with Purchasing and UIT to communicate this new policy to the Tufts community. Strategies for implementing the new policy include:

- A cover letter will be sent out to all department heads, managers, and faculty with a copy of the policy.
- An announcement about the new University proxy services and a request for a list of existing resources that are currently inaccessible from off campus. This would be mailed with the cover letter about the new policy.
- Involve Purchasing to notify the Chair of the Collections & Licensing Committee of the libraries when new contracts are received that exceed $5000.
- Establish a Web page with guidelines and checklists for licensing content resources. Publicize this resource in the policy announcement and provide links from a variety of places on the Tufts Web site.

LICENSING FAQ

University of Colorado at Boulder
University Libraries
Boulder, Colorado

Electronic information resources offer enormous benefits. They provide users faster, more convenient, 24-hour desktop access from home or campus, as well as special features such as hypertext links to related information, graphics, audio, video, and animation. These resources also offer benefits to libraries – they don't take up valuable space on library shelves, they can't be stolen or destroyed, and, depending on the license agreement, they allow more than one user to access information at the same time.

Significant portions of the five CU libraries' collection dollars are spent on electronic resources. Almost every electronic book, database, and journal provided by the CU Libraries has been licensed. Each publisher's license agreement outlines specific terms and conditions under which the resources may be used. Within each CU library and campus, licenses go through several layers of review and negotiation before they are signed. The CU Libraries Electronic Resources Task Force has prepared answers for licensing questions commonly asked by CU faculty, staff, and students.

Q. Why do libraries license information resources instead of buying them?

A. Licensing resources in electronic format allows libraries to provide access to many more titles than they could afford to purchase and shelve in paper format. These resources also provide superior indexing, retrieval, and access capabilities. Some electronic resources may only be available through a license agreement.

Q. What is a license agreement?

A. A license agreement is a contract between an intellectual property owner (or licensor) and a potential user (or licensee). Unlike print resources, libraries do not own most electronic or digital resources. Instead, a license agreement is negotiated and signed with each owner which allows the library's users to access the electronic information for a specified amount of time for a specified fee.

Q. Are there clauses and terms basic to every license or is each one different?

A. Most digital information licenses include detailed language that specifies who has the right to access the information, how the information may be used, stored, and transmitted, who is liable for violations or misuse of the information by library users, whether the information will be permanently accessible, and the charges for accessing the information.

Q. Are there restrictions on use common to most license agreements?

A. Although each license is unique, common restrictions found in licenses for digital information products include the following:

> The content may be used only for non-commercial educational, clinical, or research purposes.
> Individuals who are not affiliated with the library that has licensed the product may not use the content, or may use content only when physically at the library.
> Printing and downloading of e-resources are generally subject to copyright restrictions.
> Altering, recompiling, systematic or programmatic copying, reselling, redistributing or republishing of electronic content are typically prohibited.

Q. Who is an authorized user?

A. The definition of an authorized user depends on the terms set out in the license of a particular electronic resource. Generally authorized users are the registered students, faculty, and staff of the institution purchasing the electronic resource. In many cases, authorized users also include members of the public who use the e-resource on library premises.

Q. How do you know what license agreement is in effect for a particular e-resource and what the specific terms are?

A. Consult the reference staff at the library to find out the specific terms in effect for a particular e-resource. Some distributors of electronic content publish general license terms on the website where the content is accessed. Others block activities that violate the license terms.

Q. What constitutes a breach of license terms and what are the penalties?

A. Each individual license details uses that constitute a failure to follow the license agreement and the penalties for such violations. For example, breach of contract may occur when unauthorized users access the electronic material, or when a user prints more pages than the contract allows. Penalties usually involve suspension or termination of access to at least the violator and possibly the University. The University may add additional penalties applicable to faculty, staff or students who violate licenses.

Q. How does the library ensure that electronic information is used according to the terms and conditions of each license?

A. The library includes information on the legal use of electronic resources in class instruction sessions, on its website, and through instruction at the reference desk. The library also monitors general usage trends of each electronic resource, while respecting rights of confidentiality of library users, and works in conjunction with electronic providers to identify possible violations of licensing agreements.

Q. What happens if you violate a license agreement?

A. Distributors of electronic content use various tools to monitor types of usage but not individual usage. They look for large-scale violations, such as systematic downloading of substantial portions of an electronic title. In these cases, whether the violations occur knowingly or unknowingly, the vendor will contact the library that holds the license and may suspend the university's access to the resource. In order to have access restored libraries must take sufficient measures, such as warning the offender or department, to satisfy the provider that appropriate action has been taken to prevent future violations.

Q. Why are some e-resources available from home and others are not?

A. License agreements require libraries to screen for status before allowing access. Some e-resources require passwords for authentication. The most common strategy for authentication is to register campus IP addresses, the official Internet identification numbers for computers located on each institution's secure network. If you access e-resources from a campus computer, your IP address is recognized and access granted. If you want to access e-resources from home, you may need to do so by going through a university computer with a recognized IP address. You can do this by connecting through Virtual Private Networking (VPN), or by connecting through the campus modem pool or through the library's "proxy server." More information on these remote access connection methods can be found at http://ucblibraries.colorado.edu/research/remote.htm If you connect to the library's proxy server, please be aware that not every electronic journal title will be available full-text due to space limits on the server. Also, some publishers of electronic resources do not permit remote access and may limit use of their product to one building or one site. Some e-resources are only accessible via passwords available from the reference desk. Contact the libraries if you have trouble accessing an e-resource.

Q. Why can't I download an entire journal issue?

A. License terms do not permit copying or downloading entire issues of a journal. This is also a violation of basic copyright principles.

Q. Can I e-mail full-text articles to individuals who are not affiliated with CU?

A. As a general rule, you may not e-mail full-text articles to unauthorized users.

Q. How can I access e-resources from another CU library?

A. License terms generally restrict the use of an e-resource to a particular campus or set of campus users. There are many electronic resources available across the CU system, and the five CU libraries work cooperatively to license e-resources across the campuses when vendors and funding allow. In most cases, for e-resources that are only purchased by one CU library, faculty, staff and students from the other CU campuses must physically go to the subscribing library to access the resource. Check with the reference desk before traveling to another library to make sure you will be able to access a specific resource.

Q. Who can I contact in the Boulder campus Libraries with additional questions on licensed resources or copyright questions?

A. Contact the Faculty Director for Electronic Resources Development & Information Delivery.

University of Minnesota
University of Minnesota Libraries
Minneapolis, Minnesota

Information for Users About Open Access Computers

1. What is the difference between an open access computer and authenticated computer?

    The open access computers provide access to MNCAT (our online catalog), licensed databases, and most World Wide Web sites including federal and state government sites. Block lists have been installed on open access computers in Wilson Library to prohibit access to free e-mail, chat and gaming sites. Any patron may use the open access computers without supplying identification.

An authenticated computer provides access to LUMINA (our digital library gateway) as well as the full Internet without any blocking. Only current students, staff and faculty may use the authenticated workstations.

2. Why did we decide to authenticate and install block lists?

    We experienced a growing number of complaints that computers in Wilson Library were not available for our primary users or for researchers visiting the library from outside the University. Non-University users were monopolizing the majority of the computers and were using them for long periods of time to do personal email, chat and gaming. This is not a change in policy. We have posted signs for several years indicating that computers are reserved for research and that personal e-mail, chat and gaming are prohibited.

3. How many open access terminals are there, and how do I find them?

    Currently there are 60 public computers in Wilson Library of which 20 are open access workstations. They can be identified by yellow dots on the monitors. There are open access computers on each floor in the library. All of these open access computers have block lists installed.

4. How do the block lists work?

    The block lists prevent access to sites identified on the list. Library staff will monitor and update the list as necessary. When a user tries to access a prohibited site, a window pops up with an "access restricted" notice.

5. What does "authenticate" mean and who can authenticate?

    In this case, "authenticate" means to verify the identity of authorized users. Persons who have a current University of Minnesota User ID and password will be able to authenticate; this means all current students, faculty and staff.

6. How do people authenticate?

    They supply their University of Minnesota X.500 User ID (also called an Internet ID) and password.

7. When I authenticate, will the University be tracking my research on the workstation?

    No, the authentication software only verifies that the User ID and password are present in the University's X.500 database. It does not keep track of anyone's search history or even remember who is using the computer during the authenticated session.

8. Why aren't all taxpayers or U of MN alumni who support the University of Minnesota given the same access to library resources, computers, and the Internet?

    University of Minnesota staff and students receive a User Id and password and open access to the Internet as part of the benefits received for paying tuition or working at the University. All users have access to the collection of the University of Minnesota Libraries through LUMINA. They also have access to our licensed databases when they are in the libraries. This includes access to over six million volumes in the University of Minnesota Libraries and more than 200 research databases containing thousands of articles. Additionally, all users have access to federal and state government websites. This access is the same whether the user is on an open access computer or an authenticated computer.

9. Why can't I have open access the Internet now when I could before?

    Only current students, staff and faculty have open access to the full Internet. The authentication and blocking procedures are primarily security measures intended to prevent abuse of the Libraries' computers. See the University policy on "Appropriate Use of Computer Workstations and Electronic Resources" at http://www.lib.umn.edu/appuse.phtml.

10. What if I really need access to a blocked web site? How can I access it if I cannot authenticate?

Check with the staff at a library service desk for assistance. They assist users in locating information on the Internet. They can take suggestions for specific sites, which may be deemed appropriate to remove from the block lists.

11. I have a library card. Does that mean I can get an Internet account in order to authenticate?

No. The University Libraries' borrower card allows individuals to borrow library materials; it does not provide the opportunity for users to get mail accounts.

12. Can I buy a University of Minnesota User ID and Password?

No. The ID and password are issued to current University of Minnesota students, faculty and staff who have agreed to the University's appropriate use policies and paid the required fees. Because of the costs associated with providing computer services, and the need to ensure the best possible response times for our large University user base, e-mail accounts are not offered to patrons who are not current students, faculty and staff.

13. Is there a time limit on my use of open access computers or authenticated computers?

There is no time limit on most computers, but we ask that users respect the needs of other users if a waiting line develops. The two Open Access terminals in the basement and one computer on the second and third floors of Wilson Library have a five minute limit and should be used only for quick research like a brief search of the Libraries catalog. If staff ask a user to leave and he/she does not comply, they will notify the security monitor or call 911. There is a "time-out" on authenticated computers. If no keystrokes are made for a period of five minutes, the terminal will attempt log off automatically.

14. Can I e-mail articles from computers when using databases such as Lexis-Nexis or MNCAT?

Yes, it is possible to e-mail articles from those databases that provide such functionality. E-mailing articles from such databases works on all the workstations.

15. Where can I get open access to the Internet if not here?

Many public libraries provide Internet access to community users. Library staff will help identify the public library most convenient for user's needs. In the immediate area, the Franklin Branch of the Minneapolis Public Library, have computer labs. They also provide homework help. Ask at the reference desk for a more complete list. See our FAQ database on LUMINA.

Please note: The Electronic Library for Minnesota (ELM) provides access to many periodical databases similar to those of the University Libraries. All registered public library users can use ELM. See our Free Indexes web page on LUMINA Articles and More for links and more information.

16. Who is responsible for making the decision to install block lists on the open access workstations?

The University Libraries' Leadership Council made this decision in December 2002.

17. Where can I go to express concerns about this policy?

Concerns and complaints should be directed to ….fill out a comments form available at the Circulation Desk.

NEGOTIATION AND REVIEW GUIDELINES

Indiana University South Bend
Franklin D. Schurz Library
South Bend, Indiana

Licensing Agreements

The following provisions should be considered when negotiating and reviewing contracts with vendors:

Patron Use: Normally, there must be provisions in the agreement that all patrons of the library can use the resource, including members of the public. Under exceptional circumstances a resource will be considered which limits use by password or some other device to certain members of the IUSB community.

Cost of Access: The cost of access points and number of simultaneous users should be appropriate to the projected use of the resource. Consortial agreements may receive special consideration by the Electronic Resources Subcommittee.

Access: Agreements which allow access from remote networked locations such as homes or businesses with authentication through a proxy server are preferred.

Archiving: Strong preference should be given to agreements that allow the library to have access to, or own the content of, the last-held version of the database in perpetuity.

Fair Use: Fair use as defined by University and Library guidelines must be permitted within the context of any agreement. It is preferable that fair use provisions include interlibrary loan privileges.

Confidentiality: The confidentiality and privacy of all library patrons must be protected.

Multiple formats: Licensing Agreements should not force the Schurz library into additional purchases of the printed version of the product.

Negotiations: With the exception of resources jointly negotiated with the IU system or other consortia, agreements with electronic resource vendors are negotiated by the Head of Electronic Resources. Contracts are maintained with the Head of Electronic Resources or the Electronic Resources Administrator's office in Bloomington.

PRICING

University of Arizona
Arizona Health Science Library
Tucson, Arizona

The Current Library Environment

During the last decade rapid development of publishers' ability to supply online resources to meet the demand by users for information delivery on demand to any location has driven the trend toward the virtual library. Scientific, technical and medical publishing continues to experience rapid change. Open access publications and institutional repositories are growing in number and influence; publishers are being bought and sold until few players remain except the very large publishing houses. Publishers and database producers are consolidating electronic journals which are experiencing rapid and widespread acceptance. Much broader availability of e-books is probably not far off.

Faculty and students have expressed their need for even more electronic materials and the AHSL attempts to provide electronic access whenever feasible. At the same time, we remain attentive to the access vs. ownership issues and to efforts being undertaken worldwide to be certain that electronic content remains available.

Even before the "age of the e-journal" rising costs had become the norm. For example, in the early 1990's drastic cuts were made in print journal subscriptions in order to balance decreasing budgets and sharply increasing costs. The trend away from print subscriptions and toward license agreements for online access has not slowed these increases. On the contrary, some publishers, faced with declining numbers of print subscriptions, have attempted to impose exceptionally large annual price increases. In the most egregious cases the library refuses, whenever possible, to purchase subscriptions at vastly increased prices. However, the journals in question are often considered indispensable to the university, thus limiting price negotiability. Additionally, large corporations are buying up and consolidating publishers. Groups of journal titles are offered on an "all or nothing" basis, further weakening library negotiating positions and moving control of costs further from the library.

The availability of electronic resources brings both new opportunities and increased expectations for rapid information access in teaching, research, and patient care. Electronic resources pose new challenges in acquisition and management, often proving to be more rather than less expensive than the traditional print books and journals. In spite of increased costs and complex management issues, electronic resources are rapidly becoming critical to the success of all AHSC enterprises. The AHSL-Phoenix is being established as a primarily digital/virtual library while the AHSL-Tucson continues moving rapidly in that direction. It is important to emphasize, however, that the library acquires resources best suited to support the research, clinical, administrative and educational needs of its clients regardless of format.

Washington State Library
Olympia, Washington

COST FACTORS IN DIGITIZATION

When contemplating a digital conversion project most organizations have to face the question, "Are the resources available to do a project?" Results from the Digital Images Initiative projects conducted in 2000, 2001 and 2002, have shown that the cost of conducting a digital conversion project is well within the reach of small organizations if the project is well designed and has precisely focused goals and outcomes.

Digital Projects
Celeste Kline, Director of the Ellensburg Public Library, reported her satisfaction with their first digital project. " We have shown that it is possible for a small library to create a useful and good quality digital database from its unique collection with a reasonable amount of funding and resources, when it is supported and assisted by the larger university libraries. I am most satisfied that our project has such a nice presence on the web, due to the use of CONTENTdm software, and the use of scanning and metadata to complete the objects in the database. The cooperative parts of the project, such as sharing the CONTENTdm software and hosting by the universities, and training and consulting provided by them made this project possible."

Organizing collections, preparation for imaging and preservation of original and fragile documents will all have to be considered when computing costs of a project. When documents are prepared for scanning, physical handling, preservation tasks and packaging of originals will occur and add to workload. Organize so that you only turn the pages once, i.e. take only one image of the document. Usually you will only be able to afford to capture the image electronically one time. Cost factors vary dramatically for preparing text documents, bound books, photographs, maps, color documents, and audio tapes.

For example, a preparer must inventory, sort, and purge duplicate documents from a batch of prospective objects. Then each selected object must be set for scanning / filming which typically involves removing staples and clips, unfolding papers, repairing torn or wrinkled pages, orienting them in the stack, and noting if it will be a one-sided or two-sided scan.

Estimating cost factors can roughly be calculated by formulas like this:

> Assuming a rate of one hundred documents an hour, at minimum wage, a collection of 50,000 documents will take 500 hours and cost $2,850 for preparation alone.
> 50,000 * hours * hourly rate = total scanning cost or
> 50,000 * items * item rate = total scanning cost

Cost Categories and Estimates for Digitization: (after originals have been acquired)

Selection of materials and review of existing finding aids is a human centered activity and will be time consuming especially if the original materials are not already in good organizational order.

Cataloging/Description/Indexing:

Time will have to be budgeted to train indexing staff, create the schema and metadata templates and normalize the data to be entered.

Document / Photo Preparation:

The cost to prepare documents and photographs for scanning / filming is highly dependent upon the nature of the source objects, the way they have been stored, and the desired quality of prepared materials.

Scanning Charges:

The cost to capture an object such as a letter or photograph is dependent upon the amount of handling required and the nature of the digitized file. Papers fed through a sheet-feed scanner represent the low end of expense. Photographs or maps needing human placement on scanners represent the high end of expense. The cost per item for scanning is from fifteen cents to several dollars. If microfilming is also performed, then it is possible up to $1.25 per item will be added.

Quality Control of Images and Metadata:

Review of image quality and metadata input can be performed in a batch mode and by checking a selected percentage of the output.

Preservation/Conservation:

If any preservation or conservation activities are added to the preparation of the originals then add fifty percent more to the costs for the project.

Transportation to Capture Site:

Movement of source objects to a scanning / filming site requires additional attention beyond normal shipping practices. This includes protecting the contents from the elements, inventorying the contents for integrity of the shipment, linking their order, and assuring careful handling. Of course, if the objects are transported to the scanning site by the owners directly, this saves on movement charges.

Options to consider:

Below are referenced two digital cost studies that examine various factors to be considered when conducting digital projects.

- "Digital conversion accounts for approximately one-third of the initial costs. Other costs, primarily those connected to indexing and cataloging, administration and quality control, account for the remaining two-thirds." Steve Puglia, National Archives and Records Administration, 1999
- Puglia, Steve. "The Costs of Digital Imaging" RLG DigiNews (October 1999). http://www.rlg.org/preserv/diginews/diginews3-5.html#feature—includes several projections/cost models for the long-term maintenance of digital image files.
Stephen Chapman, Handbook For Digital Projects: Key Quality and Cost Decisions for Digitized Text pp. 108-109. (PFD version, see pages 117-120)

Project Checklist:

- Is the cost of digitization appropriate given the value of the materials and the demand for digital access?
- Where will the money come from?
- On-going costs will include the migration of media and maintenance/upgrade of infrastructure.

- Photographs are the most expensive to convert
- Avoid the hidden costs of internal development of databases and programming new systems. The cost is too high for small organizations.
- Initial project costs and ongoing costs to support digital asset management: must be estimated up-front for realistic assessment of costs.
- Consider what parts of the project will funding support? (Physical resources, hardware, software, networked access, personnel, dedicated space, vendor services, etc.)
- What about plans for maintaining access into the future (ongoing costs)? Is there a long-term institutional commitment to this project?

Chapter 9

TYPES OF MATERIAL

CDs

Neill Public Library
Pullman, Washington

Music (CDs)

Selections for the music collection are purchased in compact disc format only.

The collection is intended to cover the broad spectrum of music over time, including significant works, composers, performers and performances. The CD collection is divided into eight genres: Pop/Rock/Oldies, Folk/International/Ethnic, Jazz/Blues/Rhythm, Country/Gospel, Children's Music, Classical, Soundtracks/Show Tunes/Spoken, and Holiday. Some music by local artists and by artists who frequently visit the region may also be included. While current recordings are not precluded, in general the goal is to provide recordings of music of significant and enduring quality.

CD-ROMs

Morton Grove Public Library
Morton Grove, Illinois

Circulating CD-ROMs

The Library purchases interactive multimedia CD-ROM software on a variety of topics for children, appealing to a broad range of interests, and on limited topics for adults. In 2002, the growing number of children's CD-ROM titles forced the separation of titles into adult and children's collections. In 2002, all children's CD-ROMs were moved to the Youth Services Department. CD-ROMs purchased for the Adult Collection are incorporated into the appropriate Dewey class number and shelved with the regular book collection. Criteria for selection for CD-ROMs purchased for either Departments include materials that are informational, educational, and creative in nature. Recreational materials that meet the above criteria for selection are also purchased. Titles which operate on both PCs and Macintoshes are purchased whenever available.

Influencing Factors

The CD-ROM collection exists to serve the general informational, educational, and creative needs of the Library community. Appropriateness and expected long-term use and value to the collection are deciding factors in the selection of interactive multi-media CD-ROMS. Patron requests for specific CD-ROMs will be considered and purchased if the title is appropriate to the collection on a long-term basis. Changing technology is always a factor to be considered in the long-range development of the collection.

Selection Plan

Standard library reviewing journals, such as Library Journal and Publisher's Weekly are useful selection tools for multimedia titles with professional reviews. Lists and catalogs provided by Baker & Taylor, Ingram, and Crimson Software, other software and multimedia catalogs, and patron requests are used to identify current high-interest releases suitable for purchase.

Retention & Weeding

CD-ROMs, damaged or lost from the collection, will be withdrawn as needed and replaced, if appropriate to the changing needs of the collection. Patrons responsible for damage to CD-ROM material will be held responsible for the full replacement cost of the title. The initial loan periods for CD-ROM titles are two-weeks. Loan periods and reserve status decisions will be based on patron interest level and "turnover" considerations. Changing technology is also a factor to be considered in retention of titles and weeding of the collection.

Development Plan

The circulating CD-ROM collection continues to grow in response to community demand and interest. The emphasis is on acquiring high-interest titles and quality educational or "edutainment" programs for children. The ultimate size of the collection will be determined by long-range decisions concerning allocated funds, shelving and storage options.

DVDs AND VIDEOCASSETTES

Morton Grove Public Library
Morton Grove, Illinois

The video collection contains adult and juvenile feature titles and adult informational videos in VHS and DVD format. The collection consists of a varied selection of feature films, including current high interest, old classics, and foreign films. Informational titles include such popular subjects as travel, sports, exercise, parenting, cooking, business, language, documentaries, arts, hobbies, and home repair. Many PBS titles are purchased. Children's videos/DVDs include titles from several popular series, such as Faerie Tale Theater and Disney series. Most of the collection is currently for home use only, but the Library may puchase some public performance videos when the price is within the Library's budget. (Videos for home use are restricted to individual or family viewing. Public performance videos are those for which the Library has purchased the rights for group viewing, for either in-library programs or for organizations' use with their members.)

Influencing Factors

The video/DVD collection exists to serve the general informational, educational, and recreational needs of the Library community. Numerous local video rental stores supply recent releases of the most popular films in greater quantity than the Library. Appropriateness and expected long-term use and value to the collection are deciding factors in the selection of adult and children's videos. Closed-captioned films are purchased whenever available to meet the Library's commitment to serve the hearing-impaired. Patron requests for specific videos/DVDs will be considered and purchased if the film is appropriate to the collection for the long term. Changing technology is always a factor to be considered in the long range development of the collection.

Selection Plan

In addition to the standard selection tools, reviewing sources such as Video Review, Video Librarian, New York Times and other newspaper/journal reviews, are regularly consulted. Publishers' catalogs (Major Video Concepts, B&T Video Alert, Facets, Home Vision, etc.), ads, and patron title requests are also used to identify current high-interest releases and nonfiction films suitable for purchase. Preference is given to the purchase of new titles rather than replacements, but available titles in high demand may be replaced. Most videocassettes are replacement candidates after 150 circulations. Multiple copies may be considered for high-interest feature films only.

Retention & Weeding

The video/DVD collection is constantly growing. Weeding has been done, based on circulation counts and condition of the tape/DVD. Videos/DVDs with little or no circulation and videocassettes which circulated more than 150 times are regularly considered for withdrawal from the collection to make room for new titles. High-interest feature films may be replaced with new copies of the title, depending upon circulation history and community interest. Weeding is an ongoing process.

Development Plan

The video/DVD collection continues to grow in response to community demand and interest. The emphasis will be on acquiring high-interest feature films and quality entertainment programs for children. The ultimate size of the collection will be determined by long-range decisions affecting shelving and storage options.

Portland Community College
Portland Community College Libraries
Portland, Oregon

Non-print media, including films, videocassettes, videodiscs, audiocassettes, computer application software, multimedia software, compact discs, online subscriptions, Internet access and CD-ROMs, may be relatively expensive. Selection of these materials should emphasize support for classroom instruction, as well as the quality, effectiveness, and currency of the material.

Whenever practicable, faculty should have an opportunity to preview non-print media before a purchase decision is made. Whenever possible, selectors should negotiate a test or trial period for expensive media. For film and video previews, selectors contact the Film Booking Office. For database subscription trials, selectors work with the Electronic Resources Librarian.

Film or videocassette rental, temporary online subscription or free Internet access may be a cost-effective alternative to actual purchase.

Listed below are general issues to be considered in the selection of non-print materials.

- Content should directly support classroom instruction or be potentially useful for more than one class or department.
- Treatment and presentation of subject content should be on an appropriate academic level.
- Technical quality of color, sound, continuity, etc.
- Cost effectiveness and durability and accessibility of the format (i.e., compact disc vs. audiocassette vs. record; video vs. laser disc vs. film; floppy disk size; CD-ROM vs. on-line access; telnet vs. web; single user vs. network).
- Cost and/or availability of appropriate equipment.
- Where possible the Library will provide access to electronic media within the Library.
- Collection development staff should consult with Library Computer Specialist to determine availability of equipment prior to purchase.
- Cost and/or availability of sufficient technical support for maintenance of software and hardware.
- Collection development staff should consult with Library Computer Specialist to determine availability of support prior to purchase.

- Collection development specialists will designate electronic media as "circulating" or "reference" or "library use only" as appropriate.

Neill Public Library
Pullman, Washington

DVDs and Videocassettes

Neill Public Library currently maintains collections in both DVD and Videocassette format, but is currently adding only DVDs to the collection. The goals of the DVD and Videocassette collections are:

- To provide basic information on a variety of subjects of interest to library patrons. The collection is considered an adjunct to the print collection, with emphasis placed on purchases in which the nature of the medium adds substantially to the viewer's understanding.
- To provide children with a quality selection of preschool learning and entertainment ideas, film versions of children's literature, selected non-fiction videos that reflect areas of interest across generations (i.e. dinosaurs, animals, ancient civilizations, etc.), and award winning children's films.
- To provide patrons with entertainment DVDs and videocassettes including feature films with an emphasis on family entertainment and literature based material. The focus of the entertainment video collection is towards quality productions from such entities as PBS, BBC, and A&E and for classic television series. A representative sample of historically significant feature films, including award winning or critically acclaimed, classic American and foreign feature films, are collected, with a special bias towards those which are not easily available locally from video stores.

Additional selection criteria for Audio/Visual Materials:

- Technical quality of audio and visual reproduction
- Presentation or experience that is unique to format and provides an alternative to print
- Significance of performance or diversity in interpretation
- Critical acclaim as demonstrated in awards, nomination for awards, and/or reviews
- Suitability to be circulated or housed in a sturdy, safe and convenient manner

DVDs and videocassettes are protected by copyright and are for home use only.

Colorado College
Tutt Library
Colorado Springs, Colorado

Audiovisual materials are purchased to support the curricular needs of the college. The emphasis in the selection of audiovisual titles is placed on titles which will be directly used by the faculty for instruction or in support of instruction. Multiple copies may be required for selected titles to accommodate student and faculty use.

Emphasis in the purchasing of audiovisual materials should be in the following formats:

- DVD – Digital Video Discs
- Video recordings (VHS) – if available in no other format
- Compact discs

Audiovisual materials are replaced or updated in the latest format available.

In general, faculty members are encouraged to preview audiovisual materials prior to purchase. Selection criteria for audiovisual materials include:

- Relevance to course work

- Faculty recommendation
- Price/cost
- Favorable review in media literature
- Demand by students
- Accuracy of content
- Authority of author/director/producer
- Depth and scope of subject matter
- Availability of closed captioning (DVDs and VHS)
- (Telecourse purchasing, recording, and distribution is determined by Academic Affairs and faculty.)

Audio/Visual Materials

Video & DVD Orders

Tutt Library purchases DVDs and videos at the request of faculty for use within the classroom or as supplementary material to support a specific course. The college does not currently have the resources or the space to build a general interest AV collection or to collect AV materials exclusively for recreational use.

Format

The Library will order whichever format faculty requests, assuming it is available. We generally only order a title in one format, although for a few titles it may be appropriate for the Library to acquire one copy on DVD for classroom showing and one copy on VHS that the students may check out. Audio-visual materials circulate only to CC students, faculty and staff and are not available for interlibrary loan.

Ordering

Receiving Coordinator orders all videocassettes and DVDs for the library. Please submit your orders directly by email or use the online order form. Please include as much information as possible, including title, language, publisher, director, date, etc. Please supply us with a "needed by" date and/or block number or indicate if time is not an issue. If you wish the title to be placed on reserve please note on the order request. All Audio/Visual requests will be prioritized by the "needed by" date. Any request needed in less than four weeks will be considered a "RUSH." All requests with a "needed by" date will also be tracked by that date. If a problem or delay occurs, the requestor will be informed. Orders for Audio/Visual materials will be placed within a period of 5 working days, whether or not there is a "needed by" date.

Access & Security

All videos and DVDs that are part of the permanent collection will be cataloged, managed and maintained by the library. The library will order replacements for missing titles as determined necessary. As a security measure, the library is shelving some videos and all DVDs behind the circulation desk. These audio-visual materials are not available for browsing but are cataloged in Tiger with the location Videos – Circulation, or DVD – Circulation, and may be checked out by CC users. Closed shelf videos include titles that the library has already replaced due to theft, very expensive videos, and some rare or out of print titles.

Foreign Vendors & Formats

Videos from Europe are formatted in what is called VHS-PAL, which is incompatible with North American VHS-NTSC equipment. While we have a PAL player in the library, use of this format is limited and students certainly can't take them home and watch them. Therefore, we prefer to purchase the NTSC format whenever possible.

Owensboro Community and Technical College
Owensboro Community and Technical College Library
Owensboro, Kentucky

Ordering Videos or DVDs for Preview

Videos or DVDs that cost over $100 must be previewed before they are purchased by at least three faculty members if no reviews are available; less than three are acceptable if reviews are available. If you have a video or DVD you would like to request for purchase, send the request to Connie Johnson in the Library. She will inquire to see if previewing is allowed.

When the material arrives, you will be notified. When you pick the material up in the library, reviewing forms will be with the material along with a date to have the material back to the library. When the material is returned to the library with the forms completed, a final decision will be made on the purchase.

E-BOOKS

Texas State Library and Archives Commission
Austin, Texas

Ebooks

The TexShare collection of ebooks is selected through recommendations of the Electronic Information Working Group (EIWG), which reviews products for the TexShare program, and solicits and reviews input from member libraries. Ebook purchases are made on a subject basis and not title-by-title. Reconsiderations are governed by local library policy and practice. Ebook selection guidelines are developed each year based on:

- Usage statistics
- Areas of subject need not met by other electronic resources
- Established subject areas of collection strength
- Titles available for consortia purchase from publishers

FREE WEB-BASED RESOURCES

Florida Atlantic University
FAU Libraries
Boca Raton, Florida

Collection Development Policy: Adding Free Web/Internet Resources

Purpose

As information is increasingly being delivered over the Internet, freely available internet resources can provide unique content; they can also improve access to and enhance traditional collections, while reflecting the excellence, comprehensiveness, and authority expected in a research library. Internet Web resources will be considered for addition to the FAU Libraries' Web pages after being evaluated by librarians/selectors with expertise in the relevant subject area using the guidelines below.

The following guidelines were developed for the purpose of clarifying some factors commonly considered by those who are experienced in identifying web resources or building web pages. These guidelines are not intended to be absolute, and a specific resource does not have to meet all of the criteria to be acceptable.

Guidelines

Quality: Its uniqueness, accuracy, comprehensiveness, lack of bias, or breadth of scope indicate the quality of a web resource. High quality sites are often noted for the extent to which they include unique information and serve as a primary resource on a subject. Comprehensiveness is also indicative of a quality site.

Sites that provide information are preferred to those that simply point to other sites. Well-organized and annotated collections of links are often also judged as useful.

Relevance: The extent to which the resource satisfies the needs and is appropriate for the level and purposes of the intended users determines relevance. Language and country coverage should be appropriate for the subject involved and the intended audience.

Organization and Design: Web resources are judged both for content and visual appeal in ways that differ from the evaluation of print scholarly resources. Excellent design clearly adds value to web pages but should not be a substitute for excellent content. The design and organization of the site should be logical and visually appealing. Good organization is generally indicated by consistent graphics and style. Annotated links to other sites are considered useful to help the user move through the information.

Ease of Use: The site should be reviewed for usability to insure that it is simple, consistent, clear, and easy to load in terms of speed. If special software is required, is it linked to the site and easily located, and is it free? Navigational aids should be provided for longer pages and if searchable, the search interface should be readily understood.

Reliability and Stability: Consider the credibility, institutional affiliation, authority, status, and reputation of a site. The source of the information should be clearly identified. If the site is the creation of an individual, the individual should be considered authoritative by such measures as institutional affiliation or peer review. A name and e-mail address of a contact person or group should be available for user contact.

Maintenance: Look for evidence, such as a date or a last update, which indicates that the site is regularly maintained, and that links are active and information is current.

Access Restrictions: Consider the impact of subscription fees for commercial sites or other possible barriers to access such as registration requirements, time limitations, or stringent copyright restrictions. While such restrictions are not necessarily a basis for exclusion of a site, the impact on users should be considered. In accordance with the Americans with Disabilities Act, individuals with disabilities should be able to access all services the University offers to non-disabled individuals. Internet resources, which increase the likelihood of such access, are preferred. Such resources may include those which provide text-only options (i.e., for individuals using Screen Reader technology), large print options, or audio.

Local Orientation: Sites created by individuals or units affiliated with Florida Atlantic University and Southeast Florida will be given special consideration to the extent that they may reflect local interests, needs, or resources.

Exclusions: Exclude websites that merely advertise a service or product.

De-selection: Internet resources that are "no longer available" or "maintained" need to be removed.

INTERNET RESOURCES

University of Washington
University of Washington Libraries
Seattle, Washington

Selection Guidelines for Internet Resources

Purpose:

The mission of the University of Washington Libraries is to improve the educational, research, and service programs of the University through the dissemination of knowledge. To this end, the Libraries acquires, manages, and promotes the creation and use of knowledge in an atmosphere where information and ideas are readily accessible and freely exchanged.

Increasingly, information is being delivered over the Internet. Internet resources can provide unique content; they can also improve access to and enhance traditional collections, while reflecting the excellence, comprehensiveness, and authority expected in a research library.

Rationale:

While general collection development principles apply to all resources regardless of format, Internet resources present new and unique challenges for selectors and merit separate consideration. Most of the items available through the Internet are self-published and lack traditional editorial control. Unlike other formats that present familiar content in a new medium, the Internet provides access to millions of newly created documents and makes many items originally created in other formats newly available for collection. In addition, the fluid nature of the Internet is unprecedented. Few items in our current collection are bound together with the exponential complexity of hypertext. These and other challenges have prompted University of Washington Libraries selectors to request guidelines specific to this new environment.

Scope:

This serves as a guide for the selection of Internet resources, including paid, unpaid, serial, and monographic resources to the collection. Selection of resources simply because they are "free" should be weighed against the time necessary to describe and provide access to the site, provide registration or scripting, or other resources required to make the site available.

These selection guidelines provide a framework for selectors' decision-making when considering adding Internet resources to the collection. In keeping with the user-centered orientation of the Libraries, selectors should bear in mind the information needs of our primary clientele as they make selection decisions.

The principles and guidelines outlined herein are intended to serve as a general guide for Internet collection development decisions. It is understood that there may be exceptions, and those are left to the discretion of the appropriate selector. Issues regarding licensing of electronic resources are not addressed in these guidelines. Licensing questions should be referred to the University of Washington Libraries Principles and Guidelines for Acquiring and Licensing Electronic Information.

Access and Location:

In general, records for Internet resources will appear in the UW Libraries Catalog and OCLC.

General Selection Principles:

Selectors have primary responsibility for selecting Internet resources in their assigned areas. Due to the shared nature of these resources, selectors are encouraged to communicate selection decisions regarding interdisciplinary resources to other selectors in relevant subject areas. As with the selection of other materials, selectors should follow general collection development guidelines (Operations Manual Vol. IV, Sec. B, No. 1) as well as the existing guidelines for their areas when selecting Internet resources. The following points, as noted in the general collection development policy, also hold for Internet resources, which should:

- Support the present or potential educational, curricular, and research needs of the University of Washington and its primary audiences.
- Reflect the intellectual content, comprehensiveness, and authority expected in the Libraries' collection.
- Improve access to, or enhance, current library collections.

Specific Selection Principles:

Guidelines for selecting Internet resources fall into these categories: Authority, Content, Reliability, and Design & Access.

Authority:

Authority comprises issues dealing with the credibility, institutional affiliation, and reputation of the author or sponsor of an Internet resource. The following considerations should be weighed when selecting an Internet resource:

- Clearly identified author of the resource

- The qualifications and reputation of the author should be ascertained.
- Established and reputable sponsoring site
- In general, preference is given to academic, organizational, and governmental sites. In some disciplines or contexts, however, commercial sites may be preferred.

Content:

Content should be suitable for higher education studies, and relevant to University of Washington disciplines. The following considerations should be weighed when selecting an Internet resource:

- Amount of content provided
- In general, preference is given to sites with a significant amount of coverage. Sites that contain full-text are preferable to sites that only provide tables of contents, abstracts, advertisements, membership or contact information. If, however, there is a record for a print journal in the online catalog, it is acceptable to link to a journal site that provides only table of contents information. Sites that provide information are preferred to those that mainly provide links to other resources, although well-organized and annotated collections of links may be judged useful by selectors. For electronic journals, selectors should include a note that indicates the level of coverage, (i.e., selected or limited years).

Accuracy of the information:

The resource should document the source of its information; for example, the source of data files should be indicated. If the selector is unsure of the accuracy of a site, a comparable resource should be checked.

Comprehensiveness of the resources:

Sites providing in-depth comprehensiveness are preferred, although a collection of high-quality links is preferred to a large number of links of mixed quality.

Currency of the information:

Currency should be appropriate to the topic.

Dates of coverage:

If continued access to older data is desirable for resources that are updated either serially or continuously, ascertain if the provider plans on making all data available permanently or if there will be only limited retention. For some resources, particularly e-journals and other serially issued items, finding out the planned date coverage—if backfiles will be mounted—can also be helpful in making a selection evaluation.

Frequency of updates:

Updates should be timely and appropriate. The last update should be indicated.

Reliability:

Reliability comprises issues dealing with continued support for an Internet resource and the performance and stability of the site. The following considerations should be weighed when selecting an Internet resource:

Durability:

Non-commercial sites: Consider the reputation of the sponsor or provider and try to determine if they are likely to continue offering the resource and if they will maintain the site. Resources from academic, organizational, and governmental bodies are more likely to meet this criteria than are personal Web pages.

Commercial sites: If purchased through a vendor or other commercial provider, ascertain if the provider's business record suggests that they will continue to make the product available and if they will maintain it via updates or new versions.

Links:

Links within a resource should be active and should lead to the expected place. Well-maintained links are an indication that the resource is being supported.

Site dependability:

Sites that remain at the same address or have PURL addresses are preferable to sites whose addresses change frequently. Sites with consistently prompt response times are preferable to sites that are frequently unavailable or are slow to load.

Design and Access:

Internet resources should meet a high standard for user-friendliness and accessibility, and should be well-designed and organized. As noted in the general collection development policy, "all formats are open to evaluation but some may be more or less acceptable due to preservation considerations, cost, space requirements, or ease or difficulty of use"; these considerations especially apply to Internet resources in terms of design and access.

Design:

Well-designed and organized resources should make clear what the site is about and what the user should do next. The title and layout of the page should be an accurate indication of its content; if not, a summary note describing the resource should be supplied by the selector. Navigation tools should be easy to use. User options should be clear and understandable. Layout should not prevent printing of the page.

Compatibility:

Resources should be compatible with current hardware and software available on Libraries terminals. Resources that are not compatible are held to a higher standard of scrutiny.

Accessibility:

Accessibility for users with disabilities must be considered during selection. The value of the resource must be weighed against the access difficulties presented. Selectors will find useful information on accessible Web design, at the University of Washington DO-IT home page <http://www.washington.edu/doit/>.

Deselection Principles:

Given the dynamic and changeable nature of Internet resources, regular review of items selected is essential. Internet resources selected must remain viable and useful so that the Catalog does not become a graveyard of broken and outdated links.

Primary responsibility for review and deselection of Internet resources lies with the appropriate selector. Due to the shared nature of these resources, selectors are encouraged to communicate deselection decisions regarding interdisciplinary resources to other selectors in relevant subject areas.

Deselection Guidelines:

Selectors should deselect an Internet resource that meets any of the following criteria:
- the resource is no longer available or well-maintained
- the resource no longer offers current, reliable, or valuable information
- another resource offers superior coverage or treatment of a subject
- the resource no longer meets selection criteria as outlined in this policy

Selectors should review selected Internet sources in their subject areas on a regular basis and deselect as necessary.

In addition to the deselection criteria listed above, paid Internet resources may be cancelled for a variety of other reasons, most importantly, a shortage or reallocation of funds. In cases involving paid resources, selectors should notify other selectors with interdisciplinary interests in the product of the decision to cancel, but the decision itself lies solely with the funding selector or group of selectors.

Selector Checklist

All sites should meet the general selection guidelines concerning quality, content and the research needs of our primary audience.

Title of Site:
URL:

Content Considerations:
- Do we already have Internet or other resources covering the same subject?
- Do we have the print version of a site? URLs can be linked to the print record.
- What are the author's credentials? Is an e-mail contact provided?
- When was the site created? Is there a date of creation/revision provided? Is the site updated frequently?
- Is the site stable? Academic, governmental and organizational sites tend to be more stable.
- Is this a commercial or marketing site? [e.g. Is it simply advertising a product or itself? Generally, purely commercial sites should not be cataloged, e.g., Amazon.]
- If the site is interdisciplinary, have other selectors been consulted?

For webographies:
- Is the site sponsored by an educational organization/institution?
- Are there comparable sites that might be more useful?
- Are annotations provided?
- Are links current/active?

For e-journals:
- Does the site contain the full text of articles? Sites with just selective articles or tables of contents (toc) should generally not be cataloged but a toc link can be added to the record of a print journal.
- Will backfiles be added?
- How are previous issues archived?
- Does the site require IP verification? If so, the site needs to be in the Digital Registry so users can be authenticated via the proxy server.

Access Considerations:
- Are instructions for printing clear? Does printing work? (pdf format a problem?)
- Are navigational graphics, frames, or tables a problem?
- Have you viewed the site in Lynx and an earlier version of a browser?
- Are there clear instructions for printing (of frames, tables)?
- Is registration required?
- Does the page load quickly?
- Is a special viewer or plug-in required?
- Have you checked the accessibility of the page against usability guidelines sites, such as these?
  - http://www.useit.com/alertbox/990502.html
  - http://www.cast.org/bobby/
      Further information on accessible web design issues is available at: http://www.washington.edu/doit/Resources/web-design.html

License Considerations:

For sites requiring a license, see the University of Washington Libraries Principles and Guidelines for Acquiring and Licensing Electronic Information.

MULTIPLE FORMATS

Central Michigan University
Central Michigan Universities Libraries
Mount Pleasant, Michigan

Duplication

Acquiring an electronic resource that duplicates an existing print resource constitutes acceptable duplication when the Libraries will incur no additional fee.

The Libraries may duplicate a print resource with a fee-based electronic resource when:

- Multiple formats meet significantly different needs of user groups;
- Features or access to information is significantly improved;
- There is a cost benefit for purchasing multiple formats;
- Preservation of the original for its intrinsic value or its historical value is important

Florida Atlantic University
S.E. Wimberly Library
Boca Raton, Florida

Duplication of the print and electronic versions of a resource are generally discouraged but will be considered on a case-by-case basis. The Libraries prefer to acquire materials in electronic format if available and deemed appropriate to provide improved access to all campuses or to enhance the Libraries' current collections. Electronic access is the preferred format for serials when available.

Long Island University
B. Davis Schwartz Memorial Library
Brookville, New York

Format

The Library may provide access to both the print and electronic versions of a title. Need should be demonstrated to justify purchase of a title in more than one format by applying the following criteria: cost, scope of coverage, ease of use, ease of access, licensing requirements (whether or not online access is dependent on maintaining the print subscription), currency and frequency of updating, reliability and stability of the electronic version as related to archival or ownership issues, and value-added enhancements of the electronic product.

Rollins College
Olin Library
Winter Park, Florida

Duplication of print resources

It is preferable to avoid duplication of print resources. Electronic versions might substitute for an already-held print resource if they have advantages in accessibility, currency, or cost. Duplication may be acceptable when different formats better meet the needs of different user groups.

Welch Medical Library
Johns Hopkins University
Baltimore, Maryland

In general, the library acquires any given material in one format only. Multiple copies of a print subscription have been evolving into one institutional copy and eventually will be replaced by electronic resources as archival issues are resolved.

The number of users in a multi-user license is determined by anticipated demand and available funding. If sufficient user demand is demonstrated, additional licenses may be acquired.

University of Oregon
Knight Library
Eugene, Oregon

Duplication

Selecting an Internet resource that duplicates an existing print resource usually constitutes acceptable duplication because the site probably will incur no fee and a site's selection provides greater access than the single use point that a print resource may provide. The Library will duplicate print resources with fee-based Internet resources when:

- the resource has significant historical value
- one format is unstable
- a cost benefit for purchasing multiple formats exists
- multiple formats meet the different needs of user groups

SOUND RECORDINGS — POPULAR

Morton Grove Public Library
Morton Grove, Illinois

The popular sound recording collection includes CDs covering all varieties of music that do not fall into the classical category. This includes, but is not limited to, pop, R&B, country, jazz, reggae, world, new age, show tunes, etc.

Influencing Factors

Budget and demand dictate a strong collection of current popular mainstream recordings. Library patrons have embraced the CD technology and consequently demand is high for CDs reflecting the musical interests and pursuits of community residents and Library users.

Selection Plan

Selection tools include Billboard, Stereo Review, Chicago Tribune, and often many of the standard selection tools as well.

Retention & Weeding

Weeding should still be an ongoing process with condition and circulation statistics dictating whether or not to withdraw a title. Materials that are in poor or damaged condition are evaluated and either removed from circulation, or replaced.

Development Plan

The development goal for this collection is to have a balanced and representative collection of all types/formats of popular music. The collection is not to be a comprehensive one. Emphasis will continue to be on the CD format. However, due to changing technology in the audio field, the library must be alert and react to changes in format.

SOUND RECORDINGS—CLASSICAL

Morton Grove Public Library
Morton Grove, Illinois

The classical sound recording collection includes CDs covering the vocal and instrumental musical spectrum from baroque to ultramodern. In addition, there is a growing collection of opera recordings. Music ranges from performances by soloists through full symphonic performances.

Influencing Factors

Because of a wide variety of users, the collection should be varied and contain music that appeals to all tastes. The operas of the current Lyric season are a continuing interest of many patrons.

Selection Plan

Selection sources include Billboard, Stereo Review, CD One Stop Monthly Catalog, and standard magazines and newspapers. Special publishers catalogs or catalogs from record distributors such as Rose Records are also consulted. Unique and unusual music heard on WFMT radio station, as well as music played at live concerts, is also considered as part of the selection plan.

Retention & Weeding

Since the CD collection is fairly current, weeding should generally be limited to damaged recordings. Materials that are in poor or damaged condition are evaluated and either removed from circulation, or replaced. As the collection continues to grow, earlier performances might be replaced by CDs with higher ratings or newer technology.

Development Plan

The collection should be expanded to include more composers and more versions of well-known works.

SPOKEN WORD RECORDINGS

Morton Grove Public Library
Morton Grove, Illinois

The spoken word audiocassette and CD collection consists of both fiction and nonfiction materials. The fiction area includes contemporary and classic fiction with an emphasis on contemporary works. Works of best selling authors are represented primarily in unabridged versions. The nonfiction collection covers a range of subject areas including best sellers, instructional and self-improvement cassettes on topics such as computer use and exercise, and TOEFL preparation guides. Language instruction, with a strong demand for the Spanish language in particular, is a very popular area of this collection.

Influencing Factors

Advances in technology have given us audiocassette players that are both portable and inexpensive. The ability to have an audiocassette player both inside and outside the home broadens the patron base for this particular medium. The availability of players to all age and economic levels and the high interest levels associated with recorded books has created a large audience for spoken word sound recordings. Patron requests, circulation statistics, and budget constraints play a large part in determining purchases and buying patterns.

Selection Plan

Standard selection magazines such as Booklist, Library Journal and Publisher's Weekly include audio-cassette reviews. Bowker's On Cassette is also helpful, in both selection and verification of titles, publishers, and prices. Additional sources include publisher and vendor catalogs such as Baker & Taylor Hot Picks, G.K. Hall Audio Books, Recorded Books, Inc., and Emery Pratt. Growth areas of the collection include classics, popular fiction and non-fiction titles and language materials. MGPL's primary focus will be on ordering unabridged titles, as budget permits, in order to provide a wider selection of the preferred format for most users of spoken word/audiobooks. Factors influencing the decision to concentrate on the unabridged format include the durability and sturdy packaging of audiobooks in the unabridged format. Abridged audiobooks are packaged in flimsy cardboard and have to be re-packaged in a more durable vinyl album for library circulation, thereby increasing the cost of the abridged audiobooks and decreasing the cost differential between them and the unabridged format. Many distributors of unabridged audiobooks offer free replacements for missing or damaged tapes during the first year and charge only minimal replacement charges thereafter. In addition to their packaging limitations, abridged audiobooks do not stand up to the repetitive use patterns of the public library and, consequently, have a high damage and withdrawal rate. Consequently, the replacement policies of vendors of unabridged audiobooks offer a substantial advantage in controlling maintenance costs of the audiobooks collection. Funding for audiobooks will be expanded as budget guidelines allow.

Retention & Weeding

The spoken word audiobook collection is a rapidly expanding area of our collection development that is responsive to high demand and interest level. Therefore, at present, a primary reason for weeding would be damaged cassettes in both formats and abridged cassettes that have low circulation counts. Circulation statistics will continue to be the principal deciding factor in the replacement or withdrawal of a title from the collection. As this section continues to expand, shelf space, as well as circulation counts and new technology, will be factors to consider in the weeding process.

Development Plan

Budget and space considerations will determine how much expansion can take place with the spoken word recordings/audiobooks. The continuing focus will be on expanding the collection of titles in the unabridged format. Existing standing orders for unabridged titles should be supplemented with the selection of a wide range of individual unabridged titles, particularly classics. There should be an increase in instructional, self-help and language tapes to meet the educational and recreational needs of MGPL patrons.

Part III
Electronic Equipment and Hardware

Chapter 10

EQUIPMENT GUIDELINES

TIME LIMITS FOR COMPUTER WORKSTATIONS

South San Francisco Public Library
South San Francisco, California

The South San Francisco Public Library provides access to the Internet, Microsoft Word, Microsoft Excel, and Microsoft PowerPoint.

Access to the Internet is compatible with the Library's endorsement of the Library Bill of Rights, the Freedom to Read, and the Freedom to View statements from the American Library Association. The Internet is an unregulated network and the South San Francisco Public Library does not take responsibility for its content.

Security in an electronic environment cannot be guaranteed, thus all transactions, files and communications generated using the Library's computers are vulnerable to unauthorized access and use and should be considered public. As with all Library resources, the Library affirms the right and responsibility of parents/guardians, NOT Library staff, to determine and monitor their minor children's use of the Internet. The Library does not employ filtering software.

To assure fair and equitable access, the South San Francisco Public Library uses timing software on its public computers. This software requires patrons to have a valid library card in good standing, and allows each patron one hour of computer use per day. Accessibility patrons receive two hours of computer use per day.

Temporary access is available for patrons from outside San Mateo County upon presentation of ID.

COMPUTERS & EQUIPMENT AVAILABLE:

- 15-minute computers (no fee)
- 1-hour stations (no fee)
- 2-hour computers ($5.00 charge)
- Accessibility Computer Workstations (no fee). Accessibility users are asked to complete an application and provide documentation of disability. These stations are adjustable for wheelchair users, have special keyboards and software for vision and learning disabilities.
- Wireless access (wifi) to the Internet is available for those who bring their own laptops with wifi capability (no charge or time limit). Due to a limited number of available outlets, running on battery back up is highly recommended.
- The Library does not provide headphones; patrons may use their own headphones. Headphones are available for accessibility station users; however, use of personal headphones is highly recommended.
- 2-hour machines for fee
- Reservations—we accept reservations only for the two-hour computers. Reservations can be made up to a week in advance through the Reference Desk
- Drop-in Use—Drop-in use is available if there are no reservations (excluding dedicated accessibility stations).
- Extension—Time may be extended for an additional two hours if no one is waiting. An additional $5.00 fee will apply for the extension and only 1 extension is allowed.
- Limitations—Reservations are limited to one per day with the allowable extension if no one is waiting.

- Late Arrivals—Computers that have been reserved will be held for 10 minutes after the reservation start time.

PRINTING FILES:

Printing (black & white only) is available for $.15 per page & must be paid in advance.

SAVING FILES:

Work may be saved to a diskette or a memory stick but not to the computer hard drive. For your convenience, floppy discs are available for sale at the Reference Desk for $1 per disk. The library reserves the right to inspect any disk.

POLICY & SUGGESTIONS FOR USE:

- Assistance—Library staff will provide basic assistance. However, staff cannot provide in-depth training in the use of the software programs or personal computer use. We suggest referring to the help screens as needed. One-on-one Internet introduction classes for one hour are available by appointment.
- Reference Books—Software reference books are available for your use within the library. You may request these books from the reference librarian. Copies for checkout are also available.
- Quiet Area—In order to maintain the library as a quiet study area, no more than 2 people are allowed at each computer at a time. At the Grand Avenue Branch Library only one person at a time may use computers number 1-5 (because of limited space and in order to provide fair treatment to those waiting in line to use the computers).
- Program Installation—You may not download or copy other programs onto library computers. It is a violation of copyright laws to copy the software provided for public use in the library. Any person who attempts to copy software will be denied future use of any computers in the library.
- Closing—All computers will shut down 10 minutes before the library closes each day.
- Leaving Computer During Use—During a session, you may leave the computer for a short break by clicking on the "Lock Computer" icon on the desktop. Reference staff can assist with that function. Time away from the computer is included in the previously established session.
- The Library reserves the right to terminate a computer session that disrupts library services or that involves user behavior that violates the Library's policies.
- The user, or the parent of a minor, is responsible for his or her computer session and use of library equipment at all times.
- Parents must caution their minor children regarding personal information that should not be shared on the Internet.
- Library cards must be the sole property of the user; use of a family member's or friend's library card is not acceptable.
- Internet stations in the children's area may only be used by children; their parents or caregivers may assist them.
- Users must comply with the list of unacceptable use of computers, below.
  Unacceptable Uses of Computers include:
  - Unauthorized access, including "hacking."
  - Unauthorized disclosure, use, and dissemination of personal identification information and unlawful online activities using "chat rooms" or other forms of direct electronic communications.
  - Use of the network to make unauthorized entry into other computational, informational or communication services or resource.

- To view, print, distribute, display, send or receive images, text, or graphics that are obscene or "harmful to minors," and child pornography.
- Distribution of unsolicited advertising.
- Invasion of the privacy of others by attempting to view or read material being used by others.
- To attempt to gain unauthorized access to restricted files or networks.
- To damage or modify computer equipment or software.
- To engage in any activity that is harassing or defamatory.
- Use of the computer for any illegal activity, including violation of copyright or licensing agreements.

Response to Violations:
• Violations of Internet policy and procedures may result in loss of Internet access.
• Unlawful activities and misuse of Library computer hardware and software may result in loss to Internet and/or Library privileges and prosecution.

WARNING: USE AT YOUR OWN RISK

• The South San Francisco Public Library is not responsible for documents lost due to a virus, damaged disks, or power failure. We are not responsible for your failure to save information before your time expires, nor are we responsible if you do not save your information properly to your disk. We strongly urge you to frequently save your data on a disk. In addition, documents or files produced on outside equipment may not be compatible with our programs.
• In spite of having virus protection programs, these computers are subject to infection. Any virus infecting a disk or memory stick can infect any other computer. WE ADVISE AGAINST USING DISKS HAVING PERSONAL DATA THAT HAS NOT BEEN EITHER "VIRUS-SCANNED" OR "BACKED-UP."
• Please be aware that these are public terminals. As a result, we cannot guarantee the confidentiality of any document produced at these computers. If you are concerned about the security of the information in your documents, we strongly suggest that you use a computer at a location other than a public library.

WORKSTATION POLICIES

North Dakota State University
North Dakota State University Libraries
Fargo, North Dakota

Personally-owned Computer Equipment Policy NDSU Library employees are required to use assigned NDSU-owned computer equipment. The NDSU Library IT Department will adequately provide each employee with appropriate and suitable computing equipment required for their job functions.

It is the responsibility of the NDSU Library IT Department to support, maintain, and provide secure computing services and practices for library employees while they perform functions related to their job description. The support and maintenance of said equipment and services is only for NDSU-owned computer equipment assigned to the employee. The NDSU Library IT Department will neither support nor service personally-owned computer equipment.

As a state-owned institution, NDSU is subject to the North Dakota Public Records Law, and therefore NDSU library employees' personally-owned equipment must not be used for completion of job-related duties.

If different equipment is required to complete professional duties, the employee must use appropriate request channels for such equipment.

This policy adheres to the following policy guidelines: NDUS 1901.2, 3.1, 3.4; NDSU 158, 720.5

Chapter 11

EQUIPMENT INVENTORY

NEEDS ASSESSMENT

Greenville Public Library
Smithfield, Rhode Island

Equipment

The library has a LAN (local area network), which consists of fourteen staff workstations, forty-three public workstations, and two servers, one for files and the other for CD-ROMS. There is a virtual dvd/cd server with dual 60 gigabyte drives capable of holding the data of 190 cds, and a file server running Apple OSX Server with licenses for unlimited simultaneous users. The LAN is connected via Ethernet 10 BaseT Cat.5 wiring, two 100 mbs switches, two Apple Airport wireless servers, and equivalent network and airport cards. There is a combination of Macintosh and Wintel workstations. The offices contain Macintosh computers that run Virtual PC to access Windows programs when necessary. The public computers are also a mixture of Macintosh and Windows machines, most of which are Windows machines. Most of the public Macintosh machines are running over an Apple Airport wireless network. The Library utilizes the Apple file server as the server for its Web page.

All of our computers access the Internet and CLAN (Cooperating Libraries Automated Network) database.

There are four workstations for the public that are designated as PAC (Patron Access Catalogues) workstations. Two of these workstations are restricted to IPac and Novelist only.

There is one RapidCircIII self-checkout machine located near the circulation desk.

There are three shared printers for staff and the public in the main part of the building, one shared printer in the homework center, and one shared printer and a shared digital copier in the offices.

Chapter 12

HARDWARE AND SOFTWARE GUIDELINES

HARDWARE AND SOFTWARE MAINTENANCE AND SELECTION

Berry College
Berry College Memorial Library
Mount Berry, Georgia

Hardware, Equipment, and Software:
Selection, Installation, and Maintenance Issues

Public services librarians engaged in campus-wide instruction will recommend/select hardware and software configurations appropriate for the needs of the library's instructional services program described under the purpose statement above.

Additions or changes—either permanent or temporary—needed by other groups using the room, including installation of or removal of software on either the instructor's workstation or the participants' workstations, must be approved by Martha Reynolds or Jeremy Worsham.

Once approved, arrangements for necessary modifications will be coordinated through Jeremy Worsham, Memorial Library's Instructional and Digital Services Librarian (ext. 6707), who will determine the most efficient course of action for making the changes.

Routine maintenance, support, and service functions for all software, hardware, and other equipment in the classroom are paid for by the library and coordinated by Jeremy Worsham, working in cooperation with OIT personnel.

Notes on Current Equipment, Configurations, Hardware, and Software

Instructor's Workstation:

Full campus network/Internet connectivity; internal modem also available. Windows XP, 256.0 MB RAM, 32-bit file system. Connected to InfocusDesktop LCD projector. DVD and VCR also available.

Participants' Workstations:

10 on tables around perimeter of room, seating for 2 students per workstation. 17" monitor for each workstation; all workstations networked to Lexmark Optra S1650 Laser Printer.

Currently-loaded software (all workstations):
    Adobe Acrobat Reader Version 6.0
    Macromedia Dreamweaver MX 2004
    InfoMaker/Powersoft Version 6.0
    Internet Explorer Version 6.0
    Microsoft Word (2003)
    Microsoft Excel (2003)
    Microsoft Photo Editor

Microsoft Access (2003)
Microsoft Power Point (2003)
Microsoft Publisher (2003)
Microsoft SQL Server 6.5 Utilities
Norton Anti-Virus
Novell NetWare
NTDB (software to run CD-ROM product only)
Simmons National Consumer Survey (Choices II)

INTERFACES

Rollins College
Olin Library
Winter Park, Florida

The user interface of an electronic resource affects the quality of its results, the time users spend with it, and the willingness of users to employ the resource at all. Interfaces should be examined for user-friendliness (comprehensible and/or intuitive procedures), ease of use for novice users, advanced features for experienced users or those with relatively complex search needs, and convenient commands for printing and/or saving information to disk. Documentation, whether through on-screen instructions or accompanying manuals, is important as well. A superior interface can be a deciding factor between otherwise comparable resources.

University of North Carolina Greensboro
Greensboro, North Carolina

University Libraries' intuitive procedures provide ease of use for novice users, advanced features for experienced users or those with relatively complex search needs, and convenient commands for printing and/or saving information to disk. Documentation, whether through on-screen instructions or accompanying manuals, is important as well. A superior interface can be a deciding factor between otherwise comparable resources.

NETWORK SECURITY

Calumet College of Saint Joseph
Specker Library
Whiting, Indiana

NETWORK SECURITY POLICY

In order to promote ethical and facilitative computing, Calumet College of St. Joseph's network users must adhere to the following guidelines:

- Use of systems and/or networks in attempts to gain unauthorized access to CCSJ's network systems or remote systems is prohibited and is a punishable disciplinary offense.
- Use of systems and/or networks to harm or thwart the operations or business of the college or college activities is prohibited.
- Decryption of system or user passwords is prohibited.
- The copying of system files is prohibited.

- The copying of copyrighted materials, such as third-party software, without the express written permission of the owner or the proper license, is prohibited.
- Intentional attempts to "crash" network systems or programs are punishable disciplinary offenses.
- Running of HTTP, Email, and FTP servers is strictly prohibited on client machines.
- The willful introduction of computer "viruses" or other disruptive/destructive programs into the organizational network or into external networks is prohibited.

University of North Carolina at Greensboro
Greensboro, North Carolina

Purpose

The University of North Carolina at Greensboro's (hereinafter "University") computing and telecommunication networks, computing equipment, and computing resources are owned by the University and are provided to support the academic and administrative functions of the University.

The purpose of this policy is to support a high standard of network security. Adherence to the policy will help protect the integrity of the campus network and networked data. Enforcement actions will mitigate risks and losses associated with security threats to the network and networked data.

Federal and state law, and University policies and procedures govern the use of this equipment and technologies. Additional rules and regulations may be adopted by divisions/departments to meet specific administrative or academic needs. Any adopted requirements must be in compliance with applicable federal and state laws, and this policy.

Scope

This policy applies to all faculty, staff, students, and other authorized individuals who connect network communications devices to the University data network. It is fundamental to all information security efforts at the University.

The intent of this policy is not to change the ownership of computing and telecommunication networks, computing equipment, or computing resources.

Policy

Network Operation and Transport
Physical Connections
    The following restrictions apply:
- Only a single network communications device should be attached per Ethernet jack. If additional jacks are required, a cabling request must be submitted to ITS.
- Physical access to infrastructure network switching equipment is not permitted without specific authorization of ITS.
- Attached cables must be certified by ITS and shall not exceed 20 feet in length.
- Ethernet hubs/repeaters must not be attached.
- Ethernet switches/bridges must not be attached.
- Hardware firewall/network address translation devices must not be attached.
- Wireless enabled devices must not be attached.
- Network layer 3 (logical layer) routing devices must not be attached.
- All attached devices must have an identified owner and user.
- Logical Addressing

- UNCG has been granted Internet address spaces. ITS will exclusively provide allocation and administration of these address spaces in accordance with ITS procedures, standards, and protocols.
- All network attached devices require registration in the ITS network registration system.
- Name resolution to/from the Internet will only be provided for devices specifically identified as servers. Servers with administrative applications are subject to the Enterprise Systems Policy.
- ITS will manage additional domain name space (for example, e-mail.uncg.edu, uncg.info) in support of the University mission.
- Individuals, academic colleges/departments, or administrative departments at UNCG may not create and support an Internet domain name space without prior approval of ITS.

Quality of Service

- ITS has the authority to implement Network Quality of Service technology to control the cost of providing Internet service, ensure equal communications access for all clients, and provide differential service for enterprise applications, which may include denial of transport.

Workstation Operation

- Computer workstation users are expected to adhere to the following:
- Ensure that operating system and application software is kept up to date with manufacturer patches.
- Take all necessary precautions to avoid workstation compromise. Employees and departments are responsible for making use of the recommended security software from the ITS division as set forth in the Standards for Computer and Related Technology (Supported Products List) and for configuring the software according to ITS standards.
- Where possible, physically secure the workstation.
- Do not allow others to use a workstation when logged in with your authentication credentials.
- Ensure that data is retained and backed up if necessary.
- Store data that is classified as Restricted in the Data Classification Policy on ITS network storage facilities.
- Employ mobile device startup password protections.
- Follow ITS protocol for equipment disposal practices to ensure protection of data and licensed software.
- Take reasonable precautions to avoid actions that could deteriorate the performance of the University network or networked resources (devices connected to the UNCG network).

Server Operation

- Application server administrators are expected to adhere to the following:
- Ensure that operating system and application software is kept up to date with manufacturer patches.
- Take all necessary precautions to avoid server compromise. Employees and respective departments are responsible for making use of the recommended security software from the ITS division as set forth in the Standards for Computer and Related Technology (Supported Products List) and for configuring the software according to ITS standards.
- Physically secure the server.
- Ensure that data is backed up and retained according to the Computer Systems Backup Policy.
- Maintain system activity logs for auditing purposes.
- Equipment disposal practices must follow ITS protocols to ensure protection of data and licensed software.
- Adhere to the Enterprise Systems Policy.

Human Safety

- Network connected devices with applications directly involving human safety must be operated on a physically or logically isolated network. Examples are physical security and environmental control devices.

Wireless Computing

- The wireless communications spectrum is managed as part of the campus network. See Wireless Communications Policy.

Enterprise Passwords

- Passwords are an important aspect of computer security. Passwords represent the front line of protection for all user accounts. A poorly chosen password may compromise UNCG's entire network.

General Requirements

- System or user-level passwords must be changed on the currently recommended standard periodic basis.
- Passwords must be kept secure, and sharing of accounts is prohibited. Authorized users are responsible for the security of all assigned account and equipment activity and should follow security procedures determined by ITS standards.
- User accounts that have system-level privileges through some form of group membership, or other implementation, must have a unique password from other accounts held by that user.
- Passwords must not be inserted into e-mail messages or any other form of electronic communication.
- All manufacturer default passwords must be changed before network connection.
- The use of ITS enterprise authentication services is required.

Application Developer Requirements

- Application developers with applications containing passwords, shared secrets, or key phrases contained within should adhere to the following guidelines:
- Support authentication through ITS enterprise authentication services.
- Support authentication of individual users and not groups.
- Must not store passwords in clear text or any form that is reversible.

Remote Access

- The public sections of the University's Web site are available to any user through remote access.
- Remote access connections, whether originating from University-owned or personal equipment, should be given the same security consideration as an on-site connection.
- Faculty, staff, or students are the only ones permitted to remotely access University network resources and only through ITS-supported remote access technology.
- All remote access will be encrypted, and authenticated using ITS enterprise authentication services.
- Approaches to network traffic that threaten security are strictly prohibited.

Acceptable Encryption

- Encryption technology protects information content during network transport.
- Some data must be encrypted in conformity with the Wireless Communications Policy and the Data Classification Policy.
- ITS-supported algorithms should be selected when using encryption technology.
- Cryptographic key lengths must be of sufficient length as to prevent successful intrusion in a short time period.
- The use of proprietary encryption algorithms is not allowed for any application housing data classified as Restricted as defined by the Data Classification Policy.
- Export of encryption technologies is subject to federal law.

Non-Affiliate Access

- Visitors or non-University community members may require temporary access to computer or network resources. Non-affiliate network access is subject to the following restrictions:
- Non-affiliate network access is subject to all University policies including the Acceptable Use of Computing and Electronic Resources Policy.

- Only Deans and Department Heads can sponsor non-affiliate network access.
- Faculty, staff, and students must not use non-affiliate access procedures to gain any form of temporary computer or network access.
- Faculty and staff must not share their account information with non-affiliates.

Perimeter Security

- The perimeter of UNCG's network infrastructure is defined as the electronic border between the UNCG campus network, and the first Internet Service Provider (ISP) networking device supplying wide area network (WAN) connectivity.
- ITS maintains perimeter security for the purposes of general infrastructure protection.
- Only authorized ITS employees may modify perimeter security measures.
- All application servers must be specifically identified to ITS.

Application Service Providers

Requirements of the Sponsoring Department

- If the application is hosted on the campus, it is subject to the Enterprise Systems Policy.
- Individuals, academic colleges/departments, or administrative units must contact ITS and lodge an Application Service Provider (ASP) request.
- If the application under consideration is to be hosted outside the campus, and the data manipulated is classified as Restricted as defined by the Data Classification Policy, an ITS security review must be completed.

Requirements of the Application Service Provider

- Application service providers must adhere to ITS ASP security standards.
- ITS may request that security measures be implemented in addition to the general ITS ASP security standards.
- ASP's that do not meet the requirements may not be used for UNCG enterprise applications.

Extranet (External Network) Connections

Pre-Requisites

Security Review

All new extranet connectivity will go through an ITS security review to ensure that all access matches the business requirements in the best possible way, and that the principle of least access is followed.

Memorandum of Understanding

All new connection requests between third parties and UNCG require that the third party and UNCG representatives agree to and sign an Extranet Memorandum of Understanding. The Vice Chancellor/Chief Information Officer or his/her designee must sign this agreement, together with the Provost/Vice Chancellor of the requesting department, as well as a representative from the third party who is legally empowered to sign on behalf of the third party. The agreement must be reviewed by the Office of the University Counsel prior to signature by University officials in accordance with the UNCG Policy on Contract Review and Approval. The signed document is to be kept on file with ITS.

Point of Contact

The requesting UNCG department must designate a person to be the Point of Contact (POC) for the extranet connection. The POC acts on behalf of the department, and is responsible for those portions of this policy and the Extranet Memorandum of Understanding that pertain to it. In the event that the POC changes, ITS and the extranet organization must be informed promptly.

Establishing Connectivity

Departments within UNCG that wish to establish connectivity to a third party are to file a new site request with ITS. The sponsoring organization must provide ITS with full and complete information as to the nature of the proposed access.

All connectivity established must be based on the least-access principle, in accordance with the approved business requirements and the security review. In no case will UNCG rely upon the third party to protect UNCG's network or resources.

Modifying Connectivity

All changes in access must be accompanied by a valid business justification, and are subject to security review. Individual departments are responsible for notifying ITS when there is a material change in their originally provided information so that security and connectivity evolve accordingly.

Terminating Connectivity

When access is no longer required, UNCG departments must notify ITS, which will then terminate the access.

Compliance With Laws And Regulations Relating To Networked Data

UNCG complies with federal and state laws and regulations relating to the security of networked data. UNCG designates compliance officers for laws/regulations, as appropriate, and ITS cooperates with the designated compliance officers.

Enforcement

ITS will enforce the Security of Networks and Networked Data Policy and establish standards, procedures, and protocols in support of the policy.

Alleged violations of this policy are subject to the due process provided in existing University policies.

Any violation of this policy by a University student is subject to the Student Code of Conduct in the student handbook. For employees, any violation of this policy is "misconduct" under EPA policies (faculty and EPA non-faculty) and "unacceptable personal conduct" under SPA policies, including any appeal rights stated therein. Employees and students are required to cooperate with ITS in investigations of any alleged violations of the policy. Violations of law may also be referred for criminal or civil prosecution.

ITS has the authority to disconnect network service or modify/enhance network security without notification in the event of law violation, systems compromise involving Restricted data, or negative network communications impact affecting service for other users.

Review

The Chancellor has approved the Security of Networks and Networked Data Policy and the Information Security Committee will periodically review the policy as appropriate.

SOFTWARE WORD PROCESSING

Berkeley Heights Public Library
Berkeley Heights, New Jersey

WORD PROCESSOR POLICY & PROCEDURE

The Basics

Patrons must sign-in at the Reference Desk in order to guarantee a full one-hour session. Anyone not signing in will be asked to immediately save or print their work, sign-in properly or defer to those who are waiting.

Sign-ups are taken for the next available timeslot. Sign-ups allow five minutes between sessions. Patrons must start within 5 minutes of their established start time or risk losing their timeslot.

Reservations are not taken over the telephone.

Librarians will enter the start times. The Reference wall clock is the official time.

Users must allow time within the one-hour session to print or save their work.

Time lost due to adding paper or machine malfunction is included in the one-hour session. No additional time will be given if the next user is present.

The Fine Points

At the end of a session, if no one is waiting, the current user may sign-up for one additional session. At the end of the second session, they may continue but must promptly relinquish the computer to the next person who signs in.

During a session, a patron may leave the computer by requesting a "Computer in Use" sign from the Reference Desk to place on the keyboard. Time away from the computer is included in the previously established one-hour.

If the current user finishes early: (1) The next sign-in can start early and receive the extra time in addition to the one-hour session. If available, a second full session can be used. (2) If the next sign-in is not present, a non-sign-in can complete the remaining time and sign-in for the next available session.

Failure to adhere to the procedures and time limits may result in loss of word processing privileges.

Reference Librarians can offer basic support and assistance only.

TELECOMMUNICATIONS

Greenville Public Library
Smithfield, Rhode Island

Connection to the Internet is accomplished via two switches, one wireless Apple Airport base station, and a hub that connects the LAN to the CLAN Internet provider. The current connection is through a T1 line that is maintained by CLAN.

Lafayette Public Library
Lafayette, Louisiana

Telecommunications

A public library is in the communication and information business. Telecommunications is how we deliver much of our information to the public whether it is through the traditional telephone line, wireless services, or through digital lines.

Goal #1: Provide reliable, high speed data transmission lines to ensure reliable connectivity among our libraries and with other libraries and internet sites globally.

Strategy #5: Work with State Library in maintaining and enhancing the State network. Work with the Lafayette City/Parish Government (though its CIO) to standardize, maintain, and enhance the Library network. Monitor network utilization and upgrade bandwidth to areas as warranted by monitoring. Upgrade from Frame Relay to fiber optic connections as service becomes available if cost/benefit warrants.

Connect new facilities to the WAN via fiber optic or similar state-of-the-art technologies as affordable to meet the increasing demand of public access and staff access computing.

Strategy #6: Provide dedicated access for Distance Learning and video conferencing so that these band-width-intensive applications do not erode the available bandwidth for public and staff for Internet, ILS, Library Web site, email, and Intranet access.

Goal #2: Improve the first interaction most of the public has with the library—the telephone call.

Strategy #7: Improve the phone system, considering the newer VOIP technologies—with its ability to locally manage features and cost considerations. Improve the voice mail system—making it convenient for patrons to leave messages and easy for staff to be alerted to and retrieve messages. Consider a library-wide phone system by the time the Main Library renovations are completed. Continue to select the best long distance and phone service features for the library system, evaluating cost with efficiency.

Goal #3: Minimize technology down time.

Strategy #8: Provide paging services and / or cellular service for IT personnel.

Enhance the staff Intranet with a "help desk" site and improve the web-based submittal of technology service requests. Implement a backup generator at South Regional Library and possibly (depending on budget) at Main Library to power mission-critical technology infrastructure during power or other emergencies.

Goal #4: Improve response to facilities problems or for patron complaints that are escalated to administration or other situations requiring immediate attention.

Strategy #9: Provide paging services and / or cellular service for facilities personnel and administrative personnel.

Goal #5: Improve communication between outreach service and their users.

Strategy #10: Outreach staff is on the road 5-6 hours a day and their users often must leave a message with the receptionist. Communication with the outreach staff while on the road will allow their public to communicate with them at the public's convenience and staff to be reachable by Library personnel for communication of critical messages related to the job. Access to the Library's catalog system while the Outreach staff is on their routes will allow the staff to respond to patron queries in a timely fashion.

Chapter 13

SPECIAL EQUIPMENT GUIDELINES

DIGITAL CAMERAS

Portland Community College
Portland Community College Libraries
Portland, Oregon

Overview

Digital cameras and other equipment are paid for through technology fees, and therefore are restricted to currently registered PCC students. Cameras may be borrowed from any PCC library check out desk. A Portland Community College Equipment Use Agreement must be signed by the borrower. This agreement is kept on file in the library. All agreement terms are in force for every checkout. The borrower is responsible for the camera until it is returned to library staff and checked in.

Digital cameras are available on a first-come, first-served basis. Check out is limited to one camera per person for a 3 day period. Cameras must be returned to the check out desk staff at the same library where they were checked out.

To check out, you will need

- A signed PCC Equipment Use Agreement on file
- Current PCC Student ID with a valid term sticker
- Current photo ID such as an Oregon Driver's License

Loan period

- The loan period is 72 hours.
- Renewals are generally not allowed.

Overdue charges

Overdue charges of $5.00 per hour apply if the camera is not returned on time. There is no grace period. All charges are forwarded to the College Business Office and put directly on the student's account. Students pay charges in the Business Office.

It is the responsibility of the borrower to notify the Library check out desk of any loss, damage or defect immediately upon return of the camera.

Loan enforcement

The PCC Library reserves the right to deny checkout privileges indefinitely based on past abuses.

Printing your pictures
- You can print your pictures from any Library computer.
- You will need a GoPrint account to print (this comes with a lab account).
- Black and white printing is seven cents ($.07) a page.
- Color printing is twenty-five cents ($.25) a page.

Security

You are responsible for the camera checked out to you until it is checked back in. The Library is not responsible for loss while the camera is checked out to you.

Please do not leave the camera unattended.

Assistance

Basic directions for camera operation are available.

Student Help Desk assistants are available in the Library to answer any additional operational questions.

Library staff, other than the Student Help Desk, are not responsible for instruction in using the camera.

Report any problems with the camera to the student help desk, and in their absence to the check out desk.

Thank you for your cooperation

If you have any questions regarding the library policies, contact...

DIGITAL CRAWL RESTRICTIONS

University of Virginia Health Science
Claude Moore Health Sciences Libraries
Charlottesville, Virginia

The Claude Moore Health Sciences Library's digital signage is a promotional device to showcase Library events, services, and collections. Therefore, requests to display information unrelated to the Library are generally not accepted. Exceptions may be made when the event or activity is jointly sponsored by the Library or is complementary to a Library program or service and supports the mission of the Health System. All requests are reviewed and considered by the Library Operations Committee. In the event that an exception is made, the item's placement, wording, length, and appearance are solely under the discretion of the Library.

LAPTOP FAQ

Davidson College
Davidson College Library
Davidson, North Carolina

Borrowing a Laptop from the Circulation Desk

Q: Can anyone check out a laptop?
A. No, only Davidson students (not summer programs), faculty, and staff.
Q: Do I need to do anything other than check it out?
A. Yes, you must sign a laptop liability form that includes all equipment checked out.
Q: If the worst happens and I have to replace the laptop, what is the cost?
A. Minimum $2000.00.
Q: Can I print using a laptop?
A. Yes. Laptops print to the public printers on the main floor.
Q: If I want network connection, do I need a network cable?
A. No, wireless is available throughout the Library, and the laptop has wireless capability. However, we do have network cords if you choose to use one (or if for some reason the wireless network is down). For more information, see networking your laptop.

Q: Will I need a power cord?

A. You may request one if you wish, but it is not a necessity. A fresh battery will be placed in the laptop when you check it out (2 hour battery life). If you use a power cord, please be careful not to make the cord a tripping hazard for others.

Q: Are headphones available?

A. Yes, you may check them out at the circulation desk.

Q: Is there a CD-ROM drive?

A. Yes, and it will also play DVDs, but if you prefer a floppy drive, that will be changed out for you.

Q: May I check out a mouse?

A. No, we do not have external mice available.

Q: May I check out a Mac?

A. No, we only have Windows PCs.

Q: How long may I keep the laptop?

A. Laptops are checked out for 2 hours.

Q: May I renew the laptop?

A. Yes, if no one else has been waiting for one.

Q: Where may I use the laptop?

A. You may take it anywhere in the library. You must remain in the building with it.

Q: May I save my work to the laptop?

A. No. When the machine is turned off, all data is lost. You must save your work elsewhere (network drive, flash drive, etc).

Q: May I turn the laptop off while I have it?

A. Only if you have your data saved elsewhere. All data will be lost if turned off.

Q: May I have a drink while I have the laptop?

A. No. Even though drinks with lids are allowed in the library, you should never have one near a laptop. For more details, see the library's food and drink policy.

Q: May I keep the laptop after the Library closes for use in the 24-hour room?

A. No, it must be returned to the circulation desk before the library closes.

Q: May I take the laptop to a class for a presentation?

A. No, save your file to your network space.

Q: May I leave the laptop in my carrel while I go to the Union, class, etc.?

A. Laptops found unattended by library staff will be picked up and returned to the Circulation Desk.

LAPTOP USE GUIDELINES

College of DuPage
College of DuPage Library
Glen Ellyn, Illinois

Guidelines for Use of Library Computers and Laptop Internet Connections

Persons using Library computers shall be mindful that they are in a public environment and be respectful of others.

Use of computers and laptop Internet connections will be on a first come, first served basis. As a condition of use, patrons agree that if someone is waiting they will make the computer or laptop Internet connection available within 15 minutes of being informed by Library staff that another person is waiting.

Personal use of the computer equipment or laptop Internet connections (e.g., personal email or personal Internet browsing) are considered non-library related and will be restricted as patron use demands. Game-playing and personal (non-course-related) chatting are disallowed at all times.

DVDs marked "Home Viewing Only" may not be viewed at public computers in the Library. DVDs labeled "Home Use Only" may be viewed in the Library's Viewing Rooms if they are needed for class-related purposes. Check with Circulation Services to be assigned a room.

Non-library related use of computers and laptop Internet connections must be terminated immediately upon request of Library staff.

The Library staff will announce Library closing times 30 minutes prior to closing. Computer users must be prepared to finish their work on the computers before closing time.

Software downloaded from the Internet may contain computer viruses. Every user is responsible for maintaining virus-checking software on his/her home computer. The College of DuPage Library is not responsible for damage to any user's disk or computer, or any loss of data, damage, or liability that may occur from patron use of the Library's computers or Internet connections.

University of Virginia
University of Virginia Library
Charlottesville, Virginia

Connecting to the Network as a Guest

If you are a guest of the University wishing to connect your personal laptop to the UVa network, you will need to obtain a temporary personal identification number (PIN) to register your network card. The PIN can be obtained from the service desks in Alderman, Clemons, and Brown libraries. In addition to the PIN, you will be given special instructions for connecting your laptop to the network, as well as a copy of the UVa Computer Usage Policy. Each guest PIN is valid for seven days; when it expires, you will need to request a new PIN.

University of Virginia
University of Virginia Library
Charlottesville, Virginia

Printing from Circulating Laptops

The circulating laptops are connected to the pay-for-print public printers in the libraries.

(For additional policies, please see the accompanying CD-ROM.)

Part IV
Access to Electronic Resources

Chapter 14

ACCESS GUIDELINES

AMERICANS WITH DISABILITIES ACT (ADA) POLICIES

The University of Kansas
University of Kansas Libraries
Lawrence, Kansas

Assistance with Electronic Materials

Workstation Accessibility—All library locations have one or more workstations that are wheelchair-accessible and adaptive technology is available on designated workstations in the Watson and Anschutz libraries on the Lawrence campus and in the Regents Center Library on the Edwards campus. Please refer to the section on adaptive technology below for a complete listing of software applications currently available. Access to adaptive technology workstations requires an active KU Online ID.

Library Web site—The University of Kansas Libraries are committed to providing access to information through our Web site. While many of our Web pages and resources have been reviewed for established guidelines for accessibility, there are many legacy materials that are not yet fully compliant with those guidelines. If you have difficulty accessing one or more pages on our Web site, please contact the Library Web Services Coordinator.

Electronic journals, books, and databases—the KU Libraries subscribes to a vast number of electronic resources provided through a large number of commercial vendors and publishers and not all resources were designed for maximum accessibility. Users requiring assistance accessing these materials should contact the KU Libraries ADA Coordinator.

Adaptive Technology Available in the KU Libraries

There is one designated workstation in Anschutz, Watson and the Regents Center libraries, that serve those who need access to adaptive technology. The following is a listing of the hardware and software profiles on the designated workstations.

Anschutz Library:

Hardware Profile: Dell with Intel Core 2 processor · 1.8 GHz · 1.99 GB RAM · Cannon Scanner · accessibility stand and adaptive peripherals.

Software Profile: Microsoft Windows XP · Acrobat Reader 8 · Adobe ImageReady 7 · Adobe Photoshop 7 · ArcSoft Photobase 3 · ArcSoft Photo Studio 5 · Cannon Scanning · Connect Outloud 3 · EndNote X · insight v5.6 · iTunes · Java 2 · JAWS 8.0 · OpenBook 7.2 · QuickTime · RealPlayer · Microsoft Office 2003: Word, Excel, Access, PowerPoint · Outlook Express · Power DVD DX · RefWorks/WriteNCite · Roxio Creator DE · Windows Media Player · Windows Messenger · Browsers: Mozilla Firefox and Internet Explorer.

Watson Library:

Hardware Profile: Dell with Intel Core 2 processor · 1.8 GHz · 1.99 GB RAM · Cannon Scanner · accessibility stand and adaptive peripherals.

Software Profile: Microsoft Windows XP · Acrobat Reader 8 · Adobe ImageReady 7 · Adobe Photoshop 7 · ArcSoft Photobase 3 · ArcSoft Photo Studio 5 · Cannon Scanning · Connect Outloud 3 · EndNote X · insight v5.6 · iTunes · Java 2 · JAWS 8.0 · OpenBook 7.2 · QuickTime · RealPlayer · Microsoft Office 2003: Word, Excel, Access, PowerPoint · Outlook Express · Power DVD DX · RefWorks/WriteNCite · Roxio Creator DE · Windows Media Player · Windows Messenger · Browsers: Mozilla Firefox and Internet Explorer.

Regents Center Library:

Hardware Profile: Dell with Intel Pentium 4 dual processors · 3 GHz · 1 gig RAM · Cannon Scanner · accessibility stand and adaptive peripherals.

Software Profile: Microsoft Windows XP · Adobe Acrobat 5.0 · Acrobat Reader 7 · EndNote 8 · Roxio Easy CD Creator · IBM Via Voice in German, French, Italian, UK & US English · Java · Jaws 6.1 · Macromedia Shock Player · Microsoft Net Show Player 2.0 · Microsoft Office 2003, Word, Excel, Access, PowerPoint · Windows Journal Viewer · Mobile Option Pack · Media Player 2 · MSN Messenger · Net Meeting · OpenBook 7.0 · Outlook Express · PC Health · Quick Time · Real Player Basic · RIS Web Helper · Scheduling Agent · ShockWave · ShockWave Flash · Sound Max · Viewpoint Media Player · Win SPC 3.66 · WinZip · Yahoo Messenger · Browsers: Internet Explorer and Mozilla Firefox.

EQUITABLE USER ACCESS

Cabrillo College
Robert E. Swenson Library
Aptos, California

Equitable Access

The Library's electronic workstations and the materials to which they provide access constitute resources to be shared equitably among users.

Limiting Use

The Library supports equity of access to Internet and other electronic information resources. If and when the number of computer workstations is insufficient to meet demand, rationing service (i.e., limiting individual sessions to a certain time period and/ or limiting access to those in the primary user group) may be necessary to provide equitable access.

LIBRARY RESPONSIBILITIES

University of Minnesota
University of Minnesota Libraries
Minneapolis, Minnesota

The University's Rights and Responsibilities

As owner of the computers and networks that comprise the University's technical infrastructure, the University owns all official administrative data that resides on its systems and networks, and is responsible for taking necessary measures to ensure the security of its systems, data, and user's accounts. The University does not seek out personal misuse. However, when it becomes aware of violations, either through routine system administration activities or from a complaint, it is the University's responsibility to investigate as needed or directed, and to take necessary actions to protect its resources and/or to provide information relevant to an investigation.

Individual units within the University may define additional conditions of use for resources or facilities under their control. Such additional conditions must be consistent with this overall policy but may provide additional detail, guidelines, and/or restrictions.

Roles and responsibilities for specific University entities and individuals are defined in greater detail below.

Chief Information Officer

- Designate individuals who have the responsibility and authority for information technology resources.
- Establish and disseminate enforceable rules regarding access to and acceptable use of information technology resources.
- Establish reasonable security policies and measures to protect data and systems.
- Monitor and manage system resource usage.
- Investigate problems and alleged violations of University information technology policies.
- Refer violations to appropriate University offices such as the Office of the General Counsel and the University Police Department for resolution or disciplinary action.

Campuses, Colleges, or Departments

- Create, disseminate and enforce conditions of use that are consistent with University-wide policies for the University facilities and/or resources under their control.
- Monitor the use of University resources under their control.
- Investigate problems and alleged violations of University information technology policies.
- Refer violations to appropriate University offices such as the Office of the General Counsel and the University Police Department for resolution or disciplinary action. Possible policy violations should be reported to the appropriate entity as listed in the Contacts section of this document.

Data Custodians

- Grant authorized users appropriate access to the data and applications for which they are stewards, working with University data security and network personnel to limit access to authorized users with a legitimate role-based need.
- Review access rights of authorized users on a regular basis.
- Respond to questions from users relating to appropriate use of system/network resources.
- Implement and oversee processes to retain or purge information according to University records retention schedules.
- Determine the criticality and sensitivity of the data and/or applications for which they are stewards; determine which University data is public and private based on University definitions, in consultation with the University's Office of

Records and Information Management

- Ensure that appropriate security measures and standards are implemented and enforced for the data under their control, in a method consistent with University policies and sound business practices. The security measures implemented should be based on the criticality, sensitivity, and public or private nature of the data, and may include methodologies, change management, and operational recovery plans.
- Investigate problems and alleged violations of University information technology policies.
- Refer violations to appropriate University offices such as the Office of the General Counsel and the University Police Department for resolution or disciplinary action.

System/Network Administrator

- Take reasonable action to ensure the authorized use and security of data, networks, and the communications transiting the system or network.

- Participate and advise as requested in developing conditions of use or authorized use procedures.
- Respond to questions from users relating to appropriate use of system/network resources.
- Cooperate with appropriate University departments and law enforcement officials in investigating alleged violations of policy or law.

Office of Records and Information Management
- Assist data custodians in classifying information as public or private. Secure official rulings from the Office of the General Counsel on public and private information.

University Police Department
- Respond to alleged violations of criminal law.
- Coordinate all activities between the University and outside law enforcement agencies.

General Counsel
- Provide legal advice on official rulings on public, private and confidential information.

University Office of Information Technology Security
- Protect the University network, systems, and data. Coordinate with designated campus, collegiate, or unit technical and security staff to ensure the confidentiality, integrity, and availability of University systems and ensure that appropriate and timely action is taken. Determine if an on-site technical security evaluation is necessary and if any mitigation steps will be required. Coordinate with the unit technical/security staff to assure that appropriate diagnostic, protective, remedial, and other actions are taken as necessary to protect University resources. Coordinate with the appropriate University offices (compliance, legal, human resources, and student conduct) as well as external Internet Service Providers (ISPs) and law enforcement as necessary.

Library Responsibilities

In providing licensed electronic resources, the Libraries shall:
- whenever possible, enter only into agreements that allow access to and use of information that fully support the University's mission;
- enter into agreements that ensure user privacy, in accordance with the University's Online Privacy Statement;
- allow access only to authorized users;
- make reasonable and good faith efforts to inform authorized users of their rights and responsibilities under license agreements; and
- upon becoming aware of any breach of a license agreement, take reasonable measures to correct the breach and to prevent the breach from occurring again.

Solano Community College
Solano Community College Library
Fairfield, California

Manager Responsibilities

The unit manager is responsible for the following:
- Posting the following notice:
  - Although every effort is made by the District to secure the computer and communications systems, users cannot be assured of absolute privacy. Also, under certain circumstances, the District may access information entered on such systems.

176

- Users should be aware that it is possible for information entered on or transmitted via computer and communication systems to be retrieved, even if the information has been deleted.
- For further information, see Board Policy 2067.
• Informing users of computer and communications systems of this policy and providing copies of this policy to users, on request.
• Developing, distributing and enforcing any operational guidelines or procedures necessary are areas of classroom and public access.

The Dean of Student Services is responsible for finding Policy 2067 in the Student Handbook.

SERVICE PRIORITIES

Cumberland County Public Library and Information Center
Fayetteville, North Carolina

The Library's FY2001–2005 long range plan states as one of its main goals that "Cumberland County adults and children get the assistance they need to access, navigate, and evaluate electronic information resources so they can make full use of all technologies to communicate and learn."

The Library will provide an adequate number of computer terminals at all Library locations to facilitate public access to electronic databases and Internet resources. Although the Internet offers access to many valuable local, national and international sources of information, not all sources are accurate, complete, current or appropriate for all Library users. The Library only offers a pathway to the Internet; it does not endorse or vouch for any material transmitted through that pathway to a user.

SPECIAL STATUS ACCESS: ALUMNI, COMMUNITY, GUEST

Tulane University
Tulane University Alumni Affairs
New Orleans, Louisiana

Summary

This policy defines the boundaries of "acceptable use" of limited University electronic resources, specifically computers, networks, electronic mail services and electronic information sources, of the Tulane Alumni Association. It includes by reference a self-contained compilation of specific rules that can be modified as the electronic information environment evolves.

The policy is based on the principle that the electronic information environment of the Alumni Association is provided to support the University's mission as it relates to Alumni. Other uses are secondary. Uses that threaten the integrity of the system; the function of non-University equipment that can be accessed through the system; the privacy or actual or perceived safety of others; or that are otherwise illegal are forbidden.

By using University electronic information systems you assume personal responsibility for their appropriate use and agree to comply with this policy and other applicable University policies, as well as city, state and federal laws and regulations.

The policy defines penalties leading up to and including loss of system access. In addition some activities may lead to risk of legal liability, both civil and criminal.

Users of electronic information systems are urged in their own interest to review and understand the contents of this policy.

Purposes

Tulane Alumni Association computing resources (including, but not limited to, computer facilities and services, computers, networks, electronic mail, electronic information and data, and video and voice services) are available to Tulane Alumni, faculty, students, staff, registered guests and the general public to support the mission of Tulane Alumni Association and service missions of the University.

When demand for computing resources exceed available capacity, priorities for their use will be established and enforced. Authorized Alumni Directors and staff may set and alter priorities for exclusively local computing/networking resources.

Implied consent

Each person with access to the Alumni Association's computing resources is responsible for their appropriate use and by their use agrees to comply with all applicable University, or Alumni Association policies and regulations, and with applicable city, state and federal laws and regulations, as well as with the acceptable use policies of affiliated networks and systems.

General Standards for the Acceptable Use of Computer Resources: Failure to uphold the following General Standards for the Acceptable Use of Computer Resources constitutes a violation of this policy and may be subject to disciplinary action.

The General Standards for the Acceptable Use of Computer Resources require:

- Responsible behavior with respect to the electronic information environment at all times;
- Behavior consistent with the mission Of the University and with authorized activities of the University or members of the University community;
- Respect for the principles of open expression;
- Compliance with all applicable laws, regulations, and University policies;
- Truthfulness and honesty in personal and computer identification;
- Respect for the rights and property of others, including intellectual property rights;
- Behavior consistent with the Privacy and integrity of electronic networks, electronic data and information and electronic infrastructure and systems; and
- Respect for the value and intended use of human and electronic resources.

Enforcement, and Penalties for Violation: It may at times be necessary for authorized systems administrators to suspend someone's access to Alumni Association computing resources immediately for violations of this policy. Pending interim resolution of the situation (for example by securing a possibly compromised account and/or making the owner of an account aware in person that an activity constitutes a violation). In the case of egregious and continuing violations suspension of access may be extended until final resolution by the appropriate disciplinary body.

System owners, administrators or managers may be required to investigate violations of this policy and to ensure compliance.

Interpreting this policy

Data Stewards and Listserv Moderators

Chapter City Presidents will have the authority to monitor all transmissions over their respective Listservs. They have the duty to make the Alumni Affairs staff person assigned to the Communications Committee and the Chairperson of the Communications Committee aware of any breaches of the policy set forth heretofore.

The Communications Committee Chairman in consultation with the President of the Alumni Association has the authority to take action to attempt to stop further breaches of the heretofore Electronic Resources Policy with the most grievous action the removal of said individual from the further use of said Electronic Resources.

Specific Rules Interpreting the Policy on Acceptable Use of Electronic Resources

The following specific rules apply to all uses of Tulane Alumni Association computing resources. These rules are not an exhaustive list of proscribed behaviors, but are intended to implement and illustrate the General Standards for the Acceptable Use of Computer Resources, other relevant University policies, and applicable laws and regulations. Additional specific rules may be promulgated for the acceptable use by the Board of Directors of Tulane Alumni Association.

Content of communications

Except as provided by applicable City, State, or Federal laws, regulations or other University policies, the content of electronic communications is not by itself a basis for disciplinary action.

Unlawful communications, including threats of violence, obscenity, pornography, and harassing communications (as defined by law), are prohibited.

The use of Tulane Alumni Association computer resources for private business or commercial activities (except where such activities are otherwise permitted or authorized under applicable University policies), fundraising or advertising on behalf of non-University organizations, or the reselling of University computer resources to non-University individuals or organizations, and the unauthorized use of the University's name, are prohibited.

Identification of users

Anonymous and pseudonymous communications are not permitted except when expressly permitted by the operating guidelines or stated purpose of the guidelines or stated purposes of the electronic services to, from, or through which the communications are sent. An authorized system administrator can be directed to attempt to identify the originator of anonymous/pseudonymous messages and may refer such matters to appropriate disciplinary bodies to prevent further distribution of messages from the same source.

The following activities and behaviors are prohibited:

- Misrepresentation (including forgery) of the identity of the sender or source of an electronic communication;
- Acquiring or attempting to acquire passwords of others;
- Using or attempting to use the computer accounts of others;
- Alteration of the content of a message originating from another person or computer with intent to deceive; and
- The unauthorized deletion of another person's postings.

Access to computer resources:

- The use of restricted-access University computer resources or electronic information without or beyond one's level of authorization;
- The interception or attempted interception of communications by parties not explicitly intended to receive them;
- Making Alumni Association computing resources available to individuals not affiliated with the Tulane University or Tulane Alumni Association without approval of an authorized Alumni official;
- Making available any materials the possession or distribution of which is illegal;

- The unauthorized copying or use of licensed computer software;
- Intentionally compromising the Privacy or security of electronic information; and
- Intentionally infringing upon the intellectual property rights of others in computer programs or electronic information (including plagiarism and unauthorized use or reproductions).

Operational integrity:

The following activities and behaviors are prohibited
- Interference with or disruption of the computer or network accounts, services, or equipment of others, including, but not limited to, the propagation of computer "worms" and "viruses," the sending of electronic chain mail, and the inappropriate sending of "broadcast" messages to large numbers of individuals or hosts;
- Failure to comply with requests from appropriate Alumni officials to discontinue activities that threaten the operation or integrity of computers, systems or networks, or otherwise violate this policy;
- Revealing passwords or otherwise permitting the use by others (by intent or negligence) of personal accounts for computer and network access;
- Altering or attempting to alter files or systems without authorization;
- Unauthorized scanning of networks for security vulnerabilities;
- Attempting to alter any Alumni computing or networking components (including, but not limited to, bridges, routers, and hubs) without authorization or beyond one's level of authorization;
- Unauthorized wiring, including attempts to create unauthorized network connections, or any unauthorized extension or re-transmission of any computer or network services;
- Intentionally damaging or destroying the integrity of electronic information;
- Intentionally disrupting the use of electronic networks or information systems;
- Intentionally wasting human or electronic resources; and
- Negligence leading to the damage of University electronic information, computing/networking equipment and resources.

Applicable laws

Computer and network use is also subject to Louisiana and Federal laws and regulations. Suspected violations of applicable law are subject to investigation by Alumni Affairs and/or University and/or law enforcement officials. Among the applicable laws are:
- Federal Copyright Law: U.S. copyright law grants authors certain exclusive rights of reproduction, adaptation, distribution, performance, display, attribution and integrity to their creations, including works of literature, photographs, music, software, film and video. Violations of copyright laws include, but are not limited to, the making of unauthorized copies of any copyrighted material (such as commercial software, text, graphic images, audio and video recordings) and distributing copyrighted materials over computer networks or through other means.
- Federal Wire Fraud Law: Federal law prohibits the use of interstate communications systems (phone, wire, radio, or television transmissions) to further an illegal scheme or to defraud.
- Federal Computer Fraud and Abuse Law: Federal law prohibits unauthorized access to, or modification of information in computers containing national defense, banking, or financial information.
- Federal Child Pornography Laws: Federal laws prohibit the creation, possession, or distribution of graphic depictions of minors engaged in sexual activity, including computer graphics. Computers storing such information can be seized as evidence.
- Pyramid schemes / Chain Letters: It is a violation of the Federal Postal Lottery Statute to send chain letters which request sending money or something of value through the U.S. mail. Solicitations through electronic messaging are also illegal, if they require use of U.S. mail for sending money/something of value.

- Defamation: Someone may seek civil remedies if they can show that they were clearly identified as the subject of defamatory messages and suffered damages as a consequence. Truth is a defense against charges of defamation.
- Common law actions for invasion of privacy: Someone may take seek civil remedies for invasion of privacy on several grounds.
- Public disclosure of private facts: the widespread disclosure of facts about a person, even when true, may be deemed harmful enough to justify a lawsuit.
- False light: a person wrongfully attributes views or characteristics to another person in ways that damage that person's reputation.
- Wrongful intrusion: the law often protects those areas of a person's life in which they can reasonably expect they will not be intruded upon.

Concordia College
Ylvisaker Library
Moorhead, Minnesota

Tri-College students (NDSU and MSUM), clergy, and other community members will be allowed computer access by using the "visitor" name and password. The visitor password will be available at the Reference Desk and at the Office of Admissions. Visitors should present a current valid ID from NDSU, MSUM or a Concordia Community Card to receive the "visitor" password. Exceptions will be made for guests of the college. Visitors are not allowed access to our data ports and they cannot check out our laptops. A record/log of visitors will be kept by the Reference staff who are responsible for maintaining and appropriately purging the record/log after statistics have been compiled. Changes to the password will be made biweekly or as needed by Computer Services. (Courtesy of Concordia College Library, Moorhead, MN)

Tulane University
Howard-Tilton Memorial Library
New Orleans, Louisiana

Guests (Non-Tulane Library Users)

Guests may access the non-login computers for academic research only. Use of library computers by guests for non-academic purposes (i.e. recreation) is expressly prohibited, and guests may be asked to verify that they are using a computer for academic research purposes only. Tulane students, faculty and staff have priority over guests in cases where an insufficient number of computers are available in the library. We reserve the right to limit the amount of time that a guest may occupy a computer; normally this should not exceed two hours per day.

University of Arkansas for Medical Sciences
University of Arkansas Medical Science Library
Little Rock, Arkansas

UAMS Library Computer Use Policy for Visitors

The UAMS Library is a health sciences library. Computer use is restricted to UAMS faculty, students, and staff, and to visitors seeking health or biomedical information.

See Public Libraries listed below for other types of computer and information needs.

Computer and Internet Use:

Visitors must sign in before being logged onto a computer. By signing in visitors acknowledge that they have read, understand, and agree to this policy for computer use.

Computer use is on a first-come, first-serve basis. A visitor will only be logged onto a computer once a day. After an hour, a visitor may be required to log off the computer if another visitor is waiting for a computer.

Students enrolled in academic programs at another institution should use that institution's library as their primary library. Due to limited resources, including staff time, the UAMS Library provides very limited assistance for non-UAMS students.

The UAMS Library does not allow the use of course management tools (e.g. WebCT or Blackboard) by visitors.

Noisy or disruptive visitors will be asked to leave the Library.

Unacceptable Use:

Visitors may not use Library computers for illegal or inappropriate activities or for activities outside the scope of health and biomedical research, including:
- Misrepresenting oneself on the Internet or engaging in fraud.
- Viewing, downloading, or disseminating pornography.
- Participating in chat rooms or forums.
- Playing games.
- Issuing threats.
- Violating copyright laws or licensing agreements.
- Hacking, altering, deleting, or damaging computer software, hardware, system network, programs or data.

Children:

All persons under the age of 16 must be accompanied by a parent. A photo ID is required to verify date-of-birth. All public-access computers in the Library have full access to the Internet and there are no content filters to prevent children from accessing inappropriate materials.

Penalties

The UAMS Library staff will take appropriate action if policies are abused. This may include revoking computer access privileges, revoking library access privileges, and contacting the UAMS Police.

Public Libraries

Public libraries provide computers for Internet access, e-mail, and use of Microsoft products.

STAFF ACCESS TO RESOURCES

Cumberland County Library System
Carlisle, Pennsylvania

Electronic Mail

The purpose of this e-mail policy is to ensure the proper use of Cumberland County's Electronic Mail System by its employees. E-mail is a tool for communication and users have the responsibility to use this resource in an efficient, effective, ethical and lawful manner.

All messages composed, sent, or received on the County's e-mail system are considered to be the property of the County and are not the private property of the employee. The County has the right to monitor employees' e-mail files and will exercise its right as necessary.

The County's e-mail system generally must be used for business purposes only.

Occasional personal use is permissible but should be limited to breaks and lunch hours.

Personal use of e-mail should not interfere with business activity or employee productivity. Supervisors are responsible for monitoring the personal use of e-mail.

E-mail users are forbidden from using the county's e-mail system for the following:

1. Private business activities, amusement/entertainment purposes, or religious/political activities.
2. The creation and exchange of offensive, disruptive, discriminating, inappropriate or sexual messages of any kind regarding gender, age, race, religion or other legally protected status.
3. The exchange of proprietary, confidential or sensitive information.
4. The creation and exchange of advertisements, solicitations, chain letters, or other unsolicited e-mail.
5. The creation and exchange of information in violation of any copyright laws.
6. Subscriptions to non-business related mailing lists.

Employees may not intercept or in any way attempt to gain access to another employee's e-mail files unless specifically authorized to do so.

Violation of this policy is subject to disciplinary action determined by the Cumberland County Personnel Policy Manual, the Cumberland County Library System board and the employee's local library board.

University of Illinois at Urbana-Champaign
University of Illinois Libraries
Urbana, Illinois

Policy on Staff E-Mail Use

Context and Purpose: The use of e-mail has risen dramatically over the past several years. Indeed, the day-to-day functioning of the Library would be slowed to a snail's pace if it were not for the use of e-mail, not only to communicate with other Library staff, but to send electronic documents to one another and arrange meetings, among other things. As with other resources available to Library staff we need to seek a balance between the use of e-mail to further efficiency and effectiveness at work, on the one hand, and the abuse of e-mail for non-library purposes. The purpose of the following policy is to help us seek such a balance.

To encourage the use of e-mail:

• Each staff member is expected to check, read and respond to university e-mail at least once a day. The time spent in this activity will depend on the level and responsibility of the staff member concerned.
• Supervisors should ensure that their staff has access to e-mail and that they check it on a daily basis.

To discourage abuse of e-mail:

• Personal use of e-mail (including instant messaging) during work hours should be minimal. Within each unit each unit head will determine and set guidelines to restrict personal use.

Other considerations and policies governing e-mail: Each staff member has access to the use of e-mail by virtue of employment at the University of Illinois. This access is a privilege and because the e-mail is a University resource, it is the property of the University. (CITES policy reads: "Use [of e-mail] by University employees unrelated to their University positions must be limited in both time and resources and must not interfere in any way with University functions or the employee's duties. It is the responsibility of employees to consult their supervisors, if they have any questions in this respect. "Use of UIUCnet is a privilege, not a right, which may be suspended of terminated by CCSO when, in its judgment, this policy has been violated by the user." ... (and further) "University-supplied network identifiers (network IDs), University identification numbers, and computer sign-ons are the property of the University. The University may revoke these identifiers or sign-ons at any time.) The main purpose for a university e-mail account is university business. See Policy on Appropriate Use of Computers and Network Systems.

E-mail produced from within the University is also considered a university record and as such must be handled according to the University General Rules on records retention and disposition as well as the policies of the Illinois State Records Commission, "Destruction or Transfer of University Records."

STUDENT POPULATIONS

Long Island University
B. Davis Schwartz Memorial Library
Brookville, New York

Access to electronic resources is available to the LIU academic community, as determined by the Dean of University Libraries. Access is provided from the Library's web pages, and is implemented and maintained by the Library Webmaster in collaboration with the Database Coordinator.

User authentication for access to resources is provided through IP address whenever possible, and is arranged by the Database Coordinator in collaboration or consultation with the Library Information Technology Manager. The Library prefers access by IP address rather than by password.

Remote access is available by referring URL or by proxy server authentication, and is implemented and maintained by the Library Information Technology Manager. Remote access is available only to authorized users in the LIU academic community as determined by the Dean of University Libraries within the contractual guidelines set forth by the licensing agreements of the information providers or vendors, and subject to those legal and technical constraints.

Who can use the library?

LIU card holders (students, faculty, and staff) have access to everything: borrowing privileges, databases, interlibrary loan, etc.

Alumni, continuing education students, PLA members, and Brookville residents are allowed borrowing privileges, with an LIU card, but no access to databases or interlibrary loan.

Texas A&M Corpus Christi
Mary and Jeff Bell Library
Corpus Christi, Texas

Access: Access is fundamental consideration that is comprised of several additional criteria.

Remote Access. The ability for users to access databases from off campus continues to grow in importance given our status as a commuter campus and the continued growth of distance education. For resources that require authentication, IP recognition is preferred. Resources, especially subscription databases, that do not offer IP recognition are less desirable than those that do.

Simultaneous users. The number of users who may access a resource at a given time can have a large impact on access. Does the system have different "numbers of seats" available for on-campus or remote users? In descending order of preference, we prefer unlimited simultaneous users, a large number simultaneous users, or a small number of simultaneous users. The decision about number of simultaneous users will depend on cost but also on expected usage of the database.

Access vs. ownership. For fee-based resources, what exactly does the fee pay for? Does the fee include perpetual access to (ownership of) the content or does it only include access to the content for the duration of the subscription? If perpetual access is purchased, where will the content reside, with the publisher or with the library? Perpetual access (ownership) is preferred. The library does not own the content of freely available databases.

Interlibrary loan rights. Does the vendor/publisher permit the library's ILL department to distribute copies according to the normal and proper procedures of interlibrary loan?

License or contract. Is the library required to sign a license agreement or access contract in order to provide access to the database to users? License review and negotiation is an expensive process in terms of Library and University resources and this should be taken into consideration along with the needs of library users for timely access to databases.

Evaluation Renewal decisions are often based on the ability to assess the value of a database to users. Therefore there is a heavy preference for databases for which the vendor provides statistical data that describe how often the database is being accessed. Vendor compliance with Project COUNTER's standards for reporting usage is also preferred. Since freely available databases typically do not provide usage statistics, these databases will be evaluated on the remaining criteria in this policy.

Interoperability. The more ways in which a given resource will integrate with currently existing library resources, the better. Databases that are Open URL compliant are preferred as are databases for which MARC records are available.

USER ACCESS TO LICENSED RESOURCES

University of Minnesota
University of Minnesota Libraries
Minneapolis, Minnesota

General Information

The University Libraries provide licensed electronic resources in support of the University's three-fold mission of research and discovery, teaching and learning, and outreach and public service. In many cases, license agreements impose greater restrictions on use than does copyright law. Nonetheless, the Libraries, whenever possible, enter only into agreements that allow access to and use of information, which fully support the University's mission. Users of library-licensed resources must comply with the terms of agreements, as well as with the campus-wide policy on Acceptable Use of Information Technology Resources and related guidelines (see Supporting Information Resources below).

Users should be aware that publishers/vendors may monitor use of electronic resources to ensure compliance with licensing agreements. Breach of license may enable the publisher/vendor to turn off the University's access without warning. Therefore, users must make reasonable and good faith efforts to comply with license terms in order to help ensure access to electronic resources for the entire University community.

Authorized Users

In general, authorized users of electronic resources licensed for the University of Minnesota Libraries-Twin Cities campus are defined as:

Currently enrolled Twin Cities campus students and currently employed faculty and staff members, who are entitled to on-site and remote access; and Members of the public, who are entitled to on-site access only (i.e., within a campus library).

User Responsibilities

Users of licensed resources must comply with the terms of agreements. In doing so they are expected to:

- familiarize themselves with license terms associated with specific resources, presented at the time of access;
- limit uses to non-commercial, educational, or personal research purposes;
- not facilitate unauthorized access by others (i.e., do not share their U of M Internet account password);
- not engage in large-scale systematic downloading of licensed content (e.g., downloading entire issues of electronic journals or large-scale downloading from bibliographic files to create large databases);
- not further distribute copies of material to individuals or groups outside the University of Minnesota-Twin Cities, unless the license for the resource specifically allows it;
- not share client software used to search licensed resources with individuals or groups outside the University of Minnesota-Twin Cities; and give proper attribution when quoting from material.

Note: not all licenses allow downloading and posting of articles (or other available works) from electronic resources for use in course web sites or course reserves. It is advisable to consult with the Libraries before using licensed electronic resources for such purposes. In general, it is preferable to link to articles (via an appropriate authentication mechanism) rather than to download and post articles to a server.

Dartmouth College
Dartmouth College Library
Hanover, New Hampshire

About Licensed Resources

The Library Catalog is an index to materials owned and licensed by the Dartmouth College Library; these materials include electronic journals, digital texts and internet databases. Due to licensing agreements, many digital resources have a variety of access requirements. For example, a digital resource may be restricted to members of the Dartmouth College community; another resource may only allow access from a specific machine in a specified physical location.

Who may use licensed resources?

Licensed resources that are authenticated by IP address may be accessed by students, faculty, and staff using a computer with a Dartmouth.edu IP address. Employees of the Dartmouth-Hitchcock Medical Center in Lebanon, NH with a Hitchcock.org IP address may also access these resources. To use licensed resources when off-campus, please refer to the Web page, "Access the Dartmouth College Library from Off-Campus."

Guest borrowers and visitors may access these resources when using a computer on-campus. Access to licensed resources from off-campus is not available to guest borrowers and visitors.

Licensed resources authenticated by User Name & Password (Kerberos) may be accessed by anyone using a computer with a Dartmouth.edu IP address. Employees of the Dartmouth-Hitchcock Medical Center in Lebanon, NH with a Hitchcock.org IP address may also access these resources. To use these licensed resources, you must have Kerberos / SideCar on your computer. For more information, please refer to the Web page, "Access the Dartmouth College Library from Off-Campus : Name & Password."

Guest borrowers and visitors to the Library do not have access to these resources.

Licensed resources that are only available on a specific computer in the library include resources such as CD-ROM databases as well as some Web-based resources. If you are a guest borrower or visitor and wish to use one of these resources, please contact a Reference Librarian in advance of your visit to determine if you are permitted to use the resource.

USER ACCESS TO RESERVED MATERIALS

University of Illinois at Urbana-Champaign
University of Illinois Libraries
Urbana, Illinois

Practices for Electronic Reserves

Library practices for electronic reserve reading services are derived from the fair use provisions of the United States Copyright Act of 1976. Under the guidelines listed below, Section 107 of the Copyright Act expressly permits the making of multiple copies for classroom use. The Association of Research Libraries Bimonthly Report 232, February 2004, "Applying Fair Use in the Development of Electronic Reserves Systems," served as a model for portions of these guidelines.

The University of Illinois, Urbana-Champaign Library purchases collections for the nonprofit educational use of students and faculty. All library materials are acquired with the understanding that there will be multiple uses of a limited number of copies. The Library pays premium institutional prices for many print journal subscriptions and electronic journal license agreements—prices which are many times higher than individual subscription prices—in order to support multiple academic uses. The sole purpose of the electronic reserve service is to facilitate the making of multiple copies for classroom use by students. Considered within this context, electronic reserve services were developed by the Libraries in a manner that conforms to the fair use provisions of Section 107 of the copyright law act. Those provisions are repeated here:

Notwithstanding the provisions of sections 106 and 106a, the fair use of a copyrighted work, including such use by reproduction in copies or phonorecords or by any other means specified in that section, for purposes such as criticism, comment, news reporting, teaching (including multiple copies for classroom use), scholarship or research, is not an infringement of copyright.

In determining whether the use made of a work in any particular case is a fair use the factors to be considered shall include—

- The purpose and character of the use, including whether such use is of a commercial nature or is for nonprofit educational purposes;
- The UIUC Library has implemented our e-reserve system in support of non-profit education.
- Placement of materials on electronic reserve is at the initiative of faculty solely for non-commercial, educational purposes.
- The nature of the copyrighted work;
- The e-reserve system includes multiple formats, both factual and creative. The UIUC Library takes the character of the materials into consideration in the overall assessment.
- The amount and substantiality of the portion used in relation to the copyrighted work as a whole;
- The UIUC Library considers the relationship of the amount used to the whole of the copyright owner's work.
- Because the amount that a faculty member assigns depends on many factors, such as relevance to the teaching objective and the overall amount of material assigned, the UIUC Library may also consider whether the amount, even the entire work, in some cases, is appropriate to support the lesson or make a point.
- The effect of the use upon the potential market for or value of the copyrighted work.

Materials on electronic reserve are limited to the users of the uiuc.edu domain. Other measures may be introduced to assure that only authorized users have access to the reserve materials for that course.

Material in the electronic reserves system will only be accessible by course number (e.g. LIS390) or instructor name in the online catalog and the electronic reserves services web pages.

Whenever possible, if the Library does not already own or have licensed access to the material, it will purchase materials at a reasonable price to be copied or scanned for electronic reserves.

Additional Procedures:

Copyright notices appear on screen in the online reserve system to indicate that copyright law may cover materials.

There are no charges for access. The charge for copies made by students will be limited to the nominal cost of laser printing.

Electronic files are no longer accessible from the reserve system at the end of each semester.

The Library follows the principles of Fair Use of copyrighted materials when placing materials on reserve, including the re-use of articles or book chapters from the UIUC collections or the use of materials obtained elsewhere. When in doubt about the applicability of the Fair Use standard, the Library will seek permission from the copyright holder. Materials will be placed on reserve pending the receipt of permission.

Digitizing Information for Distance Education

Materials owned on campus may be made available electronically to those UIUC students and faculty engaged in long distance education. Documents will be password protected and available for a limited number of accesses and for a limited duration before being deleted.

Digitizing Documents Obtained Though Interlibrary Loan

Documents received through ILL services electronically may be converted to standard viewing format and posted to a secure Web space. Documents will be password protected and available for a limited number of accesses and for a limited duration before being deleted.

Copyright Law and Scanners

The Library need not enforce any special regulations on the use of scanners by library users either on or off library premises. The Copyright statement on restrictions copied below applies to any reproduction. This statement is already posted on every photocopier. It is suggested that it be posted in every library with the header "This applies to scanners too."

Warning Concerning Copyright Restrictions

The Copyright law of the United States (Title 17, United States Code) governs the making of photocopies or other reproductions of copyright material. Under certain conditions specified in the law, libraries and archives are authorized to furnish a photocopy or other reproduction. One of these specified conditions is that the photocopy or reproduction not be "used for any purposes other than private study, scholarship, or research." If a user makes a request for, or later uses, a photocopy or reproduction for purposes in excess of "fair use," that user may be liable for copyright infringement.

Document Revised August 2006

Alverno College
Alverno College Library
Milwaukee, Wisconsin

The Alverno College Library offers an electronic reserves service. Instructors may request that print materials of 30 pages or less be scanned and made available in PDF format directly from TOPCAT, the library's on-line catalog. PDF stands for Portable Document Format and is a type of image file.

Students can access the Reserve materials in PDF format from the Reserve List on TOPCAT. In order to view or print documents from the electronic reserves collection students will be required to enter their Name and Library Barcode Number . Electronic reserves are available from any networked personal computer in the Library or Computer Center. Students with personal computers and Internet access will also be able to access electronic reserves from home. Adobe Acrobat Reader is required to access the reserve documents in PDF format. Adobe Acrobat Reader may be downloaded for free via the Internet.

Suggested types of documents that are appropriate for the electronic reserves collection:

- One article from a journal issue
- One chapter from a book
- Sample lab reports
- Sample assessments, tests, quizzes
- Sample field logs
- Sample research papers
- Business plans
- Lecture notes
- Copyright and Reserves provides copyright guidelines for print and electronic reserves material.

Millersville University
Helen A. Ganser Library
Millersville, Pennsylvania

Overview

Patron authentication is required to access items made available via the electronic reserve service. The patron authentication measure is intended to ensure copyright compliance for items made accessible through this service. Requests to place items on electronic reserve are subject to the Library Reserve Policy.

If you already have an electronic file . . .

If you already have an electronic version (Microsoft Word, Microsoft Excel, pdf, gif, jpg, etc.) of the document that you would like to place on reserve, simply send the document as an attachment to library.reserve@millersville.edu and include the following information in the body of the message:

Name of the Instructor
    Example: J. Robert Buchanan

Phone Number and E-Mail for the Instructor
    Example: (123)-456-7890, Differential.Equations@Millersville.edu

Course Subject, Number
    Example: MATH 345

Course Title
    Example: Ordinary Differential Equations

Semester and Year the document is to be placed on reserve.
    Example: Fall 2001

Bibliographic Information about the Document

This should include:

> Author of the document;
>
> Title of the document;
>
> Publication;
>
> Issue Information or copyright date;
>
>> Please note: The copyright date is particularly important for book chapters and any 'articles' that have been taken from a compiled resource where the header/footer information for the particular article makes reference to the FIRST place the item appeared (say a journal), but not from where the copy in hand originated (monograph of articles in honor of ...).
>
> Publisher;
>
>> An example of what we would like to see:
>> J. Robert Buchanan
>> 872-3659, Robert.Buchanan@Millersville.edu
>> MATH 345
>> Ordinary, but Unique, Differential Equations
>> Spring 2008
>>> Gauss, The Great; The History of Extraordinary Differential Equations; Journal of Interesting Mathematical Phenomena; Vol. I, Number I, April 1797, pages 1-13; Elsevier Science.
>>> Gauss, The Great; The Story of My Life; Chapter 3.14159, Blue Ocean Press; 1842.

If you already have a physical document . . .

If you already have a physical document and you would like to place that document on Electronic Reserve, please:

- Complete the Library Reserve Request (electronic item) form. One form for each document.
- Inspect the document in your physical possession to ensure that it is not mangled or crinkled and is free from beverage and/or jelly like substance stains; is free of staples; contains ALL of the pages and the textblock is present in its entirety and is of sufficient contrast for making a copy (if it's difficult for you to read, the scanner won't do any better); and the document has at least two clean edges. Margins of about a 1/2 inch all the way around would be nice as well.
- Did we say check to make sure it doesn't have any staples?
- Attach the physical document in your possession to the form with a paperclip.
- Deliver the document(s) to a person working at the Reserve Desk located on the 1st Floor of the Library, OR send your documents to the attention of "Library Reserve" via campus mail.

If the library holds the document in its collections . . .

If the library holds the document that you would like to place on electronic reserve you should:

- Utilize the Duplication Service to secure a copy. This service is available as part of library services designed Expressly for Faculty.
- Review the item in question to ensure that it is the appropriate document and that the entire document is suitable for the intended purpose.
- Complete the steps above as "If you already have an electronic file" (if you saved your document from the webpage) or "If you already have a physical document" (if you have a hard copy).

Questions or Comments

If you have any questions or comments regarding reserve services, please feel free to contact us

USER ACCESS TO RESOURCES

Drexel University
Drexel University Libraries
Philadelphia, Pennsylvania

Access to computers in the Hagerty Library for research purposes is restricted to the following:

Drexel University—Faculty, Staff, and Students, who are required to log in

Drexel Alumni—Must show alumni card

PALCI (Faculty Members ONLY)

Faculty and Students from these cooperating institutions (must show current ID):

The Restaurant School

Temple University

University of Pennsylvania

University of the Sciences in Philadelphia

Access to computers in the Health Sciences Libraries does not currently require login, but may be restricted to members of the University community during periods of high use.

Buffalo State
State University of New York
E. H. Butler Library
Buffalo, New York

Who May Access Computers

Computers in E. H. Butler Library are for the use of Buffalo State College students, faculty, staff, and emeriti faculty and staff. Each person must have a logon username and password to access a computer.

Guest logons are available only for individuals who have a temporary educational affiliation with Buffalo State College, such as visiting scholars or students from other colleges or universities. Issuance of guest passes is at the discretion of the library.

University of Arizona
Arizona Health Science Library
Tucson, Arizona

Eligible Users

All AHS Library users may use the health information resources of the Libary Computer Lab. Priority use of resources is given to groups or individuals using those resources as part of a formal instructional (curriculum-based) activity.

Use of general purpose (i.e. non-health information) software and hardware is restricted to the following groups:

UA College of Medicine, Nursing, Pharmacy and Health Professions students, faculty and staff Arizona Cancer Center, UMC and UPI staff UA Student Health Center staff Graduate students and faculty in other health-related UA programs Health care practitioners licensed in Arizona Special Notes:

In addition to belonging to one of the above groups, each person must have a current AHS Library user ID. Certain individuals, such as visiting faculty or health sciences students from other institutions, may be temporarily granted selected computer lab privileges at the discretion of the Head of the Information Services. These individuals also must have a current AHS Library user ID and abide by all applicable policies and procedures. Computer and network resources are provided for legitimate academic, administrative and health information-related purposes which further the mission of the University. The IS computer lab is subject to the CCIT Computer and Network Usage Policy and other relevant policies. Failure to abide by this policy may result in the revocation of privileges. The library reserves the right to revoke IS computer lab privileges.

Barstow Community College
Barstow Community College Library
Barstow, California

Use of the library computers is restricted to library research only. Due to the limited number of computer stations available, primary use of these resources shall be to assist students in research related to classroom assignments. Library staff reserves the right to request that users viewing potentially offensive sites leave the library.

No E-mail, word processing, homework, online discussion groups, games or chat rooms. Computer labs are available on campus for non-research activities. The closest lab is in the computer commons.

Currently enrolled students shall have priority use of all computers. A 15-minute time limit may be imposed for any workstation when others are waiting.

Printing is available for 10 cents/page. Caution: Internet screens may comprise more than one printed page.

Individual users are responsible for using the Library's resources in an ethical, non-discriminatory and lawful manner. Failure to comply with these basic policies and responsibilities can result in the loss of access privileges.

University of Minnesota
University of Minnesota Libraries
Minneapolis, Minnesota

Entitlements for Accessing Electronic Resources Licensed for the University of Minnesota Campus

The majority of online resources not-freely available are disseminated via licenses (i.e., contractual, legal agreements). Typically, the higher education community handles such licenses based on individual campuses. The University Libraries handles the majority of University of Minnesota-Twin Cities campus licenses for electronic content.

What is a licensed resource?

A licensed electronic resource is an online database to which the University Libraries subscribe through a contractual, legal agreement. These can include primary source book/journal collections as well as secondary indexing or reference type materials. The most recent count shows over 19,000 licensed electronic journals and over 190,000 licensed electronic books.

The University Libraries typically license access for the Twin Cities campus alone, as each campus has a separate library administration and budget. However, when there are significant economies to be realized for specific titles, the Libraries share licensing and associated costs with Crookston, Duluth, and Morris.

What do most licenses say about authorized users (who they are, what they can do)?

Such licenses are legally binding documents that usually require that the University Libraries limit off-campus access to current faculty, staff, and students (in credit-earning courses) at the University of Minnesota—Twin Cities. This is a non-negotiable part of the contracts the Libraries are required to sign and there are typically no fee-for-access options for persons not affiliated as such with the University.

The University Libraries has traditionally served as a major resource for the broader community. In order to maintain access to University Libraries resources, the Libraries ensure that all licenses allow the general public to access electronic resources from within Libraries' facilities. The Libraries have structured their licensing agreements with database providers to make this possible.

While each vendor has its own unique licensing language, in general most licenses allow authorized users to:

• Print / Download / Quote for teaching/research/personal uses
• Create links to specific articles rather than a resource home page (e.g. the Libraries regularly creates such "deep links" as a convenience for faculty and students as part of its Electronic Reserves service, which makes customized web pages for specific courses/classes)
• Email articles to other authorized users

How does the library/campus ensure only authorized users have access?

Because most e-resource vendors limit access to the IP numbers of campus computers, users who wish to access library-licensed e-resources from off campus should connect by clicking on library-created login links. This allows the Libraries to issue off-campus users with credentials that are recognized by the vendor. All users who access licensed e-resources through the Libraries' web site must first log in with their University Internet ID and password.

For this login to be successful, each user must have either:

• An active staff appointment that is recorded in the University's Human Resources Management System (UM HRMS)
• A current student admission or registration that is recorded in the Office of the Registrar's web registration system (including the Graduate School zero-credit registration)

These users make up the official FTE count of U M Twin Cities students that is typically reported to library vendors as the basis for e-resource license fees. Once properly recorded by the UM HRMS or Registrar, each current staff/student will have a library access entitlement or "flag" automatically added to his/her University Internet (X.500) account.

For example, a student who is no longer registered would thus be unable to access licensed library resources remotely; he/she could, of course, use the resources inside any campus library as a member of the public. Although the University currently keeps student email accounts active (at no charge) for up to 5 years after the last registration, this extension of email privileges does not include remote access to licensed library resources.

What specifically is needed in the University's Human Resources Management System?

Each current staff member should have one of these employment categories or groups associated with his/her UM HRMS record. If a person has a current University of Minnesota—Twin Cities staff appointment, but is unable to log in to a library-licensed database, he/she should contact the departmental Human Resources office and ask that they verify that his/her UM HRMS record carries one of the following associations.

Pre-Start Hire
Regular CS/BU
Regular P&A

Regular Faculty

Temporary Posted

Temporary No-Post (CS/BU)

NASTE (CS/BU) Academic (P&A and Faculty) without salary, with appointment

Clinical Faculty without salary, with appointment

Retirees (CS/BU)

Retirees (P&A)

Retirees (Faculty)

Regents

Visiting Faculty or P&A without salary, with appointment

Note: not just any type of appointment will do; even if it is a "non-salary" appointment, the staffer in question needs to be providing a service to the University to "count." For example, a "sponsored account" does not officially document a service relationship with the University of Minnesota and is thus not eligible for remote access to the Libraries' electronic resources. Visiting Faculty (who may also be referred to as Industrial Fellows, Community-based Faculty, or similar names) can get entered into PeopleSoft in varying ways, but only those who provide a service to the University that meets the Human Resources criteria for one of the "with appointment" statuses above qualify for remote access.

If your department has already submitted a request for a PeopleSoft staff account and they need to follow up on or troubleshoot the request, or if they need assistance of any kind, they should call the University Human Resources Department's Helpline at: _____.

What about off-campus programs or more loosely affiliated individuals? Are there ways to get them access?

Distance from the Twin Cities campus does not matter. The primary requirement is that individuals have an official, properly documented service/student relationship with the University. For individuals affiliated through a University program, the relevant unit or academic department must make this determination of affiliation. Designations of affiliation can then be recorded in the UM HRMS by his/her departmental HR office.

What about summer institutes/programs run by departments?

The temporary / seasonal nature of summer programs does not matter. Any type of visiting staff must still have an official University appointment, recorded in PeopleSoft. Note that such an appointment can be "without salary, with appointment."

Any type of visiting student must still be registered through the Office of the Registrar. Departments who need assistance in setting up a registration protocol for their summer program should contact OTR directly.

Are there any "special cases"?

Though the Medical School, Duluth, and the College of Pharmacy, Duluth, are on the Duluth campus, they are integral parts of the Academic Health Center, Twin Cities. Thus Duluth's med school staff and affiliated students carry associated Twin Cities Library access privileges.

Also, some Duluth faculty are formal advisors for Twin Cities graduate students. As such, they are considered dual appointment staff and carry both Duluth and Twin Cities Library access privileges. Any faculty with multiple appointments across campuses should obtain the library privileges for each campus (e.g. a Crookston faculty member who is also a faculty member in the Twin Cities campus Extension Service thus gets both Crookston and Twin Cities access privileges).

The Rochester campus is considered administratively part of the Twin Cities, so their staff/students have the same remote access privileges as Twin Cities-based users.

I have a proxy borrowing card to do research for a faculty member. Can I also get remote access?

No. The U Libraries' Proxy Card is for checking out materials only. Borrowing privileges do not extend to library-licensed databases, which are governed by legally binding contracts with publishers. Also, bear in mind that sharing of one's U of M Internet account password with anyone is forbidden by University policy and by our database contracts.

Who is responsible for enabling access to licensed resources?

Unit

Task

Department

Assign staff/faculty affiliations as part of formal appointment process

Office of Human Resources

Record the department's staff appointments in UM HRMS

Office of Admissions

Record student admissions in UM HRMS

Office of the Registrar

Record student registrations in UM web registration system

Office of Information Technology

Assign library access entitlements in Internet X500 account based on UM HRMS data

University Libraries

Select information resources; create access links that require X500 authentication

Q. Can undergraduate students who are not currently enrolled in courses access your databases and e-journals from outside the library?

A. Unregistered undergraduate students are welcome to use the U-MN Libraries' resources on-site. The public is also welcome in our libraries for use of on-site collections and most facilities. We have structured our licensing agreements with database providers to make this possible. You do not need a card or pass to use our libraries. You may read materials in the Libraries or make photocopies of needed pages.

Q. Can graduate students who are working on their theses or dissertations but are not currently enrolled in courses check out books, use interlibrary loan, or access library databases?

A. Graduate School students holding active student status receive full library privileges, including remote access to licensed library resources.

Note that, according to the Graduate School registration policy, students must be registered every fall and spring term to maintain their active student status. The Graduate School's web site describes the registration policy and registration options (e.g., thesis credits or Grad 999—a zero-credit, zero-fee, non-graded registration option) that satisfy the registration requirement.

Students who are registered for spring term will have access during summer term, even if they are not registered during the summer.

Graduate students who do not register through the Graduate School, and who are working on a thesis or dissertation but are not currently enrolled in courses, may still be eligible to receive full library privileges. For this you will need to complete the University Libraries' "Unregistered Graduate Student" form which ultimately needs to be approved by your faculty advisor.

Although the University currently keeps student email accounts active (at no charge) for up to 5 years after the last registration, this extension of email privileges does not include remote access to licensed library resources. To comply with our binding publisher license agreements, library access rights as reflected in one's University Internet account expire at the end of the last semester for which one is registered.

Cabrillo College
Robert E. Swenson Library
Aptos, California

Primary User group

Students, faculty and staff at Cabrillo College constitute the Library's primary user group. Other library patrons may use the Library's computers and other equipment if primary user group patrons are not waiting for them.

University of Illinois at Urban-Champaign
University of Illinois Libraries
Urbana, Illinois

Definitions

Our primary user base is the UIUC community (faculty, students, and staff). This policy recognizes that there is a larger user community that is defined by University policy, consortia agreements and contractual obligations.

For the purposes of this policy electronic information is any electronic resource that is made available by the UIUC Library or that is accessible through Library workstations.

A Library workstation is a workstation that is physically located in and maintained by the UIUC Library.

USER RESOURCES DEFINITIONS

Lafayette Public Library
Lafayette, Louisiana

Definitions:

A user or patron is described by the Library as an adult or minor who uses the Library's facilities, resources, and/or materials, including both cardholders and non-cardholders.

"Child pornography" as defined in 18 U.S.C. 2256.

"Minor" is a person under the age of 17. 47 U.S.C.A. 254(h)(7)(D). "Harmful to minors" as defined in 47 U.S.C.A. 254(h)(7)(D). "Obscenity" as defined by the federal obscenity statue, 18 U.S.C. 2256.

"Sexual act" and "Sexual contact" as defined in 18 U.S.C. 2246.

Chapter 15

ACCESS OPTIONS

LOCAL AND REMOTE ACCESS

Dartmouth College
Dartmouth College Library
Hanover, New Hampshire

Remote Access to Resources

Bibliographers may also provide access to and inform users about electronic information resources located outside Dartmouth. Those resources include: catalogs; bibliographic, text, numeric, sound, image and data files; software; discussion lists, etc.

External data sources available via Telnet, Gopher, Mosaic are selected based upon expected utility and ease of access. Proven stability of the resource, and the host institution's intention to maintain an archive, are important factors for a bibliographer to consider when deciding to provide remote access. In general, if a desired resource is maintained and made accessible at a remote host site, it is preferable to provide a pointer to it within the Dartmouth College Information System rather than store archival files on-site.

In general, the provision of full bibliographic control via the library's Online Catalog is limited to materials that are owned and stored locally (including on the Library Fileserver). Resources that are pointed to will generally not be cataloged, unless the connection requires expenditure of materials funds.

A number of factors influence how access to external information is provided:

- means of access
- telnet, ftp, Gopher, Mosaic, Netscape, Wais
- hardware and software requirements to get and receive files
- file characteristics
- size, type—image, text, sound, data, etc.
- database search capabilities
- type of indexes
- expected frequency of potential use
  this may help bibliographers decide if the resource should be made available in the Navigator (implies frequent use) or in the Gopher (less-than-regular use)
- options for saving text, viewing or browsing

Bibliographers should refer identified external resources available through the Internet to the Internet Resources Subcommittee of LOSC. Subscription materials available over the Internet should be processed through normal acquisitions channels.

Dartmouth College
Dartmouth College Library
Hanover, New Hampshire

Local Access to Resources

A.1. Access via the Network

This provides the broadest access to our users. When files are mounted using the existing DCIS/DCLOS interface, it also provides a familiar method of searching. This is often the preferred method of access, but licensing fees and mainframe storage costs necessitate a discretionary selection process.

As a general rule, the Library supports network access for materials of utility to the greatest number of Dartmouth users. Interdisciplinary materials of use to a variety of users in diverse locations also receive priority treatment. Those databases which provide enhanced bibliographic access to existing library collections [i.e. Early American Imprints, Marcive, Wilson Indexes] are also appropriate for networking campuswide.

When bibliographers wish to recommend an electronic resource be networked on DCLOS, they should discuss the feasibility of mounting the resource with the Director of Library Automation. If it is more appropriate to DCIS because of the need to use PAT or another search and retrieval software, they should discuss the proposal with the DCIS Project Director. Cost estimates for both the staff resources to mount the files and the disk space to store them should be assessed. If funding is available to support the acquisition, and the material can be networked within the Dartmouth environment, a proposal detailing costs and benefits should be submitted to the CMDC sub-committee which we propose in this document.

A.2. Access via the Fileserver

The Dartmouth Fileserver predates the existence of Gopher and other Worldwide Web servers widely available today on the Internet. Computing Services have set up a Gopher and a Mosaic Home Page at Dartmouth, and the Library has experimented with their utility as document storage mechanisms and as links to other resources.

For the present, resources that are useful to have on the network, but are kept as documents and are not indexed/searchable files, may be stored on the Public Fileserver/Library folder. Materials archived in this manner should be represented in the Online Catalog, with the necessary location to link the user to the resource.

B. Access via Networked CD-ROM

Resources that are of interest to a more limited clientele, or to a group of users primarily served by an individual library within the Dartmouth College Library, should be considered in a CD-ROM format. If access via one workstation is not sufficient to meet demand, or if providing ease of access to clientele linked by an existing local network is an important factor, the Bibliographer should consider purchasing a license agreement to network the CD-ROM product.

C. Access via Stand-Alone Workstation

Electronic products of interest to a limited number of users, or those difficult to network due to the size of the data, restrictive licensing agreements, specialized software needed for operation, prohibitive cost, etc., should be considered for purchase in a stand-alone workstation environment.

Texas A&M Corpus Christi
Mary and Jeff Bell Library
Corpus Christi, Texas

Principal access points and provision of access

In order to provide consistent, useful access to electronic resources, the library designates a single, primary principal access point for each type of resource (web page, e-journal, and database).

Principal access points for databases

The principal access point for databases is the library databases page (http://rattler.tamucc.edu/elecres/index.php) where databases are presented alphabetically by title and in subject groupings and resource type groupings. The library's ability to present subject and resource type groupings will be improved (categories expanded, etc.) with the full implementation and integration of the Metalib federated search tool into the library website.

Principal access points for e-books

The principal access points for individual e-books is the library online catalog, Portal.

Principal access points for e-journals

The principal access point for e-journals is the Periodical Holdings List. With the establishment of the SFX OpenURL link resolver and the online Periodical Holdings List, providing access to e-journals, particularly online collections of e-journals is no longer necessary.

Principal access points for websites

The principal access point for web sites are subject guides and departmental web pages.

University of Minnesota
University of Minnesota Libraries
Minneapolis, Minnesota

REMOTE ACCESS TO LIBRARIES' ELECTRONIC RESOURCES

Due to vendor licensing restrictions, access to many of the Libraries' databases from outside a University library (e.g., from home or workplace) is limited to current students (in credit-earning courses), staff, and faculty at the University of Minnesota–Twin Cities. This is a non-negotiable part of the contracts we sign (and there are no fee-for-access options for persons not affiliated with the University). Although the University currently keeps student email accounts active (at no charge) for up to 5 years after the last registration, this extension of email privileges does not include remote access to licensed library resources.

Once you are listed in the U of M Student-Staff Directory as being currently registered for classes, you should once again be entitled to remote access to library databases. To comply with our binding publisher license agreements, library access rights as reflected in one's University Internet account expire at the end of the last semester for which one is registered.

Chapter 16

USER ACCESS FUNDAMENTALS

ACCEPTABLE AND UNACCEPTABLE USE OF ELECTRONIC RESOURCES

University of Dayton
Roesch Library
Dayton, Ohio

Preamble:

The purpose of this document is to establish and promote the ethical, legal, and secure use of computing and electronic communications for all members of the University community.

The University of Dayton cherishes freedom of expression, the diversity of values and perspectives inherent in an academic institution, the right to acknowledgment, and the value of privacy for all members of the UD community. At the same time, the University may find it necessary to access and disclose information from computer and network users' accounts to the extent required by law, to uphold contractual obligations or other applicable University policies, or to diagnose and correct technical problems. For these reasons, among others, the ultimate privacy of messages and files cannot be ensured. In addition, system failures may lead to loss of data, so users should not assume that their messages and files are secure.

Although the University does not typically block access to online content, it reserves the right to do so in cases where online content or activity diminishes the capacity of our network or threatens the welfare of the University of Dayton or its core academic mission. While the University does not position itself as a censor, it reserves the right to limit access to its networks or to remove material stored or posted on University computers when applicable University policies, contractual obligations, or state or federal laws are violated. Alleged violations will be treated with the same fundamental fairness as any other alleged violation of University policy, contractual obligations, or state or federal laws.

Appropriate portions of this document were developed in accordance with the Digital Millennium Copyright Act of 1998, which can be referenced at the following web site:

http://www.copyright.gov/legislation/dmca.pdf.

University of Dayton
Policy on Fair, Responsible and Acceptable Use of Electronic Resources

1. Introduction

The University of Dayton (UD) values technology as a means of communicating information and ideas to the University community and the world. In keeping with the University's commitment to utilizing technology in teaching and learning, this policy provides direction in the appropriate use of all forms of electronic resources on campus. This document articulates the University of Dayton Policy on Fair, Responsible and Acceptable Use of Electronic Resources, provides example violations and outlines procedures for reporting, addressing, sanctioning and appealing policy violations.

2. Definitions

For the purposes of this policy, electronic resources are defined as all computer-related equipment, computer systems, software/network applications, interconnecting networks, facsimile machines, voicemail and other telecommunications facilities, as well as all information contained therein (collectively, "electronic resources") owned or managed by the University.

3. General Restrictions and Disclaimers

While the use of University of Dayton electronic resources may be a requirement for coursework and work, access and use may be restricted or revoked in cases of misuse or repeated abuse. University of Dayton reserves the right to limit access to its electronic resources when applicable University policies, state and/or federal laws or contractual obligations are violated. The University does not, as a rule, monitor the content of materials transported over the University's network or information posted on University-owned computers and networks, but reserves the right to do so. Although the University does not typically block access to online content, it reserves the right to do so in cases where online content or activity diminishes the capacity of our network, or where there is a threat to the University of Dayton or its core academic mission. University of Dayton provides reasonable security against intrusion and damage to files stored on the central computing facilities, but does not guarantee that its computer systems are secure. The University of Dayton may not be held accountable for unauthorized access by other users, nor can the University guarantee protection against media failure, fire, floods, or other natural or man-made disasters.

4. Persons Covered by this Policy

This policy applies to all users of computer resources owned or managed by University of Dayton, including, but not limited to, UD faculty and visiting faculty, staff, students, external persons or organizations and individuals accessing external network services, such as the Internet and Intranet.

5. Use of Resources

All users of University of Dayton electronic resources are expected to utilize such resources in a responsible, ethical and legal manner consistent with University of Dayton mission and policies. As a user of University of Dayton electronic resources, you agree to be subject to the guidelines of this Policy on Fair, Responsible and Acceptable Use of Electronic Resources.

6. Policies on Fair, Responsible and Acceptable Use

The following policy statements, in Bold Italics, are accompanied by specific examples that highlight types of activities that constitute unfair, irresponsible or unacceptable use of UD electronic resources. That document is called "Guidelines for Interpreting the Policy." Please note that these examples are provided for the purpose of illustrating each policy's intent and are not intended to be an exhaustive list of all possible scenarios within the policy framework.

> 6a) University of Dayton electronic resources may not be used to damage, impair, disrupt or in any way cause purposeful or reckless damage to University of Dayton networks or computers or external networks or computers.

> 6b) Unauthorized access, reproduction or use of the resources of others is prohibited.

> 6c) Use of University of Dayton electronic resources to interfere with or cause impairment to the activities of other individuals is prohibited.

> 6d) Use of University of Dayton electronic resources to harass or make threats to specific individuals, or a class of individuals, is prohibited.

> 6e) Use of University of Dayton electronic resources in pursuit of unauthorized commercial activities is prohibited.

6f) Use of University of Dayton electronic resources to violate city, state, federal or international laws, rules, regulations, rulings or orders, or to otherwise violate any University rules or policies is prohibited.

7. Reporting and Response to Violations

Members of the University of Dayton community who believe they have witnessed or been a victim of a violation of the University's Policy on Fair, Responsible and Acceptable Use of Electronic Resources should notify or file a complaint with the appropriate University office as follows:

- Students should report suspected violations to the Office of Computing Ethics.
- Faculty members should report suspected violations to their Dean or the Dean's designated contact.
- Staff should report violations to their supervisor. If the unit authority determines that a violation likely has occurred, this violation should be reported as follows:
  - to the Office of the Provost (if the violation involves students or academic faculty/staff) or
  - to the Office of Human Resources (if the violation involves staff from non-academic units).

Designated persons in the Provost and Human Resources offices are responsible for recording, tracking and reporting violations to the appropriate UD officials in accordance with the University Grievance Policy and/or the Standard Judicial Process.

8. Appeal procedures

Those individuals who are found in violation of the policy may submit a written statement of appeal the same as any other grievance cases to the following:

- Students follow the Standard Judicial Process;
- Faculty and academic "staff/administrative units" can appeal to the Dean or Provost;
- Staff in non-academic units can appeal to their Supervisor or HR representative.

(For additional policies, please see the accompanying CD-ROM.)

PASSWORDS

The University of Kansas
University of Kansas Libraries
Lawrence, Kansas

Policy Title: Password Policy

Policy Purpose:

The purpose of this policy is to establish a standard for creation of strong passwords, the protection of those passwords, and the frequency of password change.

Applies To:

The scope of this policy includes: (1) all personnel who are responsible for an account (or any form of access that supports or requires a password) on any system that resides at any University of Kansas facility, (2) all individuals who have access to the University of Kansas network, and (3) all systems that store any non-public KU information.

Policy Statement:

Passwords are an essential aspect of computer security, providing important front-line protection for electronic resources by preventing unauthorized access. Passwords help the University limit unauthorized or inappropriate access to various resources at the University of Kansas, including user-level accounts, web accounts, email accounts, screen saver protection, and local router logins.

A poorly chosen password may result in the compromise of University systems, data or network. Therefore, all KU students, faculty and staff are responsible for taking the appropriate steps, as outlined below, to select appropriate passwords and protect them. Contractors and vendors with access to university systems also are expected to observe these requirements.

A department and/or system administrator may implement a more restrictive policy on local systems where deemed appropriate or necessary for the security of electronic information resources. The Information Technology Security Office can require a more restrictive policy in protection of confidential data.

Creation of Passwords

Passwords created by users of University systems, and on systems where technology makes it possible, should conform to the following guidelines:

- Must be different than the user's login name or the reverse of the name and must avoid use of knowable personal information (names of family, etc.).
- Must be at least seven characters.
- Must include digits (0-9), and both upper and lower case characters (a-z, A-Z).
- Must use a special character (for example,* & % $)

For additional assistance in creating a secure password, please refer to http://www.security.ku.edu.

These provisions will be enforced electronically whenever possible.

Changing passwords

Passwords should be changed once a semester (Fall and Spring). The new password must differ from the old password by at least three characters. Passwords are not allowed to be repeated within one year.

In addition:

Those entities that are required to be Payment Card Industry (PCI) Data Security Standard (DSS) or Health Insurance Portability and Accountability Act (HIPAA) compliant by the Information Technology Security Office shall require their user passwords to be changed at a minimum every 90 days.

Those entities that are required to be PCI/DSS or HIPAA compliant by the Information Technology Security Office shall require that their users may not use a new password that is the same as any of the last four passwords.

Protecting a password

Passwords should be treated as confidential university information.

Passwords should never be written down or posted for reference.

Passwords should not be included in email messages or other forms of electronic communication.

Sharing a password

Sharing or allowing another person to use an individual account password is a violation of this policy, unless the person is an information technology professional assisting you with a technical problem. Departmental account passwords should be shared only with appropriate departmental personnel.

Passwords may be shared via phone when necessary. However, users need to beware of "Phishing" or other social engineering scams where a user may have his or her password requested over the phone. University information technology personnel (i.e, IT Customer Service Center, Information Technology, IT

Security Office, Technical Liaisons), as a best practice, do not normally request a user's password over the phone. Phone communications may be necessary with external information technology vendors.

It is recommended that passwords be changed after allowing use as permitted in this section.

Approval of the University's IT Security Office is required prior to sharing a password with a vendor (approval may be granted on a one-time or continuing basis), and this vendor access may require implementing the appropriate technology infrastructure to accommodate the access (depending on the circumstance, and as determined by ITSO).

Reporting a password compromise
- Suspected compromises of passwords must be reported immediately to the KU Information Technology Customer Service Center at 4-8080.
- The password in question should be changed immediately.

Responsibilities of Information Technology Security Office

The ITSO may require a more restrictive policy, such as stronger passwords, in some circumstances.

The ITSO or its delegates may perform password assessments on a periodic or random basis. If a password is guessed or cracked during one of these assessments, the ITSO will promptly notify the listed contact and require that the password be changed.

Consequences

Any individual who violates this policy may lose computer or network access privileges and may be subject to disciplinary action in accordance with and subject to appropriate University policy and procedures, which may result in a range of sanctions up to and including suspension or dismissal for repeated or serious infractions.

University of Minnesota
University of Minnesota Libraries
Minneapolis, Minnesota

Using Information Technology Resources Standards

Use of IDs and Passwords

Do not share the password assigned to you.

Select an obscure password and change it frequently.

Understand that you are responsible for all activities on your username/account ID.

Ensure that others cannot learn your password.

If you have reason to believe that your username/account ID or password has been compromised, contact your System/Network Administrator immediately.

Use of Information/Data

Access only accounts, files, and data that are your own, that are publicly available, or to which you have been given authorized access. Secure information that is in your possession.

Maintain the confidentiality of information classified as private, confidential or data on decedents.

Use University information for tasks related to job responsibilities and not for personal purposes.

Never disclose information to which you have access, but for which you do not have ownership, authority, or permission to disclose. Keep your personal information/data current.

Accurately update your own records through University self-service systems and other processes provided for you.

Use of Software and Hardware

Use University e-mail, computers, and networks only for legal, authorized purposes. Unauthorized or illegal uses include but are not limited to:

- Harassment;
- Destruction of or damage to equipment, software, or data belonging to others;
- Unauthorized copying of copyrighted materials; or
- Conducting private business unrelated to University activities.

Never engage in any activity that might be harmful to systems or to any information/data stored thereon, such as:

- Creating or propagating viruses;
- Disrupting services or damaging files; or
- Making unauthorized or non-approved changes.

When vacating computer workstations, sign-off or secure the system from unauthorized use.

Use only legal versions of copyrighted software on University of Minnesota owned computer or network resources, in compliance with vendor license requirements.

Be aware of any conditions attached to or affecting the provision of University technology services:

Consult with the system administrator for any questions about system workload or performance.

Refrain from monopolizing systems, overloading systems or networks with excessive data, or wasting computer time, connect time, disk space, printer paper, manuals, or other resources.

For situations not covered here, contact your system/network administrator or departmental computer contact.

RESPONSIBLE USE OF LICENSED RESOURCES

Michigan State University
Michigan State University Libraries
East Lansing, Michigan

Notice to users of licensed databases: Prohibition of commercial use, and guidelines for acceptable use

The MSU Libraries subscribe to licensed database products to support the educational and research needs of library users. In some cases, these databases are educational versions of commercial products. Users are advised that access to these materials is controlled by license agreements: violation of license terms by individual library users potentially jeopardizes future campus access for all students and faculty, and exposes violators to sanctions.

The content of this database is made available only for the individual educational and research purposes of authorized users. By proceeding to the database itself, you as the user are indicating that you are aware of the following terms and conditions, and agree to conduct your use of this material accordingly.

Uses that are allowed:
- You may use the database for purposes of academic research or private study only.
- You may browse and search the database, and display its contents on the screen.
- You may make and save a digital copy of limited extracts from the database for academic purposes.

- You may print out copies of limited extracts from the database for academic purposes.
- You may reproduce or quote limited portions of the database contents for reports, essays, projects, and similar materials created for academic purposes, with appropriate acknowledgement of the source (such as footnotes, endnotes or other citations).

These limited extracts may be shared with other academic users.

Uses that are NOT allowed:

- You may not sell or otherwise re-distribute data to third parties without express permission.
- You may not use the database or any part of the information comprised in the database content for commercial research, for example, research that is done under a funding or consultant contract, internship, or other relationship in which the results are delivered to a for-profit organization.
- You may not engage in bulk reproduction or distribution of the licensed materials in any form.

Extensive downloading or copying, such as the use of spiders, is a violation of license terms.

Under some circumstances, violation of these guidelines could lead to loss of your right to use the campus network, in accord with MSU's Statement on Acceptable Use of Computing Systems

Michigan State University
Michigan State University Libraries
East Lansing, Michigan

Terms of Use for E-Journals and other Electronic Resources

The MSU Libraries subscribe to numerous electronic journals, databases and similar resources through licenses. The publishers and distributors of these resources require compliance with the terms and conditions of use of these products. Violation of the terms of use may result in loss of access to the resource and termination of library privileges. With some exceptions, access is limited to current MSU students, faculty and staff and to members of the general public on a walk-in basis, for non-commercial research purposes. Keep the following guidelines in mind:

TYPICAL TERMS OF USE

Generally Permitted

- making limited printed or electronic copies
- using for personal, instructional or research needs
- sharing with MSU students, faculty, and staff
- posting links to specific content

Generally Not Permitted

- systematic or substantial printing, copying or downloading (such as entire journal issues or books)
- selling or re-distributing content, or providing it to an employer
- sharing with people other than MSU students, faculty, and staff
- posting content or articles to web sites or listservs
- modifying, altering, or creating derivative works

Individual licenses and copyright law are more specific than these guidelines. Many resources post a "terms of use" link for users to view their rights. When in doubt about use or for questions, please contact Distance Learning Services or a Subject Bibliographer. All use is governed by the MSU Acceptable Use Policy and academic standards regarding plagiarism.

USER RIGHTS

Dakota State University
Karl E. Mundt Library
Madison, South Dakota

Library Patron's Rights

Library patrons have the right to confidentiality and privacy in the use of electronic information to the extent possible, given certain constraints such as proximity of other patrons and staff in public settings, security weaknesses inherent in electronic communications, and the library's need to conduct periodic use studies.

Library patrons have the right of equitable access to electronic information networks in support of the educational, research, and public service mission of the University, subject to the constraints of equipment availability.

University of Illinois at Urbana-Champaign
University of Illinois Libraries
Urbana, Illinois

Library Patron's Rights

Library patrons have the right to confidentiality and privacy in the use of electronic information to the extent possible, given certain constraints such as proximity of other patrons and staff in public settings, security weaknesses inherent in electronic communications, and the library's need to conduct periodic use studies.

Library patrons have the right of equitable access to electronic information networks in support of the educational, research, and public service mission of the University, subject to the constraints of equipment availability.

Chapter 17

WIRELESS ACCESS

GENERAL GUIDELINES

Aurora Public Library
Aurora, Colorado

Wireless Access at Aurora Public Libraries

I. WIRELESS SECURITY.

A. The Library's wireless network is an open network, and therefore not secure. The Library cannot guarantee the safety of your computer's communication across its wireless network.

B. The Library assumes no responsibility for the configurations, security or files on your laptop or wireless device resulting from connecting to the Library's network. Information sent to or from your wireless device can be intercepted by anyone else with a wireless device and appropriate software, within the range of the Library's wireless access point.

II. WIRELESS TECHNICAL SUPPORT.

A. The Library is unable to provide technical assistance to you regarding wireless access, and there is no guarantee that you will be able to make a wireless connection. If you need assistance, contact the manufacturer of your wireless device or software.

B. The Library is not responsible for any changes you make to your computer's settings, and recommends that you copy or make a note of any settings before you change them.

III. USING WIRELESS IN THE LIBRARY.

A. Aurora Public Libraries use the WiFi standard (also known as IEEE 802.11b).

B. You will need to bring your own wireless device to the Library, and it will need to have built-in WiFi or you will need to install your own WiFi netword card. The Library does not have wireless devices available for public use.

C. Most WiFi equipment will be compatible. However, the Library makes no guarantees as to compatibility of your hardware with the Library's network.

D. Printers are not part of wireless accessibility in the Library. If you need to print, you will need to save your work to a floppy disk or thumb drive, then log in to a public PC and send your print job(s) to the printer.

Orion Township Public Library
Lake Orion, Michigan

Wireless Internet Access

The Orion Township Public Library provides wireless internet access to our patrons on their laptops or other wireless-enabled mobile devices for web and email access.

As with most public wireless "hot spots," the library's wireless connection is not secure. Cautious and informed wireless users should choose not to transmit their credit card information, passwords and any other sensitive personal information while using any wireless "hot spot."

The library will not be responsible for any information (i.e. credit card) that is compromised, or for any damage caused to your hardware or software due to power surges, security issues or consequences caused by viruses or hacking. All wireless access users should have up-to-date virus protection on their laptop computers or wireless devices. Anti-virus and security protection are the responsibility of the patron.

Laptop computer users must be considerate of patrons nearby and refrain from excessive noise including the playing of music or movies on the laptop without the use of headphones.

The Library is not responsible for laptops left unattended.

Printing is not available over the wireless network. Patrons may save files to storage media and print from a Library computer.

The library does not filter the wireless access, which is available to anyone with a compatible laptop computer or other wireless-enabled mobile device, including children. Parents wishing filtered access for their children should direct their children to one of the library's public access computers or purchase filtering software for their computer.

Wireless users must comply with all provisions of the Orion Township Public Library Internet policy. Any activities deemed illegal apply to you whether you are on a Library-owned computer or your own computer.

Unacceptable uses include:

- Users shall not intentionally develop programs that harass other users or infiltrate a computer or computing system or damage or alter the software components of this or other computing systems.
- Users shall not use the Library's Internet access for any purpose that violates U.S. or State laws, to transmit threatening, obscene or harassing materials, or child pornography. Users shall not interfere with or disrupt network users, services or equipment. Disruptions include, but not limited to, distribution of unsolicited advertising, propagation of computer worms and viruses, and using the wired or wireless networks to make unauthorized entry to any other machine accessible via the network.
- Users may not represent themselves as another person.

Malicious use is not acceptable. Use of the Internet in the library in a manner that precludes or significantly hampers its use by others is not allowed.

Failure to follow guidelines of the Internet policy may result in expulsion from the library.

Boise Public Library
Boise, Idaho

Wireless Access Policy

The library provides free wireless unfiltered access points at the main library for public Internet access. These access points will allow users to connect to the Internet from their laptop computers when sitting within range of the access points.

Wireless users agree to abide by the Library's Internet Policy while using the Library's wireless network.

Users are responsible for configuring their own equipment. The library does not provide technical support for establishing or maintaining a connection nor equipment configurations. The library is not responsible for any changes made to an individual computer's settings and does not guarantee that a user's hardware will work with the library's wireless connection.

The Library is not responsible for any personal information (e.g., credit card) that is compromised, or for any damage caused to hardware or software due to electric surges, security issues or consequences caused by viruses or hacking. All wireless access users are individually responsible for maintaining up-to-date virus protection on personal laptop computers or wireless devices.

Plainfield—Guilford Township Public Library
Plainfield, Indiana

Wireless at the Library

We have a wireless network available to the public so that people with mobile devices can connect to the Internet. Please be aware that this is a "hot-spot"—there is no security in place. Just as you can pick up a radio signal on any radio, someone who is "sniffing" the wireless signals here can pick up anything being transmitted. While this is unlikely to be happening, the library's public wireless network is not the place to do your online banking. We do have filters in place to prevent a computer on the wireless network from attempting to access (hack) another computer on the same network.

River Falls Public Library
River Falls, Wisconsin

Wireless Internet Access Policy

WiFi Is Here: Wireless Internet Access at the River Falls Public Library

The River Falls Public Library now offers wireless "WiFi" access to the Library's Internet service for properly equipped laptops. When you use the Internet in the Library you are accepting the library's Internet Policy.

(Please take the time to read the policy before accessing the network.)

Advantages
- No waiting for a free PC
- No enforced time limits . . . connect as long as you like
- Spread out at a larger table in a quieter area of the building
- Fast access
- Save your files permanently on your own device

Limitations
- You must follow the library's Internet Policy.
- No printing services are available
- A WiFi network is less secure than a wired network (see below)
- Signal strength varies within the Library

802.11b, Also Known as WiFi

Your laptop must conform to the "802.11b" standard, commonly known as "WiFi". New laptops often come standard with a wireless interface. These laptops usually come automatically configured to pick up the wireless signal. Older laptops with a PCMCIA slot or USB port can be fitted with a wired/wireless network interface card (NIC) for about $80 or even less.

Where You Can Pick Up the Wireless Signal

The entire building is not wireless accessible—the library steel shelving interferes with the wireless signal. But you should be able to pick up the wireless signal in most areas of the library.

What You Will Need
- Wireless network interface card (NIC). Please note that the Library cannot assist you with your laptop, card, or configuration.
- A laptop configured to use the Library's Internet connection (see directions).

- Charged battery—the library has some accessible electrical outlets near some tables, but not all.
- Compatible headphones if you plan to use audio files. Inexpensive headphones may be available at the Reference Desk.

How Safe is WiFi?

The Internet is a public communications network, which means that there can be untrusted parties between you and anybody you communicate with. WiFi unplugs the Internet and makes personal security risks more visible. WiFi poses the same risks to your personal information that a wired network poses, as well as some new risks. WiFi users need to educate themselves about these risks, and take steps to secure their personal information. Cautious WiFi users may choose not to transmit their credit card information and passwords while using any WiFi "hotspot," including the Library's. The Library cannot assure the safety of your data when you use either our wired or wireless Internet access.

Wireless Technical Information

Wireless hardware and software varies as to the operating systems you may use on your laptop, so we can't give you precise instructions. In many cases, you need to do nothing to hook up (just click on Netscape or Internet Explorer), but you might need to check the following in your wireless software:

- In Network Neighborhood Properties (right click on Network Neighborhood and click on "Properties") click on the Wireless TCP/IP adapter setting and look at its properties. Ensure that you have checked "Obtain an IP address automatically." See directions.
- If you use Windows 2000 or XP and have more than one adaptor, you may have to disable the one you are not using.
- If you are using Windows NT, 2000, or XP, you will need to have administrative rights to change network settings.
- Some adaptors have a physical switch (very small) that must be turned on in order to connect to the Internet
- Most wireless software has an indicator that tells you a signal is being received. Make sure the link quality and signal strength are both at least "good." If not, move about the room to a location that has a stronger signal.
- Click on Netscape or Internet Explorer and the Internet should come right up!

Please note that the Library cannot assist you with your laptop, wireless network card, or configuration. The Library cannot accept the liability of handling your equipment.

Great Falls Public Library
Great Falls, Montana

The library offers free Wi-Fi (wireless) Internet access to patrons bringing in their own wireless-equipped laptops.

What you need to know about using the library's wireless network:

- You are responsible for the configuration of your own equipment
- GFPL staff will not provide any assistance or recommendations regarding configuring or troubleshooting your equipment
- No printing services are available
- Audio output must be muted or directed to your headphones
- The coverage area is approximately the whole building
- Signal strength and connection speed may vary in some areas
- A wireless connection is less secure than a wired connection

Users are responsible for understanding the risks. Great Falls Public Library cannot assure the security of your data when you use any of the publicly available PCs or the wireless network

Any activity that violates library policy regarding library-owned computers is also prohibited on user-owned equipment that is connected to the wireless network. Violation of any part of these policies may result in loss of Internet and/or library computer privileges.

Charlevoix Public Library
Charlevoix, Michigan

General Wireless Access Guidelines

Free wireless Internet access is available to laptops equipped with an 802.11b or 802.11g wireless card.

Wireless Internet access will allow you to:
- Have immediate Internet access using your own computer rather than waiting for an available library computer
- Connect to the Internet without time limits
- Download files onto your own computer
- Use your own software and have access to your own files

Be aware:
- Wireless users must comply with our Computer and Internet Policy waiting for an available library computer
- Although the wireless hub is routed through our firewall, the wireless connection is less secure than a hard-wired connection. Be a savvy user! (See below)
- Printing may be available through the wireless hub. Ask at the reference desk for a copy of the print drivers.

Be a Savvy User

The Internet is a public communications network. Public wireless networks or "hotspots" are generally not secure from your laptop to the Wireless Access Point. There can be unscrupulous parties between you and anybody you communicate with. Wireless Internet access poses the same risks to your personal information that a wired network poses, as well as some new risks because data is broadcast over radio waves. Wireless users need to take steps to secure their personal information and machines. The Library cannot assure the safety of your data.

Savvy wireless users will:
- Not transmit any important information that may be misused such as credit card number, social security numbers, home address, passwords, etc.
- Have a firewall on their personal machines
- Avoid having disks, folders and files "shared"
- Have anti-virus software installed on their machine and configured to do frequent updates automatically.
- Not leave equipment unattended.
- Do not download large files over the wireless connection
- Do not stream video or audio over the wireless connection

Configuration Information
- 802-11b or 802-11g protocol
- TCP/IP properties set to obtain an IP automatically

The Charlevoix Public Library assumes no responsibility for any loss or damage done directly or indirectly to personal data or equipment, or for any damage or injury arising from loss of privacy arising from use of its wireless connection, or connection to other Internet services.

WIRELESS NETIQUETTE

Charlevoix Public Library
Charlevoix, Michigan

Wireless Netiquette

The wireless network is intended to be a shared resource. If you use a large amount of bandwidth, you take it from others. Be considerate.

Part V
Related Library Services

Chapter 18

ELECTRONIC CLASSROOMS

GENERAL GUIDELINES

Davidson College
Davidson College Library
Davidson, North Carolina

Primary functions of the Electronic Classroom:

- Library instruction
- Course-related library instruction classes led by a librarian
- Library workshops
- Library orientation sessions
- Research consultations
- Other library activities

Secondary function of the library's Electronic Classroom:

The computers in the Electronic Classroom are usually available for use by Davidson students in the afternoons and evenings and also on weekends during the academic year.

Opening hours for student use:

Note: If there is a scheduled Library instruction session, orientation session, workshop, or consultation in the afternoon, the classroom will not open until after the session is over.

Students using the room in the evenings and on weekends should remove their belongings before the library closes each night. Items left in the classroom overnight will be placed in lost and found the following morning.

Berry College
Berry College Memorial Library
Mount Berry, Georgia

Memorial Library's electronic classroom is located on the second floor of the library. It is designed as an instructional facility for the teaching and training of students, faculty, and staff in a wide range of databases and other information retrieval systems, information management systems, and other applications essential for teaching, learning, and administration in the higher education environment.

The primary purpose of the classroom is to serve as the instructional facility for the library's ongoing instructional services program, which includes mandatory orientation for all entering students, course-related/course-integrated instructional sessions conducted by librarians at the request of teaching faculty, and workshops offered by librarians for faculty and staff. The classroom is also available for use by OIT staff members and other college personnel engaged in teaching, training, or instruction.

The room accommodates a variety of instructional approaches:

- lecture/discussion [22-25 chairs with small desktops in center of room]
- demonstration [LCD computer projector attached to PC, ELMO, DVD, and VCR at instructor's workstation]
- supervised, hands-on experience for participants [12 computers around the perimeter of the room, with space for two students per workstation to foster a collaborative environment]

ROOM USE INSTRUCTIONS

Berry College
Berry College Memorial Library
Mount Berry, Georgia

The classroom will be kept locked when not scheduled for a class. Public services library staff members are available to unlock the room for scheduled classes, workshops, and meetings.

Under no circumstances is the room to be used as an unsupervised group study area. Students or others needing group study areas when the group study rooms are full are encouraged to check with the public services librarians for other arrangements.

Public services librarians involved in campus-wide instruction determine the general arrangement and configuration of the room, and are responsible for overall maintenance and supervision of the facility.

Faculty members, OIT staff, or any other college personnel scheduling the room for any purpose are responsible for ensuring that the room is returned to its original physical configuration, should tables, chairs, etc., need rearrangement for non-library events.

Food and beverage arrangements for special occasion workshops or presentations must be coordinated with the public services librarians, who will be happy to provide advice on how to best handle arrangements in this setting.

ROOM USE PRIORITIES

Berry College
Berry College Memorial Library
Mount Berry, Georgia

Sessions in the electronic classroom are scheduled according to the following priorities:

- library instruction for students (described in purpose statement above)
- library-sponsored professional development workshops for faculty and staff of Berry College
- OIT-sponsored training sessions (may include administrative systems, continuing education)
- other class sessions (one-to-three time use) requested by faculty for their own instructional purposes
- campus committee and organization meetings requiring computer projection/network connectivity
- other uses on an as-available basis only

Semester-long classes will not be scheduled in the classroom.

Undergraduate and graduate students may not reserve the room for instructional purposes, or serve as instructors in the classroom unless a faculty/staff sponsor has accepted responsibility for adhering to the policies and procedures established.

Requests by groups other than those affiliated with Berry College will be considered on a case-by-case basis by the Head of Public and Instructional Services or the Instructional Services Librarian.

Chapter 19

LIBRARY WEB SITE

ADVERTISING ON WEB SITE

University of Virginia
University of Virginia
Charlottesville, Virginia

All University of Virginia Web pages signified by the address "virginia.edu" or within the range of Internet and Intranet protocol addresses assigned to the University of Virginia. University departments or units with Web sites based on non-University servers must comply with the terms of this policy in order to be linked from the University's home page structure.

Consistent with University and state policy on the appropriate use of University-owned equipment, the University's Web page must not be used for commercial, non-mission-related purposes.

In practice, this means that advertising space cannot be sold at any level of the Web page. "Advertising" refers to any situation in which the University or one of its units receives payment or in-kind gifts in exchange for a link or brand placement on a University Web page. Please see definitions below.

While advertising cannot be sold at any level, links to commercial vendors may be made in the following specific situations:

Licensed software required for Web viewing:

The logo or graphic represents licensed software on which a core function of the page is based, e.g., Netscape, Adobe Acrobat Reader, RealAudio, VeriSign.

Links to separately contracted vendor:

The logo or link is to a vendor or other entity separately contracted to provide services to the University, e.g., ARAmark, TIAA, Fidelity Insurance, Nike.

Sponsorship Recognition:

Within a unit's Web page, a logo or link can be displayed at that unit's second level page or below to acknowledge support of the unit's mission-related activities through sponsorship. Such logos or links are deemed to be recognition of corporate or other external sponsorship; payment may not be accepted for that link or logo. Please see definitions below.

Educational Purposes:

The text link provides information for educational or other mission-related purposes and the University has received no consideration for incorporating that link.

Guidelines for Linking and Presentation

In all of these cases, a link should provide information for educational or other mission-related purposes and the University cannot have received consideration for incorporating that link.

Such links should in no way imply endorsement of products or services offered by the external entity. Any descriptive text accompanying the link should be value-neutral. Acceptable language might include: "For more information: [link]." Unacceptable language: "Check out this great Web site [link]."

Such links should go to the home page of the entity's Web site and, wherever possible, links should not go to pages on which products or commercial services are offered for sale. The logo, text, or graphic should not include any qualitative or comparative language or descriptions of the non-University party's products, services, facilities, or company, including but not limited to price information, inducement to purchase, endorsements, savings, or value.

Particularly in cases where a group of external hyperlinks is included, the following language is recommended for inclusion: Links to Web sites external to the University of Virginia should not be considered endorsement of those Web sites or any information contained therein.

In all cases, the design of departmental or unit pages that incorporate commercial links must be consistent with established graphic and placement standards for University Web pages. (See guidelines for Web design, http://www.virginia.edu/webstandards.) For example, commercial or text logos or display material may not be placed in the "banner" area, roughly the top quarter of a page and pop-up notice of sponsorship will not be allowed under any circumstances.

Links to sponsors or other corporate recognition on a unit's home page (i.e., the third level off the University home page) will not be allowed except under special circumstances considered on a case-by-case basis by the University's Network-based Information Systems (N-BIS) editorial board. Such examples might be the University Bookstore or the University Press (selling merchandise).

The following definitions should be considered general and applicable to this policy only.

- University of Virginia Web page: A page created or maintained by or on behalf of the University of Virginia or an office, department, or division of the University of Virginia and located within the University of Virginia's information technology environment, i.e., signified by the address "virginia.edu" or within the range of Internet protocol addresses assigned to the University of Virginia. [Note: Web page and Web site may be used interchangeably.]
- Hyperlink or hypertext link: A logo, text, or other identifier incorporating a link to a Web site external to the University of Virginia, placed on a UVA Web page without compensation.
- Advertising: A logo, text, or other identifier incorporating a link to a Web site external to the University of Virginia, placed on a UVA Web page in exchange for remuneration or gifts in kind, where that placement is intended to promote or market a service, facility or product offered by the entity's Web site for a commercial purpose. Advertising includes messages containing qualitative or comparative language, price information or other indications of savings or value, an endorsement, or an inducement to purchase, sell, or use any company, service, facility or product.
- Qualified Sponsorship: A logo, text, or other identifier incorporating a link to a Web site external to the University of Virginia, placed on a UVA Web page to acknowledge donation of services, products, or financial or research support to the University of Virginia or an office, unit, center, department, or division of the University of Virginia.
- The IRS defines sponsorship as "a payment for which there is no expectation that the sponsor will receive a 'substantial return benefit,' the income received by the sponsored organization is not subject to tax as unrelated business income."
- Banner ad: A typically rectangular advertisement placed on a Web site, above, below, or to the side of the site's main content area.

E-MAIL ACCOUNTS

Lane Memorial Library
Hampton, New Hampshire

Web-Based Email Providers

The Lane Library does not provide email accounts to the public, however there are many companies that do provide email accounts for free. These accounts can be used through any of the common web browsers (such as Internet Explorer here in the library). You need to register with one of these companies to have an account. These are commercial companies with varying policies—they are not part of the Lane Library.

Among the more popular are:

- Yahoo Mail
- HotMail
- AOL Mail

There are many more available as well. You can browse through a directory of these companies here.

Calumet College of Saint Joseph
Specker Library
Whiting, Indiana

Users of Calumet College of St. Joseph's electronic mail system are assigned a user-id and password. User's names and user-ids are included in each mail message. Users are responsible for all electronic mail originating from their user-id. The following practices are not allowed:

- Forgery (or attempted forgery) of electronic mail messages.
- Attempts to read, delete, copy, or modify the electronic mail of other users.
- Attempts at sending harassing, obscene and/or other threatening email to other users.
- Attempts at sending unsolicited junk mail, "for-profit" messages or chain letters.
- Attempts to harm or thwart the operations or business of the college or college activities.

GUIDELINES FOR LINKS

University of Maryland
University of Maryland Libraries
College Park, Maryland

Guidelines for Selection of Free Web-based Reference Resources

Selection Policy:
Selection of electronic resources should follow the general guidelines developed for all electronic resources. However, recognizing that Web-based, free resources of potential value abound, suggested criteria for selection of these materials are provided here. Free, Web-based resources often lack print counterparts or established track records requiring the exercise of careful judgment by selectors.

Criteria:
Electronic resources selected as reference resources either for the general reference pages or for subject-specific pages should meet the same selection criteria as resources that are purchased. Selection should be

based on the site's ability to support and enhance the research and teaching activities of the University of Maryland. They should be of a scholarly nature or likely to assist in advancing scholarly research or university education programs. Relevance to campus teaching and research needs should be the primary selection criterion.

The quality and content of the electronic resource are likewise of great importance.

Quality indicators can include peer review of the site, review of the site by other librarians, an authoritative sponsor or producer, and evidence of ongoing support (creation of archives, mirror sites, etc.).

The amount of content provided should be significant.

In subject areas where similar sites exist, emphasis should be placed on creating a selective collection that highlights key resources rather than a comprehensive listing of all known resources.

Ease of use is also a relevant selection factor for electronic resources. Selected resources should be self-explanatory with regard to their use and offer effective support for browsing or searching.

Reliability and stability can also influence selection. Resources known to be frequently unavailable should not be selected.

If registration and/or licensing are required, licenses must be submitted for approval through the Libraries' license review process. Resources may be rejected if licensing terms are unacceptable.

Fee-based resources that are available on a free-trial basis for a limited period of time are not appropriate for selection.

Florida Atlantic University
S.E. Wimberly Library
Boca Raton, Florida

As information is increasingly being delivered over the Internet, freely available Internet resources can provide unique content; they can also improve access to and enhance traditional collections, while reflecting the excellence, comprehensiveness, and authority expected in a research library. Internet Web resources will be considered for addition to the FAU Libraries' Web pages after being evaluated by librarians/selectors with expertise in the relevant subject area using the guidelines below.

The following guidelines were developed for the purpose of clarifying some factors commonly considered by those who are experienced in identifying web resources or building web pages. These guidelines are not intended to be absolute, and a specific resource does not have to meet all of the criteria to be acceptable.

Guidelines

Quality

Its uniqueness, accuracy, comprehensiveness, lack of bias, or breadth of scope indicate the quality of a web resource. High quality sites are often noted for the extent to which they include unique information and serve as a primary resource on a subject.

Comprehensiveness is also indicative of a quality site. Sites that provide information are preferred to those that simply point to other sites. Well-organized and annotated collections of links are often also judged as useful.

Relevance

The extent to which the resource satisfies the needs and is appropriate for the level and purposes of the intended users determines relevance. Language and country coverage should be appropriate for the subject involved and the intended audience.

Organization and Design

Web resources are judged both for content and visual appeal in ways that differ from the evaluation of print scholarly resources. Excellent design clearly adds value to web pages but should not be a substitute for excellent content.

The design and organization of the site should be logical and visually appealing. Good organization is generally indicated by consistent graphics and style. Annotated links to other sites are considered useful to help the user move through the information.

Ease of Use

The site should be reviewed for usability to insure that it is simple, consistent, clear, and easy to load in terms of speed. If special software is required, is it linked to the site and easily located, and is it free? Navigational aids should be provided for longer pages and if searchable, the search interface should be readily understood.

Reliability & Stability

Consider the credibility, institutional affiliation, authority, status, and reputation of a site. The source of the information should be clearly identified. If the site is the creation of an individual, the individual should be considered authoritative by such measures as institutional affiliation or peer review. A name and e-mail address of a contact person or group should be available for user contact.

Maintenance

Look for evidence, such as a date or a last update, which indicates that the site is regularly maintained, and that links are active and information is current.

Access Restrictions

Consider the impact of subscription fees for commercial sites or other possible barriers to access such as registration requirements, time limitations, or stringent copyright restrictions. While such restrictions are not necessarily a basis for exclusion of a site, the impact on users should be considered.

In accordance with the Americans with Disabilities Act, individuals with disabilities should be able to access all services the University offers to non-disabled individuals. Internet resources, which increase the likelihood of such access, are preferred. Such resources may include those which provide text-only options (i.e., for individuals using Screen Reader technology), large print options, or audio.

Local Orientation

Sites created by individuals or units affiliated with Florida Atlantic University and Southeast Florida will be given special consideration to the extent that they may reflect local interests, needs, or resources.

Exclusions

Exclude websites that merely advertise a service or product.

De-selection

Internet resources that are "no longer available" or "maintained" need to be removed.

Electronic Collection Management Forms, Policies, Procedures, and Guidelines Manual

Appalachian State University
Belk Library and Information Commons
Boone, North Carolina

Purpose

The purpose of this document is to establish a set of criteria to be maintained in all Web pages created by the Appalachian State University Libraries. This document will be periodically revised.

Mission

In keeping with the Library's mission, Library Web pages will:

Organize and provide access to materials and resources that are integral to the educational, scholarly, and intellectual goals of the students, faculty, and staff of Appalachian State University, as well as other members of the community and region.

Web Committee

The Library Web Committee has responsibility for establishing and maintaining Library Web Page policies and procedures. This committee is chaired by the Web Services Librarian and is open to all Library staff and faculty.

General Information

Each Team at the library (i.e. reference, materials processing) will have a web editor(s) who will post pages to the server, and who will coordinate the team's web effort. The editor(s) will serve on the web committee, and the editors(s) are responsible for checking links and content regularly.

Do not post personal pages to the library server (use your vms space if you want to post personal pages). Appropriate information about employees, such as name, areas of work specialization, work phone, e-mail address, etc. will be maintained on the Library's Personnel Directory page and may also be included on team directory pages or other pages.

Content

Content should be appropriate to the mission of the Library.

Pages should be ADA compliant.

Terminology and links are to be consistent across the site.

When referring to ourselves and our services, use the phrase "Appalachian State University Libraries." References to a specific library, such as Belk, are used only when referring to specific collections and locations within that building.

Copyrighted or trademarked material should not be included without permission, and should contain a statement about permission having been granted.

Photographs, drawings, video clips or sound clips should have the following permissions: the person(s) who created or who own the rights, and those who are depicted or heard.

Layout

General | File Names | Links and Images

General
- Pages will make use of the template and CSS provided.
- Set Dreamweaver preferences to validate against XHTML strict, and in preferences, for accessibility, click the boxes "frames, media, images & tables"
- Do NOT click the boxes for use large fonts or off-screen rendering.
- Pages should have a consistent appearance across the site.
- Test your page for load time- your file should not be bigger than 40K Heavy use of graphics increases load time.
- Long pages should be broken into logical sub-pages, with a table of contents menu.

File Names and Page Titles:
- The main page of each sub-directory is named index.html
- File names should use lower case, and have no spaces (use an underscore)
- File names should have the .html extension.
- The top of the displayed page should provide a unique, descriptive title for the document (i.e., "Web Development Policy" at the top of this page).

Links and Images
- A link to the e-mail address of the person responsible for the posting content should appear at the bottom. Please use a direct mail to link, not the mail form.
    For example:
            Content editor Megan Johnson johnsnm@appstate.edu
- Images should contain ALT tag information.
- Image files should be stored in and linked from an image folder within your team's folder, if you are modifying images store the original in a png folder.

University Policies

Information providers should meet the terms set forth in the University policies governing both publications and computer use. These include:
- Appalachian State University Policy on the Use of Computers and Data Communications—located at http://www2.acs.appstate.edu/computer.htm
- Copyright and publishing law

INFORMATION ON LIBRARY WEB SITE

Duke University
William R. Perkins Library
Durham, North Carolina

Use and Reproduction Policy

The following policy applies generally to materials on Duke University Libraries web sites, unless otherwise specified on particular web pages.

The materials on this web site have been made available for use in research, teaching, and private study. You may reproduce (print, make photocopies, or download) materials from this web site without prior permission for these non-commercial purposes, on the condition that you provide proper attribution of the source in all copies (see below).

For other uses of materials from this web site, i.e., commercial products, publication, broadcast, mirroring, and anything else that doesn't fall under either "fair use" or the terms of the Creative Commons license found on most pages, we require that you contact us in advance for permission to reproduce.

Please read on for more information.

The details

Reproductions of material from Duke University Libraries web sites may be made only for non-commercial purpose such as use in research, teaching, or private study.

The recipient agrees to give proper acknowledgement to Duke University Libraries, and further agrees to secure permission in advance from Duke University Libraries to publish or broadcast any item, in whole or in part, for commercial purposes. All permissions granted by Duke are granted in so far and only in so far as the rights of Duke University Libraries are concerned. Some materials on this web site may be copyrighted by other entities, and persons wishing to reproduce such materials must assume all responsibility for identifying and satisfying any claimants of literary property rights or copyrights.

The recipient agrees to indemnify and hold harmless Duke University, its officers, employees and agents from and against all suits, claims, actions and expenses arising out of the use of reproductions provided by Duke University Libraries.

United States Copyright Law

The copyright law of the United States (Title 17, United States Code) governs the making of photocopies or other reproductions of copyrighted material.

Under certain conditions specified in the law, libraries and archives are authorized to furnish a photocopy or other reproduction. One of these specified conditions is that the photocopy or reproduction is not to be "used for any purpose other than private study, scholarship, or research." If a user makes a request for, or later uses, a photocopy or reproduction for purposes in excess of "fair use" or any other exception to the copyright law that user may be liable for infringement. This institution reserves the right to refuse to accept a copying order if, in its judgment, fulfillment of the order would involve violation of copyright law.

For more information about copyright law and how it applies to information found on the Internet, see the Copyright and Fair Use site at Stanford or the Copyright Management Center at IUPUI.

Providing attribution for materials reproduced from Duke University Libraries web sites

When using materials from the Duke University Libraries web site, please acknowledge their source by clearly stating the name of the Library, the title of the web page or resource, and the URL (web address) of the page in which you found them. Examples on how to cite web pages are available as part of the Library's guidelines for citing sources. The Guide to Citing Special Collections Materials provides further guidance on how to cite digital collections and primary source materials.

LINKS TO STUDENT GROUPS

Bryn Mawr
Bryn Mawr Library
Bryn Mawr, Pennsylvania

A personal page is a Web page about a student, faculty member or staff member created and maintained by that person himself or herself. A student-organization home page is a Web page created and maintained by a student on behalf of a student organization. Personal pages and student-organization home pages are subject to the "Home Pages" section above, except that they do not need to contain a link to the College's home page.

Although personal and student-organization home pages are neither created nor maintained by the College, people outside the College community (including high school students applying to college, their parents and Bryn Mawr alumnae) still associate these pages with the College. These pages also reflect on the author and may be viewed by prospective employers, colleagues, one's parents, Internet predators and anyone else.

Pages produced by College undergraduates and post baccalaureate premedical students must meet the standards of the Honor Code http://www.brynmawr.edu/activities/honorcode.html. Pages may not impede the efficient operation of the student Web server, nor the College's system resources. Violations of the Honor Code, policies or laws brought to the attention of the College's Web Advisory Committee may be referred to the appropriate authorities.

Personal and student-organization home pages must also contain the College's disclaimer: The content of this and subsuming pages is determined solely by the author. The presence of this page or subsuming pages on the Bryn Mawr College server does not imply endorsement by Bryn Mawr College.

Questions about this Web Site Policy should be directed to the Web Advisory Committee.

LINKS TO OUTSIDE SOURCES

Neill Public Library
Pullman, Washington

Web Links Displayed on Neill Public Library Pages

The Neill Public Library's website includes links to external websites that reflect the interests of library users. Key questions are considered before the library posts a link to a web page or web resource. These include:

- Is there a local emphasis?
- Who provides the information, and are they qualified to do so?
- Is it current and regularly maintained?
- Is it easy to use?
- Is it reliable?

Providing links to resources on the web does not mean Neill Public Library endorses the information provided. We consider the website a form of outreach to our patrons. Therefore links posted on the library website are at the discretion of the outreach staff.

3. Web Linking Policy—Choosing and Evaluating Sources

Similar to the library's materials collections, professional staff will utilize the Library's web site to identify and recommend interesting and useful Internet destinations and resources which support the library's mission and service roles. Links to information resources are based on staff's judgment of the best resources available and do not imply endorsement. Users should recognize the Library is not responsible for the content of linked sites, nor for the content of sources accessed through subsequent links. The library cannot control or monitor material that may be accessible from Internet sources because the Internet is a vast and unregulated medium with access points that change rapidly and unpredictably.

Additional selection criteria used when evaluating whether to link to a remote website:

    i.   Is the subject matter and information useful for our patrons?
    ii.   Is the remote site easily accessible?
    iii.   Is it relevant to the overall mission of the library?
    iv.   Is it a local resource?
    v.   Is the resource of sufficient quality to merit a link?
    vi.   Who has established the page? (Authority)
    vii.   Is there a sponsor?
    viii.   Is the information accurate?
    ix.   Is there a discernable bias?
    x.   Does the page have a posting and/or revision date?
    xi.   Is the site regularly maintained?

As with all collection development decisions, this policy does not replace the judgment and expertise of library staff. There will be instances when the library links to resources that may not fit all criteria. For example the "Community Resource Database" links to local resources regardless of the quality of the sites.

4. Electronic and Online Databases

NPL strives to work with consortia whenever possible in the selection of paid electronic databases and is currently working with Washington State Library as well as Whitman County Libraries. Electronic paid databases are selected according to the general selection criteria as well as applying the additional selection criteria for New and Emerging Formats.

5. Equipment

The library has a CD and DVD player available for public use in the library. A multi-media center is also available for group use in the library's Hecht Meeting Room. A personal FM system for the hearing impaired can be used in the library or checked out by groups or organizations.

6. Additional Selection Criteria for New (electronic) and Emerging Formats

    i.   Impact on equipment, staff, storage and space
    ii.   Demand for format in community
    iii.   Durability of format for library use
    iv.   Suitability for direct public access
    v.   Availability of adequate startup and continual funding
    vi.   Capability for networked distribution
    vii.   Acceptable response time
    viii.   Timeliness in updating information
    ix.   Logical operation and ease of use for public and staff

x. Technical quality of production or reproduction
xi. Capability for information to be downloaded
xii. Reduction/replacement of print or other format materials
xiii. Availability of access in-house and remotely

Aurora Public Library
Aurora, Colorado

Links from the library's web site

A "link" (hypertext reference) from the LIBRARY's home pages to other sites does not imply endorsement of the views expressed at those sites. Staff, in keeping with the general policy guidelines described above and the Website Selection Criteria is responsible for the selection of the links. Links may provide access to local community information and services. In general, the LIBRARY does not link to individual businesses, although it may include such umbrella organizations as the Chambers of Commerce. Staff may also occasionally add links to highlight particular issues or subjects that staff believes to be of interest or entertainment value to customers. Such links may be changed frequently or infrequently as may be deemed most appropriate.

Boise Public Library
Boise, Idaho

Non Library Websites

Numerous external website links are provided on www.boisepubliclibrary.org. Visitors to those sites are advised to check the privacy statements of each site and to be cautious about providing personally identifiable information without a clear understanding of how the information will be used.

River Falls Public Library
River Falls, Wisconsin

Links to Internet sites from the Library's web pages are selected to broaden, enrich, and compliment the Library's print and audio-visual collection.

The sites linked on the Library's web site are separate and independent from the Library. The Library exercises no control over the content of the information provided by the producers of those sites. Due to the vastness of the Internet, the Library web site is far from complete in any subject area. The presence or absence of a site is in no way a reflection of library policy. The linking of a site does not in any way indicate that the Library endorses, sponsors, or reviews the information provided by a particular site.

Sites are evaluated according to their credibility, quality and usefulness in order to meet the needs and interest of the Library staff and patrons.

Factors which will be considered when evaluating sites to be selected include:

- Access—stable site, no fees required, consistently available
- Design—well organized, clear instructions, easy to use, uncluttered and cleanly designed, graphics that enhance content, do not frame other sites content
- Content—authoritative, documented, verifiable, accurate, updated regularly, appropriateness of subject matter
- Preference may be given to educational (.edu), governmental (.gov), and non-profit organization sites (.org)

- Even if a site meets the above criteria, the Library may choose not to include a link to that site. Internet sites that are not linked from the Library web site may be found by using a search engine such as those listed on the Search the Internet page

Linked sites are periodically reviewed for access, design, and content. If a site no longer meets the selection criteria, or is inactive or out-of-date, it may be removed.

NOTICE: WARNING CONCERNING COPYRIGHT RESTRICTIONS

The copyright law of the United States (Title 17, United States Code) governs the making of photocopies or other reproductions of copyrighted material. Under certain circumstances, permitted by law, individuals are allowed to make copies (print, digital, or otherwise) for personal use, private study, scholarship, or research. If used for purposes other than those specified by law, or in excess of what constitutes "fair use", the individual may be liable for infringement of copyright.

Tempe Public Library
Tempe, Arizona

The Tempe Public Library, through its Internet home page and internal computer network, provides links to interesting and useful Internet destinations and resources for library users to explore. Links to recommended sites are developed with the following principles in mind:

Recommended sites are selected in accordance with the principles included in the Tempe Public Library's Collection Development Policy.

Site content should be free of charge to library users. Exceptions include, but are not limited to, sites that offer significant free content but may charge for extra information or services, and job search sites that do not charge the job seeker but rather the employer.

Site content should be kept as current as its purpose demands.

Sites should use Internet resources effectively. For sites containing primarily text, preference is given to those that are visible to text-only browsers. Sites using graphics, animation, sound, and other capabilities should use them in a manner consistent with their purpose, and use Internet resources as economically as possible.

However, due to the unregulated nature of the Internet, the Library cannot monitor the sites to which it links, nor any subsequent links, and cannot accept responsibility for the content or availability of those sites.

PURPOSE AND MISSION STATEMENTS

Bryn Mawr
Bryn Mawr Library
Bryn Mawr, Pennsylvania

Bryn Mawr College relies on the World Wide Web to support the College's teaching and research. The College's Web site is a communications vehicle for all of the College's constituencies and for the College itself.

Bryn Mawr College encourages all members of the campus community (faculty, staff and students) to create and maintain an effective Web presence. No matter the location of one's pages on the site, each participating member represents the College and herself or himself to the world. A presence on the College's site, therefore, is both a privilege and a responsibility.

USER LINK REQUESTS

Lane Memorial Library
Hampton, New Hampshire

Web Collection Development Guidelines

We've all seen places and tools on the web that we enjoy for one reason or another. These guidelines will help you determine whether a given site is a candidate for inclusion on our web site—or really just belongs in your bookmarks.

Accessibility
* Is the information clearly presented? Can you tell at a glance what the page is about?
* Is it relatively stable? Or do things seem to move around on the site?
* How concise is it? Do you have to scroll down forever to see it all?
* Does it appear on the screen quickly and reliably? Or is it often impossible to get into, slow to appear, etc.?
* Does it require additional software to use? Does it want your browser to do movies, sing, tap dance?
* Does the user have to register to use it? What information do they want from you to do so?
* Does it cost money to use?

Content
* How current is it? How regularly is it updated? How many links seem dead?
* How broad is its scope? How deep does it go? How can you tell?
* Would you consider the information reasonably authoritative? Or is it just Joe Schmoe's soapbox?
* Does the site contain original content or is it mainly just a set of links to other resources?
* Is there a way to contact the site's producer? Do they tell you why, for whom and what they hope to gain by producing this site?
* Is the information presented in a lot of jargon? Or is it clear and understandable?
* Can you distinguish the advertising from the content?

Usefulness
* Does the information add to our set of web tools? Or does it duplicate resources we already include?
* Does it add some features that may not be available in other formats?
* Does the web site's intended audience correspond with ours?
* Does it help to answer questions we're often asked? Or just those someone asks once in a rare while?

WEB SITE CONTENT

University of North Texas
University Libraries
Denton, Texas

Introduction

The web site of the UNT libraries is the interface as well as the repository for providing information about the libraries' services and resources to the academic community. In the year 2007, the UNT Libraries implemented a content management system PLONE to support the transformation from a decentralized web management model to a centralized operation.

Electronic Collection Management Forms, Policies, Procedures, and Guidelines Manual

While the web site management responsibilities are centralized to Multimedia Development Lab, the site content development will remain under control by individual units. To maintain the identity, consistency, accuracy and usability of the library site, a collaborative effort throughout the library is vital.

Multimedia Development Lab Responsibilities

- Maintain and manage the content management system
- Maintain the overall navigation of the UNT libraries' site
- Review the information throughout the site routinely
- Maintain effective communication with individual units via unit content liaison
- Ensure the site is in compliance to UNT web publishing policies and standards

With the help of the content management system, the following web publishing standards required by the university are no longer needed to be maintained by the individual unit

- Accessibility
- Web Page Standards
- HTML Coding Requirements
- Sitemap
- Site Wide Search
- Links to the following UNT Policies
  - Open Records
  - Disclaimer
  - AA/EOE/ADA
  - Privacy Statement
  - Web Accessibility Policy
  - Emergency Preparedness Information
- Links to the following UNT information pages
  - UNT Home
  - UNT News
  - UNT Events
  - Search UNT
- Links to the State of Texas

Content Creator and Contributor Responsibilities

The content reviewers of each unit are responsible for the accuracy of their web section information. Their responsibilities include:

- Using Mozzila-FireFox as the designated web browser for CMS content editing
- Understand and adhere to university web publishing policies and guidelines
- Maintain effective communication with MMDL team via unit content liaison
- Be familiar with the content management system for content creation
- Be familiar with basic html coding for better practice
- Be familiar with Adobe Acrobat
- Be familiar with image editors such as Adobe Photoshop or Firework
- Ensure all files uploaded to the CMS are free of viruses
- Respond to user inquiries
- Review and spell-proof content before publishing
- Review unit level content routinely to ensure its timeliness and accuracy
- Delete obsolete pages and files
- Fix broken links in timely manner
- Keep content updated, and modify content as needed

Request/Remove/Change CMS Access

Please submit request via email to MMDL@library.unt.edu for adding, changing, or removing employee access to the CMS. Please do not send request to individual MMDL staff's email account.

Report Site Problems

Please use "report a problem" form, or send an email to MMDL at MMDL@library.unt.edu to report a problem of using the library website.

Special Content Handling

Large files consume bandwidth resource, and will take your end-user additional time to download. Therefore, monitoring and controlling the size of the files is an important part of the web content development policy.

Meta Tags

For automatically generating the university required Meta Data by the CMS, the following fields of all content types are required to be completed

- Title: The topic or subject of the content.
- Description: A short summary of the content. A short summary should not exceed 3 or 4 sentences.
- Keyword: The words specific to the page subject. When creating new keywords, please use lowercase for all words.
- Creator: Persons who are currently responsible for this content. Please use Novell user name as the name of the creator.

Image files

The use of images for all content type of the CMS should be content related, and should not be used for decoration only. Before you publish any images please

- Ensure there are no copyright issues
- Use the images that are appropriate to the content context
- Use high quality and high resolution images as your images' source whenever it's possible
- Rescale down the images to an appropriate size that will fit screen monitors with various resolutions
- Convert the images into one of the following allowable file type: jpg, gif or png
- Minimize the image file size to be less than 200 KB, the image file that is at risk to be removed
- Minimize the number of images you display on any single page to minimize web traffic
- Provide short description (Alt Tag) for all images you display on any single page

The site administrator reserves the right to remove the images from the system if the images are not compliant to the proper use of the images. Please click here to see image policies for details.

PDF files

A link (http://www.adobe.com/products/acrobat/readstep2.html) to the Adobe Reader is required to be provided alongside of the link to the PDF file for download.

Do not use PDF simply for providing a printable document of an existing piece of web content.

Optimize the PDF for web use and minimize the file size before uploading them to the assets folder.

Microsoft Office files. Please try not to upload any Microsoft Office files to the CMS. If the upload is inevitable, please be sure it's virus free.

Tables. Tables shall be used to mark up tabular data. The structural element such as heading shall be provided.

Mark for Deletion. Content reviewers could mark their own content for deletion, and retract the content form mark for deletion before the end of each month. On the last Friday of each mouth, the MMDL will erase all contents that are marked for deletion. Those erased contents will no longer be available in the CMS.

Hours. Prior to publishing the hours page at your unit level site, each unit shall continue the current hours review process that was established between your unit and Lou Ann Bradley. Once the hours page has been published, the state of this page shall be changed from published to submit for promotion.

The MMDL will be responsible for promoting the unit hours to the library sitewide hours' page. The MMDL reserves the right to un-publish any unit's hours if the hours reviewing process with Lou Ann is not completed.

Location

Please DO NOT include links to, or local copies of UNT hosted maps. These are provided for you as links in the template itself.

Please Do Not include Mailing Address; the regular mailing address of the UNT libraries is provided for you in the template.

Please coordinate with Lou Ann Bradley on floor plan maps updates. All updated floor maps of different libraries shall live in the General Resources folder.

News and Events

Please only create and publish the news or events that are for the public. Please do not use the News and Events for internal use, such as the news for unit staff or library staff.

Once the news or event has been published, your unit level news and events will be included in the library sitewide News and Events Listing.

News and Events Home Page Promotion

If the unit would like to ask for the consideration of including a news or event to the library home page highlight area, please do the following:

- change that item's state from published to *submit for promotion* when it closes to the time for promoting this item to the home page
- complete the *effective date* and *expiration date* under properties

The MMDL will be responsible for promoting the news and events to the library home page when space is available.

Home page News and Events Highlights Display Criteria

First Priority: Administrative events, announcements, and news to the public. The starting date, duration and ending date for displaying this category's news and events will be determined by the administrative office.

Second Priority: Unit's upcoming events that cater to the UNT community. The starting date, duration and ending date for displaying these events may vary based on the quantity of the events in the queue for promotion, and the actual events date. There is no absolute guarantee that all events in this category will be displayed. In general, an immediate future event will be on top of the priority for displaying, and no event in this category will be displayed for more than a week.

Third Priority: Unit's important news about new high-profile acquisition, new exhibit, new collection and new service, etc. The starting date, duration and ending date for displaying this category of news may vary based on the quantity of the news and events from the First and Second Priority Categories. There is no absolute guarantee that all news in this category will be displayed. In general, no news in this category will be displayed for more than a week.

When all the above priorities do not occur, the news and events for the home page will be selected from the top of the news and events queue for promotion.

Front Page Photos. All units are welcome to submit high quality photos about UNT libraries to the photo pool for library home page photos display and rotation. The high quality photos shall be submitted via email MMDL@library.unt.edu or CD to MMDL.

Content Reuse. The definition of the content reuse is that when a single piece of content is written once, it can be used in multiple locations or contexts. Similarly, one change made to the source of the content will reflect throughout the site.

Benefit of Content Reuse

- Improves sitewide consistency and accuracy
- Increases site development efficiency
- Simplifies content update from multiple locations to one

Good Practice

Review the content you are about to create to identify the possibility and practicability for content reuse.

Browse or search the site to see if somebody has already created a piece of content that you intend to create. If so, instead of copying and pasting the existing content to your page, you could easily use link or alias functions to utilize this existing content.

If the content you are about to create has the potential to be reused within your department or beyond, create it as a separate object instead of part of the page content. This will make it easy to let others reuse your content.

Reusable resources within the CMS

General Resources

Images and Maps

Tutorials for Electronic Resources

Ways to reuse resources

Alias, Internal Link and Related Item.

WEB SITE EVALUATION TECHNIQUES

University of California Berkeley
Doe Library
Berkeley, California

Finding Information on the Internet: A Tutorial

http://www.lib.berkeley.edu/TeachingLib/Guides/Internet/Evaluate.html

Evaluating Web Pages:

Techniques to Apply & Questions to Ask
UC Berkeley—Teaching Library Internet Workshops
About This Tutorial | Table of Contents | Handouts | Glossary

Looking for the Web Page Evaluation Checklist PDF form?

Evaluating web pages skillfully requires you to do two things at once:

- Train your eye and your fingers to employ a series of techniques that help you quickly find what you need to know about web pages;
- Train your mind to think critically, even suspiciously, by asking a series of questions that will help you decide how much a web page is to be trusted.

This page is organized to combine the two techniques into a process that begins with looking at your search results from a search engine or other source, follows through by investigating the content of page, and extends beyond the page to what others may say about the page or its author(s).

I. What can the URL tell you?

Techniques for Web Evaluation:
1.   Before you leave the list of search results—before you click and get interested in anything written on the page—glean all you can from the URLs of each page.
2.   Then choose pages most likely to be reliable and authentic.

Questions to ask:
- What are the implications?
    - Is it somebody's personal page?
    - Read the URL carefully:
    - Look for a personal name (e.g., jbarker or barker) following a tilde (~), a percent sign (%), or the words "users," "members," or "people."
    - Is the server a commercial ISP or other provider of web page hosting (like aol.com or geocities.com)?
    - Personal pages are not necessarily "bad," but you need to investigate the author carefully.
    - For personal pages, there is no publisher or domain owner vouching for the information in the page.
- What type of domain does it come from?
    - (educational, nonprofit, commercial, government, etc.)
- Is the domain extension appropriate for the content?
    - Government sites: look for .gov, .mil
    - Educational sites: look for .edu
    - Nonprofit organizations: look for .org (though this is no longer restricted to nonprofits)
    - Many country codes, such as .us, .uk. and .de, are no longer tightly controlled and may be misused. Look at the country code, but also use the techniques in sections 2 and 4 below to see who published the web page.
- Look for appropriateness.
    - What kind of information source do you think is most reliable for your topic?
    - Is it published by an entity that makes sense?
- Who "published" the page?
    - In general, the publisher is the agency or person operating the "server" computer from which the document is issued.
    - The server is usually named in first portion of the URL (between http:// and the first /)
- Have you heard of this entity before?
    - Does it correspond to the name of the site? Should it?
    - You can rely more on information that is published by the source:
    - Look for New York Times news from www.nytimes.com
    - Look for health information from any of the agencies of the National Institute of Health on sites with nih somewhere in the domain name.

2. Scan the perimeter of the page, looking for answers to these questions:

Techniques for Web Evaluation :
1. Look for links that say "About us," "Philosophy," "Background," "Biography," etc.
2. If you cannot find any links like these, you can often find this kind of information if you Truncate back the URL.

   INSTRUCTIONS for Truncating back a URL: In the top Location Box, delete the end characters of the URL stopping just before each / (leave the slash). Press enter to see if you can see more about the author or the origins/nature of the site providing the page.

   Continue this process, one slash (/) at a time, until you reach the first single / which is preceded by the domain name portion. This is the page's server or "publisher."
3. Look for the date "last updated"—usually at the bottom of a web page.

   Check the date on all the pages on the site.

Questions to ask:
- What are the implications?
- Who wrote the page?
  - If you cannot find this, locate the publisher by truncating back the URL (see technique above). Does this publisher claim responsibility for the content? Does it explain why the page exists in any way?
  - Web pages are all created with a purpose in mind by some person or agency or entity. They do not simply "grow" on the web like mildew grows in moist corners.
  - You are looking for someone who claims accountability and responsibility for the content.
  - An e-mail address with no additional information about the author is not sufficient for assessing the author's credentials.
  - If this is all you have, try emailing the author and asking politely for more information about him/her.
- Is the page dated? Is it current enough?
  - Is it "stale" or "dusty" information on a time-sensitive or evolving topic?
  - CAUTION: Undated factual or statistical information is no better than anonymous information. Don't use it.
  - How recent the date needs to be depends on your needs.
  - For some topics you want current information.
  - For others, you want information put on the web near the time it became known.
  - In some cases, the importance of the date is to tell you whether the page author is still maintaining an interest in the page, or has abandoned it.
- What are the author's credentials on this subject?
  - Does the purported background or education look like someone who is qualified to write on this topic?
  - Might the page be by a hobbyist, self-proclaimed expert, or enthusiast?
  - Is the page merely an opinion? Is there any reason you should believe its content more than any other page?
- Is the page a rant, an extreme view, possibly distorted or exaggerated?
  - If you cannot find strong, relevant credentials, look very closely at documentation of sources (next section).
  - Anyone can put anything on the web for pennies in just a few minutes. Your task is to distinguish between the reliable and questionable.
  - Many web pages are opinion pieces offered in a vast public forum.

- You should hold the author to the same degree of credentials, authority, and documentation that you would expect from something published in a reputable print resource (book, journal article, good newspaper).

3. Look for indicators of quality information:

Techniques for Web Evaluation:
1. Look for a link called "links," "additional sites," "related links," etc.
2. In the text, if you see little footnote numbers or links that might refer to documentation, take the time to explore them.

   What kinds of publications or sites are they? Reputable? Scholarly?

   Are they real? On the web (where no publisher is editing most pages), it is possible to create totally fake references.
3. Look at the publisher of the page (first part of the URL).

   Expect a journal article, newspaper article, and some other publications that are recent to come from the original publisher IF the publication is available on the web.

   Look at the bottom of such articles for copyright information or permissions to reproduce.

Questions to ask:
- What are the implications?
- Are sources documented with footnotes or links?
  - Where did the author get the information?
  - As in published scholarly/academic journals and books, you should expect documentation.
- If there are links to other pages as sources, are they to reliable sources?
  - Do the links work?
  - In scholarly/research work, the credibility of most writings is proven through footnote documentation or other means of revealing the sources of information. Saying what you believe without documentation is not much better than just expressing an opinion or a point of view. What credibility does your research need?
  - An exception can be journalism from highly reputable newspapers. But these are not scholarly. Check with your instructor before using this type of material.
  - Links that don't work or are to other weak or fringe pages do not help strengthen the credibility of your research.
- If reproduced information (from another source), is it complete, not altered, not fake or forged?
  - Is it retyped? If so, it could easily be altered.
  - Is it reproduced from another publication?
  - Are permissions to reproduce and copyright information provided?
- Is there a reason there are not links to the original source if it is online (instead of reproducing it)?
  - You may have to find the original to be sure a copy of something is not altered and is complete.
- Look at the URL: is it from the original source?
  - If you find a legitimate article from a reputable journal or other publication, it should be accompanied by the copyright statement and/or permission to reprint. If it is not, be suspicious.
  - Try to find the source. If the URL of the document is not to the original source, it is likely that it is illegally reproduced, and the text could be altered, even with the copyright information present.
- Are there links to other resources on the topic?
  - Are the links well chosen, well organized, and/or evaluated/annotated?
  - Do the links work?
  - Do the links represent other viewpoints?

- Do the links (or absence of other viewpoints) indicate a bias?
  - Many well developed pages offer links to other pages on the same topic that they consider worthwhile. They are inviting you to compare their information with other pages.
  - Links that offer opposing viewpoints as well as their own are more likely to be balanced and unbiased than pages that offer only one view. Anything not said that could be said? And perhaps would be said if all points of view were represented?
  - Always look for bias.
  - Especially when you agree with something, check for bias.

4. What do others say?

Techniques for Web Evaluation:
1. Find out what other web pages link to this page.
   a. Use alexa.com URL information:
      Type or paste the URL into alexa.com's search box.
      Click on "Overview".
      You will see, depending on the volume of traffic to the page:
      Traffic details.
      "Related links" to other sites visited by people who visited the page.
      Sites that link to the page.
      Contact/ownership info for the domain name.
      A link to the "Wayback Machine," an archive showing what the page looked like in the past.
   b. Do a link: search in Google, Yahoo!, or another search engine where this can be done:
      1. Copy the URL of the page you are investigating (Ctrl+C in Windows).
      2. Go to the search engine site, and type link: in the search box.
      3. Paste the URL into the search box immediately following link: (no space after the colon).
         The pages listed all contain one or more links to the page you are looking for.
         If you find no links, try a shorter portion of the URL, stopping after each /.
2. Look up the title or publisher of the page in a reputable directory that evaluates its contents (Librarians' Index, Infomine, About.com, or a specialized directory you trust).
3. Look up the author's name in Google or Yahoo!
   INSTRUCTIONS in Google: Search the name three ways:
   a. without quotes—Joe Webauthor
   b. enclosed in quotes as a phrase—"Joe Webauthor"
   c. enclosed in quotes with * between the first and last name—"Joe * Webauthor" (The * can stand for any middle initial or name in Google only).

Questions to ask:
- What are the implications?
- Who links to the page?
  - Are there many links?
  - What kinds of sites link to it?
  - What do they say?
  - Sometimes a page is linked to only by other parts of its own site (not much of a recommendation).
  - Sometimes a page is linked to by its fan club, and by detractors. Read both points of view.
- Is the page listed in one or more reputable directories or pages?

239

- Good directories include a tiny fraction of the web, and inclusion in a directory is therefore noteworthy.
- But read what the directory says! It may not be 100% positive.
- What do others say about the author or responsible authoring body?
  - "Googling" someone can be revealing. Be sure to consider the source. If the viewpoint is radical or controversial, expect to find detractors.
  - Also see which blogs refer to the site, and what they say about it. Google Blog Search is a good way to do this; search on the site's name, author, or URL.

5. Does it all add up?

Techniques for Web Evaluation:
1. Step back and think about all you have learned about the page. Listen to your gut reaction. Think about why the page was created, the intentions of its author(s).

   If you have doubts, ask your instructor or come to one of the library reference desks and ask for advice.
2. Be sensitive to the possibility that you are the victim of irony, spoof, fraud, or other falsehood.
3. Ask yourself if the web is truly the best place to find resources for the research you are doing.

Questions to ask:
- So what? What are the implications?
- Why was the page put on the web?
  - Inform, give facts, give data?
  - Explain, persuade?
  - Sell, entice?
  - Share?
  - Disclose?
  - These are some of the reasons to think of. The web is a public place, open to all. You need to be aware of the entire range of human possibilities of intentions behind web pages.
  - Might it be ironic? Satire or parody?
  - Think about the "tone" of the page.
  - Humorous? Parody? Exaggerated? Overblown arguments?
  - Outrageous photographs or juxtaposition of unlikely images?
  - Arguing a viewpoint with examples that suggest that what is argued is ultimately not possible.
  - It is easy to be fooled, and this can make you look foolish in turn.
- Is this as credible and useful as the resources (books, journal articles, etc.) available in print or online through the library?
  - Are you being completely fair? Too harsh? Totally objective? Requiring the same degree of "proof" you would from a print publication?
  - Is the site good for some things and not for others?
  - Are your hopes biasing your interpretation?
  - What is your requirement (or your instructor's requirement) for the quality of reliability of your information?
  - In general, published information is considered more reliable than what is on the web. But many, many reputable agencies and publishers make great stuff available by "publishing" it on the web. This applies to most governments, most institutions and societies, many publishing houses and news sources. But take the time to check it out.
- WHY? Rationale for Evaluating What You Find on the Web

- The World Wide Web can be a great place to accomplish research on many topics. But putting documents or pages on the web is easy, cheap or free, unregulated, and unmonitored (at least in the USA). There is a famous Steiner cartoon published in the New Yorker (July 5, 1993) with two dogs sitting before a terminal looking at a computer screen; one says to the other "On the Internet, nobody knows you're a dog." The great wealth that the Internet has brought to so much of society is the ability for people to express themselves, find one another, exchange ideas, discover possible peers worldwide they never would have otherwise met, and, through hypertext links in web pages, suggest so many other people's ideas and personalities to anyone who comes and clicks. There are some real "dogs" out there, but there's also great treasure.

Therein lies the rationale for evaluating carefully whatever you find on the Web. The burden is on you—the reader—to establish the validity, authorship, timeliness, and integrity of what you find. Documents can easily be copied and falsified or copied with omissions and errors—intentional or accidental. In the general World Wide Web there are no editors (unlike most print publications) to proofread and "send it back" or "reject it" until it meets the standards of a publishing house's reputation. Most pages found in general search engines for the web are self-published or published by businesses small and large with motives to get you to buy something or believe a point of view. Even within university and library web sites, there can be many pages that the institution does not try to oversee. The web needs to be free like that!! And you, if you want to use it for serious research, need to cultivate the habit of healthy skepticism, of questioning everything you find with critical thinking.

More About Evaluating Web Sources

Evaluating Information Found on the Internet
<http://www.library.jhu.edu/researchhelp/general/evaluating/>
An excellent series of pages on this subject (from the Milton Library at Johns Hopkins University).

For annotated descriptions of many other good guides to evaluating web pages, search the subject "Evaluation of Internet Resources" in the Librarians' Internet Index <http://lii.org>.

University of Alberta
University of Alberta Libraries
Edmonton, Alberta, Canada

Critical Evaluation of Resources on the Internet

Many of the same methods used to evaluate print sources, such as journal articles and books, also apply to the evaluation of resources on the Internet. In addition, there are some evaluation criteria that are unique to Internet resources.

The following points are intended to provide assistance in evaluating resources on the Internet. Unlike most books and journal articles, which undergo a peer review process prior to publication, anyone can publish anything on the Internet. For that reason, it is imperative to critically evaluate all information taken from resources on the Internet.

Evaluation Criteria
1. Scope and Subject Matter
   What subject is covered?
   What is the purpose of the site?
   Is the site intended to be comprehensive or selective?
   Who is the intended audience? What is the intended age or academic level?

How does the site compare with other related sites? With other related print sources?

Is the information unique, or is it available in other forms?

2. Authority

    What are the credentials of the author(s)/organization who produced the site?

    Is the author/organization well regarded in the field covered by the resource?

    Is information concerning the author(s)/organization included on the site?

    Is contact information for the author(s)/organization provided?

    On which server is the site mounted?

    Is it reputable? Sponsored?

    Is there a tilde (~) in the url? This may indicate a personal web directory, thereby reflecting a personal rather than institutional viewpoint.

    Is there an obvious bias? Is this site designed for promotional purposes?

    Does the address, specifically the domain, suggest the perspective from which the site was designed and does this suit your purposes? For example, ".edu," ".com," ".gov" respectively imply education, commercial, and government origins.

    Did you link to the site from another site of which you know and trust the credentials?

    Has the site been favorably reviewed by a browser or other Internet reviewing agency?

    Have the contents been refereed?

    Have the contents been carefully edited?

    Are there grammar, punctuation, or spelling errors?

    Is appropriate attribution given where required?

3. Currency and Completeness

    When was the site created?

    When was it last updated, and is this done regularly?

    How current are the links? Do they work?

    Does the site evolve over time, or would one visit be sufficient?

    Is post-publishing editing allowed in the case of electronic journals?

    Is the document complete, or has it also been published in an expanded print version?

    Are all graphics included in the electronic format?

4. Design

    Are the resources well organized and logically presented?

    Are the text and background colour choices contrasting enough for the text to be easily read?

    Is the background plain enough for the text to be easily read?

    Are the graphics clear and representative?

    Are the graphics functional or decorative?

    Are the graphics too complex and make the page frustratingly slow to load up or to print?

    Is the page cluttered? Or does it include too much blank space which makes printing costly?

    If the site is multimedia, consider creativity, quality of the image and sound, and interactivity.

    Is multimedia appropriate for the site?

    Is an indication of size provided in kilobytes where a link leads to large volumes of data (text, images, video, or voice)?

5. Ease of Use

    Is it easy for the intended audience to connect to the site?

    Is the site user friendly with an effective interface?

    Is the design of the site linear enough so that the user can follow through and know that they have examined all components?

    Is there an option for line-mode (text) browser as well as multimedia browser?

Is there a requirement for special software and, if so, can the software be accessed or downloaded easily?

In the case of compressed files, is it clear how to gain access to the files?

Is the site open to anyone? Or do some sections require registration or payment?

In what language is the site written?

If the site is offered in translation, is the translation accurate?

Are the addresses of linking urls provided so that viewers using printed or downloaded versions of the site can still access them?

Are special needs users considered in the design? For example, are alternate text descriptions provided for the visually impaired? How will the page function for hearing impaired users?

Chapter 20

MEDIA CENTER

AUDIOVISUAL ROOMS

Barry University
Monsignor William Barry Memorial Library
Miami Shores, Florida

INDIVIDUAL USE OF AV ROOM

The first room has 2 listening stations with CD machines and 2 viewing stations with TV/VCR combos. There is 1 viewing station with a TV and DVD player. The 1st room is for individual use only. These stations are available on a first come, first serve basis. Headphones are available at Circulation Desk. They check out for 3 hours. Headphones can also be used on any of the computers in the computer lab (LIB 205.)

GROUP USE OF AV ROOM

The second room will have 1 listening station with CD machine and 1 viewing station with TV, VCR, and DVD machine. This room is for group use. This group AV room may be reserved for 2 hours at a time. There is a limit of 1 reserve period per day per student. Please contact the Circulation Desk to reserve this room. You must schedule this room with at least one day notice. No same day appointments will be accepted. A daily schedule of appointments and times will be posted in the room. When not reserved for use, this room can be used on a first come, first serve basis. There is a door that will allow privacy and noise reduction.

SLIDE PROJECTORS

There are 2 slide projectors that can be checked out at the Reserve Room. These will circulate for 3 hours. Slide projectors can be used within the library in study rooms.

GENERAL GUIDELINES

Benedict College
Benjamin F. Payton Learning Resource Center
Columbia, South Carolina

Introduction

The Media Center is located on the Court Level; various educational materials are located in this area. The function of the center is to acquire, organize and disseminate audiovisual materials that support the college curricula to maintain a well-rounded collection of a variety of AV materials and to assist the faculty and students in research.

Located in the Media Center, the Media Laboratory contains the collection of film loops, filmstrip, slides, multi-media kits, audiocassettes and other commercially produced instructional media. Faculty/staff members only may check out materials for classroom use. For students, media resources are to be used in-house only. (Materials must be requested at least three (3) days prior to the utilization date.)

Opening-Closing Hours

Monday-Friday—8:30am-12:00noon and 1:00pm-5:00pm
Saturday-Sunday—CLOSED

Facilities

The Literature Room is used for phonograph and audiotape (reel to reel, cartridge and cassette) machines. The room is available for faculty, staff, and student listening. Headphones are provided and must be used at all times.
The viewing room is for faculty, staff, and student use. The room is used for presentations and reviewing of productions.

Staff

The Media Specialist, under the supervision of the Director of Library Services, is responsible for obtaining free and rental materials for teachers upon request, consulting with individual classroom teachers, informing of available media resources, providing operators and equipment, keeping equipment and materials in repair, classifying and storing materials, training operators of audiovisual equipment, assisting curriculum committees on appropriate audiovisual materials, assisting instructors, providing delivery and pickup service for films, assisting presenters in seminars, workshops, etc. and demonstrating how to use audiovisual materials and equipment, helping classroom teachers and students with the production of simple teaching materials, producing audiovisual materials for the classroom, and directing audiovisual equipment. That person also selects and purchases new materials, with the help of faculty, staff, and students.

Functions:

- Preparing orders for materials and equipment.
- Assisting faculty, staff and students in the selection of materials.
- Providing orders for Faculty and Staff.
- Dubbing tapes.
- Circulating of materials to faculty and staff.
- Scheduling equipment and AV materials for faculty and staff.
- Repairing films and audiotapes.
- Video and audio taping.
- Serving as hostess.
- Serving as tour guide.
- Making materials equipment and space available.
- Inventorying.
- Organizing collections.
- Providing Instruction in the use of Media Resources and Services.
- Teaching library media skills to students, including knowledge of the scope and sequence of skills.
- Providing reading, viewing and listening equipment and services.
- Planning for the flexible use of facilities.

To Lecture/Make Media Presentations to Large Student Groups:
- Speaks to students to identify objectives of presentation.

- Speaks to students to explain importance of objectives.
- Discusses with students to answer students' questions.
- Translates evaluation to change presentation.
- Speaks to students in responses to student questions.

To Inform Teachers About Media:
- Confers with teachers to inform of materials and equipment.
- Assesses teaching needs to suggest appropriate materials.
- Plans small groups to demonstrate audiovisual services.

To Teach Basic Audio/Visual Course Included in the Language Arts Course
- Describes media requirement to teach use of media in instruction.
- Describes group size contingencies to teach use of media in instruction.

If the Media Center has ordered previously, the Media Specialist reminds them of their ordering history with the Educational Film Library and asks for a free preview. If a company refuses to bargain and requires a rental fee and the faculty member insists on having the film sent for preview, the faculty member's department must agree to pay the preview fee, the return shipping cost, and to return the video/film within the specified time limit.

The Media Specialist sends the invoice, which includes the shipping fee to the department. The Manager returns it to the company.

Many companies prefer to apply the rental fee to the purchase cost of the video. The logistics for applying the rental fee to the purchase cost are too convoluted and difficult to deal with in the Benedict College systems. Quite often when previewing a video, the faculty decides that the video is inappropriate and sends it back. In such a case there is no purchase price to apply the rental fee against. Therefore, the Media Center does not pay rental fees toward the purchase of a video.

Video/Film Distribution of Vendors

Whenever order requests are made for films from a company which has not been used previously (particularly when the film is expensive), the Media Specialist calls the company to learn about the company's strengths, what kind of materials are kept in inventory and to cultivate a customer service relationship. He/she shops around to see if another company has the same item for less. It is beneficial to do as much research as possible when ordering from an untried company. The Internet is used to try to locate hard-to-find distributors.

When the Media Specialists find a review or catalog ad for a video/film requested previously by a faculty member that fits in with one or more disciplines, the Media Specialist will place an order. However, films are also bought that concentrate in just a specific area to meet the needs of a particular department.

It is best to ascertain whether a company accepts a purchase order or requires prepayment. Questions are asked, such as, will the company allow returns? Prepayment is avoided if at all by a particular department.

Chapter 21

OVERDUE, LOST, OR DAMAGED ELECTRONIC MATERIALS

FINES AND FEES

Tacoma Public Library
Tacoma, Washington

Audio Books

- 21 day checkout
- 3 renewals (unless there are HOLDS)
- 20 cents per day overdue fine
- Up to 10 audio books at any one time

DVD / VHS

- 7 day checkout
- No renewals
- $1.00 per day per DVD overdue fine
- 20 cents per day per VHS overdue fine
- Up to 10 DVD / VHS at any one time

Compact Discs

- 21 day checkout
- 3 renewals (unless there are HOLDS)
- 20 cents per day overdue fine
- Up to 10 compact discs at any one time

Placing HOLDS

- 20 items on HOLD at any time in any combination within these limits.
- Up to 20 books
- Up to 10 DVD / VHS
- Up to 10 compact discs
- Up to 10 audio books.

Chapter 22

REPRODUCTION OF AUDIO, PRINT, SCANNED, AND GRAPHIC IMAGES FOR USERS

NOTE: ALL OF THE PRICES LISTED IN THIS SECTION ARE ONLY IN EFFECT UNTIL JANUARY 2, 2008. ALL PRICES ARE SUBJECT TO CHANGE.

AUDIOTAPE DUPLICATION

Portland Community College
Portland Community College Libraries
Portland, Oregon

Audiotape duplication

A number of instructors have made audiotape lessons and associated material available for duplication to interested students, staff and faculty.

Self service

Each campus library has duplication equipment set up for patrons to duplicate their own tapes. Help is available if needed. In order to avoid copyright violations duplication is limited to tapes the library provides for duplication. No other commercial or off-air programs may be duplicated.

The user must supply his/her own tape or tapes either in C-60 or C-90 formats, depending on class or program desired. Check with your instructor regarding tape length or call the library.

In special circumstances, library staff will duplicate tapes. Please ask at the check out desk to make arrangements for this service.

Tapes are processed on a first come, first served basis with guaranteed completion in 24 hours —with one exception. If tapes for an entire large lesson set are requested on one request form, time limitations may require staff to duplicate only the first 2 or 3 lessons for immediate use, processing the remainder within the next day or two. Completed tapes, sorted by patron's last name, may be picked up at the circulation desk.

Note

While master tape decks are continuously serviced and program tapes are periodically re-mastered, the audio quality on the duplicated tapes will vary. The sound quality will be affected by player brand and condition, tape brand and source of the original material supplied for the master tapes. Questions regarding sound quality should be directed to the library circulation staff.

Copyright restrictions prohibit the duplication of commercial or off-air tape programs.

PHOTOCOPYING AND PRINTING

Seattle Public Library
Seattle, Washington

FEES FOR PRINTING, PHOTOCOPYING AND FAXING

PURPOSE

To provide a policy to charge patrons for the value-added service of computer printouts, faxes and photocopies. The policy must be equitable for our patrons and support the Seattle Public Library in its efforts to be good stewards of its resources. The Library underscores its commitment to provide free basic library services. For the purposes of this policy, basic library services include, but are not limited to research and reference services and online searching of remote databases.

POLICY

It is the policy of the Seattle Public Library to charge for faxes, photocopying and printing at public-access computers to defray financial costs, conserve resources and ensure equity-of-access standards. Discretionary guidelines will be established to help staff make exceptions to this policy in a uniform, unbiased, and non-discriminatory manner.

Talbot Belmond Public Library
Belmond, Iowa

Photocopying Policy

Black & white and color copies can be made at the library.

Photocopying Charges & Policy

The library staff will make photocopies as a service to the public for the following fees:

Black & White	$ .20 (8 1/2 × 11 size)
Color	$1.00 (8 1/2 × 11 size)
	(11" × 17" size paper counts as 2 copies)

Students will be allowed to copy 5 pages free per day from the library's books or magazines if needed for a school assignment. If more than 5 pages are copied, there will be a charge of 10 cents per page.

Five (5) free black & white copies will be made for ALL patrons out of reference and other books not allowed to be checked out. Copies in excess of 5 will be ten cents each.

Adult patrons may make their own copies rather than having the staff do it if they prefer.

Colored paper is 5 cents extra per page.

The Library reserves the right to refuse to accept a copying order if, in its judgment, fulfillment of the order would involve violation of copyright law.

University of California San Francisco
Galen UCSF Digital Library
San Francisco, California

Photocopying and Cashiering Services

Information on copy rates, photocopiers, copy cards, and digital media.

Photocopying

Self-service photocopiers are available in the following locations:

Parnassus 2nd floor: Room 211

Parnassus 3rd floor: Room 327

Mission Bay Library: Copy Room

> Copiers support stapling, reduction, enlargement, and automatic two-sided copying.
> All library copiers use debit-style copy cards.
> Please recycle paper and used copy cards in the copy rooms.
> Color copying is not available in the Library. Inquire at the Circulation Desk or call . . . for information regarding color copying of non-circulating materials.
> There are no coin-operated copiers.
> The Library cannot be responsible for lost or damaged copy cards.

Copy Cards

| Cashier's Window (UCSF affiliates) | | Cashier's Window (Non-UCSF) | | Vending Machines (Non-UCSF) | |
| $0.12/copy | | $0.22/copy* | | $0.22/copy** | |
Price	# of copies	Price	# of copies	Price	Max # copies
$ 6.00	50	$ 11.94	50	$ 1.00	4
$12.00	100	$ 23.87	100	$ 5.00	20
$60.00	500	$119.35	500	$10.00	41
				$20.00	83

*   Plus tax, card price includes tax.
** Plus tax; tax charged at copier.

UCSF-Affiliate Rates

Discounted, non-taxable, copy cards for UCSF personnel and students are available at the Cashier's Window at the Parnassus Library and at the Mission Bay Library Front Desk. A valid UCSF ID is required to purchase discounted cards.

Copy Card Vending Machines (Non-UCSF rates)

Vending machines are located in Room 211 of the Parnassus Library and in the Mission Bay Library Copy Room.

- Purchase a card for $1.00 then add value to the card.
- Card dispensers do not give change.
- The vending machines accept only cards purchased at the vending machines. The cards are green.

- Please purchase only the amount needed. Refunds cannot be given.

Digital Media

The following media formats are available for purchase at the Parnassus Library:

Media type	Fee*
3.5" 1.44mb HD formatted diskette (PC or Mac)	$ 1.00
Zip disk: 100mb (PC)	$12.00
Zip disk: 250mb (PC)	$14.00
80min 700mb 1x-48x CD-R	$ 2.00
High Speed CD-RW 4x-10x 650mb	$ 3.00
Mini DV 60min	$ 6.50

* Plus tax. Returns cannot be accepted.

Staff-Mediated Photocopy

Photocopying is done by Library staff for users who do not wish to do their own photocopying. Service is provided as promptly as possible.

To request this service fill out a Staff-Mediated Photocopy Request Form (form also available at the Copy Center). Bring the form and materials to be photocopied to the Cashier's Window.

Cashiering

Fees for library services and products may be paid at the Copy Center, located on the 2nd floor of the Parnassus Library, or the Front Desk at the Mission Bay Library.

Payments accepted at Parnassus:
- cash
- pre-printed personal check drawn on a California bank (with a valid CA Driver License)
- money order
- Recharge Account number(*)
- MasterCard
- VISA
- AMEX
- Discover
- ATM cards

Payments accepted at Mission Bay:
- cash
- Recharge Account number(*)
- (*) If reimbursement is sought from a federal fund source, the customer accepts full responsibility that such costs are allowable under federal policy.

Hours for the Cashier's Window are located on the Library Hours page.

Lehigh University
Library and Technology Services
Bethlehem, Pennsylvania

Self-Service and Full-Service Photocopying

Self-Service Photocopying

Public photocopiers are available in Fairchild-Martindale and Linderman Libraries. Copies cost $.05 per page. All photocopiers only accept copy cards available at the Circulation desk. Copy cards come in set values of $5.00 and $25.00. The $5.00 charge is for a one time card cost of $1.00 and 80 copies. The $25.00 charge is for a one time card cost of $1.00 and 480 copies. Once copies are depleted on a card, the card can be recharged at the Circulation desk for any value. Cards can be purchase with cash or by charging a GoldPlus account, a personal, research or departmental bursar account.

Microform Reader Printers/Scanners

In addition to the photocopiers, there are microform reader printers and scanners located on the second floor of the Fairchild-Martindale Library. To print microform copies, the printers accept only coins; however images can be scanned and saved in the TIFF format on a personal CD or USB device.

For assistance with the photocopiers or microform readers, please ask at the Circulation Desk Fairchild-Martindale Library (ext. 8-3070 on-campus)

Full-Service Photocopy

The Library also offers a copy service for Lehigh University faculty, staff and students. To request photocopies of reports or journal articles, please fill out this ILLiad form. Most articles will be scanned and sent to you through electronic delivery (accessed from the ILLiad Login page). If needed the library will photocopy materials; you may choose to pick up the copy at the library or have them sent to you at no charge. You will be charged a fee if you specifically request a photocopy when an electronic copy is available. For an extra fee, of $1.00 per article, we will mail them to an off-campus address. For an additional fee of $3.00 per article we will fax to an off-campus address. Copy fees may be charged to a University account or to a student's Bursar bill.

Full-Service Photocopy Prices

Photocopies	$ .05 per page
Microform copies	$ .25 per page
Transparencies	$ .60 each
U.S. Mail Delivery	$1 extra per article
Off-campus Fax Delivery	$3 extra per article

Fresno County Public Library
Fresno, California

Fees & Fines

Fines: (Includes government documents, materials borrowed from outside SJVLS, microfiche, microfilm, reference materials, and 16 mm films)

Basic Overdue rate: $0.25 per item per day overdue, cumulating to a maximum of $4.00.

Special Materials: $1.00 per item per day to a maximum equal to the cost of the item.

Fees for Special Services

Computer print-out: $0.10 per page (black & white)/ $0.85 per page (color)

Faxing of information: $1.50 for the first page, plus $0.30 for each additional page, plus, for calls out of Fresno County, $0.25 for the first page and $0.15 for each additional page. No charge for FAX cover sheet.

Mailing of Information: $1.80 for the first page, plus $0.18 for each additional page.

Floppy Disc: $1.00 (includes sales tax)

Hold notices: For items borrowed from outside the San Joaquin Valley Library System, first class postage.

Information & Referral

Newsletter Subscription: $15.00

Self-Service Subscription: $77.00 (Includes sales tax)

Training Session: $10.00

Meeting Room Cleaning charge: Actual cost, not to exceed $80.00

On-Demand Book Talk: $35.00 + mileage

Photocopies (except from Microform)

    Self Serve Photocopies : $0.10 per page

    Staff-Made Photocopies : $0.20 per page

Photocopies from Microform

    Self-serve copies : $0.25

    Staff-made copies : $1.00

Rentals

    Books/Books on Tape : $0.50 for the first week and $0.25 per day thereafter (Includes sales tax)

    Videos: No charge for checkout during the life of Measure B. $ 0.25 overdue per day to a maximum of $4.00.

    Typewriter Rental : free

Photocopy and printout fees will be charged to patrons supplying their own paper.

Columbia University
Columbia University Libraries
New York, New York

Columbia University Libraries
Publication and Digital Reproduction Policy and Procedures
4/5/04

Patrons seeking to quote from or publish in any way materials held by the Columbia University Libraries should refer to the most current copyright legislation for information relating to the use of published and unpublished materials. It is the user's responsibility to adhere to the provisions of this law and, where necessary, to seek permission to publish, quote from or reproduce materials from copyright holders.

To arrange publication of Libraries' materials, a request-to-publish letter must also be sent to the Director of the distinctive collection or division holding those materials. These include:

    Avery Architecture & Fine Arts Library
    Burke Theological Library

C. V. Starr East Asian Library
Rare Book & Manuscript Library
Columbia University Archives
Art Properties Division
Oral History Research Office

For items from other collections, please contact the Director of Preservation

This letter must contain the following information:

information about the forthcoming publication (including format [for example, print, microform media, or electronic], title, expected date of publication, name of author), name of publisher clear information about the item(s) to be published (name of author or creator, name of collection, date of creation, page or item numbers, where available).

In many cases, the Columbia University Libraries can give permission only as holders of physical objects. Ordinarily, such permission covers non-exclusive, world-wide rights for a single edition in a single format and a single language for five years. Publication of paperback and hardcover editions is considered a single edition, only when publication is simultaneous. Other rights or editions or extended periods of use may require separate requests and, when relevant, additional fees.

The request-to-publish letter must be acknowledged in writing by Columbia University Libraries before publication. The appropriate form of citation will be included in the acknowledgement letter.

Please note: Materials published by the Trustees of Columbia University or held by the Columbia University Archives are not covered by this policy. Please contact the Director of University Archives at...

Publication Fees

Note: These fees do not include the costs of reproduction. A list of the fees charged by Preservation for the costs of making reproductions is available at:

http://www.columbia.edu/cu/lweb/services/preservation/reproductions.html

The fee schedule for making reproductions from the Avery Library collections may be found at:

http://www.columbia.edu/cu/lweb/indiv/avery/averepro.html

Text

No fees are charged by Columbia for the quotation of limited amounts of textual material, from works held by the Libraries in books, articles or other scholarly works in all formats, although a citation should include the source text and the name of the holding library. Permission from the copyright owner may be required, depending on whether the use to be made of the material is a "fair use" under copyright law or falls under some other exemption under the law. Fair use is a principle under copyright law that allows the public to use portions of copyrighted material, without permission from the owner, under certain circumstances. While a fair use analysis does not always provide clear answers, in general, it would allow a short quotation, such as a sentence or two, in a scholarly or other non-commercial publication, as long as appropriate citations are included. For a much fuller discussion and interpretations of fair use, and links to other sites, see:

http://fairuse.stanford.edu/

http://www.utsystem.edu/ogc/intellectualproperty/copypol2.htm

http://counsel.cua.edu/copyright/resources/guidelines/Fair_use.cfm

Whole Works

The reproduction of whole or nearly whole works in any format can be arranged, providing current copyright laws are respected. Fees for such use must be negotiated with the holding library and may include royalties or other appropriate forms of compensation.

257

Images

The Columbia University Libraries require the payment of publication use fees for the use of images from its collections in books, articles, dust jackets, brochures, album covers, catalogs, other printed material, films, video and electronic media. Such fees are used to pay for the cost of maintaining and servicing the collections.

Publication Fee Schedule for Images

Note: All fees are per image. Payment must be received in advance of publication.

PRINT PUBLICATION

Print Run

1. Books and Periodicals 1-1000 1001-2500 Above 2,500

    501C3 (non-profit) Institutions $25 $50 $100

    Dissertations $0 $0 $0

    Commercial use $50 $100 $125

2. Advertising Brochures, Jackets, Album Covers, Promotional materials, and Other

    501C3 (non-profit) Institutions $50 $100 $100

    Commercial use $100 $250 $250

    Fees will be waived for images of materials loaned by Columbia for use in exhibitions when they are included in exhibition catalogs.

ELECTRONIC PUBLICATION (CD-ROM/DVD)

Same as print publication, including additional fees for use on cover or packaging as above

[For standard Oral History Research Office audio and video rates, see below.]

INTERNET/ONLINE

per image
501C3 (non-profit) Institutions $25
Personal use $50
Dissertation $0
All other $100

AUDIO

Oral History Research Office Standard Rates:

Audio per second/minute:

Commercial, $17/second—1 minute minimum
Nonprofit Commercial, $9/second—1 minute minimum, negotiable.
Nonprofit Educational, Broadcast: $5/second—1 minute minimum, negotiable.
Nonprofit Educational Non-broadcast, Processing Fee Only.

FILM/ VIDEO/TELEVISION

$250 per image, per minute, per medium. After one minute, time is pro-rated in 15 second intervals at $67.50 per quarter minute. Minimum payment $250.

Arrangements for filming within individual libraries must be made in advance and may involve a fee to cover staff time.

For onsite commercial filming charges and procedures, contact the Manager of Special Events and Commercial Filming, at . . .

Oral History Research Office Standard Rates:

Video per second/minute:

    Commercial, $28/second—1 minute minimum.

    Nonprofit Commercial, $14/second—1 minute minimum, negotiable.

    Nonprofit Educational, Broadcast—$10/second—1 minute minimum, negotiable.

    Nonprofit Educational, Non-broadcast, Processing Fee Only.

DISCOUNTS/WAIVERS

Publication fees for images or excerpts are waived for current Columbia University faculty, staff members and students. If a whole or nearly whole work is to be published or if more than 40 illustrations are required, a royalty arrangement should be negotiated.

METHODS OF PAYMENT

Invoices will be sent when the request-to-publish letter is acknowledged. The following methods of payment may be used:

1. Checks drawn on American banks or on branches of foreign banks located in the United States and payable in U.S. dollars to Columbia University

2. Credit cards: MasterCard or Visa, only. Please send card number, name as it appears on the card, expiration date, and authorize charge with your signature either by letter or by fax.

Please enclose a copy of Columbia University Libraries' acknowledgement letter with your payment.

Longwood University
Janet D. Greenwood Library
Farmville, Virginia

STUDENT PRINTING FROM THE LIBRARY & COMPUTER LABS

In order to effectively manage Longwood's ever-growing printing costs, Academic Computing (AC) utilizes the Pharos Uniprint system for the Lab and Library laser printers. This system allows AC to track printing trends across campus.

For the Fall and Spring semesters each student is given a quota of $13.50 (the equivalent of 150 black and white pages) and $6.75 (the equivalent of 75 black and white pages) for the three summer sessions. Color printing is available at a cost of $1.00 per page. When the student print quota has been met, a charge of 9 cents for black and white or $1.00 for color per page will be incurred. The excess print charges appear on the student's Longwood University LancerNet bill.

Effective Fall 2008, students will not have the ability to print single print jobs of over 75 pages in the academic computing labs or the Library. If a job of more than 75 pages is sent to the printer, a notice will appear asking the student to break the print job into smaller jobs of 75 pages or less. This process was implemented to reduce the number of accidental print jobs reported to IT.

Any student who wishes to print in an Academic Computing lab or Library public research station PCs MUST use their Longwood University ID card.

Any questions concerning billing must be submitted hard copy to User Support Services or by email to

REPRODUCTION FEES AND CONDITIONS OF USE

Austin Public Library
Austin History Center
Austin, Texas

Custom Photo Reproduction Price List

All reproduction prices include a 5% preservation fee

	Black and White Prints:	
Size in inches	RC Paper (for publication or display) Glossy or Pearl Finish	Fiber Base Paper (higher grade for exhibition) Standard Glossy Surface
8 × 10 (or smaller)	$12.60	$24.15
11 × 14	$22.05	$35.70
16 × 20	$36.75	$48.30
20 × 24	$52.50	$68.25
24 × 36	$67.73 (pearl only)	
30 × 40	$98.77 (pearl only)	

Second B&W print of same photograph (identical size and image) is 50% of first print price.

Toning is available. Add 100% to cost and one week to delivery.

Color prints can be made; cost is subject to commercial lab fees plus a $20.00 site removal charge.

Transparencies (slides) and Inter-negatives:	
35mm slides from original material $29.00 minimum)	$6.04 each
Duplicate 35mm slides (29.00 minimum)	$3.15 each
B&W internegative where required plus standard print price	$10.50 each
4 × 5 transparencies	$24.15 each

Digitized Images	
One scanned image, any resolution or file format	$12.60 each
CD charge	$ 1.00 each

Publication/Display Fee
    Please consult handout "Fees for Publication or Display of Austin History Center Materials."
Delivery and Payment:
    Normal delivery is four to six weeks (large or complex orders may take longer). Rush service charges are as follows:

Size of Print RC Paper	Regular turnaround	Two weeks: Add 50%	One week: Add 100%	Three days: Add 200%
8 × 10	$12.60	$18.90	$25.20	$37.80

11 × 14	$22.05	$33.08	$44.10	$66.15
16 × 20	$36.75	$55.13	$73.50	$110.25
20 × 24	$52.50	$78.75	$105.00	$157.50

Rush service charges for prints over 20" × 24", fiber base paper prints, transparencies, and digitized images increase at the same rate.

Payment is required in advance by cash, check or money order made out to "Austin Public Library." 100% payment is required on all orders. Tax is added where applicable unless proof of tax-exempt status is provided.

Postage and packaging fee totaling $5.00 must be paid at the time of the order. Large orders are subject to additional packaging fees. No mailing fees will be charged if customer's express carrier account is used.

State Library of Massachusetts
George Fingold Library
Boston, Massachusetts

Fee Schedule for Digital Imaging Services

The following is a fee schedule for the creation of digital images from photographic and cartographic origi-nals, printed and non-printed materials, and pre-existing digital files of these same items.

[Fees pertain to the photographing OR scanning of original items.]
From original:
Original size = up to 11" × 17" ...... $25 per image, to 20 images.
" " = >11" × 17" .... call for quote.
Pricing will be assessed on a case-by-case basis for orders of more than 20 images.
From existing digital file:
$15 per file (jpegs only, unless otherwise determined by staff)

Thumbnails

As creating a "thumbnail" image requires the same amount of staff time to produce, the Library will not provide free or sample "thumbnail" or low-resolution images to patrons.

Image enhancement/modifications
• All scans or digital photographs are unmodified and unenhanced, except in circumstances where result-ing image is excessively dark and minor work can be done to lighten or clarify the image.
• Modifications and/or enhancements will be done only on a case-by-case basis.
• If modified or enhanced, two (2) versions of the files will be saved—unmodified and modified. (4 files total: 2 tif files, 2 jpgs)

Handling

In situations where the following apply, a handling fee of $30 per hour (minimum hour) will be assessed in addition to the image order:
• Research in excess of .5 hour
• Transportation of original to/from third-party outsourcing agents
• Conservation and other efforts to prepare original for photography, scanning or transport to third-party outsourced agents.
• Efforts to piece together images larger than 11" × 17", or those requiring multiple scans.

State Library of Massachusetts

Fee Schedule for Digital Imaging Services

Delivery

All images for the time being will be offered to the patron on a CD ROM, for an additional cost of $5. No images will be emailed.

This fee for media will be waived in the following circumstances:

- If the patron provides his or her own storage media.
- If the patron makes available to the Library a secure FTP site to which the image can be uploaded.

Shipping (See also Delivery.)

- Postage will be determined on a case-by-case basis, using the rate-finding tool available at www.usps.gov.
- For FedEx or UPS/DHL and other overnight carrier service, patron must provide the Library with a valid account number, or the fee for said service will be assessed and included in the summary of fees given in an invoice prior to signoff/approval.

Minimum turnaround

Minimum turnaround time, from the location of the original to final delivery should be between 7 and 10 business days, depending on order size and staff availability. This time does not include email or phone discussion with the patron. The Library must be in receipt of an official photo order request form, signed cost estimate/invoice, and completed permission to publish form (if applicable) in order to begin work.

Payment

Payment in full must be received before finished product will be shipped. The Library will accept payment in the form of a check, money order, or purchase order. At this time credit cards are not accepted as valid forms of payment. If using a purchase order, the number should be included in the signed/approved invoice before work can begin.

Rush

For a request that must be expedited in fewer than the minimum number of business days needed for turnaround quoted in our service guidelines, a rush fee equal to 50% of the total job (minus the costs of the media and shipping) will be assessed and added to the invoice.

Email delivery of images is available to employees of State agencies only, at the discretion of staff.

(For additional policies, please see the accompanying CD-ROM.)

Chapter 23

VIRTUAL REFERENCE

"ASK REFERENCE" GUIDELINES

Montana State University
Montana State University Libraries
Bozeman, Montana

E-Reference (Email, Chat, IM) Policies

Who can use this service?

- Our e-reference services are intended primarily for the students, faculty, and staff of Montana State University.
- We also serve the citizens of the state of Montana and anyone needing help with Montana-related topics.
- Students enrolled in the university's distance education or off-campus programs, as well as researchers with inquiries pertaining to our unique collections, are encouraged to use this service.

What kinds of questions may I ask?

- Questions of any kind may be posed through this service, but it is best suited for assistance with shorter, fact-based questions; access questions; and questions pertaining to best resource options or starting points for research.
- Reference librarians do not interpret information; provide legal, medical or financial advice; and will not provide answers for class assignments.
- Patrons requiring more involved research may be referred to private research options or encouraged to come into the MSU Libraries for additional assistance.
- Non-Montana residents posing questions unrelated to Montana or our collections at MSU-Bozeman will be encouraged to contact their local public or academic library for assistance.

How long will it take to get an answer?

- For email reference, we generally respond to questions within 24 hours during the regular work week (Monday-Friday, excluding holidays). Questions received after 5 PM on Fridays and on holidays may take as long as 72 hours to answer.
- For phone, chat, and IM reference, available whenever the reference desk is open, we usually respond within minutes. If you do not get a response, leave your email or phone number, and we'll get back to you as soon as we can.

Who will answer my question?

- MSU-Bozeman reference librarians answer all email reference questions. We are a team of faculty librarians with graduate degrees in Library and Information Science.

Electronic Collection Management Forms, Policies, Procedures, and Guidelines Manual

Longwood University
Janet D. Greenwood Library
Farmville, Virginia

Virtual Reference Services Policy

Virtual reference services are conducted on the internet using software such as instant messaging. For more information about the Greenwood Library's virtual reference services, see the Ask a Librarian page.

Eligibility

Priority is given to Longwood students, faculty, and staff for research questions.

Confidentiality

The library does not keep a log of completed reference transactions in any format—instant messaging, email, telephone, or face to face.

Use of Licensed Resources

Only authorized users (Longwood students, faculty, and staff) may be given access to material from databases with restrictive licenses.

Delivery of Material to Patrons

The library provides delivery of material to distance education patrons only, through our Document Delivery Service.

Scope of Service

The reference staff answers questions pertaining to research strategy and location of materials and services within the library. The reference staff may not:
- Answer medical, legal, or financial questions (though we will direct patrons to appropriate sources of information for such topics)
- Answer homework questions for patrons (though we will recommend information resources to help the patron complete the assignment successfully)
- Cooperate with requests for illegal material.

Patron Etiquette

In order to make the virtual reference transaction satisfying for all parties concerned, patrons should observe the following guidelines:
- Please be patient. You may need to wait if the librarian is already helping another patron at the information desk, over the phone, or via IM. If you don't have time to wait to chat with a librarian via instant messaging, you are welcome to submit your question through our Ask A Librarian email service.
- Do not type in all capital letters. It can be interpreted as YELLING.
- Harassment or misconduct of any type will not be tolerated. Common courtesies are expected and appreciated.
- The virtual reference staff reserves the right to refuse service to anyone who fails to observe these guidelines.

University of Michigan
University of Michigan Libraries
Ann Arbor, Michigan

Need Help? Ask a Librarian! Technical Information

Ask a Librarian instant messaging is a free, real-time reference service, provided by University Library reference staff on the Ann Arbor campus. Our IM reference service supports instant messaging using AOL Instant Messenger, MSN Messenger, or Yahoo! Messenger software. In addition, we use a meebo widget to provide our web-based instant messaging portion of the Ask a Librarian service.

With the meebo-based instant messaging reference service, University Library reference staff answer your questions via a chat dialog window in your web browser. When your conversation with the reference staff member is finished, click away from the Ask a Librarian web.

The meebo Ask a Librarian instant message service works best if your computer is equipped with some minimum features:

- the latest version of Internet Explorer, Safari or Firefox
- the latest version of Flash Player
- 56K modem or faster Internet connection (slower modem access will result in long delays between responses and screen refreshing)
- "cookies" and javascript enabled in your browser
- software firewall (such as Norton Internet Security) disabled

Because the responses between you and University Library reference staff on the Ann Arbor campus travel via the meebo server (located in California), some of the exchanges may seem slower than other messaging methods. Please submit your initial reference question once, and wait for University Library reference staff to reply to your chat request. Keep your web browser window; exiting your web browser may disconnect your conversation with Library reference staff.

If you experience technical problems when attempting to use this service, please submit your question via our web forms.

Our IM reference service allows us to talk to you via your AOL Instant Messenger (AIM) account, via your MSN Messenger account, or via your Yahoo! Messenger account. To use our IM service, you must have the appropriate software installed on your computer (or use your IM service's web version of their software, if available).

If you do not have an AIM screen name, an MSN Messenger account, or a Yahoo! ID/Messenger account, you need to register for an account with one of these services, and then download the free software. As soon as the IM software is installed, you can add the University Library's screen name to your personal Buddy or Contact List.

Please note: Because University Library reference staff cannot answer your technical questions about the IM software from these services, please review the service websites for instructions and hints on installing and using their IM software.

FAQs

The Alberta Library
Alberta, Ontario, Canada

What is Ask A Question (AAQ)?

Have questions about researching an assignment? Want to find out more about a subject, topic or hobby? Have a question that you have wondered about for years? Or maybe you need help finding information in the library catalogue. Whatever information you need, Ask A Question can help. This service allows you to submit your questions over the web to Alberta reference staff, who will provide help with finding the information you need and respond by e-mail.

Who can use AAQ?

Ask A Question serves the information needs of Alberta residents as well as patrons from participating post-secondary institutions, mainly students and instructors. Participating libraries have also agreed to answer questions from outside of Alberta. AAQ reserves the right to refer clients who are not Alberta residents and who are not asking a question related to Alberta to a virtual reference service closer to where you live.

What questions will AAQ answer?

For broad topics and assignments, we will direct you to resources, such as web sites, database articles, print material or other agencies where you are likely to find information on your topic. For narrow or simple questions we will provide you with an answer that is accompanied by supporting resources.

Can I ask Genealogy questions?

We accept reference questions that relate to tracing family history in Alberta. We also accept questions from Alberta residents who need genealogy research assistance. For all other types of genealogy research, we encourage you to visit your local library or consult a genealogy society. If your question requires in-depth research we will offer suggestions for web sites, books or agencies that can help you.

How do I ask my question?

Ask A Question requires you to submit:

> Your question—Please ask your question as fully as possible. Sometimes questions mean different things to different people. Providing us with as much information as you can will help us find resources appropriate to your question.

> Your email address—We need your email address so that we can email you your answer. Please double check your email address to make sure it is correct. If you haven't received a response within 72 hours of posting your question, search the archive.

If you live in Alberta, we also request:

> Your postal code—This helps us to direct your question to the most appropriate public library. If you need to request information from a particular library that is not where you live, please include the name of the library in the body of your question.

> Or

> Your educational institution and your program of study—To direct your question to your school's library and helps the library staff understand what type of information you need to answer your question.

Other questions may be asked to help us clarify what you are asking and the level of information you are looking for.

Why does AAQ need my email address?

We only use your email address for the purpose of sending an answer to you. We do not publish or disseminate your personal information or keep it for any other purpose.

Please double-check your email address when you register. If you submit it incorrectly, we cannot reply to you.

Please note that a valid email address is required in order for you to receive the answer to your question. If a valid email address is not provided, Ask A Question reserves the right to provide only a brief answer to your question.

Where is my answer?

There are three reasons why customers do not receive our answers via email:

- Most commonly is because the reply email address hasn't been entered accurately on the registration form. Please check our archive after 4 days to view your response.
- Email can also bounce if you are in a local network or behind a firewall that does not permit incoming email from our system.
- Your email account is blocking our email address due to security controls. Please ensure that the email address: aaq-admin@talonline.ca is added to your safe list.

Who answers questions?

Trained reference staff at participating public and post-secondary libraries throughout Alberta provide answers through the Ask A Question service.

How long does it take?

Upon receipt of your question, the service will send you an e-mail verifying that we have received your question. If you are asking a question of our public libraries, you will receive a response within 48 hours. If you are asking a question of our post-secondary libraries, you will receive a response within 24 hours. Questions are often answered much more quickly than our stated response times. If we are unable to provide a full answer to your question within the stated time, we will provide you with an initial starting point and provide follow-up information up to 72 hours after you have posted your question.

What will AAQ not provide?
- Advice on legal, medical or financial concerns
- Materials by fax or mail
- Detailed research
- Advice on matters of a personal nature
- Answers to homework questions (although we will help you on your way)

What is in the AAQ Archive?

Most questions submitted to Ask A Question will be saved automatically in the searchable Q & A Archive 72 hours after being submitted to Ask A Question. We reserve the right to determine if a question is not appropriate for archive purposes. If you provide personal or identifying information within the context of your question, it will be removed before entering the public archive. We do not require or collect personal information such as your name or phone number. Items will remain in the archive for six months when they will be removed because the information (especially internet based information) may become dated or the links may no longer work.

Can I evaluate AAQ?

Please give us some input! Along with our response, we will give you a link to a very short survey form. We would appreciate it if you would take a moment to send us your comments on our service. The information you give us will be used for statistical purposes only and will tell us how we are doing. Your comments will help us to improve the Ask A Question service.

Who can I contact regarding AAQ?

If you have questions or comments about the Ask A Question itself or any of its policies, please contact the administration office at aaq-admin@talonline.ca.

Please DO NOT use this email address to submit your reference or research questions. You will be redirected to the Ask A Question service.

Electronic Collection Management Forms, Policies, Procedures, and Guidelines Manual

State Library and Archives of Florida
Department of State Library and Archives of Florida
Tallahassee, Florida

FAQs

What is Ask a Librarian?

Ask a Librarian is a free online service that allows Floridians to chat live with a librarian for immediate assistance. A trained information professional can guide you to the answers you need in minutes rather than wasting hours navigating hundreds of unhelpful and irrelevant web sites. More than 90 libraries statewide collaborate to provide this service to their patrons and the patrons of other participating libraries. Ask a Librarian is a joint project of the College Center for Library Automation and the Tampa Bay Library Consortium. Ask a Librarian is funded as part of the Florida Electronic Library by a Library Services and Technology Act (LSTA) grant.

What is Ask a Librarian Mobile?

Ask a Librarian is now optimized for your handheld device. The e-mail portion of our service is available now. Visit our mobile interface http://www.askalibrarian.org/mobile, then choose your library from the list. E-mail your question anytime, and a librarian from your local library will answer you via mail. We are working on adding more features, including a live chat service.

How does Ask a Librarian work?

Watch a brief demo of the Ask a Librarian service. (1.31 meg Flash Movie)

When you click on the chat button, your question enters a queue for the on-duty librarians. Librarians answer questions in the order they receive them. Typically, depending on the expected traffic, between two and six librarians staff the Ask a Librarian desk during the hours we are available for live chat.

When the librarian accepts your question, you are able to chat one-on-one with that librarian while he or she helps you find what you need by guiding you through the myriad of resources available. The librarian might "co-browse" these resources with you. Co-browsing* is the ability to share or co-navigate resources in a Web browser, which the librarian may do while chatting with you.

If the librarian cannot answer your question during the session, he or she may suggest other sources for you to try that cannot be accessed in the online environment or ask for your contact information so he or she or your local library may follow up with you.

Once the session ends, you will be given the option to view and print your transcript or e-mail the session to yourself for later use. The transcript will provide links to all of the resources you visited during the session.

(*Co-browsing requires users to enter the chat session using broadband, with a Windows Operating System and Microsoft Internet Explorer.)

When are librarians available to answer my question?

We are available via live chat 10 a.m. to midnight Sunday through Thursday and 10 a.m. to 5 p.m. Friday and Saturday Eastern Time. E-mail assistance is available 24/7 except during scheduled maintenance.
    Holiday Schedule Live Chat E-mail
    Memorial Day Holiday May 26, 2008
    Fourth of July Holiday July 4, 2008

Am I talking to a real person?

Yes. When you use Ask a Librarian, a real Florida librarian is assisting you.

268

How many librarians are on duty?

We typically have two to four librarians monitoring questions during the hours that we are open for live chat.

How long will it take for someone to answer my question?

It should only take a few minutes for a librarian to say hello after you send your question, although your wait time could increase if we receive an unusually high number of questions. We answer questions in the order we receive them. Please be patient, and we will get to your question as soon as possible. The length of your conversation with the librarian will depend on the complexity of your question and how detailed of an answer you would like. An average chat session lasts 10 to 20 minutes.

What type of behavior is unacceptable?

Ask a Librarian has a policy of mutual respect. Our librarians will treat you with courtesy and respect and we expect the same respect in return from you. There are several types of behavior that are unacceptable and may cause you to lose the privilege to ask questions again in the future. Deliberately wasting the librarian's time or using language that is offensive, obscene or harassing will not be tolerated. To read more about our behavior policy click here.

Can the librarian on duty tell me if I have any overdue books?

Probably not. Because Ask a Librarian is a statewide service, you could be speaking with a librarian from any of our 95 participating libraries. If the librarian is not from your local library, he or she will not have access to your personal library record.

Can the librarian on duty tell me how to login to my account or provide me with my pin number?

Probably not. Because Ask a Librarian is a statewide service, you could be speaking with a librarian from any of our 95 participating libraries. If the librarian is not from your local library, he or she will not have access to your personal library record.

Why should I use Ask a Librarian instead of a search engine like Google or Yahoo?

Librarians are experts at sorting through information and finding what you need from a credible source. With over 100 million sites on the Internet, searching on Google and Yahoo can return millions of Web sites filled with information that's not quite what you were looking for. And often, those sites have questionable authority. With Ask a Librarian, you have a professional to help evaluate resources, access to great resources hidden from search engines, and access to full text journals and books. Studies prove that having a librarian assist you with your research can help you get better grades and save you time. Librarians will not only help you find information but will also help organize and evaluate that information. With so much information available, it's important to sort out fact from fiction, and librarians can help. Ask a Librarian brings this valuable resource straight to you—when and where you need it.

Should I try to save or write down all of the Web site addresses you show me during our session?

It's not necessary. When your chat session is over, you will have the option of viewing or saving your transcript session, which will include all of the Web site addresses your librarian suggested.

What are the minimum system requirements for me to use Ask a Librarian?

Your Ask a Librarian session, like all web-based applications, responds more quickly if you have a broadband connection. Using a Windows operating system and Microsoft Internet Explorer browser will allow you to enter the service in the enhanced version. All other Ask a Librarian functionality is available with any contemporary operating system or browser. For more detailed information, go to our "How It Works."

INSTANT MESSAGING

Thomas Jefferson University
Scott Memorial Library
Philadelphia, Pennsylvania

Q: When are librarians online?
A: This is a pilot service during which our hours may vary. We are generally online when the Reference Desk is open (see our hours). If we're unavailable via IM, contact us by phone or email.

Q: What kinds of questions do you answer?
A: Try us! Here are some of the questions we've answered in the past:
   How do I cite a government report in APA style?
   How many students are enrolled in JMC? How many applied?
   Is the Library open to the general public?
   Is Ovid down? It keeps telling me my account is blocked.
   Do we have the 1989 volume of Microvascular Research?
   I'm looking for information on the history of APNs in New Zealand.
   I'm wondering how to change my settings so I can access RefWorks from home.

Q: Anything else I should know?
A: Glad you asked:
   In-person requests receive priority over phone and electronic requests.
   Requests of equal priority are answered in the order they arrive.
   This is a service for Thomas Jefferson University/Hospital students, staff and faculty. You may be asked for proof of affiliation such as your Jefferson email address.
   IM is for brief communications, generally under ten minutes. For inquiries requiring more time, librarians may ask that a session be continued by phone, email, or in person.

University of Akron
University of Akron Libraries
Akron, Ohio

Instant Messaging (IM) Reference Service

IM a Bierce Librarian • IM a Science Librarian • IM a Law Librarian

Instant Messaging Service Now Available!

It is now possible to obtain research assistance from a University of Akron Librarian via our Instant Messaging (IM) Reference Service.

For science related questions, including the life and physical sciences, engineering, nursing and allied health, please contact the Science & Technology Library. For all other questions, including general information, education, business, social science, and the arts and humanities, please contact Bierce Library.

When this service is offline you may contact librarians at KnowItNow.

Getting Started with IM

What if there is no chat software on my computer?

If you do not currently subscribe to an IM service, just click on one of the Web Client links above and download IM software. If you already have a screen name from one of the above services, but are using a computer other than your own, you may IM with us using Meebo, a web portal that allows users of various IM services to connect and chat without requiring a client to be installed on the local workstation.

Who can use IM?

This service is intended primarily for University of Akron students, faculty, and staff, but questions from other users are welcome. Non-UA library users within the local community are encouraged to use the ASCPL Ask-a-Librarian service at the Akron-Summit County Public Library or the KnowItNow statewide 24/7 live online reference service.

What kinds of questions can I ask?

IM is best used for brief, factual questions, but can also be used for more in-depth research assistance as long as the response or explanation isn't too complex. IM is not a good format to conduct an extensive search for articles. For in-depth information we may suggest that you come into the library or contact the appropriate Subject Librarian via e-mail. The subject librarian will provide timely responses and may suggest an appointment for one-on-one research consultation.

Suggested uses of IM include:

- To determine which article database is most appropriate for your research
- To locate books or articles on a topic
- To obtain help in locating something on our web pages
- To find out whether or not we have a book or journal
- To get suggestions for keywords to use in your article search
- If you wish to:
- Renew a book; you can do this online at View Your Record and Renew Materials
- Ask for help with your library PIN; you can obtain help at Help Using Your Library PIN
- Ask questions about overdue fines; for these, contact the Circulation Department
- Check the status of an interlibrary loan; to do this use the ILLiad system
- Connect to Online Resources from Home, please follow these instructions

Inappropriate Behavior in E-mail, Chat, and IM

The library professionals providing this service are University of Akron employees. Please exercise good judgment by using this service in a sincere and professional manner. We reserve the right to terminate an IM session when we have judged behavior and/or language to be inappropriate. The Library's Acceptable Behavior Policy applies to all online interactions with library employees.

What about privacy?

The University Libraries respects the privacy of users, but as with any information that is transmitted electronically, we cannot guarantee the confidentiality of IM transactions. IM sessions are routinely logged for statistical purposes only and discarded at the end of each semester.

Long Beach City College
Long Beach City College Library
Long Beach, California

Instant Messaging Reference Frequently Asked Questions

Instant Messaging (IM) Reference Service

- What is Instant Messaging Reference?
- Who can use this service?
- Where can I get IM software?

- How do I IM an LBCC librarian?
- Can I use IM if the computer I'm using doesn't have Instant Messaging software installed?
- What is a screen name?
- What is a buddy list?
- What hours is IM reference service available?
- What types of questions will be answered?
- What happens to the transcripts of my IM session?
- How can I offer feedback on the Library's IM reference service?

Q. What is Instant Messaging Reference?

A. Instant messaging or IM (for short) is real-time chat over the Internet in which users type short messages back and forth, using software such as AOL Instant Messenger (AIM), Yahoo! Messenger, MSN Messenger, and Google Talk. Think of IM as being like e-mail, only faster. IM is also like a telephone conversation, except that the users communicate via text messaging instead of speech.

Q. Who can use this service?

A. The service is available to current students, faculty, and staff of Long Beach City College.

Q. Where can I get IM software?

A. IM service providers generally offer a fee IM client, which you can download—in most cases for free—and install on your computer. If you want to be able to chat over multiple messaging services from one application, try a free multi-protocol IM client, such as GAIM or Trillian. If you don't want to download anything, or you are using a computer on which you can't install software, use a Web-based IM service like meebo, which allows you to access your accounts via the Web. There are many IM service providers; however, LBCC supports the most popular ones listed below:

- AOL Instant Messenger (AIM)
- Yahoo! Messenger
- MSN Messenger
- meebo

Q. How do I IM an LBCC librarian?

A. Launch your IM application software or use the Web-based interface.
Add lbcclibref to your Buddy List.
Double-click on the Buddy name
In the message window, type your message.
Press the enter or return key on your keyboard.

Q. Can I use IM if the computer I'm using doesn't have IM software installed?

A. Yes. Most IM services provide Web interfaces that do not require client software. Examples include AIM Express, Yahoo! Web Messenger, and MSN Web Messenger. meebo is a Web-based aggregator of IM services, which allows you to connect with all your IM buddies from multiple IM services. No software download is required.

Q. What is a screen name?

A. A screen name is a name that you choose to identify yourself online when instant messaging with others. You will need to set up a screen name with an IM service before you can log in and IM a LBCC librarian. LBCC Library's screen name is "lbcclibref" with AOL, Yahoo!, MSN, and Google IM services.

Q. What is a buddy list?

A. A buddy list consists of the screen names of people you frequently IM. Add lbcclibref to your buddy list, so that you can readily IM a LBCC librarian.

Q. What hours is IM reference service available?

A. Monday through Thursday, from 11 am to 3 pm.

Q. What types of questions will be answered?
A. A specific piece of information (e.g., a fact, a date, spelling of a name)
Looking up books, journals, articles, etc., in our collection
Basic suggestions on an appropriate electronic or print resource to find information for your project or research paper
Questions about library resources and services

Q. What happens to the transcripts of my IM session?
A. The Library retains all transcripts in order to compile statistics and improve our service. Personal information, such as IP address, email, names, phone numbers, etc. that is embedded in an IM transcript, is not shared outside of the Library system.

Q. How can I offer feedback on the Library's IM reference service?
A. The Library staff welcomes your feedback. Use the suggestion form to send us your comments.

Santa Clara University
Santa Clara University Library
Santa Clara, California

Instant Messaging Reference

Frequently Asked Questions

Q. What is Instant Messaging Reference?
A. The Instant Messaging Reference service allows SCU students, faculty and staff to ask an SCU librarian basic questions about library services and resources, such as looking up a book or journal. It's a live service provided by SCU librarians.

Q. Who can use this service?
A. The service is available to current students, faculty, and staff of SCU.

Q. What types of questions will be answered?
A. A specific piece of information (e.g., a fact, a date, spelling of a name)
Looking up books, journals, articles, etc., in our collection
Basic suggestions on an appropriate electronic or print resource to find information for your project or research paper
Questions about library resources and services

Q. Who answers the questions?
A. Your questions will be answered by SCU librarians.

Q. How is my privacy or anonymity protected?
A. Privacy Statement: This privacy statement explains what we do with the personal information collected from our patrons when they use the Instant Message reference service. More specifically, it explains what personal information is collected, how it is used, and how long it is kept

We will not share your IM screen name or use it for other purposes except to provide you with this service.

The transcripts of all IM reference sessions (including screen names) are temporarily stored on our server. These transcripts are used by supervising librarians for quality control. All transcripts are permanently deleted from the system after 30 days.

Q. Is there any software required to use Instant Messaging Reference?

A. No. All you need is a free screen name from one of the IM service providers we use (AIM, Yahoo, ICQ or MSN), and an internet connection fast enough to handle IM communications. The IM Reference service does not require any installation or configuration on your part; all you need is to send us an IM.

Q. How do I get an IM screen name?

A. Simply register with any one of the IM service providers we use (they're all free):

- AIM
- Yahoo! Messenger
- ICQ
- MSN Messenger

Q. How do I send an instant message without downloading the full IM client software (for example, if I'm using a public computer)?

A. All of the IM services provide web interfaces that do not require client software:

- AIM Express
- Yahoo! Web Messenger
- ICQ2Go!
- MSN Web Messenger

MISSION ASK PRIVACY STATEMENTS

Concordia College
Ylvisaker Library
Moorhead, Minnesota

Ask a Librarian Privacy Policy

The Carl B. Ylvisaker Library staff respects our users' privacy. This policy clarifies the information collected by our IM chat service and explains how this information may be used.

The Library's IM privacy policy includes:
- What information we collect,
- Potential use of this information,
- Who has access to chat information,
- With whom chat information may be shared, and
- Your choices regarding collection, use and distribution of chat information.

Q. What information is collected by the chat service?

A. All chats are automatically logged by our IM software.

Q. For what purposes might the information be used?

A. Chat information is used to help librarians analyze the number and types of questions we are being asked. This data helps us determine appropriate staffing levels and aids in training librarians to effectively use the service.

Q. Who has access to this information?

A. This information is accessible only to faculty librarians and those library staff members who are associated with the Ask A Librarian service.

Q. With whom might the library staff share this information?

A. Individual chats are not shared with anyone outside of the library. Statistics generated from chat logs or anonymous excerpts may be used for reports or publications. However, information about specific individuals (e.g., IP address, e-mail address, personal name, phone number, etc.) included as part of a chat transcript will never be shared outside of Concordia College's library.

Q. What choices do users have regarding the collection, use and distribution of their information?

A. Any user who wants to have a record of their chat deleted may email librarian to request deletion of a chat transcript. Patrons must provide the date of their chat and their screen name.

(Courtesy of Concordia College Library, Moorhead, MN)

Chapter 24

PERSONALIZED INFORMATION SEARCHING

LIBRARY BLOG RULES AND REGULATIONS

Saint Petersburg
Saint Petersburg Libraries
Saint Petersburg, Florida

Key terms and conditions of the Creative Commons license:

- You, the blogger, retain the copyright for your own posts.
- Licensees (people who use your content in whole or in part) must:
  - Request your permission for commercial use of your posts.
  - Request your permission to create derivative works, unless their content is also licensed under the same terms as your content.
  - Keep any copyright notice intact on all copies of your work.
  - Link to the Creative Commons Attribution-NonCommercial-ShareAlike 2.5 License from copies of the work
- Licensees may not ...
  - Alter the terms of the Creative Commons license.
  - Use technology to restrict other licensees' lawful uses of the work.
- Your Creative Commons license allows licensees, provided they live up to these conditions, to take the following actions:
  - Copy the work.
  - Distribute it.
  - Display or perform it publicly.
  - Make digital public performances of it (e.g., webcasting).
  - Shift the work into another format as a verbatim copy.
- Your Creative Commons license...
  - Applies worldwide.
  - Lasts for the duration of the work's copyright.
  - Is not revocable.

Austin Public Library
Austin, Texas

Posting to the APL Blog

The Austin Public Library provides a blog on the Library's home page using Blogger, and posts the same blog on the Austin American Statesman. New blogs are posted Mondays, Wednesdays, and Fridays. Faulk Central librarians are responsible for overall blog administration. The blog's mission is to promote Austin Public Library's resources and services. Blogs include thematic item lists from our collection; topics related to today's events and news; research tips; field trips to other libraries; Texas authors and artists; and library trends.

Messages posted to the Austin Public Library blog should be relevant to the the messages to which they are attached. Messages and comments are subject to moderation by the blog administrators, who reserve the right to edit or remove any message, and to reject any comment they deem inappropriate. Inappropriate content includes (but is not limited to) personal attacks, vulgar or inflammatory language, plagiarized or copyright-protected material, private information, and commercial promotions.

Canton Public Library
Canton, Michigan

The goal of the Canton Public Library Blog is to stimulate discussion on a variety of topics, including library services and programs as well as Canton community resources and events.

Blog comments should be relevant to the specific post they are attached to. Do not post private information to the Canton Public Library Blog. All data posted to this Blog is public information. In addition to being listed on the Blog, your postings may be indexed by Internet search engines (Google, Yahoo, etc). Spam, flaming, personal attacks and off-topic comments are not permitted. The Canton Public Library reserves the right not to post any comment.

Individuals using this system without authority are subject to having their activities on this system monitored and recorded by system personnel. While monitoring individuals improperly using this system or during system maintenance, library employees may examine the activities of all authorized users. Anyone using this system agrees to such examination and is advised that if it reveals possible evidence of criminal activity, system personnel may provide this evidence to law enforcement officials.

Berkeley Heights Public Library
Berkeley Heights, New Jersey

The BHPL blog provides information on upcoming programs, library resources and services, and current library and literary news. Comments must be relevant to the topic and respectful of all BHPL patrons. In order to maintain an appropriate exchange of information, the following rules are to be followed at all times.

All comments of the BHPL blog are subject to moderation by BHPL staff and will be rejected for inappropriate content including, but not limited to, sexually-explicit material; copyrighted or plagiarized material; defamatory statements; hate speech; violent, abusive or threatening language; personal attacks; commercial promotions; and private or confidential information.

The BHPL blog may not be used for any unlawful or inappropriate purposes, including, but not limited to, transmission of any sexually-explicit material; transmission of copyrighted or plagiarized material; commercial activity; transmission of computer viruses or "spam" e-mail; harassment; or impersonation of another.

Pursuant to federal law, 47 U.S.C.A. 230, BHPL is not liable for comments posted by users. BHPL is not obligated to take any action and will not be responsible or liable for any content posted. By posting a comment, you agree to indemnify BHPL and its officers and employees from and against liabilities, judgments, damages and costs incurred that arise out of or are related to the content that you post.

Use of the BHPL blog will constitute acceptance of this policy. If you do not agree to these terms, do not access the service. This policy is subject to revision at the discretion of the BHPL. Be sure to periodically review this policy to ensure your compliance.

Saint Petersburg College
Saint Petersburg Libraries
Saint Petersburg, Florida

Bloggers

Bloggers must be affiliated with the St. Petersburg College M.M. Bennett Library, or invited guests such as SPC faculty members. Blog categories will be created—eventually.

Acceptable Use

Lively opinion and commentary are welcome in blog posts. However, it is expected that blog postings will be professional and reflect well on the St. Petersburg College community. Bloggers are strongly encouraged to check facts, cite sources, present balanced views, acknowledge and correct errors, and check spelling and grammar before making a post live.

Ad hominem attacks are not allowed, and bloggers are encouraged to put a "best foot forward" on SPC activities. SPCLB reserves the right not to post any blog post or to later remove it.

Links to related posts are encouraged, but bloggers should post original content rather than reposting entire items from other blogs or lists.

Comments

Comments are open to all but may be moderated by the blog manager. Commentary, opinion, and reaction to posts are welcome. Comments should be relevant to the specific post they are attached to. Spam, flaming, personal attacks, and off-topic comments are not permitted. SPCLB reserves the right not to post any comment.

Blog managers and/or bloggers will establish procedures for managing and moderating comments.

South San Francisco Public Library
South San Francisco, California

The South San Francisco Public Library encourages communication, self-expression and freedom of speech by providing library related blogs for public use. Blogs increase the availability of information, encourage healthy debate and make possible new connections within our community.

We respect our users' ownership of and responsibility for the content they choose to share. It is our belief that censoring this content is contrary to a service that bases itself on freedom of expression.

This policy is compatible with the Library's endorsement of the Library Bill of Rights, the Freedom to Read, and the Freedom to View statements from the American Library Association. As with all Library resources, the Library affirms the right and responsibility of parents/guardians, NOT Library staff, to determine and monitor their minor children's use of Library blogs.

In order to uphold these values, we need to curb abuses that threaten our ability to provide this service. As a result, there are some boundaries on the type of content that can be posted to SSF Library blogs. The boundaries we've defined are those that both comply with legal requirements and that serve to enhance the service as a whole.

CONTENT BOUNDARIES:
• Illegal Purposes—Library blogs may not be used for illegal purposes.

- Identity Theft and Privacy—Posts that misleadingly appropriate the identity of another person are not permitted. Users may not post other people's personally identifying or confidential information, including but not limited to credit card numbers, Social Security Numbers, and driver's and other license numbers. You may not post information such as other people's passwords, usernames, phone numbers, addresses and e-mail addresses unless already publicly accessible on the web.
- Inappropriate Content—Content including hate speech, swearing, pornography, and personal attacks may not be posted on the Library blog. This does not in any way indicate that blog entries will not be allowed because readers disagree with a person's opinion.
- Defamation/Libel—users should not publish any content that is unlawful, defamatory, or fraudulent. Note that an allegation of defamatory expression, in and of itself, does not establish defamation. The truth or falsehood of an expression is a key element in establishing defamation and we are not in a position to make that sort of fact based judgment. That said, if we have reason to believe that a particular statement is defamatory, we will remove the statement.
- Copyright—Using copyrighted material does not constitute infringement in all cases. In general, however, users should be careful when using copyrighted content without the permission of those who created it.
- Spam—We will aggressively seek to remove spam from our site. Generally, when we talk about spam, we mean content that is created for the primary purpose of manipulating search engine results or generating traffic through deceptive means.

Response to Violations:

Violations of the Blog Content Policy may result in loss of access to this service.

Unlawful activities and misuse of the Library blog may result in loss to Blog and/or Library privileges and prosecution.

PERSONAL DIGITAL ASSISTANTS (PDAS)

Duke University
Duke University Medical Center Library
Durham, North Carolina

Personal Digital Assistants (PDAs)

The growing use of PDA's (personal digital assistants) in the healthcare field as physicians, students, and clinical staff incorporate them into the patient care workflow has prompted the library to create this subject guide.

The Medical Center Library offers assistance to DUMC patrons in getting started using PDAs. We have selected resources and organized them into the following categories:

- Getting Started: PDA terminology, guidance on choosing a PDA, and information on how to put your PDA to use.
- Advanced Functions: Learn how to beam business cards, customize your PDA, and project information for presentations.
- Software—Medicine: Recommended list of software to download for Palm or Pocket PC.
- Software—Specialties: Software categorized by Nursing, Physical Therapy, and Psychiatry.
- Installing Software: Installation instructions for your Palm or Pocket PC software.
- Training: Contact information if you have questions or need some basic PDA help.

- Wireless Access: Set up wireless access and discover the resources that work over wireless connections.
- Tech Support: Get technical support within the Duke community and find links to more support pages.

University of Arizona
Arizona Health Sciences Library
Tucson, Arizona

AHSL PDA Support

PDA support is available in the Library Computer Lab at AHSL Tucson. Our technical support can assist AHSC students, staff and faculty with PDA questions, troubleshooting or related issues. A list of our services is available below, along with appropriate contact information and other pertinent information that you may find useful.

- Synchronizing
- Consultations and contact information
- Hardware
- Recommended Applications
- Links

Synchronizing
- You may synchronize your PDA in the Library Computer lab. We do not supply USB cable or cradles. Therefore, it is important that you bring your own USB cable or cradle if you wish to synchronize your PDA with one of our computers.
- The Library is open 24 hours with technical assistance between 8am and 4pm.

Hardware
We currently support the following hardware
- Palms: PalmOne, Treo, Garmin, Tapwave
- PocketPCs: HP, Dell, ASUS
- The PDA Advisor can assist students and faculty in selecting a PDA.

We are unable to support the following hardware
- Most cellular PDAs
- PalmOS: Sony Clie, Alphasmart
- PocketPC: Audiovox, Casio, Hitachi, Mitac, Motorola, Samsung, Sony Ericsson, Toshiba, Viewsonic
- RIM Blackberry

PODCASTS

Moraine Valley Community College
Moraine Valley Community College Library and Learning Resource Center
Palos Hills, Illinois

About the Library Event PodCasts

The Library Event PodCasts are intended to be a flexible, portable record of the events held within the Moraine Valley Library. As such, they are intended to enhance library programs and the larger Moraine Valley curriculum in the following ways:

- They fulfill the library's mission by "providing information literacy instruction and support across the curriculum" and "collaborating with faculty and others to develop innovative services and programs."
- They enhance the classroom experience by providing expert views on challenging and timely subjects.
- They provide an opportunity for students and community members to participate in library events even though they may not be able to visit the events in person.
- They act as an ongoing record of library events for future use.
- These events are hosted by the library in the spirit of public discussion, open debate, and intellectual growth. The views expressed by panel members, lecturers, or audience members are their own and are not necessarily the official views of the Moraine Valley Community College board of trustees, staff, faculty, or administration.

Use Policy

The Library Event Podcasts are the copyrighted intellectual property of Moraine Valley Community College. They are made freely available to students, staff, faculty, and the general public for use in the curriculum, scholarly discourse, or for personal interest. Any other retransmission, duplication, or other distribution without prior approval of Moraine Valley Community College is prohibited.

WIKIS

University of California San Francisco
Galen UCSF Digital Library
San Francisco, California

Wiki@UCSF Frequently Asked Questions (FAQ)

Q. How can I access the wiki?
A. Before you can access the wiki for the first time, your GALEN account must be added to the wiki user database. Each wiki space has a Space Administrator who can help new users with this process. If you don't know the Space Administrator for the space you want to access, please contact the Wiki@UCSF Administrators. Once you've been given access, you'll need a web browser (Internet Explorer or Mozilla Firefox) and an internet connection to start using the wiki.

Q. Do I have to be on the campus network to access Wiki@UCSF?
A. You don't have to be connected to the campus network—you can access the wiki from any computer with an internet connection. However, users located at the VA may have to use a VPN connection because of the VA's internet firewall. For more information about VPN access, visit the OAAIS website.

Q. How do I get a wiki space?
A. UCSF faculty and staff may request a space on Wiki@UCSF by completing the request form. Please read the Wiki@UCSF policies before requesting a space.

Q. Can anyone view content on the wiki?
A. No. Wiki access is limited to those who have been granted permission to access the wiki. All users must have a GALEN account and must be added to the wiki user database by an administrator before they can gain access to the wiki for the first time. Only those designated to have access to a space will be able to view it. Access is controlled by the Space Administrator and by the Wiki@UCSF Administrators who assign permissions to each space.

Q. What is a Space Administrator?

A. The person who requests the creation of a wiki space is designated as the Space Administrator for that particular space. This person decides who will be able to view/edit content in the space and can modify the overall look and feel of the space. The Space Administrator must be UCSF faculty or staff.

Q. What resources are available to help people learn how to use the wiki?

A. Within the wiki there is a Wiki Training space that's accessible to all users. It has information for users and Space Administrators, including basic and advanced editing tips. A brief wiki demonstration and training session conducted by Library staff can be arranged by contacting the Wiki@UCSF administrators.

Bridgewater State College
Bridgewater, Massachusetts

Wiki User Policy

Purpose

wiki@BSC provides the students, faculty, and administration of Bridgewater State College with wiki web page space as a means of communication and collaboration in support of the College's mission of teaching and learning and to conduct official College business. The purpose of this policy is to ensure that the wiki is used for purposes appropriate to the College's mission.

Policy Statement

Bridgewater State College provides wiki services to faculty, staff, and students. Use of the wiki@BSC service must be consistent with Bridgewater State College's mission of teaching and learning and comply with local, state, and federal laws and College policies.

Applies to

This policy applies to all students, faculty, and staff of Bridgewater State College and to all other users who are entitled to access wiki@BSC. This policy does not supersede any existing College policy.

Responsibilities

Responsible Use

Content of a wiki space must adhere to Bridgewater State College's Responsible Use of Information Technology. Respect the rights of others by complying with all College policies regarding sexual, racial and other forms of harassment.

Copyright Permissions

Wiki publishers should comply with copyright and trademark regulations. Graphics, video, audio, or text created by another person may not be placed on a page without demonstrated permission of the author or artist. Content deemed to be in violation of copyright law will be removed.

GNU Free Documentation License

The text of all wiki@BSC pages is freely licensed under the terms of the GNU Free Documentation License (GFDL). Re-users of the content must retain it under the same license, ensuring it remains free. Please read the text of the GNU Free Documentation License for full details of this license.

Images

For large images which may slow down retrieval, use a scaled-down thumbnail image and provide a link to the large image.

Storage Space

Wiki space owners must keep data space usage to a reasonable level for the purpose of their wiki.

Confidentiality of Content

wiki@BSC is a public web site. No confidential information should be contained in a wiki page.

Editing

Editing of a wiki@BSC page requires secure login with BSC user credentials. Anonymous editing is not allowed. Do not edit wiki pages that you have not created or do not have involvement with on some level. Respect the work of others.

Privacy

When editing any wiki page, recognize that your BSC username will appear in page histories next to any edits that are made.

Non-College Related Content

Wiki space is reserved solely for course and administrative work in support of the College's mission of teaching and learning, including but not limited to sanctioned clubs, sports, and other College business. Wiki sites should not be created for personal use, unless related to personal course work or College business. Personal content not consistent with Bridgewater State College's mission of teaching and learning will be removed.

Sanctions Copyright

BSC reserves the right to choose how to address or respond to any allegation of copyright infringement received including, without limitation, the choice of any defense under applicable law. Details on how BSC responds to allegations of on-line infringement of copyright are posted online at http://it.bridgew.edu/Policy/DMCA.cfm.

Responsible Use of Information Technology

Information technology users who violate this policy and/or the Responsible Use of Information Technology policy will be subject to College disciplinary processes and procedures. Privileges to use information technology may be revoked. Illegal acts may also subject users to prosecution by law enforcement authorities.

Saint Mary's University College
Saint Mary's University College Library
Calgary, Alberta, Canada

What's a wiki?

A wiki is a type of computer software that allows users to easily create, edit and link web pages. Wikis are often used to create collaborative websites, power community websites. Essentially a wiki is a type of content management system (CMS). The content managed includes computer files, image media, audio files, electronic documents and web content.

How did wikis develop?

Wiki is derived from the Hawaiian word for fast. The first wiki, WikiWikiWeb, was started by Ward Cunningham in 1994. There is some claim that its early development was inspired in part by Apple's HyperCard. This is a system that allows users to create virtual "card stacks" with supporting links between cards. Today some companies use wikis as their primary collaborative software or as a replacement for static intranets. And wikis can also be used behind firewalls and implemented with security features that are linked to an institution's or corporation's primary authentication/login protocols.

The STMU Library wiki was implemented using the open sources software package called Mediawiki. MediaWiki is a web-based wiki software application used by all projects of the Wikimedia Foundation. It was originally developed to serve the needs of development and management of the free content Wikipedia encyclopedia and other Mediawiki projects. It has also been used by corporations as an internal knowledge management solution or content management system by such companies as Novell and Intel Corporation's Intelpedia. To find out more you can consult this extensive list of examples of mediawiki in action or read about other corporate uses of wikis.

Why a wiki?

Mediawiki software is free and open source and there is a large community of programmers involved in its development. With the pervasive use of Wikipedia, which also uses the Mediawiki platform, it's likely that this tool will be around for a long time. As a CMS, the implementation of the Library Wiki functions to make various information, forms, and other documents available, inter-office and over the web, to Faculty and Administrative Staff.

The Library Wiki acts as a one stop service shop for the delivery of information & forms for Faculty and Administration. Because it is merely another website and because users are generally familiar with websites the training time required by users to access this site will be minimal.

The Library wiki:

- is remotely accessible and reasonably secure;
- allows users to login and access needed information from on-campus or remotely from home, or while at an academic conference;
- bypasses the need to use a more technically demanding File Transfer Protocol to access information and documents on the STMU servers.

The Library Wiki decentralizes delivery and management of Library services and information for Library Staff. All designated staff can make updates to the site from on-campus or remotely from another location. And it reduces the need to invest in costly software support. That is, managing this site doesn't require Dreamweaver or any other WYSIWIG "html" editor.

The Library Wiki also has these following features:

- It is self-archiving and searchable. Since Mediawiki comes with a built in search engine, any documents, pages, or other uploaded files can be easily found.
- Because uploading files and documents is relatively simple, the Library Wiki acts as an archive for things like agendas and minutes for meetings. The wiki can be used to both archive and disseminate information in a timely fashion.
- It keeps track of changes and who makes them, effectively creating an ongoing log and archive of previous versions of each wiki page. This allows for open transparency in developing collaborative content.

Chapter 25

INFORMATION LITERACY

GENERAL GUIDELINES

University of West Florida
John C. Pace Library
Pensacola, Florida

- What is Information Literacy?
- Importance of Information Literacy
- A Brief Background
- Definitions & Standards
- Programs
- Lessons & Exercises
- Contact

The University of West Florida Libraries supports information literacy throughout the university. We see it as a valuable tool for fostering critical thinking and effective use of information among students. The UWF Libraries supports information literacy initiatives through the following activities:

What is Information Literacy?

Information literacy is a set of skills that enable individuals to recognize when information is needed and to have the ability to locate, evaluate and effectively use the needed information. Information literacy focuses on 5 skills:

- Determine the extent of information needed
- Access the needed information effectively and efficiently
- Evaluate information and its sources critically
- Incorporate selected information into one's knowledge base
- Use information effectively to accomplish a specific purpose
- Understand the ethical and legal issues surrounding the use of information

In practice, information literacy utilizes critical thinking through its skills of evaluating information. Information literacy also incorporates and supplements other forms of literacy such as computer literacy, media literacy, and research literacy. Information literacy can be applied in any subject or area of study. It can be tailored to build knowledge within a specialized area, though its emphasis is to develop skills that can be put to academic, professional and personal uses.

Importance of Information Literacy

Handling Rapid Changes in Information. Information literacy emerged because increased amounts of information became available through books, journals, broadcast media, and eventually through the internet. However, the quality and reliability of such information varies. Information literacy skills enable students to effectively use and discern information they find from various sources.

Ethical Use of Information. Information can be put to positive as well as negative use, so information literacy includes skills and standards involving the ethical use of information. Students learn about plagiarism and copyright, and why they matter. Other topics may include using ethical standards defined by discipline-specific organizations, and legal, social and proprietary issues that surround the use of information.

Preparation for the workforce. Many business and industrial leaders want employees whose skills go beyond a subject area. They want employees with problem-solving skills and to be able to navigate rapid changes in information and technology. Students can learn about a discipline with information literacy, yet also acquire critical thinking and technical skills that can be applied to a variety of settings.

Lifelong Learning. Information literacy promotes lifelong learning. With information literacy skills, students are able to self-direct their learning while in school and throughout their lives. While such skills are used in classes and assignments, they are also applicable to personal decision-making.

Civic Participation. Information literacy provides skills essential for making informed decisions and effective civic involvement. It enables students to fully participate in a democracy.

A Brief Background

Information literacy has been used in higher education since the 1980s. Various education reports projected that students needed skills to adapt to the demands of a global economy and information-driven society. Additional reports, such as Reinventing Undergraduate Education by the Boyer Commission on Education, encouraged active learning where student knowledge and skills are applicable outside from school settings. As a response to such reports, educational leaders formed information literacy by synthesizing skills already taught in higher education with new developments in technology and use of information.

College libraries, which traditionally provide library instruction and subject-specific support, adopted information literacy into their instruction goals. As college libraries utilized more technology, library experts recommended that library instruction include other information sources and teach students skills needed to use a variety of information.

Many colleges and universities have incorporated information literacy in some form, ranging from less-intensive activities such as online tutorials to broader inclusion into the curriculum. Some institutions have made information literacy competencies into graduation requirements.

Definitions & Standards

Association of Colleges and Research Libraries (ACRL): Information Literacy
http://www.ala.org/ala/acrl/acrlissues/acrlinfolit/informationliteracy.htm

ACRL: Characteristics of Programs of Information Literacy that Illustrate Best Practices
http://www.ala.org/ala/acrl/acrlstandards/characteristics.htm

ACRL: Information Literacy Competency Standards for Higher Education, 2000.
href://www.ala.org/acrl/ilcomstan.html

ACRL: Information Literacy for Faculty and Administrators
http://www.ala.org/ala/acrl/acrlissues/acrlinfolit/infolitoverview/infolitforfac/infolitfaculty.htm

MISSION AND VISION STATEMENTS

Illinois State University
Milner Library
Normal, Illinois

Library Instruction Vision, Mission, Competencies and Policies

Vision

Illinois State University is acclaimed as an outstanding example of an information literate and intellectually vibrant academic community. Students develop information competence in both general and specific areas of study through library instruction and the integration of information skills throughout the curriculum and in support of lifelong learning. Milner Library faculty and staff work in collaboration with other university faculty and staff to implement information literacy instruction while also continuing to develop their own competence with information in specific disciplinary areas. Patrons value Milner Library for providing leadership of campus initiatives that support information literacy.

Mission

Milner Library's Instruction Program exists to advance the information literacy of the students, faculty, and staff at Illinois State University and the community at large. To this end, the Instruction Program teaches library users to search for, locate, retrieve, evaluate, use, and value information resources through learner-centered instructional programs, initiatives, and materials. These are developed in response to identified learning needs and through collaboration with campus faculty and staff. The Program provides independent, individual, and group instruction through point-of-use, course-integrated, web-based, and open workshop methods. The Information Literacy Competency Standards for Higher Education from the Association of College and Research Libraries provide the framework for program development and instructional objectives. The Instruction Program supports the missions of Milner Library and Illinois State University.

Adopted by the Milner Library Faculty, November 30, 2000

University of Maryland Baltimore County
Albin O. Kuhn Library
Baltimore, Maryland

What is Information Literacy? Information literacy is defined as the ability to access, evaluate, and use information from a variety of sources. The Association of College and Research Libraries (ACRL) has developed five information literacy standards, with accompanying performance indicators, and outcomes that can be used for benchmarking purposes and in program development.

The information literate student:

S1. determines the nature and extent of the information needed;

S2. accesses needed information effectively and efficiently;

S3. evaluates information and its sources critically and incorporates selected information into his or her knowledge base and value system;

S4. uses information effectively to accomplish a specific purpose; and

S5. understands many of the economic, legal, and social issues surrounding the use of information and accesses and uses information ethically and legally.[1]

What does this mean for UMBC? Library staff at UMBC believes that current campus planning and the University System of Maryland's Board of Regents (BOR) Technological Fluency mandate establish that the time is right to develop and implement an information literacy program in the context of outcomes assessment. It is believed that this effort will be most successful by using the above mentioned Standards, and teaching faculty/staff cooperation. The latter is key to program success. Recent research indicates that the relationship between the faculty and all students is critical in academic success, information literacy development, and retention at all levels.

Information Literacy at UMBC. The following goals have been identified for UMBC's information literacy program:
- To foster an awareness of the role of information literacy in lifelong learning to the University community (and beyond);
- To promote the integration of information literacy skills into the curriculum via collaboration between faculty, administrators, librarians, and students;

- To develop and foster a collaborative relationship with other colleges/universities on programs of information literacy, sharing and developing ideas and resources;
- To design intervention strategies for students/classes to facilitate the achievement of desired competencies of information literacy;
- To develop a survey instrument, based on the ACRL Standards, that assesses baseline information literacy levels in students at UMBC;
- To develop models and methods for the delivery, implementation, and communication of information literacy program initiatives (i.e., Faculty Awareness, etc.).

UMBC Information Literacy Taskforce Members:
- Head of Circulation and Media, Acting Head of Reference
- Reference and Instruction Librarian
- Services Development and Special Projects Librarian
- Reference and Instruction Librarian

Assessment. Assessment and the development of the information literacy survey are a significant part of the information literacy program. Keeping that in mind, specific goals have been identified for information literacy assessment at UMBC:

- To gather baseline data on information literacy skills of UMBC students;
- To use the data gathered to assist in the development of an information literacy program for students, faculty, and staff at UMBC.

Survey Implementation

The Information Literacy Survey will be administered in the fall of 2003. It will assess incoming freshmen and other students in core and select courses in the following disciplines:

- Biology
- Computer Science and Electrical Engineering
- English
- History
- Psychology

In addition to the assessment the Task Force will be developing and promoting the Faculty Awareness Project, to promote information literacy awareness, assist faculty, and provide support for integrating information literacy standards, objectives, and competencies into the classroom and across the curriculum at UMBC.

The Information Literacy Task Force believes that focusing Information Literacy Awareness efforts on Faculty will greatly benefit students. To that end, additional material has been developed for faculty to use in campus initiatives including the First Year Success Course. This material is also recommended for use in the First Year Seminar courses as well.

SCHEDULING INSTRUCTION

Mercer County Community College
Mercer County Community College Library
West Windsor, New Jersey

MCCC Library Information Literacy (IL) Instruction Scheduling Policy

The MCCC library provides instruction that will enhance a person's information literacy (IL) skills. This service is available to the entire MCCC community.

Types of Instruction Offered

Library Tour (15-30 minute)—A brief tour of the library that provides an overview of the physical layout of the library and the services available at the library but does not give any in-depth instruction.

General Orientation (1 or preferably 2 [50 minute] class periods)—This orientation introduces students to the wide variety of both printed and electronically accessible resources available from the library. The orientation also covers basic electronic search strategies/keywords/Boolean logic, accessing resources remotely, web search strategies, and evaluating the quality of informational resources. This class is given outside of the library in a classroom having computers for every student in the class. NOTE: given the amount of material that is covered in this class, it is often impossible to give students much hands-on time using electronic library resources when this orientation is given during a single [50 minute] class period.

Subject Orientation (usually 1 [50 minute] class period)—This orientation is given in close conjunction with the instructor and is tailored for a specific class. The expectation is that the students attending this class have previously received a general orientation from the library. This orientation gives a very brief review of the search strategies and skills covered in the General Orientation classes and focuses on search strategies and resources that have been selected jointly by both the library and course instructors. This orientation is often tied into a major research project for the course and is usually given outside of the library in a classroom having computers for every student in the class unless there is a special need to focus on printed resources.

Reference Assistance (1 or more class periods as needed)—This service is offered to classes that have recently completed a general or subject specific library orientation. Instructors sign up a time for their entire class to come to the library. During the class period, a reference librarian is assigned to assist students as they work on their research project. As the class has already received an orientation, little actual instruction will be given during this class.

Scheduling Guidelines and Advanced Notice

A. Scheduling an orientation, library tour, or reference assistance—General
    -   Faculty may request IL instruction either in person at the library, by phone, or on line at www.mccc.edu/student_library_resources_il-signup.shtml
    -   As both the number of library instructors and classroom space are limited, classes will be scheduled on a first come/first served basis.

B. Scheduling an IL orientation class
    1. For courses where the library staff has given an IL orientation in the past
        -   A minimum of 3 working days notice should be given to the library for courses that have previously been taught by the library staff within the past two (2) years.
        -   A list of these courses can be found at www.mccc.edu/student_library_resources_prev-courses.shtml
        -   Once the class is confirmed, course instructors will be notified of classroom assignments by the library.
    2. For courses that have NEVER scheduled an IL orientation class previously
        -   A minimum of 7 working days notice is requested for new courses (or courses not taught within the past 2 years).
        -   This longer notice time allows the library staff the time needed to prepare new instructional materials as a result of discussions between the faculty member and library staff person designing the IL orientation class.
        -   Once the class is confirmed, course instructors will be notified of classroom assignments by the library.

D. Scheduling library tours and reference assistance
- A minimum of 3 working days notice must be given.
- Faculty are encouraged to attend library orientations/library tours/reference assistance with their class. By attending the IL class, faculty will be able to give valuable input during the session as well as emphasizing the necessity and value of the skills covered by their presence in the class.

Part VI
Legal Safeguards

Chapter 26

COLLECTION OF USER INFORMATION

INTERNET TRACKING GUIDELINES

Duke University
William R. Perkins Library
Durham, North Carolina

Introduction

One of the cornerstones of librarianship is respect for the privacy of library users. Duke University Libraries recognize the importance of protecting your privacy and the confidentiality of the information that you share with us when you use our web sites or other library services. Described below is our policy on the collection, use, disclosure, maintenance, and protection of personal information that you provide to us.

What information is collected and how it is used

When you use this website, our web server collects certain technical information from your web browser, including your browser type, operating system type, internet address, and the web address of the page from which you linked to our site. In some cases our web server may use browser "cookies" or other technologies to maintain session and preference information or to provide other complex functionality. You may adjust your Internet browser to disable the use of cookies and other web technologies; however, some features of this website may not function properly if you block these technologies. Any information that we automatically collect via this web site is only used internally for technical troubleshooting, to improve the usability of our website, and to track aggregate statistical trends. Except for information that you choose to submit to us (through web forms, e-mail messages, chat sessions, or other communication), we do not collect any personally identifiable information (such as your name, address, phone number, age, gender, ID numbers, etc.) on our website. If you do choose to submit personally identifiable information to us, that information is used only for the purpose for which you submitted it, and will not be used for other purposes. Information from other sources is not combined with the information that we collect. While we may disclose information about use of our web site in aggregate (such as server use statistics) we will not disclose to third parties any information that could be used to identify individuals or their use of Library resources, except as required by law or appropriate law enforcement procedures.

The Library does maintain personally identifiable information for library accounts of valid library users. If you are affiliated with Duke University, the library automatically receives personally identifiable information to create and update your library account from the Registrar's Office (for students) or Human Resources (for employees). If you purchase borrowing privileges, we must obtain certain information about you in order to provide you with a library account. We will maintain confidentiality of information sought or received, and materials consulted, borrowed or acquired, including database search records, reference interviews, circulation records, interlibrary loan records, and other personally identifiable uses of library materials, facilities, or services. The Library maintains several web-based management tools, such as forms related to renewing books, asking reference questions, saving search histories or resource preferences, requesting materials, etc. The personally identifiable information collected through these tools and stored in the library's computer systems will only be used to maintain your library account and provide services to you and is not made available to any other entity outside the Library except as required by law or appropriate law enforcement procedures.

Bowdoin College
Brunswick, Maine

THE WAY BOWDOIN COLLEGE USES INFORMATION COLLECTED

Information collected by Bowdoin College "PII and/or aggregate data" may be used by Bowdoin College for:
- educational and/or research purposes;
- editorial and feedback purposes;
- promotional and recruiting purposes, including soliciting financial contributions and contacting prospective students;
- statistical analysis of a visitor's online behavior for Web site development;
- content improvement;
- analysis of the number of Web site/page "hits;" and
- Web site/page content and layout customization.

Names, postal and e-mail addresses, and phone numbers provided by visitors via online forms may added to Bowdoin's database(s). This information may be used for correspondence or other uses consistent with Bowdoin's business practices and/or academic mission. Bowdoin may also use such information to provide users with information concerning College events and other College community activities and services.

This policy provides a baseline standard; departmental privacy policies may enforce standards that are more rigorous. Some Bowdoin College departments, the College Library and the Office of Student Records for instance, have implemented very restrictive departmental privacy policies and procedures. The College also adheres to legal requirements prescribed by relevant statutes, such as the (FERPA) Family Education Rights and Privacy Act of 1974—a copy of FERPA is found in the Student Handbook.

Pickaway County District Public Library
Circleville, Ohio

The Pickaway County District Public Library uses information (collected) to help make its site more functional for visitors—to learn about the number of visitors to its site and the kinds of information they seek.

Browser and operating information allow the Pickaway County District Public Library Web site to take you to the version of site that best conforms to the capabilities of your tools.

Search results disclose whether the Pickaway County District Public Library Web site contains the kinds of information its visitors seek and are used for planning future additions to the site. These results are not linked to domain, IP, or browser data.

Bryn Mawr
Bryn Mawr Library
Bryn Mawr, Pennsylvania

Use and distribution of collected information

We use personally identifiable information to support college operations. Specific purposes may also be outlined in the space it is collected.

We will not share, sell, rent or distribute personally identifiable information submitted via the web site to other organizations or businesses except where stated or when required by law.

We may link to sites outside the Bryn Mawr College domain. We are not responsible for the content or privacy practices of those sites. Personal sites hosted by Bryn Mawr, such as those on the students.brynmawr.edu or people.brynmawr.edu servers, are the sole responsibility of those sites' owners, and Bryn Mawr is not responsible for the content or privacy practices of those sites.

If a log in is required any personal information that is gathered may not be anonymous but will be confidential.

INFORMATION COLLECTED FROM USERS

Bowdoin College
Bowdoin College Library
Brunswick, Maine

INFORMATION BOWDOIN COLLEGE COLLECTS FROM WEB SITE VISITORS

Bowdoin collects personally identifiable information at various points on College Web sites/pages. Personally identifiable information (PII) are data which contain personal information that can be associated with or traced back to an individual Web site/page visitor. This includes, for instance, a visitor's name, address, and phone number. If applicable, PII also includes a credit card number and expiration date.

Information that is not PII is often referred to as "aggregate information." This includes a user's Internet Protocol (IP) address, Web site/page traffic and other statistics, and demographic data. Most aggregate information is collected automatically.

Bowdoin College automatically collects and/or tracks the following information from visitors or individuals who communicate with College community users via e-mail:

- e-mail address;
- home server domain name and IP address;
- information knowingly provided by visitors by using online registration forms, e-mail, and surveys; and
- information regarding where, when, and how often a visitor visits College Web sites/pages.

In addition, when a visitor uses Bowdoin College's search engine, College systems may record information about the search. This information is collected and analyzed by authorized system administrators to:

- evaluate Web site navigation and accessibility;
- verify the accuracy and relevance of searches;
- solve technical issues;
- calculate usage statistics; and/or
- other uses approved by the Chief Information Officer (CIO)

Pickaway County District Public Library
Circleville, Ohio

Information Collected and Stored Automatically

If all you do is look around the Web site, read text, or download information, the Pickaway County District Public Library will gather and store certain information about your visit automatically. This information does not identify you personally.

The Pickaway County District Public Library automatically collects and stores only the following information about your visit:

- The Internet domain (for example, "aol.com" if you use a private Internet access account such as AOL) and IP address (a number automatically assigned to your computer whenever you surf the Web) from which you access the Pickaway County District Public Library Web site
- The type of browser and operating system you use
- The date and time you visit
- The pages you view
- If you linked to the Pickaway County District Public Library Web site from another Web site, the address of that Web site
- If you search the Pickaway County District Public Library Web site, the search words or phrases you use and the results of the search

INFORMATION FROM COOKIES

Bowdoin College
Brunswick, Maine

USE OF INTERNET "COOKIES" BY BOWDOIN COLLEGE

Bowdoin College may place Internet "cookies" on a visitor's computer. Cookies are files inserted automatically on the hard drive of a Web site visitor by the Web site visited. Cookies placed by the College generally do not contain PII. However, the College reserves the right to associate PII with cookies at any time.

Most browser software allows users to make choices on how cookies are set by Web sites. This includes the ability to disable cookies. User preferences also allow for the user to be notified when the Web site/page attempts to set a cookie. Setting a browser to disable cookies, however, may restrict a visitor's ability to interact with some or all information available on College Web sites/pages.

Pickaway County District Public Library
Circleville, Ohio

The Pickaway County District Public Library Web site uses Web "cookies" only when necessary to complete a transaction, and then only temporarily. The Pickaway County District Public Library does not use persistent cookies.

(For additional policies, please see the accompanying CD-ROM.)

SOCIAL SECURITY NUMBERS

University of Illinois
Urbana, Illinois

Objectives

The University of Illinois recognizes that it collects and maintains confidential information relating to its students, employees, and individuals associated with the University and is dedicated to ensuring the privacy and proper handling of this information. This should be understood as the spirit of this policy statement. The primary purpose of this Social Security number policy is to ensure that the necessary procedures and awareness exists to ensure that University employees and students comply with both the letter and the spirit of the Family Educational Rights and Privacy Act and the Privacy Act of 1974. The University is guided by the following objectives:

1. Broad awareness of the confidential nature of the Social Security number;
2. Reduced reliance upon the Social Security number for identification purposes;
3. A consistent policy towards and treatment of Social Security numbers throughout the University; and
4. Increased confidence by students and employees that Social Security numbers are handled in a confidential manner.

I. Guidelines / Regulations

I.1. Each campus, including University Administration, will assign to an existing administrator the responsibility of overseeing Social Security number usage on his or her campus. These administrators control the Social Security number and their approval will be required to use the Social Security number in any new electronic system. Specific responsibilities are spelled out in the Implementation section below (II.1). Each campus is free to choose an administrator that best fits its individual administrative model. The University Administration administrator will represent University Administration and provide an institutional perspective to all dialog between these administrators.

I.2. A University-wide Unique Identification Number (UIN) will be assigned to all students, employees, and other associated individuals, such as contractors or consultants. This UIN will be assigned at the earliest possible point of contact between the individual and the University. The UIN will be used in all future electronic and paper data systems to identify, track, and service individuals associated with the University. It will be permanently and uniquely associated with the individual to whom it is originally assigned.

I.2.1. The UIN will be considered the property of the University of Illinois, and its use and governance shall be at the discretion of the University, within the parameters of the law;

I.2.2. The UIN will be maintained and administered in accordance with the University of Illinois policy on the University Identification Number;

I.2.3. The UIN will be a component of a system that provides a mechanism for both the public identification of individuals and a method of authentication;

I.2.4. All services rendered by the University of Illinois and electronic business systems will rely on the identification and authentication services provided by this system.

I.3. The University of Illinois will adopt a phased compliance strategy with the goal of attaining complete compliance with this policy statement within five years of its adoption (see section II.4).

I.4. Grades and other pieces of personal information will not be publicly posted or displayed in a manner where either the UIN or Social Security number identifies the individual associated with the information.

I.5. Social Security numbers will be electronically transmitted only through encrypted mechanisms.

I.6. All University forms and documents that collect Social Security numbers will use the language included below (II.2) and will indicate whether request is voluntary or mandatory. Forms and documents will be modified on an as reprinted basis with full compliance by fall 2002.

I.7. Paper and electronic documents containing Social Security numbers will be disposed of in a secure fashion.

I.8. Except where the University is legally required to collect a Social Security number, individuals will not be required to provide their Social Security number, verbally or in writing, at any point of service, nor will they be denied access to those services should they refuse to provide a Social Security number. However, individuals may volunteer their Social Security number if they wish as an alternate means of locating a record.

I.9. Social Security numbers will be released by the University to entities outside the University only
I.9.1. As allowed by law;
OR
I.9.2. When permission is granted by the individual; OR
I.9.3. When the external entity is acting as the University's contractor or agent and adequate security measures are in place to prevent unauthorized dissemination to third parties; OR
I.9.4. When Legal Counsel has approved the release.
The Social Security Number Coordinators will maintain the list of approved entities.

I.10. The Social Security number may continue to be stored as a confidential attribute associated with an individual. The Social Security number will be used as
I.10.1. Allowed by law;
I.10.2. A key to identify individuals for whom a UIN is not known.

I.11. This policy does not preclude, if a primary means of identification is unavailable, University of Illinois employees from using the Social Security number as needed during the execution of their duties. The other aspects of this policy statement bind such usage.

I.12. Social Security numbers will only be collected in circumstances where the collection is mandated by a government agency.

II. Implementation

II.1. Each campus Social Security number office will have the responsibility to:
II.1.1. Oversee and ensure the implementation of this policy statement;
II.1.2. Provide support, guidance, and problem resolution for offices working with Social Security numbers;
II.1.3. Serve as an intermediary between campus units and University Legal Counsel when an opinion on the release or exchange of Social Security numbers is required;
II.1.4. Maintain a list of entities, approved by Legal Counsel, to which Social Security numbers may be released;
II.1.5. Coordinate with the other campus Social Security number offices to create an electronic system to function as the central distribution mechanism for information pertaining to Social Security number usage at the University;
II.1.6. Coordinate with the other campus Social Security number offices to produce a University-wide educational program to train employees on the handling of Social Security numbers and make students aware of their rights and responsibilities with regard to Social Security numbers;
II.1.7. Meet regularly to resolve differences in implementation procedure to ensure uniformity across the University in implementation details, and an adherence to the spirit of this policy statement;
II.1.8. Authorize the use of Social Security numbers in new electronic business systems.

II.2. All University forms and documents that collect Social Security numbers will use the language included below. It is understood that this language will be implemented on an "as reprinted" basis for existing paperwork, with a full compliance date of fall 2002. If situations arise in which the following statements are not appropriate, the administrators described in section I.1 will work with Legal Counsel to provide an appropriate alternative statement.
II.2.1.1. Student
"Use of Student Social Security numbers: Furnishing a Social Security number (SSN) is voluntary and not required for enrollment. However, the University of Illinois is required by federal law to report to the Internal Revenue Service (IRS) the name, address and SSN for persons from whom tuition and related expenses are received. Federal law also requires the University to obtain and report to the IRS the SSN for any person to whom compensation is paid. Failure to provide such

information may delay or even prevent your enrollment. The University will not disclose a SSN for any purpose not required by law without the consent of the student."

II.2.1.2. Employee

"Use of Employee Social Security numbers: The University of Illinois is required by federal law to report income along with Social Security numbers (SSNs) for all employees to whom compensation is paid. Employee SSNs are maintained and used by the University for payroll, reporting and benefits purposes and are reported to federal and state agencies in formats required by law or for benefits purposes. The University will not disclose an employee's SSN without the consent of the employee to anyone outside the University except as mandated by law or required for benefit purposes."

II.2.1.3. General Statement for student handbooks and course timetables

"The University of Illinois is committed to protecting the privacy of its students, employees, and alumni, as well as other individuals associated with it. At times the University will ask you for your Social Security number. Federal and state law requires the collection of your Social Security number for certain purposes such as those relating to employment and student loans. Whenever your Social Security number is requested the electronic or physical form used to collect your number will be clearly marked as to whether this request is voluntary or mandatory.

Why does the University ask for your Social Security number when it isn't mandatory, such as at enrollment? The University is required by the IRS to supply them with the name, address, and Social Security number of every tuition-paying student. The IRS relies on these lists to certify education related tax credits. The University cannot provide the IRS with this information without a valid Social Security number. Consequently, if you intend to take advantage of any education related deductions it is important that the University have a valid Social Security number for you.

Further, the University is required to have a valid Social Security number before an individual can be entered into any business system involving financial transactions. Thus without your Social Security number the University cannot grant an assistantship, waiver, or provide employment. Providing the University with your Social Security number in advance is the safest way to ensure that these services are available with the least delay.

Finally, many of the University's legacy computer systems (those built before the creation of the I-Card) rely on the Social Security number to track students academic and financial records. Supplying a valid Social Security number helps the University maintain these records as accurately as possible.

Social Security numbers collected by the University may be used in a variety of ways, such as but not limited to the following.

1. To identify such student records as applications for admission, registration-related documents, grade reports, transcript and certification request, medical immunization records, student financial records, financial aid records, and permanent academic records; 2. To determine eligibility, certify school attendance, and report student status; 3. To use as an identifier for grants, loans, and other financial aid programs; and 4. To identify and track employment or medical records.

The University of Illinois is working to minimize the use of Social Security numbers within its business processes. The Social Security number will not be disclosed to individuals or agencies outside the University of Illinois except as allowed by law or with permission from the individual. This statement was created for informational purposes only and may be amended or altered. For a full description of the University of Illinois' Social Security number policy, please visit http://www.ssn.uillinois.edu."

II.3. Administrative Information Technology Services (AITS) in conjunction with the campus Social Security number offices will, as part of its data management strategy, develop a set of guidelines addressing the handling of Social Security numbers in electronic systems. Adherence to these

301

guidelines in all future development will be considered a requirement of this policy statement. These guidelines will explicitly address:

II.3.1. The display of Social Security numbers on computer terminals, screens, and reports;

II.3.2. The security protocol required to access Social Security numbers when they are included in part of an electronic database;

II.3.3. Alternate mechanisms for integrating data other than the use of Social Security number;

II.3.4. The legal requirement to maintain confidentiality of the Social Security numbers imposed by the Family Educational Rights and Privacy Act and the Privacy Act of 1974;

II.3.5. Obtaining permission to include the Social Security number in a system from the administrator designated in section I.1.

II.4. Phased Compliance Strategy Timetable

II.4.1. Phase I generally consists of approving this policy, creating responsible offices, and broadly educating University personnel about Social Security number collection and usage; specifically phase I is the implementation or adoption of sections I.1, I.3, I.4, I.6, I.8, I.9, I.10, I.11, II.1, and II.3 of this policy statement.

II.4.2. Phase II prioritizes systems and services out of compliance, and begins remediating or replacing these; specifically phase II includes the definition and development of the infrastructure necessary to implement sections I.2, I.5, I.7, and I.12.

II.4.3. Phase III completes remediation or replacement of systems out of compliance, and monitors and supports existing or developing systems and procedures. Phase III will be complete when every section of this policy statement has been implemented or adopted.

III. Enforcement

III.1. On each campus, the Social Security number office will be responsible for monitoring compliance with this policy.

III.2. During the implementation of this policy the Social Security number offices will jointly produce a biennial report describing the state of adherence to this policy statement, to be presented to the Provosts and President.

III.3. An employee or student who has substantially breached the confidentiality of Social Security numbers may be subject to disciplinary action or sanctions up to and including discharge or dismissal in accordance with University and Campus policy and procedures.

IV. Definitions

IV.1. FERPA—Family Educational Rights and Privacy Act.

IV.2. Phased Compliance Strategy—A strategy that attempts to define a multi-tiered approach to achieving compliance.

IV.3. Point of Service—a physical or electronic interaction between the University and either its employees, students or other individuals, during which the University provides physical, educational, informational, or electronic services to the individual.

IV.4. Secure Fashion—In the context of the destruction of paper and electronic documents, this refers to a method that defeats both casual and deliberate attempts at theft, e.g., the shredding of documents containing Social Security numbers and the use of "confidential" recycling bins. For electronic documents this refers to explicit deletion or storage on a device protected by a password based security system.

Chapter 27

COPYRIGHT RESTRICTIONS

REPRODUCTION GUIDELINES AND PERMISSION REQUESTS

Carroll Community College
Carroll Community College and Media Center
Westminster, Maryland

How to obtain permission

When a proposed use of photocopied materials requires a faculty member to request permission, communication of complete and accurate information to the copyright owner will facilitate the request. The Association of American Publishers suggests that the following information be included to expedite the process.

- Title, author and/or editor, and edition of materials to be duplicated
- Exact material to be used, giving amount, page numbers, chapters and, if possible, a photocopy of the material
- Number of copies to be made
- Use to be made of duplicated materials
- Form of distribution (classroom, newsletter, etc.)
- Whether or not the material is to be sold
- Type of reprint (ditto, photocopy, offset, typeset)

The request should be sent, together with a self-addressed return envelope, to the permission department of the publisher in question. If the address of the publisher does not appear at the front of the material, it may be obtained from *The Literary Marketplace* (for books) or *Ulrich's International Periodicals* (for journals), both published by the R.R. Bowker Company. For purposes of proof, and to define the scope of the permission, it is important that the permission be in writing.

The process of considering permission requests requires time for the publisher to check the status and ownership of rights and related matters, and to evaluate the request. It is advisable, therefore, to allow sufficient lead time. In come instances, the publisher may assess a fee for permission, which may be passed on to the students who receive copies of the photocopied material.

Chapter 28

COPYRIGHT RULES FOR SPECIFIC MATERIALS

AUDIOVISUAL

Barry University
Barry Memorial Library
Miami Shores, Florida

Audio/Visual Materials

The Copyright Act of 1976 provides protection to "original works of authorship." Protection is extended to the holders of copyright for musical works, dramatic works, pantomimes and choreographic works, pictorial and graphic works, sculptural works, motion pictures and other audiovisual works, sound recordings, and architectural works. This protection applies equally to published and unpublished works. The holders of copyright possess the exclusive right to authorize reproduction of, distribution of copies public performance of, public display of, and preparation of derivative works based on copyrighted works. It is illegal to violate the rights of copyright holders or to direct others to do so. The penalties for violation can be severe.

As a rule, Barry University Library will not make any copies of any audiovisual material.

The library will make an audiocassette copy of a class lecture if the instructor provides written permission.

Barry University Library will make copies of a material in the collection when changing a format to reflect current technology. Only one copy will be made and the source material will be destroyed.

DISTANCE LEARNING

Bryant University
Douglas and Judith Krupp Library
Smithfield, Rhode Island

Distance Learning: Bryant University Faculty and registered students may use copyrighted materials within the classroom setting and transmit them for distance learning provided they are reasonable and limited portions of the work This use must constitute an integral part of the class session. The use of the work may mirror the use of the work in a face to face classroom setting. The Teach Act expands the fair use doctrine to the right to display for distance learning at non-profit educational institutions. After transmission the work must be retained only long enough to reasonably transmit the lecture materials. A complete lecture may be retained for future use provided it is archived and removed from the University computing system when the materials have been disseminated to the students.

Electronic Collection Management Forms, Policies, Procedures, and Guidelines Manual

College of DuPage
College of DuPage Library
Glen Ellyn, Illinois

(Proposed CONFU Guidelines)

Many of the issues covered by these proposed guidelines may have been addressed by the passage of the TEACH Act in October 2002. Keep up to date by looking at new developments.

APPENDIX I
PROPOSAL FOR EDUCATIONAL FAIR USE
GUIDELINES FOR DISTANCE LEARNING

Performance & Display of Audiovisual and Other Copyrighted Works

1.1 PREAMBLE

Fair use is a legal principle that provides certain limitations on the exclusive rights of copyright holders. The purpose of these guidelines is to provide guidance on the application of fair use principles by educational institutions, educators, scholars and students who wish to use copyrighted works for distance education under fair use rather than by seeking authorization from the copyright owners for noncommercial purposes. The guidelines apply to fair use only in the context of copyright.

There is no simple test to determine what is fair use. Section 107 of the Copyright Act sets forth the four fair use factors which should be considered in each instance, based on the particular facts of a given case, to determine whether a use is a "fair use": (1) the purpose and character of the use, including whether use is of a commercial nature or is for nonprofit educational purposes, (2) the nature of the copyrighted work, (3) the amount and substantiality of the portion used in relation to the copyrighted work as a whole, and (4) the effect of the use upon the potential market for or value of the copyrighted work.

While only the courts can authoritatively determine whether a particular use is a fair use, these guidelines represent the endorsers' consensus of conditions under which fair use should generally apply and examples of when permission is required. Uses that exceed these guidelines may or may not be fair use. The endorsers also agree that the more one exceeds these guidelines, the greater the risk that fair use does not apply.

The limitations and conditions set forth in these guidelines do not apply to works in the public domain—such as US government works or works on which the copyright has expired for which there are no copyright restrictions—or to works for which the individual or institution has obtained permission for the particular use. Also, license agreements may govern the uses of some works and users should refer to the applicable license terms for guidance.

The participants who developed these guidelines met for an extended period of time and the result represents their collective understanding in this complex area. Because digital technology is in a dynamic phase, there may come a time when it is necessary to revise these guidelines. Nothing in these guidelines should be construed to apply to the fair use privilege in any context outside of educational and scholarly uses of distance education. The guidelines do not cover non-educational or commercial digitization or use at any time, even by nonprofit educational institutions. The guidelines are not intended to cover fair use of copyrighted works in other educational contexts such as educational multimedia projects, electronic reserves or digital images which may be addressed in other fair use guidelines.

This Preamble is an integral part of these guidelines and should be included whenever the guidelines are reprinted or adopted by organizations and educational institutions. Users are encouraged to reproduce and distribute these guidelines freely without permission; no copyright protection of these guidelines is claimed by any person or entity.

1.2 BACKGROUND

Section 106 of the Copyright Act defines the right to perform or display a work as an exclusive right of the copyright holder. The Act also provides, however, some exceptions under which it is not necessary to ask the copyright holder's permission to perform or display a work. One is the fair use exception contained in Section 107, which is summarized in the preamble. Another set of exceptions, contained in Sections 110(1)-(2), permit instructors and students to perform or display copyrighted materials without permission from the copyright holder under certain carefully defined conditions.

Section 110(1) permits teachers and students in a nonprofit educational institution to perform or display any copyrighted work in the course of face-to-face teaching activities. In face-to-face instruction, such teachers and students may act out a play, read aloud a poem, display a cartoon or a slide, or play a videotape so long as the copy of the videotape was lawfully obtained. In essence, Section 110(1) permits performance and display of any kind of copyrighted work, and even a complete work, as a part of face-to-face instruction. Section 110(2) permits performance of a non-dramatic literary or musical work or display of any work as a part of a transmission in some distance learning contexts, under the specific conditions set out in that Section.

Section 110(2) does not permit performance of dramatic or audiovisual works as a part of a transmission The statute further requires that the transmission be directly related and of material assistance to the teaching content of the transmission and that the transmission be received in a classroom or other place normally devoted to instruction or by persons whose disabilities or special circumstances prevent attendance at a classroom or other place normally devoted to instruction.

The purpose of these guidelines is to provide guidance for the performance and display of copyrighted works in some of the distance learning environments that have developed since the enactment of Section 110 and that may not meet the specific conditions of Section 110(2). They permit instructors who meet the conditions of these guidelines to perform and display copyrighted works as if they were engaged in face-to-face instruction. They may, for example, perform an audiovisual work, even a complete one, in a one-time transmission to students so long as they meet the other conditions of these guidelines. They may not, however, allow such transmissions to result in copies for students unless they have permission to do so, any more than face-to-face instructors may make copies of audiovisual works for their students without permission.

The developers of these guidelines agree that these guidelines reflect the principles of fair use in combination with the specific provisions of Sections 110(1)-(2). In most respects, they expand the provisions of Section 110(2). In some cases, students and teachers in distance learning situations may want to perform and display only small portions of copyrighted works that may be permissible under the fair use doctrine even in the absence of these guidelines. Given the specific limitations set out in Section 110(2), however, the participants believe that there may be a higher burden of demonstrating that fair use under Section 107 permits performance or display of more than a small portion of a copyrighted work under circumstances not specifically authorized by Section 110(2).

1.3 DISTANCE LEARNING IN GENERAL

Broadly viewed, distance learning is an educational process that occurs when instruction is delivered to students physically remote from the location or campus of program origin, the main campus, or the primary resources that support instruction. In this process, the requirements for a course or program may be completed through remote communications with instructional and support staff including either one-way or two-way written, electronic or other media forms.

Distance education involves teaching through the use of telecommunications technologies to transmit and receive various materials through voice, video and data. These avenues of teaching often constitute instruction on a closed system limited to students who are pursuing educational opportunities as part of a systematic teaching activity or curriculum and are officially enrolled in the course. Examples of such analog and digital technologies include telecourses, audio and video teleconferences, closed broadcast and cable television systems, microwave and ITFS, compressed and full-motion video, fiber optic networks, audiographic systems, interactive videodisk, satellite-based and computer networks.

2. APPLICABILITY AND ELIGIBILITY

2.1 APPLICABILITY OF THE GUIDELINES

These guidelines apply to the performance of lawfully acquired copyrighted works not included under Section 110(2) (such as a dramatic work or an audiovisual work) as well as to uses not covered for works that are included in Section 110(2). The covered uses are (1) live interactive distance learning classes (i.e., a teacher in a live class with all or some of the students at remote locations) and (2) faculty instruction recorded without students present for later transmission. They apply to delivery via satellite, closed circuit television or a secure computer network. They do not permit circumventing anti-copying mechanisms embedded in copyrighted works.

These guidelines do not cover asynchronous delivery of distance learning over a computer network, even one that is secure and capable of limiting access to students enrolled in the course through PIN or other identification system. Although the participants believe fair use of copyrighted works applies in some aspects of such instruction, they did not develop fair use guidelines to cover these situations because the area is so unsettled. The technology is rapidly developing, educational institutions are just beginning to experiment with these courses, and publishers and other creators of copyrighted works are in the early stages of developing materials and experimenting with marketing strategies for computer network delivery of distance learning materials. Thus, consideration of whether fair use guidelines are needed for asynchronous computer network delivery of distance learning courses perhaps should be revisited in three to five years.

In some cases, the guidelines do not apply to specific materials because no permission is required, either because the material to be performed or displayed is in the public domain, or because the instructor or the institution controls all relevant copyrights. In other cases, the guidelines do not apply because the copyrighted material is already subject to a specific agreement. For example, if the material was obtained pursuant to a license, the terms of the license apply. If the institution has received permission to use copyrighted material specifically for distance learning, the terms of that permission apply.

2.2 ELIGIBILITY

2.2.1 ELIGIBLE EDUCATIONAL INSTITUTION: These guidelines apply to nonprofit educational institutions at all levels of instruction whose primary focus is supporting research and instructional activities of educators and students but only to their nonprofit activities. They also apply to government agencies that offer instruction to their employees.

2.2.2 ELIGIBLE STUDENTS: Only students officially enrolled for the course at an eligible institution may view the transmission that contains works covered by these guidelines. This may include students enrolled in the course who are currently matriculated at another eligible institution. These guidelines are also applicable to government agency employees who take the course or program offered by the agency as a part of their official duties.

3. WORKS PERFORMED FOR INSTRUCTION

3.1 RELATION TO INSTRUCTION: Works performed must be integrated into the course, must be part of systematic instruction and must be directly related and of material assistance to the teaching content of the transmission. The performance may not be for entertainment purposes.

4. TRANSMISSION AND RECEPTION

4.1 TRANSMISSION (DELIVERY): Transmission must be over a secure system with technological limitations on access to the class or program such as a PIN number, password, smartcard or other means of identification of the eligible student.

4.2 RECEPTION: Reception must be in a classroom or other similar place normally devoted to instruction or any other site where the reception can be controlled by the eligible institution. In all such locations, the institution must utilize technological means to prevent copying of the portion of the class session that contains performance of the copyrighted work.

5. LIMITATIONS:

5.1 ONE TIME USE: Performance of an entire copyrighted work or a large portion thereof may be transmitted only once for a distance learning course. For subsequent performances, displays or access, permission must be obtained.

5.2 REPRODUCTION AND ACCESS TO COPIES

5.2.1 RECEIVING INSTITUTION: The institution receiving the transmission may record or copy classes that include the performance of an entire copyrighted work, or a large portion thereof, and retain the recording or copy for up to 15 consecutive class days (i.e., days in which the institution is open for regular instruction) for viewing by students enrolled in the course.5 Access to the recording or copy for such viewing must be in a controlled environment such as a classroom, library or media center, and the institution must prevent copying by students of the portion of the class session that contains the performance of the copyrighted work. If the institution wants to retain the recording or copy of the transmission for a longer period of time, it must obtain permission from the rights holder or delete the portion which contains the performance of the copyrighted work.

5.2.2 TRANSMITTING INSTITUTION: The transmitting institution may, under the same terms, reproduce and provide access to copies of the transmission containing the performance of a copyrighted work; in addition, it can exercise reproduction rights provided in Section 112(b).

6. MULTIMEDIA

6.1 COMMERCIALLY PRODUCED MULTIMEDIA: If the copyrighted multimedia work was obtained pursuant to a license agreement, the terms of the license apply. If, however, there is no license, the performance of the copyrighted elements of the multimedia works may be transmitted in accordance with the provisions of these guidelines.

7. EXAMPLES OF WHEN PERMISSION IS REQUIRED:

7.1 Commercial uses: Any commercial use including the situation where a nonprofit educational institution is conducting courses for a for-profit corporation for a fee such as supervisory training courses or safety training for the corporation's employees.

7.2. Dissemination of recorded courses: An institution offering instruction via distance learning under these guidelines wants to further disseminate the recordings of the course or portions that contain performance of a copyrighted work.

7.3 Uncontrolled access to classes: An institution (agency) wants to offer a course or program that contains the performance of copyrighted works to non-employees.

7.4 Use beyond the 15-day limitation: An institution wishes to retain the recorded or copied class session that contains the performance of a copyrighted work not covered in Section 110(2). (It also could delete the portion of the recorded class session that contains the performance.)

APPENDIX A: ORGANIZATIONS ENDORSING THESE GUIDELINES

[To be added after endorsements are received.]

APPENDIX B: ORGANIZATIONS PARTICIPATING IN GUIDELINE DEVELOPMENT

[Being a participant does not necessarily mean that the organization has or will endorse these guidelines.]
> American Association of Community Colleges
> American Association of Law Libraries
> American Council of Learned Societies
> Association of American Publishers
> Association of American Universities
> Association of College and Research Libraries
> Association of Research Libraries
> Broadcast Music, Inc.
> Consortium of College and University Media Centers
> Creative Incentive Coalition
> Houghton Mifflin
> Indiana Partnership for Statewide Education
> John Wiley & Sons, Inc.
> Kent State University
> National Association of State Universities and Land Grant Colleges
> National Geographic Society
> National School Board Association
> Special Libraries Association
> State University of New York
> U.S. Copyright Office
> University of Texas System
> Viacom, Inc.

From: The Conference on Fair Use: Final Report to the Commissioner on the Conclusion of the Conference on Fair Use. November 1998. http://www.uspto.gov/web/offices/dcom/olia/confu/confurep.htm

IMAGES

College of DuPage
College of DuPage Library
Glen Ellyn, Illinois

(PROPOSED CONFU GUIDELINES)
PROPOSAL FOR EDUCATIONAL FAIR USE
GUIDELINES FOR DIGITAL IMAGES

TABLE OF CONTENTS:

5. Important Reminders and Fair Use Limitations Under These Guidelines.

6. Transition Period for Pre-Existing Analog Image Collections.

Appendix A: Organizations Endorsing These Guidelines.

Appendix B: Organizations Participating in Development of These Guidelines.

1. INTRODUCTION:

1.1 Preamble.

Fair use is a legal principle that provides certain limitations on the exclusive rights of copyright holders. The purpose of these guidelines is to provide guidance on the application of fair use principles by educational institutions, educators, scholars, and students who wish to digitize copyrighted visual images under fair use rather than by seeking authorization from the copyright owners for non-commercial educational purposes. These guidelines apply to fair use only in the context of copyright.

There is no simple test to determine what is fair use. Section 107 of the Copyright Act sets forth the four fair use factors which should be assessed in each instance, based on the particular facts of a given case, to determine whether a use is a "fair use": (1) the purpose and character of the use, including whether such use is of a commercial nature or is for nonprofit educational purposes, (2) the nature of the copyrighted work, (3) the amount and substantiality of the portion used in relation to the copyrighted work as a whole, and (4) the effect of the use upon the potential market for or value of the copyrighted work. While only the courts can authoritatively determine whether a particular use is fair use, these guidelines represent the endorsers' consensus of conditions under which fair use should generally apply and examples of when permission is required. Uses that exceed these guidelines may or may not be fair use. The endorsers also agree that the more one exceeds these guidelines, the greater the risk that fair use does not apply.

The limitations and conditions set forth in these guidelines do not apply to works in the public domain—such as US government works or works on which copyright has expired for which there are no copyright restrictions—or to works for which the individual or institution has obtained permission for the particular use. Also, license agreements may govern the uses of some works and users should refer to the applicable license terms for guidance.

The participants who developed these guidelines met for an extended period of time and the result represents their collective understanding in this complex area. Because digital technology is in a dynamic phase, there may come a time when it is necessary to review the guidelines. Nothing in these guidelines should be construed to apply to the fair use privilege in any context outside of educational and scholarly uses of digital images. These guidelines do not cover non-educational or commercial digitization or use at any time, even by non-profit educational institutions. These guidelines are not intended to cover fair use of copyrighted works in other educational contexts such as educational multimedia projects, distance education, or electronic reserves, which may be addressed in other fair use guidelines.

This Preamble is an integral part of these guidelines and should be included whenever the guidelines are reprinted or adopted by organizations and educational institutions. Users are encouraged to reproduce and distribute these guidelines freely without permission; no copyright protection of these guidelines is claimed by any person or entity.

1.2 Background: Rights in Visual Images.

As photographic and electronic technology has advanced, the making of high-quality reproductions of visual images has become easier, cheaper, and more widely accessible. However, the fact that images may be easily available does not automatically mean they can be reproduced and reused without permission. Confusion regarding intellectual property rights in visual images arises from the many ways that images are created and the many sources that may be related to any particular image. Clearing permission, when necessary, requires identifying the holder of the applicable rights. Determining all the holders of the rights connected with an image requires an understanding of the source of the image, the content portrayed, and the creation of the image, both for original visual images and for reproductions of images.

Visual images can be original works or reproductions of other works; in some cases, original works may incorporate reproductions of other works as well. Often, a digital image is several generations removed from the visual image it reproduces. For example, a digital image of a painting may have been scanned from a slide, which was copied from a published book that contained a printed reproduction of the work of art; this reproduction may have been made from a color transparency photographed directly from the original painting. There may be intellectual property rights in the original painting, and each additional stage of reproduction in this chain may involve another layer of rights.

A digital image can be an original visual image, a reproduction, a published reproduction, or a copy of a published reproduction. An original visual image is a work of art or an original work of authorship (or a part of a work), fixed in digital or analog form and expressed in a visual medium. Examples include graphic, sculptural, and architectural works, as well as stills from motion pictures or other audio-visual works. A reproduction is a copy of an original visual image in digital or analog form. The most common forms of reproductions are photographic, including prints, 35mm slides, and color transparencies. The original visual image shown in a reproduction is often referred to as the "underlying work." Digital images can be reproductions of either original visual images or of other reproductions. A published reproduction is a reproduction of an original visual image appearing in a work distributed in copies and made available to the public by sale or other transfer of ownership, or by rental, lease, or lending. Examples include a plate in an exhibition catalog that reproduces a work of art, and a digital image appearing in a CD-ROM or online. A copy of a published reproduction is a subsequent copy made of a published reproduction of an original visual image, for example, a 35mm slide which is a copy of an image in a book.

The rights in images in each of these layers may be held by different rightsholders; obtaining rights to one does not automatically grant rights to use another, and therefore all must be considered when analyzing the rights connected with an image. Rights to use images will vary depending not only on the identities of the layers of rightsholders, but also on other factors such as the terms of any bequest or applicable license.

1.3 Applicability of These Guidelines.

These guidelines apply to the creation of digital images and their use for educational purposes. The guidelines cover (1) pre-existing analog image collections and (2) newly acquired analog visual images. These guidelines do not apply to images acquired in digital form, or to images in the public domain, or to works for which the user has obtained the relevant and necessary rights for the particular use.

Only lawfully acquired copyrighted analog images (including original visual images, reproductions, published reproductions, and copies of published reproductions) may be digitized pursuant to these guidelines. These guidelines apply only to educational institutions, educators, scholars, students, and image collection curators engaging in instructional, research, or scholarly activities at educational institutions for educational purposes.

1.4 Definitions.

Educational institutions are defined as nonprofit organizations whose primary purpose is supporting the nonprofit instructional, research, and scholarly activities of educators, scholars, and students. Examples of educational institutions include K-12 schools, colleges, and universities; libraries, museums, hospitals, and other nonprofit institutions also are considered educational institutions under this definition when they engage in nonprofit instructional, research, or scholarly activities for educational purposes. Educational purposes are defined as non-commercial instruction or curriculum-based teaching by educators to students at nonprofit educational institutions, and research and scholarly activities, defined as planned non-commercial study or investigation directed toward making a contribution to a field of knowledge and non-commercial presentation of research findings at peer conferences, workshops, or seminars.

Educators are faculty, teachers, instructors, curators, librarians, archivists, or professional staff who engage in instructional, research, or scholarly activities for educational purposes as their assigned responsibilities at educational institutions; independent scholars also are considered educators under this definition when they offer courses at educational institutions. Students are participants in instructional, research, or scholarly activities for educational purposes at educational institutions.

A digital image is a visual work stored in binary code (bits and bytes). Examples include bitmapped images (encoded as a series of bits and bytes each representing a particular pixel or part of the image) and vector graphics (encoded as equations and/or algorithms representing lines and curves). An analog image collection is an assemblage of analog visual images systematically maintained by an educational institution for educational purposes in the form of slides, photographs, or other stand-alone visual media. A pre-existing analog image collection is one in existence as of [December 31, 1996]. A newly acquired analog visual image is one added to an institution's collection after [December 31, 1996].

A visual online catalog is a database consisting of thumbnail images of an institution's lawfully acquired image collection, together with any descriptive text including, for example, provenance and rights information that is searchable by a number of fields, such as source. A thumbnail image, as used in a visual online catalog or image browsing display to enable visual identification of records in an educational institution's image collection, is a small scale, typically low resolution, digital reproduction which has no intrinsic commercial or reproductive value.

2. IMAGE DIGITIZATION AND USE BY EDUCATIONAL INSTITUTIONS:

This Section covers digitization by educational institutions of newly acquired analog visual images and Section 6 covers digitization of pre-existing analog image collections. Refer to the applicable section depending on whether you are digitizing newly acquired or preexisting analog visual works.

2.1 Digitizing by Institutions: Newly Acquired Analog Visual Images.

An educational institution may digitize newly, lawfully, acquired analog visual images to support the permitted educational uses under these guidelines unless such images are readily available in usable digital form for purchase or license at a fair price. Images that are readily available in usable digital form for purchase or license at a fair price should not be digitized for addition to an institutional image collection without permission.

2.2 Creating Thumbnail Images.

An educational institution may create thumbnail images of lawfully acquired images for inclusion in a visual catalog for use at the institution. These thumbnail images may be combined with descriptive text in a visual catalog that is searchable by a number of fields, such as the source.

2.3 Access, Display, and Distribution on an Institution's Secure Electronic Network.

Subject to the time limitations in Section 2.4, an educational institution may display and provide access to images digitized under these guidelines through its own secure electronic network. When displaying digital images on such networks, an educational institution should implement technological controls and institutional policies to protect the rights of copyright owners, and use best efforts to make users aware of those rights. In addition, the educational institution must provide notice stating that digital images on its secure electronic network shall not be downloaded, copied, retained, printed, shared, modified, or otherwise used, except as provided for in the permitted educational uses under these guidelines.

2.3.1 Visual online catalog: An educational institution may display a visual online catalog, which includes the thumbnail images created as part of the institution's digitization process, on the institution's secure electronic network, and may provide access to such catalog by educators, scholars, and students affiliated with the educational institution.

2.3.2 Course compilations of digital images: An educational institution may display an educator's compilation of digital images (see also Section 3.1.2) on the institution's secure electronic network for classroom use, after-class review, or directed study, provided that there are technological limitations (such as a password or PIN) restricting access only to students enrolled in the course. The institution may display such images on its secure electronic network only during the semester or term in which that academic course is given.

2.3.3 Access, display, and distribution beyond the institution's secure electronic network: Electronic access to, or display or distribution of, images digitized under these guidelines, including the thumbnail images in the institution's visual online catalog, is not permitted beyond the institution's own electronic network, even for educational purposes. However, those portions of the visual online catalog which do not contain images digitized under these guidelines, such as public domain images and text, may be accessed, displayed, or distributed beyond the institution's own secure electronic network.

2.4 Time Limitations for Use of Images Digitized by Institutions from Newly Acquired Analog Visual Images.

An educational institution may use and retain in digital image collections images which are digitized from newly acquired analog visual images under these guidelines, as long as the retention and use comply with the following conditions:

2.4.1 Images digitized from a known source and not readily available in usable digital form for purchase or license at a fair price may be used for one academic term and may be retained in digital form while permission is being sought. Permission is required for uses beyond the initial use; if permission is not received, any use is outside the scope of these guidelines and subject to the four-factor fair use analysis (see Section 1.1).

2.4.2 Where the rightsholder of an image is unknown, a digitized image may be used for up to 3 years from first use, provided that a reasonable inquiry (see Section 5.2) is conducted by the institution seeking permission to digitize, retain, and reuse the digitized image. If, after 3 years, the educational institution is unable to identify sufficient information to seek permission, any further use of the image is outside the scope of these guidelines and subject to the four-factor fair use analysis (see Section 1.1).

3. USE BY EDUCATORS, SCHOLARS, AND STUDENTS:

Subject to the time limitations in Section 2.4, images digitized under these guidelines may be used by educators, scholars, and students as follows:

3.1 Educator Use of Images Digitized Under These Guidelines.

3.1.1 An educator may display digital images for educational purposes, including face-to-face teaching of curriculum-based courses, and research and scholarly activities at a non-profit educational institution.

3.1.2 An educator may compile digital images for display on the institution's secure electronic network (see also Section 2.3.2) to students enrolled in a course given by that educator for classroom use, after-class review, or directed study, during the semester or term in which the educator's related course is given.

3.2 Use of Images for Peer Conferences. Educators, scholars, and students may use or display digital images in connection with lectures or presentations in their fields, including uses at noncommercial professional development seminars, workshops, and conferences where educators meet to discuss issues relevant to their disciplines or present works they created for educational purposes in the course of research, study, or teaching.

3.3 Use of Images for Publications. These guidelines do not cover reproducing and publishing images in publications, including scholarly publications in print or digital form, for which permission is generally required. Before publishing any images under fair use, even for scholarly and critical purposes, scholars and scholarly publishers should conduct the four-factor fair use analysis (see Section 1.1).

3.4 Student Use of Images Digitized Under These Guidelines. Students may:

- Use digital images in an academic course assignment such as a term paper or thesis, or in fulfillment of degree requirements.
- Publicly display their academic work incorporating digital images in courses for which they are registered and during formal critiques at a nonprofit educational institution.
- Retain their academic work in their personal portfolios for later uses such as graduate school and employment applications.

Other student uses are outside the scope of these guidelines and are subject to the four-factor fair use analysis (see Section 1.1).

4. IMAGE DIGITIZATION BY EDUCATORS, SCHOLARS, AND STUDENTS FOR SPONTANEOUS USE:

Educators, scholars, and students may digitize lawfully acquired images to support the permitted educational uses under these guidelines if the inspiration and decision to use the work and the moment of its use for maximum teaching effectiveness are so close in time that it would be unreasonable to expect a timely reply to a request for permission. Images digitized for spontaneous use do not automatically become part of the institution's image collection. Permission must be sought for any reuse of such digitized images or their addition to the institution's image collection.

5. IMPORTANT REMINDERS AND FAIR USE LIMITATIONS UNDER THESE GUIDELINES:

5.1 Creation of Digital Image Collections.

When digitizing copyrighted images, as permitted under these guidelines, an educational institution should simultaneously conduct the process of seeking permission to retain and use the images.

Where the rightsholder is unknown, the institution should pursue and is encouraged to keep records of its reasonable inquiry (see Section 5.2). Rightsholders and others who are contacted are encouraged to respond promptly to inquiries.

5.2 Reasonable Inquiry.

A reasonable inquiry by an institution for the purpose of clearing rights to digitize and use digital images includes, but is not limited to, conducting each of the following steps: (1) checking any information within the control of the educational institution, including slide catalogs and logs, regarding the source of the image; (2) asking relevant faculty, departmental staff, and librarians, including visual resource collections administrators, for any information regarding the source of the image; (3) consulting standard reference publications and databases for information regarding the source of the image; and (4) consulting rights reproduction collectives and/or major professional associations representing image creators in the appropriate medium.

5.3 Attribution and Acknowledgment.

Educators, scholars, and students should credit the sources and display the copyright notice(s) with any copyright ownership information shown in the original source, for all images digitized by educators, scholars, and students, including those digitized under fair use. Crediting the source means adequately identifying the source of the work, giving a full bibliographic description where available (including the creator/author, title, publisher, and place and date of publication) or citing the electronic address if the work is from a network source. Educators, scholars, and students should retain any copyright notice or other proprietary rights notice placed by the copyright owner or image archive or collection on the digital image, unless they know that the work has entered the public domain or that the copyright ownership has changed. In those cases when source credits and copyright ownership information cannot be displayed on the screen with the image for educational reasons (e.g., during examinations), this information should still be linked to the image.

5.4 Licenses and Contracts.

Institutions should determine whether specific images are subject to a license or contract; a license or contract may limit the uses of those images.

5.5 Portions from Single Sources Such as Published Compilations or Motion Pictures.

When digitizing and using individual images from a single source such as a published compilation (including but not limited to books, slide sets, and digital image collections), or individual frames from motion pictures or other audiovisual works, institutions and individuals should be aware that fair use limits the number and substantiality of the images that may be used from a single source. In addition, a separate copyright in a compilation may exist. Further, fair use requires consideration of the effect of the use on the potential market for or value of the copyrighted work. The greater the number and substantiality of images taken from a single source, the greater the risk that the use will not be fair use.

5.6 Portions of Individual Images.

Although the use of entire works is usually not permitted under fair use, it is generally appropriate to use images in their entirety in order to respect the integrity of the original visual image, as long as the limitations on use under these guidelines are in place. For purposes of electronic display, however, portions of an image may be used to highlight certain details of the work for educational purposes as long as the full image is displayed or linked to the portion.

5.7 Integrity of Images: Alterations.

In order to maintain the integrity of copyrighted works, educators, scholars, and students are advised to exercise care when making any alterations in a work under fair use for educational purposes such as criticism, comment, teaching, scholarship, and research. Furthermore, educators, scholars, and students should note the nature of any changes they make to original visual images when producing their own digital images.

5.8 Caution in Downloading Images from Other Electronic Sources.

Educators, scholars, and students are advised to exercise caution in using digital images downloaded from other sources, such as the Internet. Such digital environments contain a mix of works protected by copyright and works in the public domain, and some copyrighted works may have been posted to the Internet without authorization of the copyright holder.

6. TRANSITION PERIOD FOR PREEXISTING ANALOG IMAGE COLLECTIONS:

6.1 Context.

Preexisting visual resource collections in educational institutions (referred to in these guidelines as "preexisting analog image collections") often consist of tens of thousands of images which have been acquired from a wide variety of sources over a period of many years. Many preexisting collections lack adequate source information for older images and standards for accession practices are still evolving. In addition, publishers and vendors may no longer be in business, and information about specific images may no longer be available. For many images there may also be several layers of rightsholders: the rights in an original visual image are separate from rights in a reproduction of that image and may be held by different rightsholders. All these factors complicate the process of locating rightsholders, and seeking permissions for preexisting collections will be painstaking and time consuming. However, there are significant educational benefits to be gained if preexisting analog image collections can be digitized uniformly and systematically. Digitization will allow educators to employ new technologies using the varied and numerous images necessary in their current curricula. At the same time, rightsholders and educational institutions have concerns that images in some collections may have been acquired without permission or may be subject to restricted uses. In either case, there may be rightsholders whose rights and interests are affected by digitization and other uses. The approach agreed upon by the representatives who developed these guidelines is to permit educational institutions to digitize lawfully acquired images as a collection and to begin using such images for educational purposes. At the same time, educational institutions should begin to identify the rightsholders and seek permission to retain and use the digitized images for future educational purposes. Continued use depends on the institutions' making a reasonable inquiry (see Section 5.2) to clear the rights in the digitized image. This approach seeks to strike a reasonable balance and workable solution for copyright holders and users who otherwise may not agree on precisely what constitutes fair use in the digital era.

6.2 Digitizing by Institutions: Images in Preexisting Analog Image Collections.

6.2.1 Educational institutions may digitize images from preexisting analog image collections during a reasonable transition period of 7 years (the approximate useful life of a slide) from [December 31, 1996]. In addition, educators, scholars, and students may begin to use those digitized images during the transition period to support the educational uses under these guidelines. When digitizing images during the transition period, institutions should simultaneously begin seeking the permission to digitize, retain, and reuse all such digitized images.

6.2.2 Digitization from preexisting analog image collections is subject to limitations on portions from single sources such as published compilations or motion pictures (see Section 5.5). Section 6 of these guidelines should not be interpreted to permit the systematic digitization of images from an educational institution's collections of books, films, or periodicals as part of any methodical process of digitizing images from the institution's preexisting analog image collection during the transition period.

6.2.3 If, after a reasonable inquiry (see Section 5.2), an educational institution is unable to identify sufficient information to seek appropriate permission during the transition period, continued retention and use is outside the scope of these guidelines and subject to the four-factor fair use analysis (see Section 1.1). Similarly, digitization and use of such collections after the expiration of the transition period is outside the scope of these guidelines and subject to the four-factor fair use analysis (see Section 1.1).

APPENDIX A: ORGANIZATIONS ENDORSING THESE GUIDELINES:

[To be added after endorsements are received.]

APPENDIX B: ORGANIZATIONS PARTICIPATING IN GUIDELINE DEVELOPMENT:

[Being a participant does not necessarily mean that the organization has or will endorse these guidelines.]

American Association of Community Colleges
American Association of Museums
American Council of Learned Societies
American Society of Media Photographers
American Society of Picture Professionals
Art Libraries Society of North America
Association of American Publishers
Association of American Universities
Association of Art Museum Directors
Association of College and Research Libraries
Association of Research Libraries
Coalition for Consumers' Picture Rights
College Art Association
Consortium of College and University Media Centers
Corbis Corporation
Creative Incentive Coalition
The J. Paul Getty Trust
Instructional Telecommunications Council

Library of Congress/National Digital Library Project
Medical Library Association
National Council of Teachers of Mathematics
National Endowment for the Arts
National Endowment for the Humanities
National Initiative for a Networked Cultural Heritage
National Science Teachers Association
Picture Agency Council of America
Special Libraries Association
U.S. Copyright Office
Visual Resources Association

From: The Conference on Fair Use: Final Report to the Commissioner on the Conclusion of the Conference on Fair Use. November 1998.http://www.uspto.gov/web/offices/dcom/olia/confu/confurep.pdf

MUSIC

College of DuPage
College of DuPage Library
Glen Ellyn, Illinois

Music

In April of 1976 representatives of the Music Publishers' Association of the United States, Inc., the National Music Publishers' Association, the Music Teachers National Association, the Music Educators National Conference, the National Association of Schools of Music, and the Ad Hoc Committee on Copyright Law Revision agreed upon fair use guidelines for the use of music for educational purposes. In general the guidelines stipulate that the performance of music must be

- In the course of face-to-face teaching activities
- In a nonprofit educational setting
- In a classroom or other place devoted to instruction
- With a lawfully made copy

GUIDELINES FOR EDUCATIONAL USES OF MUSIC

The purpose of the following guidelines is to state the minimum standards of educational fair use under Section 107 of H.R. 2223. The parties agree that the conditions determining the extent of permissible copying for educational purposes may change in the future; that certain types of copying permitted under these guidelines may not be permissible in the future; and conversely that in the future other types of copying may not permitted under these guidelines may be permissible under revised guidelines.

Moreover, the following statement of guidelines is not intended to limit the types of copying permitted under the standards of fair use under judicial decision and which are stated in Section 107 of the Copyright Revision Bill. There may be instances in which copying which does not fall within the guidelines stated below may nonetheless be permitted under the criteria of fair use.

A. Permissible Uses
  1. Emergency copying to replace purchased copies that for any reason are not available for an imminent performance, provided purchased replacement copies are substituted in due course.

2. a) For academic purposes other than performance, multiple copies of excerpts of works may be made, provided that the excerpts do not comprise a part of the whole which would constitute a performable unit such as a section, movement or aria, but in no case more than 10% of the whole work. The number of copies may not exceed one copy per student.

   b) For academic purposes other than performance, a single copy of an entire performable unit (section, movement, aria, etc.) that is (1) confirmed by the copyright proprietor to be out of print, or (2) unavailable except in a larger work may be made by or for a teacher solely for the purpose of his or her scholarly research or in preparation to teach a class.

3. Printed copies that have been purchased may be edited or simplified, provided that the fundamental character of the work is not distorted, that the lyrics (if any) are not altered, and that no lyrics are added, if none exist.

4. A single copy of recordings of performances by students may be made for evaluation or rehearsal purposes and may be retained by the educational institution or individual teacher.

5. A single copy of a sound recording (such as a tape, disc or cassette) of copyrighted music may be made from sound recordings owned by an educational institution or an individual teacher for the purpose of constructing aural exercises or examinations and may be retained by the educational institution or individual teacher. (This permitted copying pertains only to the copyright of the music itself and not to any copyright which may exist in the sound recording.)

B. Prohibitions

1. Copying to create or to replace or substitute for anthologies, compilations or collective works.

2. Copying of or from works intended to be "consumable" in the course of study or of teaching such as workbooks, exercises, standardized tests and answer sheets and like material.

3. Copying for the purpose of performance, except as in A(1) above.

4. Copying for the purpose of substituting for the purchase of music, except as in A.1 and A.2 above.

5. Copying without inclusion of the copyright notice which appears on the printed copy.

Pennsylvania State University
Walter and Doris Goldstein
Music and Media Center
University Park, Pennsylvania

Audio Electronic Reserves is a course-related audio service of the University Libraries and Digital Library Technologies. This service employs audio streaming technology to provide Penn State students and instructors access to music and other audio being studied in courses at Penn State University. The techniques employed in providing this service are intended to comply with the Fair Use provisions of Copyright Law. The Penn State University Libraries observe the guidelines for this type of service established by the Association of Research Libraries and by the Music Library Association.

Some key characteristics of this compliance are:

• Use for non-profit, educational purposes.
• Restriction of access to authorized Penn State users.
• Limitation of the service to requests made by faculty to support classroom activities.
• Access via course-specific links only, and only for the duration of the semester the course is taught.
• Streaming only, with measures taken to prevent downloading.
• Low fidelity (streamed at 32 Kbps, FM-radio quality).
• Purchase of requested audio recordings for the library when they have not already been purchased by the University Libraries.
• Exclusion of content marketed to students for student consumption (e.g., audio that accompanies textbooks).

319

MULTIMEDIA PRODUCTIONS

College of DuPage
College of DuPage Library
Glen Ellyn, Illinois

(Proposed CONFU Guidelines)

Basically students may incorporate another's work into their multimedia production and perform or display them for academic purposes. Faculty may incorporate another's work in their multimedia productions to produce curriculum materials. These materials may be made available to students in distance learning so long as it is restricted to only those students. The multimedia work may be used for educational purposes for two years, after which time copyright permission must be obtained. Faculty may also demonstrate their multimedia productions at professional meetings and may keep a copy for their portfolio.

There are very specific limits of the amounts.

Motion media (video, etc.)—up to 10% or three minutes, whichever is less.
Text—up to 10% or 1,000 words, whichever is less.
Poems—up to 250 words. Only three poems per poet and no more than five poems from an anthology.
Music—up to 10% or 30 seconds, whichever is less.
Photos or images—up to 5 works from one author and up to 10% or 15 works, whichever is less, from a collection.
Database information—up to 10% or 2,500 fields or cell entries, whichever is less.

Fair Use Guidelines for Educational Multimedia

PROPOSAL FOR FAIR USE GUIDELINES FOR EDUCATIONAL MULTIMEDIA

TABLE OF CONTENTS

1. INTRODUCTION

1.1 Preamble

Fair use is a legal principle that provides certain limitations on the exclusive rights of copyright holders. The purpose of these guidelines is to provide guidance on the application of fair use principles by educators, scholars and students who develop multimedia projects using portions of copyrighted works under fair use rather than by seeking authorization for non-commercial educational uses. These guidelines apply only to fair use in the context of copyright and to no other rights.

There is no simple test to determine what is fair use. Section 107 of the Copyright Act sets forth the four fair use factors which should be considered in each instance, based on particular facts of a given case, to determine whether a use is a "fair use": (1) the purpose and character of use, including whether such use is of a commercial nature or is for nonprofit educational purposes, (2) the nature of the copyrighted work, (3) the amount and substantiality of the portion used in relation to the copyrighted work as a whole, and (4) the effect of the use upon the potential market for or value of the copyrighted work.

While only the courts can authoritatively determine whether a particular use is fair use, these guidelines represent the endorsers' consensus of conditions under which fair use should generally apply and examples of when permission is required. Uses that exceed these guidelines may or may not be fair use. The endorsers also agree that the more one exceeds these guidelines, the greater the risk that fair use does not apply.

The limitations and conditions set forth in these guidelines do not apply to works in the public domain—such as U.S. Government works or works on which copyright has expired for which there are no copyright restrictions—or to works for which the individual or institution has obtained permission for the particular use. Also, license agreements may govern the uses of some works and users should refer to the applicable license terms for guidance.

The participants who developed these guidelines met for an extended period of time and the result represents their collective understanding in this complex area. Because digital technology is in a dynamic phase, there may come a time when it is necessary to review the guidelines. Nothing in these guidelines shall be construed to apply to the fair use privilege in any context outside of educational and scholarly uses of educational multimedia projects. These guidelines do not cover noneducational or commercial digitization or use at any time, even by non-profit educational institutions. These guidelines are not intended to cover fair use of copyrighted works in other educational contexts such as digital images or archives, distance education, or electronic reserves, which may be addressed in other fair use guidelines.

This Preamble is an integral part of these guidelines and should be included whenever the guidelines are reprinted or adopted by organizations and educational institutions. Users are encouraged to reproduce and distribute these guidelines freely without permission; no copyright protection of these guidelines is claimed by any person or entity.

1.2 Background

These guidelines clarify the application of fair use of copyrighted works as teaching methods are adapted to new learning environments. Educators have traditionally brought copyrighted books, videos, slides, sound recordings and other media into the classroom, along with accompanying projection and playback equipment. Multimedia creators integrated these individual instructional resources with their own original works in a meaningful way, providing compact educational tools that allow great flexibility in teaching and learning. Material is stored so that it may be retrieved in a nonlinear fashion, depending on the needs or interests of learners. Educators can use multimedia projects to respond spontaneously to students' questions by referring quickly to relevant portions. In addition, students can use multimedia projects to pursue independent study according to their needs or at a pace appropriate to their capabilities. Educators and students want guidance about the application of fair use principles when creating their own multimedia projects to meet specific instructional objectives.

1.3 Applicability of These Guidelines (Certain basic terms are identified in bold and defined in this section.)

These guidelines apply to the use, without permission, of portions of lawfully acquired copyrighted works in educational multimedia projects which are created by educators or students as part of a systematic learning activity by nonprofit educational institutions. Educational multimedia projects created under these guidelines incorporate students' or educators' original material, such as course notes or commentary, together with various copyrighted media formats including but not limited to, motion media, music, text material, graphics, illustrations, photographs and digital software which are combined into an integrated presentation. Educational institutions are defined as nonprofit organizations whose primary focus is supporting research and instructional activities of educators and students for noncommercial purposes.

For the purposes of these guidelines, educators include faculty, teachers, instructors and others who engage in scholarly, research and instructional activities for educational institutions. The copyrighted works used under these guidelines are lawfully acquired if obtained by the institution or individual through lawful means such as purchase, gift or license agreement but not pirated copies. Educational multimedia projects which incorporate portions of copyrighted works under these guidelines may be used only for educational purposes in systematic learning activities including use in connection with non-commercial curriculum-based learning and teaching activities by educators to students enrolled in courses at nonprofit educational institutions or otherwise permitted under Section 3. While these guidelines refer to the creation and use of educational multimedia projects, readers are advised that in some instances other fair use guidelines such as those for off-air taping may be relevant.

2. PREPARATION OF EDUCATIONAL MULTIMEDIA PROJECTS USING PORTIONS OF COPY-RIGHTED WORKS

These uses are subject to the Portion Limitations listed in Section 4. They should include proper attribution and citation as defined in Sections 6.2.

2.1 By Students:

Students may incorporate portions of lawfully acquired copyrighted works when producing their own educational multimedia projects for a specific course.

2.2 By Educators for Curriculum-Based Instruction:

Educators may incorporate portions of lawfully acquired copyrighted works when producing their own educational multimedia projects for their own teaching tools in support of curriculum-based instructional activities at educational institutions.

3. PERMITTED USES OF EDUCATIONAL MULTIMEDIA PROJECTS CREATED UNDER THESE GUIDELINES

Uses of educational multimedia projects created under these guidelines are subject to the Time, Portion, Copying and Distribution Limitations listed in Section 4.

3.1 Student Use:

Students may perform and display their own educational multimedia projects created under Section 2 of these guidelines for educational uses in the course for which they were created and may use them in their own portfolios as examples of their academic work for later personal uses such as job and graduate school interviews.

3.2 Educator Use for Curriculum-Based Instruction:

Educators may perform and display their own educational multimedia projects created under Section 2 for curriculum-based instruction to students in the following situations:

- 3.2.1 for face-to-face instruction,
- 3.2.2 assigned to students for directed self-study,
- 3.2.3 for remote instruction to students enrolled in curriculum-based courses and located at remote sites, provided over the educational institution's secure electronic network in real-time, or for after class review or directed self-study, provided there are technological limitations on access to the network and educational multimedia project (such as a password or PIN) and provided further that the technology prevents the making of copies of copyrighted material.

If the educational institution's network or technology used to access the educational multimedia project created under Section 2 of these guidelines cannot prevent duplication of copyrighted material, students or educators may use the multimedia educational projects over an otherwise secure network for a period of only 15 days after its initial real-time remote use in the course of instruction or 15 days after its assignment for directed self-study. After that period, one of the two use copies of the educational multimedia project may be placed on reserve in a learning resource center, library or similar facility for on-site use by students enrolled in the course. Students shall be advised that they are not permitted to make their own copies of the educational multimedia project.

3.3 Educator Use for Peer Conferences:

Educators may perform or display their own educational multimedia projects created under Section 2 of these guidelines in presentations to their peers, for example, at workshops and conferences.

3.4 Educator Use for Professional Portfolio

Educators may retain educational multimedia projects created under Section 2 of these guidelines in their personal portfolios for later personal uses such as tenure review or job interviews.

4. LIMITATIONS—TIME, PORTION, COPYING AND DISTRIBUTION

The preparation of educational multimedia projects incorporating copyrighted works under Section 2, and the use of such projects under Section 3, are subject to the limitations noted below.

4.1 Time Limitations

Educators may use their educational multimedia projects created for educational purposes under Section 2 of these guidelines for teaching courses, for a period of up to two years after the first instructional use with a class. Use beyond that time period, even for educational purposes, requires permission for each copyrighted portion incorporated in the production. Students may use their educational multimedia projects as noted in Section 3.1.

4.2 Portion Limitations

Portion limitations mean the amount of a copyrighted work that can reasonably be used in educational multimedia projects under these guidelines regardless of the original medium from which the copyrighted works are taken. In the aggregate means the total amount of copyrighted material from a single copyrighted work that is permitted to be used in an educational multimedia project without permission under these guidelines. These limitations apply cumulatively to each educator's or student's multimedia project(s) for the same academic semester, cycle or term. All students should be instructed about the reasons for copyright protection and the need to follow these guidelines. It is understood, however, that students in kindergarten through grade six may not be able to adhere rigidly to the portion limitations in this section in their independent development of educational multimedia projects. In any event, each such project retained under Sections 3.1 and 4.3 should comply with the portion limitations in this section.

4.2.1 Motion Media

Up to 10% or 3 minutes, whichever is less, in the aggregate of a copyrighted motion media work may be reproduced or otherwise incorporated as part of an educational multimedia project created under Section 2 of these guidelines.

4.2.2 Text Material

Up to 10% or 1000 words, whichever is less, in the aggregate of a copyrighted work consisting of text material may be reproduced or otherwise incorporated as part of an educational multimedia project created under Section 2 of these guidelines. An entire poem of less than 250 words may be used, but no more than three poems by one poet, or five poems by different poets from any anthology may be used. For poems of greater length, 250 words may be used but no more than three excerpts by a poet, or five excerpts by different poets from a single anthology may be used.

4.2.3 Music, Lyrics, and Music Video

Up to 10%, but in no event more than 30 seconds, of the music and lyrics from an individual musical work (or in the aggregate of extracts from an individual work), whether the musical work is embodied in copies, or audio or audiovisual works, may be reproduced or otherwise incorporated as a part of a multimedia project created under Section 2. Any alterations to a musical work shall not change the basic melody or the fundamental character of the work.

4.2.4 Illustrations and Photographs

The reproduction or incorporation of photographs and illustrations is more difficult to define with regard to fair use because fair use usually precludes the use of an entire work. Under these guidelines a photograph or illustration may be used in its entirety but no more than 5 images by an artist or photographer may be reproduced or otherwise incorporated as part of an educational multimedia project created under Section 2. When using photographs and illustrations from a published collective work, not more than 10% or 15 images, whichever is less, may be reproduced or otherwise incorporated as part of an educational multimedia project created under Section 2.

4.2.5 Numerical Data Sets

Up to 10% or 2500 fields or cell entries, whichever is less, from a copyrighted database or data table may be reproduced or otherwise incorporated as part of an educational multimedia project created under Section 2 of these guidelines. A field entry is defined as a specific item of information, such as a name or Social Security number, in a record of a database file. A cell entry is defined as the intersection where a row and a column meet on a spreadsheet.

4.3 Copying and Distribution Limitations

Only a limited number of copies, including the original, may be made of an educator's educational multimedia project. For all of the uses permitted by Section 3, there may be no more that two use copies only one of which may be placed on reserve as described in Section 3.2.3. An additional copy may be made for preservation purposes but may only be used or copied to replace a use copy that has been lost, stolen, or damaged. In the case of a jointly created educational multimedia project, each principal creator may retain one copy but only for the purposes described in Sections 3.3 and 3.4 for educators and in Section 3.1 for students.

5. EXAMPLES OF WHEN PERMISSION IS REQUIRED

5.1 Using Multimedia Projects for Non-Educational or Commercial Purposes

Educators and students must seek individual permissions (licenses) before using copyrighted works in educational multimedia projects for commercial reproduction and distribution.

5.2 Duplication of Multimedia Projects Beyond Limitations Listed in These Guidelines

Even for educational uses, educators and students must seek individual permissions for all copyrighted works incorporated in their personally created educational multimedia projects before replicating or distributing beyond the limitations listed in Section 4.3.

5.3 Distribution of Multimedia Projects Beyond Limitations Listed in These Guidelines

Educators and students may not use their personally created educational multimedia projects over electronic networks, except for uses as described in Section 3.2.3, without obtaining permissions for all copyrighted works incorporated in the program.

6. IMPORTANT REMINDERS

6.1 Caution in Downloading Material from the Internet

Educators and students are advised to exercise caution in using digital material downloaded from the Internet in producing their own educational multimedia projects, because there is a mix of works protected by copyright and works in the public domain on the network. Access to works on the Internet does not automatically mean that these can be reproduced and reused without permission or royalty payment and, furthermore, some copyrighted works may have been posted to the Internet without authorization of the copyright holder.

6.2 Attribution and Acknowledgment

Educators and students are reminded to credit the sources and display the copyright notice and copyright ownership information if this is shown in the original source, for all works incorporated as part of educational multimedia projects prepared by educators and students, including those prepared under fair use. Crediting the source must adequately identify the source of the work, giving a full bibliographic description where available (including author, title, publisher, and place and date of publication). The copyright ownership information includes the copyright notice (©, year of first publication and name of the copyright holder).

The credit and copyright notice information may be combined and shown in a separate section of the educational multimedia project (e.g., credit section) except for images incorporated into the project for the uses described in Section 3.2.3. In such cases, the copyright notice and the name of the creator of the image must be incorporated into the image when, and to the extent, such information is reasonably available; credit and copyright notice information is considered incorporated" if it is attached to the image file and appears on the screen when the image is viewed. In those cases when displaying source credits and copyright ownership information on the screen with the image would be mutually exclusive with an instructional objective (e.g. during examinations in which the source credits and/or copyright information would be relevant to the examination questions), those images may be displayed without such information being simultaneously displayed on the screen. In such cases, this information should be linked to the image in a manner compatible with such instructional objectives.

6.3 Notice of Use Restrictions

Educators and students are advised that they must include on the opening screen of their multimedia project and any accompanying print material a notice that certain materials are included under the fair use exemption of the U.S. Copyright Law and have been prepared according to the educational multi-media fair use guidelines and are restricted from further use.

6.4 Future Uses Beyond Fair Use

Educators and students are advised to note that if there is a possibility that their own educational multimedia project incorporating copyrighted works under fair use could later result in broader dissemination, whether or not as commercial product, it is strongly recommended that they take steps to obtain permissions during the development process for all copyrighted portions rather than waiting until after completion of the project.

6.5 Integrity of Copyrighted Works: Alterations

Educators and students may make alterations in the portions of the copyrighted works they incorporate as part of an educational multimedia project only if the alterations support specific instructional objectives. Educators and students are advised to note that alterations have been made.

6.6 Reproduction or Decompilation of Copyrighted Computer Programs

Educators and students should be aware that reproduction or decompilation of copyrighted computer programs and portions thereof, for example the transfer of underlying code or control mechanisms, even for educational uses, are outside the scope of these guidelines.

6.7 Licenses and Contracts

Educators and students should determine whether specific copyrighted works, or other data or information are subject to a license or contract. Fair use and these guidelines shall not preempt or supersede licenses and contractual obligations.

APPENDIX A: (Endorsements and letters of support received as of November 25, 1996)

I. ORGANIZATIONS ENDORSING THESE GUIDELINES:

Agency for Instructional Technology (AIT)

American Association of Community Colleges (AACC)
American Society of Journalists and Authors (ASJA)
American Society of Media Photographers, Inc. (ASMP)
American Society of Composers, Authors and Publishers (ASCAP)
Association for Educational Communications and Technology (AECT)
Association for Information Media and Equipment (AIME)
Association of American Publishers (AAP)
Association of American Colleges and Universities (AAC&U)
Association of American University Presses, Inc. (AAUP)
Broadcast Music, Inc. (BMI)
Consortium of College and University Media Centers (CCUMC)
Creative Incentive Coalition (CIC)
Information Industry Association (IIA)
Instructional Telecommunications Council (ITC)
Maricopa Community Colleges/Phoenix
Motion Picture Association of America (MPAA)
Music Publishers' Association of the United States (MPA)
Recording Industry Association of America (RIAA)
Software Publishers Association (SPA)

2. COMPANIES AND INSTITUTIONS ENDORSING THESE GUIDELINES:

Houghton Mifflin
John Wiley & Sons, Inc.
McGraw-Hill
Time Warner, Inc.

3. US GOVERNMENTAL AGENCIES SUPPORTING THESE GUIDELINES:

US National Endowment for the Arts (NEA)
US Copyright Office
US Patent and Trademark Office

APPENDIX B: ORGANIZATIONS PARTICIPATING IN GUIDELINE DEVELOPMENT:

[Being a participant does not necessarily mean the organization has or will endorse these guidelines.]

Agency for Instructional Technology (AIT)
American Association of Community Colleges (AACC)
American Association for Higher Education (AAHE)
American Library Association (ALA)
American Society of Journalists and Authors (ASJA)
American Society of Media Photographers (ASMP)
Artists Rights Foundation
Association of American Colleges and Universities (AAC&U)
Association of American Publishers (AAP)
  – Harvard University Press
  – Houghton Mifflin
  – McGraw-Hill
  – Simon and Schuster
  – Worth Publishers
Association of College and Research Libraries (ACRL)
Association for Educational Communications and Technology (AECT)
Association for Information Media and Equipment (AIME)

Association of Research Libraries (ARL)
Authors Guild, Inc.
Broadcast Music, Inc. (BMI)
Consortium of College and University Media Centers (CCUMC)
Copyright Clearance Center (CCC)
Creative Incentive Coalition (CIC)
Directors Guild of America (DGA)
European American Music Distributors Corp.
Educational institutions participating in guideline discussion
  – American University
  – Carnegie Mellon University
  – City College/City University of New York
  – Kent State University
  – Maricopa Community Colleges/Phoenix
  – Pennsylvania State University
  – University of Delaware
Information Industry Association (IIA)
Instructional Telecommunications Council (ITC)
International Association of Scientific, Technical and Medical Publishers
Motion Picture Association of America (MPAA)
Music Publishers Association (MPA)
National Association of State Universities and Land-Grant Colleges (NASULGC)
National Council of Teachers of Mathematics (NCTM)
National Educational Association (NEA)
National Music Publishers Association (NMPA)
National School Boards Association (NSBA)
National Science Teachers Association (NSTA)
National Video Resources (NVR)
Public Broadcasting System (PBS)
Recording Industry Association of America (RIAA)
Software Publishers Association (SPA)
Time Warner, Inc.
US Copyright Office
US National Endowment for the Arts (NEA)
Viacom, Inc.

Prepared by the Educational Multimedia Fair Use Guidelines Development Committee, July 17, 1996

INFORMATION RELATED TO THE FAIR USE GUIDELINES FOR EDUCATIONAL MULTIMEDIA

The Association of American Publishers (AAP) membership includes over 200 publishers.

The Information Industry Association (IIA) membership includes companies involved in the creation, distribution and use of information products, services and technologies.

The Software Publishers Association (SPA) membership includes 1200 software publishers.

The Creative Incentive Coalition membership includes the following organizations:

Association of American Publishers
Association of Independent Television Stations
Association of Test Publishers
Business Software Alliance

General Instrument Corporation
Information Industry Association
Information Technology Industry Council
Interactive Digital Software Association
Magazine Publishers of America
The McGraw-Hill Companies
Microsoft Corporation
Motion Picture Association of America, Inc.
National Cable Television Association
National Music Publisher's Association
Newspaper Association of America
Recording Industry Association of America
Seagram/MCA, Inc.
Software Publishers Association
Time Warner, Inc.
Turner Broadcasting System, Inc.
West Publishing Company
Viacom, Inc.

MULTIMEDIA GUIDELINES WEB SITES. The Proposal for Fair Use Guidelines for Educational Multimedia Document with a current list of endorsers can be found on the following web site: http://www.libraries.psu.edu/avs/

From: The Conference on Fair Use: Final Report to the Commissioner on the Conclusion of the Conference on Fair Use. November 1998. http://www.uspto.gov/web/offices/dcom/olia/confu/confurep.htm

Carroll Community College
Carroll Community College and Media Center
Westminster, Maryland

Multimedia:

Students and teachers may use limited amounts of copyrighted materials (generally 10% of the whole work) for classroom multimedia projects with proper attribution.

Photographs and/or illustrations are permissible, but within the limitation of 10% (or 15 images) from a collected work.

Multimedia projects may be shown in class or conference-like settings for 2 years.

Projects may be used for personal portfolios for review.

Projects may be performed or displayed over a secure network.

OFF-AIR RECORDINGS

Cabrillo College
Robert E. Swenson Library
Aptos, California

The recording of a televised broadcast program by a non-profit educational institution results in an "OFF AIR RECORDING" that may be used and viewed within the following copyright guidelines.

At the request of a teacher an OFF AIR RECORDING used in the classroom may be made by Cabrillo College Media Services.

The program being recorded may be recorded only one time regardless of televised reruns.

A limited number of copies of this OFF AIR RECORDING may be made as necessary.

The content of the recording may not be altered in any way.

The copy must contain the copyright notice.

Cabrillo College Media Services is responsible for maintaining copyright control in this area.

The copy may be kept for evaluation no more than 45 days after which it must be erased.

An OFF AIR RECORDING may be viewed in a classroom a maximum of two times only during the first 10 days only of the 45 day limit period.

College of DuPage
College of DuPage Library
Glen Ellyn, Illinois

GUIDELINES FOR OFF-AIR RECORDING OF BROADCAST PROGRAMMING FOR EDUCATIONAL PURPOSES

(1) The guidelines were developed to apply only to off-air recording by nonprofit educational institutions.

(2) A broadcast program may be recorded off-air simultaneously with broadcast transmission (including simultaneous cable transmission) and retained by a nonprofit educational institution for a period not to exceed the first forty-five (45) consecutive calendar days after date of recording. Upon conclusion of such retention period, all off-air recording must be erased and destroyed immediately. "Broadcast programs" are television programs transmitted by television stations for reception by the general public with charge.

(3) Off-air recordings may be used once by individual teachers in the course of relevant teaching activities, and repeated once only when instructional reinforcement is necessary, in classroom and similar places devoted to instruction within a single building, cluster, or campus, as well as in the homes of students receiving formalized home instruction, during the first ten (10) consecutive school days in the forty-five (45) day calendar day retention period. "School days" are school session days—not counting weekends, holidays, examination periods, or other scheduled interruptions—within the forty-five (45) calendar day retention period.

(4) Off-air recordings may be made only at the request of and used by, individual teachers, and may not be regularly recorded in anticipation of requests. No broadcast program may be recorded off-air more than once at the request of the same teacher, regardless of the number of times the program may be broadcast.

(5) A limited number of copies may be reproduced from each off-air recording to meet the legitimate needs of teachers under these guidelines. Each such additional copy shall be subject to all provisions governing the original recording.

(6) After the first ten (10) consecutive school days, off-air recording may be used up to the end of the forty-five (45) calendar day retention period only for teacher evaluation purposes, i.e., to determine whether or not to include the broadcast program in the teaching curriculum, and may not be used in the recording institution for student exhibition or any other non-evaluative purpose without authorization.

(7) Off-air recordings need not be used in their entirety, but the recorded programs may not be altered from their original content. Off-air recordings may not be physically or electronically combined or merged to constitute teaching anthologies or compilation.

(8) All copies of off-air recordings must include the copyright notice on the broadcast program as recorded.

(9) Educational institutions are expected to establish appropriate control procedures to maintain the integrity of these guidelines.

RESERVES

College of DuPage
College of DuPage Library
Glen Ellyn, Illinois

Electronic Reserves

The principles for electronic reserves are not very different, with the exception that access to items placed on electronic reserves should only be available to students enrolled in the class. The COD Library is just beginning to implement electronic reserves. Below are the CONFU guidelines for electronic reserves.

FAIR-USE GUIDELINES FOR ELECTRONIC RESERVE SYSTEMS

Prepared by the Conference on Fair Use (CONFU), sponsored by the Information Infrastructure Task Force's Working Group on Intellectual Property Rights

Revised: March 5, 1996

INTRODUCTION Many college, university, and school libraries have established reserve operations for readings and other materials that support the instructional requirements of specific courses. Some educational institutions are now providing electronic reserve systems that allow storage of electronic versions of materials that students may retrieve on a computer screen, and from which they may print a copy for their personal study. When materials are included as a matter of fair use, electronic reserve systems should constitute an ad hoc or supplemental source of information for students, beyond a textbook or other materials. If included with permission from the copyright owner, however, the scope and range of materials is potentially unlimited, depending upon the permission granted. Although fair use is determined on a case-by-case basis, the following guidelines identify an understanding of fair use for the reproduction, distribution, display, and performance of materials in the context of creating and using an electronic reserve system.

Making materials accessible through electronic reserve systems raises significant copyright issues. Electronic reserve operations include the making of a digital version of text, the distribution and display of that version at workstations, and downloading and printing of copies. The complexities of the electronic environment, and the growing potential for implicating copyright infringements, raise the need for a fresh understanding of fair use. These guidelines are not intended to burden the facilitation of reserves unduly, but instead offer a workable path that educators and librarians may follow in order to exercise a meaningful application of fair use, while also acknowledging and respecting the interests of copyright owners.

These guidelines focus generally on the traditional domain of reserve rooms, particularly copies of journal articles and book chapters, and their accompanying graphics. Nevertheless, they are not meant to apply exclusively to textual materials and may be instructive for the fair use of other media. The guidelines also focus on the use of the complete article or the entire book chapter. Using only brief excerpts from such works would most likely also be fair use, possibly without all of the restrictions or conditions set forth in these guidelines. Operators of reserve systems should also provide safeguards for the integrity of the text and the author's reputation, including verification that the text is correctly scanned.

The guidelines address only those materials protected by copyright and for which the institution has not obtained permission before including them in an electronic reserve system. The limitations and conditions set forth in these guidelines need not apply to materials in the public domain—such as works of the U.S. government or works on which copyright has expired—or to works for which the institution has obtained permission for inclusion in the electronic reserve system. License agreements may govern the uses of some materials. Persons responsible for electronic reserve systems should refer to applicable license terms for guidance. If an instructor arranges for students to acquire a work by some means that includes permission from the copyright owner, the instructor should not include that same work on an electronic reserve system as a matter of fair use. These guidelines are the outgrowth of negotiations among diverse parties attending the Conference on Fair Use ("CONFU") meetings sponsored by the Information Infrastructure Task Force's Working Group on Intellectual Property Rights. While endorsement of any guidelines by all conference participants is unlikely, these guidelines have been endorsed by the organizations whose names appear at the end. These guidelines are in furtherance of the Working Group's objective of encouraging negotiated guidelines of fair use.

This introduction is an integral part of these guidelines and should be included with the guidelines wherever they may be reprinted or adopted by a library, academic institution, or other organization or association. No copyright protection of these guidelines is claimed by any person or entity, and anyone is free to reproduce and distribute this document without permission.

A. SCOPE OF MATERIAL

1. In accordance with fair use (Section 107 of the US Copyright Act), electronic reserve systems may include copyrighted materials at the request of a course instructor.

2. Electronic reserve systems may include short items (such as an article from a journal, a chapter from a book or conference proceedings, or a poem from a collected work) or excerpts from longer items. "Longer items" may include articles, chapters, poems, and other works that are of such length as to constitute a substantial portion of a book, journal, or other work of which they may be a part. "Short items" may include articles, chapters, poems, and other works of a customary length and structure as to be a small part of a book, journal, or other work, even if that work may be marketed individually.

3. Electronic reserve systems should not include any material unless the instructor, the library, or another unit of the educational institution possesses a lawfully obtained copy.

4. The total amount of material included in electronic reserve systems for a specific course as a matter of fair use should be a small proportion of the total assigned reading for a particular course.

B. NOTICES AND ATTRIBUTIONS

1. On a preliminary or introductory screen, electronic reserve systems should display a notice, consistent with the notice described in Section 108(f)(1) of the Copyright Act. The notice should include additional language cautioning against further electronic distribution of the digital work.

2. If a notice of copyright appears on the copy of a work that is included in an electronic reserve system, the following statement shall appear at some place where users will likely see it in connection with access to the particular work:

> "The work from which this copy is made includes this notice: [restate the elements of the statutory copyright notice: e.g., Copyright 1996, XXX Corp.]"

3. Materials included in electronic reserve systems should include appropriate citations or attributions to their sources.

C. ACCESS AND USE

1. Electronic reserve systems should be structured to limit access to students registered in the course for which the items have been placed on reserve, and to instructors and staff responsible for the course or the electronic system.

2. The appropriate methods for limiting access will depend on available technology. Solely to suggest and not to prescribe options for implementation, possible methods for limiting access may include one or more of the following or other appropriate methods:

    (a)   individual password controls or verification of a student's registration status; or

    (b)   password system for each class; or

    (c)   retrieval of works by course number or instructor name, but not by author or title of the work; or

    (d)   access limited to workstations that are ordinarily used by, or are accessible to, only enrolled students or appropriate staff or faculty.

3. Students should not be charged specifically or directly for access to electronic reserve systems.

D. STORAGE AND REUSE

1. Permission from the copyright holder is required if the item is to be reused in a subsequent academic term for the same course offered by the same instructor, or if the item is a standard assigned or optional reading for an individual course taught in multiple sections by many instructors.

2. Material may be retained in electronic form while permission is being sought or until the next academic term in which the material might be used, but in no event for more than three calendar years, including the year in which the materials are last used.

3. Short-term access to materials included on electronic reserve systems in previous academic terms may be provided to students who have not completed the course.

The CONFU guidelines are currently under review by the following organizations:

    American Association of Law Libraries
    American Council of Learned Societies
    Association of Academic Health Science Library Directors
    Association of American Universities
    Association of American University Presses
    Association of College and Research Libraries
    Association of Research Libraries
    Indiana Partnership for Statewide Education
    Medical Library Association
    Music Library Association
    National School Board Association
    Special Libraries Association

UNIVERSITY LOGO REPRODUCTION

University of Arizona Health Science
University of Arizona Health Science Library
Tucson, Arizona

Website Standards

All websites that represent Arizona Health Sciences Library must comply with the minimum design standards outlined below:

- Have the official AHSL Logo. Provide contact information for both Tucson and Phoenix Libraries including:
   - Library name

- Street address
- Mailing address with zip code
- Area code and phone number
- Provide a link to an electronic form as a means to contact AHSL Provide a link to the homepage. Meet current web accessibility standards.
- Be functional in all 4.x & 5.x and text-only browsers. Users must be able to navigate the website, view information, and print from the web site. Provide up-to-date and well-maintained information. Abide by the UA policies including Code of Conduct, Copyright, Advertising, and the Approved Use of University Computing and Communication Equipment policy. Official identity of the Arizona Health Science Library
- One of the following images must appear on all AHSL-related websites/pages.
  - Official AHSL logo
  - AHSL acronym
  - AHSL one line wordmark
    These images are a visual representation of AHSL and should be used consistently to help represent our identity. The following guidelines will help to ensure consistent use.
- The fonts may not be changed. The size may be re-proportioned, but retain legibility. The font of the AHSL Logo and Acronym is: Madison Avenue. The font of the Line Logo is: Opcivet-Light. The font of the Tucson & Phoenix is: Friz Quadrata. The official colors used in the AHSL logos are cardinal red and navy blue. Please follow the guide below for assistance.
  - AHSL red (web safe color)
  - RGB 153, 0, 0
  - Hex value 990000
  - AHSL blue (web safe color)
  - RGB 0, 51, 102
  - Hex value 003366
    Exceptions can be made to these colors ONLY for project specific reasons like inter-departmental use and other Library affiliated presentations or documentation. Any color changes must be approved by the AHSL Web Editorial Board.

VIDEOS

Brown University
Brown University Libraries
Providence, Rhode Island

Rules and Permissions for Audio-visual Media Copyright law and audio-visual materials

Copyright owners have the exclusive right to display and perform their works, including the projection of a film or videotape. However, educators may show films or video-tapes without explicit permission from the copyright owner if the showings are for educational purposes and are in accordance with Congressional guidelines. The film or video must be directly related to instruction and shown in the course of face-to-face teaching activities in a nonprofit education institution. In addition, the film or video must be a legally acquired or legally duplicated copy of the work.

In order to know which uses of audiovisual materials are permitted and prohibited by the Copyright Act, educators need to understand two key terms: performance and display. Under Section 101 of the Copyright Act in the case of a motion picture or other audiovisual work, these terms are defined as follows:

- To display a work means to show individual images non-sequentially.

- To perform a work means to show its images in sequence or to make the sounds accompanying it audible.

For example, in lay terms, one displays pictures of audio-visual frames of a film or videotape, whereas one performs an audiovisual work by running all or part of it through the projector or player.

Permissible Uses

The display or performance of audiovisual works in non-profit institutions is permissible, provided the following conditions are met:

- They must be shown as part of the instructional program.
- They must be shown by students, instructors or guest lecturers.
- They must be shown either in a classroom or other location devoted to instruction such as a studio, library, or auditorium if it is used for instruction.
- They must be shown either in a face-to-face setting or where students and faculty are in the same building or general area.
- They must be shown only to students and/or educators.
- They must be using a legitimate (that is, legally reproduced) copy with the copyright notice included.

Prohibited Uses

Displays and performances of audiovisual works are prohibited in nonprofit educational institutions when:

- They are used for entertainment, or for their cultural or intellectual value but unrelated to a teaching activity.
- They are shown in a public performance, to an audience not confined to students, and not related to educational instruction, such as a sporting event, graduation ceremony or community arts or lecture series.
- They involve an illegally acquired or illegally duplicated copy of the work.
- They are transmitted by radio or television (either closed or open circuit) from an outside location.

The "For Home Use Only" Warning on Videotapes

Educators should understand that the "For Home Use Only" warning on the labels of many videotapes is unlikely to preclude using such tapes in the classroom.

However, the restrictions are applicable to public performances held on the educational institution's property such as an evening event or weekend event open to the public, for entertainment or for cultural purposes. Such public performances do not include instructional activities in an educational institution which are limited to students.

Libraries and Videotapes

The libraries of educational institutions can allow videotapes to be viewed by the faculty or students, provided that such viewing is for instructional purposes. Presumably this applies to viewing by an individual or small groups of students as part of a class assignment or project

Random viewing in the library or media services that is not related to instruction may be questionable unless media services or library personnel obtain permission through license or contract, so it's best to only allow the viewing of copyrighted videotapes in library carrels or rooms for direct instructional purposes.

As with books, libraries may loan videotapes to faculty for use in their own home and libraries have the right to sell, or otherwise dispose of their copies.

Reproduction of video tapes by media services/libraries is limited by Section 108 of the copyright law. Reproduction of copyrighted videotapes may occur only to replace a work that is lost, stolen or damaged and that cannot otherwise be replaced at a fair price.

Guidelines For Taping Broadcast Programming (10-Day Fair Use)

There are a number of restrictions placed on the use of videotapes made from broadcasted television programs. The two most critical limitations are:

- Videotaped recordings maybe kept for no more than 45 calendar days after the recording date, at which time the tapes must be erased.
- Videotaped recordings may be shown to students only within the first 10 school days of the 45-day retention period.

Additional restrictions include:

- If recorded at an educational institution the off-air recordings must be made at the request of an individual faculty member for instructional purposes.
- The recordings are to be shown to students no more than two times during the 10-day period and the second time only for necessary instructional reinforcement.
- The tape recordings may be viewed after the 10-day period only by the faculty for evaluation purposes, that is, to determine whether to include the broadcast program in the curriculum in the future.
- All copies of off-air recordings must include the copyright notice on the broadcast program as recorded.
- The "off-air recordings" may not be physically or electronically altered or combined with others to form anthologies. Also off-air recordings need not be used or shown in their entirety.
- If several faculty request the videotaping of the same program, duplication is permitted but all copies are subject to restrictions of the original recording.

These guidelines apply only to nonprofit educational institutions.

Remember that the above guidelines are for commercial television broadcasts and some public television broadcasts, unless there are other negotiated rights or licensing agreements.

Public Broadcasting Service/Programs

Many of the programs and series distributed by PBS include a 7-day rerecord right. The 7-day rerecord rights allow:

- Only a single copy of the program may be recorded by an educational institution and it may not be duplicated.
- Programs may be recorded with prior request from a faculty member and may be recorded and shown each time a program is broadcast.
- The program may be retained for 7 consecutive days following the broadcast but must be erased at the end of the 7th day.
- The program may be transmitted on closed circuit systems, closed cable systems or ITFS systems.
- The program may be shown as often as needed during the 7-day period.

Videotape Distribution and Duplication

Rights to make multiple copies of a program and distribution of those programs beyond the institution can vary from program to program and from series to series. An educational institution should not make assumptions and should obtain exact information about what rights are available.

Distribution and duplication rights may have to be purchased from the producer or the distributor.

Sometimes there are no rights available from any source at any cost.

And sometimes those rights may only be available to the agency granted those rights by a distributor or producer.

Cabrillo College
Robert E. Swenson Library
Aptos, California

Copyright Law as granted by 17 USC Section110(1) states that students and teachers may show any legally obtained copyrighted video in a classroom, as part of instruction, when the following conditions are true:

- The video must be made from a legitimate copy
- Attendance must be limited to the teacher and pupils
- The video must be part of a systematic course of instruction and not for entertainment or recreation
- The showing must be part of the teaching activities of a nonprofit institution
- The showing must take place in a classroom or place intended for instruction

College of DuPage
College of DuPage Library
Glen Ellyn, Illinois

There are no special guidelines for the use of videos in the classroom; instead the provisions of Section 110(1) and (2) apply. This means that a video, even a feature film or one marked Home Use Only, may be shown in a classroom if it

- Is part of the face to face teaching activities
- In a non-profit educational institution
- Takes place in a classroom or other place of instruction
- Uses a lawfully made copy
- Is a regular part of the instruction and is directly related to the teaching content

Libraries may make copies of videos under certain provisions.

The user must document that a reasonable effort has been made to obtain a copy and that

- The publisher is out of business or
- The publisher does not have a copy available in another format and the equipment is obsolete or
- A copy is not available at a reasonable price and
- The original copy has been legally obtained.

Obsolete is defined in the code as "no linger manufactured or no longer reasonably available in the commercial marketplace."

Chapter 29

FAIR USE POLICIES

GUIDELINES FOR DOWNLOADING

Bryant University
Douglas and Judith Krupp Library
Smithfield, Rhode Island

Downloading: Downloading of music is limited to the license granted. You may not download music and retransmit it over any medium unless you have a license that allows multiple transmissions, whether for profit or for free. Streaming video and unauthorized downloading as well as peer to peer unauthorized downloading by any member of the University Community is prohibited.

POLICY STATEMENTS

Carroll Community College
Carroll Community College and Media Center
Westminster, Maryland

DEFINITIONS

Brevity

Poetry: (a) A complete poem if less than 250 words and if printed on not more than two pages, or (b) from a longer poem, an excerpt of not more than 250 words

Prose: (a) Either a complete article, story of essay of less than 2,500 words, or (b) an excerpt from any prose work of not more than 1,000 words or 10% of the work, whichever is less, but in any event a minimum of 500 words. (Each of the limits stated in i. and ii. may be expanded to permit completion of a prose paragraph.)

Illustration: One chart, graph, diagram, drawing, cartoon or picture per book or per periodical issue.

"Special" works: Certain works in poetry, prose or in "poetic prose" which often combine language with illustrations and which are intended sometimes for children and at other times for a more general audience and which fall short of 2,500 words in their entirety. Paragraph ii above notwithstanding such "special" works may not be reproduced in their entirety: however, an excerpt containing not more than 10% of the words found in the text thereof may be reproduced.

Spontaneity

The copying is at the instance and inspiration of the individual teacher, and The inspiration and decision to use the work and the moment of its use for maximum teaching effectiveness are so close in time that it would be unreasonable to expect a timely reply to a request for permission.

Cumulative Effect

The copying of the materials is for only one course in which the copies are made.

Not more than one short poem, article, story, essay or two excerpts may be copies from the same author, not more than three from the same collective work or periodical volume during one class term.

There shall not be more than nine instances of such multiple copying for one course during one class term.

(The limitations stated in "ii" and "iii" above shall not apply to current news periodicals and newspapers and current news sections of other periodicals.

Framingham State College
Henry Whittemore Library
Framingham, Massachusetts

Fair Use and Copyright Guidelines

The Whittemore Library at Framingham State College offers access to its collections in order to support and facilitate education, research and scholarship. Within the parameters of that access, it is presumed that certain materials may be made available for reproduction for use in the classroom, for course reserves, or the Internet or World Wide Web. Many such materials in the Library's collections are protected by the U.S. Copyright Act of 1976 (Title 17, U.S.C., Sec. 101 et seq.). Additionally, the use or reproduction of certain materials may be restricted by terms of gift, privacy and publicity rights, and College policy.

It is recommended that scholars and researchers desiring to copy and reproduce materials available from the Library for educational, research and scholarship purposes consult the guidelines below. The purpose of these guidelines is to provide guidance for educators, scholars and students to reproduce copyrighted works for use in educational contexts under the fair use principles of current copyright law, including Section 107 of the U.S. Copyright Act.

Reproduction or transmission of protected items beyond that allowed under fair use exemptions to the U.S. Copyright Law requires the written permission of the copyright owner. In addition to print, copyright protections also govern the use of audio, video, and images, as well as text and images on the Internet and World Wide Web (WWW). It is the obligation of the educator or researcher to determine and satisfy copyright or other use restrictions when distributing copyrighted materials. The limitations and conditions listed herein do not apply to works in the public domain, including U.S. Government works such as judicial opinions and administrative rulings, current newspaper or periodical articles, or very old works on which copyright has expired. Also to be considered are license agreements that govern the use of some works, such as audio recordings or photographic images.

Fair Use

There is no strict definition of fair use that is universally accepted, and copyright law is constantly evolving and changing. However, generally speaking, the more one exceeds these guidelines; there is greater risk that copyright violations will apply. The individual who wants to use a copyrighted work must weigh several factors:

- The purpose and character of the use: is the copyrighted work to be used for educational or nonprofit purposes?
- The nature of the copyrighted work: is it published or unpublished, out of print, factual or artistic? If a work is published and factual, it is more likely to be considered fair use than if it is not.

- The amount and substantiality of the portion used: does the amount used exceed reasonable proportions to the rest of the work, and would it adversely affect the author's or creator's economic benefit?
- The effect of use on the potential market for the copyrighted work: if the copyrighted work is to be incorporated into a project with a final end product, the more the new work differs from the original, the less likely it will be considered an infringement.

Fair use guidelines for instructors:

- Copying by teachers must meet the tests of brevity and spontaneity:
- Brevity refers to how much of the work can be copied.
- Spontaneity refers to how many times the work can be copied.
- The copies are to be used only for one course at one school.
- The expectation is that permission to use a copyrighted work will be sought as soon as it is possible.
- No more than 9 instances of multiple copying for 1 course during 1 semester are permitted. Newspapers and current news periodicals are excluded from this restriction.
- Fair use for instructional purposes prohibits copying without permission if:
- Copying is done to create, replace or substitute for whole anthologies, collective works, etc.
- Copying substitutes for the purchase of books or periodicals.
- Copying is repeated term to term by the same instructor.
- Copying is of consumables, e.g., workbooks, standardized tests, etc.
- Fair use of multiple copies for classroom use:
- Cannot exceed 1 per pupil per class.
- Must be made by or for the course instructor.
- Must include a notice of copyright on each copy acknowledging the author of the work.

What can be copied?

- A chapter from a book (never the entire book).
- An article from a periodical or newspaper.
- A short story, essay, or poem. Not more than one short poem, article, essay and not more than two excerpts by a single author may be copied.
- Not more than 3 excerpts from the same collective work, such as an anthology, or periodical volume may be copied in 1 class term. (Newspapers and current news periodicals are excluded).
- A chart, graph, diagram, drawing, cartoon or picture from a book, periodical, or newspaper.
- Poetry: Multiple copies of a poem of 250 words or less that exist on two pages or less or 250 words from a longer poem.
- Prose: Multiple copies of an article, story or essay that are 2,500 words or less. If the work is more than 2,500 words, excerpts up to 1,000 words or 10 percent of the total work may be copied, whichever is less. No more than two excerpts by a single author can be copied.
- Illustrations: Multiple copies of a chart, graph, diagram, drawing, cartoon, or picture contained in a book or periodical issue.
- Special works: works that combine text and illustrations; a children's book is an example. Special works should never be copied in their entirety. An excerpt of no more than two pages or 10 percent, whichever is less.

What should be avoided?

- Making multiple copies of different works that could substitute for the purchase of books, publisher's reprints, or periodicals.
- Copying the same works from semester to semester.
- Copying the same material for several different courses at the same or different institutions.

When is permission required?

- When you intend to use the materials for commercial purposes.

- When you want to use the materials repeatedly.
- When you want to use a work in its entirety and it is longer than 2,500 words.

How do I get permission?

Permission to use copyrighted materials can be ordered from a commercial enterprise. The Copyright Clearance Center (http://www.copyright.com/) is commonly used in higher education. Permission can also be obtained by directly contacting the copyright holder.

For materials to be used outside of Framingham State College courses, you must obtain permission yourself directly from the copyright holder.

Copyright and electronic publishing

The same protections that exist for traditional copyrighted works exist for works that are in an electronic format, e.g. a database, CD-ROM, bulletin board, or on the Internet.

If copies are made from an electronic source, such as the Internet or WWW, for noncommercial educational uses, it is likely to be seen as fair use.

There are both non-copyrighted and copyrighted materials available on the Internet. Always assume a work is copyrighted.

Tips for the Internet

Always credit the source of your information.

Find out if the author of a work (e.g., video, audio, graphic, icon) provides information on how to use his or her work. If explicit guidelines exist, follow them.

Whenever feasible, ask the owner of the copyright for permission. Keep a copy of the request for permission and the permission received.

Motion media: video/DVD/film

Legal possession of any of these formats does not confer the right to show them in a public setting. However, in the case of educational, nonprofit educational institutions, these media may be used if certain criteria are met:

- Display is to a class.
  The media is legal (not pirated) and a copyright notice is included.
- Copying of videos/DVD/film
  Copying of these media is strictly forbidden. The single exception is a library that wishes to replace a work that has been damaged or lost and cannot purchase it at a reasonable price.
- Off-air recordings of broadcasts
  - Licenses may be obtained for copying broadcasts. In the absence of a formal agreement, copies may be made under the following guidelines:
  - Copied recordings may not be kept more than 45 calendar days after the recording date. At that time recordings must be erased or discarded.
  - Copies may be shown to students only within the first 10 school days of the 45-day retention period.
  - Off-air recordings may not be altered or combined with others to form anthologies.
- Educational Multimedia Project Guidelines
  The guidelines provide guidance for the use, without permission, of portions of lawfully acquired copyrighted works for multimedia projects produced by educators and scholars.

Definitions

The guidelines are intended to apply to educational multimedia projects that incorporate educators' original material, such as course notes or commentary, together with various copyrighted media formats, including motion media, music, text material, and graphics illustrations.

The guidelines are voluntary and do not have the force of law.

If you follow the guidelines, it is highly likely that your use is fair use.

The guidelines are safe minimums.

The newly created work that includes copyrighted material may only be used for education-related activities. Other uses, such as selling the work commercially, require permission.

Student guidelines:

Students may incorporate portions of copyrighted materials when producing a project for a specific course.

Students may perform and display their own projects and use them in their portfolio or use the project for job interviews or as supporting materials for application to graduate school.

Faculty guidelines

Faculty may include portions of copyrighted works when producing their own multimedia project for their teaching in support of curriculum-based instructional activities at Framingham State College.

Faculty may use their project for:

- assignments for student self-study
- for remote instruction, provided the network is secure and is designed to prevent unlawful copying
- for conferences, presentations, or workshops
- for their professional portfolio

Time restrictions

The fair use of copyrighted material in multimedia projects lasts for two years only. After two years, obtain permission before using the project again.

Types of media and permissible amounts

Motion media:
- up to 10 percent of the total or three minutes, whichever is less.

Text material:
- up to 10 percent of the total or 1,000 words, whichever is less.
- a complete poem of less than 250 words, or, if a longer poem, an excerpt of no more than 250 words may be used. No more than three poems by one poet or five poems by different authors from an anthology may be used.

Music, lyrics, and music video:
- up to 10 percent of the work but no more than 30 seconds of the music or lyrics from an individual musical work.

Illustrations or photographs:
- no more than five images from one artist or photographer.
- no more than 10% or 15 images, whichever is less, from a collection.

Numerical data sets:
- up to 10 percent or 2,500 fields or cell entries, whichever is less, from a copyrighted database or data table.

Copying of a multimedia project:
- no more than two copies may be made of a project.

When should you get permission?

- When you intend to use the project for commercial or non-educational purposes.
- When you intend to duplicate the project beyond the two copies allowed by the guidelines.
- When you plan to distribute the project beyond the scope of the guidelines.

Library Reserve Policy

Materials which may be placed on Reserve without obtaining copyright permission:
- Exams
- Lecture notes
- Most government publications

Portions of copyrighted materials that may be photocopied or scanned and placed on electronic reserve:
- A chapter from a book
- An article from a periodical or newspaper
- A short story, essay, or short poem
- A chart, graph, diagram, drawing, cartoon or picture from a book, periodical or newspaper

Copyrighted materials that may not be photocopied or scanned and placed on reserve:
- Pages from works intended to be "consumable" in course of study or teaching. These include workbooks, exercises, standardized tests, test booklets and answer sheets.
- An entire book, whether in print or out-of-print

Length of time photocopied/scanned materials may be on reserve:

Photocopies of copyrighted materials may be placed on reserve one semester only without permission. If the instructor wishes to keep these materials on reserve for more than one consecutive semester, permission from the copyright holder must be requested. Once the request has been made the material can remain on reserve pursuant to the copyright holder's response. If permission is not granted than the material must be taken off reserve.

When copyright permission is needed:

- When a journal article, book chapter or portion of a work is on reserve for consecutive semesters.
- When multiple articles from one issue of a journal are needed for reserve during the same semester.
- When multiple chapters from a book are needed during one semester.

Chapter 30

LIBRARY POLICIES

COMPLIANCE WITH POLICIES

University of Michigan
University of Michigan Libraries
Ann Arbor, Michigan

Overview of the University of Michigan Copyright Policy

The following is a brief outline of the principles of the University of Michigan Copyright Policy as it relates to the copyrighted work of faculty, staff, and students, as well as work by independent contractors or other non-employees.

Read the official policy regarding ownership of copyrighted works created at The University of Michigan.

1) Faculty. As a general rule, faculty (including adjuncts, part-time faculty, and emeriti) hold the rights to the scholarly works they produce, both research papers and teaching materials. There are three main exceptions where the University may own the copyright. The first is material (scholarly or administrative) that has been directly assigned or has been created as a specific duty of employment. The second is material created with the support of external grants (government or foundation), in which case the terms of the grant are controlling as far as copyright ownership is concerned. The third is material created with the support of "unusual" University resources, where "unusual" refers to money or facilities provided by the University which in quantity or kind go beyond what is normally made available to one's cohorts in one's department or other academic unit.

If you are unsure whether the support was "unusual" and therefore whether you are entitled to the copyright in your work, you should ask your department chair or unit director for a determination, preferably in writing. If you disagree and are unable to resolve the matter informally, you are entitled to file a formal appeal with the Office of Provost.

2) Staff. Materials created by staff as part of their job responsibilities are considered "work made for hire." The copyright in such work automatically belongs to the University.

3) Students. The copyright on academic materials (term papers, theses, etc.) created by students in their capacity as students belongs to them. If students create material as a result of employment with the University, for example as graduate student instructors or research assistants, the copyright in such work belongs to the University.

4) Others. U-M's general policy is to claim copyright ownership of materials created for the University by persons who are not U-M faculty, staff, or students. However, this is subject to contractual agreement to be worked out between the parties. Any such copyright agreement must be in writing and signed by the University and the other party.

Boise Public Library
Boise, Idaho

Electronic information is considered constitutionally protected unless determined otherwise by a court with appropriate jurisdiction. Copyright issues and protection are covered under this statement. All efforts will be made by the library to ensure that the security of the library's computing resources and network are not breached and the integrity of the data available is not compromised.

DEPARTMENTAL DISCLAIMERS

W. Walworth Harrison Library
Greenville, Texas

As with access to other materials and services of the Library, supervision of minors with respect to the use of the Internet and other electronic resources is the responsibility of the minor's parents or legal guardians. Parents or guardians concerned about their child's use of the Internet are encouraged to read and share with their children "My Rules of Online Safety." This is included in an excellent publication from the National Center for Missing and Exploited children, entitled "Child Safety on the Information Superhighway." Parents who are concerned about their children's use of electronic resources should provide guidance to their children.

Disclaimer

The Internet is a global network of computers with no central organizational structure or control. It provides a gateway to millions of local, national, and international sources of information. While the Internet generally provides access to a wealth of information that is valuable and enlightening, the user may find information that is controversial, offensive, disturbing, erroneous, or illegal. It is the responsibility of the user to determine the appropriateness, accuracy, and usefulness of the information accessed through the Internet. The provision of access to electronic information by the Library does not imply sponsorship or endorsement of the information.

Aurora Public Library
Aurora, Colorado

Library Disclaimers

1. Internet Customer Usage Statement

The Aurora Public Library strives to meet the challenge of the multi-cultural community's continually changing needs by developing appropriate collections, resources and services. The provision of Internet resources is one of many valuable services the Aurora Public Library provides to library users. Because Internet terminals are open to the public, users should be cautious about accessing sensitive data, such as private documents or personal financial information. The Aurora Public Library will not be held liable for Internet usage or access. In addition, utilization of Aurora Public Library Internet access for illegal, criminal or other unauthorized purposes will not be tolerated, and may result in the loss of library privileges and/or criminal prosecution or other legal action.

2. External Link Disclaimer

The Aurora Public Library provides links to external websites as a convenience to our customers and for informational purposes only. These links do not constitute an endorsement or favoring by the LIBRARY or by the City of Aurora of any of the products, services or opinions represented by the external Websites. Use of any information contained in these Websites is voluntary on the part of the individual accessing them. While the LIBRARY does its best to select sites that will be most useful for our customers, the Aurora Public Library bears no responsibility for the accuracy, legality or content of external websites or for that of subsequent links. Users should contact the external website with questions or concerns regarding its content. (approved by City Attorney's office)

Texas State Library and Archives Commission
Austin, Texas

Statement of Responsibility

The TexShare Core Databases offer access to a wealth of material that is personally, professionally, and culturally enriching to Texans of all ages Professional librarians select the TexShare core databases by a process involving a statewide effort over an extended period of time. The purchase of electronic databases and ebooks by the Texas State Library and Archives Commission does not constitute an endorsement of the ideas or opinions expressed in the content of those databases and ebooks. Use of all library resources is governed by local library policies and procedures.

ENFORCEMENT AND SANCTIONS

Northeast Community College
Northeast Community College Library
Norfolk, Nebraska

Existing Legal Context

Users may be held accountable for their conduct under any applicable College policies, procedures, or regulations. Complaints alleging misuse of NECC electronic resources will be directed to those responsible for taking appropriate disciplinary action as specified under the Enforcement section. Misuse of electronic resources may result in the loss of access to electronic resources and prosecution under applicable statutes. Illegal reproduction of software and associated documentation licensed to the college is protected by U.S. Copyright Law and is subject to civil damages and criminal penalties including fines and imprisonment. All existing laws (federal and state) and College regulations and policies apply, including not only those laws and regulations that are specific to computers and networks, and other electronic resources, but also those that may apply generally to personal conduct.

When accessing remote resources from NECC facilities, users are responsible for obeying both the policies set forth in this document and the policies of the other organizations.

This policy is effective at all College locations and represents the minimum requirements that must be in place. Individual areas that have electronic resources and networks may have additional controls and security, but they are in addition to this policy. A notice may be posted in computer laboratories to provide further information in regard to procedures, restrictions, or use of facilities that are in effect at that particular location.

Enforcement

Northeast students discovered in violation of the above will be reported to the Vice President of Student Services.

Violation of any provision of this policy may result in (a) a limitation on a user's access to some or all College systems, (b) the initiation of legal action by the College, including, but not limited to, criminal prosecution under appropriate State and Federal laws, (c) the requirement of the violator to provide restitution for any improper use of service, and (d) disciplinary sanctions, which may include suspension or expulsion from a class or the college.

Ames Public Library
Ames, Iowa

Ames Public Library provides a safe, comfortable environment conducive to the use of library materials and facilities. The library is intended for the use of all members of the public. Customers are expected to observe the rights of other customers and staff members and to use the library for its intended purposes. Misconduct will not be allowed in the library.

Neill Public Library
Pullman, Washington

Internet stations are to be used in a legal and ethical manner. Violations may result in the loss of library privileges and/or criminal prosecution or other legal actions. If a patron is a minor his/her parents/guardians will be notified. First violation: Warning note will be placed on patron's record. Second violation: Situation will be referred to the Library Director for appropriate action, which may include loss of Internet privileges and reporting of the violation to the police.

Aurora Public Library
Aurora, Colorado

Enforcement and Consequences

No one, minor or adult, has the right to use public property to commit crimes. At the same time, no policy can ensure that crimes will never be committed. If customers are found to be accessing materials that may be, at the discretion of the LIBRARY, obscene or illegal, they will be first be asked to immediately exit the site. Non-compliance will result in the individual's ejection from the library facility and they may be barred from future use of library resources.

Bryant University
Douglas and Judith Krupp Library
Smithfield, Rhode Island

Warning and Take Down Policy: In the event a Bryant University User is found to be infringing, the user will be immediately warned of the alleged infringement. Failure to cease and desist from any and all infringing action will cause the IT Department to "take down" the user from the Bryant University network and the user's privilege to use the network will be terminated in accordance with Bryant University's obligations under the Digital Millennium Copyright Act.

Bowdoin College
Brunswick, Maine

Response Protocol to Infringement Claims

Protocol for response to a complaint regarding copyrighted materials:
- If any Bowdoin College employee or agent is informed about a copyright infringement complaint, he/she will send the entire complaint to the designated agent for Bowdoin College.
- The designated agent will determine the identity of the individual involved in the complaint and the status of the individual (student, faculty or staff member).
- There are two protocols that take place depending upon whether the individual has a previous record on file with the designated agent.

- If this is a first complaint against the individual, the designated agent or his designee will send the individual an e-mail notice requesting that all questionable materials be removed from his/her computer and that the individual notify the designated agent via e-mail within 72 hours that the materials have been removed.
- If the individual is a student, copies of the letter and the complaint will be automatically forwarded to the Dean of Student Affairs for appropriate action. The Dean of Student Affairs or his designee will inform the student of this policy. The Office of the Dean of Student Affairs will maintain a database of students and keep track of the number of violations for purposes of taking disciplinary action, if any.
- If the individual is a faculty member, copies of the letter and the complaint will also be forwarded to the appropriate academic department chair and the Dean for Academic Affairs for appropriate action.
- If the individual is a staff member, copies of the letter and the complaint will also be forwarded to the supervisor and department head for appropriate action.
- If the involved person complies with the request to remove questionable materials within 72 hours, the designated agent will notify the complainant of the institutional resolution.

Orion Township Public Library
Lake Orion, Michigan

Notice of Claimed Copyright Infringement

Users and subscribers of this system are required to respect the legal protection provided by copyright and license to programs and data. If you believe that your work has been copied, adapted, reproduced, or exhibited on this website (http://www.orion.lib.mi.us/) in a way that constitutes copyright infringement, please provide written notice of the claimed infringing activity to the Orion Township Public Library's designated agent, in accordance with the requirements of the Digital Millennium Copyright Act, 17 U.S.C. ß 512.

A notice of claimed copyright infringement must include the following information:

1. An electronic or physical signature of the copyright owner or a person authorized to act on behalf of the owner of an exclusive right that is allegedly infringed.

2. Identification of the copyrighted work claimed to have been infringed, or if multiple copyrighted works at a single online site are covered by a single notice, a representative list of such works at that site.

3. Identification of the material that is claimed to be infringing or to be the subject of infringing activity and that is to be removed or access to which is to be disabled, and information reasonably sufficient to permit the Orion Township Public Library to locate the material.

4. Information reasonably sufficient to permit the Orion Township Public Library to contact the complaining party, such as an address, telephone number, and, if available, an electronic mail address at which the complaining party may be contacted.

5. A statement that the complaining party has a good faith belief that use of the material in the matter complained of is not authorized by the copyright owner, its agent, or the law.

6. A statement that the information in the notice is accurate, and under penalty of perjury, that the complaining party is authorized to act on behalf of the owner of an exclusive right that is allegedly infringed.

Designation of Agent to Receive Notification of Claimed Infringement

A notification of claimed copyright infringement must be provided in writing to the Orion Township Public Library's designated agent. The designated agent to receive notification of claimed infringement under Title II of the Digital Millennium Copyright Act (17 U.S.C. ß 512) is:

Upon receipt of notification of claimed copyright infringement, the Orion Township Public Library will follow the procedures outlined in Title II of the Digital Millennium Copyright Act (17 U.S.C. ß 512).

Notice and Takedown Procedure

It is expected that all users of this system will comply with applicable copyright laws. However, if the Orion Township Public Library is notified of claimed copyright infringement, or otherwise becomes aware of facts and circumstances from which infringement is apparent, it will respond expeditiously by removing, or disabling access to, the material that is claimed to be infringing or to be the subject of infringing activity.

Repeat Infringers

Under appropriate circumstances, the Orion Township Public Library may, in its discretion, terminate the accounts of subscribers and account holders of its system or network who are repeat infringers.

Accommodation of Standard Technical Measures

It is the Orion Township Public Library's policy to accommodate and not interfere with standard technical measures, i.e., technical measures that are used by copyright owners to identify or protect copyrighted works and (1) have been developed pursuant to a broad consensus of copyright owners and service providers in an open, fair, voluntary, multi-industry standards process; (2) are available to any person on reasonable and nondiscriminatory terms; and (3) do not impose substantial costs on service providers or substantial burdens on their systems or networks.

LIBRARY LIMITATION OF LIABILITIES

College of DuPage
College of DuPage Library
Glen Ellyn, Illinois

User Responsibilities

The user agrees to hold the Library harmless from any claims, losses, damages, obligations, or liabilities relating to the use of information obtained from the Library's electronic information system.

Chapter 31

PRINCIPLES

INTELLECTUAL FREEDOM GUIDELINES

Northcentral University
Northcentral University Library
Prescott Valley, Arizona

The Library of Northcentral University supports the American Library Association's Bill Of Rights and the Freedom To Read Statement. The Library follows the "Intellectual Freedom Principles for Academic Libraries." For this policy, the Library has adopted sections of the Library Bill of Rights applicable to collection development as approved by the ACRL Board of Directors. The general principles set forth in the Library Bill of Rights form an indispensable framework for building collections, services, and policies that serve the entire academic community. A strong intellectual freedom perspective is critical to the development of academic library collections and services that subjectively meet the education and research needs of a college or university community. The purpose of this statement is to outline how and where intellectual freedom principles fit into an academic library setting, thereby raising consciousness of the intellectual freedom context within which academic librarians work. The following principles should be reflected in all relevant library policy documents. The development of library collections in support of an institution's instruction and research programs should transcend the personal values of the selector. In the interests of research and learning, it is essential that collections contain materials representing a variety of perspectives on subjects that may be considered controversial. A service philosophy should be promoted that affords equal access to information for all in the academic community with no discrimination on the basis of race, values, gender, sexual orientation, cultural or ethnic background, physical or learning disability, economic status, religious beliefs, or views. The Library acquires materials that represent differing opinions and without censorship in regard to controversial issues.

Calumet College of Saint Joseph
Specker Library
Whiting, Indiana

Free expression of ideas is central to the academic process. The computer system administrator will not remove any information from individual accounts or from electronic bulletin boards maintained on them unless the administrator finds that:

* The presence of the information involves illegality (e.g. copyrighted material, software in violation of a license agreement).
* The information in some way endangers computing resources or the information of other users (e.g. a computer worm, virus, or other destructive program).
* The information is inconsistent with the mission of the college, involves the harassment of others including the use of obscene, bigoted, or abusive language or images, or is otherwise not in compliance with legal and ethical usage listed below.

University of Maryland
University of Maryland Libraries
College Park, Maryland

Primary Principles: Freedom of Expression and Personal Responsibility

Freedom of expression and an open environment to pursue scholarly inquiry and for sharing of information are encouraged, supported, and protected at the University of Maryland. These values lie at the core of our academic community. Censorship is not compatible with the tradition and goals of the university. While some computing resources are dedicated to specific research, teaching, or administrative tasks that would limit their use, freedom of expression must, in general, be protected. The university does not limit access to information because of its content when it meets the standard of legality. The university's policy of freedom of expression applies to computing resources.

Concomitant with free expression are personal obligations of each member of our community to use computing resources responsibly, ethically, and in a manner which accords both with the law and the rights of others. The university depends first upon a spirit of mutual respect and cooperation to create and maintain an open community of responsible users.

FREEDOM OF SPEECH GUIDELINES

Tempe Public Library
Tempe, Arizona

The Tempe Public Library believes strongly in the free flow of information and makes every effort to comply with the First Amendment of the United States Constitution and Article II, Section 6 of the Arizona Constitution. Accordingly, any visitor to the Library who uses the electronic information resources and reasonably believes that the Library's filtering software has unnecessarily blocked a Web site, can seek to have it reviewed expeditiously by Library staff. If the Library staff determines the Web site to be in violation of the policy, the visitor can request further expeditious review by staff at the Tempe City Attorney's Office. If the staff at the Tempe City Attorney's Office determines the Web site to be in violation of the policy, the visitor can request expeditious judicial review of said Web site. If the Library staff or City Attorney's Office determines that the Web site is not in violation of the policy, Library staff will promptly submit a request to the Information Technology Division to modify the filter so that it will permit access to the site in question. If a visitor to the Library using the Library's electronic resources finds a Web site that he or she feels is in violation of the policy and that has not been blocked by the filter, the visitor can seek to have it reviewed expeditiously by Library staff. If the Library staff or City Attorney's Office determines that the reported Web site is in violation of the policy, Library staff will promptly submit a request to the Information Technology Division to modify the filter so that it will not permit access to the site in question. The aforementioned procedural safeguards are not a license to purposely offend Library staff, and any attempt to do so may result in the loss of library privileges.

Bryn Mawr
Bryn Mawr Library
Bryn Mawr, Pennsylvania

Free Speech

The constitutional right of free speech applies to all citizens of the electronic community. Bryn Mawr College respects the right to freedom of expression within the context of the shared values of its community.

Members of the community are expected to behave ethically and to respect the diversity and privacy of other people.

RECORDS AND THE USA PATRIOT ACT

College of DuPage
College of DuPage Library
Glen Ellyn, Illinois

Policy and Procedures for Responding to Search Warrants and Subpoenas

PRIVACY OF LIBRARY RECORDS with reference to the USA PATRIOT Act

The College of DuPage Library is committed to ensuring the confidentiality of all personally identifiable information about Library users. In accordance with the Illinois Library Records Confidentiality Act (75 ILCS 70/1) all borrowers' registration, circulation, and use records are confidential and may not be revealed to the public except by court order.

The Library interprets this Act to include:

* Patron name, address, telephone number, and place of employment.
* A listing of items which a patron has checked out.
* The identity of a patron with a particular item checked out.
* Any patron debts owed to the Library.
* Use records of any Library equipment such as computer equipment.

The above information will only be disclosed to the patron directly. Such information will not be disclosed to any other patron, family member, or College of DuPage staff except as detailed below.

In order to comply with this Act, requests for release of one's own information by a patron should be made in person. The patron requesting his/her information must present two forms of identification, one of which must be a picture ID. If written or phone requests are made, the information requested will be mailed only to the patron's address of record.

This Act does not preclude the Library's use of patron records for purposes of recovering Library materials, fines, or other charges related to the use of Library property, even if that includes release of necessary information to a college official, collection agency, or law enforcement agency. The Library also recognizes that there may be occasions when records regarding Library users will be requested through lawfully issued subpoenas and search warrants. It is the policy of the Library that confidential Library records should not be released or made available in any form to a federal agent, law enforcement officer, or other person unless a court order in proper form has been entered by a court of competent jurisdiction after a showing of good cause by the law enforcement agency or person seeking the records.

If the court order is a search warrant issued pursuant to the Uniting and Strengthening America by Providing Appropriate Tools Required to Intercept and Obstruct Terrorism Act of 2001 ("USA PATRIOT Act" or "Patriot Act"), special requirements must be followed. The USA PATRIOT Act became law on October 26, 2001 and expanded the authority of law enforcement to gain access to business records, medical records, educational records and Library records, including stored electronic data and communications. It also expanded the laws governing wiretaps and "trap and trace" phone devices to Internet and electronic communications. The Act allows law enforcement agents or officers to obtain a search warrant for "any tangible thing," which can include books, records, papers, floppy disks, data tapes, and computers with hard drives.

The USA Patriot Act also stipulates that law enforcement agents can obtain a court order allowing the monitoring of Internet and e-mail use, or requiring that the Library provide the information about such use to law enforcement from the Library's records. If an order of this type is received, the Library shall cooperate with law enforcement in setting up monitoring devices or providing information.

Pursuant to the Patriot Act, the Library is prohibited from disclosing to the Library user or any other party that communications are being monitored or records have been obtained.

In order to respond appropriately to request for patron's records, the Library hereby adopts appropriate procedures.

Madison Public Library
Madison, Wisconsin

USA Patriot Act and Madison Public Library Records

See also Board Resolution on the USA Patriot Act and Related Measures that Infringe on the Rights of Library Users

HR-3162, known as the USA Patriot Act, became Public Law 107-56 in response to the events of 9/11/01. The full title of the law is: Uniting and Strengthening America by Providing Appropriate Tools Required to Intercept and Obstruct Terrorism Act of 2001. For information on the 2005 Reauthorization see: USA PATRIOT IMPROVEMENT AND REAUTHORIZATION ACT OF 2005

The Act provides law enforcement broader boundaries when investigating information accessed and transmitted by patrons with regards to national security concerns. The law provides federal officials the authority to conduct searches of business records, including library and bookstore records, with a court order issued by a federal court, and requires that, if such a search is conducted, no one involved will divulge that the search has taken place.

The confidentiality of patron's library use is taken very seriously by public libraries. As a result of the USA Patriot Act, public libraries face a dilemma of having the responsibility of protecting the privacy of library users while responding to legitimate national security concerns. Madison Public Library recognizes the confidentiality of information sought or received and materials consulted, borrowed or acquired by a library user, and that is reflected in Madison Public Library Confidentiality Policy revised March, 2003, as follows:

All Madison Public Library circulation and other records which indicate the identity of library users, especially as they connect library users with material or services used, are confidential. This confidentiality extends to information sought or received, including library materials consulted or borrowed, database search records, reference interviews, circulation records, registration records and all other personally identifiable uses of library materials, facilities or services.

Such information may not be disclosed, except to:

• Persons acting within the scope of their duties in the administration of the library or library system.
• An agency or individual or any local, state or federal government, pursuant to a process, subpoena or court order authorized pursuant to a federal, state, or local law relating to civil, criminal, administrative or legislative investigative power. Library staff will seek legal counsel from the City Attorney's Office in the event of such request for release of library records, and will respond to the request according to advice of counsel.
• Persons authorized by the individual to inspect the individual's record.

The policy cites Wisconsin Statute 43.30, Public Library Records, and a statement from the American Library Association on release of records. (Print copies of either of these will be made available upon request.)

Madison Public Library Records and the USA Patriot Act:

Madison Public Library has in place guidelines regarding information access and confidentiality for specific library records, which include the following:

- The Library does not retain records of individual user activity with personally identifiable information except those required for the efficient operation of the Library, in accordance with WI Statute 43.30.
- The Library does not create unnecessary records containing a user's personally identifiable information—except those required for the efficient operation of the Library.

Specific existing library records:

Database Search Records: Searches of the collection using LINKcat, the on-line catalog, are conducted by using the library's automated circulation system, Dynix. Once a search is conducted, the software does not retain a copy of the search. Records of the search no longer exist. The library also does not retain searches of other databases, such as newspaper, magazine or automobile repair databases, licensed by the library or library system.

Circulation Records: Data matching items with patrons is stored on the LINK system while the material is checked out to the patron. When an item is returned and any fees and fines are paid, it is removed from the borrower's file but a link from the item to the borrower is maintained until: 1) the item is loaned to the next borrower, or 2) 30 days elapse.

Copies of the operating system, application software and databases, and transaction records of the LINK integrated library system are stored on backup media. Nightly backups are stored for one month. The information is retained in the event that a catastrophic hardware or software failure would require restoration of software or data files.

Home Service Circulation Records: Records are kept of books checked out and delivered to those physically unable to come to the library who use the volunteer supported home delivery program. These records allow staff to provide new titles for the patron. The maintenance of these records is required in order to serve the participants in this special program.

Computer Use Records: Madison Public Libraries offer computers for public access to the Internet. Software is used to manage the high demand for Internet access. Internet users enter their library card, or an Internet-access card, to reserve a computer. Reservation information is retained for ten days. Patron information is then deleted.

Inter-Library Loan Records: Patrons may borrow items not owned by South Central Library System libraries from other libraries worldwide via Inter-Library Loan (ILL). Madison Public Library tracks items being borrowed and generates a paper record with patron information. The Library keeps records for one year.

Reference Interviews: A reference interview occurs when a patron looking for information approaches library staff and staff interacts with the patron in order to narrow down the specific information needed. No paper record is kept during the interview that has any patron information on it. If a patron name and number is taken by phone, and patron information is written down, as soon as the requested information is delivered, the paper record is destroyed.

AskAway Online Reference Service: Reports from this new service are kept for many months for reporting purposes. However, if a patron provides an email address and/or name, this information, along with an IP address, is stripped from the transcript of the session after 33 days. If, however, an email address or name is referenced in the chat portion of the session, those items may be retained longer than 33 days. If a patron logs in as "anonymous," there is no way to link them to any personal information after 33 days.

For more information: The American Library Association has posted information on the USA Patriot Act and libraries. The Department of Homeland Security's site has more information (Search by "USA Patriot").

Sharon Public Library
Sharon, Massachusetts

Sharon Public Library & the USA PATRIOT Act of 2001: Patron Confidentiality & Privacy, a Statement of Operations & Procedures

The Sharon Public Library strives to create a library environment that is:
- A place where patrons can ask any question and discuss any topic
- A place for learning and pursuing knowledge and information on any topic
- A safe place
- Crime free

The Sharon Public Library recognizes the confidentiality of information sought or received and materials consulted, borrowed or acquired by a library user. The Library will do its utmost to uphold the privacy and confidentiality of patrons' free access to information. The library will rely on existing laws and library policies to control behavior that involves public safety or criminal behavior.

Sharon Public Library adheres to Massachusetts General Laws Chapter 78, Section 7 which states that library records shall be confidential and shall not be disclosed except that such records may be disclosed to the extent necessary for the proper operation of such library and shall be disclosed upon request or consent of the user or pursuant to subpoena, court order or where otherwise required by statute. Sharon Public Library will not sell, lease or otherwise share any personal information to outside parties unless required by law. Sharon Public Library considers circulation and registration records identifying the names, addresses, email addresses, and telephone numbers of library patrons, as well as materials borrowed or accessed electronically, not to be part of the public record.

The USA PATRIOT Act of 2001

Public Law 107-56 was passed in response to the events of 9/11/2001. The full title of the law is: Uniting and Strengthening America by Providing Appropriate Tools Required to Intercept and Obstruct Terrorism Act of 2001.

This Act provides law enforcement with broader boundaries when investigating information accessed and transmitted by library patrons with regard to national security concerns.

Under the USA PATRIOT Act, government access to patron information may include but not be limited to:

Database Search Records
- Circulation Records
- Computer Use Records
- E-mail Records
- Inter-Library Loan Records
- Reference Interviews

How Sharon Public Library attempts to maintain patron confidentiality and privacy in light of this Act is detailed below:

Sharon Public Library Statement of Operations & Procedures Regarding Patron Confidentiality and Privacy

Database Search Records: These records refer to the searches of the library's and consortia members' collections which a patron may conduct using the Online Public Access Catalog (OPAC) terminals or from home via the Internet. These searches are conducted by utilizing the library's automated library catalog system, iBistro. iBistro is a product of SIRSI Systems. Once a search is conducted and completed, the software does not retain a copy of the search. Any records of the search will not exist unless a patron prints or emails a copy of the search for his/her own use.

Circulation Records: Patron material is circulated via the SIRSI WorkFlows system. The circulation software tracks materials currently checked out and until any/all outstanding fines and fees are resolved. Old Colony Library Network retains a list of items that a patron has borrowed as "My Favorites." Items recorded as "My Favorites" are deleted after 180 days. Instructions for disabling "My Favorites" are available on the OCLN homepage and at OCLN member libraries.

Computer Use Records: The Sharon Public Library has numerous public use computers available to surf the Internet and/or perform word processing functions. Patrons reserve the use time for most of these computers by writing his/her name on a reservation form. The daily reservation form does contain the user's name and which computer he/she signed up for. However, the use statistics are totaled daily from the reservation forms and are then destroyed; no paper record with the patron's name or other information is retained by the library. The only statistic gathered is the total hours the computers were in use. Periodically, the computer's Internet cache is cleared of all web pages visited and documents inadvertently saved to the computer's hard drive are removed.

Sharon Public Library's Internet service is provided through the Old Colony Library Network whose connection is supported with funding from the Massachusetts Board of Library Commissioners and member communities. OCLN and Sharon Public Library keep no permanent record of Internet sites visited by library patrons, the electronic databases accessed, or the searches performed by individual patrons. OCLN counts the number of viewers of different web pages within the sites it hosts (OCLN.org) and Sharon Public Library does the same for the pages it hosts (SharonPublicLibrary.org). This information is collected in order to improve the content offered on those sites and may be used to compile statistical reports. These logs do not include names, phone numbers, addresses, email addresses or other identifying personal information.

NOTE: Sharon Public Library cannot and does not guarantee that every task completed on any computer connected to its local and/or OCLN wide area network is private. Patrons are advised that they have no expectation of privacy in library computers and, therefore, any information or data viewed or stored on library computers may be accessed by others.

E-Mail Records: E-mail messages sent to any Sharon Public Library and/or Old Colony Library Network address may be stored or forwarded to others within the Library, OCLN, or to other libraries' staff in order to respond to a request for information.

Library patrons may supply the Library with an email address to receive periodic mailings about new acquisitions, upcoming events, items about to fall due or items being held. This service can be discontinued by contacting the adult and/or children's circulation desks.

Inter-Library Loan Records: Patrons may borrow items not owned by the Sharon Public Library from other libraries worldwide via Interlibrary Loan (ILL). The Sharon Public Library tracks items currently being borrowed and generates a paper record with patron information. Once the materials are returned and all appropriate fines and/or fees are paid, the paper record is destroyed. Only usage statistics are retained, not names of borrowers. For U.S. copyright purposes, titles of items may be kept but the borrower's name is not attached to this record.

Reference Interviews: A reference interview occurs when a patron looking for information approaches a library staff and staff questions or interviews the patron in order to narrow down the specific information needed. Normally, no paper record is kept during the interview that has any patron information on it. However, if a request for information requires the librarian to contact the patron at a later time, which happens with an involved request or at busy times, for example, a patron name and number is taken and patron information is written down. As soon as the requested information is delivered to the requesting patron, the paper record is destroyed.

NOTE: For further information and related policies please review the following: OCLN Privacy Policy, OCLN Internet Use Policy, SPL Internet Access Policy, SPL Electronic Information Access Policy, SPL Rules for Use of Public Access Computers, SPL Library Behavior Policy, SPL Safety of Children in Library Policy, and the USA PATRIOT Act of 2001.

Sharon Public Library Staff Procedures for Complying with Law Enforcement

The Sharon Public Library staff will comply with law enforcement when supplied with legal subpoena or warrant.

Staff Procedures:

If anyone approaches you alleging to be a law enforcement official requesting information, do not disclose to that individual any information. Immediately contact a supervisor, department head, assistant director, or director.

The supervisor, department head, assistant director, or director will ask to see official identification and will photocopy the ID and/or request business card and/or record badge number and other pertinent ID information.

If law enforcement presents a subpoena, library staff should direct that person to their supervisor, department head, assistant director, or director; who will in turn direct the subpoena to legal counsel.

If library staff is presented with a warrant, do not interfere with their search and seizure. Contact your supervisor, department head, assistant director or director as soon as possible.

Keep a record of all legal requests.

Keep a record of all costs incurred by any search and/or seizures.

If a "gag order" is not in effect, director will notify the patron(s) affected, library trustees, town administration, the American Library Association, and other officials as deemed appropriate.

Emergency Situations

If, in the normal course of business, a library staff member observes what can be reasonably construed to be a threat of imminent danger to the library, staff, or patrons, he/she is to contact law enforcement officials immediately. He/She should then contact/inform his/her supervisor, department head, assistant director or director.

Athol Public Library
Athol, Massachusetts

ATHOL PUBLIC LIBRARY
USA PATRIOT ACT OF 2001 POLICY

Policy and Procedures in Response to the USA Patriot Act of 2001

The Athol Public Library (APL) supports the President of the United States and congressional leaders in our nation's efforts to preserve and protect the many hard-fought freedoms we enjoy as Americans.

Public libraries are facing a dilemma of having the responsibility of protecting the privacy of our patrons while responding to legitimate national security concerns. The APL recognizes the confidentiality of information sought or received and materials consulted, borrowed or acquired by a library user.

The APL strives to create a library environment that is:

- Crime free
- A safe place
- A place for learning and pursuit of knowledge and information on any topic
- A place where patrons can ask any question and discuss any topic

The library will do its utmost to uphold the privacy and confidentiality of patrons' free access to information. The library will rely on existing laws and library policies to control behavior that involves public safety or criminal behavior.

About the USA Patriot Act of 2001

HR-3162 became Public Law 107-56 in response to the events of 9/11/01. The full title of the law is: Uniting and Strengthening America by Providing Appropriate Tools Required to Intercept and Obstruct Terrorism Act of 2001.

The Act may provide law enforcement broader boundaries when investigating information accessed and transmitted by patrons with regards to national security concerns.

Access to patron information may include but not be limited to:

- Database Search Records
- Circulation Records
- Computer Use Records
- Inter-Library Loan Records
- Reference Interviews

The APL Policy & Procedures Regarding Information Access and Confidentiality

Database Search Records: These records refer to the searches of the collection a patron may conduct on the Online Public Access Terminals (OPAC). These searches are conducted by utilizing the library's automated circulation system, Follett Software. Once a search is conducted, the software does not retain a copy of the search. Any records of the search will not exist.

Circulation Records: Patron material is circulated via the Follett system. The circulation software tracks materials currently checked out, automatically erasing a reader's borrowing record once a book is returned and all fines are paid.

Computer Use Records: The library system is equipped with Dell computers and computers supplied via a grant by the Bill and Melinda Gates Foundation. Patrons use their library card to check out computers while using them. The daily booking sheet is destroyed. When the patron logs off of a Gates computer, the software erases all history of their research and activity.

Inter-Library Loan Records: Patrons may borrow items not owned by the APL from other libraries worldwide via Inter-Library Loan (ILL). The APL tracks items currently being borrowed and generates a paper record with patron information. Once the materials are returned and all appropriate fines and/or fees are paid, the record is destroyed.

Reference Interviews: A reference interview occurs when a patron looking for information approaches a library staff member and the staff questions or interviews the patron in order to narrow down the specific information needed. No paper record is kept during the interview that has any patron information on it. If a patron name and number is taken by phone, and patron information is written down, as soon as the requested information is delivered, the paper record is destroyed.

The APL Policy & Procedures for Complying with Law Enforcement

The APL staff will comply with law enforcement when supplied with legal subpoena or warrant.

Staff Procedures:

- If anyone approaches you alleging to be a law enforcement official requesting information, do not disclose to that individual any information. Immediately contact a supervisor, Assistant Director, Director or the Town Manager.
- The supervisor, Assistant Director, Director or the Town Manager will ask to see official identification and will photocopy the ID.
- If the law enforcement official presents a subpoena, library staff should direct that person to a supervisor, Assistant Director, Director or the Town Manager; who will in turn direct the subpoena to legal council for a review of the document's legal sufficiency. Tell the law enforcement officer of this procedure.
- If library staff is presented with a warrant, do not interfere with their search and seizure. Contact your supervisor, department head, assistant director or director as soon as possible.
- Keep a record of all legal requests.
- Keep a record of all cost incurred by any search and/or seizures.
- If a "Gag Order" is not in effect, director will notify the American Library Association.

Recap:

Requests for information or subpoenas – do not give out information until legal council has reviewed.

Search warrant—may be executed immediately by officer.

Emergency Disclosures of Communication

If in the normal course of business, the library staff observes what can be reasonably construed to be a threat of imminent danger to life and limb they are to contact law enforcement immediately. They should then contact their supervisor, department head, assistant director or director and fill out an Incident Report form.

Approved by the Athol Public Library Board of Trustees on: 19 March 2003

STAFF RESPONSIBILITIES TO ENSURE COMPLIANCE

W. Walworth Harrison Library
Greenville, Texas

Responsibility and Authority

Final responsibility and authority for Internet and electronic information access rests with the Director of Library Services, who will operate within a framework of policies and principles approved by the W. Walworth Harrison Public Library Board. The staff will operate under the Director's delegated authority. The Library is authorized to develop such procedures, guidelines, and rules as may be necessary to carry out these policies. Further, the Library is authorized to utilize appropriate technologies to address the implementation of these policies.

Chapter 32

USER PRIVACY PROTECTIONS

ACCESS TO USER INFORMATION LIMITATIONS

University of Illinois
Urbana, Illinois

Rule on Sharing of Information

The University of Illinois uses the University Web for business purposes and is committed to ensuring the privacy of personal information. Use of the University Web is subject to all applicable state and federal laws, as well as general University and campus policies. It is the University's usual practice not to share any personal information with those outside the University. However, when circumstances arise for the need to share information gathered from its University Web servers, the University may share as:

* authorized by law,
* permitted under University and campus policies,
* authorized by an approved University of Illinois contract,
* clearly stated at a University Web site that such information will be shared and the user indicates consent by providing the information,
* consent is otherwise given,
* available, certain student and employee demographic information with the University of Illinois Alumni Association, the University of Illinois Foundation, applicant students' high schools and other educational institutions with questions about students who have been admitted or earned a degree from the University, or
* authorized for good cause by the Chancellor for each campus or the Vice President for Academic Affairs of the University of Illinois.

Exceptions to Rule

The University Web consists of hundreds of University Web servers. Some servers hosted by the University of Illinois may adopt different privacy notices as their specific needs require. If another University Web server has a privacy notice that is different from this notice, then that notice must be approved by the campus Chief Information Officer or equivalent administrator responsible for that domain, and it must be posted on the site that has adopted the different notice. However, those sites cannot adopt a privacy notice that in any way supersedes federal or state laws or regulations or University or campus policies.

GENERAL GUIDELINES

University of Michigan
University of Michigan Libraries
Ann Arbor, Michigan

User Privacy Policy of the University Library

It is the policy of the University Library that the privacy of all users shall be respected in compliance with federal and state laws and professional standards. The Library will not reveal the identities of individual users or reveal what information sources or services they consult. This policy applies to all resources regardless of their format or means of delivery as well as to all services offered by the Library.

To aid understanding of the use or value of resources and services the Library may aggregate and retain user data for a reasonable period of time. It will, however, neither collect nor retain information identifying individuals except during the period when and only for the purpose that such record is necessary to furnish a specific service (for example, loaning a book, ordering a report, recording user service preferences, or for internal service evaluation). Data on individuals will not be shared with third parties unless if required by law.

For examples of how this policy applies to specific services or programs, please refer to the Practice Guidelines that follow.

Circulation

It is the policy of the Library that the privacy of all borrowers of library materials shall be respected. The Library will not reveal the names of individual borrowers nor reveal what books are, or have been, charged to any individual.

When library users need books that are on loan, the units with circulation responsibility will assist them by calling in those books as soon as the guaranteed loan period (usually three weeks) has ended. If the books desired are in a renewal period, they will be recalled immediately.

Collection Development and Resource Management

Comments, purchase recommendations, gifts-in-kind, and special requests from users make an important contribution to building and shaping the Library's collections. Purchase, transfer, and related collection management requests linked to individual users—or even group of users (e.g., the History Department)—are deemed confidential reader information and not shared outside the Library. Within the Library, user names are temporarily attached to internal records and shared among relevant staff to facilitate notification of Library actions and follow-through.

Contracts and Licenses for Information Resources

Consistent with its user privacy policy the Library expects its information service providers to follow the same standards in the performance of the products they license, lease or sell to the Library. Contracts, licenses, agreements and arrangements that the Library enters shall accordingly and as the standard practice protect the identity of individual users and the information they use.

To provide additional personalized services (for example, help in using resources, and profiling user interests for subsequent notification) service providers may require users to identify themselves. Such identification will be only at the user's discretion and will require the user to follow clearly indicated procedures before the service is activated. The service provider may not sell, lease, or loan information identifying individual users or the information they use to third parties unless authorized in advance by each user. To aid understanding of the use or value of resources and services, service providers may aggregate and retain anonymized user data.

Interlibrary Loan/Document Delivery

Requestors of interlibrary loan and document delivery services receive the same protection in terms of confidentiality of their requests. In some cases, information about requests is shared with other library staff for collection development purposes; it remains confidential within the library. Documentation of requests may be retained as necessary for the Library to comply with auditing, copyright or other regulations.

Library Surveys/Assessment Projects

Information and data obtained by the Library or its units through surveys (group or individual interviews or other means) in support of assessment of services, collections, facilities, resources, etc., or in support of research related to library and information services, are considered confidential and will not be shared except in aggregations, to protect the privacy of individual participants.

Public Access Digital Systems

The Library's access systems (e.g., Mirlyn, the Library's website, and discovery tools maintained by the Library) frequently track or "log" the actions performed by users of those systems. In some cases, specialized services or enhancements to system functionality require retaining the transaction logging. Users may request that the Library not retain their individual records, but a user who does so will be unable to use the associated services. In other cases, data that can be tied to individuals will be kept intact only for a limited period of time. Its use will be restricted to trouble-shooting and problem resolution related to system functions and service transactions. It is the Library's policy that no transaction logging containing personal information will be shared with third parties.

Information from transaction logs may be aggregated for reporting on types of use and use of materials. For this purpose, information regarding individual identities or the source of the transaction will be removed. In the case of logs kept for a limited period of time (i.e., where transaction logging is not retained for services or enhancements), the precise duration of the period needed for storing full transaction level logging will be determined on a case-by-case basis. When the information is no longer reasonably useful for problem resolution, the original transaction logging information will be destroyed, and backups and other stored forms of the data will not be retained.

Dartmouth College
Dartmouth College Library
Hanover, New Hampshire

Members of the Dartmouth community have reasonable expectations of privacy in their use of information resources, in accordance with this policy. State and federal law, and Dartmouth policy, prohibits unauthorized access to computer and telephone systems. No one should use aliases, nicknames, pointers, or other electronic means to capture information intended for others without permission of the intended recipient. Attempts to gain unauthorized access to machines or computer records, to decrypt encrypted materials, to monitor other individuals' computer or network use, to attempt to obtain their passwords, or to obtain privileges or information to which the user is not entitled, are prohibited.

Information stored on an individual's account is presumed to be private unless the account holder has made the information available to others. If, for example, the account holder allows public access to files via file sharing, it is presumed that the account holder has waived his or her privacy rights to those files.

Systems operators, supervisors, and other College officials may access information resources to locate business information, maintain the system and network, comply with legal requirements, or administer this or other Dartmouth policies.

Local area networks and local resources, including personal computers, workstations, file servers, printers, and similar devices, shall be subject to the same rights to privacy and confidentiality afforded centralized computer systems, regardless of whether those local resources are connected to any of Dartmouth's central information technology networks.

Some programs and networked services gather information about the people who use them. If such information could directly or indirectly identify a person using the program, then each user should be warned and given a chance to leave the program or service before data collection begins, a procedure referred to as a "privacy warning." To avoid issuing excessive numbers of warning messages, an exception is made for host operating systems and some networked utilities used by Computing Services that collect identifying information as part of their normal operation. A list of these exempted programs and services and the data that they collect is available from Computing Services and is provided in the Appendix. The provider of any program or service that gathers information about those who use it must either install a privacy warning or request Computing Services to place the program or service on the list of exempted programs.

PRIVACY/NO PRIVACY DISCLAIMERS

Solano Community College
Solano Community College Library
Fairfield, California

Although every effort is made by the District to secure the computer and communications systems, users cannot be assured of absolute privacy because of potential abuse of the systems.

Users should be aware that it is possible for information entered on or transmitted via computer and communication systems to be retrieved, even if the information has been deleted.

Transmitted information may potentially be subject to subpoena or discovery in litigation.

The District shall have the right to access all communication systems to ensure integrity and security.

In response to a report or discovery of an alleged violation of law, this policy, or other District policies and procedures, the Superintendent/President (in his/her absence see Board Policy 2040) shall direct the appropriate systems administrator to provide the person responsible for the investigation with access to the information relevant to the investigation. If the Superintendent/President is the subject of the investigation, the President of the Governing Board shall authorize the investigation. Prior to the commencement of any investigation, the individual authorizing the investigation shall:

- Complete and sign, in writing, a form identifying the alleged violation and specify the information sought.
- Present the signed form in person to the employee at the time of the investigation or, if the employee is not present, deliver it via certified mail, return receipt requested.

University of Arizona
Arizona Health Science Library
Tucson, Arizona

Privacy

Activities on University-owned workstations cannot be guaranteed any right to privacy. Users should not transmit personal information regarding themselves or others via workstation computers, nor should they transmit other sensitive information. Library staff are frequently in the workstation area assisting patrons. If Library staff observes a violation of policy, or if another customer complains of a violation, such violations will be addressed pursuant to this policy or other applicable policy or law.

Boise Public Library
Boise, Idaho

As in all other library resources and services, Boise Public Library patrons have the right to confidentiality involving their individual legal use of electronic resources and services. The library attempts to maintain patron confidentiality at all times, but cannot guarantee the confidentiality of information sent by a patron onto the Internet.

University of Arkansas for Medical Sciences
University of Arkansas Medical Science Library
Little Rock, Arkansas

Please read the following carefully before accessing or using the University of Arkansas for Medical Sciences (UAMS) Library Web Sites. By accessing and using the UAMS Library Web Sites, you acknowledge that you agree to be bound by the terms and conditions set forth below. Do not use this site if you do not agree with these terms. UAMS Library may modify the agreement at any time, and such modifications shall be effective immediately upon posting. You should review the agreement periodically to be aware of such modifications. By continuing to access this site, you indicate your acceptance of the modified agreement.

The UAMS Library takes your privacy, rights, and online security seriously. If you have any concerns regarding these issues please contact Library Director.

Privacy Statement

UAMS Library's web sites do not automatically collect personal information. Such information is gathered and recorded only if you supply the information to us via an e-mail or one of our online forms (such as the InterLibrary Loan form). This information is only used to record, process and track loan requests, comments about our web site, and other recommendations or requests for information by the user.

All user information will be confidential while maintaining the ability for authorized UAMS Library staff to quickly and effectively access this information when required for operational purposes. No user information will be sold or otherwise made known to any individual or company where this information is not required for the operation of UAMS Library.

User ID and user passwords (as applicable) are confidential and will not be made available to any person or company outside of the University of Arkansas for Medical Sciences (UAMS) for any reason whatsoever.

The network at UAMS is monitored to identify unauthorized attempts to upload or change information, or otherwise cause damage. Unauthorized attempts to upload information or change information on this service are strictly prohibited and disciplinary action for violating the code shall be governed by the applicable provisions of student handbooks, faculty and staff handbooks, personnel policy manuals for UAMS, and UAMS Operating Policies.

UAMS Library may log http requests to our server for statistical purposes. No Privacy Act information, such as name and address, is collected or used.

Use of "cookies:" Cookies are small files which are used to store information on your computer, such as a user ID and password for entering a site or user identification information used during web applications (ex. online forms). Any use of cookies will be only while you are in a site requiring a user ID and password or a site requiring user identification for processing a user request (ex. online forms). We do not use cookies to track what other sites you have visited, and we do not use cookies to obtain any personal or confidential information other than that which we ask for up front.

While UAMS Library will cooperate with law enforcement personnel and legal investigations of our users, all user information will be held private unless ordered by a court to surrender this information.

University of Illinois
Urbana, Illinois

LEGAL NOTICES OF TERMS AND CONDITIONS

Access to the University Web is provided subject to the following terms and conditions. Please read these terms carefully as use of the University Web constitutes acceptance of all of the following terms and conditions:

Disclaimer of Liability

Neither the University of Illinois, nor any of its units, programs, employees, agents or individual trustees, shall be held liable for any improper or incorrect use of the information described and/or contained in the University Web and assumes no responsibility for anyone's use of the information. In no event shall the University Web, the University of Illinois or its units, programs, employees, agents or individual trustees be liable for any direct, indirect, incidental, special, exemplary, or consequential damages (including, but not limited to, procurement or substitute goods or services; loss of use, data, or profits; or business interruption) however caused and on any theory of liability, whether in contract, strict liability, or tort (including negligence or otherwise) arising in any way out of the use of this system, even if advised of the possibility of such damage. This disclaimer of liability applies to any damages or injury, including but not limited to those caused by any failure of performance, error, omission, interruption, deletion, defect, delay in operation or transmission, computer virus, communication line failure, theft or destruction or unauthorized access to, alteration of, or use of record, whether for breach of contract, tortuous behavior, negligence or under any other cause of action.

Disclaimer of Warranties and Accuracy of Data

Although the data found using the University of Illinois' access systems have been produced and processed from sources believed to be reliable, no warranty, express or implied, is made regarding accuracy, adequacy, completeness, legality, reliability or usefulness of any information. This disclaimer applies to both isolated and aggregate uses of the information. The University of Illinois provides this information on an "as is" basis. All warranties of any kind, express or implied, including but not limited to the implied warranties of merchantability, fitness for a particular purpose, freedom from contamination by computer viruses and non-infringement of proprietary rights are disclaimed. Changes may be periodically made to the information herein; these changes may or may not be incorporated in any new version of the publication. If a user has obtained information from any of the University Web pages via a source other than the University of Illinois pages, be aware that electronic data can be altered subsequent to original distribution. Data can also quickly become out of date. It is recommended that careful attention be paid to the contents of any data associated with a file, and that the originator of the data or information be contacted with any questions regarding appropriate use. If a user finds any errors or omissions, please report them to:

Disclaimer of Endorsement

The University of Illinois is a distributor of content sometimes supplied by third parties and users. Any opinions, advice, statements, services, offers, or other information or content expressed or made available by third parties, including information providers, users, or others, are those of the respective author(s) or distributor(s) and do not necessarily state or reflect those of the University of Illinois and shall not be used for advertising or product endorsement purposes. Reference herein to any specific commercial products, process, or service by trade name, trademark, manufacturer, or otherwise, does not constitute or imply its endorsement, recommendation, or favoring by the University of Illinois.

Disclaimer for External Links

The University Web has links to other Web sites. These include links to Web sites operated by Illinois agencies and officials, other government agencies, nonprofit organizations and private businesses. When a user leaves the University Web and visits another site, the user is subject to the privacy policy of that new site. The University of Illinois is not responsible for the contents of any off-site pages referenced. The user specifically acknowledges that the University of Illinois is not liable for the defamatory, negligent, inaccurate, offensive, or illegal conduct of other users, links, or third parties and that the risk of injury from the foregoing rests entirely with the user. Links from University Web pages on the World Wide Web to other sites do not constitute an endorsement from the University of Illinois. These links are provided as an information service only. It is the responsibility of the user to evaluate the content and usefulness of information obtained from other sites. The University Web contains links to other related World Wide Web sites and resources. Since the University of Illinois and its Web site is not responsible for the availability of these outside resources or their contents, the user should direct any concerns regarding any external link to its site administrator or webmaster.

Disclaimer of Duty to Continue Provision of Data

Due to the dynamic nature of the Internet, resources that are free and publicly available one day may require a fee or restricted access the next, and the location of items may change as menus, pages, and files are reorganized. The user expressly agrees that use of the University Web is at the user's sole risk. The University of Illinois does not warrant that the service will be uninterrupted or error free. The documents and related graphics published on this Web or server could contain technical inaccuracies or typographical errors. Changes are periodically added to the information herein. The University of Illinois and/or its respective units and programs may make improvements and/or changes in the information and/or programs described herein at any time.

Duke University
William R. Perkins Library
Durham, North Carolina

Transmissions made on the Internet are generally not secure, since the information is transferred in clear text. In some cases transactions made via our web site are conducted using a SSL (Secure Socket Layer protocol) connection in order to provide increased security to the information as it is transmitted. Only authorized library staff with assigned password may access personally identifiable information stored in the library's computer systems and then only for the purpose of performing library work. We use industry-standard security measures to protect any personal information that you may provide to us. However, we cannot guarantee that your submissions to our website, any content residing on our servers, or any transmissions from our server will be completely secure.

Tempe Public Library
Tempe, Arizona

Data downloaded from external computers and networks, including the Internet, may contain computer viruses that could be potentially harmful to the computer systems of Library users. The Tempe Public Library is not responsible for damage to any user's storage media or computer, or any loss of data, damage, or liability that may occur from a library user's utilization of the Library's electronic information resources. The Library recommends that users maintain checking and scanning software to identify and eliminate viruses in any data, files, or programs they obtain from external computers and networks.

Use of the library's wireless network is entirely at the risk of the user and the Tempe Public Library disclaims all liability for any damage that may occur to one's computer and/or loss of confidential information or other damages resulting from that loss. As with most public "hot spots," the library's connection is not secure. Users accessing the wireless network should have personal firewall and updated virus protection software installed on their computers to protect their privacy and to provide for their own security. Users should be aware that there can be untrustworthy parties between them and anyone with whom they communicate. Any information being sent or received could potentially be intercepted by another wireless user. Users should avoid entering credit card numbers, passwords or any other confidential information unless they are certain that the Web site with which they are interacting provides its own security mechanism such as Secure Sockets Layer "SSL" encoding. An SSL protected web page is usually indicated by a small lock icon display along the lower edge of the browser window.

Part VII
Issues of Special Interest to Public Libraries

Chapter 33

INTERNET USE

CHILDREN'S INTERNET PROTECTION ACT

Aurora Public Library
Aurora, Colorado

Access by Minors to Internet Resources

The LIBRARY will make all reasonable effort to limit access by minors to Internet resources that are obscene or illegal. As specified by state and federal laws (HB 04-1004 Internet Protection in Public Librar-ies, C.R.S. 24-90-601-606 and Children's Internet Protection Act (CIPA), Pub. L. No. 106-554) the LIBRARY will filter all public Internet-capable computers, defaulting always on children's-use workstations to the highest level of filtering appropriate by the filtering software in place.

LIBRARY efforts toward the above objective include:

1. Utilization of electronic filtering software;

2. Classes offered to instruct parents and children on how to search the Internet safely and effectively;

3. Supervision of public space. Minors, like adults, are expected to behave in a civil and appropriate man-ner in the library. The display of visual material that is sexual in nature or that might be considered immediately offensive to others constitutes rude behavior in many circumstances. In such circum-stances, at the discretion of staff, customers will be asked to cease such behavior. If they do not, they may be ejected from the library, and risk the loss of future library privileges.

4. Supervision of public space by the placement of Internet workstations, where possible, in direct line of sight of staff. LIBRARY staff will investigate all complaints lodged by other customers.

5. Limitation of access on Internet workstations by supervising their use through observation and by employing an "internet protection measure." Technology and various technological tools are changing rapidly. Staff shall seek to remain current concerning various options, but it is understood that no tech-nology has proved to be 100% effective in allowing only "good" content and blocking only "bad."

6. Creation of web pages designed to direct minors to positive, high quality sites, created or reviewed by librarians.

Parental Responsibility

1. To address issues of safety and security of minors when using electronic mail, chat rooms and other forms of electronic communication, parents and legal guardians are encouraged to urge minors to fol-low basic safety guidelines: never give out personal information (name, address, phone number, etc.), never arrange via a computer to meet someone and never respond to messages that are threatening or suggestive, remembering that people online may not be who they say they are.

2. Instruction of minors in the safe and effective use of Internet resources is highly encouraged.

3. Parents are advised to have their children use Internet PCs in the children's service areas where filter-ing is at a higher level than that for PCs in the adult areas.

CHILDREN'S INTERNET USE POLICIES

Toronto Public Library
Toronto, Ontario, Canada

At Toronto Public Library we try to give you information in many different forms. The Internet is a good way to get information from places in your own community and from places all over the world. How you use the Internet is up to you and your parents or guardians.

The Internet is not controlled by anyone. This means that anyone in the world could put information on an Internet site. The Internet contains lots of great information and fun stuff, but it also contains information that may not be true or may make you uncomfortable. Be careful when you use the Internet, because it is sometimes possible for other people to get information about you and what you are doing on the Internet.

Toronto Public Library has a home page for children. We are very careful about choosing links to other information on the Internet, but we have no way of controlling the information on Internet sites created by other people. We are only responsible for information on our Home Page.

We want to do everything we can to make you feel safe, comfortable and welcome when you come to the library. One way we do this is by giving you your own "Kids' Space Workstations" in many of our libraries. The computers in these workstations will stop many of the Internet sites with words or images that might make you feel uncomfortable, afraid or sad; but there is no way for us to stop everything that might make you uncomfortable.

You need to learn to protect yourself when you are on the Internet. If you see something you don't like, click the back arrow on your browser to get away from the image or words quickly, just as you would change the channel on TV if you saw something you didn't want to watch. If the back button doesn't work, ask someone who works at the library to help you get away from that site. If you see something on the Internet that bothers you, your parents or guardians are the best people to talk to.

We have rules to make sure people can get on the Internet at the library if they want to. We also have Rules of Conduct that remind you what you can and cannot do in the library. When using the Internet please respect the other people around you.

Copying information from the Internet and showing it to other people can sometimes be against the law. It is up to you to make sure you do not break these copyright laws. If you have questions about what you can or cannot copy, or about how to use the Internet, ask someone who works at the library. If you are not sure about what you should or should not do on the Internet, ask your parents or guardians.

PARENTS AND CHILDREN

Larchmont Public Library
Larchmont, New York

The Library affirms the right and responsibility of parents and legal guardians to guide their children's use of all library resources, including the Internet. Parents are encouraged to take an active role in their children's use of the Internet and to convey their expectations for their children's use of this resource. Filters are not used on the Library's computers, in part because they have been shown to be ineffective at blocking access to information that might be deemed objectionable while also blocking access to valid and useful information.

Orland Park Public Library
Orland Park, Illinois

Children's Access to Electronic Information Networks

The Orland Park Public Library supports the right of all library users to access information and will not deny access to electronic information networks based solely on age. The Library recognizes that electronic information networks, such as the Internet, contain material inappropriate for children. As with other library materials, supervision of a child's access to electronic information networks is the responsibility of the parent or legal guardian. Children age nine and under must be accompanied by an adult or other guardian during use of the electronic information networks. The library provides filtered and unfiltered access to the electronic information networks and it's the responsibility of the parent/guardian to choose the type of access for their children under the age of 10. Due to the nature of the Internet and current technology limitations, the Library cannot guarantee that filtered Children's Internet access will prevent the access of inappropriate material. Parents are encouraged to discuss with their children issues of safe and appropriate use of electronic resources. Library staff cannot monitor children's use.

Plainfield—Guilford Township Public Library
Plainfield, Indiana

"My Rules for Online Safety": Guidelines for Children's Internet Safety

I will not give out personal information such as my address, telephone number, parent's work address or telephone number, or the name and location of my school without my parent's permission.

I will tell my parent right away if I come across any information that makes me feel uncomfortable.

I will never agree to get together with someone I "meet" online without first checking with my parents. If my parents agree to the meeting, I will be sure that it is in a public place and I will bring my mother or father along.

I will never send a person my picture or anything else without first checking with my parents.

I will not respond to any messages that are mean or in any way make me feel uncomfortable. It is not my fault if I get a message like that. If I do, I will tell my parents right away so that they can contact the online service.

I will talk with my parents so that we can set up rules for going online. We will decide on the time of day that I can be online, the length of time I can be online, and the appropriate areas for me to visit. I will not access other areas or break these rules without their permission.

Porter County Public Library System
Valparaiso, Indiana

*****Various versions of this policy are available on many Web sites. It is fortunate that we as librarians continue to share what works for us. If you see your hand in this, all librarians thank you.*****

Youth Information Highway Rules of the Road

I agree to follow these rules when using the Internet:

- I will not give out personal information such as my address, telephone number, parent's work address, telephone number, or the name and location of my school without my parent's permission.

- I will tell my parents or a librarian right away if I find something that makes me worried or scared. I will not visit sites that are only for adults.
- I will not use bad language, scare, or try to hurt anyone through my actions online.
- I will not try to enter files or systems that are restricted.
- I will not try to enter my own programs or materials onto the public terminals.
- I will follow the rules for signing up and leave promptly when my time is up.

I understand that breaking these rules means I will lose Internet use in the library.

Chapter 34

VIRTUAL REFERENCE

SAFETY ISSUES

Bowdoin College
Brunswick, Maine

BOWDOIN'S COMMITMENT TO CHILDREN'S PRIVACY

In most cases, Bowdoin College neither collects nor attempts to collect PII from children known to be under the age of thirteen (13). However, Bowdoin College cannot always determine if a visitor is a child. In general, the subject matter provided on the College's Web site(s) is not directed toward children under the age of thirteen (13).

Pickaway County District Public Library
Circleville, Ohio

Information from Children

The Pickaway County District Public Library is especially concerned about protecting children's privacy and encourages parents and teachers to be involved in children's Internet explorations, particularly when they're asked to provide personal information online. The Pickaway County District Public Library requests that children get their parents' or guardian's permission before providing any information online—at the Pickaway County District Public Library site or any other site. Most importantly, when children do provide information through the Pickaway County District Public Library Web site, it is only used to enable the Pickaway County District Public Library to respond to the writer. The Pickaway County District Public Library does not create profiles of children.

THIRD-PARTY ISSUES

Duke University
William R. Perkins Library
Durham, North Carolina

Services provided by third parties

This website contains links to websites and licensed databases that are not maintained or supported by Duke University Libraries. In some cases library services may be provided via third party tools (chat or search widgets, for example). While you may reach these services via library web sites, the Library is not responsible for the privacy practices or the content of these third parties, and we encourage users of these services to familiarize themselves with their policies before using them.

Bowdoin College
Brunswick, Maine

DISCLOSURE OF PERSONAL DATA TO THIRD PARTIES

Bowdoin College occasionally retains the services of third parties to process information, financial transactions, or other purposes approved by members of Bowdoin's senior management. The College may also, on a very limited basis, share, rent, sell, or otherwise discloses PII to carefully screened third parties. The College will not disclose to third parties any PII collected by Bowdoin if the third party fails to meet and maintain the College's electronic privacy policies.

Before providing PII to a third party, Bowdoin College will obtain a non-disclosure and confidentiality agreement from the third party. Aggregate information and/or information that is publicly available is not subject to such agreements.

Tempe Public Library
Tempe, Arizona

Transaction logs and any other information that can be used to identify a user with specific data, files, or programs, or other electronic materials are considered by the Tempe Public Library to be confidential and shall not be divulged to anyone other than the user, except as otherwise noted herein.

Pursuant to Arizona law (A.R.S. §41-1354), the Tempe Public Library shall not disclose any record or information which identifies a user of library services as requesting or obtaining specific materials or services or as otherwise using the Library. Records may be disclosed only in the following circumstances:

- If necessary for the reasonable operation of the Library, as determined by the Deputy Community Services Manager responsible for the Library Division.
- On the written consent of the library user.
- On receipt of a court order.
- If required by law.

Any person who knowingly discloses any record in violation of this section is guilty of a class 3 misdemeanor.

Chapter 35

WEB SITE HOME PAGE FOR CHILDREN

FILTERS

W. Walworth Harrison Library
Greenville, Texas

For the purposes of this policy children are defined as being 12 years of age and under and young adults are defined as being 13 to 17 years of age. Adults are defined as patrons 18 years of age and older. The W. Walworth Harrison Public Library uses filtering software on all Internet computers designated for use by minors. It is used to assist in preventing access to sites which may be harmful to minors and violate Texas Law: PC 43.24, Sale, Distribution, or Display of Harmful Material to Minor. The current filter settings for the children's computers block sites featuring chat, nudity, pornography, graphic violence, and vulgar text. The current filter settings for computers designated for young adult use block sites featuring nudity, pornography, and graphic violence. The software also allows the Library staff to override a block or to place a block. Upon request librarians may override blocked sites deemed not to be in violation of the criteria set forth in the user guidelines section of the W. Walworth Harrison Public Library Internet Policy. Parents and guardians are advised that filtering software is not comprehensive and minors may be exposed to materials found to be personally offensive or inappropriate. W. Walworth Harrison Public Library provides both filtered and unfiltered Internet access for adults.

Cumberland County Library System
Carlisle, Pennsylvania

Internet Filtering:

To comply with Federal laws requiring that Internet access be filtered for children age 16 and younger, the Library System filters all of its computers. In addition, Federal law also requires Internet filtering even if a child is accompanied by a parent or guardian.

Web sites are filtered to prevent minors from viewing material that is

1. obscene,
2. child pornography or
3. harmful to minors.

The term "harmful to minors" is defined by the Communications Act of 1934 (47 USC Section 254 [h] [7]), as meaning any picture, image, graphic image file, or other visual depiction that:

1. taken as a whole and with respect to minors, appeals to a prurient interest in nudity, sex, or excretion;
2. depicts, describes, or represents, in a patently offensive way with respect to what is suitable for minors, an actual or simulated sexual act or sexual contact, actual or simulated normal or perverted sexual acts, or a lewd exhibition of the genitals;
3. taken as a whole, lacks serious literary, artistic, political, or scientific value as to minors.

As necessary for bona fide research or other lawful purposes, people age 17 and older may have filtering disabled by a library staff member. Computers located in children's library areas cannot be unfiltered.

Filters are not foolproof. They can give people a false sense of security that they are protected from harmful material. Filters can also block sites that may be considered inoffensive or useful. Thus, if you do not find what you need, please ask a library staff person for help.

Boise Public Library
Boise, Idaho

The library filters all public Internet stations in the children's area in compliance with the Children's Internet Protection Act (CIPA). Parents are responsible for providing guidance to their own children. Through special software, the library offers individual choice and parental choice for their own minor children among options for filtered, unfiltered, or no Internet access. Library users who do not have borrowing privileges will be offered the same Internet access choices. The library currently uses commercial filtering software with an access management system to provide Internet access choices. Links to filtered search sites are offered from the library's web site for those who wish to use them. The library accepts no responsibility for failures of the filtering software to block specific sites.

Great Falls Public Library
Great Falls, Montana

The Internet is a dynamic resource containing vast amounts of information and a small percentage of potentially offensive sites. Because of the nature of the way filters operate, there currently is no filter which does not inadvertently block constitutionally protected material. Many of these unintentionally blocked sites contain valid and valuable information. Nor do filters block all potentially offensive sites. Therefore, the GFPL does not use filters for Internet stations located in the non-fiction area.

However, if a patron wishes to use a filter, it is possible to activate one from some of the major search engines on the Internet. If you need help with this, you can inquire at the Information Desk.

Web Junction
State Library and Archives of Florida
Department of State Library and Archives of Florida
Tallahassee, Florida

Guidelines from an article by Web Junction:

Filter? Yes, we do.

Before the CDA, before COPA and before CIPA, the Board of Trustees of the Carroll County Public Library voted to accept a LSTA grant. The 1995 grant project, to provide Internet service to local government via the library's computers, demonstrated the application of new technology. At first it was simple; we were dealing with text-based Pine email. Not long into the project, however, "Mosaic" emerged, which made both text and graphics available through something called the World Wide Web. Soon Mosaic, the first browser, was eclipsed by Netscape as the WWW became increasingly commercial and gained in popularity.

By 1997, it was time to discuss with the Board the success of our LSTA grant and our plan for going forward. WWW sites were growing exponentially. Information available on the web was a fabulous addition to library resources. Patron information needs could be served in ways we only dreamed about in library school.

When staff met to plan our presentation to the Board of Trustees, we knew we needed to explain the entire range of information and "other stuff" available on the Web. We explored some of the "other" sites ourselves, and knew we had a problem. The problem, of course, was what could be called up on the screen: porn. How to explain to the Board, in light of our Collection Development Policy, the kind of "stuff" easily accessible to library patrons on our computers?

Our Collection Development Policy, like those of other public libraries, is a lengthy, weighty document that cites many ALA positions like the Library Bill of Rights, and adheres to intellectual freedom principles. After reading over our Collection Development Policy many times, I just couldn't justify making "stuff" that we wouldn't purchase for our print collection available on library computers. There were a few other issues, too: Library Internet users must comply with the same behavior standards we expect all patrons to meet; staff has better things to do than monitor porn viewers; and filters can be easily disabled on request. Therefore, I recommended that we purchase an inexpensive filtering system for our branch Internet access computers. Although my recommendation to filter was approved, several Board members were uncomfortable with the decision (and remained so until the recent U.S. Supreme Court decision on CIPA).

Objections to Internet sites have not been a major issue in Maryland libraries, whether they filter or not. So, we kept on keeping on with our filters. Meanwhile, staff responsible for applying for e-rate discounts took their job seriously. Subsequently we have received a substantial return in e-rate money for their work. By the time e-rate discounts became part of the court case that resulted in CIPA, we were already filtering and spending e-rate money on services to our patrons—without apology. Knowing how the media loves a First Amendment story, and standing on the lonely side of the filtering issue, it did not surprise us to hear from national reporters every time there was a complaint about porn in libraries.

We revisited our filtering decision with the Board several times between 1996 and the CIPA ruling. Two years ago, we installed Guardianet software on Internet computers in one of our branches. Guardianet is now known as PAMS and is owned by 3M. The software works through a chip on a library card to perform several tasks: it schedules patron Internet use, works as a debit card to recover copy costs, saves patron search "favorites," and enables the patron to choose an individual Internet filter level. I told the Board that as soon as I could find funds, I planned to install Guardianet-like software system-wide so that any Internet filtering decision would be made by the individual patron rather than Board policy. In other words, Internet access from library computers would be unfiltered; the insertion of the individual's card would specify their predetermined level of filtering.

This was a great plan until CIPA. With the CIPA ruling I think the basic filter will remain throughout the system. Adult patrons can choose to turn off the filter for their entire session, but the filter will automatically resume at the start of the next session.

The U.S. Supreme Court clearly said that because the filters can be removed, public libraries are not infringing on free speech. The Court also stated that our own Collection Development Policies limit our claim to public forums, and that if we don't need the money we don't need to filter. At Carroll County Public Library, we will abide by the Court's ruling on free speech and the public forum argument, and then I will spend the e-rate money on improving service to patrons.

PURPOSE AND MISSION STATEMENTS

Ouachita Parish Public Library
Monroe, Louisiana

Electronic Access / Internet Policy

I. Mission

"Freedom of expression is an inalienable human right and the foundation for self-government. Freedom of expression encompasses the freedom of speech and the corollary right to receive information. These rights extend to children as well as adults. Libraries and librarians exist to facilitate these rights by providing access to, identifying, retrieving, organizing, and preserving recorded expression regardless of the formats or technologies in which that expression is recorded." (ALA Draft Version 1.1, Access to Electronic Information, Services, and Networks)

The library's mission is to provide patrons with the best and most current possible resources. It is the library's desire to offer access to the electronic resource environment for the use of all of the citizens of Ouachita Parish.

II. Electronic Resources and Users Responsibility

Use of electronic resources is considered a privilege and is intended primarily for information and research. Equal access to that information is a cornerstone of the library's mission. These online resources contain a wealth of valuable information resources. However, users should be aware that some information may be inaccurate, outdated, or offensive. Your use of these resources carries with it a responsibility to evaluate the quality of the information accessed. Parents, not the library, are responsible for the use of these resources by their children.

Berkeley Heights Public Library
Berkeley Heights, New Jersey

To be used in conjunction with BHPL's Responsible and Courteous Use of the Internet

Berkeley Heights Public Library is pleased to offer patron access to the wealth of information available through the Internet as part of the Library's goal of providing quality service in meeting the educational and recreational needs of its public.

Berkeley Heights Public Library endorses the American Library Association Library Bill of Rights and Access to Electronic Information, Services, and Networks: an Interpretation of the Library Bill of Rights.

Berkeley Heights Public Library does not endorse the viewpoints or vouch for the authenticity of information accessed via the Internet. Users must determine what information is appropriate and must evaluate for themselves the accuracy of the information accessed.

Responsibility for (and any restriction of) a child's use of the Internet rests solely with his or her parents or legal guardians. Internet access computers in the Children's Department are filtered. Because no commercially available filtering software is effective in all cases, BHPL cannot unequivocally state that all objectionable materials will be filtered. Internet access computers in the Children's Department are limited to students up through 8th grade, parents/caregivers accompanied by young children, and parents assisting children.

All Library users have the right to confidentiality in their research and use of services provided by Berkeley Heights Public Library. However, users are advised that because of the open nature of the Internet, both technical aspects and physical/space constraints, the Library cannot guarantee the privacy of searching conducted at public access computers.

Berkeley Heights Public Library reserves the right to terminate a patron's Internet session at any time and to enforce the guidelines expressed in the attached document, Responsible and Courteous Use of the Internet. At the Director's and/or Board of Trustees discretion, repeated abuse of this policy will result in a loss of Internet use for a specified period of time based upon the severity and frequency of the offense.

Illegal activity involving BHPL's Internet resources will be subject to prosecution by the appropriate authorities.

Berkeley Heights Public Library expressly disclaims any liability or responsibility arising from access to or use of information obtained through its electronic information resources, or any consequences thereof.

Neill Public Library
Pullman, Washington

The mission of Neill Public Library is to provide free access to the widest possible variety of ideas, information and opinions in an open and nonjudgmental environment. The library has made information available in a variety of formats to meet the diverse needs of our community. To expand and enhance its information sources, Neill Public Library is providing Internet access.

Neill Public Library affirms the right of each individual to have access to constitutionally protected material. The Board subscribes to the ideas enunciated in the American Library Association's Library Bill of Rights as interpreted for access to electronic information, services, and networks.

The Internet, as a global electronic network, enables individuals to search for ideas and information beyond the confines of the library collection. Currently, the Internet is an unregulated medium; it provides a wealth of enriching material but also some that may be erroneous, out-of-date, illegal, or offensive. Library users are the final selectors in using the Internet and are responsible for their individual choices and decisions.

The library also affirms the right and responsibility of parents to determine and monitor their children's use of library materials and resources, including the Internet. If a parent or guardian does not wish their child to have Internet access at the library, they may ask the library to deny access. (The library will note the restriction in the patron record.)

Aurora Public Library
Aurora, Colorado

The primary mission of the Aurora Public Library [the LIBRARY] is to provide public information by means of a variety of resources, including Internet access. Toward this end, it is the intent of the LIBRARY to provide free and equitable public access to Internet resources. This access honors the fundamental library principle of intellectual freedom, an abiding respect for the dignity and privacy of individual inquiry.

In addition to general access to the resources of the Internet, the LIBRARY strives toward:

1. The development and/or purchase of information resources as reasonable and appropriate, such as the catalog of LIBRARY collection holdings, databases, other text files and databases of local or regional interest, including information about the LIBRARY;

2. The identification and organization of links to resources the LIBRARY believes fit general collection policies.

Part VIII
Today's Top Job
Descriptions

Chapter 36

ADMINISTRATIVE

ADULT SERVICES SUPERVISOR/AUTOMATION COORDINATOR

Concord Public Library
Concord, New Hampshire

REPORTS TO: LIBRARY DIRECTOR

JOB SUMMARY:

Manages and oversees the library's Adult Services Division and its integrated automation system. Is responsible for the overall goal setting, planning, development and implementation of services in the Adult Services Division, which includes both reference and circulation services. Supervises Adult Services staff. Performs professional work analyzing and responding to the informational and recreational needs of the public. Works with library management team to implement the library's technology plans. Serves as system administrator for library's integrated automation system, serves as liaison with hardware and software vendors; oversees maintenance of system hardware and software; coordinates staff training; and troubleshoots computer problems for users.

ESSENTIAL JOB FUNCTIONS:

As Adult Services Supervisor:

- Carries out supervisory responsibility for reference librarians, circulation staff, and others in Adult Services Division in accordance with City policies, procedures and applicable laws including: scheduling, training in job skills; planning, assigning and directing work; appraising performance; addressing complaints and resolving problems.
- Is responsible for the overall goal setting, planning, development and implementation of services in the Adult Services Division.
- Reviews progress, accomplishments, budgets and strategies for the Adult Services Division.
- Acts as member of management team. Confers with upper management to keep them informed on key issues and progress toward objectives and to gain their support and approval; makes recommendations to assist management in making needed improvements.
- Coordinates and oversees the development of the adult collection.
- Develops an annual plan to allocate book and AV funds for the whole library.
- Prepares reports, memos, and correspondence concerning areas of responsibility.
- Serves the public at reference desk as needed to assist patrons in finding information and to recommend books for leisure reading, to reserve books, to retrieve materials, or to teach on-line catalogue use.
- Analyzes users requests and searches for and locates needed resources.
- Directs patrons in using library equipment and services.
- Locates appropriate agencies or organizations and refers patrons to them.
- Trains public in use of resource materials and equipment.
- Oversees overdue materials procedures. Assigns overdue tasks to circulation staff.
- Keeps abreast of professional library literature.
- Maintains education in library science; attends courses, workshops, and conferences.
- Belongs to and is active in local and state library organizations.

- Interprets and explains library policies and procedures.
- Participates significantly in the development and implementation of library policies, procedures and long-range plans.

As Automation Coordinator:

- Oversees system maintenance operations on hardware and software, such as conducting system back-ups, tracking communication error logs, adding and modifying user and password files; and reviewing and modifying system profiles.
- Works as system administrator for library's integrated automation system; serves as liaison with vendor for hardware and software support; responds directly to staff for hardware and software support, evaluating problems, and when necessary consulting with the vendor for assistance per the maintenance contract.
- Implements new system features; oversees system upgrades and enhancements; evaluates new software modules offered by the vendor, etc.
- Compiles reports, statistics, and notices associated with library's integrated automation system.
- Interprets and monitors performance of vendor contracts; reviews bills from vendors.
- Maintains and updates databases, including creating tables, performing queries, uploading and downloading files, creating forms, defining and maintaining feature attributes and the like.
- Serves as system administrator for local or wide area networks; maintains databases and files; installs and configures software; maintains levels of security; ensures daily system backup.
- Troubleshoots hardware and software problems for users; provides training for users on the operation of various software.
- Serves as liaison for department with school system on mainframe computer needs and with the City's data processing department.
- Develops long range automation goals and technology plans.
- Maintains education in computer field; attends courses, workshops, and conferences.

Other:

- Prepares budget in each of assigned areas.
- Performs duties of Library Director in his/her absence.
- Performs other related duties as assigned.

MATERIAL AND EQUIPMENT USED:
- Personal computer and/or terminal CD-ROM equipment Printers
- Microfilm/microfiche reader/printers Barcode readers Audiovisual equipment
- General Office Equipment

MINIMUM QUALIFICATIONS REQUIRED:

Education and Experience:

Master's degree in Library/Information Science accredited by the American Library Association; three years of progressively responsible related experience or any combination of education, training and experience that provides the knowledge, skills and abilities required for the job. Licenses and Certifications: None.

KNOWLEDGE, SKILLS AND ABILITIES:

Knowledge of:

- Library operations and administration.
- Professional library principles and practices.
- Modern practices of library automation.
- Computer hardware and peripheral devices.

- Various software applications programs.
- Various software operating systems.
- Design, operation, and configuration of local or wide area networks.
- Principles of supervision, training and performance evaluation.
- Principles and practices of budgeting.
- Principles and practices of marketing.
- Wide variety of public and scholarly information sources.
- Trends relating to publishing, computers and media.
- All department policies, rules and regulations.
- In-house library collection as well as networked resources worldwide.
- All client groups and the community as a whole and its various needs.
- Policies, functions and administrative operations related to area of assignment.

Skills in:

- Communicating clearly and effectively, both orally and in writing.
- Operating computer equipment and peripheral devices.
- Maintaining database files.
- Maintaining computer system hardware and software, including troubleshooting problems.
- Reading, understanding and interpreting technical information regarding computer operations.
- Skills of supervision and management: planning, organizing, assigning, directing, reviewing and evaluating work of those supervised and providing leadership.
- Tact, discretion, initiative and independent judgment.
- Compiling statistics and analyzing data.
- Effective interviewing techniques.
- Independently organizing work, setting priorities and following up assignments.
- Preparing reports and correspondence.
- Formulating goals, objectives and methods of evaluation.
- Determining client needs.
- Information retrieval.
- Database searching skills.

Mental and Physical Abilities to:

- Establish and maintain effective working relationships with staff, patrons, and other city departments.
- Translate library requirements into data processing requirements.
- Speak effectively before public groups and respond to questions.
- Write reports, correspondence and procedure manuals.
- See and read a variety of complex information concerning hardware and software specifications and instructions.
- Read, analyze, and interpret professional periodicals and journals.
- Effectively utilize a wide range of information resources and technology, in-house and remote.
- Analyze information needs and select effective course of research.
- Apply logical thinking to solve problems and accomplish tasks.
- While performing the essential functions of this job, the incumbent is regularly required to use hands to finger, handle or feel objects, and to reach with hands and arms. While performing the essential functions of this job, the incumbent is frequently required to lift and/or move objects up to 20 pounds.

Working Conditions:

Incumbent's working conditions are moderately quiet.

This class specification should not be interpreted as all inclusive. It is intended to identify the essential functions and requirements of this job. Incumbents may be requested to perform job-related responsibilities and tasks other than those stated in this specification. Any essential function or requirement of this class will be evaluated as necessary should an incumbent/applicant be unable to perform the function or requirement due to a disability as defined by the Americans with Disabilities Act (ADA). Reasonable accommodation for the specific disability will be made for the incumbent/applicant when possible.

ASSISTANT DEAN FOR TECHNOLOGY STRATEGY

University of Arizona
University of Arizona Libraries
Tucson, Arizona

Job description:

The University of Arizona Libraries' 4.7 million volume collection are housed in five primary facilities, the intellectual crossroads of the university, where students and scholars from all disciplines meet. We are a diverse, team-based organization which affords unique opportunities to work with team-mates and learn continuously. The UA Libraries are proud to be recognized for inspiring trends and technological achievements in information service.

Surrounded by mountains and the high Sonoran desert, Tucson's population of over 750,000 residents Tucson enjoy more than 300 days of sunshine each year. The metro area boasts diverse multicultural and international influences reflecting the richness of the Southwest. With a growing economic, cultural and recreational community, Tucson provides an exciting backdrop for a university and an exceptional quality of life for its residents.

LIBRARY MISSION STATEMENT:

The University of Arizona Libraries and Center for Creative Photography advance the University's mission through the active contributions of knowledgeable staff who choose cost effective methods of acquiring, curating, managing, and connecting customers to information services and resources and providing education in their use.

All Library staff members are charged with advancing the vision and mission of the Libraries through system-wide thinking and shared responsibility for successful teams. Individuals are responsible and accountable for problem solving, processes improvement, maintaining quality standards and are empowered to make decisions at appropriate levels. Staff members are encouraged to take satisfaction in their accomplishments in an atmosphere of cooperation and to have a balance of personal and professional lives. The University of Arizona Libraries and CCP are part of a dynamic, team-based, learning organization dedicated to a customer centered philosophy. We work in an environment of shared authority, responsibility and decision-making among a diverse group of colleagues committed to support of the learning and research activities of a comprehensive research university.

POSITION SUMMARY:

The Assistant Dean for Technology Strategy will serve as the Chief Technology Strategist for the Libraries and CCP in development of a shared information technology strategy that supports the mission of the University and is responsive to the changing information needs of its constituents. The Strategist will collaborate with Library functional and cross-functional teams and team leaders, the University Information Technology Services and other partners within and beyond the University. The incumbent will research and assess information about information technology trends and innovations that will impact the directions of the digital library and enhance the customers experience with information resources and share the information and recommendations with the Libraries. The Assistant Dean will work closely with the Digital Library and Information Systems Team on implementation of new technology projects and innovations. The Strategist will contribute to and be active in local, consortia, regional and national meetings to stay abreast of technology and program developments and trends and represent the positions and interests of the University and the Libraries. The Assistant Dean for Technology Strategy reports directly to the Dean of Libraries and CCP.

DUTIES, RESPONSIBILITIES and EXPECTATIONS:

1. Participates in the development of a shared vision and strategy for the Libraries that supports the mission of the University and is responsive to the changing information needs of customers.
2. Collaborates with the Strategic Long Range Planning Team to create and articulate an evolving technology strategy to support the Libraries' vision.
3. Creates and articulates an evolving technology strategy to support the Libraries' and University's technology vision, with ongoing input and feedback from key stakeholders.
4. Assesses information technology developments, trends and innovations that will impact the Library and its goals, and shares the information with the staff and administrators.
5. Actively coordinates and leads efforts to integrate Library and University technology strategies into programs to enhance the Libraries' support to our customers.
6. Researches, recommends and coordinates on implementations of new technologies to enhance and transform the user experience with information resources.
7. Develops a strong relationship and collaborates with team leaders to support customers' needs and digital library development given the increasing overlap of workload and responsibilities among teams.
8. In alignment with the Libraries' strategic plan, directs collaborative research and development efforts with University Information Technology Services (UITS) and other appropriate partners with and beyond the University.
9. Ensures good project management processes are used in providing services to the Libraries and customers.
10. Understands, advocates, communicates and exhibits commitment to the Libraries' mission, vision, values and goals, and effectively conveys the broader context in which the Libraries operate.
11. Anticipates, initiates and responds to changes in the environment, and keeps abreast of trends that impact higher education and the library profession that ensure the Libraries and the University achieve their goals.
12. Cultivates external relationships with deans, associate deans, faculty and donors to assess needs, leverage opportunities, and build future collaborations. Educates and promotes the Libraries as a campus-wide resource.
13. Expands the Libraries' contributions to e-research and provides leadership in the development of a University cyber-infrastructure.
14. Represents the Libraries in collaborative technology initiatives across the University and in national and international efforts.
15. Enhances the Libraries' reputation as a leading research library for the future.
16. Identifies needs and explores options for grant funding from federal and private funding sources.

MINIMUM REQUIREMENTS:

- Master's degree in library/information science from an ALA-accredited institution.
- Must have record of achievement which would allow continuing status.
- Five years of progressively responsible experience in information technology in a major academic and research University Library.

PREFERRED QUALIFICATIONS:

- Demonstrated knowledge of emerging trends in digital library services, ability to assess the market place, and translate knowledge into vision and strategy. Possesses a commitment to proactively continue tracking trends and innovations and incorporating findings into the Libraries' information technology strategy.
- Experience with developing digital library technologies and institutional repositories and integrating library systems.
- Demonstrated command of trends in digital libraries, information policy, collaborative technologies and the storage, management, preservation and delivery of information.
- Effective skills in facilitation, consensus building, creative problem solving and a team-based approach to achieving success.
- Demonstrated success in the leading and managing of a significant program or project.
- Possesses a thorough understanding of trends away from print toward digital content/resources and tools as a preference and reality for the future in this library and nationally. Ability to communicate the changes, requirements and benefits to faculty, students and researchers across campus.
- Ability to lead in a team-based environment and work with diverse people and serve a diverse population.
- Must be a systems thinker with a collaborative style and entrepreneurial spirit in developing strategies for the future of the digital library.
- Extensive skills in strategic planning and translating the resulting strategies into programs or projects that can be implemented to further all library goals. Willingness to use a library and University-wide view, rather than a parochial view, in developing strategies to achieve goals.
- Excellent communication skills and the ability to interact effectively with customers, colleagues, campus administrators and local, regional, consortial and national partners and organizations.
- Commitment to the Libraries' vision, mission, values and goals and the ability to communicate them clearly and persuasively in a variety of contexts to the library and campus.
- Ability to liaise with various campus, state and community organizations to develop and implement workable programs, enhances service to customers, and communicates the Library strategic goals and directions.
- Demonstrated ability to develop collaborations to enhance and fulfill the mission of the Libraries, the University and external organizations.
- Demonstrated commitment to risk taking and continuous improvement.

STANDARD PRE-EMPLOYMENT SCREENING: The University of Arizona conducts pre-employment screening for all positions, which includes a criminal background check, verification of academic credentials, licenses, certifications, and work history.

As an equal opportunity and affirmative action employer, the University of Arizona recognizes the power of a diverse community and encourages applications from individuals with varied experiences and backgrounds. The University of Arizona is an EEO/AA Employer-M/V/D/V.

ASSOCIATE DIRECTOR FOR DIGITAL INITIATIVES

University of Saint Thomas Minnesota
University of Saint Thomas Libraries
Saint Paul, Minnesota

Responsibilities include: planning, developing, implementing and sustaining the UST Libraries' digital environment; conducting hands-on leadership in building, configuring and maintaining the UST Libraries' website; coordinating library technology projects using formal project management processes; analyzing and assessing the usage and effectiveness of electronic resources and technologies; working with campus colleagues on the development of library technologies in the context of university wide planning; collaborating with library staff and university faculty on the development and management of electronic content; coordinating and developing standards of technical training for UST Libraries' staff.

Qualifications: MLS or equivalent and 5 years professional experience, preferably in a higher education setting. High level of skill and experience in systems development and the implementation of web and database solutions including learning/content/asset management and portal technologies. Preferred experience with some of the following programming languages: CFML, ASP, J2EE, J2SE, JSP, XML, DHTML, HTML, CSS, JavaScript, SQL.

Have skills in planning, implementing, monitoring and improving library services; in the use of automated library systems and in instructing others in the use of library systems and in research; leading and managing information resources and technology programs in a team based and collaborative environment.

AUTOMATED SERVICES COORDINATOR

Cumberland County Library System
Carlisle, Pennsylvania

AUTOMATED SERVICES COORDINATOR (Library System) Position Description Grade 19 Exempt

OVERALL OBJECTIVE OF JOB: To coordinate the development, implementation, operation and maintenance of the library system's automated services.

ESSENTIAL FUNCTIONS OF JOB: 1. Serves as system administrator for all County library system automated systems and performs/provides new installations, ongoing system maintenance, system upgrades, and database security. 2. Coordinates the planning, development, implementation and evaluation of Countywide library automation services. 3. Performs administrative functions associated with Cumberland County Library Services automated systems, including recommending an automated services budget, suggesting cost-saving solutions, and regular automated services reports. 4. Supervises and evaluates automated services staff. 5. Coordinates staff and vendors to investigate, troubleshoot and resolve automated library service computer hardware and software problems. Handles emergencies as required. 6. Develops, coordinates and provides automated library service training for staff. Trains local system administrators to perform basic system maintenance. 7. Acts as liaison with automated system vendors and computer support vendors. 8. Works with system libraries and system director to develop and coordinate automated library service policies and procedures. 9. Works with system libraries to develop automation training materials for the public. 10. Works with technical services coordinator to develop and maintain database maintenance standards.

OTHER DUTIES OF JOB: 1. Attends meetings, training seminars as required. 2. Represents the library system's computer capabilities to county officials, the community and other libraries. 3. Offers technical assistance to member libraries automating unique local library functions. 4. Performs other job-related duties as needed. SUPERVISION RECEIVED: Receives minimal instruction and some supervision from System Director in regard to daily work duties.

SUPERVISION GIVEN: Supervises Automated Services Assistant and LAN Services Technician.

WORKING CONDITIONS: 1.Works indoors in adequate work space, with adequate temperatures, ventilation and lighting. 2. Above normal exposure to noise, stress, and disruptions. 3. Periodically will work on-call or as emergencies arise. 4. Must possess a valid Pennsylvania driver's license and be able to visit member library facilities, using one's own vehicle. 5. Full-time position, 37.5 hours per week. The Cumberland County Library System office is open 8:00 AM-4:30 PM, Monday through Friday.

PHYSICAL/MENTAL CONDITIONS: 1. Must possess ability to record, convey and present information, explain procedures and follow instructions. 2. Must be able to sit for long periods throughout the workday, with intermittent periods of standing, walking, bending, twisting, reaching to carry out essential duties of job. 3. Coordinated movements of fingers/hand; and simple movements of feet/legs and torso. 4. Medium work, with occasional lifting/carrying of objects with weights of twenty to fifty pounds. 5. Must be able to pay close attention to details and concentrate on work.

QUALIFICATIONS:

A. EDUCATION/TRAINING: Masters degree in library or information science from an ALA-accredited institution and/or certification as public librarian in Pennsylvania.

B. WORK EXPERIENCE: 2-4 years working experience in public library automation field; preferably some experience with Microsoft computer networks and epixtech library automation software, as well as some supervisory experience.

KNOWLEDGE, SKILLS AND ABILITIES REQUIRED: 1. Must be able to speak and understand the English language in an understandable manner in order to carry out essential functions of job. 2. Must possess ability to communicate effectively. 3. Must possess ability to function independently, have flexibility and the ability to work effectively with clients, co-workers and others. 4. Must possess the technical knowledge of operating personal computers and other office equipment with accuracy and reasonable speed. 5. Must possess the ability to troubleshoot computer problems and make needed repairs/adjustments.

AUTOMATION AND INFORMATION TECHNOLOGY MANAGER

Manitowoc Public Library
Manitowoc, Wisconsin

Automation & Information Technology Manager

CLASSIFICATION: Manager

DEPARTMENT: Automation & Information Technology

REPORTS TO:

UNION STATUS: Non-represented FLSA STATUS: Exempt

POSITION HOURS: Salaried full-time, typically working at least 80 hours per two-week pay period on a flexible schedule which may vary from week to week. May be scheduled to work days, evenings, Saturdays, and Sundays. Must return to duty whenever needed. Works more than a 40-hour week, when necessary, with or without compensatory time.

BROAD SCOPE OF POSITION: Under the general direction of the Library Director, administers the Automation & Information Technology Department and its program of services. Administers the integrated library system (currently SirsiDynix Unicorn), LAN/WAN, and Manitowoc Public Library's digital phone system. Plans, develops, implements and evaluates staff technology training. Shares webmaster responsibility. Plans, develops, implements and evaluates the program of automation and information technology services by budgeting and expending resources (personnel, space, money, etc.), with appropriate approval. Guides overall functions and direction of the department. Analyzes technological advances and recommends appropriate applications. Participates on the Library's management team and assists in administration of the Library. Supervises, schedules and evaluates departmental staff. Makes hiring and disciplinary action recommendations to Library Director. May provide direct service to the public. Handles large-scale, ongoing projects for the Library as assigned.

PRINCIPAL DUTIES AND RESPONSIBILITIES: The following list identifies principal duties and responsibilities of the job. It is not a definitive list and other similar duties may be assigned. An asterisk (*) before any of the following items indicates duties and responsibilities which are not "essential functions" of the job as defined by the Americans with Disabilities Act. Principal duties may be performed for any combination of the following as assigned:

1. Plans, develops, implements and evaluates the program of automation and information technology services by budgeting and expending resources (personnel, space, money, etc.). Guides overall functions and direction of the department. Coordinates departmental plans within Library's goals, objectives and policies, and establishes departmental priorities. Administers and manages departmental budget and plan of departmental services. Directs development and implementation of departmental procedures and routines. Writes project proposals and grants, and implements programs.

2. Administers the integrated library system, LAN/WAN, and digital phone system. May be contracted to functions as system administrator for LARS, the Library Automated Resource Sharing consortium. Plans, develops, implements and evaluates staff technology training. Shares responsibility as webmaster with PR Manager. Assists with administration of the facility's automated systems, such as HVAC and security system. Must return to work, if needed, to operate and monitor any of the automated systems.

3. Supervises and schedules department staff. Evaluates staff in conjunction with Director. Team interviews and makes hiring recommendations to Library Director. Develops and implements plans for training departmental staff, and involves staff from other departments, as appropriate. When necessary, handles progressive discipline of staff through the level of written warnings and makes recommendations for further discipline, up to and including firing, to the Library Director.

4. Analyzes technological advances and recommends appropriate applications. May provide technical analyses for Manitowoc Calumet Library System (MCLS) and other LARS libraries as directed.

5. Participates on the Library's management team and assists in administration of the Library. Attends meetings and communicates decisions with staff, as appropriate. Provides professional and managerial support to Library Director and other members of the management team. Assists in establishing and meeting goals and objectives for the Library. Recommends policies and administrative actions to Library Director. Communicates with other members of the management team about departmental issues and priorities.

6. May provide direct service to the public. May assist patrons at the Reference, Youth and/or Circulation Desks, as occasionally scheduled or as needed. Interprets policy and procedures for patrons, particularly those who express concerns about routines or practices; refers issues to Library Director when appropriate. Deals with problem patrons, particularly those who disrupt normal use or operation of the Library, or attempt to unlawfully remove library materials from premises. Assists with maintenance of building security. Writes Incident Reports when necessary or appropriate.

7. Handles large-scale, ongoing projects for the Library, as assigned. Acts as liaison between the Library and community groups, as initiated and/or assigned. Participates on Library's Disaster Team. Participates in planning efforts, as assigned. May participate on City's Emergency Response Team and City's Data Processing Committee, as delegated or assigned.

8. May perform work of another member of the Library's management team, as assigned. Performs work of other departmental staff, as needed.

JOB SPECIFICATIONS:

1. Knowledge of technical services practices as well as public library administrative and managerial practices, and ability to apply these to the automation and information technology department. Willingness to contribute to ongoing development of Library-wide philosophy, mission and services, and ability to lead development of departmental philosophy, goals and services.

2. Skill at functioning as system administrator of integrated library system, LAN/WAN, various automated systems controlling library building functions, and other automated systems. Skill in using computers and related software. Skill at setting up, configuring, installing and maintaining software, hardware and peripherals. Knowledge of or ability to quickly acquire knowledge of phone system, HVAC control program, clock system program, MicroLite system, etc. Initiative and ability to apply problem-solving skills when troubleshooting equipment software or hardware issues.

3. Skill at providing training and support for end users, particularly newly hired library staff and those staff who require training. Ability to develop user-friendly training modules. Ability to communicate technical information effectively.

4. Knowledge of public library planning and role-setting practices and their application to automation and information technology. Ability to analyze and evaluate current conditions and make logical evaluations of future needs. Ability to develop and execute short-range plans. Ability to synthesize and creatively adapt trends in information technology. Skill in negotiating for resources to meet departmental needs.

5. Ability to assume a leadership role in a group setting. Ability to establish and maintain effective working relationships with the Library Director, other library staff members, and member library staff, ILS vendor representatives, sales and service representatives, community officials, agency representatives, and the public. Ability to work in the Library's team setting. Willingness to assist and support coworkers, contribute ideas, and maintain flexibility. Ability to adapt to a rapidly changing environment.

6. Commitment to and skill in supervising people. Knowledge of supervisory and training techniques. Willingness and ability to provide a positive managerial example. Willingness and ability to foster environment in which employees and volunteers are self-motivated and can exhibit high morale. Capacity to recognize and utilize talents of others. Fairness when distributing workload, responsibility, and authority. Ability to identify proper work assignments for subordinates and willingness to follow-up to ensure proper completion.

7. Ability to set realistic standards for employees and to encourage productive and efficient performance. Conscientiousness when appraising performance, counseling employees, writing and administering performance appraisals, and making personnel recommendations.

8. Skill in managing departmental workflow, including ability to identify, negotiate, establish, communicate, and apply priorities. Ability to schedule and oversee work performed by vendors and contractors. Skill in performing and supervising routine and non-routine procedures involving many steps. Ability to give and follow complex written and/or verbal instructions and to pay close attention to detail. Willingness to provide professional and managerial support to the Director and other members of the Management Team. Ability to accept delegation and to work under general supervisory direction.

9. Ability to make realistic budget proposals, to operate within established budgetary guidelines, and to identify and analyze budgetary impact of services. Ability to analyze and evaluate current conditions and to make logical evaluations of future needs. Ability to plan and execute short-range plans. Skill in negotiating for resources to meet departmental needs.

*10. Physical capacity and skill at installing and maintaining equipment. Minimum skill level: Physical capacity to lift and maneuver monitors, servers, and other equipment often weighing up to 50 lbs. Physical capacity to crawl beneath desks and to reach up behind desks to attach cables, plug in computers, etc. Physical capacity to climb ladders to reach cable raceways in ceiling. Physical capacity to pull cable. Manual dexterity to install cable ends, network cards, modems, etc.

11. Ability to communicate effectively in English, both orally and in writing. Skill in interpersonal communication. Capacity to hear and to be easily understood on voice telephone. Ability to do technical writing for procedures, proposals, reports, etc. Ability to read, understand and interpret policy and procedure.

12. Visual capacity, including close vision, color vision, depth perception, and the ability to adjust focus.

13. Initiative and resourcefulness to take acceptable risks, make appropriate decisions, and exercise proper authority. Ability to present clear explanations of established policies and procedures. Ability to think and act appropriately under pressure. Willingness and ability to grant logical exceptions to Library policies and procedures when warranted. Willingness to maintain confidentiality when appropriate.

14. Ability to provide courteous and timely public service to patrons of various ages, interests, backgrounds, and levels of library expertise. Ability to conduct a reference interview in English to determine patron needs. Capacity to be easily understood on voice telephone. General knowledge of reference tools, methodologies, and philosophy. Ability to provide instruction and encouragement in use of library resources to patrons individually and in groups.

15. Must comply with the Library's "Drug-Free Workplace" policy.

16. Ability to develop work-related goals and objectives. Willingness to develop job-related abilities, skills and knowledge. Willingness and ability to keep abreast of changing technologies and procedures and to assume responsibilities required by introduction of different services and equipment.

17. Willingness and ability to understand and support the fundamental principles of library services, such as: open access to library materials for people of all ages; the library's obligation to provide materials representing as many points of view as possible; and a patron's right to privacy in dealings with the library and with respect to records maintained by library.

WORKING CONDITIONS: 1. Usually (up to 100% of work time) works in close proximity with computers and other similar electronic equipment. 2. Usually (up to 100% of work time) works in shared-office environment with considerable staff and public contact. 3. Usually (up to 100% of work time) maintains work environment. For example: vacuuming computer areas, dusting, recycling paper; cleaning up after programs. Infrequently (as situation requires) assists with building emergencies which may involve cleaning up snow, bodily fluids, etc. 4. Usually (up to 100% of work time) performs routines with many rapid, repeated motions.

DIGITAL LIBRARY MANAGER

Worthington Library
Worthington, Ohio

FLSA STATUS: Exempt
REPORTS TO: Director of Technology Services
DEPARTMENT: Technology
POSITIONS SUPERVISED: Webmaster

PURPOSE:

Under direction, the Digital Library Manager coordinates the design, content and implementation of web sites hosted by Worthington Libraries including interactive applications available now and those yet to be developed, in order to provide essential library services through electronic digital technologies.

ESSENTIAL POSITION FUNCTIONS:

1. Works with the Webmaster in the overall development, design and maintenance of Worthington Libraries Online (WLO) and other sites hosted by WLO

2. Develops and implements procedures for the ongoing revision of WLO

3. Monitors sites for accuracy and relevance

4. Assists with technology planning and visioning for the Library

5. Works with end users on projects, problems and ideas

6. Oversees the development, implementation, and support of essential library services based on the Web and other Internet technologies, including but not limited to the library's catalog

7. Oversees the electronic publication of library information and resources

8. Assesses community needs and interprets them into digital library services

9. Evaluates digital library services, equipment and support

10. Works with schools to introduce and test products and services

11. Creates and adds content to WLO

12. Monitors new trends in web development and implements, as appropriate

13. Conducts usability testing with staff and patrons

14. Supervisory duties

REQUIRED QUALIFICATIONS:

Education, Training and/or Experience

1. Master's degree in Library Science from an American Library Association accredited school

2. A minimum of two (2) years of experience in planning and contributing to website content development

3. A minimum of one (1) year of experience in usability testing

Knowledge, Skills, Abilities and Personal Characteristics

1. Ability to maintain confidentiality and use appropriate judgement in handling information and records

2. Ability to work accurately with attention to detail

3. Ability to arrange items in alphanumeric and/or subject order

4. Knowledge of computer operations and software applications

5. Skill in video and audio editing

6. Ability to deliver presentations and speak before groups in a variety of settings

7. Basic knowledge of application standards, including but not limited to HTML, XML and graphic formats

8. Ability to inspire and motivate staff within the organization

9. Ability to interpret and apply laws, regulations and policies

10. Knowledge of state and federal employment laws

11. Ability to define problems, collect data, establish facts and draw valid conclusions

12. Proficient in the use of Microsoft Office applications including Outlook, Word, Excel, Access and PowerPoint

Certifications, Licenses, Registrations: None

PREFERRED QUALIFICATIONS:

1. Experience in the design and implementation of interactive Web content

2. Supervisory experience

PHYSICAL DEMANDS:
- Ability to sit and use computer for extended periods and operate standard office equipment, daily
- Ability to lift and move up to fifty (50) pounds, occasionally
- Travel by automobile is required occasionally

WORKING CONDITIONS:
- Majority of work performed in general office/library environment
- Requires availability for extended hours as needed
- Requires periodic participation and attendance at events and training

This position description is not intended to be a complete list of all responsibilities, skills or working conditions associated with this position and is subject to review and change at any time in accordance with the needs of Worthington Libraries. Reasonable accommodations may be made to enable someone with a qualifying disability to perform the essential functions of the position.

CORE COMPETENCIES: Core Competencies are the knowledge, skills, attitudes, values and behaviors that all employees are expected to demonstrate. The Worthington Libraries Core Values are indicated in italicized text.

Competency	Definition	Demonstrated Behaviors
Adaptability *Future Oriented* *We respond appropriately to emerging practices and technologies in library and information science and related fields, and anticipate changes in our community's needs.*	The ability to adjust to changing situations and take calculated risks.	• Interprets and responds quickly to new or changed responsibilities, methods and procedures • Learns and applies new skills • Remains positive and productive
Customer Service *Quality Service* *We anticipate needs and exceed expectations in delivering service.* **Diversity** *We strive to be inclusive, and we recognize the dignity of all people from all backgrounds; we value contributions and ideas from all members of our diverse community.* **Intellectual Freedom** *We are committed to providing open access to library resources which interest, inform and enlighten all people in our community.*	The ability to appreciate the variety of patrons and staff and accommodate their diverse needs to the highest extent possible.	• Welcomes interactions • Consistently greets patrons and staff with a smile • Strives to make library resources accessible to all members of the community • Proactively anticipates and addresses patron and staff expectations and needs • Knows when it is appropriate to bend the rules and explains positively when denials are required
Communication *Communication* *We engage in the open exchange of information as a critical process for creating synergy of ideas within our library and with our community.*	The ability, through both verbal and written methods, to provide concise, timely and accurate information, internally and externally, among all organizational levels and with all of the appropriate people.	• Listens to others and verifies understanding of the message • Uses a variety of communication methods in the most appropriate form, in the manner that best enables the message to be understood • Responds to the comments and questions of others in a timely manner • Uses appropriate language

		• Proficient in the use of Microsoft Outlook • Knows how to find and use information on the Staff Intranet
Organizational Awareness	The ability to support the library's mission, vision, culture and structure.	• Understands and identifies with the goals and values of the Library and models and actively communicates them effectively • Knows and appropriately follows the library's hierarchy • Knows, understands and appropriately applies policies and procedures • Keeps current on information sent by Administration
Technology	The ability to use equipment, materials, and processes to do work.	• Readily uses technology that is necessary to the position • Keeps current on changes in technology that are necessary to the position
Teamwork ***Teamwork*** *We work together in a spirit of cooperation, supporting each others' efforts to achieve organizational excellence and provide quality service.*	The ability to work collaboratively with others.	• Willingly assists others by sharing expertise and time • Prepared to complete assigned tasks • Respects the ideas and opinions of others • Gives and accepts feedback in a positive manner • Proactively involves others to solve problems and achieve results which meet the needs of the Library
Problem Solving	The ability to understand the entire perspective on a situation or issue, identify patterns or connections between situations, assess problems and troubleshoot in order to identify effective solutions.	• Acquires new information and applies knowledge to analyze issues and resolve problems • Breaks problems down into components to identify required tasks or activities • Formulates new and imaginative solutions that reflect careful consideration of patron and library needs and goals • Considers risks, benefits, and impact of solution on the present and future library environment • Transfers learning from one situation to solve a problem in another • Consults with appropriate staff members before implementing solutions

Personal Responsibility *Integrity* *We act with honesty and fairness as we conduct our business with patrons and each other; we assume personal responsibility for accomplishing the goals of the organization.*	The commitment to take appropriate action to meet patron and library goals and needs.	• Ensures accuracy and completeness of work • Accepts responsibility for accomplishments and seeks to correct and learn from mistakes • Continually seeks opportunities for learning and training • Evaluates own strengths and weaknesses and seeks feedback from others for self-improvement • Reports to work as scheduled and provides acceptable notice when unable to do so • Is prepared to commence work activities at the assigned time • Adheres to break and lunch schedules • Utilizes time efficiently, eliminates unnecessary activities and does not waste efforts and time of patrons, co-workers or supervisor

---

POSITION SPECIFIC COMPETENCIES: The skills, knowledge, attitudes, values and behaviors necessary to an individual's success in a position and to the overall success of an organization

Competency	Definition	Demonstrated Behaviors
Applied Library Knowledge	The ability to evaluate, package and manage collection formats, instruct and support patrons in the pursuit of lifelong learning and provide equal access to information.	• Develops, provides and/or manages convenient, accessible and patron-oriented information services • Recommends materials appropriate to various user levels and interests • Possesses knowledge of collection development, resources and formats • Works to build a balanced collection in a variety of formats to fill the needs of patrons
Effective Supervision	The ability to provide leadership, coaching and guidance to staff in fulfilling their responsibilities and building positive relationships.	• Determines necessary staffing levels and distribution of work • Interviews and selects candidates for hire • Ensures that staff receive orientation, training and development • Coordinates work schedules, reviews time sheets and approves leave requests • Assigns work and ensures that it is completed properly and in a timely manner

		• Monitors and manages performance, including the administration of corrective action • Ensures effective communication of information • Interprets and enforces policies and procedures • Reviews policies and procedures and recommends changes
Marketing and Public Relations	The ability to identify, develop and implement successful marketing and public relations strategies that effectively communicate the value of the library and its services to the community served.	• Understands and uses the basic concepts of marketing and public relations as they relate to one's position • Develops, creates and coordinates the distribution of promotional materials designed to meet the needs of diverse audiences • Communicates with various populations (children, teens, adults, etc.) to explain how the library's services meet specific information and educational needs • Promotes value of products and services within the library and throughout the community
Project/Program Management	The ability to plan, oversee and/or implement tasks resulting in projects or programs that are completed on time, within budget, and that meet or exceed expectations.	• Assesses needs, plans and implements programs or projects that are consistent with the library's mission, values, goals and objectives • Utilizes the library's tools, processes and models effectively, such as forms, statistics, guidelines, etc. • Evaluates programs and projects for effectiveness • Provides written and oral reports on both routine and special projects • Participates in or leads project specific teams or performs special tasks
Resource Management	The ability to effectively allocate or use resources to meet library goals and objectives, including risk assessment, cost/benefit analysis and the justification of expenditures.	• Determines core and non-core programs and services • Manages or uses human, financial and physical resources to maximize results • Establishes prudent budgets • Develops strategic plans and establishes long and short range goals • Involves staff appropriately in planning, decision making and problem solving

DIGITAL PROJECTS LIBRARIAN AND INSTRUCTIONAL REPOSITORY COORDINATOR

University of Connecticut
University of Connecticut Libraries
Storrs, Connecticut

University Librarian II, Digital Projects Librarian and Institutional Repository Coordinator—(UCP 7)
The University of Connecticut Libraries

Job Summary: Reporting to the Preservation Librarian, this position serves two main functions: Digital Projects Librarian and Institutional Repository Coordinator. The Digital Projects Librarian is responsible for managing digital reformatting operations that preserve and improve access to the University of Connecticut's library and archival collections in all information formats (text, image, audio, video). As Institutional Repository Coordinator, this position oversees the day-to-day management, public education, marketing and promotion, and long-term planning for UConn's institutional repository (IR), Digital Commons @UConn.

Minimum Qualifications: A graduate degree in Library or Information Science from a program accredited by the American Library Association; two years experience using technology to deliver digital content in an academic research library or other cultural institution, or in a service bureau contracted to such an institution; demonstrated broad knowledge of current digital reformatting and digital conversion trends including issues relating to the application of metadata to digital objects; demonstrated knowledge of digital reformatting and digital conversion policies and technical procedures, including cost factors and productivity issues; basic knowledge of copyright issues as they relate to digital reformatting and scholarly communication; excellent analytical and problem-solving skills; evidence of excellent communication skills, including effective presentation and promotional abilities; evidence of participation in professional development activities.

Preferred Qualifications: Working knowledge of a range of computing platforms, storage environments, and digital library metadata frameworks (such as METS, MIX, and PREMIS, as well as the OAIS model) and operational experience with any of the following tools: CONTENTdm, XTF, DAITSS, FEDORA, SHERPA/RoMEO; Demonstrated initiative and commitment to public service; Experience with photography and scanning in a library or archival environment sufficient to be fluently conversant with image capture and manipulation issues; knowledge about scholarly communication issues and strong interest in pursuing the development of alternative publishing venues for faculty and students; preservation experience in an academic research library or other cultural institution, or in a service bureau contracted to such an institution; experience with grant writing and fund procurement.

INFORMATION RESOURCE MANAGER

MOBIUS Consortium
Columbia, Missouri

CLASS TITLE: INFORMATION RESOURCE MANAGER—MOBIUS
BASIC FUNCTION AND RESPONSIBILITY

This position is responsible for acquiring and managing the information resource services for the MOBIUS Consortium Office (MCO). MOBIUS is a consortium serving academic and public libraries. The incumbent will serve as the administrative point of contact for internal and external groups regarding electronic resources and collection development services. Work emphasis is placed on improving the organization's functions through identifying, developing, and delivering end-products resulting from strategic initiatives; on project administrative and resource development needed to sustain strategic initiatives; and the timely delivery of these services. The position reports to the Executive Director of MOBIUS. The incumbent will function as a member of the organization's senior management and routinely interact with clientele, funding representatives and host institution personnel.

CHARACTERISTIC DUTIES

Consortium—General Operations
- Assist the MOBIUS Executive Director in planning MCO's goals, objectives and budgets.
- Assist in the evaluation of MCO programs, including the development of evaluative tools and procedures and the analysis of statistical and other data.
- Participate in consortium wide planning with Executive Director and MOBIUS members.
- Assume responsibility and authority for the MCO as assigned in the absence of the Executive Director.

Fiscal Responsibilities
- Participate in the development and implementation of the electronic resources and collection development budget. Provide the Executive Director with current financial information in accordance with established fiscal policy and guidelines.
- Monitor spending during the year to ensure that it is reasonable and directly supports the department's mission.
- Review and approve operating expenditures related to electronic resources and collection development.
- Work with the Executive Director to pursue grants and other funding opportunities.

Electronic Resources
- Coordinate the annual cycle of evaluation and assessment of new electronic information products.
- Solicit initial and renewal price quotes from vendors.
- Coordinate vendor demos, evaluations, and trials.
- Negotiate contracts and manage licenses following University of Missouri policies and procedures.
- Responsible for ensuring that orders are placed with selected vendors.
- Responsible for ensuring that billing is sent to appropriate member institutions.
- Working with vendors and individual members addresses technical issues such as authentication, access control, and customization of individual institution interfaces configurations.
- Develop and manage information tools to track license and vendor files; ensures compliance with licensing agreement by communicating terms of contract to appropriate member institutions.
- Stay abreast of issues, trends, and best practices in electronic resources.

Collection Management
- Leverage the capabilities of Common Library Platform (CLP) for collection management and access
- Identify potential opportunities for further development and/or institutional collection development collaboration
- Working with consortium members develop strategies, policies and programs for the future management of library collections, both digital and print formats
- Manage consortium collection development contracts; evaluating service performance and resolving MOBIUS member complaints.
- Stay abreast of issues, trends, and best practices in collection management

Institutional Assessment
- Track, analyze and report on cost trends in scholarly resources and the economic and service benefits that accrue to consortium members through participation in cooperative licensing

- Study the behavior and attitudes of users when using MOBIUS products and services
- Coordinate the benchmarking of MOBIUS library collections and services against peer institutions
- Coordinate the collection and organization of usage data and statistics; prepare reports on trends in overall usage
- Stay abreast of issues, trends, and best practices in library management and scholarly communication.

Consortium Membership Communication
- Serve on MOBIUS committees and task forces as directed by Executive Director.
- Act as the MCO liaison to MOBIUS Collection Development Advisory Committee and MOBIUS Electronic Resource Advisory Committee.
- Act as the MCO liaison to other MOBIUS Advisory Committees as designated by Executive Director.
- Represent the MCO at meetings or events when designated by Executive Director.
- Maintain effective and proactive communications with appropriate outside groups to develop, implement and monitor effective electronic resources/collection management solutions for MOBIUS members.

SUPERVISION RECEIVED

Direction is received from the MOBIUS Executive Director

SUPERVISION EXERCISED

None

QUALIFICATIONS

- Master's Degree in Librarianship (MLS), from an ALA-accredited library school program.
- Experience in both public service and technical service areas of a library—preferred.
- Demonstrated expertise with electronic information resources, search systems and supporting technology—both hardware and software.
- Minimum of one year's experience negotiating and administering contracts, including knowledge of Digital Rights Management and copyright.
- Ability to work in a business oriented environment.
- Demonstrates strong analytical and time management skills to plan, sustain and achieve positive outcomes.
- History of achieving high levels of personal productivity.

LIBRARY INNOVATION AND TECHNOLOGY MANAGER

Boulder Public Library
Boulder, Colorado

CITY OF BOULDER
POSITION DESCRIPTION
POSITION TITLE: LIBRARY INNOVATION & TECHNOLOGY MANAGER

EMPLOYEE GROUP: MGMT/Non-union

DEPARTMENT/DIVISION: Library & Arts/Innovation and Technology

POSITION VISIONARY STATEMENT

The Library Innovation and Technology (LIT) Manager will be a visionary, energetic member of Boulder Public Library's Leadership Team. The Manager will be responsible for supporting leading-edge technology and digital services into the fabric of the library's mission and on-going activities. A strong dedication to innovation and rapid integration of services is necessary. The LIT Manager will work with all Public Library departments to maximize the resources of the public library in order to create meaningful and remarkable services, programs and experiences for internal and external customers.

OVERALL JOB OBJECTIVE

Under limited supervision, the LIT Manager leads the library in strategy building, planning, and implementing all aspects of electronic media and innovative practices associated with technology. Working with the Library Senior Leadership Team, the LIT Manager is responsible for ongoing improvements and progress of web technologies and e-learning throughout the Library. Advancing a commitment to interdepartmental collaboration, the LIT Manager ensures the ongoing development integration of library services and programs with current technologies and Web 2.0 practices. The LIT Manager works to optimize the Library's technology resources, systems and network infrastructure to deliver outstanding customer support.

ABOUT THE LIBRARY INNOVATION & TECHNOLOGY DEPARTMENT

The Boulder Public Library is a department of the city of Boulder and includes its own information systems department (Library Innovation & Technology Department) focused on client support, PC hardware and software maintenance, and library application administration. The Public Library does utilize the city's central network backbone, but is otherwise independent.

The LIT Manager reports to the Director of Library & Arts. The position supervises the department, which works in four main areas of focus:

- Network Services: PC and end-user support, Help Desk, network server, systems and database administration. Establishes and maintains a secure environment for all network services.
- Application Services: Application development and enterprise "Commercial off the Shelf" software application administration and support
- Library Innovation: Research, prototyping and integration of fresh practices in the fields of Libraries, Technology an innovative business practices. Ensures that the Public Library supports a culture of curiosity, learning and ongoing implementation of innovative practices.
- Administrative Services: Department financial management and support with leadership and administrative service

DUTIES AND RESPONSIBILITIES

1. Manages the Library Innovation & Technology Department. The successful candidate will have a high level of organizational skills to lead a staff of three technology specialists, one web developer, as well as contract employees. Evaluates and prioritizes tasks and projects on a daily as well as long-range basis. Administers staff reviews, hiring, coaching and daily support needs to create a high-performing and innovative department.

2. Serves as a member of the Library Leadership Team, which is responsible for implementing new initiatives while maintaining effective core services. Advices senior leadership team members as well as staff system-wide.

3. Develops and implements a visionary technology and innovation plan that aligns with the vision and mission of the Public Library and the city of Boulder.

4. Collaborates with library departments as well as city of Boulder Information Technology Department to ensure a high level of professionalism, efficiency, functionality, style, and consistency in library brand and mission.

5. Researches, evaluates, recommends and acquires emerging systems for digital service delivery. Prototypes new software and applications that benefit staff and the public on an ongoing basis.

6. Directs the technology operations and developments in support of 200 User LAN/WAN collectively known as the Flatirons Library Consortium, comprised of the Boulder Public Library and neighboring

libraries—Louisville Public and Mamie Dowd Eisenhower Public in Broomfield. The responsibilities in this area include the following:

- Overall design, support and maintenance of the workstations, servers, Web site and network technologies within the Library & Arts Department.
- Work with Integrated Library Systems Specialist and ILS Vendor to manage and enable the mission critical task of technical support and maintenance of the Flatirons Library Consortium's ILS at all locations during operational hours.
- Guide special upgrades and projects involving new systems, programs, and innovative practices in the Library.

7. Actively participates in library and non-library professional opportunities and openly shares learning and innovative practices with library staff through trainings, learning sessions and ongoing implementation.

8. Advises the Director of Libraries & Arts in matters regarding technology and digital services. Prepares reports and presentations for staff, Library Commission and city officials as needed.

9. Maintains open flow of communication within the Library & Arts Department as well as pursues creative, innovative ways to convey information to our public through digital services.

10. Performs other duties related to technology and library leadership. Shows a commitment to ongoing education, staying current in the field of libraries and technology, advancements in integration of services as well as serving on teams, project staffs and advisory committees.

11. Other considerations
- Performs related duties as required to meet the needs of the city.
- Takes proper safety precautions to prevent accidents. Responsible for the safety of self, others, materials, and equipment. Uses all required safety equipment and follows all safety regulations, policies and procedures. Reports all accidents and damage to city property.
- Responsible for knowing and complying with all city and department policies; participating in professional trainings and development; and adhering to attendance and workplace attire policies.

Please note:

The city of Boulder is committed to hiring employees who provide excellent customer service. Our employees act with a high level of integrity and take responsibility for their words and actions.

City of Boulder employees strive to respect and appreciate each individual's differences, and to work effectively with all people and their diverse backgrounds. We support candid and honest interactions, which respect other points of view, and are sensitive to communication differences. We achieve organizational goals through inclusive problem solving, planning, and decision-making. Community partnerships are included in this effort.

This position is a management/supervisory level position. All city supervisors are responsible for understanding and enforcing relevant collective bargaining agreements and management policies; hiring and firing supervised employees or making related recommendations; ensuring employees are trained initially and on an ongoing basis, as needed providing appropriate feedback to employees by monitoring day-to-day performance; completing performance evaluations on time; correcting problems in employee work habits or performance in a timely manner; prioritizing and scheduling work functions and vacations; ensuring adherence to established safety standards; ensuring the timely completion and submission of all paperwork required by the city to process employee transactions, insurance or injury claims, etc.; maintaining related records; and ensuring the accuracy of reported time use.

CHAIN OF SUPERVISION

1. Title of immediate supervisor: Director of Library & Arts

2. Titles of positions over which this position has direct supervision:

Web Services Specialist (1); Technology Specialist (3); Contract Employee (1)

REQUIREMENTS

- Education: Bachelor's Degree in Computer Science, Information Systems, Telecommunications or a related field.
- Experience: At least five years of experience managing a department or organization with a digital/technology focus. Extensive experience with Windows XP, Windows Vista, Windows Server 2003, Internet Information Services Microsoft Exchange/Outlook, MS Office 2003 and 2007.
- At least three years of supervisory experience of Information Technology professionals in a library, university, municipal or county environment.
- Equivalent combination: Or an equivalent combination of education and experience.
- Other Requirements: Proven ability to manage projects involving departmental and interdepartmental collaboration. Ability to clearly articulate ideas, procedures and directions through daily interactions as well as formal presentations. Knowledge of online social networking applications such as Facebook, flickr, twitter and meebo. Effectively listens and communicates both verbally and in writing with a diverse group of people, including library staff, managers, colleagues, vendors and customers. Job offers, and continued employment if hired, are subject to acceptable background information including criminal conviction record and credit history.

DESIRED QUALIFICATIONS

- Master's Degree in Library Science or Library & Information Studies.
- Strong knowledge of public library services and operations.
- Experience working with database vendors and content management systems such as Drupal.
- Awareness and interest in open source development.
- Proven track record of successful project management.
- Dedication to leadership and progressive career challenges.
- Ability to process new information and implement in a timely manner.
- Commitment to service excellence with both internal and external customers.
- Active participation in relevant associations and organizations.
- Strong online presence or proven support for Web 2.0 applications within a library or other organization.

WORKING CONDITIONS

Physical Demands: Primarily sedentary physical work requiring the ability to lift a maximum of 10 pounds; occasional lifting, carrying, walking and standing; frequent hand/eye coordination to operate personal computer and office equipment; vision for reading, recording and interpreting information; speech communication and hearing to maintain communication with employees and the public.

Work Environment: Works primarily in clean, comfortable environment.

Machines and equipment used: These include but are not limited to the following—frequently uses standard office equipment including personal computers, telephones, calculators and copy/fax machines. Also uses LAN Analyzer equipment CISCO routers, Windows 2003 Server, Microsoft SMS Server, Windows XP/Vista workstations, Sun Server, and all related devices.

NETWORK ADMINISTRATOR

Worthington Library
Worthington, Ohio

FLSA STATUS: Exempt
REPORTS TO: Director of Technology Services
DEPARTMENT: Technology

POSITIONS SUPERVISED: Technology Trainer

PURPOSE:

Under direction, the Network Administrator manages the LAN, WAN and WLAN; manages hardware and software maintenance and licensing; installs software; documents the network; and performs related tasks.

ESSENTIAL POSITION FUNCTIONS:

1. Manages, troubleshoots and repairs Microsoft Windows (Windows) systems and hardware
2. Maintains the security of the network
3. Implements system hardware and software upgrades and licensing
4. Researches new and improved technologies
5. Monitors system usage and ensures system availability
6. Ensures physical security of equipment rooms
7. Ensures proper operations of phone and automatic door lock systems
8. Works to create ways to improve services to both staff and patrons
9. Manages the LAN, WAN and WLAN
10. Provides "help desk" service to staff and the public
11. Supervisory duties

REQUIRED QUALIFICATIONS

Education, Training and/or Experience

1. Bachelor's degree in Computer Science or a related degree
2. A minimum of one (1) year of experience with integrated online systems, Cisco-based LANs, WANs and WLANs, telecommunications networks and application software
3. A minimum of one (1) year of experience with Windows NT (2000), Windows XP, Microsoft Exchange, Microsoft Office Professional and Internet applications, OR
4. An equivalent combination of education, training, and experience

Knowledge, Skills, Abilities and Personal Characteristics

1. Ability to maintain confidentiality and use appropriate judgment in handling information and records
2. Ability to work accurately with attention to detail
3. Ability to arrange items in alphanumeric and/or subject order
4. Knowledge of registration of domain names
5. Ability to define problems, collect data, establish facts and draw valid conclusions

Certification, Licenses, Registrations

- Microsoft Certified Systems Administrator (Windows 2000 or Windows Server 2003)—may be acquired after hire

PREFERRED QUALIFICATIONS

1. One (1) year of experience with Active Directory
2. Cisco Certified network Associate
3. Supervisory experience

PHYSICAL DEMANDS

- Ability to sit and use computer for extended periods and operate standard office equipment, daily
- Ability to lift and move up to fifty (50) pounds, daily

- Ability to disassemble and reassemble computer hardware, daily
- Ability to stand for extended periods, daily
- Travel by automobile is required frequently

WORKING CONDITIONS

- Majority of work performed in general office/library environment
- On call evenings and weekends, in coordination with the Technology Trainer
- Requires periodic participation and attendance at events and training

This position description is not intended to be a complete list of all responsibilities, skills or working conditions associated with this position and is subject to review and change at any time in accordance with the needs of Worthington Libraries. Reasonable accommodations may be made to enable someone with a qualifying disability to perform the essential functions of the position.

CORE COMPETENCIES: Core Competencies are the knowledge, skills, attitudes, values and behaviors that all employees are expected to demonstrate. The Worthington Libraries Core Values are indicated in italicized text.

Competency	Definition	Demonstrated Behaviors
Adaptability ***Future Oriented*** *We respond appropriately to emerging practices and technologies in library and information science and related fields, and anticipate changes in our community's needs.*	The ability to adjust to changing situations and take calculated risks.	• Interprets and responds quickly to new or changed responsibilities, methods and procedures • Learns and applies new skills • Remains positive and productive
Customer Service ***Quality Service*** *We anticipate needs and exceed expectations in delivering service.* ***Diversity*** *We strive to be inclusive, and we recognize the dignity of all people from all backgrounds; we value contributions and ideas from all members of our diverse community.* ***Intellectual Freedom*** *We are committed to providing open access to library resources which interest, inform and enlighten all people in our community.*	The ability to appreciate the variety of patrons and staff and accommodate their diverse needs to the highest extent possible.	• Welcomes interactions • Consistently greets patrons and staff with a smile • Strives to make library resources accessible to all members of the community • Proactively anticipates and addresses patron and staff expectations and needs • Knows when it is appropriate to bend the rules and explains positively when denials are required
Communication ***Communication*** *We engage in the open exchange of information as a critical process for creating synergy of ideas within our library and with our community.*	The ability, through both verbal and written methods, to provide concise, timely and accurate information, internally and externally, among all organizational levels and with all of the appropriate people.	• Listens to others and verifies understanding of the message • Uses a variety of communication methods in the most appropriate form, in the manner that best enables the message to be understood

		• Responds to the comments and questions of others in a timely manner
		• Uses appropriate language
		• Proficient in the use of Microsoft Outlook
		• Knows how to find and use information on the Staff Intranet
Organizational Awareness	The ability to support the library's mission, vision, culture and structure.	• Understands and identifies with the goals and values of the Library and models and actively communicates them effectively
		• Knows and appropriately follows the library's hierarchy
		• Knows, understands and appropriately applies policies and procedures
		• Keeps current on information sent by Administration
Technology	The ability to use equipment, materials, and processes to do work.	• Readily uses technology that is necessary to the position
		• Keeps current on changes in technology that are necessary to the position
Teamwork **Teamwork** *We work together in a spirit of cooperation, supporting each others' efforts to achieve organizational excellence and provide quality service.*	The ability to work collaboratively with others.	• Willingly assists others by sharing expertise and time
		• Prepared to complete assigned tasks
		• Respects the ideas and opinions of others
		• Gives and accepts feedback in a positive manner
		• Proactively involves others to solve problems and achieve results which meet the needs of the Library
Problem Solving	The ability to understand the entire perspective on a situation or issue, identify patterns or connections between situations, assess problems and troubleshoot in order to identify effective solutions.	• Acquires new information and applies knowledge to analyze issues and resolve problems
		• Breaks problems down into components to identify required tasks or activities
		• Formulates new and imaginative solutions that reflect careful consideration of patron and library needs and goals
		• Considers risks, benefits, and impact of solution on the present and future library environment

		• Transfers learning from one situation to solve a problem in another
		• Consults with appropriate staff members before implementing solutions
Personal Responsibility *Integrity* *We act with honesty and fairness as we conduct our business with patrons and each other; we assume personal responsibility for accomplishing the goals of the organization.*	The commitment to take appropriate action to meet patron and library goals and needs.	• Ensures accuracy and completeness of work • Accepts responsibility for accomplishments and seeks to correct and learn from mistakes • Continually seeks opportunities for learning and training • Evaluates own strengths and weaknesses and seeks feedback from others for self-improvement • Reports to work as scheduled and provides acceptable notice when unable to do so • Is prepared to commence work activities at the assigned time • Adheres to break and lunch schedules • Utilizes time efficiently, eliminates unnecessary activities and does not waste efforts and time of patrons, co-workers or supervisor

---

POSITION SPECIFIC COMPETENCIES: The skills, knowledge, attitudes, values and behaviors necessary to an individual's success in a position and to the overall success of an organization

Competency	Definition	Demonstrated Behaviors
Effective Supervision	The ability to provide leadership, coaching and guidance to staff in fulfilling their responsibilities and building positive relationships.	• Determines necessary staffing levels and distribution of work • Interviews and selects candidates for hire • Ensures that staff receive orientation, training and development • Coordinates work schedules, reviews time sheets and approves leave requests • Assigns work and ensures that it is completed properly and in a timely manner • Monitors and manages performance, including the administration of corrective action • Ensures effective communication of information • Interprets and enforces policies and procedures

		• Reviews policies and procedures and recommends changes
Project/Program Management	The ability to plan, oversee and/or implement tasks resulting in projects or programs that are completed on time, within budget, and that meet or exceed expectations.	• Assesses needs, plans and implements programs or projects that are consistent with the library's mission, values, goals and objectives • Utilizes the library's tools, processes and models effectively, such as forms, statistics, guidelines, etc. • Evaluates programs and projects for effectiveness • Provides written and oral reports on both routine and special projects • Participates in or leads project specific teams or performs special tasks
Resource Management	The ability to effectively allocate or use resources to meet library goals and objectives, including risk assessment, cost/benefit analysis and the justification of expenditures.	• Determines core and non-core programs and services • Manages or uses human, financial and physical resources to maximize results • Establishes prudent budgets • Develops strategic plans and establishes long and short range goals • Involves staff appropriately in planning, decision making and problem solving

V-CAT ADMINISTRATOR/TECHNOLOGY COORDINATOR

Wisconsin Valley Library Service
Wausau, Wisconsin

Definition of Position

The V-CAT Administrator/Technology Coordinator is responsible for administrating the integrated library system; coordinating WVLS' technology efforts in cooperation with WVLS Tech Team members and program managers; maintaining the V-CAT Informational web site; and maintaining and managing a mission-critical WAN with 32 service outlets (currently using Unix/Windows servers, Cisco products). The V-CAT Administrator/Technology Coordinator is supervised by the Director and is responsible for reporting regularly to the Director.

Responsibilities/Examples of Work

(The list below is intended to describe the general content of and major responsibilities for performance of the position. It is not intended to be an exhaustive statement of job duties or requirements.)

- Serve as administrator of the V-CAT shared automation system and coordinate V-CAT operations.

- Assist the Migration Committee in defining system needs for future growth and development.
- Draft annual V-CAT budgets and present to the V-CAT Council and WVLS Board of Trustees.
- Oversee the development and installation of recommended computer configurations to optimize V-CAT Council member libraries' use of the library automation software.
- Recommend, plan and coordinate upgrades to the library automation software.
- Prepare information packets for V-CAT Council, Migration Committee, and Network Committee meetings.
- Attend V-CAT Council, Migration Committee, and Network Committee meetings and present information and reports as necessary.
- Work with the WVLS Tech Team, V-CAT Council and Network Committee to ensure the security of data
- Redesign and maintain the V-CAT Informational web site.
- Coordinate the installation, configuration, maintenance, and diagnostic support for network.
- Monitor servers, network bandwidth and network hardware for health and security.
- Recommend network enhancements of potential benefit to V-CAT Council, WAN members and Director for consideration.
- Work with WVLS Tech Team, WVLS Network Committee and outside consultants to ensure optimal network design and maximum uptime.
- Visit libraries and attend local library board meetings as necessary.
- Represent system and V-CAT Council at state-level and national-level meetings.
- Work with WVLS staff to support system programs and services.
- Write proposals and grants for technology projects.
- Negotiate V-CAT/WAN-related contracts with vendors.
- Regularly engage in activities that promote professional development.
- Perform other duties as assigned.

Knowledge and Abilities

- Considerable knowledge of automated systems, computer applications, telecommunication networks, databases and search methods.
- Ability to understand library policies and procedures and apply them to the WVLS operation.
- Ability to install, maintain and troubleshoot hardware, software and peripherals.
- Ability to read, analyze and interpret general periodicals, professional journals, and technical procedures.
- Ability to effectively present information in non-technical terms and respond to questions/concerns from WVLS staff, library staff, trustees and other members of the library community.
- Professional, upbeat manner and a sense of humor.
- Commitment to quality, accuracy and efficiency.
- Strong initiative, self-directed, energetic.
- Strong customer service orientation and skills.
- Ability to work comfortably, patiently, and helpfully with people whose computer skills range from negligible to advanced.
- Ability to work in a collaborative, team-oriented environment.
- Ability to perform assigned tasks with minimal supervision.
- Willingness to maintain skills in above mentioned areas through active participation in continuing education activities.
- Valid Wisconsin driver's license, means of transportation, and willingness to travel.
- Willingness to work flexible hours, including some evenings or weekends and perform emergency tasks during off-hours.

Education and Experience

- Master's Degree in Library Science or an equivalent combination of education and experience.
- Bachelor's Degree in Computer Science, Information Systems or a related field or equivalent combination of education and experience.
- Three years experience managing wide area networks and local area networks preferred.
- Experience managing a library automation system, including SirsiDynix Horizon software, desirable
- Knowledge of web site design principles and practical experience designing/creating web sites required. Experience in the use of Microsoft Expression Web 2.0 preferred.
- Familiarity with variety of automation software products and service options is highly desirable.
- Experience in training people in computer applications desirable.
- Experience working in a multi-institutional environment desirable.

Mental Requirements

- Analytical skills: resolve novel and diverse work problems on a daily basis; identify problems and potential areas for improvement; utilize available information sources in decision making; develop feasible, realistic solutions to problems; able to deal with abstract and concrete variables.
- Planning and organizational skills: develop long-range plans and establish methods for accomplishing goals.
- Communication skills: effectively communicate ideas and information both in written and oral forms and in Standard English.
- Reading ability: effectively read and understand information contained in professional resources, memoranda, reports and bulletins.
- Mathematical ability: calculate basic arithmetic problems [addition, subtraction, multiplication, division] without the aid of a calculator; ability to compute rate, ratio, percentage, and to draw and interpret bar graphs; ability to work with mathematical concepts such as probability and statistical inference.
- Time management: manage multiple projects, set priorities and meet project and assigned deadlines.

Physical Demands

- While performing the duties of this job, the employee is occasionally required to: sit; use hands to write, grasp and keyboard; talk; hear; stand, kneel and crouch; walk and reach with hands and arms; and, lift and/or move up to 50 pounds.
- Specific vision abilities required for this job include close vision, distance vision, color vision, depth perception, and ability to adjust focus.
- Ability to work in confined spaces.

Work Environment

- Heated and air conditioned office environment. Noise level is usually low to moderate.
- Works in close proximity to computer terminals and electronic equipment.
- Flexible work hours, including some nights and weekends.
- Requires travel.

Chapter 37

LIBRARIANS

ADULT AND ELECTRONIC SERVICES LIBRARIAN

Wasilla Public Library
Wasilla, Alaska

Job Title: Adult and Electronic Services Librarian

Department: Library

Reports To: Library Director

Classification: Non-Exempt

Summary: Assists with the planning, coordination and delivery of adult services, including circulation, reference and readers advisory programs. Coordinates duties with other staff to deliver quality public library service.

Scope and Accountability: Coordinates with network support staff to plan and maintain integration of automated and electronic resources with traditional library operations and services. Provides training for staff and public on use of library resources, including online catalog, CD-ROM materials, the Internet and other electronic resources. Acts as second in command of the library staff. The Adult and Electronic Services Librarian will become the acting Library Director in the absence of the Library Director. Supervises one full time employee and four part time employees. Responsible for scheduling employees under the supervision of the Adult and Electronic Services Librarian. Works with the Children's Librarian to set shift schedules. Responsible for employee evaluations under the supervision of the Adult and Electronic Services Librarian.

Essential Functions: The responsibilities listed below are illustrative of the various types of duties that may be performed with or without reasonable accommodation.

- Provides reference and reader advisory services to public.
- Develops, implements, and/or coordinates training on audiovisual equipment, computer equipment and applications for staff and public with adherence to established policies and procedures with minimal impact on daily operations and public service.
- Evaluates automation applications and innovations for libraries, recommending changes, long-range plans, and upgrades in accordance with community needs.
- Serves as liaison and single point of contact with automation and equipment vendors and with network support staff.
- Troubleshoots and arranges repair of computer hardware, software applications, telecommunications equipment, peripherals and audiovisual equipment.
- Manages the maintenance of computer hardware/software and audiovisual equipment preparing reports, adhering to required procedures.
- Works with other libraries and agencies to cost-effectively enhance access to resources and to maintain efficient use of hardware/software.
- Performs all functions related to circulation of library material according to established policies and procedures.
- Coordinates access to community resource information, including Internal Revenue Service forms, voter registration forms, and community schedules.

- Develops and evaluates policies and procedures designed for effective information services and technology applications for use by staff and public.

Secondary Functions:

- Recommends additions, deletions, reclassification and circulation of print and non-print material for library collection development based upon use of the existing collection and public needs.
- Seeks continuing education opportunities for self and staff related to information services delivery within limits of available time and funds.
- Coordinates reviews, and stores material for the annual book sale sponsored and organized by the Friends of the Library.
- Assists in evaluating library interns/volunteers on performing their job duties.
- Perform other duties and special projects as assigned.

Knowledge, Skills, and Abilities: Bachelor's Degree required. Master's Degree, Library Science desirable.

DIGITAL INITIATIVES LIBRARIAN

The University of Toledo
Ward M. Canaday Center for Special Collections,
University of Toledo Libraries

This position is a full-time tenure track position that holds the rank of Assistant Professor of Library Administration.

Primary Duties:

The Digital Initiatives Librarian will have a primary assignment in the Ward M. Canaday Center to develop, manage, and expand the digital collections of the Canaday Center. This position will also serve as the lead position for digital initiatives for the University Libraries and represent The University of Toledo regarding OhioLINK's Digital Resource Commons and regional collaborations. The position will also consult with other university constituencies on developing and managing digital assets, including the Mulford Library on UT's Health Sciences Campus.

Duties will include creating and managing digital collections based upon existing paper-based collections of the Canaday Center, including University Archives; helping to set policies and priorities regarding digital collections; establishing best practices and procedures for the production and management of digital content; and working with other university constituencies to support the development of digital collections and manage content. Individual will be responsible for the content development and management of Toledo's Attic, a virtual museum of 20th century Toledo history, in cooperation with the other community partners. This includes working closely with WGTE Public Broadcasting, which provides the technical support for the project.

Working with the University Archivist, this position will also take the lead in coordinating initiatives related to the management and preservation of the university's electronic records, including providing guidance on issues such as authenticity, reliability, trustworthiness, and digital preservation. Position will recommend policies to ensure long-term preservation and access to university electronic records of historical value in accordance with state public records laws and professional best practice. This position will oversee UT's participation in OhioLINK's Digital Resource Commons, including the creation and maintenance of metadata records in coordination with the Technical Services Department.

As a faculty position, the individual will meet the requirements for appointment as an assistant professor and the requirements for a tenure-track position as stated in the UT-AAUP Collective Bargaining Agreement.

Required:

Master's degree in library or information science from an ALA-accredited program with specialized training or experience in archives administration.

Preferred:

Specialized training in archives administration ALA-accredited program. Experience in archives administration. Experience in managing digital collections and/or managing electronic records desirable.

DIGITAL PROJECTS LIBRARIAN

University of Notre Dame
Hesburgh Library
Notre Dame, Indiana

Responsibilities

The primary job responsibilities include:
- Writing documentation for requirements, standards, portal protocols, portal architecture, instructions for participating libraries, and "about the portal."
- Planning the implementation schedule for future development.
- Communicating project activities to participating libraries, CRRA committee members, and project sponsors.
- Training and instructing on the creation of Encoded Archival Description (EAD) files to participating libraries based on current best practices as well as CRRA metadata standards, requirements, and protocols.
- Serving as a member of Team Catholic Portal.

The successful candidate will initially be appointed for a two year term with every expectation that the position will become ongoing. The individual will be housed in the Digital Access and Information Architecture Department and administratively report to the Head of the Department. Team Catholic Portal is responsible for the overall management of the portal.

Environment

The CRRA is a collaborative effort initiated by eight Catholic colleges and universities to share their resources electronically with librarians, archivists, researchers, scholars interested in the Catholic experience, and the general public. The CRRA was founded by the libraries at Boston College, The Catholic University of America, Georgetown University, Marquette University, University of Notre Dame, Seton Hall University, University of San Diego and St. Edward's University. More information as well as a demonstration portal is accessible at http://www.catholicresearch.net/. On behalf of the CRRA, the University of Notre Dame serves as the current secretariat where the project staff will be housed.

The University of Notre Dame is a highly selective national Catholic teaching and research university located in South Bend, Indiana. Approximately 8,200 undergraduates and 3,100 graduate students pursue a broad range of studies. The Hesburgh Libraries hold about 3 million volumes and provide access to the content of about 60,000 serials. The Libraries have approximately 140 staff and 55 librarians. The Libraries are a member of the Academic Libraries of Indiana, the Association of Research Libraries, INCOLSA, the Michiana Academic Library Consortium, the Center for Research Libraries, and the North East Research Libraries.

The University of Notre Dame is open to and enriched by the presence of diverse scholars. As such, we welcome and encourage applications and nominations from women and minorities.

Qualifications

ALA-accredited master's degree in library, archival and/or information science, or appropriate equivalent. Knowledge of metadata and archival encoding standards, including but not limited to EAD, MARC, XML, and Dublin Core. Analytical and organizational skills such as meeting deadlines, setting priorities, etc. A demonstrated ability to work collaboratively and train others is critical. An understanding of the importance of rare and archival special collections is desirable. Evidence of critical thinking and excellent oral and written communication skills are required.

DIGITAL RESOURCES LIBRARIAN

University of Wyoming
University of Wyoming Libraries
Laramie, Wyoming

RESPONSIBILITIES:

The Digital Resources Librarian will coordinate a broad range of digital activities and projects that combine traditional library activities with digital initiatives. Create, integrate, and ensure long-term access to digitized information services and resources that support the teaching, learning, and research missions of the University of Wyoming. Collaborate with the university community to develop policies and procedures for management of the University's digital intellectual output, and the digital conversion of library and archival collections. Work with various partners to build an Institutional Repository of scholarly digital materials. Function as the library authority for digital library issues and technologies, and coordinate with the appropriate library departments during digital project implementation. Maintain best practice documentation for all areas of digitization. Develop and oversee grant applications to fund digital projects. Pursue an active and ongoing program of professional development, scholarship, and service. Supervise one staff position and non-benefitted student positions. Report to the Head of Library Systems.

REQUIRED: MLS from an ALA accredited institution; minimum five years professional experience; demonstrated ability in the development and management of digital collections and knowledge of current digital library technologies, standards, and best practices; familiarity with current trends in the conversion of analog to digital resources, born-digital resources, and the long term management and preservation of digital objects; knowledge of current metadata schemes; experience with digital asset management systems; excellent interpersonal, organizational, communication and presentation skills; strong leadership skills, including creativity and initiative in planning and facilitating projects; experience collaborating with librarians and a variety of information technology professionals on complex projects; strong customer service orientation.

PREFERRED: Experience in an academic library; experience in systems administration, analysis and/or management; experience in public service and/or user education; experience with grant writing and solicitation; experience with digital archival methodology and best practices.

Digital Services Librarian

Tulane University
Howard-Tilton Memorial Library
New Orleans, Louisiana

Job description:

Howard-Tilton Memorial Library seeks a creative, dynamic librarian to serve as Digital Services Librarian.

RESPONSIBILITIES: The Digital Services Librarian is an innovative and service-oriented librarian who takes overall responsibility for the Library's main website, including oversight of content and design; plans future redesigns and innovations to the site; engages in usability testing and other assessments of the website; and coordinates and facilitates the development of access to web content and services from library departments. The librarian works closely with a Web Steering Committee comprised of representatives from units around the library, and supervises a full-time web programmer. This librarian also coordinates digitization projects library-wide, setting standards for the creation of content and metadata, and represents the library to other groups around campus and the region engaged in the creation of digital collections. Reporting to the Director of Public Services, the librarian shares reference duties with other librarians and participates in the library's instruction program. The librarian may also participate in collection development.

REQUIREMENTS: ALA-accredited MLS or equivalent; knowledge and experience with web design, metadata, and information architecture; some web coding and programming experience such as PHP, JavaScript, XHTML, and CSS; background in developing digital initiatives such as archival projects or database-backed dynamic websites; working knowledge of metadata standards such as Dublin Core as well as digital preservation standards; working knowledge of relevant Web 2.0 technologies for digital content delivery; skill in translating student and faculty needs into web functions; experience in assisting library users with online resources in an academic library; knowledge of current copyright and licensing issues; project management skills; potential for leadership in a collaborative setting; effective communication and teaching skills; enthusiasm for an innovative and changing environment; willingness to participate in professional development and in the shared governance of the library and the university.

PREFERRED: One year or more of post-MLS experience. Experience with ColdFusion and/or CommonSpot content management system. Experience with library instruction, outreach, and reference services. Familiarity with collection development in an academic library.

ENVIRONMENT: Tulane University is an AAU/Carnegie Research I institution with its main campus located in picturesque uptown New Orleans. Howard-Tilton Memorial Library is the university's main library, an ARL research collection supporting programs in the humanities, social sciences, and the sciences. Recently, the library has been reorganizing, building its collections, and developing an architectural plan for expanded library facilities. The library is also engaging in a website redesign which includes migration to the university's content management system. During this period of dynamic change, the library seeks to build its professional staff by recruiting talented, energetic librarians interested in participating in the recovery of Tulane and New Orleans.

Tulane University is an ADA/AA/EO employer. Women, minorities and veterans are encouraged to apply.

DIGITAL TECHNOLOGY/REFERENCE LIBRARIAN

Kettering University
Kettering University Library
Flint, Michigan

Required Qualifications:

- Master's Degree in Library Science (MLS) or Information Science.
- Demonstrated knowledge of evolving information technology and digital content to include Web design, online databases, and vendor software.
- Ability to analyze and assess the usage and effectiveness of electronic resources and technologies.
- Knowledge of methods for designing, integrating, and improving digital services in support of library users.
- Demonstrated experience utilizing strong human relations skills as well as analytical and conceptual skills to handle the duties of this position.
- Demonstrated effective interpersonal, verbal and written communication skills.
- Demonstrated flexibility and the ability to work independently as well as in a team environment where consultation, collaboration, and cooperation are essential.
- Willingness to work flexible hours, including nights and weekends.

Preferred Qualifications:

Experience with SirsiDynix automation system preferred.

Job Duties:

- Collaborate with library staff and university faculty on the development of digital technology and digital content.
- Design, update, and maintain library digital initiatives including blogs, wikis, web pages, RSS feeds, and digital image databases.
- Analyze and assess the usage and effectiveness of electronic resources and technologies.
- Conduct hands-on leadership and training in the use of library electronic databases and other technology.
- Research, evaluate, test, and recommend methods, standards and software used in the creation of digital collections.
- Assist with vendor pricing and licensing agreements for digital content.
- Prepare necessary documentation and reports relating to digital collections.
- Collaborate and serve as a member of the Reference Team by performing public services duties at the reference desk.
- Instruct and assist library patrons in the use of electronic resources and the application of digital content in teaching, learning, and research.
- Perform other duties as assigned.

ELECTRONIC RESOURCES LIBRARIAN

Montana State University Bozeman
Montana State University Libraries
Bozeman, Montana

Departmental Information:

Montana State University, the state's land-grant institution, is located at Bozeman in the beautiful Gallatin Valley of southwestern Montana, 90 miles north of Yellowstone National Park. The University has an enrollment of over 12,000 students and an emphasis in agriculture, engineering, and the sciences. MSU has 14 doctoral programs, 40 masters programs, and is recognized by the Carnegie Foundation as one of 96 top tier universities with very high research activity. Montana State University Libraries is committed to providing and promoting information resources to ensure student and faculty success. We value team-work, creativity, and an entrepreneurial spirit. Our librarians are leaders in university affairs as well as within state, regional, and national library communities.

The MSU Libraries plays an integral role in the teaching, research, and outreach missions of the University. With 21 faculty and professionals, 31 staff, and 27 student employees, we are committed to providing optimal information access and delivery through both traditional and electronic formats to patrons on and off-campus. The Libraries' collections include over 730,000 volumes, 9,700 serial subscriptions, and nearly 7,000 DVDs and videos. The Libraries is positioned to continue to move forward in a dynamic electronic, team-oriented environment.

Duties and Responsibilities:

MSU Libraries seeks an Electronic Resources Librarian who is responsible for managing and negotiating subscriptions to electronic resources. This position provides leadership and expertise in the evaluation, selection, promotion, and accessibility of electronic resources, especially serials. This person will work with OpenURL linking technologies, budgeting, and consortia agreements. The Electronic Resources Librarian is a member of the Information Resources Development Team and collaborates with library staff and faculty as well as faculty across campus. Additional opportunities may include staff supervision, liaison responsibilities, reference desk, and instruction duties. Library faculty are expected to meet the research and service requirements for promotion and tenure. We seek an innovative, detail-oriented, dynamic individual who can provide leadership in planning, organizing, implementing, and supporting ongoing access to electronic resources within the Libraries and the University.

Required Qualifications:

1. Masters degree from an ALA (American Library Association) accredited graduate program.
2. Demonstrated familiarity with electronic serial linking technologies.
3. Demonstrated analytical, organizational, time, and project management skills.
4. Knowledge of vendors, publishers, and library consortia.

Preferred Qualifications:

1. Experience managing electronic resources.
2. Experience in academic libraries.
3. Experience with subscription vendors (e.g. EBSCO, Blackwell, etc.).

4.   Familiarity with EDI and electronic resources management technologies.
5.   Experience with budgeting and serials invoicing.
6.   Experience with negotiation contracts and licenses.
7.   Familiarity using relational databases.

INFORMATION TECHNOLOGY/INTERLIBRARY LOAN/REFERENCE LIBRARIAN

Town of Williston
Dorothy Alling Memorial Library
Williston, Vermont

JOB SUMMARY:

The Information Technology/Interlibrary Loan/Reference Librarian, under the direction of the Library Director and Assistant Director, is responsible for maintaining the library computer network and training staff and patrons in its use. This position also provides interlibrary loan service and maintains the reference collection and assists patrons with reference queries. This position oversees the circulation desk in the absence of the Circulation Librarian.

DUTIES INCLUDE BUT ARE NOT LIMITED TO:

-   Assists library patrons before other duties
-   Maintains the computer network, including working with vendors and/or consultants, and arranges outside technical assistance if necessary
-   Provides instruction in the use of library resources and technologies to groups and individuals
-   Orders and installs new technology equipment
-   Resolves technical problems for staff and patrons
-   Maintains the library web site and electronic newsletter
-   Assists Director with technology planning & upgrades
-   Provides staff training in library technology and electronic resources
-   Stays abreast of new technologies and suggests ways of integrating technology with traditional library services
-   Provides reference services to patrons and instructs staff in the use of reference resources including online information
-   Maintains and updates the reference collection
-   Oversees the circulation desk in the absence of the circulation librarian
-   Provides Interlibrary Loan services, including borrowing and lending materials using the VALS (Vermont Automated Library System) database, OCLC and other resources
-   Attends workshops and keeps abreast of changes in library science
-   Assumes additional duties as required

PHYSICAL REQUIREMENTS:

Must be able to carry 30 lb. boxes.

EDUCATION AND EXPERIENCE:

A Bachelor's degree in the Liberal Arts and an MLS from an ALA accredited library program is preferred, otherwise a Vermont Certificate of Librarianship or in active pursuit thereof. Public library experience preferred. Knowledge of information technology and library automation systems, excellent communication skills, and an ability to work well with people of all ages is required.

INFORMATION RESOURCES LIBRARIAN

University of Washington
University of Washington Libraries
Seattle, Washington

Job description:

Among the largest academic research libraries in North America, the University of Washington Libraries has a collection of more than seven million cataloged volumes, an equal number in microform format, more than 50,000 serial titles, and several million items in other formats. Students and faculty recognize the value provided by the Libraries and rank the Libraries as the most important source of information for their work. The Libraries also receives the highest satisfaction rating of any academic service on the surveys of graduating seniors conducted by the Office of Educational Assessment.

THE UNIT:

Collection Management Services (CMS) provides leadership and support for the development and management of the Libraries' information resources. The unit coordinates the development of Libraries-wide selection policies and strategies, and interprets and helps to implement them in daily operations. CMS fosters cooperative collection development within the UW Libraries and beyond it, and manages the Libraries' consortia purchasing relationships.

THE POSITION:

Under the general direction of the Director, Information Resources and Scholarly Communication, works in a team environment within CMS to provide support for collection and electronic resource management activities. Key position responsibilities will include stewardship of the Libraries' electronic resource usage data, gathering and presentation of other quantitative information, management of license information, and support and assistance in managing information resources in various formats.

SPECIFIC RESPONSIBILITIES AND DUTIES:

- Coordinates and manages intake and reporting of electronic resource usage data from multiple sources, and is responsible for integrity and organization of usage data archive and supporting documentation.
- Works with other CMS staff to obtain, analyze, and present quantitative information to support budget allocation and selection work, and for general informational purposes; assists in collection of data to respond to surveys, such as those from ARL and other professional organizations; utilizes the Innovative Interfaces ILS to provide collection management information for subject liaisons/selectors and others, and assists in developing related training and support materials.

- Assists in the management of licensing and license files. Assists in reviewing proposed vendor/publisher license terms, identifying problem areas for follow-up and negotiation; mark-up and input license details into Innovative Interfaces E-Resource Module; manages digitizing of license documents and digitized files in D-space repository; contributes to policies and procedures for management of licenses and license information.
- Provides general support for electronic resources, including administrative configurations and profiling, troubleshooting access and data problems, and supporting pre-purchase review, such as organizing trials and gathering pricing and product information.
- Supervises student assistant(s). Manages recruitment, hiring, and ongoing procedures such as timekeeping and budgets. In consultation with other librarians in CMS, assigns responsibilities, provides training and oversees activity.
- Responds to user purchase requests received through the Libraries' gateway, initiating order requests and/or contacting subject liaisons/selectors according to unit guidelines.
- In consultation with other CMS staff, manages and contributes to the ongoing development of the CMS web pages and the related "Selectors' Portal." Assists the Collection Development Librarian in creating and maintaining subject web pages for Comparative Religion, General International Studies, and Latin American Studies.
- Contributes to Innovative Interfaces staff training as needed for Millennium Acquisitions overview, Millennium Create Lists, and Millennium Electronic Resource Management.
- According to interests and background, may perform activities in one or more of the following areas: research and instructional services; subject liaison/selector for one or more subject areas; monographic or serials acquisitions support.
- Assumes other responsibilities as assigned; performs other duties as required.

QUALIFICATIONS:

Required:
- Graduate degree from a program accredited by the American Library Association or an equivalent graduate library science/information studies degree.
- Demonstrated commitment to diversity and understanding of the contributions a diverse workforce brings to the workplace.
- Minimum of one year successful post-MLS professional experience supporting electronic resources in an academic or research library.
- Experience with an integrated library system.
- Proficiency in using a variety of software, including spreadsheets and databases (MS-Excel and MS-Access).
- Excellent communication, interpersonal, organizational and analytical skills; ability to present information clearly and succinctly to a variety of audiences.
- Ability to function well in a changing environment, work effectively within a large organization, and exercise initiative in a collaborative framework.

Preferred:
- Experience with Innovative Interfaces integrated library system.
- Demonstrated strong quantitative skills and interests.
- Experience analyzing usage data of digital resources.
- Direct experience working with publishers/providers of electronic resources.
- Knowledge of licensing, rights management, or other intellectual property issues.

The University of Washington, an Equal Opportunity and Affirmative Action Employer, is building a culturally diverse staff and strongly encourages applications from female and minority candidates.

In compliance with the Immigration Reform and Control Act of 1986, the University is required to verify and document the citizenship or employment authorization of each new employee.

INFORMATION SERVICES LIBRARIAN

Ames Public Library
Ames, Iowa

Immediate Supervisor:

Library Information Services Coordinator

Position Description:

Under the direction of the Library Information Services Coordinator, plays a lead role in the development and management of the library's electronic services; performs professional library tasks including reference services; adult readers' advisory and programming that support the mission of the library; assists the IT Systems Administrator as needed.

JOB FUNCTIONS:

Examples of Essential Job Functions: Develops the library's electronic services including databases, blogs, wikis, and other current and emerging technologies. Develops and manages the electronic resources budget. Develops and maintains a budget for non-print collections. In collaboration with other staff members, identifies, evaluates, selects and maintains the library's non-print collection. Identifies, evaluates, selects and maintains other areas of the library collection as assigned.

Provides reference and readers' advisory services to the public in person, by telephone, fax, correspondence, and via the Internet using a wide array of resources including print and electronic sources, people, organizations, government and other agencies. Assists in planning, presenting and evaluating library programs. Evaluates information and service needs of library customers through the development and application of appropriate needs assessment methodologies. Makes changes in services or policies as appropriate based on data collected. Has responsibility for reading professional journals for selection of materials.

Performs senior staff duties on a regular basis including responsibility for building safety and security, responding to emergencies, and interpreting library policy and procedure for the staff and public. Researches and analyzes trends in library services, collections, and programs. Participates in library-wide problem-solving; develops and reviews policies, strategic planning, service programs, and collections. Participates in library-wide public relations and marketing efforts. Participates in professional organizations and continuing education activities.

Other professional duties include producing reports, grant applications, newspaper columns, bibliographies; promoting collections and services; leading and facilitating library-sponsored book groups and programs; teaching information literacy skills to customers and staff through classes, tutorials, and individual instruction. Full job description at the following link: Job Description.

EMPLOYMENT STANDARDS:

Education and Experience: Master's degree in library science from an ALA accredited institution.
Licenses and Certificates: Eligible for Professional Librarian certification by the State of Iowa.

Knowledge, Abilities and Skills:

Extensive knowledge of the philosophy and principles of public library services, intellectual freedom, library materials and collections, policies and procedures. Knowledge of the principles of public relations and promotion.

Skill in oral and written communication. Skill in training staff, volunteers, and customers. Skill in customer service. Skill in creative problem solving. Skill in developing search strategies and in using Internet search engines and other reference tools.

Knowledge of integrated library systems, Microsoft Office Suite, HTML and web-editing software. Strong commitment to customer service and information access. Demonstrated commitment to continuous improvement and professional development.

Ability to develop curriculum and to teach information literacy skills. Ability to tolerate ambiguity. Ability to evaluate the effectiveness of library collections, services, and programs. Ability to initiate and implement new services and programs. Ability to be proactive in problem solving and trouble-shooting. Ability to assess and prioritize multiple tasks, projects and deadlines. Ability to develop effective relationships with co-workers, fellow City employees, and the public.

City of Ames—Excellence Through People (ETP):

Employees must continually strive to bring shared values to life, through our Excellence Through People organizational culture. Values include continuous improvement, respect for others, customer focused, data-driven decisions, positive attitude, teaming environment, creativity, and employee involvement. ETP assures that exceptional services are delivered to the public and employees experience an enjoyable and stimulating work environment.

LIBRARY SERVICES LIBRARIAN FOR TECHNICAL SERVICES

University of Massachusetts Boston
Joseph P. Healey Library
Boston, Massachusetts

Job Description:

The Digital Library Services Librarian for Technical Services assumes overall responsibility for digital library services metadata development, cataloging, and quality control policy development and maintenance in coordination with Fenway Library Online (FLO) standards and expectations. The incumbent trains, supervises, and develops all primary technical services functions in a network environment with FLO in accordance with new developing modes to acquire, access, and store information resources. This position is part of the Digital Library Services (DLS) management team which coordinates departmental policies, procedures and workflows, including technical services and how DLS functions related to other library operations and services, particularly Reference Outreach and Instruction. The incumbent supports access to Healey Library's print and digital collections, including e-journals, e-books, blogs, pod-casts, 3-D images, virtual environments, and other web content as selected by faculty, librarians, and other stakeholders. S/he also assists in the development and maintenance of the library's web portal. The incumbent works in coordination with the Acquisitions Coordinator and the Electronic Resources Librarian to ensure efficient and effective delivery of electronic resources to the campus community, and to develop and provide access to information and materials that support research and public needs and meet the outreach goals of the Library. S/he participates in preparing grant submissions for additional projects and maintains statistics and produces monthly reports.

Requirements:

ALA-accredited masters level degree in library or information science, or its equivalent is required. Minimum two years relevant experience in a library, museum, archive or information center, including experience with evolving standards of cataloging e-books and other electronic resources, issues related to the loading and integration of MARC records. Knowledge of current cataloging rules and standards, relational database management, and use of technology in a technical services library environment. Knowledge of cataloging operations for all formats, LC and Dewey classification schemes, authority and subject heading systems, and the use of bibliographic utilities. Evidence of supervisory experience. Demonstrated successful project management experience.

Demonstrated ability to participate in a team environment to create innovative cataloging workflows that contribute to quality customer service. Evidence of innovation using emerging information technologies, including the ability to develop concepts from idea to implementation. Demonstrated familiarity and experience with integrated library systems (i.e. Voyager, ExLibris) and metadata schemas and tools (such as MARC, TEI, EAD, DC or OAI/PMH, XML, Dublin Core, MODS, METS, etc.). Ability to work collaboratively with faculty, librarians, staff, students and administrators. Familiarity with relational database management structures and SQL queries.

LICENSING AND INFORMATION CONTENT LIBRARIAN

University of Texas at Arlington
University of Texas at Arlington Libraries
Arlington, Texas

Purpose of position:

To develop, assess, & manage the collections & electronic resources in support of teaching & research in assigned subject disciplines (business). Serves as primary negotiator of licenses for new electronic resources in all disciplines.

Essential functions:

Reviews & negotiates vendor licenses for potential new digital resources using guidelines from the UT System. Reviews existing agreements to align to current needs & best practices. Serves as resource person on use of database content. Identifies & selects resources for purchase or lease in assigned subjects. Works closely with subject liaison librarians in assigned areas. Works with vendors to establish trials for electronic products under consideration. Determines budget priorities, allocates funds & monitors expenditures in assigned disciplines. Establishes, monitors & refines approval plan profiles; creates & maintains policy statements for each discipline. Uses quantitative & qualitative measures to assess existing collections & to determine utility to existing & planned degree programs & research interests. Participates in unit & library-wide planning, goal-setting & implementation of services; serves on library, university & professional committees & organizations. Monitors trends in publishing, serials, copyright & licensing; participates in unit planning & goal setting.

Marginal/Incidental functions:

Other functions as assigned.

Required qualifications:

American Library Association accredited Master's degree. 2 years post-MLS experience in an academic library. Competence with MS Office suite, especially Excel. Demonstrated ability to work independently & collaboratively. Excellent verbal & written communication skills. Applicants must include in their online resume the following information: 1) Employment history: name of company, period employed (from month/year to month/year), job title, summary of job duties and 2) Education: If no high school diploma or GED, list highest grade completed; If some college or college degree, list school name, degree type, major, graduated or not, and hours completed if not graduated. Finalist(s) will be asked to give a presentation on a library related topic. Equivalent combination of relevant education and experience may be substituted as appropriate.

Preferred qualifications:

Academic library experience working with electronic resources in acquisitions or collection management. Experience reviewing & negotiating licenses. Significant coursework in one or more of the assigned disciplines. Knowledge of emerging trends in publishing, scholarly communication & information delivery. Knowledge of principles of resource management & assessment in the digital environment.

Working conditions:

May work around standard office conditions. Repetitive use of a keyboard at a workstation. Use of manual dexterity. Lifting and moving. Security Sensitive; criminal background check conducted.

Occasional night or weekend work as needed to complete projects. Professional development and training may require some overnight travel.

MEDIA CATALOGING/METADATA LIBRARIAN

University of Washington
University of Washington Libraries
Seattle, Washington

Among the largest academic research libraries in North America, the University of Washington Libraries has a collection of more than six million cataloged volumes, an equal number in microform format, more than 50,000 serial titles, and a combined media collection of well over 27,000 items. Located on the Pacific Rim, the University has a great interest in Asia. The Libraries have significant collections in South and Southeast Asia, Near East, Slavic and Eastern Europe, Central Asia, and East Asia. As scholarship shifts from print to a broader range of formats for primary and secondary sources, the Libraries' media collections for these areas of the world are growing rapidly.

THE MONOGRAPHIC SERVICES DIVISION:

The Monographic Services Division is one of two technical services units within the Resource Acquisitions and Description/Information Technology Services department of the University of Washington Libraries. It acquires and catalogs monographs and integrating resources for the Seattle, Bothell and Tacoma campuses of the University. The Division handles a growing volume of non-book materials, in particular film and sound recordings, in a wide range of languages and scripts. It also creates digital collections, provides subject analysis and authority work for them, and plays a lead role in setting cataloging policy and in developing metadata standards and applications within the Libraries.

THE POSITION:

As a member of the Special Materials Cataloging Section, which functions as a self-managing unit of the Monographic Services Division, classifies and provides subject analysis for monographs in a variety of formats. Participates in the creation of metadata for digital collections using a variety of metadata schema.

SPECIFIC RESPONSIBILITIES AND DUTIES:

- Performs descriptive and subject cataloging and classification of monographs in non-book formats in all subject areas and languages, in particular for DVDs and VHS, using current Anglo-American Cataloging Rules, Library of Congress classification and subject headings and OCLC/MARC tagging, in accordance with local policies.
- Coordinates and performs cataloging of International Studies media materials. Contributes to the cataloging of media in languages with which the incumbent is not familiar, using team cataloging as necessary.
- Serves on the Metadata Implementation Group, helping organize and implement digital projects as needed. Implementation may involve the application of non-traditional metadata schema; the Libraries currently employs Dublin Core, EAD, and MARCXML, with work developing on other standards.
- Participates in all aspects of team management.
- When serving as a member of the division's Management Team, participates in the development, communication, implementation and evaluation of new policies and procedures. Cooperatively prepares reports, studies and surveys as required. Works with other team members to plan new initiatives, adjust staffing and workflow, and meet changing circumstances and goals. Assists and substitutes for the other team members when necessary.
- When serving as Personnel Coordinator of the section, conducts performance evaluations for one librarian and four library specialists; evaluates temporary staff as circumstances require; acts upon travel and leave requests.
- Serves as liaison between the Division and other library units as assigned to resolve cataloging problems or questions.
- Accepts responsibility for communication with coworkers and supervisors.
- Participates in library committees and meetings as appropriate.
- Performs other duties as assigned.

REQUIRED QUALIFICATIONS:

- Graduate degree from a program accredited by the American Library Association or an equivalent graduate library science/information studies degree.
- Demonstrated commitment to diversity and understanding of the contributions a diverse workforce brings to the workplace.
- Minimum of two years of experience cataloging using AACR2 and LCRI, MARC and LCSH.
- Experience cataloging media materials, specifically video and sound recordings.
- Knowledge of metadata standards, in particular Dublin Core.
- Ability to work in a self-managing section.
- Excellent oral and written communications skills. Analytic and problem-solving skills.
- Ability to work effectively with individuals and with groups. Ability to function well in a changing environment, to work effectively within a large organization, and to exercise initiative in a collaborative framework.
- Commitment to professional development and service.

PREFERRED QUALIFICATIONS:

- Reading knowledge of one or more foreign languages from among the Slavic languages, and/or Arabic, Persian, Turkish, Vietnamese, Thai, Indonesian, or Hindi.
- NACO, SACO or BIBCO experience.
- Work experience in a research library.
- Experience assigning metadata in Dublin Core or another non-MARC schema.

The University of Washington, an Equal Opportunity and Affirmative Action Employer, is building culturally diverse staff and strongly encourages applications from female and minority candidates.

In compliance with the Immigration Reform and Control Act of 1986, the University is required to verify and document the citizenship or employment authorization of each new employee.

METADATA LIBRARIAN

University of Miami
Otto G. Richter Library
Coral Gables, Florida

Job description:

The University of Miami Libraries seek a creative, enthusiastic professional for the position of Metadata Librarian. Reporting to the Head of Cataloging & Metadata Services, the Metadata Librarian provides leadership and guidance in the planning, development, creation, and implementation of metadata standards for the Libraries, and actively participates as a resource and liaison to the University community in regards to metadata practices.

THE UNIVERSITY: The University of Miami is one of the nation's leading research universities in a community of extraordinary diversity and international vitality. The University is privately supported, non-sectarian institution, located in Coral Gables, Florida, on a 260-acre subtropical campus. The University comprises 11 degree granting schools and colleges, including Architecture, Arts and Sciences, Business Administration, Communication, Education, Engineering, Law, Medicine, Music, Nursing, and Marine and Atmospheric Science (www.miami.edu).

THE LIBRARY: The University of Miami Libraries (www.library.miami.edu) ranks among the top 50 research libraries in North America with a combined collection of approximately 3 million volumes, 45,000 current serials, and over 29,000 E-journal titles. The University of Miami Libraries include, the Otto G. Richter Library which lies in the heart of the Gables campus, the Paul Buisson Architecture Library, the Judi Prokop Newman Business Information Resource Center, and the Marta & Austin Weeks Music Library, and the Marine and Atmospheric Science Library located at the Virginia Key campus. The campus also has an independent Medical and Law library. The Libraries provide support and services for approx. 10,100 undergraduates, 5,100 graduate students, and 10,000 full and part time faculty and staff. The Libraries has a staff of 37 Librarians and 86 support staff and is a member of ARL, ASERL, CLIR, NERL, OCLC, and SOLINET.

POSITION: Reporting to Head of Cataloging & Metadata Services and working collaboratively with all library units, the Metadata Librarian plays a major role in the Libraries' digital projects; is responsible for the creation of metadata for a variety of digital collections; serves as the local authority for metadata standards, keeping abreast of developments in metadata standards and practices; documents and implements adopted metadata standards, practices, and workflows; provides training to the Libraries' faculty and staff in metadata creation; participates in quality control activities for the Libraries' bibliographic and metadata repositories; works closely with the Digital Initiatives, Resources, and Services, and other stakeholders to plan digital collections and projects; networks, collaborates and actively participates in local, regional, national, or international organizations regarding issues in librarianship, metadata services, and the development of resource discovery tools and services; serves as the Libraries' metadata liaison to the University; serves on/participates in University and Libraries committees, task forces, and teams as appropriate.

QUALIFICATIONS: Required: Master's degree from an ALA accredited program or foreign equivalent, or Ph.D. with required library experience. Working knowledge and experience with two or more metadata schema and protocols such as Dublin Core, EAD, VRA Core, MODS, METS, etc.; Knowledge of cataloging rules, standards, and controlled vocabularies; awareness of current issues and trends in metadata and digital library development; demonstrated ability to work quickly and accurately in a service and production-oriented environment and adapt to a fast paced rapidly changing environment; ability to plan and implement routines and processes that ensure optimum production, and monitor projects through to completion in a cost-effective manner; demonstrated ability to work independently, as well as collaboratively with diverse constituencies; Effective oral, written and interpersonal communication skills.

Highly desirable: Experience with applying metadata standards to describe digital collections using CONTENTdm or other digital management system(s); Familiarity with related XML technology such as XSLT or XLINK; Familiarity with relational database structure; Experience with archives and archival practice; One year of experience in a medium to large research library or similar organization; Cataloging experience in an academic library; Reading knowledge of Spanish.

The University of Miami is an Equal Opportunity Affirmative Action Employer. The University has a strong commitment to diversity and encourages applications from candidates of diverse cultural backgrounds.

REFERENCE EMERGING TECHNOLOGIES LIBRARIAN

Coastal Carolina University
Kimbel Library
Conway, South Carolina

Job description:

Coastal Carolina University's Kimbel Library is seeking an energetic, innovative, and service-oriented librarian for a new position to lead the libraries' new technology initiatives. The Reference Emerging Technologies Librarian will serve as an explorer of, and champion for, the use of evolving and existing technologies as part of the Public Services Team and will participate in planning and implementing the new Learning Commons. He/she will collaborate with and support colleagues across Coastal Carolina University in discovering (or creating), assessing, and evaluating new digital learning materials to enhance the effectiveness of the libraries' instructional initiatives and of student learning.

Responsibilities: The Reference Emerging Technologies Librarian reports to the Head of Public Services to plan and direct the work of incorporating new and emerging technologies into the library services. He/she will take an active role in defining the new Learning Commons and will participate in planning and implementing this new facility. As part of the Reference team, he/she will participate in teaching and developing informational and instructional materials, reference, collection development and serve as a department liaison. Kimbel Library has a strong team environment and he/she will be expected to work collaboratively with all library departments on a wide variety of projects and library committees. The Reference Emerging Technologies Librarian will be expected to take a strong role in developing relationships with the Coastal

Carolina departments involved in the new Learning Commons. He/she will participate in the daily, nightly, and weekend reference desk rotation.

Required Qualifications:

- ALA-accredited master's degree in library or information science.
- Excellent interpersonal and communication skills.
- Ability to work in a team environment and with diverse clientele.
- Strong commitment to public service.
- Ability and interest in fulfilling tenure and promotion requirements for job performance, scholarship, professional development and service.

Preferred:

- Experience with technological applications including multi media technologies.
- Reference experience.
- Instructional experience.
- Demonstrated ability for problem solving.

Coastal Carolina University is a public mid-sized, comprehensive liberal arts-oriented institution. Coastal Carolina University is located in Conway, South Carolina, just nine miles from the Atlantic coastal resort Myrtle Beach, one of the fastest-growing metropolitan areas in the nation. It has an enrollment of 8,400 students and is expected to have continued growth for the next several years. Coastal Carolina University is a part of the South Carolina system of public education and has close ties with its founders, the Horry County Higher Education Commission.

Review of application materials will begin immediately and continue until the position is filled. Interested candidates should submit: a letter of application, curriculum vitae, and names and contact information for at least three (3) professional references electronically at: http://jobs.coastal.edu.

Coastal Carolina University is an EO/AA employer.

SYSTEMS LIBRARIAN

University of Texas at El Paso
University of Texas at El Paso Libraries
El Paso, Texas

Summary: Maintains the library's network stability and integrity.

Essential Duties and Responsibilities: include the following. Other duties may be assigned.

- Maintains the Local Area Network, computers, servers and related peripherals within the library.
- Delivers responsive services rapidly and effectively to meet the needs of library users and staff.
- Provides training associated with the introduction of new technologies.
- Provides quality PC hardware and software support; prepares user documentation.
- Performs system upgrades, new installations, backups, and distributes computer technology assets.
- Consults with other staff members regarding projects that involve existing computer technology or planned implementation of new technology and library systems.
- Participates in library-wide planning and policy development.
- Performs periodic maintenance of the library website to include updates, enhancements, and functionality.

- Tests and evaluates new electronic products.
- Participates in policy and procedure development for the use of networked microcomputers.
- Acts as liaison between internal/external customers and vendors.
- Serves on committees as needed.
- Complies with all State and University policies.

Qualifications: To perform this job successfully, an individual must be able to perform each essential duty satisfactorily. The requirements listed below are representative of the knowledge, skill, and ability required. Reasonable accommodations may be made to enable individuals with disabilities to perform the essential functions.

Education and Experience:

Master's in Library Science or master's degree within area of assigned responsibility; and one to two years related experience and training.

Communication Skills:

Ability to read, analyze, and interpret common scientific and technical journals, financial reports and legal documents. Ability to respond to common inquiries or complaints from customers, regulatory agencies, or members of the business community. Ability to effectively present information and respond to questions from groups of managers, clients, customers and the general public.

Mathematical Skills:

Ability to add, subtract, multiply, and divide in all units of measure, using whole numbers, common fractions, and decimals. Ability to compute rate, ratio, and percent.

Reasoning Ability:

Ability to solve practical problems and deal with a variety of concrete variables in situations where limited standardization exists. Ability to interpret a variety of Instructions in written, oral, diagram, or schedule form.

Computer Skills:

Preferred computer knowledge within area of assigned responsibility or the ability to learn.

Certificates, Licenses, Registrations:

Professional Certifications, Licenses, or Registrations within area of assigned responsibility preferred.

Other Qualifications:

Bilingual (English and Spanish) preferred. Occasional travel may be required.

Physical Demands:

The physical demands described here are representative of those that must be met by an employee to successfully perform the essential functions of this job. Reasonable accommodations may be made to enable individuals with disabilities to perform the essential functions.

While performing the duties of this job, the employee must frequently sit; use hands to feel; reach with hands and arms; and talk or hear. The employee must occasionally walk and stand; and climb or balance. The employee may occasionally lift and move up to 50 pounds.

Work Environment: The work environment characteristics described here are representative of those an employee encounters while performing the essential functions of this job. Reasonable accommodations may be made to enable individuals with disabilities to perform the essential functions.

The noise level in the work environment is usually quiet.

This position is security-sensitive and subject to Education Code §51.215, which authorizes the employer to obtain criminal history record information.

Lima Public Library
Lima, Ohio

Job Classification
Systems Librarian IV 40 hours per week

Minimum Qualifications

Master of Library Science or Information Science from an ALA Accredited program or comparable education/experience. Bachelor's degree or equivalent education/experience in computer science a strong plus. Ability to read, write, and follow oral and written instructions. An individual who may pose a direct threat to the health and/or safety of him/herself, staff, trustees, or the public in the work place will be considered not qualified for this position.

Required Knowledge, Skills and Abilities

Ability to: read and write effectively, and communicate in both written and oral form; work extensively with automated information in a detailed and accurate manner for extended periods of time. Knowledge of and interest in personal computers, printers, modem, and other hardware required. Analytical ability to assist staff with hardware and software problems. Ability to explain and train "non-technical" individuals in the effective use of all relevant systems. Above average manual dexterity to use computer key boards, repair hardware, and work with system peripherals. Ability to climb ladders, bend and stoop, and to lift and/or move computer equipment weighing 40 lbs. Ability to work with minimum supervision.

Responsibilities

Trouble shoots software and hardware problem systems wide for the Library's automated systems. Diagnoses technological problem and communicates problems to appropriate administrative level. Installs, maintains, and performs repairs on personal computers, terminals, printers and peripheral Performs system analysis on an on going basis. Works with the library automation staff, public service departments, library vendors, and software suppliers in a positive and pleasant manner. Advises Administration of system wide needs and concerns.

Typical Duties

- Performs a wide range of automated services duties.
- Supervises the daily operation of the computer system.

- Installs and trouble shoots new hardware/software, including telecommunications devices and data lines.
- Assists Department Heads with the selection and evaluation appropriate electronic resources.
- Assists Administrative Staff with purchase of compatible hardware, software, licensing and network agreements.
- Performs routine computer system functions, diagnostics, and maintenance routines.
- Generates and interprets statistical survey, and diagnostic and reports.
- Trains library staff and develops computer documentation and procedures.
- Develops mining components for patron use of resources.
- Assists automation staff, library vendors, and software providers with development and implementation programs, upgrades, and maintenance work.
- Maintains awareness of developments and trends in public service, library computer systems through professional journals, in service workshops, meetings conferences and training programs.
- Maintains various files and indices.
- Assists in public service as necessary.
- May serve as supervisor in the absence of a Department Head.
- Performs additional duties, as assigned.

(For additional policies, please see the accompanying CD-ROM.)

VIRTUAL LIBRARIAN

Naperville Public Library
Naperville, Illinois

INFORMATION TECHNOLOGY

Collaborates with the Webmaster to plan and develop library web applications to create a dynamic virtual library.

Explains, demonstrates, and assists patrons in the use of electronic resources including computer databases and the Internet, as well as print reference resources.

Utilizes and accesses information using a broad spectrum of resources (print, electronic, referral, etc.).

Builds consensus and communicates effectively with librarians and staff to collaboratively design and offer innovative Web and electronic services.

Maintains current knowledge of new and developing technologies, identifying new trends, tools, and practices, and their library applications.

Provides leadership, training, and guidance to staff and the public for online resources, as well as developing technologies.

Coordinates online reference services. Monitors online activities, assists with problems as necessary, and ensures superior public services.

Performs other related duties as assigned.

Performs functions for delivering web-based services and providing technical expertise in the selection, development, and implementation of new information technologies and their library applications. Also performs functions to assist library patrons, in person and virtually.

Under general direction:

VIRTUAL LIBRARIAN
- Collaborates with other staff to provide community development and outreach regarding our virtual services.
- Prepares statistics and reports for management review.
- Troubleshoots minor personal computer problems for patrons and staff.
- Uses personal computer and other common office equipment.
- Researches, recommends, and implements new and developing technologies such as IM, podcasting, and streaming audio/video.
- Assists with management of online materials and services and technology collection through recommendation of new library materials and services in traditional and electronic formats.

Chapter 38

SUPPORT STAFF

COMPUTER AND NETWORK TECHNICIAN

Public Library of Youngstown and Mahoning County
Youngstown, Ohio

Title: Computer and Network Technician

Purpose: Maintains computer equipment and networks to ensure optimum performance

Function: Under general supervision provides support for computer systems and networks of the Public Library of Youngstown and Mahoning County.

Typical Duties and Responsibilities:

- Configures and installs computer, peripheral and network equipment.
- Maintains security of systems by running antivirus software, deleting unused files, securing equipment to its location, and by other appropriate means.
- Troubleshoots computer hardware and software problems.
- Maintains hardware and software service, inventory and license records.
- Makes backup tapes and performs recovery of equipment and system failures.
- Provides technical support to staff in the use of computer systems.
- Assists staff in understanding operation of computer, peripheral and network equipment.
- Recommends hardware and software upgrades.

Required Skills and Abilities:

- Knowledge of current computing practices, standards and equipment
- Prior working experience with computers, peripherals and with Windows 95 and DOS
- Experience with Windows NT highly desired
- Ability to operate personal computers, networking equipment printers and barcode readers
- Ability to prepare accurate reports and to provide quick and innovative solutions to computing problems
- Knowledge of software diagnostic tools and their use
- Ability to remove and reinstall hardware components
- Ability to move heavy equipment (50 lbs) daily
- Ability to establish and maintain helpful and friendly atmosphere for computer and network support
- Ability to establish and maintain an effective working relationship with staff
- Employee training skills
- Good organization and time-management skills
- Good communication skills
- Ability to work with frequent interruptions
- Must be able to work some evenings and weekends and to be available on short notice to resolve problems
- Ability to drive a car and travel to different sites

Minimum Education and Experience:

- Course work in electronics and/or electrical engineering. Completion of 2-year technical school or 2-years of college or university credits in core subject area. One to two years prior computer, networking, telecommunications and/or electronic data processing experience.

Note: The preceding statements describe the nature and level of assignments normally given incumbents. They are not an exhaustive list of duties. Additional duties may be assigned.

COMPUTER EQUIPMENT TECHNICIAN

Cuyahoga County Public Library
Parma, Ohio

Reports To: Computer Hardware and Network Supervisor

General Summary:

Under general direction, performs computer equipment repair. Work involves installing, maintaining and repairing computer and data communications equipment throughout the library system. Worker troubleshoots, diagnoses, and repairs equipment; arranges for outside repairs as necessary; and oversees the work of contractors.

Essential Job Functions

(Note: The following functions represent the essential duties and outputs of the position.)
- Complies with work scheduling and attendance requirements according to reasonable policy and practices. Staffing for branch and regional libraries and some headquarters (HQS) departments requires rotational scheduling, which includes evening and weekend (Saturday & Sunday) hours. Most HQS departments are weekday operations.
- Installs computer equipment and devices such as terminals, keyboards, printers, desktop computers, and communications hardware; lays cables, installs connectors, assembles and tests equipment, installs software.
- Maintains and repairs equipment by tracing and diagnosing malfunctions, repairing or replacing components, adjusting settings, and testing equipment and communications hardware and networks for satisfactory operation.
- Uses electronic and computer test equipment, tools, supplies and materials.

Other Duties

(Duties listed are not intended to be all inclusive nor to limit duties that might reasonably be assigned.)
- Directs and inspects work done by contractors.
- Explains and demonstrates use of equipment to users.
- Maintains supply of spare parts and equipment.
- Maintains files on vendors, purchases and accounts.
- Contacts vendors regarding equipment and supply purchases.
- Maintains liaison with telephone company regarding data communications services.

Knowledge, Ability and Skills

(The following knowledge, abilities and skills (KASs) represent the KASs needed at time of appointment to perform Essential Job Functions.)

Knowledge of
- Electronic theory and practice as applied to the installation, maintenance and repair of computers and related equipment.
- Network communications hardware and systems.

Ability to

Install, troubleshoot, diagnose and repair computers and related equipment including network communications hardware and systems.

Skill in

Use of electronic and computer test equipment and tools of the trade.

Qualifications

(Note: Any acceptable combination of education, training and experience that provides the above KASs may be substituted for those listed.)

Education and Training:

Graduation from high school or possession of a GED certificate and completion of technical school training in electronics and computer repair.

Experience:

Two years of experience in the installation, maintenance and repair of computers and related equipment.

Licenses:

A valid Ohio Driver's license is required to operate library owned vehicles and a clean driving record must be maintained at all times.

Other:

Due to the physical exertion required to perform the essential duties of this job, the decision to hire is contingent on job candidate passing a pre-employment medical exam through a medical provider contracted by the library.

Work involves strenuous manual effort, exposure to electrical hazards, and worker is subject to emergency callbacks.

Exempt/Nonexempt: Position is nonexempt from FLSA.

COMPUTER SERVICES TECHNICIAN

Cumberland County Public Library
Carlisle, Pennsylvania

COMPUTER SERVICES TECHNICIAN (Library Systems) Position Description Grade 16 Non-Exempt

OVERALL OBJECTIVE OF JOB: To install, troubleshoot and diagnose hardware, software and network problems, and to serve as network administrator for local and wide area networks in the library system.

ESSENTIAL FUNCTIONS OF JOB: 1. Serves as network administrator for local and wide area networks for library and administrative functions. 2. Installs, troubleshoots and diagnoses personal computer and library network hardware. Provides hardware or network related maintenance. 3. Maintains Internet/Web server and NT server to ensure continuity of service. 4. Manages the library system's telecommunications hardware, including Internet connection. 5. Develops and maintains a System Policy and Procedures manual that documents server and network configurations, backup procedures, etc. 6. Serves as liaison between computer vendors and library system for hardware and network-related problems. 7. Maintains a hardware/software license inventory including hardware repair records for the library system. 8. Advises library system on emerging technologies; recommends cost saving alternatives. 9. Provides library staff with basic instruction on use of personal computers, hardware, software, networking, and computer security. 10. Coordinates and serves as primary public contact for hardware donations. 11. Advises library system on distribution, upgrading, and replacement of equipment.

OTHER DUTIES OF JOB: 1. Offers technical expertise to member libraries. 2. Represents the library system's computer hardware and software capabilities to county officials, the community and other libraries. 3. Performs other job related duties as required or assigned. SUPERVISION RECEIVED: Receives minimal instruction and supervision from Automated Services Coordinator in regard to daily work duties. SUPERVISION GIVEN: None.

WORKING CONDITIONS: 1. Works indoors in adequate work space, with adequate temperatures, ventilation and lighting. 2. Normal office exposure to noise, stress and disruptions. 3. Must be on-call for evening and weekend network-related problems. 4. Must possess a valid Pennsylvania driver's license and be able to visit member library facilities, using one's own vehicle. 5. Full-time position, 37.5 hours per week. The Cumberland County Library System office is open 8:00 AM-4:30 PM, Monday through Friday.

PHYSICAL/MENTAL CONDITIONS: 1. Must possess ability to record, convey and present information, explain procedures and follow instructions. 2. Must be able to sit for long periods throughout the workday, with intermittent periods of standing, walking, bending, twisting and reaching to carry out essential job duties. 3. Coordinated movements of fingers/hands; and simple movements of feet/legs and torso. 4. Medium work, with occasional lifting/carrying of objects with weights of twenty to fifty pounds. 5. Must be able to pay close attention to details and concentrate on work.

QUALIFICATIONS:

A.   EDUCATION/TRAINING: Associate degree in computer science including training/ knowledge in computer hardware, local area networking and telecommunications equipment.
B: WORK EXPERIENCE: 2-4 years working experience in computer field.

KNOWLEDGE, SKILLS AND ABILITIES REQUIRED: 1. Must be able to coherently speak and understand the English language in an understandable manner in order to carry out essential job functions. 2. Must possess highly effective communication and interpersonal skills. 3. Must possess ability to function independently, have flexibility and the ability to work effectively with clients, co-workers and others. 4. Must possess the technical knowledge of operating personal computers and other office equipment with accuracy and reasonable speed. 5. Must possess requisite knowledge and ability to install computer programs. 6. Must possess the ability to troubleshoot computer problems and make needed repairs/adjustments. 7. Must possess knowledge of various computer programs and the ability to instruct others in use of a variety of computer operating systems and software applications.

INFORMATION SYSTEMS TECHNICIAN

Saint John the Baptist Parish Library
LaPlace, Louisiana

Information Systems Technician

Primary Duties:

- To assist with the installation, maintenance and repair of all public and staff computers and printers, the Online Public Access Catalog (OPAC), wiring, servers, switches, routers and firewalls.
- To evaluate the need for training on various technology-related topics, including Microsoft Office products, online databases, Internet resources and the OPAC, and to design, implement and teach computer instruction programs that will effectively meet those needs for the general public and for library staff.
- To develop and design innovative and effective training tools including web pages, PowerPoint Presentations, lesson plans and other documents on various technology and computer topics for staff and patrons.
- To work with the Systems Administrator and the Director in short-term and long-range planning for technological growth.
- To analyze and implement procedures in order to ensure the security and integrity of the library network and provide system monitoring.
- To provide backup administration of Microsoft Exchange Server.
- To supervise and implement network backup systems.
- To assist in the preparation of reports and applications for eRate funding and grants and all other external sources of funding.
- To maintain inventory of all library computer equipment
- To stay abreast of advances in computer technology by attending continuing education programs and making recommendations for improvements in technology.
- To work cooperatively and in professional harmony with staff members, administrators, and patrons
- To perform other duties and assignments.
- To follow all library policies and procedures.

Minimum Qualifications

- Associate Degree in computer technology or related field
- Two years (post degree) of directly related experience installing, configuring and supporting a Windows network
- Proven experience in the configuration, installation, and troubleshooting of computer software, including Microsoft Windows XP, Windows Server 2003, Microsoft Exchange Server, Microsoft Office Suite, Symantec Antivirus software and cloning software.
- Demonstrated knowledge of Microsoft Active Directory, firewall technology (specifically Cisco PIX), SPAM and Antivirus software, DNS, DHCP, remote access software, WAN technology and wireless networking.
- Strong background in the configuration and troubleshooting of computer hardware including desktops, printers, servers, laptops, UPS systems, etc.
- Strong background in the configuration and troubleshooting of network hardware including routers, firewalls, switches, etc.
- Proven experience in providing training on Microsoft Office products and Internet Access.

- Effective written and oral communication skills.
- Ability to convey and teach technical information in terms that are understandable to any audience.
- Ability to work well in groups and individually with little supervision.
- Excellent technical troubleshooting skills.
- Other combinations of experience and training which provides the required knowledge, skills, and abilities to perform job duties will also be considered.
- Ability to lift and move items and materials up to 40 pounds in weight.

SENIOR LIBRARY TECHNICIAN

Longmont Public Library
Longmont, Colorado

DEFINITION: Performs responsible administrative, public service and technical tasks in support of the Longmont Public Library computer services and functions.

PRINCIPAL DUTIES: Provide computer technical support to staff. Assist in the repair, maintenance, and installation of library personal computer hardware, software and peripheral equipment including routine maintenance and troubleshooting of the Library's personal computer networks, Internet, and SirsiDynix computer system. Oversee personal computer security system. Maintain documentation related to personal computer hardware and software. Develop technical specifications and recommend personal computer related purchases. Maintain effective working relationships with supervisors, co-workers, and the public. Collaborate with other Library staff to provide effective customer service. Supervise employees and volunteers in the Computer Lab including assisting in the selection process, preparing work schedules, designing and conducting training, problem resolution, ensuring staff coverage, and performance evaluation. Provide direct assistance to customers in the Computer Lab. Assist and interview Library patrons by telephone or in person to determine needs and locate desired information or library materials using the computerized databases, library materials, other reference tools, or contacts with other libraries. Assist Library patrons (children, teens, or adults) with personal computers, providing instruction in using reference sources, word processing, and the Internet and assisting with problems. Attend weekly Library management and monthly staff meetings as directed. Compile monthly and yearly statistical reports. Recommend and assist in updating procedural and training manuals in areas of assignment.

WORKING ENVIRONMENT: Work is performed in a standard library environment, which includes exposure to dust. Requires the ability to move around the building and to access materials on shelves. Work requires light lifting/carrying (up to 15 lbs.) standing, walking, bending/stooping, reaching, pushing/pulling, twisting, kneeling, and squatting, and sufficient visual and physical capabilities to work on computers and associated equipment. Work requires repetitive motion to enter data on keyboard. Requires skill in working productively independently as well as with a group and communicating effectively with co-workers and public of diverse age, nationality, education, and socioeconomic backgrounds. Irregular work schedule required including days, evenings, Saturdays and Sundays.

QUALIFICATIONS: Any combination of education and experience equivalent to an Associate's Degree from an accredited college or university. Knowledge of library computer systems. General supervisory experience is desirable. Bilingual English/Spanish proficiency desirable. Knowledge of routine procedures of public libraries desirable. Ability to establish and maintain effective working relationships with other City employees, representatives of other agencies and organizations, other City departments, and members of the community.

TECHNOLOGY CENTER ASSISTANT

Westerville Public Library
Westerville, Ohio

Position Title: Technology Center Assistant
Job Classification: Part-Time Library Associate/Adult
Reports To: Manager, Adult Services Department

SUMMARY OF RESPONSIBILITIES

Provides library service to the public and performs specific tasks related to library service in accordance with the goals and objectives established by the library board. Primary responsibilities include instructing patrons in the use of technology; clerical duties. Responsible to the department manager.

RESPONSIBILITIES TO THE PUBLIC

- Assist patrons in the Technology Center.
- Answer questions regarding locating an internet site using a LTRL or search engine.
- Answer questions regarding creating a document using the word processors.
- Answer questions regarding printing and the use of the debit card system.
- Answer questions regarding the use of the microfilm reader/printers.
- Re-logon to computers whenever necessary.
- Ensure that computers, printers, microfilm reader/printers, etc. have necessary supplies.
- Troubleshoot and report machine failures to the Adult Services staff or the Computer Services staff.
- Assist in training classes and/or demonstrations for the public.
- Assist in writing search guides.
- Other duties as assigned.

RESPONSIBILITIES TO THE MANAGER

- Recommend policy, procedure, and signage.
- Gather department transaction statistics
- Attend monthly department meeting.
- Participate in annual performance appraisal and individual conferences during the year.
- Attend annual in service day.
- Participate in training sessions for professional development

RESPONSIBILITIES TO THE ADMINISTRATION

Explain and implement library policy.

RESPONSIBILITIES TO THE STAFF

Interact with department personnel in a positive, consistent, friendly and professional manner.

POSITION REQUIREMENTS

- College degree or equivalent education and experience.

- Ability to work independently with little supervision.
- Ability to interact with the public in a consistent, friendly and professional manner.
- Commitment to provide quality customer service.
- A positive attitude and a willingness to accept change.
- Ability to learn and operate complex computer applications and programs.
- Ability to stoop, bend, and lift.

Chapter 39

TECHNOLOGY AND WEB SITE PERSONNEL

TECHNOLOGY TRAINER

Worthington Library
Worthington, Ohio

FLSA STATUS: Non-Exempt
REPORTS TO: Network Administrator
DEPARTMENT: Technology
POSITIONS SUPERVISED: None

PURPOSE:
Under direction, the Technology Trainer is responsible for developing and conducting staff and patron technology training opportunities.

ESSENTIAL POSITION FUNCTIONS:

1. Develops and conducts staff and patron technology training opportunities and materials
2. Serves as an internal consultant on technology training issues
3. Assists librarians in the preparation of technology training programs
4. Assists the Network Administrator in basic network support
5. Provides "Help Desk" service to staff and the public

REQUIRED QUALIFICATIONS:

Education, Training and/or Experience

1. Bachelor's degree
2. A minimum of one (1) year of experience in various methods of training
3. A minimum of one (1) year of experience with and significant interest in electronic resources, Windows XP, Microsoft Office and Internet applications, OR
4. An equivalent combination of education, training and experience

Knowledge, Skills, Abilities and Personal Characteristics

1. Ability to maintain confidentiality and use appropriate judgment in handling information and records
2. Ability to work accurately with attention to detail
3. Ability to arrange items in alphanumeric and/or subject order
4. Experience with development of individual and group training programs
5. Ability to train "non-technical" persons in the effective use of on-line network systems
6. Knowledge of adult learning theory and styles
7. Ability to define problems, collect data, establish facts and draw valid conclusions

Certifications, licenses, Registrations: None

PREFERRED QUALIFICATIONS:

A minimum of one (1) year of experience in developing and delivering technology training programs

PHYSICAL DEMANDS:
- Ability to sit and use computer for extended periods and operate standard office equipment, daily
- Ability to lift and move up to fifty (50) pounds, frequently
- Ability to disassemble and reassemble computer hardware, frequently
- Ability to stand for extended periods, frequently
- Travel by automobile is required frequently

WORKING CONDITIONS:
- Majority of work performed in general office/library environment
- On call evenings and weekends, in coordination with the Network Administrator
- Requires periodic participation and attendance at events and training

This position description is not intended to be a complete list of all responsibilities, skills or working conditions associated with this position and is subject to review and change at any time in accordance with the needs of Worthington Libraries. Reasonable accommodations may be made to enable someone with a qualifying disability to perform the essential functions of the position.

CORE COMPETENCIES: Core Competencies are the knowledge, skills, attitudes, values and behaviors that all employees are expected to demonstrate. The Worthington Libraries Core Values are indicated in italicized text.

Competency	Definition	Demonstrated Behaviors
Adaptability **Future Oriented** *We respond appropriately to emerging practices and technologies in library and information science and related fields, and anticipate changes in our community's needs.*	The ability to adjust to changing situations and take calculated risks.	• Interprets and responds quickly to new or changed responsibilities, methods and procedures • Learns and applies new skills • Remains positive and productive
Customer Service **Quality Service** *We anticipate needs and exceed expectations in delivering service.* **Diversity** *We strive to be inclusive, and we recognize the dignity of all people from all backgrounds; we value contributions and ideas from all members of our diverse community.* **Intellectual Freedom** *We are committed to providing open access to library resources which interest, inform and enlighten all people in our community.*	The ability to appreciate the variety of patrons and staff and accommodate their diverse needs to the highest extent possible.	• Welcomes interactions • Consistently greets patrons and staff with a smile • Strives to make library resources accessible to all members of the community • Proactively anticipates and addresses patron and staff expectations and needs • Knows when it is appropriate to bend the rules and explains positively when denials are required

Communication *Communication* *We engage in the open exchange of information as a critical process for creating synergy of ideas within our library and with our community.*	The ability, through both verbal and written methods, to provide concise, timely and accurate information, internally and externally, among all organizational levels and with all of the appropriate people.	• Listens to others and verifies understanding of the message • Uses a variety of communication methods in the most appropriate form, in the manner that best enables the message to be understood • Responds to the comments and questions of others in a timely manner • Uses appropriate language • Proficient in the use of Microsoft Outlook • Knows how to find and use information on the Staff Intranet
Organizational Awareness	The ability to support the library's mission, vision, culture and structure.	• Understands and identifies with the goals and values of the Library and models and actively communicates them effectively • Knows and appropriately follows the library's hierarchy • Knows, understands and appropriately applies policies and procedures • Keeps current on information sent by Administration
Technology	The ability to use equipment, materials, and processes to do work.	• Readily uses technology that is necessary to the position • Keeps current on changes in technology that are necessary to the position
Teamwork *Teamwork* *We work together in a spirit of cooperation, supporting each others' efforts to achieve organizational excellence and provide quality service.*	The ability to work collaboratively with others.	• Willingly assists others by sharing expertise and time • Prepared to complete assigned tasks • Respects the ideas and opinions of others • Gives and accepts feedback in a positive manner • Proactively involves others to solve problems and achieve results which meet the needs of the Library
Problem Solving	The ability to understand the entire perspective on a situation or issue, identify patterns or connections between situations, assess problems and troubleshoot in order to identify effective solutions.	• Acquires new information and applies knowledge to analyze issues and resolve problems • Breaks problems down into components to identify required tasks or activities

445

		• Formulates new and imaginative solutions that reflect careful consideration of patron and library needs and goals
		• Considers risks, benefits, and impact of solution on the present and future library environment
		• Transfers learning from one situation to solve a problem in another
		• Consults with appropriate staff members before implementing solutions
Personal Responsibility *Integrity* *We act with honesty and fairness as we conduct our business with patrons and each other; we assume personal responsibility for accomplishing the goals of the organization.*	The commitment to take appropriate action to meet patron and library goals and needs.	• Ensures accuracy and completeness of work • Accepts responsibility for accomplishments and seeks to correct and learn from mistakes • Continually seeks opportunities for learning and training • Evaluates own strengths and weaknesses and seeks feedback from others for self-improvement

POSITION SPECIFIC COMPETENCIES: The skills, knowledge, attitudes, values and behaviors necessary to an individual's success in a position and to the overall success of an organization.

Competency	Definition	Demonstrated Behaviors
Applied Library Knowledge	The ability to evaluate, package and manage collection formats, instruct and support patrons in the pursuit of lifelong learning and provide equal access to information.	• Develops, provides and/or manages convenient, accessible and patron-oriented information services • Recommends materials appropriate to various user levels and interests • Possesses knowledge of collection development, resources and formats • Works to build a balanced collection in a variety of formats to fill the needs of patrons
Project/Program Management	The ability to plan, oversee and/or implement tasks resulting in projects or programs that are completed on time, within budget, and that meet or exceed expectations.	• Assesses needs, plans and implements programs or projects that are consistent with the library's mission, values, goals and objectives • Utilizes the library's tools, processes and models effectively, such as forms, statistics, guidelines, etc. • Evaluates programs and projects for effectiveness

WEBMASTER

Municipal Research and Service Center of Washington
Seattle, Washington

WEBMASTER, City of Spokane, Washington, 2001 Job Description

NATURE OF WORK:

Performs professional work in development, implementation, and management of the City's World Wide Web sites and intranet applications. Duties require independent judgment and the ability to analyze facts to determine the proper course of action. Few checks and controls exist and errors, if not detected, could cause considerable loss of time or embarrassment to the City. Employee has regular contact with employees of other departments of a policy making nature, and with professionals outside the City to obtain and supply factual information.

SUPERVISION:

Employee works under general direction from the MIS Director; plans and arranges own work, and refers only unusual cases to the supervisor. On a project basis, provides direction to a multi-discipline team in developing new web applications.

ESSENTIAL JOB FUNCTIONS:

Develops enterprise-wide web applications using Hypertext Markup Language (HTML). Maintains the City Home Page and directly surrounding layers of Hypertext files. Manages the evolution of the City's Web sites, web related work, and technical applications. Provides technical support for problem resolution.

- Configures servers and sets communication parameters which ensure timely delivery of information. Ensures servers and browsers are configured so that all City web sites are visible to the largest possible audience. Configures network security so that publications are served only to the intended audience.
- Ensures presentation of a consistent visual image on the City's web sites by promoting uniform fonts, formatting icons, images, layout techniques, and modularization. Promotes proper use of HTML language and stays abreast of developing HTML standards.
- Promotes the City web site to appropriate internal and external audiences. Establishes pointers from other relevant sites and WWW search sites. Organizes information seminars and encourages promotion of the site through other departmental communications vehicles. Provides publisher and user support and coordinates training for publishers, etc. Represents the City on external working and advisory committees.
- Maintains HTML template/image archives and related records as required.
- Performs related work as required.

REQUIREMENTS OF WORK:

- Considerable knowledge of the World Wide Web as a system and of the principles and practices of good web site design from both server and client perspectives.
- Considerable knowledge of, and ability to develop, web site architecture and applications using Hypertext Markup Language.

- Considerable knowledge of TCP/IP, systems administration, CGI gateways, security/firewalls, data-bases, and database linking.
- Knowledge of relevant hardware, software applications, and techniques used in web site design, development, and maintenance.
- Knowledge of, and ability to work with the various computer operating systems.
- Ability to learn complex technical materials and adapt in a rapidly changing technological area.
- Ability to communicate effectively, both orally and in writing.
- Ability to establish and maintain effective working relationships with other employees and outside contacts.

PHYSICAL REQUIREMENTS:

- Ability to see well enough to read fine print displayed on a computer screen.
- Ability to hear and speak well enough to converse on the telephone.
- Ability to use office equipment, particularly computers.
- Enough body mobility to move about the office.

MINIMUM EDUCATION AND EXPERIENCE:

Open Entry Requirements: Graduation from an accredited four-year college or university with a degree in Computer Science, Engineering, or related field; AND one year of experience in internet/intranet site development, implementation, and maintenance; OR, two-year (associate) degree from an accredited college in information systems, computer science, or closely related field; and two years of experience in internet/intranet site development, implementation, and maintenance

WEB PROGRAMMER

Tri-College Libraries Web Programmer
Bryn Mawr, Haverford, and Swarthmore College Libraries

Dynamic, creative, and highly knowledgeable Web Developer. If you fit this description, then this may be the position for you.

Tri-College Library Consortium of Bryn Mawr, Haverford, and Swarthmore Colleges is looking for a web developer with 3-5 years experience. The web developer will be responsible for library technologies to enhance the Tri-College Libraries' digital services. Library technologies include: information search and retrieval; digital content creation, access and delivery; and administrative tools for library staff. Duties include web programming, systems and applications support, data mining, and some training. This position will support the implementation, operation, and enhancement of core information systems such as the integrated library system, inter-library loan/document delivery software and systems, digital asset management systems, institutional repositories, and other centrally-served technologies. While the position will report directly to the Head of Information and Acquisition Delivery Services at Bryn Mawr College, frequent interaction and involvement with Haverford and Swarthmore library staff as well as a strong working relationship with the IT Departments of all three institutions is part of the Tri-College culture.

Required: BA/BS or advanced degree in computer or information science or related field; proficient in current programming and/or scripting languages or technologies including JavaScript, PHP, SQL; demonstrated knowledge of Web design and development languages including HTML, CSS, SML, and XSLT; working knowledge of data migration and crosswalks; strong analytic and problem solving skills; strong written and oral communication skills and a creative outlook on the use of technology.

Desired: Experience with Linux and/or Unix web servers and database application configuration (MySQL, Oracle, and/or Postgres a plus); programming experience using Python, Java, Perl, or Ruby; experience with standard metadata formats, such as the Dublin Core; some knowledge of Photoshop or other graphic design tools. Coursework or experience in Library or Information Science or familiarity with academic library technologies would be beneficial.

Part IX
Treasury of Recommended Forms

DATABASE SEARCH REQUEST

Thomas Jefferson University
Scott Memorial Library
Philadelphia, Pennsylvania

- The AISR Information Services Department makes every effort to provide accurate and complete database search results. However, it assumes no liability for information retrieved, its interpretation, applications or omissions.
- Search request privileges are available to TJU faculty, students, staff, alumni, staff at affiliated hospitals, and corporate members. See Database Search Services for policy, fee, and other background information.
- Normal searches are performed within 48 hours of request. Rush service is available for patient care or bonafide emergencies at no extra cost. The highest priority is always given to patient care information.
- Search results are available in print or electronic form suitable for word processing applications or personal bibliographic software. Electronic results may also be send via email, upon request.
- Topics will be searched on all appropriate TJU subscription databases, based on the request below. For cost estimates on searches of other literature, please consult directly with a librarian by phone or ask a librarian.

REQUESTED BY [   ]

PHONE [   ]

EMAIL [   ]

If this form is being completed by an assistant or colleague, please give your name and contact information as well: [   ]

REQUESTER'S AFFILIATION *(Please check all that apply)*

○ Jefferson

   Department: [   ]

   University Division: ○ CHP   ○ JMC   ○ CGS   ○ TJU Hospital

   ○ Methodist Hospital   ○ Other TJU

   Status: ○ Faculty   ○ Student   ○ Staff   ○ Resident   ○ Other [   ]

○ Affiliated Hospital: [   ]

○ Other: [   ]

PAYMENT METHOD

○ Interdepartmental Charge Code: [   ]

○ Cash or Check, Due Upon Delivery: *(Give billing name and address)*

[   ]

PURPOSE OF SEARCH

☐ Research ☐ Publication ☐ Education ☐ Patient Care

TOPIC OF SEARCH

Please type a sentence or phrase describing the subject(s) of your search (e.g., recent articles on the effects of gamma-rays on man-in-the-moon marigolds). For each subject, please also give any keywords, synonyms, phrases, acronyms or abbreviations to be included. Be sure to indicate any relationships between multiple topics.

SEARCH LIMITATIONS

Language of Output *(Please choose one)*

○ English Only   ○ All Languages   ○ Only These: [＿＿＿＿]

Dates to Cover: [＿＿＿] to [＿＿＿]   *(e.g., 1993 to 2003)*

Age Groups: [＿＿＿＿＿＿]

Population *(Please check all that apply)*:

☐ Human

○ Male

○ Female

☐ Animal Experiments

Any specific animals? [＿＿＿＿＿＿]

Amount of Output:

How many articles are you expecting to find on this topic? [＿＿＿]
What kind of articles do you want to see? *(Please check all that apply)*

○ All Types—a comprehensive search

○ Review Articles

○ Few, Highly Relevant Articles

DELIVERY METHOD *(Please check only one)*

○ Pick Up at Circulation Desk

○ TJU Mail *(Give campus address)* [＿＿＿＿＿＿]

○ Electronic Mail *(Give email address)* [＿＿＿＿＿＿]

○ U.S. Mail *(Give complete address)*

OUTPUT FORMAT *(Please check only one)*

- ○ Paper Printout
- ○ Disk *(Please specify Mac or IBM format, 3 1/2" or 5 1/4", and whether a specific output format is needed to support bibliographic management software)*

> [Clear the Form and Try Again]

DISTANCE LEARNING LIBRARY INSTRUCTION REQUEST FORM

Appalachian State University
Belk Library and Information Commons
Boone, North Carolina

To schedule a library instruction session at an off-campus site, please complete and submit the form below.

You will be contacted to confirm the session date and time. Questions? Email . . . or phone . . .

* Required Fields

Preferred Date for Library Instruction:

*1st Choice *date:* [   ]   Day of week: [   ]   *Time: [   ]

*2nd Choice *date:* [   ]   Day of week: [   ]   *Time: [   ]

Librarians request an hour to an hour-and-a-half to allow sufficient time to cover resources and research strategies.

Faculty Requestor:
* Name: [   ]

* E-mail: [   ]

* Phone *(for confirmation):* [   ]

Cell Phone *(helpful if a librarian needs to reach you the day/evening of the class):* [   ]

Off-site Location:
* Community college (or other location): [   ]

City: [   ]

* Building Name: [   ]

* Room #: [   ]

Does classroom have:
  • computers for students?

      O Yes   O No   O Not sure at this
                         moment

  • a teacher computer workstation?

      O Yes   O No   O Not sure at this
                         moment

Course Description:
* Program or Cohort: [   ]

* Course Name: [   ]

* Course Number: [   ]

Number of Students: *(If not known, please estimate)* [   ]

Preferences/Notes:
* If any of your students have special needs please indicate that here.

* Please provide a general description of the skills and resources you would like the librarian to address:

[   ]

Please describe any research-related activities or assignments related to this session:

[   ]

| Submit this Form | Reset this Form | Return to Top |

E-JOURNAL REQUEST

Florida Atlantic University
S.E. Wimberly Library
Boca Raton, Florida

PLEASE CHECK THE CATALOG BEFORE SUBMITTING A REQUEST. WE MAY ALREADY OWN THE ITEM.

E-journals: For Faculty Only. Students who would like to should contact a faculty member and have him or her complete this form.

Item suggested

Note: There is a limit of 10 electronic requests per month. If you need to request more than 10 items per month, please contact Maris Hayashi for paper order request forms.

Check one:

○ E-book/CD-ROMs   ○ E-journal   ○ E-database/E-resource   ○ CD-ROM Subscription

Title:

Author: (E-books)

Provider/Publisher:

Date of Publication:

ISBN/ISSN:

URL:

Price:

Source of Information:

○ Sample Issue   ○ Review   ○ Other:

Priority Level:

○ Nice if we owned it   ○ Highly desirable   ○ Essential for a class

Benefit to the FAU Libraries' Collection and other information:

Please consult with

Contact Information
* Indicates required fields

Your Name:*

Status: ○ Faculty   ○ Student   ○ Staff   ○ Other

Department:

E-mail Address:*

Campus Address:

Daytime Telephone:

[Submit Request] [Clear Form]

EQUIPMENT RENTAL AGREEMENT

Portland Community College
Portland Community College Libraries
Portland, Oregon

Last Name: _____ First Name: _____
　　　　　　　　(Please Print)　　　　　　　　　　　　　　　　　　　　　　(Please Print)

Student ID Number **G** _____

Drivers License # _____　　**Staff Signature** _____

Portland Community College Equipment Use Agreement

Checking out a piece of equipment from any Portland Community College Library indicates that the borrower will inspect the equipment before <u>every checkout session</u> and confirm it to be in proper working order and that all pieces are included. (The checkout process will ask for verification of the number of pieces checked out). Equipment is intended for academic purposes.

The borrower will reimburse Portland Community College Library for the reasonable cost of repairs, parts and replacement arising because of damage or loss of equipment occurring while it is checked out to the borrower. If any piece of equipment is damaged beyond repair while in the borrower's possession the borrower will reimburse Portland Community College Library in an amount equal to the replacement cost of the equipment. The borrower will cooperate in filing and processing appropriate insurance claims with either PCC insurers or borrower's insurers. The borrower understands that the equipment cannot be used in violation of the law or of Portland Community College policies.

The equipment shall be returned to the PCC Campus Library it was borrowed from, on time and in as good condition as when received except for normal wear and tear. PCC is not responsible for damage to any removable disk or loss of data that may occur due to malfunctioning hardware or software.

Overdue charges accrue at $5.00 per hour. There is no grace period.

Equipment checkout may be denied to people who abuse equipment, repeatedly return equipment late or otherwise interfere with the provision of equipment to PCC students.

I understand that the replacement cost for the

_____　**Laptop Computer** will be no less than $1,700 (includes Laptop, AC Power Adapter, Removable
(initial)　Drive, Battery).

_____　**Digital Camera** will be no less than $350 (includes Camera, Carrying Case, Battery, Battery
(initial)　Charger, Video Cables, Memory card, Instruction sheet).

_____　**Digital Video Camera** will be no less than $500 (includes Camera, Carrying Case, Battery, Battery
(initial)　Charger, Video Cable, Audio Adapter, Instruction sheet).

_____　**LCD Projector** will be no less than $1500 (includes projector, Carrying Case, bulb, remote, Video
(initial)　Cables, Audio Adapter, Instruction sheet).

This agreement will last through last day of the school year _____.
　　　　　　　　　　　　　　　　　　　　　　　　　　　　　　　　(date)

I have read this entire document and my signature below indicates my agreement with the above statements.

X _____　Date: ___/___/___

IM Reference Service Survey

Thomas Jefferson University
Scott Memorial Library
Philadelphia, Pennsylvania

AIM

1. Are you already an AOL Instant Messenger (AIM) user?

○ Yes

○ No

2. Do you use other IM networks?

○ Yes

○ No

3. If so, which? (check all that apply)

☐ Yahoo!

☐ MSN

☐ ICQ

☐ TJUH JeffNet

☐ Other: [   ]

4. What is your affiliation with Jefferson? (please check all that apply)

☐ Student

☐ Resident/Fellow

☐ Faculty

☐ Staff

☐ Alumni

☐ Affiliate

☐ None

☐ Other: [   ]

5. Have you used the Library's reference service in the past three months? (please check all that apply)

☐ in person at the Reference Desk (2nd floor Scott building)

☐ by phone

☐ by email or Web (AskALibrarian, search request, etc.)

☐ by instant messaging (AIM)

6. Have you used the Library's AIM *chat* reference service?

○ yes, this was my first time

○ yes, more than once

○ no, but I will consider it in the future

○ no, I won't use it. Why not? [_____]

7. If you've used our *chat* reference service, how satisfied were you with the experience?

○ very satisfied

○ somewhat satisfied

○ neutral

○ somewhat dissatisfied

○ very dissatisfied

8. Would you use the service again?

○ Yes

○ No

9. What hours are you most likely to use the service? (please check all that apply)

☐ 9 AM–11 AM

☐ 11 AM–1 PM

☐ 1 PM–3 PM

☐ 3 PM–5 PM

☐ 5 PM–8 PM

☐ Other: [_____]

10. Please add any additional comments and suggestions about the *chat* reference service.

[_____]

[Submit Survey]

Thank you!

INFORMATION LITERACY INSTRUCTION REQUEST E-MAIL FORM

University of Texas at Arlington
Arlington, Texas

Request an Instruction Session

Please request an instruction session at least 3 days in advance in order for UT Arlington Library to prepare a customized session for your group.

You may be entitled to know what information The University of Texas at Arlington (UT Arlington) collects concerning you. You may review and have UT Arlington correct this information according to procedures set forth in UTS 139. The law is found in sections 552.021, 552.023, and 559.004 of the Texas Government Code. For more information, see our Internet Privacy Policy.

Contact Name: ☐

Dept./Organization: ☐

Phone: ☐

E-mail: ☐

UT Arlington Course (if applicable): ☐

Number of Participants: ☐

Session Time: ☐

Session Length: ☐

Session Date: ☐

Level of Participants (choose all that apply):

☐ Freshman   ☐ Adult Group

☐ Sophomore   ☐ Elementary School Group

☐ Junior   ☐ Middle School Group

☐ Senior   ☐ High School Group

☐ Graduate Students

Location/Type of Facility Preferred:

☐ Library Hands-on Classroom (B21)   ☐ Your Classroom ☐

☐ Library Classroom (315A)   ☐ Other ☐

Topics for Instruction (choose all that apply):

☐ UT Arlington Library Catalog Searching   ☐ Research Process

☐ Library Database Searching   ☐ Citing/Plagiarism

☐ Internet Searching/Evaluating   ☐ Library Tour

☐ Library Services   ☐ Library Assignment

☐ Library Resources

Other Topics (list below):

Additional Services for your class/group (choose all that apply):

☐ Course Page designed to meet library needs of your class/group

☐ Library Assignment designed to test skills of your class/group

Please describe briefly the assignment or course to which the session relates (include links to syllabus or assignment if available):

Additional Comments (including Special Accommodations if needed):

I would like an e-mail copy of this request:
(if yes, be sure to include your e-mail address above)

☐ Yes   ☐ No

| Submit Instruction Request | Reset |

You will be contacted by a librarian within three working days. If you do not receive a response after three days . . .

LAB REQUEST FORM

Hunter College
Hunter College Library
New York, New York

PCS Lab Request Form	
FACULTY and STAFF Use Only	**Date:**
○ Fall 2007 ○ Spring 2008 ○ Summer 2008 ○ Fall 2008 ○ Spring 2009	
This Request is for:	
☐ Windows Labs (1001HN) ☐ Windows Labs (TH 403/402)	☐ Macintosh Lab (1001HN)
Please fill out all text boxes before submitting your request, (including the Comments field). * For Summer 2008 requests, please indicate Session I or Session II in the Comments field.	
Instructor (or contact person) Name:	
Department and room number:	
Hunter College Telephone number:	
Alternate phone number:	
Email address:	
Course title:	
Course number and section:	
Number of students anticipated:	
Will this class be held in the computer lab every week throughout the entire semester? YES ○ NO ○	
If YES, list the day(s) of the week and times of classes:	**Days or Dates:**
If NO, list the specific dates and times you need the lab: (PCS will only honor requests that specify exact dates.)	**Times:**

Will you be using PCS-supported software?*	YES ○ NO ○
If yes, which software (see the list below)	
Comments (If none, Type "none")	

PCS-supported software:	
Windows XP:	MS Office 2003-(Word, Excel, PowerPoint, Access) Netscape 7.x, Internet Explorer 6.x, Acrobat Pro 7.x, CUNY+Plus, SPSS 13, SPSS 14, SAS 8.2, Mathematica 5.x, Stata Quest, ArcGIS 8.3, Map Info 5.5, SSH 3.2.9, C++ Builder 6
Macintosh-10.x:	BetterTelnet, Adobe Creative Suite-(Photoshop, Illustrator, Acrobat 6.x, InDesign), Mathematica 5.x, Netscape 7, Safari, QuarkXpress 7, MS Office 2004 (Word, Excel, PowerPoint), Flash MX, Dreamweaver MX

*If you will not be using PCS-supported software, you must contact Chris Thompson at ext. 3289 to coordinate installation and testing of non-PCS software at least two weeks prior to class date(s). Instructors are responsible for testing out their software after it has been installed in our labs. Site licenses, documentation, instruction, and support must be provided for non-PCS Software.

Before you Press the Submit Button, print this page for your records.

Press the **Submit** button:	Submit	Reset
For further information contact:		

465

Laptop Liability Form

Hunter College
Jacqueline Grennan Wexler Library
New York, New York

HUNTER COLLEGE LIBRARIES
68th St/Wexler library
LAPTOP LIABILITY FORM

Library Staff: Fill out top section.

Date/time borrowed _____   Time due _____

Library Staff at borrowing _____   Library Staff at return _____

Computer # _____   Checklist completed OUT_____ IN_____

Accessories Borrowed _____

Borrower: Please read this agreement, and sign it.

Print Name _____   email _____

I understand that I may use this lap top only in the library and for a maximum of 3 hours, with no renewal.

- I accept full responsibility for the laptop computer and accessories I am borrowing.
- I will reimburse Hunter College for the cost of repairing or replacing this laptop, and/or accessories if they are damaged, lost, stolen, or not returned while checked out in my name.
- I understand that the replacement cost for this laptop computer will be no less than **$2000** plus accrued overdue fine(s).
- I will pay an overdue fine of $40 per hour and $10 per 15 minute period or portion thereof, if I fail to return this laptop and all accessories to the Library's Reserve Desk at the time due indicated above.
- I have witnessed the physical inspection of the Laptop computer and its components and accessories. All checked parts and accessories are present and appear to be functioning.
- I understand that any abuse of laptop loan privileges may also result in disciplinary action and the inability to borrow laptop computers in the future.
- I understand that all charges that are accrued as a result of violations of these policies will be sent to the Bursar's Office and will prevent me from registering for classes, from obtaining diploma/transcript(s) and/or graduating until paid in full.
- I understand that failure to return the laptop within the allotted time will be considered theft of Hunter College property and appropriate action will be taken.
- I understand that I am not to perform any illegal activities with this laptop (i.e., hacking, pirating, downloading illegal materials, etc.) or any activities inconsistent with the CUNY Policy on Acceptable Use of Computer Resources.
- I understand that if I perform any illegal activities or any activities that violate the CUNY Policy on Acceptable Use of Computer Resources with this laptop, I will be subject to the disciplinary rules and regulations of Hunter College and perhaps, those of the City University of New York, which may result in the possibility of arrest.
- I do hereby verify that I have read and understand the Use and Liability Agreement as it pertains to the loan of a Hunter College laptop computer.
- I agree to abide by this and related laptop loan policies.

LIBRARY INSTRUCTION STUDENT EVALUATION

Texas Tech Universitsy
Texas Tech University Libraries
Lubbock, Texas

Library Instruction Student Evaluation

Please help us by taking a few moments to complete this form. All comments are welcome and will help us improve our Library Instruction Program.

Items in red are required. Use NA instead of leaving a required item blank.	
Current Date/Time	Monday, October 13, 2008, 4:40 PM
Date of Course	13 Oct 2008
Librarian-Instructor Name	
Name/Number of Course	
After this class, how confident are you that you can find a book on your topic in the online catalog?	○ Very Confident ○ Confident ○ Not Confident ○ I am Lost ○ NA
After this class, how confident are you that you can find a newspaper in the online catalog?	○ Very Confident ○ Confident ○ Not Confident ○ I'm Lost ○ NA
After this class, how confident are you that you can find a journal article on your topic in the online catalog?	○ Very Confident ○ Confident ○ Not Confident ○ I'm Lost ○ NA

After this class, how confident are you that you can find the library's journal holdings?	O Very Confident O Confident O Not Confident O I'm Lost O NA
Overall, how effective do you think this class will be in helping you do library research on your topic?	O Very Effective O Effective O Not Effective O I'm Lost O NA
Would you like to learn more about any of the following topics?	☐ Choosing and using general databases ☐ Choosing and using subject-specific databases ☐ Choosing and using print resources like journals ☐ Finding Internet sources and evaluating them ☐ Finding scholarly resources ☐ How to use the catalog more effectively ☐ How to broaden or narrow my search ☐ How to develop keywords and/or concepts
Comments	
The librarian who led this class was well-prepared and organized.	O Strongly Agree O Agree O Neutral O Disagree O Strongly Disagree O NA

The librarian who led this class made the subject clear and understandable.	○ Strongly Agree ○ Agree ○ Neutral ○ Disagree ○ Strongly Disagree ○ NA
The librarian who led this class provided helpful handouts.	○ Strongly Agree ○ Agree ○ Neutral ○ Disagree ○ Strongly Disagree ○ NA
The librarian who led this class encouraged the class to participate.	○ Strongly Agree ○ Agree ○ Neutral ○ Disagree ○ Strongly Disagree ○ NA
Comments	
What color is an orange? (Helps prevent automated Spam)	
	Send

MINOR CONSENT TO USE INTERNET FORM

Stillwater Public Library
Stillwater, Oklahoma

LIBRARY COMPUTER USAGE CONSENT FORM FOR MINORS

PLEASE SELECT ONE INTERNET OPTION FOR MINOR CHILD:

_____ HIGH FILTER (Computers in children's area only; no access to email or chat)

_____ LOW FILTER (May use any computer in the Library; access to email & to chat)

_____ NO ACCESS

☐ I have read the Stillwater Public Library's Computer Usage Policy and agree to its terms and conditions. I understand that the Library has no responsibility or obligation to restrict access to material on the Internet that I may find personally offensive.

☐ I understand that the Library is unable to monitor use of the Internet by children regardless of the presence of filtering software and that responsibility remains with the parent or legal guardian.

☐ I agree not to use the Library's Internet terminals or word processing computers to libel, harass or threaten others, to engage in unlawful activities or to tamper with hardware or software belonging to the Library or the City of Stillwater.

In consideration of the privilege of using the Stillwater Public Library's Internet terminals and for having access to the free information contained within it, I hereby release and hold harmless the City of Stillwater, its officers, agents, servants, or employees, volunteers, representatives, or advisors from any and all legal liability or responsibility for any and all claims, damages, losses, costs or expenses arising either directly or indirectly from the use of the Library's Internet terminals or word processing computers, whether or not caused in whole or in part, by alleged negligence of the City of Stillwater, its officers, agents, servants, employees, volunteers, representatives or advisors.

Child's signature _____
(Child MUST sign)

Child's printed name _____

Parent's Name _____
(Please Print)

Parent's Signature _____
(Parent MUST sign)

Non-UC Scanning Request and Digital Submission Agreement

University of California, Santa Barbara
Map and Imagery Laboratory, Davidson Library
Santa Barbara, California

The time needed to complete your request will vary depending upon number of sheets to be scanned, work already scheduled, and staff available. Average time frame: 2-4 weeks. MIL staff will contact you with estimated date of completion, and also when scanning is complete.

Item Call Number: _____

Item Name & Number: (e.g., Elba B-25-IV) _____

Your Name: (please print) _____

Email Address: _____ Phone: _____

Mailing address: _____

If shipping other than U.S. mail is required, specify shipping firm (e.g., UPS; FedEx; DHL; etc.) and your charge number:

Firm's name: _____ Charge number: _____

The Copyright Law of the United States (Title 17, U.S. Code) governs the making of photocopies or other reproductions of copyrighted material. Photocopies or other reproductions may be furnished only under certain specified conditions. One condition is that the photocopy or reproduction is not to be "used for any purpose other than private study, scholarship or research." Use of the reproduction may make the user liable for copyright infringement.

Signature: _____ Date: _____

The Map and Imagery Lab (MIL) may refuse to accept a copying request if, in its judgment, fulfillment of the request would violate copyright law.

____ Material is or may be within copyright by other than The Regents; requestor must obtain copyright release from copyright holder. Email/Webpage for copyright holder: _____

____ Copyright to material, and therefore to the scans, is held by The Regents. Publication (in, e.g., dissertations; journal articles; books) requires release from MIL.

____ Material is in the public domain. UC policy requires payment by non-UC users for a copy of these scan(s). The scans are for educational and non-commercial research purposes only; scans are not to be posted on the Web or published in any way without permission by the Map and Imagery Laboratory.

____ Material does not have any copyright statement or symbol on it, but may be copyrighted; requestor should obtain copyright release from author of material before publishing it.

Scanning specifications: 300ppi (maps); RGB or grey-scale; .tif file with no compression, written to disc.

Scan request approved by: _____

Date: _____

Notes: _____

SCANNING BY Map and Imagery Lab STAFF FOR NON-UC USERS

Interested in getting a scan of a map or aerial photograph held by the Map & Imagery Lab (MIL)? Plan ahead. This process can take up to four weeks, to schedule time on scanners and for you to obtain copyright release when required. ONLY MIL MATERIALS WILL BE SCANNED.

PRICES

The MIL receives no funding for services to persons not affiliated with the University of California, or for non-UC work done by persons who are student, faculty or staff of the University of California. Fees have therefore been implemented to cover the cost of staff time, maintenance of collections and equipment, and overhead. Rates are subject to change without notice. For items 11" x 17" or smaller: $18

For items larger than 11" x 17": $29

COPYRIGHT

Is the item copyrighted or not? Items that are copyrighted often but not always include the copyright symbol (c) or the word "Copyright" plus the name of the copyright holder and a date. Sometimes the copyright statement does not appear on the item; it is best to consider that the item is copyrighted unless you are sure it is not.

Copyright law – U.S.; foreign countries

U.S.: A rule of thumb for items with U.S. copyright is that items published prior to 1923 are not within copyright.

Foreign countries: Copyright law is very complex and differs from country to country. Check with MIL staff about ways of finding out what copyright law in non-U.S. countries is.

If the item is within copyright and copyright is not held by the University of California:

1. Get a copyright release from the copyright holder. The quickest way to do that is to find the copyright holder's website to get an email to send an enquiry. If you can't find a website, then send a hard-copy letter in snail mail. Write your request in the language of the copyright holder. Often, copyright holders will give permission for scanning only if the scan will be for personal use only and will not be published in any form – either on the Web or in a hard-copy publication. Copyright holders very often charge a fee for commercial/business use. Your enquiry should state clearly exactly how you intend to use the scan, and what map you are interested in having scanned—give author, title, scale, place of publication, publisher, and date of publication.

2. When you have obtained a written copyright release, bring it in to MIL, attached to a filled-out form (blank form is on the other side of this page).

3. If you decide at a later date that you would like to publish the scan or any portion of the scan, get in touch with the copyright holder and request permission.

If the item is within copyright and either copyright or reproduction rights are held by the University of California:

1. Is the item an uncopyrighted map to which the Regents hold reproduction rights? Request permission for any form of commercial use or publication from the Map and Imagery Lab by sending an email, with publication information, to milrefdesk@library.ucsb.edu.edu . Both a brief citation and a credit line should be given with the illustration when it is published. This is generally citation information, plus: "from collections of the Map and Imagery Laboratory, Davidson Library, University of California, Santa Barbara. Copyright 2007 The Regents of the University of California. All rights reserved."

2. Citing the original item:
   Use this general form: Author. Title. Scale. Place of publication: Publisher, date. (Series if any)

MIL has more detailed instructions if you need them, in a publication kept at the reference desk: Cartographic Citations (MIL-REF GA 108.7 C55 1992).

Permission Granted Form

Michigan State University
Michigan State University Libraries
East Lansing, Michigan

I grant Michigan State University (MSU) permission to audiotape, videotape and/or photograph my image and/or voice at my presentation on _____ or use in research, educational, and public service
Month/Day/Year
programs, including, but not limited to, Web Access as part of the collections of the MSU Libraries.

I grant MSU non-exclusive permission to edit, duplicate, distribute, reproduce, reformat and translate into other languages these audio, video, film and/or print images, in any manner, without payment of fee, in perpetuity.

I represent and warrant that the aforementioned material does not infringe on any existing copyright or other legal right.

None of these permissions shall be construed as a transfer of copyright ownership.

Print Name: _____

Signature: _____

Event Name: _____

Event Location/Building: _____

Presentation Title: _____

Date: _____

Address: _____

City: _____ State: _____ Zip Code: _____

Phone: _____

Email: _____

Please fill in the appropriate blanks. Sign the form where indicated and fax or mail a copy to:

473

PERMISSION REQUEST SAMPLE LETTER

Carroll Community College
Carroll Community College and Media Center
Westminster, Maryland

(Date)

(Name & address of addressee)

Dear _____,

(If you contacted the owner by phone, begin the letter): This letter will confirm our recent telephone conversation. I am _____ at Carroll Community College. I would like your permission to (explain your intended use in detail) reprint the following article for use in a course lecture dealing with _____. I will be using the article during the _____ semesters for my Introduction to _____ course. I will be making approximately _____ copies for student and instructional use.

(Insert full citation to the original work.)

Please indicate your approval of this permission by signing the letter where indicated below and returning it to me as soon as possible. My fax number is _____. By signing this letter, you are confirming that you own (or your company owns) the copyright to the above described material.

Thank you very much.

Sincerely,

(Your name and signature)

_____

PERMISSION GRANTED FOR THE USE REQUESTED ABOVE:

(Type name of addressee below signature line)

_____

(signature)

Date: _____

RECOMMEND A BOOK, JOURNAL, OR DIGITAL RESOURCE FOR PURCHASE

University of Maryland, Baltimore
University of Maryland Health Sciences and Human Services Library
Baltimore, Maryland

The Library welcomes suggestions for books, journals, and digital resources. The Library reserves the right to make all decisions on what to purchase but will try to fulfill as many appropriate requests as possible. Please check **CatalogUSMAI** to verify that the Library does not already own the item before submitting a recommendation for purchase. For more information on how the Library makes purchasing decisions, consult the **Library's Collection Development Policy**. If you have questions, please call or e-mail.

---

* - Indicates required fields.

Personal Information

Name: [   ] * Required!

Email: [   ] * Required!

Phone Number: [   ]

Affiliation: [<Select>   ] * Required!

Status: [<Select>] * Required!

Resource Information Resource Type: [<Select>   ] * Required!

Author(s)/Editor(s): [   ]

Title: [   ] * Required!

Publisher: [   ]

Year of Publication: [   ]

Series (if any): [   ]

ISBN/ISSN: [   ]

Comments: [   ]

For Book and Electronic Requests Is this for course reserve? ○ Yes ○ No

Would you like to be notified when available? ○ Yes ○ No

[Recommend]

RECOMMEND A CD PURCHASE

Longwood University
Janet D. Greenwood Library
Farmville, Virginia

Recommend a CD purchase

To recommend a CD for the Library to purchase, please complete the following. Items marked * are required. Faculty should contact their departmental librarian liaison directly for class-related materials.

---

*Your Longwood status or academic standing:

○ Freshman ○ Sophomore ○ Junior ○ Senior ○ Graduate ○ Faculty ○ Staff

*Title: [   ]

*Artist: [   ]

Any other helpful information: [   ]

Optional Information: (required if you wish to be notified about the status of your request)

Your Name: [   ]

Your Telephone Number: [   ]

Your E-Mail Address: [   ]

[Submit suggestion] [Clear] NOTE: Ordering is subject to availability of funds. At this time, due to the tightness of the library materials budget, we will hold your request but we will not be purchasing titles that do not support the academic curriculum until further notice.

REQUEST FOR INSTRUCTION

Texas State University
Albert B. Alkek Library
San Marcos, Texas

Request Instruction

Submit this form to schedule library instruction sessions. You will be contacted by an Instruction Librarian in order to confirm appointments. Required fields below are marked with an asterisk (*). An online instruction calendar is available.

Please note that submitting this form does not guarantee an appointment. All requests must be scheduled & confirmed by an Instruction Librarian.

Name: *

Department * Please select:

Email Address:

Phone Number:

Date, 1st Choice: *

Date, 2nd Choice: *

Time of Day (begining and ending class times): *

Course Title or Number: *

Number of Persons: *

Assignment: *

Assignment Due Date:

Additional Comments:

Name of Person Submitting this Request and Today's Date: *

Send Request

REQUEST FORMS FOR REPRODUCTION

Jefferson County Public Library
Lakewood, Colorado

Request for Photo-duplication
Jefferson County Public Library Historical Collections
Arvada Historical Society Collection (Arvada Library)

Photocopies and photo-prints of materials in the collections are provided as a service to expedite research and lessen wear on documents, and are made solely for the personal use of the individual researcher requesting them. Photocopies and photo-prints may not be transferred to another individual or organization, deposited at another institution, or reduplicated without proper credit. Purchase of photocopies or photo-prints constitutes agreement to comply with the following conditions:

Reproduction of photographs requires written permission of the Jefferson County Public Library. Jefferson County Public Library gives no exclusive rights for use of graphic material. Permission for reproduction is granted for one-time use only. Any subsequent use requires written permission. The Library reserves all other rights in full.

Duplication by the Department in no way transfers either the copyright or property right, nor does it constitute permission to publish in excess of "Fair Use." Researchers assume full responsibility for complying with any copyright, libel or literary rights applicable to their use of any Historical Collections or Library materials.

The library reserves the right to restrict the use or reproduction of rare or valuable material; and to charge a higher reproduction fee for materials requiring special handling. The requesting patron is responsible for fees based on the cost of reproduction by means of photocopying and photo printing.

The aforementioned procedures and policies also apply to reproductions made from digital images.

The library reserves the right to deny the use of any photograph to a patron at the discretion of the Library Manager or Department Head.

Each reproduced copy must be credited as follows and as appropriate:
- Courtesy Jefferson County Public Library, Arvada Historical Society Collection
- Courtesy Jefferson County Public Library Historical Collections.
- Arvada Historical Society Collection

The library reserves the right to limit the number of photographic copies.

Library staff provides all photocopying. Colorado Camera conducts all photo printing. Photo printing is not an immediate process, plan accordingly. An additional fee will be required if a copy negative is needed. The library retains all negatives.

Two complimentary copies of any published work using a library photograph will be provided to the Jefferson County Public Library Historical Collections.

To obtain a photocopy or photo-print:
1. Read the copyright warning below and sign your name.
2. Complete the order form on the back of this sheet. Indicate special instructions.
3. Give the order to a reference staff person. Orders will be filled as staff time permits.

Golden Historical Collection- Richard A. Ronzio Collection
Warning Concerning Copyright Restriction
Insert the warning here

I have read and abide by the rules stated above.

Name: _____

Date: _____

RESERVE REQUEST FOR ELECTRONIC ACCESS

Millersville University
Helen A. Ganser Library
Millersville, Pennsylvania

Priority _____ of _____

Semester Reserve Request (Electronic access)

Please complete the following information and then attach the physical document in your possession to this page with a PAPERCLIP (not a staple). One form for each document. Thank you.

PLEASE NOTE: If you are submitting MORE than two items at the same time,

PLEASE provide us with relative priority of each of the items in question by noting the priority in the upper right hand corner of this form. This prioritization allows more timely access to materials for students.

Instructor's Name: _____

Instructor's Phone Number: _____

Instructor's E-Mail: _____

Course(s) for which the item is to be placed on semester reserve: _____

Course Subject & Number: _____

Official Course Title: _____

Course Subject & Number: _____

Official Course Title: _____

Semester and Year the document is to be placed on reserve: _____

Bibliographic Information about the Document: _____

Author of the document: _____

Title of the document: _____

Publication: _____

Issue Info/ copyright date: _____

Publisher: _____

Anything else you would like to tell us: _____

For Library Use Only:

Date Received at Library: _____ Scanned by: _____ Scan Date: _____

Filename: _____

SOFTWARE REQUEST

Central Michigan University
Central Michigan Universities Libraries
Mount Pleasant, Michigan

CMU Library Public Workstation

Software Request Form

Email completed form to: _____

Date of Request: _____

Requestor's Name: _____

Department: _____

Phone Number: _____

E-mail Address: _____

Software Title: _____

Publisher/Distributor (if known): _____

Version Number: _____

Description: What is the purpose of this software? What type of information/data does it contain or provide access to? _____

Reason for Request: _____

Funding Source: _____

Number of Students expected to use this software: _____

Dates required (Expected length of use): _____

LIBRARY USE ONLY:

Library action: (   ) Approved   (   ) Not Approved

Date: _____

Retention Decision: (   ) Permanent   (   ) To be reviewed   (   ) To be removed

Date to be Reviewed / Removed: _____

Survey on Library Hours

University of Dayton
Roesch Library
Dayton, Ohio

Your Opinion Counts!

During this semester the Library experimented with longer hours, closing at 5:00 a.m. instead of 3:00 a.m. What should we do next year?

_____ Continue staying open until 5:00 a.m.

_____ Closing at 3:00 a.m. suits my needs

_____ I would prefer a later closing time or a 24/7 area

_____ I have no opinion; I do not study at the library after midnight.

WEB SITES OF CONTRIBUTING LIBRARIES

The Alberta Library
Alberta, Ontario, Canada
http://askaquestion.ab.ca.FAQ.html (accessed
December 6, 2008)

Alexandria Library
Alexandria, Virginia
http://www.alexandria.lib.va.us/lhsc_online
_collection_guides/photo/sellpix.html (accessed
October 14, 2008)

Alverno College
Alverno College Library
Milwaukee, Wisconsin
http://depts.alverno.edu/library/ersvs2.html
(accessed July 19, 2008)

Ames Public Library
Ames, Iowa
http://www.amespubliclibrary.org/aboutlibrary/
amespubliclibraryjobs-librarian.asp (accessed
September 24, 2008)
http://www.amespubliclibrary.org/Docs_PDFs/
Policy/ConductintheLibrary.pdf (accessed March
31, 2009)

Appalachian State University
Belk Library and Information Commons
Boone, North Carolina
http://www.library.appstate.edu/admin/policy/web
_policy.html (accessed June 30, 2008)

Athol Public Library
Athol, Massachusetts
http://www.cmrls.org/policies/policies/Policies_%
20Patriot_%20Act_Athol.pdf (accessed
December 4, 2008)

Aurora Public Library
Aurora, Colorado
http://auroralibrary.org/screens/about/policies/
polInternetAccess.html (accessed July 19, 2008)
http://auroralibrary.org/screens/about/policies/
polWireless.html (accessed July 19, 2008)

Austin History Center
Austin, Texas
http://www.ci.austin.tx.us/library/ahc/pricelist.htm
(accessed October 14, 2008)

Austin Public Library
Austin, Texas
http://www.cityofaustin.org/library/blogpost.htm
(accessed June 30, 2008)

Barstow Community College
Barstow Community College Library
Barstow, California
http://www.barstow.edu/LRC/Library/policies.asp
(accessed July 20, 2008)

Baruch College/CUNY
William and Anita Newman Library
New York, New York
http://newman.baruch.cuny.edu/about/eresource
_guidelines.html (accessed June 30, 2008)
http://portal.cuny.edu/cms/id/cuny/documents/level
_3_page/001171.htm (accessed June 30, 2008)

Benedict College
Benedict College Learning Resource Center
Columbia, South Carolina
http://www.benedict.edu/divisions/acadaf/lrc/policy
_n_proc/bc_lrc_manual_of_policies_n
_procedures06_mc.html#mc (accessed July 17,
2008)
http://www.benedict.edu/divisions/acadaf/lrc/policy
_n_proc/bc_lrc_manual_of_policies_n_
procedures03_ref.html#erc-pol (accessed July
17, 2008)

Berkeley Heights Public Library
Berkeley Heights, New Jersey
http://bhplnjbookgroup.blogspot.com/ (accessed
June 30, 2008)
http://www.youseemore.com/BerkeleyHeights/
about.asp?p=8 (accessed June 30, 2008)
http://www.youseemore.com/BerkeleyHeights/
about.asp?p=6 (accessed June 30, 2008)

Berry College
Berry College Memorial Library
Mount Berry, Georgia
http://www.berry.edu/library/instruct/elecroom.asp
(accessed July 20, 2008)

Boise Public Library
Boise, Idaho
http://www.boisepubliclibrary.org/About_BPL/
Policies_and_Plans/privacy.shtml (accessed July
21, 2008)
http://www.boisepubliclibrary.org/About_BPL/
Policies_and_Plans/Policy_manual.pdf (accessed
July 21, 2008)

Boulder Public Library
Boulder, Colorado
http://innopacusers.org/jobs/2008)/04/24/systems
-librarian-boulder-public-library/ (accessed
September 24, 2008)

Bowdoin College
Bowdoin College Library
Brunswick, Maine
http://www.bowdoin.edu/it/contact/privacy.shtml
(accessed July 1, 2008)
http://www.bowdoin.edu/it/contact/dmca-policy
.shtml (accessed July 1, 2008)

Bridgewater State College
Bridgewater, Massachusetts
http://it.bridgew.edu/Policy/wiki.cfm (accessed
October 15, 2008)

Brown University
Providence, Rhode Island
http://www.brown.edu/Administration/Copyright/
media.html (accessed March 31, 2009)

Bryant University
Douglas and Judith Krupp Library
Smithfield, Rhode Island
http://www.bryant.edu/wps/wcm/connect/Bryant/
Divisions/Information%20Systems/Library_New/
Library%20Information/Technology%20Plan
(accessed July 1, 2008)
http://www.bryant.edu/wps/wcmresources/libfiles/
library/copyright/CopyrightPolicy.pdf (accessed
July 1, 2008)

Bryn Mawr
Bryn Mawr Library
Bryn Mawr, Pennsylvania
http://www.brynmawr.edu/computing/docs/
flexlaptop.shtml (accessed July 27, 2008)

http://www.brynmawr.edu/computing/policy/policy
-web.shtml (accessed July 27, 2008)
http://www.brynmawr.edu/computing/policy/policy
-webprivacy.shtml (accessed July 27, 2008)

Buffalo State
State University of New York
E. H. Butler Library
Buffalo, New York
http://www.buffalostate.edu/library/about/policies
.asp (accessed June 30, 2008)

Cabrillo College
Robert E. Swenson Library
Aptos, California
http://libwww.cabrillo.edu/about/technologyplan
.html (accessed June 23, 2008)
http://libwww.cabrillo.edu/about/laptops.html
(accessed June 23, 2008)
http://libwww.cabrillo.edu/about/PolicySheetSpecial
.html (accessed June 23, 2008)
http://libwww.cabrillo.edu/about/copyright.html
(accessed June 23, 2008)

Calumet College of Saint Joseph
Specker Library
Whiting, Indiana
http://www.ccsj.edu/library/policies.shtml#pcuse
(accessed July 26, 2008)

Canton Public Library
Canton, Michigan
http://www.cantonpl.org/blog/bloginfo.html
(accessed June 30, 2008)

Carnegie Library of Pittsburgh
Pittsburgh, Pennsylvania
http://www.clpgh.org/locations/pennsylvania/ppl
.html (accessed October 14, 2008)

Carroll Community College
Carroll Community College and Media Center
Westminster, Maryland
http://www.carrollcc.edu/library/policies/
collectiondev.asp (accessed June 23, 2008)
http://www.carrollcc.edu/library/research/
copyrightinfo/copyright_guidelines.asp (accessed
June 23, 2008)
http://www.carrollcc.edu/library/research/
copyrightinfo/letter.asp (accessed June 23, 2008)

Central Michigan University
Central Michigan Universities Libraries
Mount Pleasant, Michigan
http://www.lib.cmich.edu/policies/e-only-serials.htm
(accessed June 23, 2008)
http://www.lib.cmich.edu/policies/electronic.htm
(accessed June 23, 2008)

Charlevoix Public Library
Charlevoix, Michigan
http://www.charlevoixlibrary.org/about/about-pol
-computer.htm (accessed July 26, 2008)

Clemson University
R. M. Cooper Library
Clemson, South Carolina
http://www.slis.indiana.edu/careers/view_job
_specific.php?job_id=4331 (accessed September
11, 2008)

Coastal Carolina University
Kimbel Library
Conway, South Carolina
http://www.slis.indiana.edu/careers/view_job
_specific.php?job_id=4262 (accessed September
12, 2008)

College of DuPage
College of DuPage Library
Glen Ellyn, Illinois
http://www.cod.edu/library/services/copyright/
guidelines.htm#Video (accessed July 28, 2008)
http://codlibrary.org/index.php?title=Library
_Policies#The_Internet (accessed July 28, 2008)

Colorado College
Tutt Library
Colorado Springs, Colorado
http://www.coloradocollege.edu/library/index.php/
policies/acquisitions-policies (accessed June 23,
2008)

Columbia College
Columbia College Library
Chicago, Illinois
http://www.lib.colum.edu/about/
ecollectiondevelopment.php (accessed June 23,
2008)

Columbia University
Columbia University Libraries
New York, New York
http://www.columbia.edu/cu/lweb/data/services/
preservation/dlpolicy.pdf (accessed June 24, 2008)
http://www.columbia.edu/cu/lweb/services/
preservation/publicationsPolicy.html (accessed
Oct 5, 2008)

Concord Public Library
Concord, New Hampshire
http://www.onconcord.com/PERSONNEL/CLASS
SPECS/ADULT%20SERVICES%20SUPVR%
20AUTOMATION%20COORDINATOR.pdf
(accessed September 26, 2008)

Concordia College
Carl B. Ylvisaker Library
Moorhead, Minnesota
http://library.cord.edu/about/policies/computers
.html (accessed June 24, 2008)
http://library.cord.edu/askus/privacy.html (accessed
June 24, 2008)

Connecticut State Library
Douglas Lord
Hartford, Connecticut
http://ct.webjunction.org/techplan-writing/articles/
content/2943729 (accessed October 16, 2008)

Cumberland County Library System
Carlisle, Pennsylvania
http://www.pacounties.org/cumberland/lib/
cumberland/ls/ccls-doc-policy_manual.pdf
(accessed June 30, 2008)
http://www.statelibrary.state.pa.us/libraries/lib/
libraries/ComputerServicesTechnician.pdf
(accessed September 13, 2008)
http://www.pde.state.pa.us/libraries/lib/libraries/
AutomatedServicesCoord.pdf (accessed
September 13, 3008)
http://dsf.pacounties.org/cumberland/lib/cumberland/
ls/ccls-doc-policy_manual.pdf (accessed March
31, 2009)

Cuyahoga County Public Library
Parma, Ohio
http://winslo.state.oh.us/publib/jobauto7.html
(accessed September 12, 2000)

Dakota State University
Karl E. Mundt Library
Madison, South Dakota
http://www.departments.dsu.edu/hr/newsite/policies/
015100.htm (accessed June 24, 2008)

Dartmouth College
Dartmouth College Library
Hanover, New Hampshire
http://www.dartmouth.edu/~cmdc/cdp/electronic
.html (accessed June 25, 2008)
http://www.dartmouth.edu/~cmdc/index.html
(accessed June 25, 2008)
http://www.dartmouth.edu/~library/home/help/
libcat/licensed.html (accessed June 25, 2008)
http://www.dartmouth.edu/comp/about/policies/
general/itpolicy/privacy.html (accessed June 25,
2008)

Davidson College
Davidson College Library
Davidson, North Carolina
http://www3.davidson.edu/cms/x6494.xml
(accessed December 6, 2008)

Drexel University
Drexel University Libraries
Philadelphia, Pennsylvania
http://www.library.drexel.edu/about/computerpolicies
.html (accessed June 25, 2008)

Duke University
Duke University Medical Center Library
Durham, North Carolina
http://www.mclibrary.duke.edu/training/pda
(accessed October 13, 2008)

Duke University
William R. Perkins Library
Durham, North Carolina
http://library.duke.edu/about/collections/eonly.html
(accessed June 25, 2008)
http://library.duke.edu/about/privacy.html (accessed
June 25, 2008)
http://library.duke.edu/about/copyright.html
(accessed June 25, 2008)

East Knox High School
Karen McLachlan
Howard, Ohio
http://www.cyberbee.com/content.pdf (accessed
October 14, 2008)
mclachlan_k@treca.org

Florida Atlantic University
S.E. Wimberly Library
Boca Raton, Florida
http://www.library.fau.edu/policies/cd_fau.htm#
formats (accessed June 25, 2008)
http://www.library.fau.edu/policies/cd_e
-resources.htm (accessed June 25, 2008)
http://www.library.fau.edu/eforms/elecreq.htm
(accessed June 25, 2008)

Florida Atlantic University Libraries
http://www.library.fau.edu/policies/cd_free_
e-resources.htm (accessed March 31, 2009)

Fresno County Public Library
Fresno, California
http://www.fresnolibrary.org/card/fees.html
(accessed October 14, 2008)

Great Falls Public Library
Great Falls, Montana
http://www.greatfallslibrary.org/filter.html
(accessed July 21, 2008)

Greenville Public Library
Smithfield, Rhode Island
http://www.yourlibrary.ws/TechnologyPlan/
Technology%20Plan%202006Revised.pdf
(accessed June 24, 2008)

W. Walworth Harrison Library
Greenville, Texas
http://www.youseemore.com/harrison/about.asp?
p=19 (accessed June 24, 2008)

Highline Community College
Highline Community College Library
Des Moines, Washington
http://flightline.highline.edu/libraryadmin/a_policies/
Appendix3.html (accessed June 25, 2008)

Hunter College
Jacqueline Grennan Wexler Library
New York, New York
http://library.hunter.cuny.edu/pdf/laptop_loan
_policies.pdf (accessed June 26, 2008)
http://library.hunter.cuny.edu/laptop_loan.htm
(accessed June 26, 2008)

Illinois State University
Milner Library
Normal, Illinois
http://www.scu.edu/library/services/reference/rs/
imfaq.cfm (accessed November 21, 2008)

Indiana University – Purdue University Fort Wayne
Walter E. Helmke
Fort Wayne, Indiana
http://www.lib.ipfw.edu/1272.0.html (accessed
October 13, 2008)

Jefferson County Public Library
Lakewood, Colorado
http://jefferson.lib.co.us/pdf/Request_for
_Photoduplication.pdf (accessed October 14,
2008)

Johns Hopkins University
Sheridan Libraries
Baltimore, Maryland
http://www.library.jhu.edu/researchhelp/general/
evaluating/index.html (accessed October 13,
2008)

Johns Hopkins University
Welch Medical Library
Baltimore, Maryland
http://www.welch.jhu.edu/about/ecdpolicy.html
    (accessed July 21, 2008)

Kettering University
Kettering University Library
Flint, Michigan
http://www.slis.indiana.edu/careers/view_job
    _specific.php?job_id=4535 (accessed September
    12, 2008)

Lafayette Public Library
Lafayette, Louisiana
http://www.lafayette.lib.la.us/docs/LPLTechnology
    Plan2008).pdf date access June 24, 2008)
http://www.lafayette.lib.la.us/docs/Electronic
    ResourcesPolicy.pdf (accessed June 24, 2008)

Lane Memorial Library
Hampton, New Hampshire
http://www.hampton.lib.nh.us/library/policies/
    webcolldev.htm (accessed June 24, 2008)
http://www.hampton.lib.nh.us/faqs/email.htm
    (accessed June 24, 2008)

Larchmont Public Library
Larchmont, New York
http://www.larchmontlibrary.org/internetpolicy
    .html#childrenandparents (accessed June 24, 2008)

Lehigh University Libraries
Lending Services
Bethlehem, Pennsylvania
http://www.lehigh.edu/library/services/copyinh
    .shtml (accessed October 14, 2008)

Long Beach City College
Long Beach City College Library
Long Beach, California
http://lib.lbcc.edu/services/im-faq.html (accessed
    October 13, 2008)

Long Island University
B. Davis Schwartz Memorial Library
Brookville, New York
http://www.liu.edu/cwis/cwp/library/acq/policy
    .htm#1110 (accessed June 26, 2008)

Longmont Public Library
Longmont, Colorado
http://www.ci.longmont.co.us/human_resources/
    jobs/descriptions.htm#SLT (accessed September
    10, 2008)

Longwood University
Janet D. Greenwood Library
Farmville, Virginia
http://www.longwood.edu/library/sug_cd.htm
    (accessed September 2, 2008)
http://www.longwood.edu/helpdesk/support/
    studenttechhndbk.htm#STUDENT%
    20PRINTING%20FROM%20THE%20LIBRARY%
    20&%20COMPUTER%20LABS (accessed
    September 2, 2008)
http://www.longwood.edu/library/sug_cd.htm
    (accessed September 2, 2008)
http://www.longwood.edu/library/about/policy/chat
    .htm (accessed September 2, 2008)

Lorain Public Library
Lorain, Ohio
http://winslo.state.oh.us/publib/jobauto11.html
    (accessed September 13, 2008)

Madison Public Library
Madison, Wisconsin
http://www.madisonpubliclibrary.org/about/patriot
    .html (accessed July 28, 2008)

Manitowoc Public Library
Manitowoc, Wisconsin
http://74.125.95.104/search?q=cache:pyj1Oo7ItF0J:
    www.manitowoc.lib.wi.us/AboutourLibrary/
    Employment%20Info/IT%20Manager%207
    -08.pdf+library+job+description+network+
    administrator&hl=en&ct=clnk&cd=11&gl=us
    (accessed September 15, 2008)

Mercer County Community College
Mercer County Community College Library
West Windsor, New Jersey
http://www.mccc.edu/student_library_resources
    _il-policy.shtml (accessed October 13, 2008)

Michigan State University
Michigan State University Libraries
East Lansing, Michigan
http://guides.lib.msu.edu/page.phtml?page_id=1069
    (accessed June 26, 2008)
http://www2.lib.msu.edu//resources/licdbnotice.jsp
    (accessed June 26, 2008)

Middle Georgia Regional Library
Technology Services Department
Macon, Georgia
http://www.georgialibraries.org/lib/erate/techplans/
    large_system_tech_plan.pdf (accessed July 2,
    2008)

Millersville University
Helen A. Ganser Library
Millersville, Pennsylvania
http://www.library.millersville.edu/guide.cfm?Parent
=644 (accessed July 2, 2008)
http://www.library.millersville.edu/pdf_forms/
FORM_e_reserve_31102001.pdf (accessed
February 11, 2009)

Montana State University
Montana State University Libraries
Bozeman, Montana
http://www.lib.montana.edu/digital/about.php
(accessed July 14, 2008)
http://www.lib.montana.edu/ask/erefpolicy.php
(accessed July 14, 2008)
http://www.montana.edu/cgi-bin/msuinfo/fpview/f/
8584-2 (accessed September 13, 2008)

Moraine Valley Community College
Moraine Valley Community College Libraries
Palos Hills, Illinois
http://www2.morainevalley.edu/defaultasp?SiteId=
10&PageId=1496 (accessed July 2, 2008)

Morton Grove Public Library
Morton Grove, Illinois
http://www.webrary.org/inside/colldevadultcirccdr
.html (accessed July 2, 2008)
http://www.webrary.org/inside/colldevadultvideos
.html (accessed July 2, 2008)
http://www.webrary.org/inside/colldevadultclass
.html (accessed July 2, 2008)
http://www.webrary.org/inside/colldevadultpop
.html (accessed July 2, 2008)
http://www.webrary.org/inside/colldevadultspk.html
(accessed July 2, 2008)

Municipal Research and Service Center of
Washington
Seattle, Washington
http://www.mrsc.org/jobdesc/S73WEBMAST.aspx
(accessed September 9, 2008)

Naperville Public Library
Naperville, Illinois
http://www.naperville-lib.org/atl/job/virtual
_librarian.PDF (accessed September 24, 2008)

Neill Public Library
Pullman, Washington
http://www.neill-
lib.org/Departments/Library/DrawOnePage
.aspx?PageID=112 (accessed July 2, 2008)
http://www.neill-lib.org/Departments/Library/
DrawOnePage.aspx?PageID=113#iuse (accessed
July 2, 2008)

North Dakota State University
North Dakota State University Libraries
Fargo, North Dakota
http://xavier.lib.ndsu.nodak.edu/groups/policies/wiki/
61712/Personally-owned_Computer_Equipment
_Policy.html (accessed September 12, 2008)

Northcentral University
Northcentral University Library
Prescott Valley, Arizona
http://ncu.edu/library/policy/ncu/default.asp?pol
_num=6#Electronic%20Collection%
20Development (accessed July 3, 2008)
http://ncu.edu/library/policy/ncu/default.asp?pol
_num=7#NCU%20Library (accessed July 3,
2008)

Northeast Community College
Northeast Community College Library
Norfolk, Nebraska
http://www.northeastcollege.com/AN/Policies/PDF/
5000/5090a.pdf (accessed July 3, 2008)

Northwestern University
Northwestern University Library
Evanston, Illinois
http://staffweb.library.northwestern.edu/dl/
documents/DLCScopeDocumentSept1603.pdf
(accessed July 2, 2008)
http://staffweb.library.northwestern.edu/dl/
documents/DLC-AFF-finalreport-july03.pdf
(accessed July 2, 2008)

Orbis Cascade Alliance
Eugene, Oregon
http://orbiscascade.org/index/electronic-resources-
committee (accessed March 31, 2009)

Orion Township Public Library
Lake Orion, Michigan
http://www.orion.lib.mi.us/general/internetpolicy
.htm (accessed July 19, 2008)
http://www.orion.lib.mi.us/general/copyright.htm
(accessed July 19, 2008)

Orland Park Public Library
Orland Park, Illinois
http://www.orlandparklibrary.org/documents/
policies/internet_policy.pdf (accessed July 2,
2008)
http://www.orlandparklibrary.org/computerpolicy
.htm (accessed July 2, 2008)

Ouachita Parish Public Library
Monroe, Louisiana
http://www.ouachita.lib.la.us/elecaccpol.htm
(accessed March 31, 2009)

Owensboro Community and Technical College
Owensboro Community and Technical College
  Library
Owensboro, Kentucky
www.octc.kctcs.edu/library/FacultyServices.htm
  (accessed July 17, 2008)
http://www.octc.kctcs.edu/library/CollectionPolicies
  _ElectronicResources.htm (accessed July 17, 2008)

Pasadena Public Library
Pasadena California
http://www.ci.pasadena.ca.us/library/policy.asp
  (accessed July 21, 2008)
http://www.ci.pasadena.ca.us/library/collection.asp#
  Electronic-Databases (accessed July 21, 2008)
http://www.ci.pasadena.ca.us/library/photoorder
  .asp (accessed October 14, 2008)

Pennsylvania State University
Pennsylvania State University Libraries
University Park, Pennsylvania
http://www.libraries.psu.edu/psul/artshumanities/
  musicaudio/audio_electronic_reserves.html
  (accessed March 31, 2009)

Pickaway County District Public Library
Circleville, Ohio
http://www.pickaway.lib.oh.us/privacy.php
  (accessed July 2, 2008)

Plainfield–Guilford Township Public Library
Plainfield, Indiana
http://www.plainfieldlibrary.net/librarybasics/
  librarypolicies.html (accessed July 21, 2008)
http://www.plainfieldlibrary.net/librarybasics/
  wireless.html (accessed July 21, 2008)

Porter County Public Library System
Valparaiso, Indiana
http://www.pcpls.lib.in.us/PC_Internet_Policies.htm
  #Youth_Information_Highway_Rules_of_the
  _Road (accessed July 21, 2008)

Portland Community College
Portland Community College Libraries
Portland, Oregon
http://www.pcc.edu/library/policies/duplication.htm
  (accessed July 3, 2008)
http://www.pcc.edu/library/policies/laptop.htm
  (accessed July 3, 2008)
http://www.pcc.edu/library/policies/digcamera.htm
  (accessed July 3, 2008)
http://www.pcc.edu/library/policies/equipment_use
  _agreement.pdf (accessed July 3, 2008)
http://www.pcc.edu/library/policies/collection.htm#
  av (accessed July 3, 2008)

Public Library of Youngstown and Mahoning
  County
Youngstown, Ohio
http://winslo.state.oh.us/publib/jobauto3.html
  (accessed September 11, 2008)

Purchase College
http://dlist.sir.arizona.edu/206/ (accessed July 3,
  2008)

River Falls Public Library
River Falls, Wisconsin
http://www.rfcity.org/library/policies/web.html
  (accessed July 21, 2008)
http://www.rfcity.org/library/policies/wireless.html
  (accessed July 21, 2008)

Rollins College
Olin Library
Winter Park, Florida
http://www.rollins.edu/olin/techsrvcs/acquisitions/
  Electronic%20ResourcesCollectionDevelopment
  Policy.doc (accessed July 3, 2008)

Rutgers University
Rutgers University Libraries
New Brunswick, New Jersey
http://www.libraries.rutgers.edu/rul/rr_gateway/res
  earch_guides/copyright/boyle_licensing_terms
  .pdf (accessed September 23, 2008)

Saint John the Baptist Parish Library
LaPlace, Louisiana
http://www.state.lib.la.us/la_dyn_templ.cfm?doc_id
  =965 (accessed September 10, 2008)

Saint Louis University
Saint Louis University Libraries
Saint Louis, Missouri
http://libraries.slu.edu/about/policies/approuse.html
  (accessed July 11, 2008)

Saint Mary's University College
Saint Mary's University College Library
Calgary, Alberta, Canada
http://library.stmu.ab.ca/services/serv_faculty.htm
  (accessed October 15, 2008)

Saint Petersburg
Saint Petersburg Libraries
Saint Petersburg, Florida
http://www.spcollege.edu/central/libonline/book
  _image/spclbpolicystatement.htm (accessed July
  11, 2008)
http://www.spcollege.edu/central/libonline/book
  _image/SPCLBcopyrightstatement.htm (accessed
  July 11, 2008)

Sandusky Library
Follett House Museum
Sandusky, Ohio
http://www.sandusky.lib.oh.us/archives/policies.php
   (accessed October 14, 2008)

Santa Clara University
Santa Clara University Library
Santa Clara, California
http://www.scu.edu/library/services/reference/rs/
   imfaq.cfm (accessed October 13, 2008)

Saskatchewan Library Association
Regina, Saskatchewan, Canada
http://www.lib.sk.ca/staff/virtref/projectplan.html
   (accessed July 21, 2008)

Satilla Regional Library System
Douglas, Georgia
http://www.srlsys.org/policies.htm (accessed March
   31, 2009)
http://www.srlsys.org/SRLSCollectionDev.htm
   (accessed July 21, 2008)
http://www.srlsys.org/SRLSCollectionDev.htm
   (accessed October 4, 2008)

Seattle Public Library
Seattle, Washington
http://www.spl.org/default.asp?pageID=about_policies
   _printingfees (accessed October 14, 2008)

Sharon Public Library
Sharon, Massachusetts
http://www.sharonpubliclibrary.org/about
   _policypatriot.htm (accessed July 28, 2008)

Solano Community College
Solano Community College Library
Fairfield, California
http://www.solano.edu/tech_learn_resources/
   techplan/library.html (accessed July 11, 2008)

South San Francisco Public Library
South San Francisco, California
http://www.ssflibrary.net/files/southsanfrancisco/
   Blog%20Policy.pdf (accessed July 21, 2008)

State Library and Archives of Florida
Department of State Library and Archives of
   Florida
Tallahassee, Florida
http://info.askalibrarian.org/faq.asp (accessed July
   11, 2008)

State Library of Massachusetts
George Fingold Library
Boston, Massachusetts
http://www.mass.gov/lib/services/reproform.htm
   (accessed October 14, 2008)
http://www.mass.gov/lib/services/Fee%20Schedule-
   v%200.pdf (accessed October 14, 2008)

Stillwater Public Library
Stillwater, Oklahoma
http://library.stillwater.org/Policies/tech.pdf
   (accessed July 21, 2008)
http://library.stillwater.org/Policies/internet.pdf
   (accessed July 21, 2008)

Tacoma Public Library
Tacoma, Washington
http://www.tpl.lib.wa.us/Page.aspx?nid=36
   (accessed October 14, 2008)

Talbot Belmond Public Library
Belmond, Iowa
http://www.belmond.lib.ia.us/library-information/
   policies/photocopy (accessed October 14, 2008)

Tempe Public Library
Tempe, Arizona
http://www.tempe.gov/library/admin/policies/accept
   use.htm (accessed July 21, 2008)

Texas A&M Corpus Christi
Mary and Jeff Bell Library
Corpus Christi, Texas
http://rattler.tamucc.edu/policy/ERCollDevPolicy_8
   _Dec_2006.pdf (accessed July 14, 2008)

Texas State Library and Archives Commission
Austin, Texas
http://www.texshare.edu/programs/academicdb/
   collectionpolicy.html (accessed July 17, 2008)

Texas State University
Albert B. Alkek Library
San Marcos, Texas
http://www.library.txstate.edu/about/departments/
   instruction/request-instruction.html (accessed
   October 13, 2008)

Texas Tech University
Texas Tech University Libraries
Lubbock, Texas
http://library.ttu.edu/forms/?li_eval (accessed
   October 13, 2008)

Thomas Jefferson University
Scott Memorial Library
Philadelphia, Pennsylvania
http://jeffline.jefferson.edu/SML/reference/aim.html
(accessed August 11, 2008)
http://jeffline.jefferson.edu/SML/reference/
searchrequest.html (accessed August 11, 2008)
http://jeffline.jefferson.edu/SML/policies/cd/index
.html (accessed August 12, 2008)

Tri-College Libraries
Bryn Mawr, Haverford, and Swarthmore College
Libraries
http://www.brynmawr.edu/Library/jobs.shtml
(accessed September 10, 2008)

Toronto Public Library
Toronto, Ontario, Canada
http://kidsspace.torontopubliclibrary.ca/privacy
.html (accessed July 21, 2008)

Town of Williston
Dorothy Alling Memorial Library
Williston, Vermont
http://www.town.williston.vt.us/website/index.php?
option=com_content&task=view&id=370&Itemid=
32 (accessed September 26, 2008)

Tufts University
Tisch Library
Medford, Massachusetts
http://uit.tufts.edu/?pid=175&c=110 (accessed July
29, 2008)
http://www.library.tufts.edu/Tisch/blc_policies.htm
(accessed July 29, 2008)

Tulane University
Howard-Tilton Memorial Library
New Orleans, Louisiana
http://library.tulane.edu/about/library_policies/
computer_use.php (accessed July 29, 2008)
http://www.slis.indiana.edu/careers/view_job
_specific.php?job_id=4434 (accessed September
11, 2008)

Tulane University
Tulane University Alumni Affairs
New Orleans, Louisiana
http://alumni.tulane.edu/E-mailpolicy.html (accessed
July 29, 2008)

United States Department of Agriculture
National Agriculture Library
Beltsville, Maryland
http://www.nal.usda.gov/about/policy/coll_dev
_add2.shtml (accessed July 17, 2008)

University of Alberta
University of Alberta Libraries
Edmonton, Alberta, Canada
http://www.library.ualberta.ca/guides/
criticalevaluation/index.cfm (accessed October
13, 2008)

University of Arizona
Arizona Health Science Library
Tucson, Arizona
http://www.ahsl.arizona.edu/policies/CollDevPol20
06.cfm (accessed July 19, 2008)
http://www.ahsl.arizona.edu/policies/usepolicy.cfm
(accessed July 19, 2008)
http://www.ahsl.arizona.edu/about/guidelines/index
.cfm (accessed July 19, 2008)
http://www.ahls.arizona.edu/computing/labs/
instructor_info.cfm (accessed November 19,
2008)

University of Arizona
University of Arizona Libraries
Tucson, Arizona
http://www.slis.indiana.edu/careers/view_job
_specific.php?job_id=4242 (accessed September
12, 2008)

University of Arkansas for Medical Sciences
University of Arkansas Medical Science Library
Little Rock, Arkansas
http://www.library.uams.edu/policy/privacy.aspx
(accessed September 2, 2008)
http://www.library.uams.edu/policy/visitcomp.aspx
(accessed September 2, 2008)
http://www.lib.berkeley.edu/TeachingLib/Guides/
Internet/Evaluate.html (accessed October 13,
2008)

University of California, San Francisco
Galen UCSF Digital Library
San Francisco, California
http://www.library.ucsf.edu/info/copycash.html
(accessed October 14, 2008)
http://www.library.ucsf.edu/edtech/wiki/faq.html
(accessed October 14, 2008)

University of California, Santa Barbara
Map and Imagery Laboratory, Davidson Library
Santa Barbara, California
http://www.sdc.ucsb.edu/services/repro_options
_NON-UC.htm (accessed October 14, 2008)

University of Colorado at Boulder
University Libraries
Boulder, Colorado
http://www-libraries.colorado.edu/services/
electronic.htm (accessed September 2, 2008)

University of Connecticut
University of Connecticut Libraries
Storrs, Connecticut
http://ctlibraryjobs.blogspot.com/2007/10/digital-projects-librarian-and.html (accessed September 9, 2008)

University of Dayton
Roesch Library
Dayton, Ohio
http://udit.udayton.edu/digitalAssets/878_fraup_policy.pdf (accessed September 18, 2008)
http://library.udayton.edu/ (accessed April 24, 2008)

University of Illinois
Urbana, Illinois
http://www.vpaa.uillinois.edu/policies/web_privacy.cfm (accessed May 24, 2008)

University of Illinois at Urbana-Champaign
University of Illinois Libraries
Urbana, Illinois
http://www.library.uiuc.edu/administration/services/policies/electro_reserve.html (accessed May 24, 2008)
http://www.library.uiuc.edu/administration/services/policies/electro_info.html (accessed September 18, 2008)
http://www.library.uiuc.edu/administration/services/policies/email.html (accessed September 18, 2008)
http://clips.lis.uiuc.edu/2005_07.htm (accessed October 13, 2008)

University of Iowa
University of Iowa Libraries
Iowa City, Iowa
http://www.lib.uiowa.edu/collections/policy.html (accessed April 24, 2008) September 19, 2008)
http://www.lib.uiowa.edu/dls/mission.html (accessed September 23, 2008)
http://www.lib.uiowa.edu/dls/principles1.html (accessed September 23, 2008)
http://www.lib.uiowa.edu/dls/goals2.html (accessed September 23, 2008)

The University of Kansas
University of Kansas Libraries
Lawrence, Kansas
http://www.lib.ku.edu/services/ada/ (accessed September 19, 2008)
https://documents.ku.edu/policies/Information_Services/Information_Technology/Password%20Policy/Password%20Policy.htm (accessed September 19, 2008)

University of Maryland
University of Maryland Libraries
College Park, Maryland
http://www.diversejobs.net/candidate/processcandviewjob?docid=A2343-0073&source=search (accessed September 10, 2008)
http://www.lib.umd.edu/CLMD/COLL.Policies/selection-freeweb.html (accessed September 19, 2008)
http://www.lib.umd.edu/CLMD/COLL.Policies/elecrescdp.html (accessed September 19, 2008)
http://www.lib.umd.edu/ETC/ejournalfaq.html (accessed September 19, 2008)
http://www.nethics.umd.edu/aup/ (accessed September 19, 2008)

University of Maryland, Baltimore
University of Maryland Health Sciences and Human Services Library
Baltimore, Maryland
http://www.hshsl.umaryland.edu/general/about/policies/colldev.html#elect (accessed May 31, 2008)
http://www.hshsl.umaryland.edu/resources/bookquest.html (accessed September 23, 2008)
http://www.hshsl.umaryland.edu/general/about/policies/elecdev.html#implementation (accessed September 23, 2008)
http://www.hshsl.umaryland.edu/general/about/policies/elecdev.html#implementation (accessed September 23, 2008)

University of Maryland, Baltimore County
Albin O. Kuhn Library
Baltimore, Maryland
http://aok.lib.umbc.edu/informationliteracy/infoliteracy.php (accessed October 13, 2008)
http://aok.lib.umbc.edu/informationliteracy/libinstrform.php (accessed October 13, 2008)

University of Massachusetts, Boston
Joseph P. Healey Library
Boston, Massachusetts
http://umb.interviewexchange.com/jobofferdetails.jsp;jsessionid=334BA6145C5F7644ED4A92216E6CA9A4?JOBID=10867 (accessed September 13, 2008)

University of Miami
Otto G. Richter Library
Coral Gables, Florida
http://www.slis.indiana.edu/careers/view_job_specific.php?job_id=4522 (accessed September 12, 2008)

University of Michigan
University of Michigan Libraries
Ann Arbor, Michigan
http://www.lib.umich.edu/policies/eresources.html (accessed September 24, 2008)
http://www.lib.umich.edu/lit/dlps/about.html (accessed September 24, 2008)
http://www.copyright.umich.edu/policy_intro.html (accessed September 24, 2008)
http://www.lib.umich.edu/policies/privacy.html (accessed September 24, 2008)
http://www.lib.umich.edu/ask/technicalstuff.html (accessed October 13, 2008)

University of Minnesota
University of Minnesota Libraries
Minneapolis, Minnesota
http://www.lib.umn.edu/copyright/licensed-std.phtml (accessed September 24, 2008)
http://www.fpd.finop.umn.edu/groups/ppd/documents/appendix/useguidelines.cfm (accessed September 24, 2008)
http://www.fpd.finop.umn.edu/groups/ppd/documents/policy/acceptable_use.cfm (accessed September 24, 2008)
http://faq.lib.umn.edu/public/showRecord.pl?kbrecordid=115&results=115&mode=public (accessed October 4, 2008)
http://faq.lib.umn.edu/public/showRecord.pl?kbrecordid=321&results=186,187,321&mode=public (accessed October 4, 2008)
http://www.lib.umn.edu/site/authentication.phtml (accessed October 4, 2008)
http://www.lib.umn.edu/site/authenticationfaq.phtml (accessed October 4, 2008)

University of Minnesota Law School
University of Minnesota Law Library
Minneapolis, Minnesota
http://local.law.umn.edu/uploads/images/992/E_Res_CD_Policy.pdf (accessed September 24, 2008)

University of North Carolina Greensboro
University Libraries
Greensboro, North Carolina
http://its.uncg.edu/Policy_Manual/Network_Security/ (accessed September 26, 2008)

University of North Texas
University of North Texas Libraries
Denton, Texas
http://www.library.unt.edu (accessed March 31, 2009)

University of Northern Iowa
Rod Library
Cedar Falls, Iowa
http://www.library.uni.edu/cmss/electronic_resources.shtml (accessed September 24, 2008)

University of Notre Dame
Hesburgh Library
Notre Dame, Indiana
http://www.slis.indiana.edu/careers/view_job_specific.php?job_id=4606 (accessed September 15, 2008)

University of Oregon
Knight Library
Eugene, Oregon
http://libweb.uoregon.edu/colldev/cdpolicies/internet.html (accessed September 26, 2008)
http://libweb.uoregon.edu/colldev/cdpolicies/ejournals.html (accessed September 26, 2008)
http://libweb.uoregon.edu/colldev/cdpolicies/eresources.html (accessed September 26, 2008)

University of Ottawa
University of Ottawa Library
Ottawa, Ontario, Canada
http://www.biblio.uottawa.ca/content-page.php?g=en&s=biblio&c=abt-ptq-numeriq (accessed September 23, 2008)

University of Saint Thomas Minnesota
University of Saint Thomas Libraries
Saint Paul, Minnesota
http://innopacusers.org/jobs/2007/11/28/associate-director-for-digital-initiatives-university-of-st-thomas/ (accessed September 15, 2008)

University of the Southwest
Scarborough Memorial Library
Hobbs, New Mexico
http://www.csw.edu/203900.ihtml (accessed June 23, 2008)

University of Texas at Arlington
University of Texas at Arlington Libraries
Arlington, Texas
http://www.higheredjobs.com/details.cfm?JobCode=175334311 (accessed September 10, 2008)
https://library.uta.edu/instructionServices/scheduleInstruction.jsp (accessed March 31, 2009)

University of Texas at Austin
Research Services Division
University of Texas Libraries
Austin, Texas
http://www.lib.utexas.edu/admin/cird/policies/
subjects/framework.html (accessed September
23, 2008)

University of Texas at El Paso
University of Texas at El Paso Libraries
El Paso, Texas
http://admin.utep.edu/Default.aspx?tabid=25820
(accessed September 10, 2008)

The University of Toledo
Ward M. Canaday Center for Special Collections,
University of Toledo Libraries
http://www.utoledo.edu/library/info/jobs/
DigitalLibrarian.pdf (accessed September 15, 2008)

University of Virginia
University of Virginia Library
Charlottesville, Virginia
http://www.virginia.edu/copyright.html#advertising
(accessed July 26, 2008)
http://www.lib.virginia.edu/laptops.html#guest
(accessed July 26, 2008)

University of Virginia Health Science
Claude Moore Health Sciences Library
Charlottesville, Virginia
http://www.hsl.virginia.edu/admin/policy/collection-
toc.cfm (accessed July 26, 2008)
http://www.hsl.virginia.edu/admin/policy/digital
_signage.cfm (accessed July 26, 2008)

University of Washington
University of Washington Libraries
Seattle, Washington
http://www.slis.indiana.edu/careers/view_job
_specific.php?job_id=4293 (accessed September
12, 2008)
http://www.slis.indiana.edu/careers/view_job
_specific.php?job_id=4238 (accessed September
12, 2008)
http://www.lib.washington.edu/msd/internetselguide
.html (accessed May 23, 2008)

University of West Florida
John C. Pace Library
Pensacola, Florida
http://library.uwf.edu/Research/InformationLiteracy
/Literacy.htm (accessed October 13, 2008)

University of Wyoming
University of Wyoming Libraries
Laramie, Wyoming
http://www.wyla.org/jobboard.shtml (accessed
September 26, 2008)

Washington State Library
Olympia, Washington
http://digitalwa.statelib.wa.gov/newsite/projectmgmt/
costfactors.htm (accessed July 17, 2008)
http://digitalwa.statelib.wa.gov/newsite/collection/
preservation.htm (accessed July 17, 2008)
http://digitalwa.statelib.wa.gov/newsite/funding/
pursue.htm (accessed July 17, 2008)

Wasilla Public Library
Wasilla, Alaska
http://www.cityofwasilla.com/content/files/HR%20-
%20Job%20Description%20Adult%20and%
20Electronic%20Services%20Librarian%
20Revised%20103.pdf (accessed September 15,
2008)

Web Junction
OCLC Online Computer Center
Library Center
Dublin, Ohio
http://www.webjunction.org/cipa/articles/content/
432245 (accessed November 6, 2008)
http://www.webjunction.org/cipa/articles/content/
432255 (accessed November 6, 2008)

Westerville Public Library
Westerville, Ohio
http://winslo.state.oh.us/publib/jobauto15.html
(accessed September 13, 2008)

Wisconsin Valley Library Service
Wausau, Wisconsin
http://wvls.lib.wi.us/jobs/jobopp.html (accessed
September 15, 2008)

Worthington Library
Worthington, Ohio
http://winslo.state.oh.us/publib/TechnologyTrainer
.pdf (accessed September 11, 2008)
http://winslo.state.oh.us/publib/DigitalLibraryMgr
.pdf (accessed September 11, 2008)
http://winslo.state.oh.us/publib/
NetworkAdministrator.pdf (accessed September
11, 2008)

INDEX